The Papers of Josiah Bartlett

The Papers of

Josiah Bartlett

Frank C. Mevers, Editor

Published for the New Hampshire Historical Society

by the University Press of New England

Hanover, New Hampshire 1979

This publication meets standards established
by the National Historical Publications and
Records Commission of the General Services
Administration and was produced with its assistance
and that of the New Hampshire American
Revolution Bicentennial Commission and
the New Hampshire Historical Society.

Frontispiece: Josiah Bartlett
Pencil sketch by John Trumbull, 1790.
New Hampshire Historical Society

The signature used in the title is a facsimile
of that on the Declaration of Independence.

To The Memory of ELWIN L. PAGE *(1876–1974)*

Editorial Advisory Board

Foreword

Established by the General Court during the legislative session of 1969, the New Hampshire American Revolution Bicentennial Commission, comprised of twenty-five residents of the state appointed by the Governor, was organized in the early summer of 1970. Having been named Chairman at the Commission's first meeting, much of my time and energy have subsequently been expended in seeking to carry out a far-reaching program of Bicentennial activities in New Hampshire and the nation. Fortunately, I have had the loyal support of the members of the Commission and of a small but highly competent staff.

An emphasis which seemed wise to all of us on the Commission was to undertake efforts that would have an enduring effect upon thoughtful minds in our state and in the nation as a whole. One such effort, we decided early in 1973, would be to arrange for the collection and publication of a comprehensive edition of the papers of Dr. Josiah Bartlett. At the time of the American Revolution Dr. Bartlett was a citizen of Kingston, and already a figure of repute in New Hampshire. When the crisis came in 1775, he soon became one of the leaders among that galaxy of notable Americans who led in the successful struggle for national independence. When he died, he left behind him an unknown number of papers and records which, until now, have remained scattered and inaccessible. It was altogether fitting and proper, we felt, to make such a collection one of the chief endeavors of the New Hampshire American Revolution Bicentennial Commission.

Having reached this conclusion, we joined with the New Hampshire Historical Society, which, we learned, had already evolved a plan for gathering, editing, and publishing all extant Bartlett papers. The Historical Society, which had in its archives a mass of Bartlett manuscripts, agreed to cosponsor the project. In the summer of 1974, with substantial financial backing from both the New Hampshire Commission and the National Historical Publications and Records Commission, the effort began. We were fortunate to secure the services of Frank C. Mevers, a scholar with particular interest in the American Revolution, to direct the work. With the advantage of professional training in manuscript research, collation, and editing, he undertook the exciting task of finding and organizing Bartlett material. Combing both private and public collections, writing letters to scores of persons in this country and abroad, the editor has completed a microfilm edition of several thousand items, many previously unknown, and has edited and annotated several hundred for this selective letterpress edition.

As these lines are being written, twentieth-century Americans are proudly observing the adoption of the Articles of Confederation. On

November 15, 1777, this document, the first constitution for the United States of America, was approved by the Continental Congress, then meeting at York, Pennsylvania. Josiah Bartlett was on the Congressional committee appointed in June of 1776 to prepare the text for the Articles. Thanks to his knowledge and diplomatic skill, he helped to get the draft constitution accepted by Congress. Early in 1778 he similarly persuaded the New Hampshire legislature to endorse the Articles. On July 9, 1778, while again representing New Hampshire in Congress, he officially signed the new Constitution.

All students of New Hampshire and United States history will share with me a sense of pride in the work which has been done. Dr. Bartlett needs to be better known by those interested in the history of the state and nation. Physician, jurist, soldier, farmer, developer of scores of worthy community causes, member of the Continental Congress, Signer of the Declaration of Independence, President of New Hampshire for three terms, the first governor of New Hampshire, founder of the New Hampshire Medical Society, Josiah Bartlett was a worthy colleague of John Adams, Benjamin Franklin, Thomas Jefferson, and many of our nation's founding fathers. To read his writings is better to understand him and the part that he played two hundred years ago; to understand him is to learn how much there is to admire in him; to learn to admire him is to experience one of the lasting joys of our American Bicentennial.

New London, N.H.
15 November 1977

J. Duane Squires
Chairman, New Hampshire
American Revolution
Bicentennial Commission

Contents

A section of illustrations follows page 240

Acknowledgments

As is the case with any such project, this one depended on the good will and assistance of a multitude of individuals and organizations. John F. Page, as Director of the New Hampshire Historical Society, has strongly supported the endeavor from its inception. His guiding principles have led to efficient execution of the project, while his precise literary criticisms have saved the editor from grievous errors. He has watched and commented on every phase of the project in a manner that has been not only meaningful but also extraordinarily helpful. The staff of the Historical Society and its trustees, members, and friends have likewise continually lent their enthusiastic effort; they have made the work a pleasant experience. The citizens of New Hampshire, to whom the Historical Society looks for much of its support, can be proud of its library of approximately 85,000 books, which has made possible the comprehensiveness of this volume.

Dr. J. Duane Squires, as Chairman of the New Hampshire American Revolution Bicentennial Commission, has kept a vigilant and helpful eye on the entire project on behalf of the Commission members. Appreciation is also extended to Gilbert S. Center and the Commission staff.

Frank G. Burke, Director, and Roger A. Bruns, Richard N. Sheldon, Sara Dunlap Jackson, Mary Giunta, and others on the staff of the National Historical Publications and Records Commission have been cordial as well as helpful on the many occasions they have been called upon for assistance.

Appreciation is extended to the Director of the Essex Institute, Bryant F. Tolles, Jr., who, as Assistant Director of the New Hampshire Historical Society in 1974, played a large role in constructing the project.

None took so active a personal interest as did Harriet S. Lacy, former manuscripts librarian of the Historical Society. Though officially retired, she has volunteered many months of her time to share her knowledge and abilities in practically every phase of the project. In particular, it should be noted that Mrs. Lacy compiled the chronology and the genealogy, in addition to researching much of the biographical information presented in the annotation.

Laura L. Hall, assistant to the project for more than two years, accomplished a superb feat in transcribing, collating, and retyping documents to be printed. She filed, organized, and proofread—all on a part-time basis. Her special interest in Mary Bartlett helped solve several problems and will lead to a broader knowledge of the role of women in Revolutionary New Hampshire.

Members of the Bartlett family, now spread across the United States, have been most cooperative. A note of special appreciation is extended to Mr. and Mrs. Rodney M. Wilson of Kingston, New Hampshire, for their generous cooperation. Mrs. Wilson (née Gertrude Bartlett), a great-granddaughter of Dr. Bartlett, has been one of the project's most enthusiastic supporters.

For their unstinting efforts thanks go also to Kenneth C. Cramer and the staff of the Baker Library at Dartmouth College; to Avis Duckworth, Stella J. Scheckter, and the staff of the New Hampshire State Library; and to Director Robert A. Lauze and the staff of the New Hampshire Division of Records Management and Archives. Other institutions which provided copies of their papers are listed with location symbols and with each document printed. Sincere thanks are extended to the many persons on those staffs whose interest made the project successful. The project also extends appreciation to Francis W. Bartlett, Sol Feinstone, Robert I. Hinkley, S. Bartlett Howard, Warren A. Reeder, J. Duane Squires, Robert A. Stein, Captain J. G. M. Stone, Ronald von Klaussen, Lloyd L. Wells, and Mr. and Mrs. Rodney M. Wilson for permission to print copies of manuscripts in their possession.

Leon W. Anderson, John A. Archer, Eric C. Bagan, Edward C. Brummer, Helen L. Cripe, John W. Durel, J. Worth Estes, Joseph W. P. Frost, Donna-Belle Garvin, John K. Gemmill, Mrs. Ferne Goonan, Mrs. Harriet K. Greer, Harold J. Hayes, William House, Hannah Lacy, Kathryn H. Mevers, Ruth C. Page, Dana Parks, Marius B. Pélàdeau, Hamilton S. Putnam, David G. Stahl, Sara Stone, Mrs. Samuel S. Sverdlik, Donald M. D. Thurber, and Paul W. Wilderson all deserve special mention for various contributions to the project.

Members of the Advisory Board have given generously of their time, knowledge, and talents when called upon at several critical stages. The photography for the volume is the fine production of Bill Finney of Concord. David Horne, Director, and the staff of the University Press of New England have made publication a pleasant experience.

To all those who have lent their support in so many ways to the success of the project the editor will remain eternally grateful.

Concord, New Hampshire   *Frank C. Mevers*
September 1978

Introduction

Josiah Bartlett—signer of the Declaration of Independence, first constitutional governor of New Hampshire, founder of the New Hampshire Medical Society—left a significant number of papers, many of which have enhanced our understanding of New Hampshire and the nation during the period of the American Revolution. In the belief that Bartlett's papers deserve to be made available to a wider audience, the New Hampshire Historical Society decided to edit them as part of its contribution to the nation's Bicentennial observance.

The three-year project was proposed in 1973. With support from the New Hampshire American Revolution Bicentennial Commission and from the National Historical Publications Commission, it was begun in September 1974 under the general sponsorship of the New Hampshire Historical Society. The objective was to bring together originals or copies of all extant papers written by or to Josiah Bartlett, or signed by him, for reproduction first on microfilm and then in a "letterpress" edition of selected items. Major collections of Bartlett papers were known to exist in New Hampshire and in Washington, D.C. In the expectation that others lay hidden elsewhere, inquiries were sent to several hundred repositories. It was originally estimated that approximately 1,800 documents might be found; by the time the microfilm was completed, nearly twice that number had been located. All were photographed on seven rolls of microfilm as described in the *Guide to the Microfilm Edition of the Papers of Josiah Bartlett*, 1976 (MJB). The publication of the present volume of selected items concludes the project.

The disposition of Bartlett's papers over the past two centuries is only generally known. Many early documents were destroyed along with the Bartlett house when it burned in February 1774. Some were saved and remain with other family papers at the Kingston house, which was rebuilt in 1774 and has been occupied continuously by Bartlett's descendants. Most of the Bartlett material now at the New Hampshire Historical Society came as gifts from Richard Bartlett in the nineteenth century and from Mrs. John Watt in the twentieth; both were family members. Through marriage, some papers were acquired by the Wingate family of Stratham, New Hampshire; in 1903 they were presented by J. C. A. Wingate to the New Hampshire State Library. Other papers (mainly congressional correspondence) were given by the Haverhill, New Hampshire, branch of the family to the Northern Academy of Arts and Sciences at Hanover in 1841. When the Academy was dissolved in 1903 its library was sold to Dartmouth College, where the collection is now housed. It is available at Baker Library on a single roll of microfilm. A number of documents, known to have been sold from Kingston around the turn of the century, are now scattered among collections throughout the United States, and most of the public documents remain in the New Hampshire Archives. Selected items have left Kingston with various members of the Bartlett family. A collection of family papers at the Library of Congress consists principally of nineteenth-century items beyond the purview of this project.

Bartlett's contemporaries often relied upon him to write legislative committee reports and official papers, perhaps owing in part to the legibility of his handwriting and the clarity of his expression. During periods of service in the Continental Congress his correspondence reached its peak as he endeavored to keep in touch with colleagues, friends, and family who more often than not answered his letters. Bartlett did not systematically make copies of his letters. Most of those found are originals, the letters actually received by the addressee. This is especially true of the letters between Bartlett and his wife Mary.

One of the revelations of the project has been the enthusiasm found in Mary Bartlett's letters to her husband while he was attending Congress. Her letters went from Kingston nearly every week carrying news of family and community health, the weather, crops, and significant local events —comments of interest to Josiah and to us as well because they contain many observations on eighteenth-century and Revolutionary domestic life not otherwise available. Mary's letters, composed while managing the farm and a growing family, show not only that she had acquired some education, but also that she can be included among the women who vigorously supported their husbands and the Revolution.

From 1778 on, Bartlett maintained correspondence with many of New Hampshire's delegates to the Continental and United States Congresses. His extensive travel in New England offered him frequent opportunities for personal contact with colleagues, thus obviating the need for written communication with them. His correspondence during the 1790s dealt chiefly with matters pertaining to state government. In these later years, while chief executive of the state, he received more letters from New Hampshire's federal congressmen than he took time to answer.

If his papers reflect his character, Bartlett was a sober, pragmatic man, given to prodigious work, frugality, and moral rectitude. Sincere concern for the well-being of his fellow man, rather than personal ambition, appears to have been the motivation that spurred him to leadership. He was able and willing to give of his time and talents wherever they were needed at a specific moment. These rare qualities so consistently put forward made him a man not only known but also admired by most of the people of New Hampshire as well as by many in the new nation. The stern, intellectual, yet compassionate face drawn by John Trumbull in 1790 is similar in quality to those of his contemporaries, with whom he can be listed as one of the Founding Fathers of the United States.

Josiah Bartlett was born in Amesbury, Massachusetts, on 21 November 1729, the last of the seven children of Stephen Bartlett, a shoemaker who lived on the Merrimack River near the ferry landing. Josiah obtained some formal education from the schoolmaster supported by the town, evidence of which appears in his copy book. Kept when he was fourteen years old and dated 1743, this was the earliest item found among his papers. According to his son Levi's memoir, Bartlett early displayed a keen interest in the library and profession of a relative in Amesbury, Dr. Nehemiah Ordway. Financially unable to attend college, Josiah began an apprenticeship under Dr. Ordway about 1747. In 1750, with a few essentials provided by his father, young Dr. Bartlett set out for Kingston, New Hampshire, then a community still relatively near the frontier. Here he hoped to establish a medical practice. The increasing number of entries in his account books, begun in 1750, attests to his success.

He continued to practice medicine—in the very broad eighteenth-century sense of that term—for the next forty years, even while busy in public service. Only a few years after settling in Kingston he was well known for his ability to use quinine, or peruvian bark, and for his application of cooling liquids to temper fever. This latter treatment he apparently used first on himself when, against the orders of his own physician, he persuaded his attendants to give him cool cider instead of warm. To the astonishment of everyone, Bartlett immediately began to recover.

Bartlett augmented his medical income through land transactions, marketing the produce of a small farm and dealing in wood and lumber. His marriage in 1754 to a cousin, Mary Bartlett of Newton, New Hampshire, led to a sizable family. Mary gave birth to twelve children, eight of whom lived to adulthood. (A brief genealogy follows on p. xxiii). As Bartlett's family grew, so did his influence in the community; he was elected a selectman of Kingston for the first time in 1757. Because of his active interest in the settlement of the frontier, he was made an original proprietor in the new towns of Warren and Wentworth. At a later date he purchased rights in Perrystown (now Sutton) and Salisbury.

In 1765 Governor Benning Wentworth commissioned Bartlett a justice of the peace, a natural promotion for an influential man. The commission was reissued by Governor John Wentworth in 1767; he later made Bartlett a lieutenant commander of the seventh regiment of militia. By then Bartlett was a member of the legislature, having been elected to represent Kingston in the spring of 1765. He was continuously reelected until the General Court's dissolution in 1775. His two royal commissions were rescinded in February 1775, apparently in retaliation for the raids on Fort William and Mary, though Bartlett took no direct part in those actions. The factors that prompted Bartlett to side with the Revolutionaries in defiance of British authority are not discussed in his papers. We can conclude, however, that he joined in the view that Parliamentary acts in regard to America were unjust, and that he was outraged by certain British activities in the colonies.

Bartlett cemented his Revolutionary connection by representing Kingston in the extralegal Provincial Congresses during 1774 and 1775. Although unable to accept his selection by the Provincial Congress to represent New Hampshire in the Continental Congress in 1774, Bartlett did accept the appointment the following year and left for Philadelphia in September 1775 with his fellow delegate, John Langdon. There he was among the more active delegates, serving on a multitude of committees, including those on secret correspondence, marine affairs, medicine, clothing, and qualifications of army officers.

The high points of Bartlett's congressional service, as might be expected, were the signing of the Declaration of Independence, in August 1776, and the Articles of Confederation, in July 1778. His letters comment only briefly on the Declaration but enough to show that he was anxious for its adoption by 1776. Some have suggested that Bartlett was the first delegate to sign the Declaration. The available evidence does not settle this question, but it is more likely that he was second, following the bold signature of John Hancock and signing in the lower right corner just as he invariably signed his own correspondence. Bartlett was older than William Whipple, the other New Hampshire delegate then present; and New Hampshire, always given first vote as the northernmost province, was probably allowed to sign before the others, as it did in the case of other congressional documents. We may be fairly certain that Bartlett was the first to vote for independence on 2 July and the first to vote in favor of the draft on 4 July. The signing of the Declaration had to be put off until 2 August, when a Philadelphia engrosser finally presented a fair copy. In addition to Bartlett and Whipple, Dr. Matthew Thornton of Londonderry also signed for New Hampshire, but not until his arrival in Philadelphia in November 1776. As for the Articles of Confederation, Bartlett was a member of the original committee appointed in June 1776 to draft them. He was not in Congress at the time of their adoption in November 1777, but had no qualms about signing them in 1778. He served in Congress throughout 1776 and returned for six months in 1778.

Meanwhile, in New Hampshire, a constitutional form of government was adopted in January 1776. The newly created General Court, consisting of a House of Representatives and an Executive Council, elected Bartlett to the Council and commissioned him a justice of the Inferior Court of Common Pleas for Rockingham County and a colonel in the militia. It also made him a member of the Committee of Safety which had governing power in the state during adjournments of the General Court.

Upon his return from Philadelphia in November 1776, Bartlett immediately entered into these local commitments. He attended meetings of the Executive Council at Exeter, and sessions of the Court of Common Pleas at Exeter in February and July and at Portsmouth in May and November. He also attended the Court of Quarter Sessions, sitting automatically by virtue of his Council seat and judgeship. When not present at Council meetings or Court, Bartlett sat on the Committee of Safety. Its records reveal that he missed few meetings during the war years, and sometimes served as chairman when the health of Chairman Meshech Weare deteriorated.

Bartlett traveled to western New Hampshire, to Hartford, Connecticut, and elsewhere to attend conferences on economic policy or boundary questions on behalf of the state government. In August 1777 he was called upon to attend the wounded from the battle of Bennington. Back in Kingston, he maintained his leadership of the local militia regiment, grappling with the complicated administrative problems which that post entailed. His account books attest that the remainder of his time was spent profitably at home. The War of American Independence demanded great sacrifices from the Bartletts, as from most Americans, in time, energy, and, perhaps, prosperity.

The conclusion of the war in 1781–1782 brought relief from incessant activity. The members of the General Court, recognizing Bartlett's stature in the state, appointed him to the Superior Court, then the state's highest tribunal. The 1784 constitution required that he relinquish his other duties to hold this post, which involved traveling to the five county seats for court sessions each spring and autumn. The Court, established by acts of 1692 and 1699, consisted of a chief justice and three associate justices who heard criminal and civil cases above the value of twenty pounds, and cases relating to land titles. The circuit was a rigorous exercise, even after session dates were consolidated by the terms of a 1785 law recommended and perhaps written by Bartlett. He attended every session for which records exist, and was appointed chief justice in January 1790.

Perhaps this promotion resulted in part from Bartlett's activity at the state convention on the Federal Constitution in February and June 1788. He served as temporary chairman to open the first meeting and then worked for ratification, which was obtained at Concord on 21 June 1788. New Hampshire was the ninth state to ratify. Also to Bartlett's credit in the 1780s was his active membership on a committee appointed by the General Court to settle disputed lands in the Mason Patent. Within six months of his appointment as chief justice, he found himself chief executive of the state. In the spring election of 1790 he allowed his name to be placed on the ballot for president. The populace did not give any candidate a majority, and in fact Bartlett received the third highest number of votes. However, such was his prestige with the General Court that, of the top four candidates, it picked Bartlett.

As president he had limited authority, but conducted the state's affairs cautiously. One of his principal achievements was the chartering of the New Hampshire Medical Society in February 1791. Bartlett thus fulfilled his long-desired goal to bring the medical profession together and establish standards to ensure the quality of medical care given to citizens of New Hampshire. There is evidence in his memoirs that the Society evolved from informal gatherings of area physicians in the Bartlett home for the exchange of ideas and medical experiences. Service as president of the Medical Society from 1791 to 1793 capped his medical career.

Bartlett had urged the revision of the state's 1784 constitution to provide for a stronger executive, and under the leadership of William Plumer such an instrument was written and adopted. The revisions took effect in 1793, with the result that upon his fourth consecutive election Bartlett became the first constitutionally elected New Hampshire chief executive to bear the title of governor.

Josiah Bartlett retired from public life in June 1794. His health had failed steadily since the sudden death of his wife in 1789. He died on 19 May 1795, within twelve months of leaving office.

Bartlett's love of family, friendship with neighbors, respect for colleagues, and faith in God are apparent in his letters. His frugal nature reacted against the high prices of commodities in Philadelphia, and his sound economic policies worked in New Hampshire's behalf in the troubled period of the 1780s and 1790s. The filth left behind in Philadelphia when the British evacuated in 1778 incurred the wrath of Bartlett the physician. His decision to be inoculated against smallpox in 1775 illustrates his ability to accept rational new concepts. His love of country engendered a willingness to tax and to be taxed so that the battle for independence and individual rights could continue. His papers show that he was extremely responsible in the realm of personal finance. He eventually paid his commitments without imposing on his creditors, and accumulated a moderate amount of property, which he dispersed equitably in his will; he advised contemporaries who were experiencing personal financial problems. Bartlett held education in high esteem and saw to it that his children received as much of it as possible. He supported Dartmouth College, from which he received two honorary degrees, and was of help in Jeremy Belknap's attempt to publish New Hampshire's history.

These characteristics have not been forgotten during the intervening two hundred years. Bartlett's native town of Amesbury, Massachusetts, raised a statue to him on 4 July 1888, on which occasion John Greenleaf Whittier composed "One of the Signers." The poem captures the "proud memory" of "the fathers of the Old Thirteen" and begs that we, their heirs, see to it that their "sculptured lips shall not be dumb." Their work, done for the world, continues, and is now being documented permanently through this project and scores of others like it. It is hoped that this volume will help to perpetuate the spirit of honest enthusiasm with which Bartlett and his colleagues pursued liberty and set in motion the new nation. Bartlett will continue to speak, through this volume, through the publication of many of his papers in the *Naval Documents of the American Revolution*, and through his writings now being published as part of the *Letters of Delegates to Congress, 1774–1789.*

This volume cannot reflect Bartlett's tremendous influence on New Hampshire's legal and judicial system, nor can it adequately describe his medical practice or his legislative involvement. The reader is urged to judge Bartlett for himself—from the papers and notes published here and from the papers on microfilm. Additional insights may be gained from a memoir compiled by Levi Bartlett, which is included in the microfilm edition, and from a manuscript biography at the New Hampshire Historical

Society, "Rider for Freedom: Josiah Bartlett, 1729–1795," by Elwin L. Page. Page, an attorney and judge of the state Supreme Court, was long an officer of the Society. An historian by avocation, he published widely in the field of New Hampshire history. So great is the editor's obligation to Judge Page's research on Josiah Bartlett that this volume could be dedicated to no one else.

Family of Josiah and Mary Bartlett

1. MARY: b. 28 Dec. 1754; d. 7 July 1826; m. 12 Mar. 1780 Jonathan Greeley. Children: (1) Mary, b. 1 Apr. 1781; d. 1782; (2) Polly, b. 20 Oct. 1783; (3) Jonathan B., b. 10 July 1785; (4) Josiah, b. 23 Aug. 1789.

2. LOIS: b. 2 June 1756; d. 28 Feb. 1798. Unmarried.

3. MIRIAM: b. 19 June 1758; d. 27 Aug. 1785; m. 28 June 1781 Joseph Calef. Children: (1) Josiah, b. 21 May 1782; (2) Miriam, b. 20 May 1784; (3) Judith, b. —.

4. RHODA: b. 22 May 1760; d. 28 Sept. 1794; m. 22 Feb. 1789 Reuben True. Children: (1) Levi, d. 19 Oct. 1790; (2) Josiah B., d. 1831.

5. HANNAH: b. 31 Aug. 1762; d. 7 Sept. 1762.

6. LEVI: b. 2 Sept. 1763; d. 30 Jan. 1828; m. 1st Sally Hook, who d. with child, Levi, 1793; m. 2nd 18 Apr. 1807 Abigail Stevens. Children: (1) Luella Julietta, b. 30 Dec. 1807; (2) Junia Loretta b. 1 June 1810; (3) Levi Stevens b. 3 Dec. 1811.

7. JOSIAH: b. 20 Aug. 1765; d. 30 Dec. 1765.

8. DOROTHY: b. 9 June 1767, stillborn.

9. JOSIAH: b. 29 Aug. 1769; d. 16 Apr. 1838; m. 1st 1792 Sarah Wingate; 2nd April 1812 Hannah Weeks. No children.

10. EZRA: b. 13 Sept. 1770; d. 5 Dec. 1848; m. 31 Jan. 1799 Hannah Gale. Children: (1) Laura S., b. 20 Oct. 1799; (2) Josiah, b. 1801; d. 1802; (3) Josiah, b. 3 May 1803; (4) Hannah, b. 7 Jan. 1805; (5) Levi, b. 4 Oct. 1806; (6) Mary, b. 23 Aug. 1808; (7) Sarah, b. 23 Apr. 1810; (8) Ezra, b. 28 Sept. 1811; (9) Amos Gilman, b. 14 Jan. 1814; (10) Albert Gallatin, b. 23 May 1815; (11) Stephen Madison b. 22 June 1817.

11. SARAH: b. 29 July 1773; d. 19 Oct. 1847; m. 24 Apr. 1796 Dr. Amos Gale, Jr. Children: (1) Ezra, b. 13 Oct. 1797; (2) Levi, b. 29 Aug. 1800; (3) Josiah, b. 11 Jan. 1803; (4) Amos Gilman, b. 17 Feb. 1807; (5) Stephen Madison, b. 20 Oct. 1809; (6) Sarah Bartlett, b. 5 Sept. 1811; (7) Mary Bartlett, b. 20 Aug. 1815.

12. HANNAH: b. 13 Dec. 1776; d. 17 Apr. 1777.

Editorial Method

The "letterpress" phase of the project called for the printing of only selected items. Selection, seldom a simple task, was made more difficult by the profusion of items that lent themselves to publication. It was quickly determined to print correspondence with a few other items of particular interest. Of the correspondence, that written by Bartlett was first selected and then those letters written to him which were judged to have significant value to the researcher and to be of special interest to the general reader. A few letters were omitted because they have recently been printed in full or are currently being edited and printed elsewhere, such as letters written from the Continental Congress. Enough has been included here, however, to maintain the sense of the correspondence printed. Other correspondence is included in the Calendar, which indicates the general nature and microfilm reference of each item. It is anticipated that researchers having specific interests will refer to the more inclusive microfilm.

The project has generally followed patterns established by ongoing editions of papers of Thomas Jefferson, James Madison, Daniel Webster, and others. General notes or headnotes are interspersed between the texts, especially in chronological gaps or upon significant events, to support the documents. The documents are printed in chronological order, letters by Bartlett being placed ahead of those addressed to him bearing the same date. The date and point of origin are uniformly placed in the top right corner in the style written on the manuscript. The heading is left as on the document, but the complimentary close is run continuously with the last line of text. When a signature exists, it is printed as written.

The text of each document is fully reproduced from the original or the copy closest to the original. Where more than one manuscript copy is cited, the first is the one printed. Copies from printed sources are reproduced exactly, except that the italics in Peter Force's *American Archives* have been omitted. Original spelling has been rigorously followed, with the exception of "ye," which has been transcribed "the" where so intended. Obvious slips of the pen (such as an ungrammatical repetition of a word) have been silently corrected. Names of ships are in italics: all other italics are the writer's unless otherwise indicated. Punctuation has most often been left as it appears, though in a few cases colons and dashes—eighteenth-century devices for breaking continuity—have been silently transcribed as periods. All sentences are begun with a capital letter. Superscripts have been brought down to the line, interlineated material has been transcribed in its intended place, crossed out matter has been omitted or noted where significant, and abbreviations have been left as found except where the modern reader might experience confusion, in which cases the modern form of the abbreviation is rendered.

Square brackets [ ] either enclose material inserted by the editor or indicate damage to or deterioration of the manuscript. Up to five characters have been supplied when absent because of damage and when the writer's intention is obvious. Blanks left by the writer appear as blanks in the volume.

Enclosures are occasionally printed, immediately following the document. Those not printed are cited if known. The descriptive note following each document indicates the type of manuscript, its location, and other pertinent information about the document itself. Addresses and dockets in the usual form are not noted.

Annotation has been kept minimal. It is used to assist in understanding points brought up in the text and as a guide to other sources. Identification of all persons named in the text appears usually upon the first appearance of the name. When the editor has been unable to identify an individual, there is no citation. Bold face type in the index indicates references to identifications. Members of the Continental Congress and the United States Congress are so identified, with the understanding that each is included in the *Biographical Directory of the American Congress.* That source and the *Dictionary of American Biography* are not cited in the annotation. It has seemed appropriate to cite genealogical studies and local histories, which are often the only source of information about an individual. These, as all sources, have been used with care and should be accepted with caution. The term "not printed" refers only to this volume: many Bartlett papers have been printed previously, but limitations on the project prohibited a comprehensive search for and citation of them.

The Bibliography, necessarily selective because of space limitations, gives full citations only to those works cited in this volume. Other sources were consulted, many of which were helpful, although often indirectly, in providing information for the annotation.

Terminology has posed few problems. Unless otherwise indicated, "Committee of Safety" refers to the New Hampshire Committee of Safety; the terms "legislature," "General Court" and "General Assembly" all refer to the New Hampshire legislature; "Superior Court" refers to the New Hampshire Superior Court; and "Court of Common Pleas" refers to the Inferior Court of Common Pleas for Rockingham County. Place names without a state throughout are for places in New Hampshire. State names are supplied for places outside of New Hampshire except for such well-known cities as Boston, New York, Philadelphia, and Annapolis. Names of persons have been transcribed as they appear, sometimes in various forms (e.g., Calef and Calfe; Hoyt, Hoit, and Hoitt; Clap and Clapp).

The abbreviation JB refers to Josiah Bartlett.

Symbols and Abbreviations

The following symbols are used to describe and give the location of each document in the unnumbered note following it. Where more than one descriptive symbol appears, the first describes the document reproduced.

MnHi	Minnesota Historical Society, St. Paul
N	New York State Library, Albany
Nh	New Hampshire State Library, Concord
Nh-Ar	New Hampshire Division of Records Management and Archives, Concord
NhD	Dartmouth College, Baker Library, Hanover, N.H.
NhExP	Philips Exeter Academy, Exeter, N.H.
NhHi	New Hampshire Historical Society, Concord. Also NHHS.
NHi	New York Historical Society, New York City
NN	New York Public Library, Astor, Lenox, and Tilden Foundations, Manuscript Division, New York City
NNPM	Pierpont Morgan Library, New York City
OCHi	Cincinnati Historical Society, Cincinnati, Ohio
OClWHi	Western Reserve Historical Society, Cleveland, Ohio
PHC	Haverford College Library, Haverford, Pa.
PHi	Historical Society of Pennsylvania, Philadelphia
PP	Free Library of Philadelphia
PPAmP	American Philosophical Society, Philadelphia
PPL	Library Company of Philadelphia
R-Ar	Rhode Island State Archives, Providence
RHi	Rhode Island Historical Society, Providence
RPJCB	The John Carter Brown Library, Brown University, Providence, R.I.
VtHi	Vermont Historical Society, Montpelier

ABBREVIATIONS

BDEB	Sobel, Robert, ed. *Biographical Directory of the United States Executive Branch, 1774–1791.* Westport, Conn.: Greenwood Publishing Co., 1971.
DNB	Stephen, Leslie, et al., eds. *Dictionary of National Biography.* 63 vols. + 7 supplements. New York: Macmillan and Co., 1885–1971.
JCC	Ford, Worthington C., et al., eds. *Journals of the Continental Congress, 1774–1789.* 34 vols. Washington, D.C.: Government Printing Office, 1904–1937.
MJB	"The Papers of Josiah Bartlett." Microfilm, 7 rolls. New Hampshire Historical Society, 1976. [See *Guide to the Microfilm Edition of the Papers of Josiah Bartlett (1729–1795),* Edited by Frank C. Mevers. Concord: New Hampshire Historical Society, 1976.]
NDAR	Clark, William B., and Morgan, William J., eds. *Naval Documents of the American Revolution.* 7 vols. to date. Washington, D.C.: Government Printing Office, 1964– .

NEHGR   *New England Historical and Genealogical Register.* 131 vols. to date. 1847– .

NHGR   *New Hampshire Genealogical Record.* 7 vols. 1903–1910.

NHHS   New Hampshire Historical Society.

NHSP   Bouton, Nathaniel, et al., eds. *Documents and Records Relating to New Hampshire.* 40 vols. Concord and Manchester, 1867–1940. [New Hampshire State Papers.]

PCC   Papers of the Continental Congress. DNA.

RG   Record Group.

WGW   Fitzpatrick, John C., ed. *The Writings of George Washington from the Original Manuscript Sources, 1745–1799.* 39 vols. Washington: Government Printing Office, 1931–1944.

Josiah Bartlett Chronology 1729–1795

1729

November 21   Born in Amesbury, Mass., seventh and youngest child of Deacon Stephen and Hannah (Webster) Bartlett.

1745

Apprenticed to study medicine with Dr. Nehemiah Ordway of Amesbury.

1750

Settled in Kingston, N.H., to practice medicine.

1751

October 15   Purchased twelve acres and house from Thomas Turner.

1754

January 15   Married his cousin Mary Bartlett of Newton, N.H., daughter of Joseph and Sarah (Hoyt) Bartlett.

1757

March   Elected selectman of Kingston; reelected 1761, 1764, 1768, 1769, 1773, 1774.

1763

July 14   Named as an original grantee of Warren, N.H. Was also a grantee of Sudbury, Vt., and Wentworth, N.H., and a proprietor in Salisbury and Perrystown (now Sutton), N.H.

1765

Commissioned justice of the peace by Gov. Benning Wentworth.

May 21–
July 4   Served as member from Kingston in N.H. legislature. Subsequently reelected, he attended all sessions until Gov. John Wentworth prorogued the General Assembly in September 1775.

June 25   Entered into three-year partnership with Dr. Amos Gale for medical practice in Kingston.

1767

July 2
Gov. John Wentworth assumed office and addressed House of Representatives.

September 3
Appointed to legislative committee to review and propose method of regulation of province laws.

September 30
Appointed justice of the peace by Gov. Wentworth.

1770

March 23
Appointed to legislative committee to establish an equitable method of taxation.

November 11
Commissioned lieutenant colonel of 7th militia regiment—Kingston, East Kingston, Hawke (now Danville), Sandown, Hampstead, Salem, Plaistow, Atkinson, Newton. Jonathan Greeley was colonel, Jacob Gale, major.

1774

January 14
On legislative committee to examine expired laws.

February 27
House in Kingston burned.

May 28
Appointed to legislative committee on correspondence. Legislature concerned about closing port of Boston.

July 21
Attended First Provincial Congress, Exeter. On committee to draft instructions to delegates to First Continental Congress.

December 14
Raid on Fort William and Mary, Portsmouth harbor. JB did not take direct part, but alerted militia after learning that attack had been carried out.

1775

January 25
Second Provincial Congress met. JB on committee to call another when necessary and on committee of correspondence.

February 22
Dismissed from offices of justice of the peace and lieutenant colonel of militia.

April 21–
May 2
Third Provincial Congress met in response to clashes at Lexington and Concord, Mass. JB on committee to draft answer to a letter from Massachusetts Congress.

May 4–6
General Assembly met, Portsmouth. JB on committee to draft answer to governor's speech.

May 17–
June 10
Fourth Provincial Congress met, Exeter. JB appointed to Committee of Safety on which he served until 1784.

June 27– July 7	Provincial Congress met, Exeter. JB on committee to plan for emission of paper money.
July 11, 14, 17, 18	General Assembly met for last time, Portsmouth. JB on committee *re* treasurer's accounts and governor's message.
August 22– September 2	Provincial Congress met, Exeter. JB elected delegate to Continental Congress; put on committee to draft instructions to delegates; appointed colonel of 7th militia regiment.
September 4	Left Kingston for Continental Congress.
September 15	Arrived at Philadelphia; served in Congress to March 18, 1776. Sat on Secret Committee and other standing and temporary committees.

1776

January 5	New Hampshire adopted a constitution providing for a house of representatives which was to elect a council of 12 members. The house and council legislated simultaneously as the General Court.
January 6–27	First General Court met, Exeter. JB appointed to Congress for coming year; elected member of Council, reappointed colonel of 7th militia regiment, and commissioned justice of Court of Common Pleas for Rockingham County, *in absentia*. Served as justice of Court of Common Pleas until 1782, on Council until 1784.
February 29	Credentials of reappointment read in Congress.
March 18	Left Philadelphia on leave of absence; in Kingston March 28 to c. May 7.
May 17	Arrived in Philadelphia; in Congress to October 26.
June 12	On committee to draft form of confederation.
July 2	Voted with Congress to declare independence.
July 4	Voted with Congress to accept draft of Declaration.
August 2	Signed engrossed copy of Declaration of Independence.
October 26– November 9	Journeyed from Philadelphia to Kingston.
December 16	Mustered 7th militia regiment; prepared men to march to Rhode Island.

December 23	Elected to Congress. Declined in March 1777.
December 25– January 2	Attended conference at Providence on military and economic policies for New England.

1777

January 15	New Hampshire Grants declared themselves to be independent state of New Connecticut.
February 13	JB with committee to settle grievances in Grafton County, met with 28 delegates from 12 towns at Lebanon. Committee left Exeter on January 28.
July 30– August 5	With Nathaniel Peabody attended currency conference at Springfield, Mass.
August 23	Ordered, with Peabody, to attend those wounded at Battle of Bennington.
September 18	Chaired legislative committee on tax reapportionment.
November 11, 13	Chaired legislative committees on state tax and grievances of towns in Grafton County.

1778

February 24	Chaired legislative committee of the whole to debate Articles of Confederation. House approved Articles on March 4.
March 12	Appointed delegate to Congress; asked to be excused; motion denied.
May 21	Presented credentials to Congress, York, Pa.
June 10	Elected *in absentia* by Kingston as delegate to state constitutional convention.
July 2	Followed Congress from York to Philadelphia.
July 9	Signed Articles of Confederation as adopted November 15, 1777.
August 14	Appointed *in absentia* as delegate to Congress for following year. Later declined.
October 31	Granted leave of absence by Congress; left Philadelphia November 3, arrived Kingston 16th.
November 21–25	Chaired legislative committee to reactivate courts of Cheshire County. On committee to name Loyalists whose estates should be confiscated.

1779

March 16	Resigned as colonel of 7th militia regiment.
April 2	Submitted legislative committee report on New Hampshire Grants.
June 5	Attended constitutional convention at Concord. On committee to print and distribute proposed constitution.
October 20–November 2	Attended economic convention at Hartford, Ct.

1780

March 15	On legislative committee to consider sale of Gov. John Wentworth's estate.
June 22	Appointed by Committee of Safety to muster soldiers at Kingston.

1781

October 19	Cornwallis surrendered at Yorktown, Va. War effort slackened.

1782

March 19	Chaired committee on courts in Grafton County.
November 14	Appointed justice of Superior Court. Served until 1790.

1783

January 20	Preliminary Articles of Peace signed at Versailles.
February 26	Appointed delegate to Congress. Declined.
June 20	As chairman of Committee of Safety signed *An Address to the People of New Hampshire concerning charges of war and changes in the 8th Article of Confederation.*

1784

June 2	New state constitution took effect providing for separation of legislative, executive, and judicial branches. As a judge JB had to relinquish his Council seat. He kept closely in touch with the work of the legislature but never again served in it.
June 2–15	First General Court met at Concord. JB attended as senior member of preceding Council, presided over

the first meeting, and swore in new senators and representatives.

June 12   Served with Samuel Livermore and John Sullivan on committee to revise state laws.

1785
February 24   Served with legislative committee to examine accounts of treasurer, board of war, and collector of rum tax.

June 4   Received 720 votes for president of N.H. of 7,079 votes cast.

1787
January 16   Agreed to serve with committee to establish the Masonian line and ascertain what waste lands belonged to state. Reported for committee June 6.

June 7   Received 628 votes for president of 9,285 cast.

1788
February 13–22   Federal Constitutional Convention met at Exeter. JB chosen temporary chairman.

June 18–21   Federal Constitutional Convention met at Concord. JB on committee to consider articles to be prepared as amendments.

November 12   Elected to U.S. Senate. Declined.

1789
June 4   Received 968 votes for president of 8,534 cast.

July 14   Mary Bartlett died at Kingston.

July 16   Received nomination for chief justice.

1790
January 18   Received appointment as chief justice of Superior Court.

June 3   Received 1,676 votes for presidency; 7,762 votes cast; no majority.

June 5   Elected by Senate as President of New Hampshire. Delivered acceptance address and took oath of office June 8. Delivered inaugural address June 9.

June 16   Town of Bartlett, N.H., incorporated. Named for JB.

July 1	Notified that as Presdient he was ex officio trustee of Dartmouth College.
July 7, 8	Meeting of President and Council, Kingston. John Pickering appointed Chief Justice.
August	Awarded honorary A.M. degree by Dartmouth.

1791

January 6	Recommended legislation to General Court.
February 16	New Hampshire Medical Society incorporated. JB elected president.
June 2	Elected President by popular vote of 8,679. Gave inaugural address June 3.

1792

June 8	Elected President with 8,092 votes. Gave inaugural address June 9.
August	Awarded honorary M.D. degree by Dartmouth.
September 5–6	Constitutional convention met at Concord, approved revised Constitution providing for office of Governor.
November 23	Appointed elector for U.S. President and Vice President.

1793

June 6	Received 7,388 votes of 9,854 cast for Governor. Took oath of office as first Governor of New Hampshire June 7, delivered inaugural address June 8.
June 19	Resigned as president of New Hampshire Medical Society.
September 27	Elected member of Massachusetts Agricultural Society.

1794

January 29	Notified General Court of his wish to retire in June.
February 7	Sent letter of resignation to House.
February 21	General Court accepted JB's resignation.

1795

May 19	Died in Kingston.

One of the Signers

by John Greenleaf Whittier

O Storied vale of Merrimac,
    Rejoice through all thy shade and shine,
And from his century's sleep call back
    A brave and honored son of thine.

Unveil his effigy between
    The living and the dead to-day;
The fathers of the Old Thirteen
    Shall witness bear as spirits may.

    .   .   .   .

Be thine henceforth a pride of place
    Beyond thy namesake's over-sea,
Where scarce a stone is left to trace
    The Holy House of Amesbury.

    .   .   .   .

Among those picked and chosen men
    Than his, who here first drew his breath,
No firmer fingers held the pen
    Which wrote for liberty or death.

Not for their hearths and homes alone,
    But for the world their work was done:
On all the winds their thought has flown
    Through all the circuit of the sun.

    .   .   .   .

O hills that watched his boyhood's home,
    O earth and air that nursed him, give,
In this memorial semblance, room
    To him who shall its bronze outlive!

And thou, O Land he loved, rejoice
    That in the countless years to come,
Whenever Freedom needs a voice,
    These sculptured lips shall not be dumb!

Written for the dedication of the Bartlett statue
at Amesbury, Massachusetts, 4 July 1888.

The Papers of Josiah Bartlett

The earliest of JB's extant papers is a school copy book dated 1743 when he would have been a boy of fourteen in Amesbury. MJB 1. There is nothing further until he had moved to Kingston and was setting up a medical practice according to training received from Dr. Nehemiah Ordway. In these early years the papers deal with the purchase of drugs and materials. As a selectman and justice of the peace JB witnessed several deeds and signed several public papers. See MJB.

FROM HANAH KENT[1]

DOCT. BARTLETT

Sir   Newbury May 15 1751

I Recd yours and am dermind to take Hampshir mony dd[2] in yr province. If you will keep it till I send for it or if I shod order any into your hands shall be obligd to you if you will take care of it for me but I must charge you something dearer for Medsins in that mony which I hope you will be willing to allow. I am sir yr obligd friend & humle servt.   Hanah Kent

4 oz. Bacci lau	@ 1/5------0	6	0
4 oz. curama	@ 2/6------	10	
4 oz. gention	@ 1/6------	6	
1 oz. slo sal Amm[3]	------	6	
2 oz. spice	1/6------	3	
	viol----------------	1	6
		1 12	6

RC (Mr. and Mrs. Rodney M. Wilson, Kingston, N.H., 1975).

1. Hanah Kent (c. 1691–1758) was the widow and apparent business successor of merchant Richard Kent (d. 1740) of Newbury, Mass. Briggs, *Kent Genealogies*, 249.

2. Delivered *or* upon delivery.

3. Bacci laurus (laurel berries), used as a sedative for nerves; curcuma (tumeric), used as a stimulant and for treatment of jaundice; gentian, used to treat dyspepsia; sal ammoniac (ammonium chloride), still being used as a diuretic.

FROM JOSEPH MANNING[1]

DOCT. BARTLET SR   Ipswich Sept the 23d 1751

I have Sent Some Medicines by My Son. I would Acquaint that if any of them Suite you you Shall be welcome to have them and pay in merchantable Goods at any landing in almsbury[2] And any other article that I can Serve you in which is all from your friend and humble Servant.

Joseph Manning

RC (Mr. and Mrs. Rodney M. Wilson, Kingston, N.H., 1975).

1. Joseph Manning (1704–1784) graduated from Harvard in 1725. He practiced medicine and conducted business from his home and wharf in Ipswich, Mass.

Shipton, *Harvard Graduates*, 7:544–45; Waters, *Ipswich*, 1:458; 2:269.

2. Amesbury, Massachusetts.

TO [AMOS TOPPAN?]

Sir   Kingston, February the   1760[1]

These Lines Comes with my Good will & Respects hoping they will find you well as by GODs Goodness I & mine are at this time. As to our Parish affairs we seem very much Devided Since you Left us, what method to take in order to settle a minister Peaceably among us. Many People being unwilling to Lay aside the Tho'ts of your Setling with us they Think that your Settlement with us is the Likeliest way to Unite us, as we were so well United in you & the Settlement was the only Stick with the most of the opposers and as it appears that the Greater Part of that would be Paid by Private subscriptions So Could they Know that there was a Probability; Your affairs would be Bro't on again, with as much or more Zeal than Before, or on the Contrary that you are Engaged or fully Resolved not settle with us the minds of your friends (as I may Call them) would be turned some other way & so a Greater Likelihood of uniting in some other man than there is at Present. And if sir you would Do me the Pleasure to write a Line wither it is best to Carry matters any farther upon that Head you would Do an acceptable Piece of service to the Parish in General as well as to your friend & Humble Servant

Josiah Bartlett

P.S. If what you should write you should think not proper to be shewn openly to others, your orders therein shall be Complied with & Please to Let this Letter Remain with you alone at Present.

Draft (Mr. and Mrs. Rodney M. Wilson, Kingston, N.H., 1975).

1. The year 1760 was added at a later date by JB and should be 1762. Following the death of the Reverend Joseph Secombe of Kingston in September 1760, a committee of the town invited a number of recent Harvard graduates (including William Pike, John Treadwell, Thomas Rice, Paul Coffin, Samuel Cotton, and Jonathan Livermore) to preach. Job Whitney (d. 13 June 1761) received a call, but declined. In March 1761 JB was elected selectman and wrote the call to Amos Toppan (1735–1771) of Newbury, Mass., on 8 Feb. 1762. On 19 April Toppan accepted the call, and he was ordained on 18 Aug. 1762. Kingston Town Records, 2:121, 125–27, 150, 155; 3:92–98; Kingston Church Records, 1725–1844, 97; Shipton, *Harvard Graduates*, 14:74–77, 196, 346–51, 365–66, 403–10, 648–49.

FROM WILLIAM PARKER[1]

Sir   Portsmouth, Feb. 16th 1762

As to the Case of the Young Woman which you put, So far as She has proceeded Seems to be right, but all this will not Oblige the Man to pay a farthing, unless She proceeds to Conviction of the Man at Court, So far as to Obtain Sentence against him as the Putative Father. All that has been done is only preparative to that, & if it rests here, there can be no fruit of it. As the Child lived So Short a time, the Charge cant be very great, it may be worth while to Consider it in a Prudential View, as any party at Law always Spends more than is Recoverd in the Cost, whether she had best proceed or not, for Such Small Damages as its likely she woud Recover now. For you must note, that in these Cases, where a Man is Convicted, he is to Hand Chargd with the Maintenance, with the Assistance of the Mother, Says the Law.[2] Therefore the Man is Adjudgd Generally to pay only half what is Supposd to be a Competent Support & Consequently as to the Damages past, he will be Sentenc'd if Convicted to pay half, which will Enable her to Judge, whether it is not better to pay the whole herself, which She is Obligd to if able, than to take the trouble of proceeding, or if she is not able, whether the Town which must bear the Charge in that Case, had best assist her in the prosecution for what is like to be Recoverd.

As to your 2d Case. A man coming into a Town & living there three Months, without Warning gains a Settlement. That warning–which was given (if any) being Suspended three Months, is as if there had been none. But a Warning given Returnd to the Court as the Law Directs, and Renewd once in three Months, will Prevent a Man from being a Legal Inhabitant, that is from gaining a Settlement, & Save the Town from the Charge of his Support notwithstanding his Residence.[3] Now you may as well Rate a Man of another Town at 50 Miles Distance, as one *in the Town*, whom you have Excluded from becoming an Inhabitant, tho' he may Reside there, & it woud be an hard Case to Subject a Man to the burden, & deny him the benefit of being a Inhabitant. In Short you have nothing to do with one You warn out of Town, while that warning Operates. All that is here Said is meant of One who has no Estate in the Town. I am Sir Your most Humble Servt. William Parker

RC (Mr. and Mrs. Rodney M. Wilson, Kingston, N.H., 1975).

1. William Parker (1703–1781), a Portsmouth attorney, was register of probate for Rockingham County prior to the Revolution. He served also as a surrogate judge of admiralty, as a representative to the General Court, 1764–1775, and as an associate justice on the Superior Court, 1771–1775. Attacks of gout limited his activity after 1775. Bell, *Bench and Bar*, 26–28.

2. See "An Act for the Punishment of Criminall Offenders," passed 14 June 1701, in *Laws of N.H.*, 1:677–78 .

3. See "An Act for Regulating Townships, Choice of Town Officers & Setting Forth Their Power," passed 2 May 1719, ibid., 2:340–45.

FROM DANIEL ROGERS[1]

Sir   Portsmo. 14 Sept. 1762

I rec'd yours of this date and agreable to your request have sent the Articles wrote for: the Bill pbl. on the other side which wish safe to hand & Content. From yr Obliged hl. sevt. Danl Rogers

[Bill on reverse side]
Doct. Josiah Bartlet

Portsmo 14 Septr. 1762

Bot of Danl Rogers

Viz. 3 3/4 oz. Sp. Lavand[2]	£ 1:10:00	
4 1/4 oz. Sal Ammon	1:14:00	
1 1/4 oz. Ol Anisi[3]	3:02:06	
1 oz. Rad Rhis[4]	1:15:00	
4 oz. Rad Salopii[5]	2:05:00	
4 oz. G. Cambog[6]	3:04:00	
2 oz. Pulv Ipecaeuanh[7]	5:00:00	
1/2 lb. Flor Sulph[8]	10:00	
1 Doz. Phials	2:00:00	
3 Doz. Corks	7:06	
1/2 lb. G. Aloes Shepert[9]	3:00:00	
4 oz. Rad Curcum	15:00	
1/2 lb. Gentian[10]	12:00	
2 oz. Cort. Aurantior[11]	10.00	
Glasses	12.00	

Ol Tenor £ 26.17.00

RC (Mr. and Mrs. Rodney M. Wilson, Kingston, N.H., 1975). In addition to assistance from J. Worth Estes, M.D., reference was made to *Steadman's Medical Dictionary*, 21st ed. (Baltimore, 1966), for identification of drugs.

1. Daniel Rogers (1715–1795), an apothecary of Portsmouth, was referred to as "Dr. Daniel Rogers" in his obituary. Agnes Bartlett, "Portsmouth Families"; *N.H. Gazette*, 20 Oct. 1795.

2. Spirits of Lavandula (lavender), used as a perfume or poultice.

3. Oil of Anise, used to prevent passing of wind.

4. Radix Rhus (sumac root), used to treat urinary incontinence.

5. Radix Salopii (root of a species of orchid from Turkey), used to soften stools.

6. Gum Cambogia, a cathartic made from gum resin grown in Cambodia and the East Indies.

7. Pulverized Ipecachuanha (ipecac), a potent emetic.

8. Flor Sulphur (flowers of sulfur, or evaporated sulfur), used as a cathartic, for skin conditions, and for arthritides.

9. Gum Aloes Shepert. Aloes was used as a cathartic and for treating worms. "Shepert" probably refers to a species or preparation which is not readily identifiable.

10. Curcuma and Gentian are identified in Hanah Kent to JB, 15 May 1751.

11. Cortex Aurantius (orange peel), used as a flavoring.

FROM JOSIAH GILMAN [1]

Sr.

Exeter Nov. 26. 1762

I have sent Your things all but the Mace and not so much of Ol Tereb.[2] that being made in this Country did not Import it, but shall soon have more. Was forct to use boxes instead of Gally-potts not being Yet supplyd. They write me from England that some things are Just now very dear occasioned by Scarcity of them as Opium Cantharides Cort. Peru[3] Croc Ang. & some other things but shall Charge my things as low as possibly I can in order to make quick sale ·& should take it as a favour if You would Encourage Others as you may have Oppertunity to trade with me as I am Newly beginning. I have the prices they are sold in Boston & will sell as cheap as they do there for their sort of money & hoping you will receive your things Safe. I remain Your Humbl. Servt.

Josiah Gilman

RC (Mr. and Mrs. Rodney M. Wilson, Kingston, N.H., 1975).

1. Josiah Gilman (1740–1801), a merchant of Exeter, served in the militia and as a justice of the peace. Gilman, *Gilman Family*, 92.

2. Mace, a spice of the dried outer covering of the nutmeg. "Ol Tereb," turpentine oil.

3. Cantharides, the pharmaceutical name of the dried beetle or Spanish Fly. Cort. Peru, peruvian bark or quinine.

The following articles of agreement between Bartlett and Amos Gale (1744–1813) possibly represent the first contractual medical partnership in American history. Bartlett, having been elected to represent Kingston in the General Court in the spring of 1765, felt an obligation to provide medical care for his patients. His confidence in Gale arose from Gale's apprenticeship under Bartlett in the early 1760s and from Gale's intimate knowledge of the Kingston community. Eventually Gale's son, Amos Gale, Jr., married Sarah Bartlett, one of JB's daughters. NEHGR, 1:97; Gale, Gale Family, 205–06. The account book covering the three-year partnership is in the collections of NhHi and is reproduced on MJB 4564–4732.

ARTICLES OF AGREEMENT BETWEEN
DRS. BARTLETT AND GALE

This Indenture, made the 25 Day of June in the fifth Year of the Reign of our Sovereign Lord George the third by the Grace of God of Great-Britain France & Ireland King Defender of the Faith &c. Annoque Domini 1765 Between Josiah Bartlett of Kingston in the Province of New Hampshire Esqr. of the one Part, & Amos Gale of said Kingston Physician of the other part Witnesseth that the said Bartlett & Gale having had experience of each others Care & Fidelity & in Confidence thereof have agreed upon a Copartnership in Carrying on the Practice of Physic & Surgery & therefore Each of them Respectively & for their several & Respective Executors & Administrators Doth Covenant promise & agree to & with the other of them his Executors & Administrators by these Presents That from & after the Day of the Date hereof they the said Bartlett & Gale shall & will be & Continue Copartners in the said Practice of the Arts & Mysteries of Physic & Surgery & all things incident thereunto for & during the Term of Three years thence forth to be fully Compleat & Ended if they shall Both so long live, And to that End each of the said Parties doth Covenant Promise & agree with the other of them in manner following, that is, that the said Bartlett shall & will at his own Cost & Charge find provide & procure two third parts of all such medicines drugs materials & things (excepting Instruments which each shall find for himself) that is or shall be necessary for the practice aforsaid Seasonably & in such Quantities as shall best serve the Jointly Interest in said Practice & the said Gale at his own Cost & Charge shall & will in like manner find & provide the other third part & that they will Each of them use apply & Employ the same honestly for the Good of each of their Patients & the partnership & jointly Interest aforsaid—& that they shall & will be just & true & faithfull to each other in all their Buyings Sellings Accounts Reckonings Disbursements & Dealings Concerning the said Copartnership & Shall each of them as far as is in their power endeavour to promote the Interest of the same by all just Care & Attendance on the said Practice. And that the said Bartlett his Executors or Administrators shall have the full Right & property of in & unto two third parts of the said Jointly Stock of medicines Drugs & other things belonging to the said Copartnership & also of in & unto two third parts of all the Gains Profits & Increase which shall arise happen accrue or be made thereby or by the ordering or Employing of the same or by any Business by them Done as Copartners & shall bear & pay two thirds of all Losses Costs Expences & damages which shall happen arise come be Expended or laid out in about or concerning the Joint Practice & Copartnership aforsaid in any Wise whatsoever. And that the said Gale in like manner shall be Interested & Suffer in one third Part thereof. That fitting & Convenient Books shall be kept wherin shall be faithfully entered all accounts relative to the said Copartnership of which said Books the said parties & Either of them their Executors or Administrators shall freely at all times as well During the Continuance of the said Partnership as afterwards have the sight & Perusal when & as often as it shall be desired & shall have liberty to Copy out all & any Part thereof without let hindrance or Denial. Also that notice shall be given by the said parties Respectively of all sum & sums of money & other things that each of them shall receive on account of the said practice unto the other of them & all such sum & sums of money & other things that each of them shall receive take & apply to his own Particular Use shall be fairly entered in an account to be thereof Kept in the Books aforsaid. And the said Parties shall & will once every year yearly & if either Desire the same once every six months from the Date hereof reckon adjust & settle the said account of all monies & other things which each of the said parties shall have had received & taken belonging to the said Joint Practice & arising & growing thereby to the End that each of them may have his full proportion in manner as aforsaid.

And that neither of the said Parties shall contract any Debt for any matter or thing whatever upon the Credit of the said Copartnership. And that if either of the said parties shall at any time during the Continuance of said Copartnership be absent out of Town upon other than the Business of said Copartnership, the person so absent shall for each Days absence become Indebted to said Company in the sum of two shillings Proclamation money & enter the same in the Books accordingly. And neither of the said Parties to these Presents without the Consent of the other shall release or Discharge any debt duty sum or sums of money or other things which shall be Due owing & belonging to the said Jointly Accompt or any part thereof but only so much as Shall be actually Received nor shall Compound or agree to receive any part for the whole. And it is further agreed by & Between the said Parties to these Presents & it is hereby declared to be their true Intent & meaning that if either of the said Parties shall die During the Continuance of the said Copartnership yet Nevertheless no Benefit of Survivorship shall accrue unto or be had or taken by the Survivor of them in any wise whatsoever but the full part of the ready money stock Debts & Effects things whatsoever belonging to the said Copartnership shall Come & be to the Executor or Administrator of the party who shall so Decease or to such person or persons as he shall dispose thereof to & the other part thereof to the Survivor in the proportion before mentioned. And it is further agreed by & between the said parties that within Forty Days next after the End & Determination of the said Copartnership if both the said parties shall be living a final account Partition & Division shall be made by & between the said Copartners for & Concerning all such money stock & effects as they shall then have in Possession or in the hand of them & each of them belonging to the joint Interest & Copartnership & all out standing Debts then Due to them as Copartners shall be Collected in the name of the said Copartners Divided & Settled in said proportion between them as such debts shall be recovered & received & all losses by bad Debts or otherwise shall be sustained by them in the Proportion aformentioned. For the well & true Performance of the above articles the Parties to these Presents Do bind themselves & their heirs &c. Each to the other in Witness whereof they have hereunto interchangeable set their hands & seals the 25th Day of June 1765 first mentioned.

Signed Sealed & Delivered   Amos Gale
In Presence of
Peter Abbot
Jonathan Hutchinson

 MS (Mr. and Mrs. Rodney M. Wilson, Kingston, N.H., 1975). Written and signed by Gale.

FROM JOHN WENTWORTH[1]

Sirs,   Portsmouth October 15th: 1773.

I am to request of you, an exact List of the inhabitants of the Town of Kingston distinguish'd into different Ranks or Classes, according to the Schedule on the other side; which I shall be glad to have return'd to me, authenticated; as soon as possible.[2]   J Wentworth

RC (DLC: Peter Force Papers). Addressed to the selectmen of Kingston. Franked: "(On his Majestys Service)."

1. John Wentworth (1737–1820) followed his uncle, Benning Wentworth, as royal governor of New Hamphire in 1767. In June 1775, unable to stem the tide of popular sentiment against British authority, he retreated to the protection of Fort William and Mary until August when he left the province for Boston, returning in September to the Isles of Shoals to issue a proclamation proroguing the General Court. From 1778 to 1783 he resided in London. He returned to Halifax in 1783 where he served as surveyor-general of the King's woods and then as

lieutenant governor. He died in Halifax on 8 April 1820. John Wentworth was a son of Mark Hunking Wentworth of Portsmouth, N.H., and should not be confused with his cousin, John Wentworth, Jr., who achieved influence with the Revolutionary faction of New Hampshire. Wentworth, *Genealogy*, 1:536–50. See also Mayo, *John Wentworth*, and Wilderson, "Protagonist of Prudence."

2. The census signed by selectmen JB and John Wadleigh shows a population of 989. MJB 501. Printed in *NHSP*, 10: 626.

FROM WENTWORTH CHESWILL[1]

Sir,   New Markett 19th May 1774

Your Friend Mr. John Burleigh[2] sends you gratis a Box, Containing

1 m 20d Nails	1 Stock Lock
2 m 10d. do.	1 Brass Knob Lock
2 m 6d. do.	1 Pulback Lock
6 m 4d do.	4 Yds. Hollon[3]
2 m Brads	

By his direction I have sent them to Colo. Saml. Folsom's[4] at Exeter, where please to send for them. I wish them safe to Hand & am Sir in Mr. Burleighs behalf Your most obt. Humbl. Servt.   Wentworth Cheswill

RC (MiU-C). Note with address: "leave it at Col. S. Folsoms, Exeter."

1. Wentworth Cheswill (1746–1817), a successful merchant of Newmarket, had been educated at Dummer Academy. He was also a noted scrivener. George, *Old Newmarket*, 55–57.

2. John Burleigh (1717–1776), a native of Ipswich, Mass., was a selectman of Newmarket in 1765. He had served with JB in the House of Representatives in 1765, 1767, and 1770. Burleigh, *Burleigh Family*, 14–15; George, *Old Newmarket*, 21–22; *NHSP*, 7:60, 105, 149, 239, 240.

3. In February 1774 fire destroyed JB's house. He rebuilt it during the summer and fall and was therefore forced to decline appointment by the provincial congress to represent New Hampshire in the First Continental Congress.

4. Samuel Folsom (1732–1790), an innkeeper in Exeter, like his brother, Gen. Nathaniel Folsom, was active in the Revolutionary affairs of Exeter. Folsom, *Genealogy*, 1:113–15.

JB continued to represent Kingston in both the General Assembly and the provincial congresses during 1774 in spite of the extra burden imposed by the necessity of rebuilding his house. On 28 May he was appointed with John Wentworth, Samuel Cutts, John Giddinge, Clement March, Henry Prescott, and John Pickering to a committee of correspondence for the House. This committee carried on some business after Gov. John Wentworth dissolved the Assembly on 8 July 1774, leaving the province without a legitimate legislature until a new one convened on 4 May 1775. NHSP, 7:366–71.

FROM JOHN PICKERING[1]

Sir   Portsmo. June 21st 1774

In Consequence of letters of the greatest importence from our Sister Colonies, proposing a Congress of Deputies from the Colonies, friday next is appointed, for the Committee of Correspondence for the House of Representatives to meet at Capt. Tiltons in this Town,[2] four O Clock P.M: as the Matters then to be considered and determined by the Committee are very enteresting & Momentous, it is hoped that every Member will be very punctual in his Attendence.[3] By Order of the Committee.

John Pickering Ju.

RC (PPAmP). In clerk's hand.

1. John Pickering (c. 1738–1805), an attorney, graduated from Harvard in 1761 and settled in Portsmouth in 1771. He was a state legislator, chief justice of the Superior Court, and a judge on the U.S. District Court beginning in 1795. Shipton, *Harvard Graduates*, 15:91–96.

2. Jacob Tilton (1734–1776) kept an inn "At the sign of the Marquis of Rockingham" in Portsmouth. Tilton, *His-*

tory, 1, no. 8, 244–45; Scott, "Colonial Innkeepers," 21, 43.

3. On 21 July 1774 eighty-five men met at Exeter as New Hampshire's first provincial congress. They elected John Sullivan and Nathaniel Folsom to attend the intercolonial congress at Philadelphia that September. JB and Pickering helped draft instructions for the delegates. *NHSP*, 7:407–08.

During the remainder of 1774 JB tended to local business as a justice of the peace. He was on the Kingston committee that sent one hundred sheep as a gesture of sympathy to Boston in September (MJB 553). In December, in reaction to news that the British were sending reinforcements to Fort William and Mary in Portsmouth harbor, four hundred citizens captured the garrison, defended only by Capt. John Cochran and a contingent of five men. Parsons, "The Capture of Fort William and Mary," 18–47; and Wilderson, "Raids on Fort William and Mary," 178–202.

TO THE CITIZENS OF SANDOWN

Gentlemen   Kingstown December 15th 1774

Last Night about Eleven of the Clock I Received a Letter by Express from the Committe of Correspondance at Exeter[1] informing that it was Expected that the Regulars would forthwith take Possession of the Fort at Portsmouth in which there is a large Quantity of Powder & other military Stores. The Town of Portsmouth have notified the Neighbouring Towns. Exeter was to be Ready to go to their Assistance this morning. This Town & the East parish are meeting to Consult upon the Occasion. As it is a matter of the utmost importance I Should think it would be best to Consult on the affair among yourselves. I am in haste your Humble Servt. Josiah Bartlett

To Jethro Sanborn Esqr.   Collins Mr. Moses Hook[2]
 Capt. Sleeper Capt. Joseph   and any & every of the
 Tilton Lt. Sanborn Ensign   Inhabitants of Sandown

RC (NhHi). Addressed "To Capt. Joseph Tilton, Lieut. Samuel Sanborn, or Mr. Moses Hook in Sandown."

1. Letter not found.

2. Jethro Sanborn (1738–1811), moderator of the town meeting, David Sleeper (1721–1780), Joseph Tilton (1710-1777), Samuel Sanborn (b. 1730), Robert Collins (b. 1733), and Moses Hook (1737–1796) appear to have been Sanborn's unofficial committee of correspondence. This letter resulted in a notice the following day for the militia to appear at Tilton's and "there to attend till further orders." Sanborn, *Genealogy*, 124, 129; Tilton, *History*, 1, no. 6, 159; Stearns, *Genealogical*, 2:811; Greeley, *Genealogy*, 74, 139; Sandown Town Records, 1:157, 167, 174; Kingston Vital Records, 23.

FROM JOHN GIDDINGE[1]

Sir   Exeter, 15th. Decbr. 1774

This Town is at this time happily furnished with seventy two barrils of Powder—part of which think might be well deposited with the Patriotick sons of Liberty in Kingstown. The personal Attendance of a Number of them at Exeter to Consult & Advise with the sons of Freedom here I think would be very necessary & pleasent. The Manner of the Powders being here, with some Other Accounts of procedure—Refer You to the verbal Intelligence of Dr. Gale. I am Sr. Your Most Obt.   John Giddinge

RC (NhD).

1. John Giddinge (1728–c. 1785), physician and merchant, represented Exeter in the General Court, served on the committee of correspondence with JB, and took part in the raid on Fort William and Mary. Bell, *Exeter*, 380; NHSP, 7:366.

FROM GEORGE KING[1]

Sir,   [Portsmouth,] 22 Feby 1775

I am commanded by his Excellency the Governor to acquaint you that he has thought proper (with advice of the Honble. his Majestys Council) to dismiss you from being Lieutenant Colonel of the Regiment of Militia commanded by Colonel Jonathan [Greeley].[2] I am sir, Your most hble Servant.[3]   Geo: King D Secy

RC (Mr. S. Bartlett Howard, San Mateo, Calif., 1975).

1. George King (d. 1788), a Portsmouth shipper, was clerk of the Superior Court and deputy secretary of the Council. In 1779 he took the name of Atkinson to comply with provisions in the will of Theodore Atkinson. King held several responsible positions in state government during the war. Wentworth, *Genealogy*, 1:300; NHSP, 7:324, 368, 375, 415; 8:15, 61, 465.

2. Jonathan Greeley (b. 1718) was a taverner in Kingston. His weak support of the patriot cause evoked charges of treason during the war. Greeley, *Genealogy*, 66–67; NHSP, 7:577.

3. Governor Wentworth also retracted JB's justice of the peace commission. See Isaac Rindge to JB, 22 Feb. 1775, MJB 586.

TO NATHANIEL FOLSOM[1]

Sir   Kingstown June 18th 1775

This moment one Mr. Moretone has Come Express from Cambridge, has Brought a Letter from the Continental to our Congress which I shall send to the President.[2] He Came from thence last Evening has Rode all night & informs that the Regulars Came out of Boston yesterday, to Charlestown & had Begun an Engagment that he is well assured that Charlestown is Burnt & that our people were flocking Down all last night to the army.[3] I shall send to the president to be at Exeter to morrow morning. Desire that the Rest of the Committe be notifid. Your prudence will Direct you about marching our men.[4] In Great Haste I am &c.

Josiah Bartlett

RC (MeHi: The John S. H. Fogg Autograph Collection). On the reverse side of the letter are notes, dated "June 18th, 1775, 11 oClock AM," concerning officers and units ordered to march.

1. Nathaniel Folsom (1726–1790), a merchant of Exeter, commanded the New Hampshire militia as a major general during the Revolution, served in the Continental Congress in 1774 and again in 1777–1780, and was a member of the N.H. Committee of Safety. Merrill, "Nathaniel Folsom," 24.

2. The letter from Congress transmitted resolves of 10 June. NHSP, 7:512–13. Matthew Thornton was chairman of the Committee of Safety.

3. The engagement was the Battle of Bunker Hill fought on 17 June. This show

of courage against British regular troops "caused renewed enthusiasm among the radicals in New Hampshire." Upton, *Revolutionary New Hampshire*, 65.

4. In addition to Thornton, JB, and Folsom, William Whipple and Ebenezer Thompson sat on the Committee of Safety, which promptly ordered Col. Enoch Poor to march his regiment, except for the company of Capt. Henry Elkins, "immediately to Cambridge." Bouton, "Committee of Safety," 6. Poor's regiment is listed in NHSP, 14:107–58.

In the next letter JB makes reference to New Hampshire's Fourth Provincial Congress. The first had met on 21 July 1774. A second met on 25 Jan. 1775 and a third on 21 April. The principal purpose of these early extralegal assemblies had been to deal with intercolonial correspondence relating to dissatisfactions with British authority and to select representatives to the Continental Congresses called at Philadelphia in September 1774 and May 1775. JB represented Kingston in each Provincial Congress. The Third Congress appointed JB, Nathaniel Folsom and Samuel Hobart as a committee to wait on the Massachusetts congress then meeting in Concord, Mass., with a letter expressing their intention to assist in the emergency resulting from the skirmishes at Lexington and Concord. The Massachusetts congress sent back a letter asserting its confidence that the New Hampshire congress scheduled to meet on 17 May would "take such effectual steps as the present exigency of public affairs requires, and the Continent of America must necessarily approve." NHSP, 7:442, 452, 461–62, 465.

The meeting scheduled for 17 May was the first of four sessions of the Fourth Provincial Congress which would convene during 1775: 17 May–10 June, 27 June–7 July, 22 August–2 September, and 31 October–15 November. On 20 May the congress appointed a committee of safety, consisting of Matthew Thornton, JB, William Whipple, Nathaniel Fol-

som, and Ebenezer Thompson, with authority to carry on most provincial business during congressional recesses. NHSP, 7:468–661, 478, 485. JB attended the congress until he set out in early September for the Continental Congress.

TO [JOHN SULLIVAN[1] AND JOHN LANGDON]

Gentlemen   Kingstown June 29th 1775

This Colony Chose Deputies who met in Congress[2] at Exeter the 17th Day of may last and agreed to raise 2000 men for the Common Defence of the Colonies, which men are now Chiefly raised and are at medford under the Command of General Nathaniel Folsom. The Cost of Raising so many men, purchasing provisions Blankets &c. &c. you will Readily see to be a very Difficult task for so Small a Colony & without any money to Begin with. We have wrote to you & to the Congress on the Situation of our affairs But Receiving no Directions we have ordered & are now Striking off for the present Emergency 10050 £ L:M: in notes of hand on the Credit of this Colony to be paid within 3 years with Six pr Cent: Intrest. If some Resolve of the american Congress were published giving Such notes a Currency it would be of Great service. We are anxious to Know the Result of your Deliberations in order to Know how to Conduct the affairs of the Colony which at this time are in Great Confusion the people not Suffering any affairs to proceed in the usual form and no other being adopted. The Ships of war already Stop & Seize all vessels laden with Provisions Salt or molasses which very much Distress the Eastern parts: they have Destroyed fort Wm. & Mary and have this week taken the Guns & Carried them to Boston Except 8 that were Brought from Jerry's Point[3] some time ago. The General Court met the 4th of may Did no Business were adjourned to the 12th Instant when the Governor laid before us Lord Norths famous plan of accomodation on which nothing was or will be acted without Directions from the american Congress. The assembly now is adjourned to the 11th of July: Previous to the adjournment Col. John Fenton (who you may Remember was Chosen as a member for Plymouth by the Kings writ without the Consent of the assembly) made his appearance in the House Tho he had for sometime before Kept on Board the man of war in the Harbour. The House took into Consideration his Election & vacated his seat. The people of the Town Greatly Exasperated at his Conduct obliged him to Surrender tho he had taken shelter in the Governors House; and he has Since been Kept under Guard.[4] The Governor & his Lady[5] went off that Evening to Capt. Cochrans[6] at the fort under the protection of the man of war. Please to write us by Every oppertunity and let us Know as much of affairs as you are permitted. You may Direct for the Congress or Committe of Safety at Exeter one of which will be Constantly Sitting. We are Greatly Concerned about Amunitons as we have Scarce any Except what was taken out of the fort last winter Some of which we were forced to send to our western frontiers & Some to the army Before Boston. We hope some plan is laid for Bringing it in to the southern Colonies for New England is so guarded that there is but little hope gitting it in here.

Draft (NhHi). In JB's hand, but unsigned. (At some point, JB's signature was clipped from another document and attached to this one. See MJB 616.) Probably written for the Committee of Safety.

1. John Sullivan (1740–1795) had practiced law in Durham since 1760. He represented New Hampshire in the Continental Congress, 1774–1775, and 1780–1781, was a brigadier general under George Washington, 1775–1780, was attorney general and then president of New Hampshire during the 1780s, and sat as judge of the U.S. District Court of New Hampshire from 1789 to 1795. In the Continental Army Sullivan commanded brigades at Bunker Hill, Long Island, Princeton, Germantown, in Rhode Island, and against the Iroquois. At this time he was in command of New Hampshire's brigade at Cambridge. Winter Hill was Sullivan's headquarters. Whittemore, *John Sullivan.*

2. JB refers to New Hampshire's Fourth Provincial Congress. The General Court mentioned later was the legal legislative body under Royal Governor John Wentworth. JB served in both simultaneously.

3. A fortification in Portsmouth Harbor.

4. John Fenton (d. 1785) was a British army officer who had lived in Plymouth since 1771 and held several royal appointments. On a King's writ Plymouth elected Fenton to the May 1775 session of the General Court, an election not accepted by the Court. Fenton's advice to his constituents to remain peaceable, combined with his overt loyalty to Governor Wentworth, led to his arrest by the Provincial Congress. American authorities sent Fenton to army headquarters, and then to Hartford, Conn. There he obtained a release and sailed to Great Britain. Mayo, *John Wentworth,* 149–56; Stearns, *Plymouth,* 1:68–79; NHSP, 7:445–80, 543–44. See also N.H. Loyalists Transcripts, 2:515–47.

5. Frances "Lady" Wentworth (1745–1813), widow of Theodore Atkinson, Jr., married Gov. John Wentworth in 1769. Wentworth, *Genealogy,* 1:318. For her account of the summer of 1775 see Daniell, "Lady Wentworth's Last Days in New Hampshire," 14–25.

6. John Cochran, commander of Fort William and Mary, left New Hampshire with Governor Wentworth on the *Scarborough* in August 1775. Cochran's estate was confiscated in 1778. NHSP, 8:811–14; N.H. Loyalists Transcripts, 1:319–51; *Laws of N.H.,* 4:177–80.

FROM NATHANIEL PEABODY[1]

Sir   Atkinson Augt 30th, 1775

The agreable acquaintance I have had, the Honr. of, with you in time past; and the Candour you have ever discovered; assures me that you will not take umbrage at the freedom I now Take. I am not insensible Sir—of the indefatigable endeavours of J—W—h and Some Others, from whom better things might Justly be expected, to render my person, Character & performances—in the most Odious Colour imaginable, as they have not the least regard for Truth, where a lie will by any means suit their Turn. I want but Time & oppertunity to Demonstrate to you the Matchless deceit, of Those persons. Please to Enquire of Capt Webster, who will probably wait on you Concerning the State of the militia here, and you will find Things very different from what said J. W.h Has informd you. You will find that the people here even to a man Sincerely regard you & dont wish to be Governed by, a better or, any other person if the Regt is not Divided—but They are Steadfastly determined Never to be Governed by J.__W__h. let the Consequences of refusal be ever so destressing—and upon the whole Sir, you will find in the *People* in these parts an irreconciliable aversion to the late proposed plan for Settling the militia.

It is the General Opinion of the people in this, and the adjacent Towns that it would be much better to have the Regt. Divided—but if it Should not be Divided—they are a full in the Opinion that they Ought to have the Nomination of the 2d. in Command in the Regt—if we Should be able to find a man qualified for a Lt. Colo. in this part of the Regt—but if not Rather than to loose the Chance we would Send one or Two of our best men to School to Majrs Gale & Welch for a while Till they have Just learn'd to Cobble up an old Shoe, or a Dung fork & such like qualli-fications & then no doubt we Shall Stand Something of a Chance with Such curious artificers—as those Gent. Now are! Upon the whole Sir I hope you will parden my Nonsence, & give me leave Just to Say that you will find it would lend Greatly to the peace & good order of the militia here, if the Commissiong the above mentioned Gent. might be deferred Till the People shall have opportunity to make their minds Known in Some decent way & manner about the premises. But however I submit to your better Determination upon the matter as I have Nothing in view at this Time, but to promote the General Good of mankind & that peace & tranquility may ever attend all your military undertakings.[2] Sir I heartily Congratulate you on acct. of your being Chose a member for the Continental Congress[3]—& wish all your Councills for the weal of this Country may be Crowned with Success. I am Sir your assured friend most Obedt. & very Humbl Servt.

Nathl Peabody

N.B. It is Now 4 Ck. in the morning & pray excuse me & my Jargon.
RC (Nh).

1. Peabody was a physician of Atkinson. See Committee of Safety to JB and Peabody, 23 Aug. 1777, n.1.

2. On 24 Aug. 1775 the provincial congress had voted JB to be colonel of the 7th militia regiment. Jacob Gale was appointed lieutenant colonel, Joseph Welch first major, and John Webster second major. *NHSP*, 7:577.

3. The provincial congress on 23 August selected JB to attend the Continental Congress with John Langdon on behalf of New Hampshire. *NHSP*, 7:575.

FROM MATTHEW THORNTON[1]
Gentlemen

In Provincial Congress
Exeter Septr 1st. 1775

We are fully satisfied, that you have just Apprehensions of the excellency of the English Constitution as originally formed for securing to all their just Rights & Liberties, & the Necessity of opposing by every proper Method, the Schemes & Devices of those who seek our Ruin, manifestly calculated to destroy the fundamental Principles of our happy Constitution. The Zeal you have always shewn & the Services you have done for supporting the essential Principles of Liberty & opposing those cruel Measures which have been devised for enslaving America, leave us no

Room to doubt of your steady Perseverance therein, which makes it unnecessary particularly to direct you respecting a Matter of which you are so fully acquainted.

In transacting the Business you are appointed to you will remember that you are entrusted, as well on the behalf of the whole united Colonies, as of this in particular; you will therefore aim at Such a Plan for settling the present unhappy Dispute on such a Basis that the essential Principles of Liberty & Freedom be firmly established throughout the American Colonies—particularly that no Taxes be imposed but by their own Representatives—That the Right of Trial by Juries be fully maintained—That the officers for the Administration of Justice be appointed & supported in such a way as may most probably prevent their Judgment from being biased—And that the despotic Court of Admiralty be no longer.

And if it should happen that a Plan for the establishing a form of Government in the respective Colonies should come under your Consideration—You will have a particular Regard to this Colony—That our Establishment may be such as shall secure our essential Rights, as fully as in the other Colonies—Especially that a full & equitable Representation be secured to us And that the Court of Appeals, whereby the Trial by Juries is in many Instances superseded, be abolished.

And we would have you immediately use your utmost Endeavour to obtain the Advice & Direction of the Congress with Respect to a Method for our administering Justice & regulating our civil Police. We press you not to delay this Matter as its being speedily done, (your own knowledge of our Circumstances must inform you) will probably prevent the greatest Confusion among us.

We need not mention that from Time to Time you give us the earliest Advice of such of your Proceedings as you are allowed to disclose.

Matthew Thornton, President

The foregoing was voted for Instructions to our Delegates Josiah Bartlett and John Langdon Esqrs appointed to represent This Colony at the Continental Congress.[2]   Attest E. Thompson Secretry[3]

FC (NhExP).

1. Matthew Thornton (c. 1714–1803), physician of Londonderry, served as a provincial legislator, 1758–1775, as president of the fourth provincial congress in 1775, and as a chairman of the N.H. Committee of Safety. He attended the Continental Congress from November 1776 to May 1777, sat as an associate justice on the Superior Court, 1776–1782, and served the state again from 1783 to 1785. He spent his last years in Merrimack. Estes, "Honest Dr. Thornton," 70–98.

2. John Langdon (1741–1819), a merchant of Portsmouth, sat in the General Court with JB prior to the Revolution and represented New Hampshire at the Continental Congress in 1775–1776 and 1786–1787. Langdon served as president of the state twice, 1785 and 1788, as governor twice, 1805–1809, and 1810–1812, as a member of both the constitutional convention at Philadelphia and the state ratifying convention at Concord, and as a U.S. Senator, 1789–1801. Mayo, *John Langdon*. Langdon and JB had been elected to Congress by the General Court on 23 Aug. 1775. *NHSP*, 7:575.

3. Ebenezer Thompson (1737–1802), a Durham physician, was a member of the N.H. Committee of Safety and the Council. He was clerk and then judge of the Court of Common Pleas in Strafford County, and secretary of New Hampshire, 1775–1786. Thompson, *Memoir of Judge Ebenezer Thompson*; Bell, *Bench and Bar*, 48–50; NHSP, 22:852–54.

TO MARY BARTLETT[1]

My Dear   Woburn 5th Septembr 1775

We Lodged at Haverhil last night and have had a fine ride to Day to this place by half after 12 o'Clock.[2] Am in good health and make no Doubt by the Leave of providence I shall have a pleasant Jorney & a safe Return perhaps by the Begining of Novembr next and hope to find you all in good health. At present the Greatest uneasiness I have is leaving my family for so long a time But shall Endeavor to make my self as Easy as possible and Return as soon as I Can.

I hope neither you nor the Children will make themselves uneasy about me as I shall take all possible Care of my self and I hope you will not be afraid of any Cost that may be wanting to make you or the family Comfortable in my absence. Capt. Calfe[3] will frequently Call to see how you Do and will be ready to assist you. I shall write to you as often as possible. In haste I Remain yours &c.   Josiah Bartlett

P.S. I Expect to Do our Business at winter hill & Cambridge to Day and Get to watertown to night and then proceed on our jorney without any more stops. I Should have Defered writing till night but am afraid I shall not have an oppertunity Either to write or send it then.   J: B:

RC (NhHi).

1. Mary Bartlett Bartlett (1730–1789), a daughter of Joseph Bartlett of Newton, was JB's wife.

2. JB was traveling to the Continental Congress, having left Kingston on 4 September. See his itinerary, 18 Mar. 1776.

3. John Calef (1731–1806), a Kingston tanner, served as a captain of a company on Great Island in 1775. He later attained a colonelcy. His son Joseph married JB's daughter Miriam in 1781. Boardman, *Robert Calef*, 53–54, 76. The surname appears variously as Calef and Calfe throughout the papers.

TO MARY BARTLETT

My Dear

Philadelphia
Saturday Septembr 16th 1775

I Arrived yesterday at this place about noon, after a pretty agreeable Jorney having had no rain Since the Day I set out till a Small Shower last thursday. After we got in yesterday it rained most of the afternoon. I hope & trust that you & my family are well as nothing will give me So much Uneasiness as to hear any of you are Dangerously Sick in my absence But I hope & trust kind Providence will bring us all togather again in safety. I am well Except something of a Cough as is usual after a Great Cold that I took on my Jorney. The Small Pox is in the City. Some of the members of the Congress are now under Innoculation & some have taken [   ] as hitherto to Escape it. Which I Shall Do I am not fully

Determined, altho all agree there is no Danger in Innoculation, yet it will hinder me at least a fortnight from my Duty at Congress. I have nothing new to inform you of Except that the Storm [   ] we had the Sabbath before I Set out from home was very severe in New york, new Jersey & Pensylvania doing great Damage tearing Down trees &c. &c. an accont of which you will probably see in the Publick Prints. I wrote you from woborn [   ] from windsor in Connecticut[1] both of which I hope you have Received. Remember my Love to my Children and to all Enquiring friends Particularly to Lieut Pearson[2] & Capt. Calef and their families. I shall frequently write to you and want to hear from you & my family. Hope you will not neglect to write now I am here and you know where they will find me. I am yours &c.   Josiah Bartlett

RC (NhHi). Bracketed spaces indicate illegible or deteriorated portions of the manuscript.

1. No letter to Mary written from Windsor has been found. JB and John Langdon did send a letter from Windsor to the N.H. Committee of Safety dated 9 Sept. 1775. MJB 686.

2. John Pearson was a taverner in Kingston. MJB 439.

TO MATTHEW THORNTON

Dear Sir   Philadelphia Septembr 20th 1775

Yesterday it was moved in Congress to Discharge Col. Fenton from his Confinement. It Seems that he living at Hartford had oppurtunity to See Several of the members as they passed to & from the army & by his politeness & address and by telling how much he had Suffered had prejudiced Some of them that he had been hardly Dealt with by us. The Copy of a Letter from General Putnam[1] was also Produced wherein he Says "that the Populace had Siezed him and Carried him before the Congress of N. Hampshire and that after a full hearing they Could not find that he had Done any thing against the Liberties of america in *Word* or *Deed* but for fear that he might, had ordered him to be Confined" But as we knew the whole of that affair we Convinced the Congress that our Convention had Done right. The Congress then passed a Resolve to this Affect "That whereas the Convention of the Colony of New hampshire had *prudently* & *Justly* ordered Col. John Fenton to be Confined and that he being now Desirous to Remove to Great Britain or Ireland therefore Resolved that General Washington be Directed to allow Col. Fenton to Repair forthwith to New york and from thence to Great Brittain or Ireland on his giving his Parole not to take up arms against america" which order your Delegates Consented to thinking it better than Keeping him Confined at the publick Expence.[2]

As to Publick news you will See it in the Publick prints and we have no other that we Can at present Communicate. We should be glad to Receive from you all possible Intelligence of our affairs and shall think it our Duty to write you often Even tho it were only to tell you we have nothing to new to inform you of. We are your most obedient Humble Servts.

Josiah Bartlett
John Langdon

RC (Nh-Ar). In JB's hand; signed also by Langdon. Addressed to "Matthew Thornton Esqr. Chairman of the Committe of Safey N. Hampshire to be Communicated."

1. Israel Putnam (1718–1790), Connecticut farmer, had served with the rangers of Robert Rogers in the French and Indian War. Congress commissioned Putnam a major general in June 1775, and he served with Washington's army until crippled by a paralytic stroke in December 1779. *JCC*, 2:99.

2. *JCC*, 2:255.

TO MARY BARTLETT

My Dear wife & family   Philadelphia October 2nd 1775

I Can now with pleasure inform you that I have been Inoculated for the Small Pox and am almost Got well of it. I had it very favorable not above 20 Pock or thereabout tho I was Confined by the fever to the House 5 or 6 Days.[1] It is 4 weeks this Day Since I left Kingstown and have not heard from you Since I Saw you. I want very much to hear from you Tho I Know you have the Same almighty preserver in my absence as when I was with you So I Endeavor to rest Satisfied Knowing that my Uneasiness will Do you no good.

This is the fourth Letter I have Sent you Since I Left home and hope within a few Days I shall Receive one from you. When I shall Return I Can give no better account than when I left you But as soon as I Can you may be Sure I Shall Return with great pleasure. The Living in So Grand a City without the pleasure of a free Country air is not very agreable to me.[2] I have nothing of Publick news more than you will See Dayly in the Publick papers and private affairs I may not Communicate. Gideon George is well.[3] Remember me to all my acquaintance. You need be under no fear of the Small Pox by this Letter Tho it would be very Safe to hold all my Letters over the Smoke a Little before you handle them much as the Small Pox is very frequent in the City. I am &c.   Josiah Bartlett

RC (NhHi).

1. Smallpox inoculation had begun on a large scale in 1721 and was used widely until modified by Edward Jenner's "vaccination" about 1800. Shryock, *Medicine in America*, 7–8.

2. According to a census taken for General Cornwallis in 1777, Philadelphia had 5,470 houses and 21,767 inhabitants. Greene and Harrington, *American Population*, 118.

3. Gideon George (b. 1737), a Kingston tailor, accompanied JB to Philadelphia. *Vital Records of Haverhill, Mass.*, 1:136; N.H. Deeds, 70:140; MJB 816.

TO [MATTHEW THORNTON][1]

Sr.   [Philadelphia, 2 October 1775]

Agreable to your desire, that we should write, as often as may be, have taken this early oppertunity, tho' little or nothing to Communicate.

Before this Comes to hand, doubtless, you'll Receive letter from our President desire'g your attendance at head Quarters, to Consult with a Committee from this Congress Relative to the Army—Doctr. Franklin, Mr. Lynch and Colonal Harrison, are the Committee.[2]

We humbly beg leave here to suggest whether it would not be good oppertunity to mention the Convud[3] state of our Colony and the Absolute Necessaty of Govermt and also to forward by them a petition from our Convention, to take Government. We have Consulted many of the members on the Matter and as soon as Colonal Bartlet is able to Attend the house, which will be in a few days as he's almost well of the Small Pox, shall Motion, for leave to take the same goverment as Massachusets Bay. You'll also give us leave to urge the forwarding of our Accts. Against the Continent immediately otherwise, there may not be money in the Continental Treasury as great Sums are dayly Drawing from thence; the Consequence of which will be, shall be Obliged to wait for another emition.

There has nothing been Transacted in Congress as yet that we are at Liberty to Communicate. The Journals are not yet Printed, tho' ready for the press, but will be soon. You'll give us leave to Repeat our Desire that our Convention, or Committee of Safety will forward a Petition for government seting forth the Absolute Necessaty of it the impossablity of Tax'g with out which is a thing that must be done, as it would Ruin us to be emitting paper on every Occasion. You'll pardon us for throw'g out these hints. We are Sr. your mo. obt Serts.

Josiah Bartlett
John Langdon

RC (Nh-Ar). In Langdon's hand, signed also by JB.

1. Thornton served as chairman of the N.H. Committee of Safety from 10 May through December 1775. Bouton, "Committee of Safety," 1, 36.

2. On 30 September the Continental Congress appointed Benjamin Franklin, Thomas Lynch, and Benjamin Harrison as a committee to confer in Cambridge with George Washington and representatives from each New England state "touching the most effectual method of continuing, supporting, and regulating a continental army." Thornton being unable to attend, the N.H. Committee of Safety asked Meshech Weare and Nathaniel Folsom to meet the congressmen. The meeting took place from 15 to 25 October. *JCC*, 3:265–66; Bouton, "Committee of Safety," 22; Burnett, *Continental Congress*, 105–06.

3. Convulsed.

FROM JOHN SULLIVAN

Gentlemen: Winter Hill, October 4th, 1775

You will by this Post Receive Intelligence from head-Quarters of Dr. Church'es having been detected in holding a Treasonable Correspondence with the Enemy.[1] His Behaviour Towards our Sick & wounded long since Convinced me that he either was void of humanity and Judgment, or that he was Determined by untimely Removals & Neglect of Duty to Let all those under his care breathe their Last within the walls of his Detestable General Hospital. His Conduct with respect to my Brigade has been very regular, for he has Regularly Killed most or all those he has taken from us. I will mention Two Instances of the wounded: one was the well known instance of Mr. Simpson, who was shot in the foot—an amputation was necessary. Doctor Jackson,[2] who every one must allow to be Infinitely his Superior, was there, & had every thing prepared to take off the Limb. Doctor Church happened to come in—forbid him to proceed & ordered the man to be sent to the Hospital. He went home himself—Eat his Dinner—Drank his Glass—then went to meet the wounded voluntier who, by the Loss of Blood, The Tearing and Lacerating his flesh by the Fractured Bone had become happy by growing Insensible of his pain. Jackson had fortold this, but Church Determining to Kill the man Secundem Artem, called his *Subs* around him—assigns each one his post, and then requests Jackson to take off the Limb. He Refused, Informing them that the only reason was that the Man's life could not be saved by amputating the Limb or by any other methods, & agreeable to his predictions the Man Died on the Second day. The other was an instance of a man in my Brigade who, while we were throwing up our last Redoubts, was wounded in the Leg. Dr. Jackson was by—said his Leg must be taken off, but he did not dare to do it till Church was sent for. He sent down two of his Subs, who Complimented Jackson with the Liberty of using the Saw. One of them was to cut the flesh—the other to take up the Arteries. The first failed, leaving some of the muscles untouched, & the other would not if left to himself have taken up the Arteries till the man had Bled to Death. Jackson was obliged to take the knife from one & the needle from the other—performed the operation—Drest the man & tended him three Days. Every symptom was favourable & Doubtless the man would have soon Recovered, but on the Fourth day Doctor Church sent for him & ordered him to the Hospital. Jackson told them that the fourth being the Day on which the Inflammation was at the highest he would assuredly die if removed. He was not regarded—the man was removed & died accordingly. I could give you more instances, but hope the Inclosed Copy of a Petition presented to me by the Field Officers in my Brigade will suffice to show their & my sense of the Hospital Proceedings.

I now entreat you, Gentlemen, to solicit an appointment for Dr. Jackson, in whom every Officer & Soldier has great Confidence, & whose skill is even ackowledged by Dr. Church himself—many valuable lives may Depend upon this appointment. Sure I am that I could more boldly enter the field if so able a Surgeon as Jackson was at hand to dress the wounds which perchance I might receive. Gentlemen, I am with great respect Y'r very Humble Ser'vt.   John Sullivan

P.S. I have called the General Hospital a most Detestable one. I will now assign my reason: in the first place—it is detested by every person seeming to have an aversion to it—in the second place every person must allow that has the least acquaintance with such matters that a number of

Sick persons being brought together in one hospital will Render the Air so putrid that it will not only be pernicous to the Neighbouring Inhabitants but must prove Fatal to the Patients themselves. Another reason is that the Soldiers are Taken from among their friends and acquaintances & put among persons with whom they have no sort of Acquaintance & under Physicians they never saw.

I most sincerely wish we had hospitals for the several Brigades or one for two adjoining Brigades or in such case a Trustty Person might have been appointed to Inspect each Hospital, an emulation would have been raised to bring in their accounts as low as possible & to exceed each other in the care of their Patients. The Regimental Surgeons could take the whole business upon them & prevent the enormous expense of an Inspector General with a vast number of others unconnected with the Regiments & who endeavour to Render useless the Regimental Surgeons who by the way are to be paid whether they act or not: add to this that Patients are even more Likely to recover under the care of Physicians in whom they have Confidence than a stranger even though his skill should exceed the other. Gentlemen I am extreme haste y'r most obed't Ser'vt.

Jno. Sullivan

Reprinted from *Letters by Josiah Bartlett*, 34–37. TR (DLC: Force Transcripts). Addressed to JB and John Langdon.

1. Benjamin Church (1734–1776) was elected chief physician of the army by Congress in 1775, but in October he was convicted of treason for having furnished military information to the British. The ship on which he sailed to London was lost at sea. Shipton, *Harvard Graduates*, 13:380–98.

2. Hall Jackson (1739–1797) of Portsmouth introduced the foxglove, or digitalis, to America in 1786. By 1775 Jackson had already achieved renown for his skill in cataract operations, obstetrics, and surgery. Thacher, *American Medical Biography*, 1:311–13; Estes, "An Account of the Foxglove in America," 394–408.

COMMITTEE OF SAFETY TO JB AND JOHN LANGDON

Gentlemen   Exeter Octr 12 1775

On the 2d of this Inst. the Ship *Prince George* Richard Emms Master from Bristol bound to Boston with 1892 Barrels of Flour for the use of Genl. Gages Army[1] came into our Harbour & was boarded by a number of men under the command of Leiut Pickering of the Matross Company[2] and Bro't up to Portsmouth where she is detained.[3] Genl. Washington has been consulted concerning her and has desired that the Cargo may be sent to the army, and has promised to write of it to the congress for their directions in what manner her Cargo should be disposed of and what should be allowed the Captors &c.

As there is not a Barrel of Flour to be sold in this Colony & we were under a Necessity of taking a Hundred Barrels of the Flour for the Support of our Soldiers & workmen at the Battery's erecting on Seavys & Pierces Islands there being upwards of a hundred Soldiers besides workmen &c. employed thereon which we have since represented to Gen.

Washn. with a proposal to sell 500 Barrels to the Insptr. of Ports & deposit the money Safely until directions from the Congress should be obtained.[4]

Our Batteries are almost compleated the Work done on them will Surpass your Imagination Several Hundreds of Men from the Country round about having Voluntarily laboured thereon a considerable part of the time—since they were begars. We have lately had a Requisition from Genl Washington to pay our Troops Wages up to the 4th of August which was quite unexpected & will Occasion our Emitting more Money and of Course hinder our Accounts from being forwarded some time. The numbering the Inhabitants of this Colony is in hand & when compleated we shall transmit you an account thereof.

We have Nothing to communicate to you new, our Publick affairs continuing much as they were when you left home, but must desire your diligent Endeavours to procure something to be done relative to our Civil Government.

P.S. If thro the Multiplicity of his affairs Gen. Washg. should omit to write fully concerning the Said Ship & Cargo we desire you to lay the Matter before the Congress & procure their directions concerning it to be transmitted to us as soon as possible.

Draft (Nh-Ar). Endorsed, "Copy of a Letter to Messrs. Bartlet & Langdon Octr 12th 1775." Words deleted by the author have been omitted. See MJB 699.

1. Thomas Gage (1721–1787) commanded the British army in North America from 1763 to 10 Oct. 1775, when he sailed for England leaving the command to Gen. William Howe. *DNB*, 20:355–56. See also *General Gage*.

2. Thomas Pickering served in Capt. Titus Salter's militia company at Fort Washington on Pierce's Island. Titus Salter (c. 1722–1798), a Portsmouth merchant, had been given command of a matross company in September. *NHSP*, 14:227; Emery, *Salters*, 34–39.

3. JB and Langdon probably already knew of the capture through Thomas Thompson. Thompson to Langdon, 3 Oct. 1775, in *NDAR*, 2:277.

4. Upon receiving the committee's letter, Washington requested Congress to direct him how to dispose of ship and cargo. Congress received the letter on 13 October and referred it to the Naval Committee. In the meantime, on 11 October the N.H. Committee of Safety asked the General's permission to use the flour to feed its militia at Portsmouth. Washington agreed. *NDAR*, 2:267, 301, 397–98, 461, 502–03; *JCC*, 3:293.

TO MARY BARTLETT

My Dear   Philadelphia October 25th 1775

I had the pleasure this morning to Receive yours of the 13th of this month[1] informing me that you & the Rest of my family were well altho Molly & Ezra had been Sick. I hope you will take good Care of your & the family's health as nothing will give me greater pain than to know any of you were Dangerously sick in my absence. I am by the Goodness of GOD in a Good State of health; have got my Strength and have not So much of the Head ach as usual. When I Shall be able to Return I Cannot inform you But am in hopes I Shall be at home Sometime in December. I Expect it will be very Difficult going Such a jorney in the winter. As Soon as Business will admit you may be asured I Shall Return with all Speed.

I Begin to fear I Shall Soon want Exercise as we are obliged to Set Every Day Except Sunday from 9 in the morning till near 4 in the afternoon and by that time we have Dined or Supped Call it which you please it is night and So have no time for Riding out.

Last Sunday Mr. Randolph member of Congress from Virginia & late President of the Congress was taken at table with an Apoplexy & Died in a few hours and was yesterday Buried attended by the Congress, the Assembly of this Province, the ministers of all Denominations in this City, 3 Regiments Consisting of about 2000 men in their Regimentals with Drums muffled &c. and it is thought 12 or 15 Thousand other Inhabitants; in Short it is Supposed to be much the Greatest funeral that Ever was in America.[2]

I hope you will take particular Care to lay in wood and other necessaries for winter to make you Comfortable and if in want of money apply for the money Due from the Town as I mentioned. Remember my Love to all the Children, and tell Polly I Received her letter and Shall be very Careful not to Bring home the Small Pox to my family as Col. Moulton[3] Did to his. I think my Self & Cloaths Clear of it at this time. Remember me to all friends. I wrote you 3 times already this month viz the 4th the 10th & 14th[4] all which I hope you have Received. Yours &c.

Josiah Bartlett

P.S. Give my Regards to Mr. Thurstain.[5] Fryday night 27th this Letter Sealed to be sent tomorrow morning. Am now well.

RC (NhHi).

1. Not found.

2. Peyton Randolph (c. 1721 to 22 Oct. 1775), an attorney from Williamsburg, Va., had presided over the Continental Congress in 1774 and May of 1775.

3. Jonathan Moulton (c. 1726–1787), a merchant of Hampton, was colonel of the 3rd regiment of militia throughout the Revolution. Dow, *Hampton*, 1:278–79, 536, 550; 2:866, 870; Potter, *Military*

History, 1:194, 274, 331.

4. None found.

5. Benjamin Thurston (1753–1804) graduated from Harvard in 1774, was considered as Congregational clergyman at Kingston in 1773 and settled in North Hampton in 1784. French, *Reminiscences*, 13–14; Thurston, *Genealogies* (rev. ed.), 72.

JB AND JOHN LANGDON TO WILLIAM WHIPPLE

Sr.   Philad. 26th October 1775

Your favor, in Committee of the 12th. Instant is now before us in answer to which we say that General Washington had laid the affair of the flower ship, before the Congress some days before your favor Came to hand, but nothing has been concluded. We urged, that the Ship and her Cargo belonged to the Colony as she was taken by our men in Provincial pay; and not by Continental forces. That we had suffer'd and were still suffering many losses by the takeing of our Ships inward and outward bound; and that before the takeing of this flower ship—As soon as this matter is settled shall inform you.[1]

We are greatly Rejoyce'd to hear that the Batteries are in such Readyness as we have expected to hear that Portsmouth was Canonaded. Capt. George Hastins (who built a Ship at Kennebeck last year and loaded with masts at Portsmouth) is now here, haveing been cast away on the Jersey shore, in a transport from Boston, bound to New York, with Capt. Duncan Chambel & Leiut Simes, and number of men, who were imploy'd to Inlist Scotchmen in the Back parts of New York, to Reinforce the Ministerial Army. They are all Close Prisoners Except Capt. Hastins; a quantity of goods &c. is saved out of the ship.[2]

I saw Capt. Hastings Yesterday and as I was Acquainted with him he ventured to informe me, that when he saild from Boston, 6th Instant, Capt. Mowatt[3] (Scotchman) with three Armed Transports, were almost Ready to go round to Portsmouth, for the purpose of burning the Town, therefore (for God sake be ye ready). You mention Powder; there is a Secret Committee for Procuring that article, of which Mr. Langdon is one; every Precausion is takeing for Ample Supplies; but as the whole Continent is to be supplied, as well as the two Armies, it makes it uncertain when can send you any. We beg leave here to suggest, that the greatest Attention should be paid to the use of powder, that no Cannon be fired unless Drove to the last extremity. We were sorry to see that you Intended to emitt more paper money, but as Genl. Washington's Requisition Demanded it, must be done. The House is now Crowded with Motions, otherwise should have move'd for a grant of a Certain sum to our Colony, which would have Answer'd our purpose without emitt'g—shall do it first oppertunity, but fear the want of our Acct. will prevent the grant.

We some time since made motion for the Regulation of our Civil Government, and this day a Committee was appointed to Consider the Motion and Report thereon;[4] Could have wished for a Petition from our Congress Sett'g forth all the Reasons &c. had been transmitted us, which would have help'd the matter much. Committee has been appointed to Collect the Depredations, committed by the Sons of Tyranny, thro' the Continent who you'll hear from.[5] We are with Respect your most Obt Servts.   Josiah Bartlett   John Langdon
P.S. Inclosed is Resolution of Congress Respect'g Powder.[6]

RC (Nh-Ar). Written by Langdon, signed by JB and Langdon. Addressed "To William Whipple Esqr., Chairman P. T. of Committee of Safety–at Exeter, New Hampshire."

1. See letter of 12 Oct. 1775, and n. 4.

2. Capt. Duncan Campbell and Lt. James Smith Sims, officers of the Royal Highland Regiment of Emigrants, were on a recruiting mission on board the transport *Rebecca and Francis*, George Hastings master, when the vessel went aground at Brigantine Beach, about sixty miles from Philadelphia, on 17 October. *NDAR*, 2:545, 558, 597, 1170; *JCC*, 3:305.

3. Captain Henry Mowat of H. M. Armed Vessel *Canceaux* led a squadron to attack and burn Falmouth (Maine) on 17 October. *NDAR*, 2:500–02; Fowler, *Rebels*, 33–34.

4. The motion was made on 18 October. Members of the committee were John Rutledge, John Adams, Samuel Ward, Richard Henry Lee, and Roger Sherman. *JCC*, 3:298, 307.

5. The committee of Silas Deane, John Adams, and George Wythe, appointed on 18 October, sent a circular letter to each committee of safety requesting "clear,

distinct, full, and circumstantial details of the hostile and destructive acts, and the captures or seizures, and depredations in your Colony." *JCC*, 3:298–99; Force, *American Archives*, 4th ser., 3:1105.

6. Enclosure not found. On 26 October Congress resolved to print its resolution of 15 July permitting the importation of gunpowder, saltpeter, and sulphur. *JCC*, 2:184–85; 3:306.

TO [MATTHEW THORNTON]

Sr.   Philad. 3d Novr. 1775

This serves to Inclose a Resolve of the Congress Relative to Civil Government for the Colony of New Hampshire, by which you'll see, they Recommend such a form as shall be agreable to a free Representation of the People, in short such a government as shall be most Agreable to the Province.[1] The arguments on this matter, (being the first of the kind as we had no Charter) were Truely Ciceronial, the eminent Speakers, did honour to themselves and the Continent; Carried by very great Majority.

The Power is ample and full even to the Choice of governor, if the Colony should think it necessary but that, we humbly Conceive worthy of Consideration. You'll see that the goverment is Limited to the Present Contest to ease the minds of some few, persons, who were fearful of Independance. We tho't it Adviseable not to oppose that part too much, for once we had taken, any sort of goverment, nothing but Negociation with Great Britain, can alter it.

We would here beg leave to suggest whether a government somewhat simelar to the Massachust would not be best—A free Representation of the Province tho', not too many, as they may be increased at any time, but it would be hard to Diminish; those Representatives to Chose a Counsel, of proper number; say 15 these two Branches to Act in all Cases whatever and not to Proceed so far as govenor at Present, tho' the Door may be left open for that purpose. We throw out these hints with great submission to the Honbl. Convention.

We think can say, (without boasting) have done our duty in this matter, by paying constant attention, for long time, not only in the House but in Private Conversation with members, to clear up any doubt they might have on this head. We can't help Rejoice'g to see this as a ground work of our goverment, and hope by the Blessing of Divine Providence, never to Return to our former Despotick state.

Inclosed is also Resolves Respect'g Trade which we had order to Transmit.[2]

We have also the Pleasure to inform you that an, express has just arrived from St. John's, with advice that our men has taken the fortress at Chamble, and have sent the standard Coulours of the Seventh Regiment to this Congress took six Tons of Powder, and many Valuable stores abt 100 Prisoners, hope to have Possession of St. John's Soon.[3] Mr. Langdon Expects to set out in few days for Canada, being one of a Committee for that Place.[4] We are your most obt. Servts.

                                                     John Langdon
                                                     Josiah Bartlett

The Sooner government is Set abt the Better.

RC (Nh-Ar). In Langdon's hand; signed by Langdon and JB.

1. The enclosed resolve appears in MJB 704 and is printed in *JCC*, 3:319.

2. Enclosure not found. This was a resolve of 1 November prohibiting exportation of produce. *JCC*, 3:314.

3. The Northern Army, under Generals Richard Montgomery and Philip Schuyler, was advancing from Fort Ticonderoga to Montreal and Quebec. The fortress at

Chambly was taken on 18 October, St. Johns on 3 November, and Montreal on 12 November. Wallace, *Appeal to Arms*, 67–70; Carrington, *Battles*, 127–29.

4. Congress had appointed Langdon, Robert Treat Paine, and Eliphalet Dyer as a committee to confer with General Schuyler. *JCC*, 3:317.

TO THE COMMITTEE OF SAFETY

Gentn   Philadelphia Novr 13th 1775

Enclosed I transmit to you the Letter Directed to the Speaker of our House of assembly.[1] I Suppose it Came from England Sent by the agents who presented the late Petition of Congress; By it you will be able to Guess what will be the fate of that Petition.[2] I also send you a Duplicate of the vote of Congress Concerning our Civil affairs, the first Copy of the vote was sent Novr 6th.[3] Yesterday Capt. Langdon Set off on his Jorney to Canada So that I am left here alone to act in Behalf of our Colony. I Dont Expect him here any more During this session of the Congress. When the Congress will rise I Cant say But fear it Cant till winter, if it Can before spring.

The affair of the Ships taken at Portsmouth has not been Considered by Congress, by reason of urgent Business, But I Expect soon that that & several other Captures will be taken under Consideration & Some General rules adopted. When any thing is Determined on it, will inform you by the first oppertunity.

I am Directed by the Congress to Send you the Inclosed Resolves for making Salt Petre and I would Earnestly Recomend the puting them in practice.[4] It appears from Several Experiments in this Colony that the Surface of the Earth that has been for Some years Kept from the rain will produce Salt petre. The floor of a meeting House being taken up, the Earth under it produced one pound from Every Bushel; under Barns Stables &c. much more. There appears to be no more art in making it, than in making pot ash. When the Liquor is properly Boiled and put into Pans to Cool it Shoots & Sticks to the Bottom & Sides very Beautifully, the Liquor may then be Easily Drained off and Either Boyled over again or put on another mash.

Tho probably the Continent will be well supplied with Powder in the spring yet it is best by all means to put it out of the power of our Enemies to Defeat us of that necessary article by Supplying our selves and if we have a Double or treble Quantity it will be no Damage and in future Save our Cash from being sent abroad after it. I am Gentlemen your friend & Humble servt.   Josiah Bartlett

RC (Nh-Ar).

1. Not found.

2. A petition to George III, adopted by Congress on 6 July, was presented to the government by the colonial agents in London. Congress learned on 9 November that the king had spurned the document. Burnett, *Continental Congress*, 86–87, 115.

3. JB meant the 3rd.

4. A congressional committee recommended on 10 November that each state appoint certain persons "whose business it shall be to employ and set to work so many persons as they may think proper, both to work up such earth as is now fit for making salt petre, and to collect together and place in beds or walls under sheds, all such earth and composition of materials as are suitable to produce salt petre, after being duly exposed to the air, in order to encrease the produce of it, and that the delegates of the respective colonies be directed to send this resolve, together with the resolve of last session respecting salt petre, to their respective colonies, and cause them to be printed and made public there." *JCC*, 3:296, 345–49.

FROM WILLIAM WHIPPLE

Gentlemen,

In Committee of Safety
at Portsmouth, 21 November 1775

The Committee of Supplies & others concerned in supplying & paying our Troops, have not as yet been able to close their accounts in such a manner, as that we could make out the Colony Account against the Continent. But have proceeded so far as to be sure, that supplying and paying our Troops in the Continental Army under General Washington to the 4th. of August, with what we advanced to those gone in Collo. Arnolds Detachment, and those now in Canada under the command of General Scuyler, will amount to upwards of Twenty Thousand Pounds Lawful Money.[1]

To avoid the Necessity of Emitting more paper Money for our own Internal Charges, we desire you would request the Honbe. Congress to make as a Grant of such a part of the aforesaid Sum as they shall see fit, and our Accounts shall be Transmitted, as soon as a Settlement can be made with the Persons who has Transacted the Business.

The Numbers of the Inhabitants in the several Towns in this Colony, directed by our Congress, to be taken by the several & respective Selectmen as returned under Oath, has chiefly been compleated. We send you inclosed the List as Returned, except those where only the Column for the sum total are filled up, which not being Returned we have set down by the best information we could obtain, and are confident we have done it very near the true number.[2] However shall forward those wanting when they come to hand (which we daily expect) that the whole may be compleated by the Selectmens Returns. By Order of the Committee.

Wm: Whipple Prest P. T.

RC (DNA: RG 360, Miscellaneous Papers of the Continental Congress). Addressed to JB and Langdon.

1. At least 88 New Hampshire men with Capts. Henry Dearborn and Samuel Ward were moving toward Quebec in the contingent being led by Col. Benedict Arnold through Maine. At the same time 195 New Hampshire men were marching with Col. Timothy Bedel in General Schuyler's northern army toward the

Canadian fortress via Lake Champlain. *NHSP*, 14:209–22.

2. On 25 August the provincial congress ordered the selectmen of each town to return a census as soon as possible.

Estimated figures for the towns which had not yet reported are included on the draft of this letter (Nh-Ar), which is reproduced in MJB 713. See also the census report in NHSP, 7:724–81.

TO NATHANIEL FOLSOM

Sir   Philadelphia Novembr 23d 1775

When I left New Hampshire I was in hopes to have been favored by my friends, who had the Care of publick affairs; with frequent accounts of Every thing of a public nature transacted in the Colony. You must be sensible that besides my anxious Desire of Knowing Every thing that Relates to the welfare of the Colony; it is highly necessary as your Delegate that I Should be well & Early informed of all its publick affairs. Somethings that perhaps you would think of Little Consequence would have been of great service if I had been informed of them. Every other Delegate Every week Receives Regular accounts from their Congresses, Committes of Safety & private Gentlemen, so as to be able to give a particular account of their Respective Colonies; while I Know but very Little of our Colony affairs Since I left it.

The Publick papers have informed us that Portsmouth has been threatned by the Tools of tyranny and that the Colony had Exerted themselves for its Defence. I want to be informed what is Done, what Batteries, how many guns mounted, what No. of men Constantly Kept there; what No. of men has been employed about Building the Batteries &c. whither the Inhabitants have moved out their Effects, whither the province is making more paper Bills, if So how much & when Redeemable. Whither a new Convention is Called, and when to meet. Whither a new Committe of Safety is appointed, and if So who are the members. How the people like the Resolve of the Congress Concerning Civil goverment, and what is Done in Consequence of it. Whither the Colony has undertaken to procure themselves any Powder. Whither any Salt petre is made or any body Engaging in that Business. Whither the firearms voted by the Covention are made. Whither the people in General are peacable & orderly or not. I should be very Glad to be informed of these and of Every other public affair, as soon & as often as possible, and hope that you and my other friends will frequently write to me. If it Does no other good (that is if Some of the letters should not Convey me any material public intelligence) it will at least give me great pleasure to hear from my friends in our Colony, while (as I Expect) I am Confined here the Ensuing winter. In order to Encourge intelligence being Conveyed to & from the Delegates while the Congress is Setting, they have ordered that all letters from & to them be Carried post free as you will see by the publick prints.[1]

I hope our Colony will omit nothing in their power to put themselves in a good State of Defence for unless good providence interpose, I Believe the ministry will use their greatest Efforts the spring and Summer

Coming to Subdue us to slavery thus it appears by the latest & best accounts.

If we Can Stand our ground one year more I make no Doubt things will turn to our minds.

Capt. Langdon went off to Ticonderoga the 12th Inst so I am left here alone in behalf of our Colony & am obliged to attend Constanly otherwise the Colony will have no vote. We frequently leave off so late as Scarely to Dine by Daylight. I am in good Health hope this will find you & your family So too. Remember me to all friends. I am sir your friend and servant.   Josiah Bartlett

P.S. Please to inform me how the Gentlemen at Portsmouth behaved in the late Surprize there[2] and Excuse my incorrectness & Blotings as I have not time to Copy it and write in haste by Candle light.   J. B.

RC (PHi).

1. The resolution of 8 November was printed two days later in the *Pennsylvania Packet. JCC*, 3:342.

2. The "late Surprize" was a scare that Portsmouth would be attacked, as was Falmouth in mid-October. During late October and early November Portsmouth built defenses to meet "the late sudden alarming emergency." *N.H. Gazette*, 2 Nov. 1775; *NHSP*, 7:651; Brighton, *They Came to Fish*, 1:64–65.

TO MARY BARTLETT

My Dear   Philadelphia Decembr 4th 1775

Yesterday I Received yours of the 17th Instant[1] and have the Satisfaction to be informed you are well (Except Colds). I am well Tho I have lately had Something more of my old headach than I had for Sometime after I got well of the Smallpox. I had that Distemper So very favorable that no person would Suspect I have had it by my looks; have but a few pock in my face & them So Small as not to be seen unless Carefully looked for.

When I Shall be able to return I Can inform you no more than when I wrote you last. Some news of Governor Dunmores Behavior in virginia will I See Detain me here longer than I was in hopes of,[2] However Still hope I Shall be able to Set out from hence by Christmas if not Sooner: Of this one thing you may be Assured that as Soon as I Can return with propriety I shall immediately Set out, for I am Sure you Cannot be more Desirous of Seing me than I am of Seeing you & the family. But as providence has Called me here I Cannot Return (and I Believe you would not Desire I Should) till the Business will permit me to Do it with honor. In the meantime whither I return Soon or not before Spring (which must in a great Measure Depend on what news we Receive) I hope and trust kind providence will order all things for the best, that our lives & healths may be preserved and we brought to See Each other again in health & Safety. Let us Endeavor to make our lives as Comfortable as we Can and be Contented with the allotments of providence.

I have wrote you Every week last month & Shall Continue to write Every week while I tary here be it longer or shorter. Hope not to write you from hence above once or twice more. As to my affairs at home I must leave them to your Direction till my return. Hope if you want any advice or assistance the Neighbours will not be backward. Give Peter a particular Charge to take good Care of the Cattle & not to waste the hay and Encourage him to behave well till my Return.[3]

Give my Compliments to Mr. Thurstin & to all that ask after me. Remember my love to all the Children: I think a good Deal of them all, particularly poor Ezra; hope he is as well as when I left you otherwise think you would have wrote to me.

Tell my Daughters I Recd their letter[4] & that I want to see them as much as they Do me. I Believe the account of the rising in England is not to be Depended on. Doctr Church is not to be Brought here at present but Confined in Conecticut till further order. I Believe no very great number of Regulars will be Sent from England this fall but think they may be Some Expected in the Spring. I hope the news they mention of the Gentleman at Exeter is not true. I Shall be very Sorry if it is. In haste I Still Remain yours.   Josiah Bartlett

Decembr 4th 1775

P.S. George is well. The weather here is Cold & the ground froze.

RC (NhHi).

1. Not found.

2. In October and November John Murray, Earl of Dunmore and governor of Virginia, had dispersed American forces at Norfolk and offered freedom to the slaves. Wallace, *Appeal to Arms*, 89; Boyd, *Papers of Jefferson*, 1:261n.

3. Peter, a Negro servant, did not always behave. On 13 Feb. 1776 Mary was forced to request public assistance to locate the runaway Peter whom she described as "thick Set about Seventeen Years of age." (NhHi).

4. Not found.

TO THE COMMITTEE OF SAFETY

Gentm.   Philadelphia Decembr 4th 1775

Yesterday I Received yours of the 21st Ultmo Requesting the Congress to grant a Sum of money to our Colony towards what we have advancd on account of the Continent. I took the oppertunity this morning to lay the Same before Congress, who have voted us the Sum of forty Thousand Dollars as you will See by the inclosed Extract from their minutes.[1] I fear it will not be ready in less than three or four weeks from this time, as all that has been Emitted is Expended, and Several grants, previous to ours, made on the next Emission, which was ordered by Congress near a month ago. But the Committe has been retarded for want of proper paper; they now Say they Shall begin in a few Days. If the Congress Should not rise before the money is ready (which is at present uncertain) I will use my best Endeavors to Send it as Soon as possible by Some Safe Conveyance. Perhaps I may send it to Cambridge and inform you that you may Send for it there. If the Congress Shall rise before it Can be procured I will to give orders to have it Sent as Soon as may be; unless by tarrying a Short time I Can bring it with me. I am Gentm. with great Respect your very Humble Servt.   Josiah Bartlett

RC (Nh-Ar). Docketed: "recd 20th Decr." Enclosure not found.
  1. The resolve is printed in *JCC*, 3:403.

TO THE COMMITTEE OF SAFETY

Gentm.   Philadelphia December 21st 1775

The Congress having Determined to Build at Continental Expence a number of Ships of war in the united Colonies to be ready for Sea if possible by the last of march next: Have agreed that one, of the Inclosed Dementions, to Cary 32 guns, be Built in our Colony. It is proposed that one or 2 persons well Skilled in Ship building, of approved Integrity, be forthwith appointed to provide the materials, Employ workmen, oversee the Business, to Keep Exact & Regular accounts of the whole to Draw on the Marine Committe of Congress for money to Cary on the Business, and to be accountable to Said Committe; for all which they will be handsomely Rewarded. As the Ship Building business is out of my sphere I am unwilling to nominate the Said overseers: I am therefore Directed by Said Committe to Desire you immediately to Consider of proper overseers also of a proper place for Building Said vessel, both for safety & Convenience of Materials & workmen. She will be about 700 tons; an Exact Draught will be sent forward in a few Days. In the mean time it will be necessary for the overseers to Buy up without Loss of time, Every necessary for Building & fitting out said ship, and what Cant be had in our Colony must [   ] notified to the marine Committe at Philadelphia [   ] they may provide it. The marine Comtte [   ] of one Delegate from Each Colony.[1]

You will take Care to name Such Suitable persons [   ] our Ship may be as well Built, as Soon & as Cheap [   ] any of the Colonies and that as Soon as the draught of the ship shall arrive they may be ready to proceed on the Business immediately.

Four vessels are purchased by the Congress and are now ready for sea. One Carries 20 guns the others less.[2] The ships that are to be Built are 5 of 32 guns 5 of 28 Do. 3 of 24 Do. one to be Built New Hampshire 2 Massachusetts 2 Rhode Island one Conecticut two New York four Pensylvania one Maryland. I hope you have Recd mine enclosing the vote of Congress Concerning our Civil Goverment Tho I have Recd no account of it. In my last I informed you that the Congress had voted our Colony forty thousand Dollars in part of our Demand till the account Can be setled. The money is yet not ready to be sent. I am Gentm. your friend and Humble Servt.   Josiah Bartlett

P.S. I have Sent a printed Copy of the Journals of last session of Congress.

This was wrote to sent[3] to the Comtte before Mr. Langdon's arrival from Ticonderoga.[4] On his return before sending off the letter at his Request I appointed him to build the Ship and he returned home for that purpose.

RC (NhD). Franked. This letter and address are entirely crossed through; but the final note, written on the address side of the paper, presented here following the postscript, indicates that perhaps John Langdon conveyed the letter to the Committee of Safety or the General Court. Bracketed spaces indicate a large tear in the manuscript.

1. On 13 December Congress resolved to construct thirteen naval frigates, including one to be built in New Hampshire. The following day Congress created a permanent committee of one delegate from each province to manage naval operations. JB was New Hampshire's first member of this Marine Committee. *JCC*, 3:425–28.

2. The four–ships *Alfred* and *Columbus* and brigs *Andrew Doria* and *Cabot*—joined by two sloops and two schooners, all under Commodore Esek Hopkins, made up this first Continental fleet. The Naval Committee of seven congressmen

had directed the organization of this force during the fall of 1775. Though ready to sail at this time, the fleet remained hemmed in the Delaware River by ice until mid–February. Mevers, "Congress," 14–40.

3. JB evidently meant either "to be sent" or "to send."

4. The committee to Ticonderoga returned during the weekend of Saturday, 21 December, and submitted its lengthy report to Congress on Monday. *JCC*, 3:446–52. Langdon had set out for New Hampshire by the end of 1775. See JB to Mary Bartlett, 1 Jan. 1776.

TO MARY BARTLETT   Philadelphia Decembr 25th 1775
My Dear   10 of the Clock in the Evening

I this moment Receivd yours of the 7th Instant[1] and with pleasure hear you & the family are well. But am Sorry to inform you that I Cannot return to you at present. So much Business lays before the Congres; I fear it wont rise for Some time, when it Does rise, one Delegate from Each Colony must tarry to transact the Publick Business in the recess, So that I think I shall not be able to return till towards Spring. Capt. Langdon is returned here from Ticonderoga, and I Expect he will return to Pourtsmouth in a few Days and George will return with him. I will Endeavor to send by him the things you mention in your letter and by George shall write you more fully.

I am Extremely Sorry for the Disappointment we both have in my not returning so soon as I Expected & gave you reason to Expect, But I hope all will turn out for the best. Who Knows but that if I had Set out this very Severe weather it might have been the means of my Death and so hinder my being Ever able to see you; in short I desingn to make my self as Easy as possible and hope you will Do the Same and make your life as Comfortable as you Can.

I intend to send you Some mony by George and hope you will lay it out for what you want. I am in good health but very tender by being Confined here for above 3 months with but little Exercise; this Day being Christmas the Congress Did not set, so I had an oppertunity to ride about 6 or 7 miles out of town in a sley. Yesterday and the Day before we had a severe Cold Storm of Snow which is now about Six inches Deep. Desire Capt. Calef to look me out a good faithful Steady hand & hire him for me for 9 months or a year to assist in my farming Business. I am Determined to return as soon as I Can with propriety. Give my Kind regards to Capt. Calef Col. Grely Leut Pearson and all friends. I remain yours &c.

Josiah Bartlett

I had rather Capt. Calef should give something Extraordinary than not have a good hand. Ebenr Hills has the Small pox by innoculation pretty favorable as his Doctr tells me.[2]   JB:

RC (NhHi). On the verso is a letter from Mary dated 9 Feb. 1776.
    1. Not found.
    2. Probably Ebenezer Hills (1748–c. 1806) of Malden, Mass., a brother of John Hills (1752–1787). John, a graduate of Harvard College in 1772, was recorded as living in Kingston in 1774 and taught

school there for several years. On 4 May 1776 JB recorded the settling of an account with Ebenezer Hills. Hills, *Hills Family*, 271, 292; MJB 5029. See also JB to Mary Bartlett, 1 Jan. 1776.

TO MARY BARTLETT

My Dear   Philadelphia January first 1776
   This will be Delivered you by Gideon George, who I have Consented should return home without me. Capt. Langdon & his man returns with him, So that I shall be now here without any body from Newhampshire. I was, till lately in hopes I should be able to return with him; but to my great Disappointment I now find Publick Business will not permit me to leave this place till our Newhampshire Convention appoint & send another Delegate to take my place here: I shall write to our Convention for that purpose. The time will Seem long, but if providence favor us with health we must make our selves Easy.
   I have wrote to Capt. Calef to Desire his assistance in purchasing any necessaries you may want, and to hire a hand for me for nine months or a year. Some things that I would have taken Care of, in the farming Business, I have mentioned in the Enclosed paper.[1] As I Dont Know what want you may have of money, I have sent you Enclosed the value of [illegible] Dollars which you will make use of as you may find necessary. Last Sunday morning at 3 o'Clock we were alarmed with the Cry of fire when a printing office &c. were burnt. For any particulars of this or any other affairs in this City George Can give you good information. I have given orders to George about sending the horse he rides home to Capt. Page—what Cost you are at about it must be Kept account of.[2]
   I have sent you Some few things which will be named in the Enclosed paper. I fear I shall not hear from you for some time, as you have looked for me home and I suppose not wrote to me, but I hope from the time you Receive this till my Return you will write to me Every week. The last letter I receivd was yours of the 7th of December. I have wrote a letter to be Delivered to Capt. Page with the horse. Any particular things you may be Desirous of being informed of & knowing my mind about before my return you will I hope mention to me in your letters. I shall Constantly write to you nearly Every week.[3] Remember me to all that ask after me. Remember me to James Procter.[4]
   If you have any school I should be glad to have Levi attend it as much as Possible. If not let Mr. Hills[5] or Dr. Gale write him some Copies & let him write. I hope he will take Care to get as much Learning as possible

and not Idle away his time now he is young so as to be a great Dunce when he grows up. Let me Know particularly how Ezra is. I Remain as usual yours &c.   Josiah Bartlett

RC (NhHi).

1. The enclosure gives more explicit instructions on managing the farm and lists the items JB is sending back with Gideon George. MJB 736.

2. Caleb Page (1705–1785) of Dunbarton had obtained two horses from Capt. Robert Wilson of Chester for JB's journey to Philadelphia. Both Page and Wilson were representatives to the fourth provincial congress in May 1775. Stark, *Dunbarton*, 181–89; NHSP, 7:468–70; MJB 820.

3. Judging by later performance, it can be presumed that JB wrote every week. If so, however, many of his letters are lost.

4. James Proctor (1722–1776), Kingston blacksmith, was a neighbor of JB. Proctor, *Genealogy*, 23; N.H. Deeds, 63:107; 71:382; 97:30.

5. Probably John Hills. See JB to Mary, 25 Dec. 1775, n. 2.

TO JOHN LANGDON

Sir,   Philadelphia Jany 13th 1776

I wrote you 9th inst[1] per post informing you of a contract for importing goods for the use of the Army to the amount of ten thousand dollars which the Secret Committee are willing to make with you which letter I hope will come safe to your hands, and that you will answer it as soon as may be.

Last evening the draughts of the several ships of war were laid before the Marine Committee and approved of; and they have ordered one for each of the Contractors to be forthwith made out. But it is so large I know not how to send it to you: it cannot be sent in a letter and what other way to contrive I know not, but will do the best I can as soon as I can procure it.

This morning I see in the newspaper (which by the way is almost the only way I hear from our Colony) that Portsmouth had appointed Messrs Cutts, Sherburne and Long, to represent that town in Provincial Convention, and by the Instructions I find the town is very much afraid of the idea conveyed by the frightful word *Independence*![2] This week a pamphlet on that subject was printed here, and greedily bought up and read by all ranks of people.[3] I shall send you one of them, which you will please to lend round to the people; perhaps on consideration there may not appear any thing so terrible in that thought as they might at first apprehend, if Britain should force us to break off all connections with her. Give my compliments to Col. Whipple[4] who I see is left out by the Town in their choice of Delegates for the Provincial Convention. I am Sir your friend and Servt.   Josiah Bartlett

P.S. The 57 tons of salt petre which arrived here last week was this day by order of Congress purchased by the Secret Committee for the use of the Continent and three tons of powder this day arrived here from the Jersies.   J. B.

Pray write me a full account of our affairs and don't forget to put the Colony in mind to send Delegates here as soon as may be that I may return to my family.

TR (DLC:Force Transcripts).

1. Not found, but see JB to Committee of Safety, 9 January.

2. Samuel Cutts (d. 1801), Samuel Sherburne (1744–1826), and Pierse Long (c. 1739–1789), all Portsmouth merchants, were elected to the fifth provincial congress, which met on 21 Dec. 1775. *NHSP*, 7:690; Bartlett, "Portsmouth Families"; Shipton, *Harvard Graduates*, 16:231–34.

3. This was Thomas Paine's pamphlet *Common Sense: Addressed to the Inhabitants of America*. In Philadelphia's bookstalls by 9 Jan. 1776, it had probably sold 150,000 copies by the end of the year. Hawke, *Paine*, 44–47.

4. William Whipple (1730–1785), Portsmouth merchant, served in the Continental Congress in 1775, 1776, and 1778, as a brigadier general in 1777, and as a judge on the New Hampshire Superior Court. Dorothy M. Vaughan, *This Was a Man* (n.p., 1964); Obituary, *N.H. Gazette*, 9 Dec. 1785.

TO THE COMMITTEE OF SAFETY

Gentlemen   Philadelphia Jany 20th 1776

The Congress on the 8th Inst voted to raise one Regiment in the western parts of our Province for the Service in Canada: The news of the Misfortune at Quebeck arriving here last thursday,[1] They voted yesterday to give the men a Bounty of forty shillings and one months pay advance, to Encourage the Speedy inlisting & sending forward Said Regiment, and I hope you will do every thing in your power to hasten it, as the taking & Securing Canada this winter or Early in the Spring before the arrival of Brittish troops, will be of almost Infinite advantage to the Continent, more Especially to New England and to our Colony in particular. One Regiment will begin to march from this place for Canada in a few Days, and one Regiment from New Jersey in 8 or ten Days; orders are also given to raise as Soon as possible for the Same Service; (Beside those in Newhampshire) one more Regiment in Pensylvania, one Do. New Jersey, One Do. on the western parts of New york, and One Do. in Conecticut, and this Day I Expect one will be ordered to be raised in Massachusetts, for the same purpose: no Cost or pains must be Spared to Secure the important Province of Canada.[2]

I Beg leave to renew my request, that Delegates may be appointed & Sent here as Soon as may be, as in my opinion the Representation of a Colony at this important Crisis is too weighty and important to be intrusted to any one person. That you may See the necessity of a larger Representation of our Colony, I would inform you, that Beside Committees for Special purposes that are frequently Chosen, there are four or five Standing Committees appointed, Some for Secrecy, Some for Dispatch, Some of which Committees are Entrusted with large powers and that there may be no Cause of Complaint, Those Committees Consist of one Delegate from Each Colony; Sometimes two, Sometimes 3, of those Committees Set at the Same time. So that tho I attend Some one of the Committees almost Every night & morning before & after Congress yet some Business of Consequence is transacted by them without our Colony being Represented, and sometimes the Committees Set while the Congress is Seting so that our Colony must be unrepresented in one of them, while Every other Colony may be represented in Both.

I have been here almost five months a great part of the time without a Coleague. I really find that I never knew what Confinement with Business was before; and that I want more Exercise of Body & less of mind, at least for Sometime. I please my self with hopes I shall soon see Delegates here from our Colony and that I may return to my family, and with my Domestick affairs relax and unbend my fatigued mind.

The Sum of 12500 Dollars which the Congress ordered to be Sent to you, to be used in raising our Regiment for Canada, I shall Send forward as Soon as I Can.[3] Please to acquaint me with the Publick affairs of our Colony as often as Convenient, and in particular of your Success from time to time in raising the Regiment. As the Congress have Entrusted you with appointing the officers, I know you will Do the best you Can to appoint proper persons, and hope you will be so fortunate as to give general Satisfaction.[4] I am Gentln your most obedient servant.

Josiah Bartlett

RC (Nh-Ar).

1. During November and December of 1775 two American forces—one from Cambridge under Benedict Arnold and one from Fort Ticonderoga under Gen. Richard Montgomery—marched toward Quebec. The forces attacked early on 31 December during a raging snowstorm. Under Gen. Guy Carleton's leadership the British repulsed the attack, killing Montgomery and taking many American prisoners. Wallace, *Appeal to Arms*, 76–84.

2. See *JCC*, 4:70–71.

3. JB sent the money on 24 January. MJB 754.

4. On that day, 20 January, Congress had ordered that the New Hampshire General Court or Committee of Safety be entrusted with blank commissions for appointing field officers to command the battalion raised for the invasion of Canada. *JCC*, 4:74–75.

TO MARY BARTLETT

My Dear Philadelphia Janry 24th 1776

Yours of the 6th Inst:[1] I Received the 22nd & as I had not Received any letter from you Since yours of the 7th of December, it gave me great pleasure to hear you & my family were well the 6th of this month; I hope you & they Still Continue So. I am by the favor of kind providence in health at this time: I have been lately a little troubled with a pain in my head, owing I suppose to my being So long Confined without any Bodily Exercise: as the Days grow longer I Design Every Day before or after Congress to ride or walk an hour or two; I have 2 or 3 Days this week, after the Congress rose walked from 5 to 6 of the Clock. At four the Congress Comonly rise, Dine by 5, walk till Six, then on a Committe till 8, 9 or 10: this is Comonly my Business Every Day.

I have wrote to our Convention at Exeter to request them to send Delegates here, which I hope they will Comply with; as soon as they arrive here, I shall prepare to return home. Remember me to All the Children, to Col. Greely, Mr. Procter, and all friends. I hope Capt. Calef has hired me a good faithful hand: give my Kind regards to him and tell him I am glad to hear he has Success in making Salt petre. Tell Polly & Lois I Recd their letter[2] and shall write to Mr. Sweat about the powder mill. I am yours &c.   Josiah Bartlett

P.S. The Express is going so soon I Can't write to Samll Sweat[3] but will Endeavor to next week.

RC (NhHi).

1. Not found.
2. Not found.
3. Samuel Sweat (1744–1792), a joiner of Kingston and son of Deacon Benjamin Sweat, signed a petition for bounty on the manufacture of saltpeter on 12 March

1776. Sweat had worked on JB's house and kept a diary of his activities over several years. Stackpole, *Swett Genealogy*, 35–36; *NHSP*, 17:42–43; Lacy, "Samuel Sweat's Diary, 1772–1774."

FROM EBENEZER THOMPSON

Dear Sir   Durham Janry. 29th. 1776

I Acknowledge my fault in not writing to you since November, but must plead in excuse that I expected you would not remain at Philadelphia much longer after that time, until Capt. Langdon came home and told you had consented to tarry until Spring. Since his arrival I have been much Hurried in Public Business, however I now engage to write often, if it is only to let you know there is such a place as New Hampshire remaining.

Before the Dissolution of our late Congress a Plan for a General Representation was agreed upon to consist of 89 Persons; in consequence of which Writs Issued, and the Delegates chosen were Impowered by their Constituents, in case a Recommendation should be sent us from the Continental Congress for taking up Government to Resolve themselves into a House of Representatives & proceed as Recommended.[1]

Before the Meeting of the new Congress the Recommendation about Government arrived, and when met they proceeded on the Business, several Members being of Opinion that the best way was for the Congress to remain under that name and Assume the Power of appointing all Publick Officers; but it was carried by a Majority of Two to one for forming two Branches, in the manner you will see by the inclosed Resolve.[2] The Minority did not appear very much displeased when the Resolve passed, but after the choice of the Council a Violent opposition appeared. Ten Members protested against the proceedings, and about as many Towns Petitioned for a reconsideration urging that taking up Government in that way savoured too much of Independantcy. However Mr. Langdons coming has Abated the Noise and I hope it will pass over without much Difficulty if some new mull Wind dont blow up the Smothered

Coals; as I beleive it all arose from Disappointment: which I expected beforehand wou'd be the case, as every one could not be chosen to such offices as they desired.

Our Batteries on Sevey's, and Pierce's Islands were finished last Fall, Twenty Three Cannon are Mounted in both, some 32 & some 24 pounders among them. A Magazine, that is Bomb proof in one of them, tho' very little Powder in it. Also Barracks to Lodge 200 Matrosses in & near both. Two Hundred Matrosses are constantly kept at the two forts and they have lately Enlisted for a Year. Since the Burning Falmouth we have had a Considerable Body of soldiers posted at Portsmouth & New Castle, about three Weeks there were 1400 since for a considerable time about 700, and at this time none except Matrosses they having been sent down to Head Quarters to tarry a while until they can form their new army— But a considerable number of Troops must be soon raised and sined at our Harbour, considering our Vicinity to Boston, and with what Ease a Descent may be made upon us from thence for which reasons I could wish your Congress would order a Battalion of Troops in our Colony as they have Done in Others, more able & less exposed than we.

Three vessels from Portsmouth Laden with Beef, & Some Cash on Board, Sailed about a Month past in Quest of Powder at the Colony Risque.

The making Salt Petre, begins to make considerable progress & I verily believe before Spring Great Quantity's will be made in this Colony, It is but lately began, and suceeds so well that I hear one Capt. Calfe of Kingtown has made 200 weight & several others 100 Pounds, & upwards each and Scarce a Town but what they are beginning and in some Towns great numbers, in Short all the Pot ash works in the Colony are or I believe will be employed therein. The Method used here is Simple and Easy, the same that it is likely you have seen published by the Massachusetts Committee.

Upon hearing the news of the unhappy Defeat at Quebeck, this Colony, (the Court being then Setting) the same day ordered a regiment to be raised with all possible dispatch to march there & tarry for a year, Coll. Bedel[3] Commands it and will be ready to march soon I expect, as most of the men I hear is Enlisted, tho' the fitting this Regiment will be prodigious Expensive.

The Ensuing Summer, I expect will Determine the Fate of this great Struggle, that at the end of which you & I may see America crowned with Laurels is above all other things the hearty and Inveriable wishes of your most Humble Sevt. E. Thompson

P.S. Since writing the above, I received yours of the 9th. of Janry. for which I am really Obliged to you. And am Glad the Raising of the Canada Regiment happens to be done so consistent with the mind of Congress. I forgot to let you know, That yourself, Capt. Langdon & Coll. Whipple are appointed Delegates for the Ensueing years.[4] Coll. Whipple Intends very soon to set out to relieve you. ET

RC (NhD). Dated clearly; but docketed: "Decembr 29 1776."

1. The plan for representation had been adopted on 14 Nov. 1775. *NHSP*, 7:657–60.

2. The fifth provincial congress met in Exeter on 21 Dec. 1775. On the twenty-seventh it voted to take up a new form of government, and on the twenty-eighth appointed a committee to draft a constitution. *NHSP*, 7:690, 703–04. As adopted on 5 Jan. 1776 the constitution established a government of two branches—a house of representatives and a twelve-member executive council. The enclosed resolve was a copy of the constitution as embodied in the journals of the House of Representatives. JB was elected to the Council. *NHSP*, 8:1–4, 6.

3. Timothy Bedel (d. 1787) of Bath and Haverhill had fought in the French and Indian War. He represented Bath in New Hampshire's fourth provincial congress, which appointed him colonel of a regiment of provincial Rangers in 1775. On 20 Jan. 1776 he was commissioned colonel of the New Hampshire regiment for the army under General Schuyler. *NHSP*, 7:655; 8:45; Heitman, *Historical Register*, 95.

4. On 23 January the General Court (i.e., the House of Representatives and the Executive Council, according to the constitution of 5 January) had appointed JB, John Langdon, and William Whipple as delegates to the Continental Congress for 1776. *NHSP*, 8:51; MJB 751.

TO JOHN LANGDON

Dear Sir,   Philadelphia Feby 3d 1776

Your's of the 22d ultimo[1] I recd the first inst:, and am glad to hear you got home well and in good order. I perceive by your letter that our Colony have taken up Govt: as you say a "Committee of both Houses waited on you" and "that some difficulties had arose which you hoped would be soon ended." I wish you had been a little more particular, as I am very desirous of knowing how things go on in our Province. I am glad to hear that delegates are like to be soon sent here to relieve me; hope good hearty Sons of Liberty will be appointed. I hope the Gentn you say has the same as he had in the Militia will be taken proper notice of in the appointments—Quere—whether the office of High Sheriff of the County of Rockingham might not be agreeable to him.

I have not been able to procure the draft of the ship till last night, shall send it as soon as possible and shall enclose in this letter some directions about building. I enquired of the Committee concerning the bigness of the masts; they say they know of no stated rule so it must be left to your and the carpenter's discretion. I sent you a contract with the Secret Committee for ten thousand dollars for importing sail cloth, blankets &c. which I hope you have rec'd.[2] I have the pleasure to inform you that Mifflin's brig arrived in this river yesterday with sixty tons of salt petre and seven tons and a half of powder on account of the contract and five tons and a half of powder and 1297 complete stands of arms as a private adventure; and this day the Secret Committee have sent down to Reedy Island to land the cargo and bring it up by land as the ice hinders her getting up any further.

While I tarry here I shall expect to hear from you every week and hope you will if you have time be a little more particular, and if it should be in my power to serve you, I shall do it with great pleasure.

Capt. Hazzen of Canada who came here with the news of the fate of poor Montgomery is appointed Col. of a regiment of Canadians and is returned to raise them. Col. Bull's regt are gone off for Canada; the first company has I hope got to Albany by this time.[3] I hope our Colony will use their utmost to raise and send forward the regt for Canada that Quebec may be taken before the enemy arrives in the Spring.

General Prescot for his conduct with regard to Col. Allen is by order of Congress confined in close gaol in this city.[4]

Our men of war fell down the river the fore part of last month but stopping about 30 miles down to take in supplies were stopped by the ice and have not yet sailed.[5]

Col. Gadsen is returned home. The draft is so big I cannot send it by the post. Mr. Hancock will send it with those for their Province in a few days. The dimensions for the *Pallas* frigate is sent by Govr Hopkins desire: he says it may be of some advantage.[6] I am your sincere friend.

Josiah Bartlett

TR: (DLC: Force Transcripts).
1. Not found.
2. Not found.
3. Moses Hazen (d. 1803), who had been a lieutenant in the British army, was appointed on 22 January. Maj. Gen. Richard Montgomery (1735–1775), who had served in the French and Indian War, was killed in the attack on Quebec, 31 Dec. 1775. John Bull (d. 1824) had resigned command of the first Pennsylvania battalion on 20 January. Heitman, *Historical Register*, 131, 282; JCC, 4:72–73, 78.
4. See JCC, 4:22–23, 78, for the charges against British Gen. Richard Prescott. Ethan Allen (1738–1789) was the leader

of the Green Mountain Boys in Vermont. See Pell, *Ethan Allen*.
5. The naval fleet was delayed at Reedy Island. See 21 Dec. 1775, n. 2.
6. Christopher Gadsden (1723–1805), a merchant and political leader of South Carolina, served in the Continental Congress in 1774 and from May 1775 to January 1776. John Hancock (1736–1793) was president of Congress from May 1775 to October 1776. Stephen Hopkins (1707–1785), senior member of Congress in 1776, had served as a colonial governor of Rhode Island and was highly influential in establishing the Continental Navy.

FROM MESHECH WEARE

Sr   Exeter Feby 8th. 1776

Your favours of the 9th & 20th Ulto. we acknowledge the Receipt of,[1] And are heartily Sorry for the Loss at Quebec—especially of General Montgomery. But previous to the Receipt of any Letter from Philledelphia, And at the Request of his Excelly General Washington, we had given Orders to Raise a Regiment in the upper part of our Colony which is now nearly Compleated, and Some part of them Already marched of, Who are under the Command of Collo. Beedel. We differ'd a little in our Encouragement to the Soldiers, which was to have been Two months advance pay But Since the Receipt of a Letter from your President, we have followed his Directions and given 4 of Bounty and One months pay advance, agreable to the Resolves of Congress.[2] Nothing has been wanting in us, in having Said Regimt Raised and in forwarding the Same—Who We hope may arrive in Time, And that all Canada may fall into our hands, Without which we are to expect Every difficulty on the frontiers, And on ours in Particular, Which Convinces us that no Cost Ought to be

Spared to Secure the Same. Your hint was hardly in Season, to put us in Mind of Choosing another delagate to attend the Congress. As that business was done before your favour Came to hand—We concluded it was Necessary, especially as we found One of ours was for Some time out of the way, And will Necessairly be detained here. Our Colonys Poverty you are Perfectly acquainted with, Therefore its Needless to inform you that was Reason which Confined us to the Choice of one Only By whom you will Receive this—And pray you would assist him in Getting a Credit for as much Money of the Congress as will Procure 1000 Barrels of Flowr, And have the Same Shipped to this Port as Soon as may be. We are Convinced its the hardest of Labours to be Confined So much as you are, But if your health, Should not be impared thereby, you will Still Perservere In the Arduous Task, And in the End Receive the Plaudets of Your Country men for your good Services. The money you mention to be order'd to be Sent to us by the Congress for the Use of the Northern Army, we have not as yet Received, And at the Same time Remind you, it is much Less than what we have advanc'd them. We are preparing our accounts of Expences as well Provincial as Continental, And when Compleated Shall be forwarded, which we hope wont be Long first. As to other Public matters they Stand with us much as per last Only that we are convinced that it wont be above one Month, before we Shall be under the Necessity of Raising a Number of Men, for the Defence of our Metropolis: At least One Battalion, And have taken the Liberty to petition the Congress to fix them as Continentals, Which we are Very desirous of having Granted, And ask your Intrest in getting the Same Accomplished. We likewise acknowledge the Receipt of Common Sence for which we are much obliged to you.

We cannot find by the Records that there has been any Petitions forwarded to Great Britain, Since The Commencement of these Time's. By Order of the Committee I am sr Your mt hum. Sev.   Meshech Weare

RC (MeHi: The John S. H. Fogg Autograph Collection). In clerk's hand; signed by Weare.

1. Meshech Weare (1713–1786), a farmer and jurist of Hampton Falls, was chairman of the N.H. Committee of Safety. He had served in the General Court since 1745 and during the Revolution was the state's leader as chairman of the Committee of Safety and of the Executive Council under the constitution of 1776. Butters, "New Hampshire History and the Public Career of Meshech Weare, 1713–1786."

2. Washington's letter of 19 January and Hancock's of the twelfth, both to the Committee of Safety, are printed in NHSP, 8:38–39.

The following is the first of forty-two extant letters from Mary Bartlett to JB while he attended Congress in 1776 and again in 1778. Most of these letters reflect routine problems of the Bartlett family and Kingston community. Available on microfilm to the specific audience they address, only a few of Mary's letters could be selected for publication here. The letters appear in several different handwritings. Mary's daughters could write, and it is conjectured that either Mary (Polly) or Lois, the elder daughters, wrote most of their mother's letters. (Polly's writing is especially apparent in her postscript to JB's letter to Levi Bartlett, 22 Sept. 1777. MJB 1244.) Enough handwriting of her elder sons, Levi and Josiah, is evident to conclude that they did not write Mary's letters. It is quite possible that Mary, in the midst of her unceasing activities as parent, homemaker, and businesswoman, dictated her thoughts while one of her daughters wrote them out. An attempt is made here to identify the writer of each letter printed.

FROM MARY BARTLETT

My Dear   feb 9 1776

I heaving an oppertynity to send a Letter by Collel Whippel which I expect will be the Last I shall send to you as I expect you will set out for home as soon as he arrives at phaledelphia. He wrote to me he should set out the 12th of febuary from portsmouth.

I hope you will prepare your self for your journey both for your health & for your Defence. I would advise you not to take your jorney to tegous of as to worry you. If you have a mind I should send a man to meet you as far as Cambridge, watertown or Connecticut if you Can write & Describe the time when & place where he shall meet you I will endeavour to send a man. I hope these Lins will find you in good helth & may you continue so. My self & the rest of the family by the favour of Devine Providance are very Comfortably at this time.

Draft (NhHi). In Mary's hand, written on the reverse of JB's letter of 25 Dec. 1775.

FROM MESHECH WEARE

Gentn.   Exeter, 10 February 1776

Inclosed in this Packet you will find a Representation of the taking up Government and Difficultys that have arisen with Several Copies relating thereto.[1] We desire you would lay them before the Congress, And Endeavour to Obtain their Oppinion thereon as we Expect uneasiness will remain untill the Same is Obtained, which we hope will Settle the dust and desire you will be Assiduous in Getting it decided and forwarded as soon as may be. By order of the Committee I am Gentn Your most hum Servt.   M Weare Chairman

RC (NhD). In clerk's hand; signed by Weare. Addressed to JB and William Whipple.

1. Enclosed in the packet were petitions from several New Hampshire towns and a remonstrance signed by some members of the House of Representatives protesting adoption of the state constitution (Nh-Ar). A long letter, also signed by Weare, covering these documents was addressed to the "Honourable Congress of the United Colonies of North America" and is printed in *NHSP*, 8:65–66. See also Upton, *Revolutionary New Hampshire*, 178–79.

On this date Receiver General Nicholas Gilman issued a receipt to Jared Tracey for $12,500 brought from Congress for the use of New Hampshire (Nh).

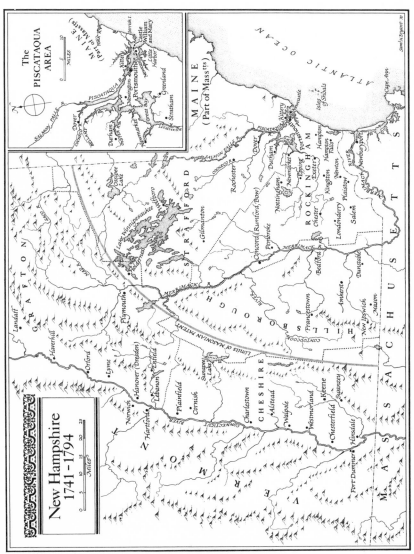

Josiah Bartlett's New Hampshire as drawn by Samuel H. Bryant, 1970.
Courtesy of Jere R. Daniell.

TO JOHN LANGDON

Dear Sir,   Philadelphia Feby 13th 1776

I have rec'd your's of the 29th ulto[1] which is now before me and in answer would inform you that I have last week sent you all the votes of the Committee that you will want that are already passed. The draft goes this day with the money to the Camp at Cambridge.[2]

As to your being further impowered, I have took the opinion of many of the Committee separately (for there has been no meeting since I rec'd yours) and they are all of opinion that you are already authorised to build, rig, equip and fit for sea the ship to be built in our Colony and that you will do it according to your discretion, except where you have particular orders: what orders are sent to you are the same that are sent to the other builders and where any thing cannot be supplied in the Colony they will inform the Committee by a letter to the Chairman. Hemp and cordage you say are high; as to that I would inform you that Mr. Lewis[3] has procured a considerable quantity: Russia hemp at 65s. and this country do. from 56s. to 58s. per hundred york money so you will see whether it is best to buy with you or send to New York.

I expect the Committee will meet tomorrow evening; when they meet I will try to procure an order for more money to be sent you and hope to send it off this week and will enquire concerning the length of cable and weight of anchors—as for cannon I believe a Committee of Congress have contracted for them. By order of Congress a detachment of this City Associators equal to one battalion, is ordered to march to New York. Col. Dickinson takes the command: Major Patton goes Major of the detachment and Mr. Dean will go: so I shall be left alone at my lodgings.[4] I expect to see Col. Whipple here the latter end of this week as you say he was to set out the next week when you wrote. I expect to write to you again in a few days, and am your friend &c.   Josiah Bartlett

TR (DLC: Force Transcripts).

1. Not found.

2. This was the draft for the *Raleigh* as approved by the Marine Committee of Congress.

3. Francis Lewis (1713–1803), a delegate from New York, was a member of the Marine Committee. He remained interested in naval affairs throughout the war.

4. Philemon Dickinson (1739–1809) of New Jersey and Delaware was the commander of the New Jersey militia. He

later served in the Continental Congress and in the U.S. Senate. John Patten (1746–1800) of Delaware served in battles from Long Island to Camden and later represented his state in Congress. Congressional delegate Silas Deane (1737–1789) of Connecticut was going home for a brief respite before journeying to France as a representative of Congress. Heitman, *Historical Register*, 197, 429; *JCC*, 4:133; Clark, *Silas Deane*, 37, 42–43.

TO MARY BARTLETT

My Dear   Philadelphia Febry 19th 1776

Yours of the 2nd Inst:[1] I Recd this morning and with pleasure, am informed that you and the family were then well. I think it a great favor, that so large a family, Should be Blessed with health, for so long a time. I hope it will Continue till it Shall please God, to return me home in health. When that will be I know not; But if life and health permit, I hope to be at home before the middle of April, for as Soon as the going is any thing like, I design to Come home, Even if I should be obliged to return again to this City after a short Stay with you.

When I read at the Close of your letter, an account of the Death of my good friend, John Wadleigh, it very sensibly affected me, as I had received no account of his being worse than when I left home. I had really a great value for him, and think the Town & Especially that part of it, have met with a great loss in his Death. I Cant help Calling to mind, the many hours, pleasant Conversation I have had with him, and tho' he had Some Sentiments Different from mine, yet I really Loved & Esteemed him, and I Despise the Bigot, who Can have no Esteem or friendship for any man, whose religious opinions are Different from his own.[2]

This Day Dr. Smith[3] of this City Delivered a funeral Oration, to the Memory of General Montgomery and the other Brave men, who fell in the attack on Quebeck; the oration was Delivered in a large and Beautiful & Elegant Dutch Church. The Congress the General Assembly of this province, the Committes of Safety & inspection, and about 30 Clergymen of the Different Denominations in this City, with other Gentlemen, walked from the Court house, in a Body, to the Church, on Each Side, walked three Regiments of the City Associators. The musick was very solemn & mournful, and Composed with the organs, Bass viol, 8 or 10 violins, german flutes, french horns &c., the whole was Conducted with great order & Decency. The solemnity of the Ocasion, with the news of the Death of my friend Wadleigh, or Something Else, seems to have Setled my Spirits at least a peg too low. I Know that troubles & Disappointments, are the Common lot of all men, and that the Supreme Disposer of all Events, Can, and I really believe, will, over rule all things for the best. That is my greatest Comfort when things Seem to look with a Dark and Dismal Countenance, Either of a publick or private nature.

I am sorry to hear that the post from Cambridge to Exeter, is not likely to Continue riding, as I fear, it will put us under a Difficulty, of gitting Each others letters, but I shall nevertheless Continue to write to you weekly. The weather here has been very pleasant till yesterday, it is now very Cold for this place tho not Equal to Some in Newhampshire.

I am in good health at this time. Remember my love to the Children, and my Regards to all friends.

February 21st I am now very well and Still Remain your   Josiah Bartlett

RC (NhHi).

1. Not found.

2. John Wadleigh (1730–1776), blacksmith, lived in South Kingston, a tax district in Kingston. Although he did not pay the minister's tax and probably was a Quaker, he was chosen a selectman of the town in 1773 and 1775. Kingston Town Records, 3:161; Kingston Vital Records, 18, 80.

3. William Smith (1727–1803) was a controversial Anglican minister of Trinity Church, Oxford, Pa. The preceding June Smith had created a sensation in the colony when he preached to Congress on American affairs.

TO JOHN LANGDON

Dear Sir   Philadelphia Febry 19th 1776

Yours of the first Inst:[1] is now before me, and would inform you, that the Marine Committe look on you as fully Authorised, to Build the Ship to be Built in Newhampshire and finish her fit for the Sea; if any thing is wanted that you Cannot procure, they Expect you will Give them timely notice. The Draught is sent forward & you will no Doubt receive it before this Comes to hand; I Enquired Concerning the length and Bigness of Cables & weight of anchors, but the Committe has not Determined on it: Govr Hopkins Says he told their Contractor that the Cables must be fifteen Inches, & 120 fathoms Long at least, and had sent them the Dementions of the *Pallas* frigate as a rule for the masts & yards of the 32 gun ships; However the Committe advised to apply to the Comissioners for Building the ships in this City, to know their Determination on those articles which as soon as I can procure I will send you.

The Marine Committe have given me an order in your favor, for twenty Thousand Dollars, which I was to have sent by a man who is to take some money for the Ships to be built in Massachusetts. But as you inform me, you have Drawn one and are likely to Draw more orders here, I Believe I shall not send the whole by that oppertunity.

In yours of the 29th ulto.[2] you informed me that Col. Willm. Whipple was to Set out for this place the then next week, and in Consequence I now look out Sharp for him, & hope he will be here this week, as I am Extremely anxious not only for his assistance but to be informed of what nature the Difficulties are which you say have unaccountably turned up in regard of the Civil goverment of the Colony. What you have hinted, has given me vast uneasiness and Could wish you had mentioned the particular Difficulties, for I am greatly at a loss to Guess at them: I am greatly Surprized to hear, that there is Danger, that the poison of Toryism, will spread in the Colony of Newhampshire. If you had informed me of the Danger of the Small pox or *plague* Spreading, it would not have given me half the Concern, as the one is only temporal, and the other in a sense Eternal, for if our rights & privileges are now given up, they are gone forever. I think it very strange that the Committe of Safety, nor any one of them, have wrote me a line of the Situations of the affairs of the Colony, nor answered any of my letters for above three months past. What is the reason I Know not, how Disagreable it must seem, you know by Experience in some measure, however I hope soon to be informed by my worthy Colleagues.

The pamphlet *Comon Sense* has already had three Editions in this city. In the last there is an apendix and large additions, it has also been reprinted at N: York by the best information it has had a Great Effect on the minds of many here & to the southward.

General Lee is ordered for Canada and Schuyler to New York;[3] Col. Dickinson was countermanded Just as he was on the march, hearing that Clinton had sailed. The Common opinion here is, that Comissioners are Coming from England to treat with the Congress. I think it not unlikely, but fear no good will accrue to the Colonies from that measure; if no hurt I Shall be glad.

Dr. Franklin, Mr. Chace & one Caryl of Maryland are going as Deputies from the Congress to Canada.[4] As to an Agent being appointed in the Several Colonies, I Believe it will be a useful Expedient for the Continent, But as yet nothing is Done about it in any of the Colonies.[5] When any thing of that Kind is Done by the Congress in any of the Colonies I will take Care that the Same be Done for us, and make no Doubt you will be appointed, But think it not proper to move it till I see a proper time and things ripe for it. At this time I am Sure it would answer no good end.

Febry 21st. Last Evening the Secret Committe met, Signed the Contract &c. which I shall Enclose to you. They have likewise drawn an order for the Money, which order I have taken and have given my recept that I have recd it for you, but how to Conduct the affair I Know not, whither the treasurers, if I should Desire it, will be willing to Deliver me the money as I have no order from you to Receive it I know not and if I should Receive it without order, and send it Down & any mishap befall it, I may bring my self into Difficulty, without any prospect of advantage. How or when I shall have a safe opertunity to send Down so large a Sum as 30,000 Dollars I know not; The man that Mr. Hancock Expected is not Come and when he Does I am uncertain whither he will be willing to take Charge of it. I Could wish you had given some more particular orders about the money as I am puzzeled how to Conduct for the best. I shall write you again in a few Days.

Yesterday Mr. Lynch was taken with an apoplectic fit and was thought to be near his end, but is something better to Day.

I Believe it is certain the British parliament, has ordered all American vessels to be Seized, as you will see by the publick papers. Two of the outward bound vessels fitted out by the Secret Committe, for the purpose of necessaries, are taken and carried into the West Indies, the master of one has got back. In short we have nothing to Expect from Brittain, but war & Bloodshed, notwithstanding the pretence of sending Commissioners here to treat.

I am this Day informed that a petition to the Congress, is Signing fast by the Inhabitants of this City, for Leave to fit out privateers, and make reprisals on all Brittish vessels, to indemnify them for the Losses they have Sustained by the Depredations of Brittish men of war. Indeed it seems very hard that Brittain is Seizing all American vessels and the Americans are not permitted to return the compliment. The late measure has I think (*sub rosa*) much altered the minds of the people here and in the C———ss too. Give my Compliments to all Enquiring friends, & believe me to be *your* friend.   Josiah Bartlett

P.S. By the latest account it seems the Parliament has altered their measure of treating, and the Comissrs. are to treat with Each Colony separate, which will Certainly, and unfailingly, Destroy the whole, for I am sure no Colony will, at this time, treat seperately; I think I may venture to

Engage for Newhampshire. J: B:

The Invoice of the goods you are to procure with your Contract and the weight of anchors &c. I Shall send in my next.

RC (Capt. J. G. M. Stone Private Collection, Annapolis, Md., 1976).

1. Not found.

2. Not found.

3. Charles Lee (1731–1782), one of the officers originally commissioned a major general in June 1775, had been given command of the Continental Army in Canada. Schuyler's appointment was made the same day, 17 February. Congress subsequently countermanded the order to Lee on 28 February and 1 March. JCC, 4:157, 175, 180–81. See JB to Folsom, 1 July 1776 and notes.

Philip Schuyler (1733–1804), a New York landholder, had been commissioned a major general in the Continental Army in June 1775. As commander of the Northern Department, he organized the 1775 expedition to Canada. He resigned his commission in 1779, but continued in public service until 1798. Bush, *Revolu-*

tionary Enigma.

4. Franklin, Samuel Chase (1741–1811), of Maryland, and Charles Carroll of Carrollton (1737–1832), of Maryland, were appointed commissioners on 15 February. Congress did not complete the draft of their instructions until 23 March. JCC, 4:151–52, 233.

5. Most of the naval agents were appointed in April. Their duties included all dealings with prize vessels taken by the navy or by privateers, supplying naval vessels with all necessities, being of all possible service to naval officers, and maintaining records for and correspondence with the Congress through the Marine Committee. Mevers, "Congress," 67–82; [Morgan], *Maritime Dimensions,* 6–7.

TO JOHN LANGDON

Dear Sir,   Philadelphia March 5 1776

Yours of the 19th ulto[1] is now before me and am very sorry that any person in New Hampshire could pretend to write and print so ridiculous a piece as that you mention; I had the reading of it, being enclosed to Col. Whipple. I think your Committee acted wisely in putting a stop to it, though the chief hurt that will arise from the publishing such trifling inconsistent and puerile pieces is to make the persons and the place producing them mean and ridiculous to every sensible reader. I am extremely sorry that our Colony, who has hitherto stood high in the esteem of the whole Continent, for their manly and spirited exertions in the cause of liberty should by such productions added to some late manoeuvres of Portsmouth and some other towns in regard to taking up govt, fall to the lowest depth of ignominy and contempt, which unless a stop is put it will certainly be the case. The packet containing the whole of the affairs of taking up civil govt. we carried in the evening to the President, who opened it while we were present; after reading the whole to himself for some time, he asked us what was the question the Colony wanted to have put to the Congress for their answer as he said he could not find out by reading the papers, and neither Col. Whipple nor I could inform him; for the order of Congress to take up civil Govt. in such a manner as the Colony should think proper nobody can deny, and that the Colony had taken up Such a form as was most agreeable to majority, is not disputed; that a number disliked it and protested against it is set forth, but what the Congress can say in the matter I am at a loss to guess, consistent with their constant declaration not to interfere with internal Govt of any of the Colonies, any further than to recommend to them to adopt such forms, as they shall think best calculated, to promote the quiet and peace of the Society, leaving every Colony to take such govt. as is most agreeable to the majority, during the present dispute. However as it was directed to the Congress, it was the next day publicly read together with the petition for a regt. to be stationed at Portsmouth; the whole was committed to Dr. Franklin, Mr. Wythe and Mr. Braxton, a new member from Virginia; what or when they will report is uncertain,[2] but for the honor of the Province I wish it had been kept at home.

The protestor's insinuation that it was unfairly obtained, I think (and they are not alone in it) reflects highly in the Congress in general as well as the delegates of New Hampshire, which the whole Congress know is illiberal and unjust. According to the best of remembrance (as well as of some others that I have asked) not more than one Colony voted against it (if one): however I hope the difficulty will soon subside, and by the future good conduct of the Colony, they will regain their former esteem; their spirit and activity in raising the regt. for Canada is highly commenced.

The twenty thousand dollars for which the Marine Committee gave me an order, as mentioned in my last, I have rec'd and have agreed with Mr.   (who is to take some money down for Mr. Cushing) to take fifteen thousand dollars for you. I have taken up your order to Mr. Dalton for 1333 1/3 dollars, the remaining 3666 2/3 dollars, I shall leave with Col. Whipple to answer such orders as you may draw on him, or the Marine Committee.[3]

I enclose you an account of the goods you are to purchase with your contract, the money cannot be sent till you empower somebody to draw it for you.

The order of the Secret Committee (a copy of which I shall enclose) I shall leave with Col. Whipple and you will send him a power to draw it for you and to pay it to such persons or send it down to you as you think best. Yesterday a vessel arrived here with twenty seven tons and a half of powder 5 tons of salt petre, 300 stand of arms.

I expect in 10 or 15 days to set out for New Hampshire to see how affairs go on with you, when I hope to have the pleasure to see you well. I am Sir your friend.   Josiah Bartlett

P.S. This letter goes by the Express: the money will set off this afternoon by Mr. Avery and will be sent to the care of Mr. Thomas Cushing where you must send for it.[4]   J. B.

TR (DLC: Force Transcripts).

1. Not found.
2. The New Hampshire material was committed on 1 March. *JCC*, 4:179.
3. Thomas Cushing (1725–1788) of Boston was a member of Congress 1774–

1775 and then, like John Langdon, built ships for the Continental Navy. Tristram Dalton (1738–1817), a wealthy Newburyport merchant, was employed by the province to sell prizes, fit out men of war, and buy ammunition and provisions. He was a U.S. senator, 1789–1791. Shipton, *Harvard Graduates*, 11:377–95; 13: 569–78.

4. John Avery (1739–1806), a Boston merchant like his father-in-law Thomas Cushing, was employed for some months as a messenger by both the Massachusetts provincial congress and the Continental Congress. He was later secretary of state of Massachusetts. Shipton, *Harvard Graduates*, 14:384–89.

JB's journey from Philadelphia to Kingston can be followed in this itinerary. At home he attended principally to domestic affairs until the first of May, when he again set out for Congress. His few papers and his day book attest that he was busy working on his farm, tending to his medical practice, and settling accounts. MJB 5028–29.

ITINERARY: PHILADELPHIA TO KINGSTON
[18–28 March 1776]

	miles
From Philadelphia to	
the Sign of the wheat sheaf	9
to Bristol	11
to Trenttown ferry	8
to the Sign of the Star trentown	2
Princtown Whiteheads	12
to Kents tavern near Sign of Hudibrass	
6 mile run	11
to Brunswick ferry	7
to Woodbridge Congers tavern	5
to the Blazeing Star at Stratton	
Island over a ferry	11
to Bergen point ferry	5
to Powles's Hook ferry	9
thence over the ferry to Kingsbridge	15
to Rye Hunts	15
to horseneck Knapps	9
to norwalk Bett's	15
to fairfield Penfield's	12
to Stratford ferry	10
to Milford Bryants	3
Newhaven Beers	10
Wallingsford	13
to Midletown Biggelows	14
to Hartford	15
to windsor Chaffe's	6
to Suffield Kent's	10
to springfield ferry	10
to Palmer Graves's	14
to Brookfield Rice's	15

to Spencer	Martin's		9
to Worcester	Jones's		11
to Northbury	Wid: Martin's		12
Sudbury	Barker's		17
Wilbraham & Watertown		Bravers	9
to woborn by Cambridge & Mistick			12
to Haverhil ferry			22
to Kingstown N: H:			12

MS (NhHi).

FROM WILLIAM WHIPPLE

Dear Sir   Philadelphia 28th. March 1776

I am just return'd from attending the remains of our worthy Friend Gov: Ward to the place appointed for all the Human race.[1] His better part took its flight to world of Spirits on Tuesday morning. This loss will be felt by Congress, and no doubt greatly lamented by the Colony he so faithfully represented. The Corps was first carried to the meeting house in Arch Street where an excellent Sermon well suited to the Maloncoly occation was deliver'd by Mr: Stilman from thence to Mr: Stilmans Meeting house where it was depossited.[2]

My last was by Express to Cambridge inclosing Bill Loading & invoice of your flower, which I wish safe to hand, but am somthing doubtful of it as the Coast is much infested with pirates. Its reported that a 40 Gun ship is at the Capes. The *Lexington* is gone down, The M. C. have bot another ship which will be ready to sail in a weak.[3] The Battery goes down to her station to morrow & the Province ship will follow her in a few days. We have a report that our fleet is at South Carolina, but no certain advice of it. I suppose you visited Boston in your way, pray give me a perticular accot how you found matters there. I have not yet receiv'd a line from any body concern'd in publick affairs in N. Hampshire. I shall be glad to know what I have done to deserve such neglect, however I shall expect better things of you while you tarry, which I hope will not be long. Settle your affairs as soon as possible and come away, for I expect them Devils from the other side the water very soon. Its said they will certainly be here by the middle of April.

There is nothing new in papers however I send you one. Congress have not yet had time to take up the report on New-Hampshire matters. I am with great Respect Your real Friend & Humle Sert. Wm Whipple

RC (PHi).

1. Samuel Ward (1725 to 26 March 1776), a former governor of Rhode Island, had sat in Congress with JB since September 1775.

2. Samuel Stillman (1737–1807), a minister of the First Baptist Church in Boston, had retired with his family to Philadelphia at the outbreak of the Revo-

lution. The Congress requested him to preach the funeral sermon for Ward. Stillman's sermon "Death, the Last Enemy, Destroyed by Christ," was printed by Joseph Crukshank in Philadelphia. *JCC*, 4:237; Shipton, *Harvard Graduates*, 14:216–25; Sprague, *Annals*, 6:71–79.

3. The naval brigantine *Lexington* was

commanded by Capt. John Barry. On 28 March Congress authorized the Marine Committee to purchase the *Molly*, which became the *Reprisal. JCC*, 4:238; *NDAR*, 4:547–48.

EXPENSE ACCOUNT WITH NEW HAMPSHIRE

[ca. 30 March 1776]

The Colony of Newhampshire to Josiah Bartlett

Septr 1775	Dtr		
To Expences on his jorney to Philadelphia			8:10:7
paid Fredrick Bull of Hartford for his horse to New york & Keeping one of mine	3:0:0		
paid Mr. Newstead of New york for his horse to Philadelphia	1:11:6		
for sending his horse back to N york	0:18:0		7:15:6
for Bringing my horse to Philadela and his Keeping	2:6:0		
paid to a farrier for one of the horses for the Jorney of 2 horses to Philadelphia			0:18:0
paid for horse keeping at Philadelphia from the 15th of septembr 1775 to the 18th of March 1776			26:11:3
for shoeing horses			1:6:10
My Expences Innoculating for the small pox			4:12:0
for my own & my servants Board from the 15th of septembr to the first of January			27:6:0
for my board from the 1st of Janry to 18th march			13:5:8
My washer woman bills			2:14:3
Barber's Bills			2:12:6
paid to my waiter for four months & an half service from septr 3d to Janry 19th			10:16:0
paid for Mr. Lovewell of Boston			0:18:0
to Expences for a waiter from the first of Janry to the 18th of march			3:6:0
To Sundry Expences on Committees & riding out postage of Letters paper &c. &c. &c. &c. at least 15 Dollars			4:10:0
for Col. Whipples Horse & servant from Philadelphia to Newhampshire			
for my Expences Returning from Philadelphia			8:3:7
To my own time from the 3d of septembr 1775 to the 30th of march 1776 fitting myself out &c. 209 Days			

Creditr

To Cash Recd of Nicholas Gilman Esqr Colony Treasurer August 1775	140:0:0
To Cash Recd at Philadelphia as per Receipt Dated	120:0:0

to 36 Dollars Recd of the Continental
      Treasure to reimburse the Colony for   10:16:0
      so much paid to Jared Tracy for Carrying
      money from Philadelphia to N. Hampshire

                                           £ 270:16:0

MS (NhHi). A similar MS is in Nh. See MJB 610.

FROM WILLIAM WHIPPLE

My Dear Sir   Philadelphia 5th Apl 1776
I hope this days post will advise me of your arrival 'tho I don't fully depend on it but shall the next. By the time this reaches you I hope You'll be preparing to set out, have not yet got the New Hampshire matters pass'd in Congress, have been ever since your departure on the Privateering business, & Regulation of Trade. The latter was finish'd Yesterday, shall send them to you next post.[1] I have given over all thots of hearing from any body concerned in the Legislature of New-Hampshire. I have been now near two months from thence & have not received a single line 'tho the Genl: Court has been seting almost a month.

A schooner arrived this weak from Guadalupe with 1200 Cask Powder but they are small the whole content no more then 7 or 8 Tons. The *Wasp* arriv'd the 3d inst she parted from the fleet about 12 days ago off Bermudas where they had been cruising for the transports from the West Indies. They have on board 90 or 100 Cannon from 18 to 42 pounders a large Quantity of shot & one Ton Powder taken from New Providence have also Brot off the Gov: Lieut Gov. & an Officer belonging to Pensecola.[2] The Capt. of the *Wasp* says the fleet are bound to New England suppose Road I. If so you'll hear of them before I shall. A Piolet Boat which was taken some time ago by the *Roebuck* (now Laying at the Cape) was a few days ago retaken near Lewis-town with a Leiut. & 3 or 4 men belonging to the *Roebuck*. No late news from Canada. I am with great Esteem Yours   Wm. Whipple

RC (NhD).
1. Whipple was writing on Good Friday, Congress being adjourned for the day. Congress had heard the committee's resolutions on trade on the fourth but had tabled the matter. *JCC*, 4:256–57.
2. These captures resulted from the American navy's first successful venture, an expedition of eight vessels to New Providence in the Bahama Islands. On the return voyage William Hallock, captain of the schooner *Wasp*, was sent into Philadelphia, while the remainder of the squadron continued on to Rhode Island. Fowler, *Rebels*, 96–99; Morgan, *Captains to the Northward*, 33–43.

FROM THOMAS RICE [1]

                    Pownalborough in the County of
                    Lincoln, Colony of the
Sir   Massachusetts Bay   April 18, 1776
The delegates of this County now met in Convention having taken

into their most serious Consideration the state of this County distressed as well by the common Calamities of the Times, of which it feels a full Share, as by Difficulties its local Sictuation and the Circumstances of its Settlements render peculiar to it, beg leave to avail themselves of an invaluable Priviledge in which no part of the Continent more cordially rejoices, Recourse to the Honorable Congress (of which you are a Member) as the fairest Representatives & therefore the fittest Guardians of the Rights of all America.

Amidst the accumulated hardships conspiring to necessitate an address to that august Body, one that demands their earliest Attention and occasions you the Trouble of this letter, is their being cut off from all Means of publick Inteligence by the Regulations established on the suppression of the Provincial post Office.[2]

Before that Time the peculiar Legislative of this Colony had thot it proper to extend the Circuit of the Post to Georgetown in said County, and the Inhabitants were well assured it should be extended in a short Time to St. Georges, if the publick Weal permitted that Institution to continue under their Controul. This Limitation was accounted sufficiently contracted as it comprehended but about Eighty Miles out of three hundred & ten which the Sea-Coasts of this County includes, and which already forms a continued Chain of Settlements from Kennebeck to St. Croix each of which being annually on the increase, must e'er long contribute its Quota, as to the defraying the publick Expence in general, so especially towards raising a Sum necessary to make the Incomes of the general Post Office equal to the Expence of it, should those Incomes be insufficient of themselves, and therefore presume they ought not to be deprived of so valuable a Priviledge common to all other Parts of the united Colonies, maintained at the common Charge and absolutely necessary for their Order and safety: especially as this Distance from the seat of Legislation and Ordinary Scene of publick Action is such, as makes the Cost of their Letters a Revenue to the Post-Office vastly greater in proportion to their Numbers, than that of any other County where the Course of the Post now lies.

But on the Post-Office's being taken into the hands of the Continent this Line was cut off at Falmouth in the County of Cumberland, by which no Means of publick Information was suffered to enter the Bound of this or Ferfax County by Land, and the Suppression of our Navigation forbids all wonted access to proper Information by Water, hence this County tho' the weakest in the Colony, is reduced to the necessity of maintaining constant Expresses at its own Expence, while it contributes its Mile to provide Inteligence for the ablest Parts of the Continent, of whose advantage in that respect it can enjoy no Share; or sits down under all the Inconveniences of Ignorance both of its Duty & its Danger, whilst its Inhabitants can receive no benefit from the friendly Charges & necessary Warnings of the Legislative, and its several Committees are in hazard of continually violating the Orders of Congress & Court which none would more Ardently wish to obey,—and an uniformity of Conduct in its several Towns & Settlements is rendered impossible.

This Convention mean not to insinuate that these Difficulties arose from any designed neglect in the Honble. Congress, but merely from the Case being passed without mention by us who were most concerned, while a multitude of more important Objects engrossed the Attention of that venerable Body.

In Remedy of this they have therefore forwarded a Petition to the Honorable Congress[3] praying an Extension of the Limits of the Post-Office from Falmouth in the County of Cumberland to St. Georges in this County, and having credible Information that in your return from Philadelphia in Conference with a Member of this Convention at Watertown, you were pleased to engage your Influence in favour of such a Petition, we therefore take the Liberty of requesting your kind Offices for carrying to Effect this our earnest desire as soon as may be; we have written on the Subject to the Honble. John Hancock with whom as well as with the other worthy Delegates from this Colony you will be pleased to confer on the Occasion;—and if the Distance, of the County should cause any Difficulties respecting Roads, Distances, or Persons to be employed, we would inform you that the whole Distance is but about Eighty Miles all on a Direct Road, no cross or by Roads being included therein. That from Falmouth to Georgetown is about forty Miles where one Deputy Post-Office would be needed; from thence to Newcastle is about twenty Miles where it would be convenient to have another appointed, from thence to St. Georges is about twenty Miles more;—and if no other Persons are known to the Congress by whom the publick Interest might be better servd, the Convention would recommend John Wood as a Post Master in Georgetown, Samuel Nickels in Newcastle, and Michael Packard in St. Georges;—Moses Copeland as Post Rider from St. Georges to Georgetown, and Joseph Bucker from thence to Falmouth.

After begging your kind attention to this Matter, and your Pardon for this Intrusion which our Confidence in you & the Encouragement aforementioned, has prompted us to offer, we conclude having the honor to be with the greatest Respect Sir your most Obedient & very humble Servants.

Signed in behalf of the Convention of the County of Lincoln.

Thos. Rice Chairman

RC (NhD).

1. Thomas Rice (1734–1812) of Pownalborough, Massachusetts (now Wiscasset, Maine), was a physician, town officer, representative to the Massachusetts provincial congress, 1774–1775, justice on the Court of Common Pleas for Lincoln County, and later chief justice. JB knew Rice, for he was among those invited to preach in Kingston in 1761. Rice later abandoned the ministry to study medicine under Dr. Oliver Prescott of Groton. Shipton, *Harvard Graduates*, 14:74–77; Chase, *Wiscasset in Pownalborough*, 507–08; see also JB's letter of February 1762 and note.

2. On 26 July 1775 Congress had established a line of post offices between Falmouth (some miles south of Pownal-

borough) and Savannah, Ga. *JCC*, 2:208.   ably by JB, on 25 May. *JCC*, 4:390.
   3. The petition was presented, prob-

FROM PIERSE LONG

Respected Sir,   .   Portsmo. May 7th. 1776

I hope this will meet you Safe Arrived at Philledelphia. And that the Honble. Congress have got Over every difficulty That prevented there declaration of Independency. I am Truely Sorry That This Place has been So much Cencered, As it appears to me to have been, As that protest and the Cause of it, Then appeared to us to have been a duty We Owed our Constituants. But I must Acknowledge at the Time We forwarded it to you, It had a Different Aspect,[1] And I Very believe that Should you Cut the Knot, That Every Person here (Old Counceller &c. Excepted) Would Acquiese therein. We are this day Called to meet in Committee of Safety to Consult on some thing that is necessary to be done towards Raising More men. Collo. Weare Recd An Express from the Committee of the General Court of the Massachusetts Requesting our holding a Number of Militia or Others in Readiness, To Assist them, in Repulsing a fleet of Hessians To the Amount of 12,000, which were Seen the 12th. day of April Bound for Boston.[2] This Intelligence Came by Cap. Jon. Ley of Newby.[3] from Bilboa Out 29 days Who was on board a Brig from Falmouth, Bound to Newfoundland, Who 3 days before Parted with them. Should George too Choice of Britons to foreign Realms apply And madly arm half Europe, yet still we would defy Turk Russian Jew & Infidel and All those powers in One While &c. &c. &c.

I am fully perswaded they will find more than there Match in us. He further says he Read an English Paper on Board Sd Brig., which gave an account of the Parliaments Voting pay for Said Troops, As also for 4000 Hanoverians who Sailed about the Same time under the Command of General Borgoine,[4] Bound for Quebec. Likewise That the King of Prussia's demands on England had been paid. All the Powder Vessels are at Last Arrived. Greenough and Trefethern were the Last.[5] They got in Two days past, But with no Powder. Capt. Trefethern about 12 days ago In the Lattitude of 29 No. and Long. 66 W. fell in with upwards of Twenty Sail of Ships Stearing N. W. He Supposed Bound for Virginia, But dare not go Very Near them. Governor Cook of Rhoade Island[6] had a Vessel at Martinico near Ready to Sail, with 8000 powder, and a quantity of Canvis. Youl please to make my Complyments Acceptable to Collo. Whipple. I know nothing to the Contrary But that all your and his friends are well. I am with Much Respect Sr Your most hum. Sevt.

Pierse Long

N.B. Lord How has the Command of the Hessian Troops, And in Sd fleet are 27 Commissioners. Should they arrive at Philledelphia I think it would be advisable to Hang them Emmeadiately for there impudence in Coming, Especially with Troops.

RC (NhD).

1. Long, a member of the House, had signed a petition from Portsmouth protesting adoption of the state constitution. The Committee of Safety had appointed him naval officer of Portsmouth on 26 April. *NHSP*, 8:14–15, 121–22.

2. The Committee of Safety directed state militia Gen. Nathaniel Folsom to maintain several regiments in Rockingham, Strafford, and Hillsborough counties "to hold themselves in readiness to march in case of an invasion." Weare informed Massachusetts of the preparations in a letter of 13 May to Thomas Cushing. Bouton, "Records of the Committee of Safety," 45; *NHSP*, 8:123–24.

3. John Lee (1728–1812), a sea captain engaged in privateering and sailed ships for the Tracy family of Newburyport.

Lee, *John Leigh*, 41; Currier, *Newburyport*, 1:638–39, 643, 646.

4. John Burgoyne (1722–1792) had come to America in 1775 as a top British commander. In 1777 he led the expedition south from Canada which resulted in the Battle of Bennington and finally in the British surrender at Saratoga. He later commanded troops in Ireland. *DNB*, 7:340–42.

5. Epes Greenough and William Trefethen were Portsmouth sea captains. Portsmouth Town Records, 18:151; 20: 607.

6. Nicholas Cooke (1717–1782) was governor of Rhode Island, 1775–1778. Long had advised Cooke on 6 May of the arrival of his sloop *Diamond*. *NDAR*, 4:1417–18.

FROM MARY BARTLETT
My Dear

Kingstown May 17th 1776
8 oclock in the evening

Your's of the 10th Instant[1] I recd the 16th Day & I am thankfull to hear you had arrived as far as Rhode Island safe & in health. I hope by this time you have arrived as far as Philadelphia in health & without Difficulty & may you be kept from all Evil; tho' I hear Some British Lord's have Laid a Plan to attack Philadelphia by Land if Impraticable by Sea—however I Beleive they can Plan more than they will be suffer'd to accomplish. These Lines Leave, me & the Rest of the family well. Levi Sent me a Letter last Saterday. He was well then.

Leiut Pearson is Better of all his Disorder's hiccup's left him Last thursday morning; he is very weak tho' he is able to walk the house with a Staff; I hope he will Recover & be able to write to you in a Little time. No Death's in this Parish Except the widdow Fowler Who was buried last Sunday. Their has been near 30 Person's Sick with the Canker & all like to Recover. Sally Hook has been very bad with the Canker (the Doctor almost Gave her over) But now in a fare way of Recovery.[2] I think it a Great favour of Divine Providence that we are in health when So many are Sick among us.

The weather very much alter'd Since you left us. Warm Rain's & Shine's by turn's which has Brought the peach trees Cherry & other Plumb trees in full Blossom—apple trees Begining to Blossom they Do not appear to Bloom So thick as they Did Last year. We have almost Done Plantain.

I wrote to you last week & Shall write every week if I have an opertunity to Send. I Shall be Glad to hear from you as often as I Can. I wish you would be Pleased to mention in your Letter's the number of your Letter's & When Dated & when you Recd mine & then we Shall Know when we Receive all that we Sent. I Shall be Glad you will write any new's you think you may. No more at Present. I Remain yours &c.

Mary Bartlett
2nd Letter

RC (NhHi). In Polly's hand; signed by Mary. Docketed: "Recd June 1st 1776."

1. Not found.
2. Sarah Hook (1759–1793), daughter of Jacob Hook of Hawke (now Danville),

married Levi Bartlett on 6 Nov. 1791. Kingston Vital Records, 55; Bartlett, *Genealogical*, 57.

TO MARY BARTLETT

My Dear   Philadelphia May 18th 1776

Yesterday afternoon I arrived here in good health after a very fatigueing Journey: the weather has been, this week uncommonly hot and Coming so suddenly after the Cold weather made it very uncomfortable both to horse & man. I wrote you by Col. Gale which no Doubt you have Recd.[1] After I left him I went by Norwich & New London to Newhaven; went to meeting Sunday afternoon at Brandford, and rode after meeting to Newhaven, on Monday rode from Newhaven to Horseneck. Tuesday morning I understood the Eastern post was to Call there that morning & Breakfast, which I thought was a good oppertunity to write to you, but while I was in another room writing & Sealing a Letter he Came, left his papers and was gone. So I was Disappointed of sending it at last. When I got to New york on tuesday I found that General Sullivan and all the Newhampshire Regiments were Marched off for Canada, the two last Regiments had been gone about a fortnight.[2] The account of the *Roebuck* & *Liverpool* men of war Coming up Deleware within 30 miles of this City & the Engagement of the Philadelphia Gondalos[3] with them you will no Doubt see in the newspapers. The Gondalos had much the advantage of the men of war & obliged them to sheer off; when the men of war were Coming up the people here were much frighted & many of them sent out their goods into the Country. The Congress have sent out a General Recommendation to all the Colonies to take up a new form of Goverment.[4]

You Desired me to write, you how much forwarder the spring was this way than with us; the people all the way as I Came Complain of the Backwardness of the spring till this week. At the South part of Connecticut last monday the apple trees were in full Blossom peach trees & Cherry trees out of the Blossom: from New york to this City the trees all out of the Blossom & Cherries of Some Bigness the winter Rye cured out to its full heights. However the people all the way were planting Indian Corn. I want to hear from you & in particular from Lieut Pearson. Hope one or more of your letters are on the road here. I shall now Constantly write to you Every week and at present Direct them to be left at Newbury Port. Tell Mrs. Burbank that the Regiment her son is in was Encamped at some Distance from New york so that I Could not see him, but I Saw a Captain that Belonged to the Same Encampment and I Gave him the letter & he promised me to find him out & give him the letter. The Company where Mr. Flagg's Son is was stationed at Stratton Island four or five miles from New york but I took the best Care to Convey it to him. I am yours &c.   Josiah Bartlett

RC (NhHi).

1. Letter not found. Jacob Gale (1736–1784) of East Kingston was JB's lieutenant commander of the 7th militia regiment and a brother of Dr. Amos Gale of Kingston. "Gale Family Records," 16, 19; *NHSP*, 7:577.

2. Sullivan's brigade had moved from Cambridge to New York in late March. At the beginning of May, Washington ordered Sullivan to reinforce Gen. Philip Schuyler's army at Fort Ticonderoga. The New Hampshire troops reached Albany about 10 May. See George Washington to Nicholas Cooke, 1 Apr. 1776, *WGW*, 4:458; Sullivan to Schuyler, 10 May 1776, Hammond, *Sullivan Papers*, 1:197.

3. Large, flat-bottomed river boats, used as gunboats by the Americans on bays, rivers, and lakes.

4. The resolution was passed on 10 May, the preamble on the 15th. *JCC*, 4: 342, 357–58.

TO JOHN LANGDON

Dear Sir,   Philadelphia May 19th 1776

Last Friday afternoon I arrived here all well, and on Saturday we rec'd a sad, but very imperfect account of affairs at Quebeck; according to the account rec'd it seems there was a most shocking and unaccountable misconduct in the whole affair[1]—however cannot help hoping that affairs are not so bad as has been reported and if they are that the Generals and soldiers who had not joined the army will in a great measure retrieve matters, and that things there will soon be in a better situation.

Hard money is very much wanted in Canada, and unless considerable sums are forthwith sent there, our affairs will suffer very much on that account: you will receive directions from the Chairman of the Secret Committee relative to what you have in your hands.[2]

The order of Congress concerning taking up govt under the people, which Col. Whipple sent forward, has made a great noise in this Province. Enclosed I send you an address to the people of Pennsylvania[3] and an order for the meeting of the City and Liberties tomorrow—what will be the consequence I know not, but think the Assembly will be dissolved and a Convention called. As to other affairs I have had no time to be informed myself and Col. Whipple tells me he has wrote you from time to time fully; as to the Agency affair I shall make one more trial when that matter comes on. The order of Congress for raising a regt for the defence of our Colony you will receive before this comes to hand. I hope good officers will be recommended and every thing put in the best posture of defence and the courage and resolution of the people kept up as I have great reason to think we shall have a severe trial this summer with Britons, Hessians, Hanoverians, Indians, negroes and every other butcher the gracious King of Britain can hire against us. If we can stand it out this year (and I have no doubt, we can, by divine assistance) I think there will be a final end of British Tyranny and this country soon enjoy peace, liberty and safety. Use your best endeavors to keep up the spirit of the people; for our all is at stake, life liberty and fortune. We have nothing to hope for, if conquered, and our misfortune in the war ought to animate us the more to diligence, firmness and resolution; to conquer is better than life, to be subdued infinitely worse than death.

I have resolved punctually to answer all letters wrote to me from any persons in our Colony, but never to write a second to any person who does not answer mine—except what I am obliged to write officially to the Colony or Committee of Safety.

By an express rec'd from General Lee we are informed a number of transports had arrived at Cape Fear with troops from England but had not landed when the express came away.

May 21st Yesterday the City met agreeable to notification in the field before the State House, a stage being erected for the Moderator (Col. Roberdeau) and the chief speakers (Mr. McKean &c.).[4] I am told they unanimously voted that the present House of Assembly are not competent to changing the form of Govt and have given orders for calling a Convention: Pennsylvania Assembly was to meet yesterday—I fear some convulsions in the Colony, the *infamous* instructions given by the Assembly to their Delegates which they, at their last meeting refused to alter, is the cause of their loosing their confidence of the people.[5]

One of the rifle men taken at Quebeck, last fall is arrived in this City last evening. I am told he has brought letters sewed up in his clothes for the Congress and that he left England the 24th of March last.[6] I saw him last evening, when he first came in the Coffee House. I expect to know more at Congress as the letters are sent to the President, but the post is now setting off, so must conclude by assuring you I am Your steady and sincere friend.   Josiah Bartlett

P.S. Col. Whipple has enclosed one of the Addresses.

TR (DLC: Force Transcripts).

1. Following their unsuccessful New Year's Eve attack on Quebec, the troops under Benedict Arnold, though ill-equipped, kept the British garrison under siege through the winter. On 1 April Arnold relinquished command to Gen. David Wooster who a month later turned it over to Gen. John Thomas. Within a few days the Americans raised the siege and retreated southward toward Lake Champlain. The letters received by Congress were from its commissioners then in Canada reviewing the situation. Wallace, *Appeal to Arms*, 84–85; *JCC*, 4:362.

2. New Hampshire sent £1145:15:10. *NHSP*, 8:161.

3. The address probably was not enclosed: see postscript. It was probably either an address of the committee of inspection for the county of Philadelphia to the Pennsylvania General Assembly, or

an address "To the worthy Inhabitants of the Province of Pennsylvania," signed by "The Forester" (Thomas Paine), and published in the *Pennsylvania Packet*. Burnett, *Letters*, 1:485, n. 3. See also JB's continuation of this letter, dated 21 May.

4. Daniel Roberdeau (1727–1795), a brigadier general of the Pennsylvania militia, served in Congress, 1777–1779. Thomas McKean (1734–1817) represented Delaware in Congress.

5. Public reaction led the Pennsylvania Assembly to reconsider its instructions regarding independence. On 8 June the Assembly removed certain restrictions on Pennsylvania's congressional delegates thereby allowing them to concur with delegates of other colonies in certain endeavors. Burnett, *Continental Congress*, 177.

6. The rifleman was George Merchant,

who had escaped from prison and made his way with a number of important documents to John Langdon. Langdon had sent Merchant and his papers to

Washington, and Washington had sent him on to Congress. JB obviously knew nothing as yet about Langdon's involvement. *WGW*, 5:57.

TO MESHECH WEARE

Sir Philadelphia, 28th: May 1776

We have obtain'd an order for 10500 Dols: for defraying the expences of raising & advancing a month pay to the Regiment, to be station'd at Portsmo. which we only wait for an opportunity to send forward.[1] Flour & salt Provisions may be suppli'd from Boston where a much larger Quantity was left by the Commisary Genl: then will be wanted by the troops station'd there. We are extreamly sorry that the Colony, we have the Honour to Represent which has had so high a place in the esteem of the whole Continent, for its forwardness, & great exertions, in the Glorious Contest, in which we are now engag'd, sho'd be lessen'd by the delay of the Regiment, order'd last winter into Canada. Our misfortune in that Country is imputed to tardiness of that & two other N. England Regiments. If that Regiment, had March'd at the time we expected, & frequently asserted, the evil might have been averted. We hope (for the Honor of the Colony) there will be a strict inquirey made and the cause of the delay fully investigated, that the Officers, (if they are faulty) may be brought to justice.[2]

The Convention of Virginia have instructed their delegates to use their endeavors that Congress sho'd declare the United Colonies a Free independent state, North Carolina have signified the same desires, S. Carolina & Georgia will readily Acceed. The Proprietary Govts will be the last to agree to this necessary step, the disafect'd in them are now exerting themselves but there exertions are no more then the last strugles of expiring faction. We hope in a few months Civil Governments will be establish'd in all the United Colonies on a firm & permanent Basis. We sho'd be glad to know the sentiments of our Colony on the importat subject of a total seperation from Great Britain. Let our own opinions be what they may, we think ourselves in duty bound to act agreeable to the sentiments of our constituents. We are with great Respect Your Most Obt Sevts.

Josiah Bartlett
Wm: Whipple

RC (DLC: Peter Force Collection). In Whipple's hand; signed also by JB.

1. Congress agreed to the $10,500 order on 22 May. On the fourteenth, Congress had voted to allow New Hampshire to raise a battalion at Continental expense. *JCC*, 4:357, 380.

2. Col. Timothy Bedel had raised the regiment in January. See Meshech Weare to JB, 8 Feb. 1776.

TO MARY BARTLETT

My Dear Philadelphia June 3rd 1776

Last Saturday I recd your 2nd letter Dated 17th May and am very thankful to hear that you and my family are well and that my friend Lieut Pearson is Recovering his health again. I hope this will find you and yours well as it leaves me and that we may all retain our health till by the leave of Providence we meet again in Safety.

This is the 4th. letter I have wrote you from this place, beside the one I wrote by Col. Gale. The Dates are May 18th., 21st & 28th all which I hope are come safe to hand.[1] That of the 21st I sent by the way of Portsmouth, the other two directed to be left at Newbury Port. I want much to know whether those sent to Newbury come Seasonably to you. The post takes your letters from Newbury sometimes on tuesday & the next Saturday week they arrive here. The weather here pleasant and Seasonable tho' two nights last week so cold I am told there was a white frost here. All last week there was plenty of green peas in the market here—strawberries and cherries just begin to be brought in. We have recd certain intelligence that Brittain is Determined to use her utmost Endeavers this year to subdue us. The Congress have Determined to oppose them with all their power and have agreed to send 8 Regiments of Militia of 750 men each to joyn our army in Canada: one of the Regiments is to be raised in the western parts of our Province, four in Massachusetts, 2 in Connecticut, & one in N. Y. and 25 thousand men more are to be raised by turn New Hampshire & Maryland viz in Mass., Conn., N. Y., N. J., Penn. & Maryland for the Defense of the Sea Coasts.[2] As to the Enemy attacking this place I am in no fear of it, nay I rather wish it for the Difficulties will be so great that I am almost sure they must be Defeated. It is said that Canada & New York will be their principal objects, tho it is likely they will make attacks on some other places. I hope the Americans will play the man for their country & for their all, and that kind Providence will give us success & victory that the wickedness and villany of our Enemies will fall on their own heads, and that America may be forever seperated from the tyranny of Brittain.

French vessels frequently arrive here two came up to this city yesterday their loading chiefly cotton, molasses, sugar, coffee, canvass &c. Last Saturday an American vessel arrived from the french west Indies with 7400 lb. of powder 149 stand of arms beside a large quantity of other articles.

I hope you wont fail to write to me every week for receiving letters from you is next to seeing you.

Tell Polly & Lois I recd. their's[3] and am glad to hear they are well. Remember my Love to them & to all the children. Give my regards, to Mr. Thayer[4] Lieut Pearson, Capt. Calef, James Procter and all my friends. I am yours &c.   Josiah Bartlett

p.s. I shall for the present write to you by tuesdays post which will convey them to Newbury the next friday week. This goes off this Day the 4th & I expect will get to Newbury the 14th & to you the 15th. the same day I expect to Receive yours which will leave Newbury to Day or to morrow morning. I am now well.   J. B.

TR (Mr. and Mrs. Rodney M. Wilson, Kingston, N.H., 1975).

1. That of 28 May has not been found.
2. See *JCC*, 4:399–401, 410–14.
3. Not found.
4. Elihu Thayer (1747–1812) had graduated from Princeton in 1769; he settled in the ministry at Kingston in 1776 until

his death. He was president of the N.H. Missionary Society, 1801–1811, and received an honorary D.D. degree from Dartmouth in 1807. He preached JB's funeral sermon in 1795. Sprague, *Annals*, 2:104–05; MJB 3515.

In the following letter Bartlett notes the receipt of news from the Cedars, news which eventually caused great consternation in New Hampshire as well as in Congress. The Cedars is a point of land projecting into the St. Lawrence River about forty-three miles north of Montreal. Toward the middle of May 1776 New Hampshire's Colonel Timothy Bedel had temporarily established his regiment there. On the fifteenth of that month the command was surprised and overtaken by a force of British and Indians. Bedel was absent at the time, ostensibly recuperating from a case of smallpox, having left Major Isaac Butterfield in charge. When attacked, Butterfield sent for Major Henry Sherburne; but Sherburne was taken prisoner, and his unit arrived too late to stave off the attack. Bedel was charged with having purposely quit the post knowing that the attack was imminent. The dispute that ensued became bitter and eventually involved the testimony of several officers and civilians. In the end it was Butterfield, not Bedel, who was stripped of his commission, Bedel being forced only to give up his current command. Bedel returned to active service in November 1777. Carrington, Battles, 164; Aldrich, "The Affair of the Cedars," 194–231.

TO JOHN LANGDON

My dear Sir   Philada. June 3rd. 1776

Yours of the 21st. ulto[1] is come to hand. I hope you have had good luck in lanching the Ship. The Circumstances of Affairs in Canada and the certainty of a large body of Hessians &c. being hired and designed soon to attack the United Colonies has so engrossed the attention of Congress to be prepared for them, that it is not possible to get them to attend to smaller matters: The affair of the Agency lays dormant. Capt. Thompson is nominated by the Marine Committee for the command of your ship but not yet confirmed by Congress.[2] The Generals Washington, Gates, and Mifflin are here to consult the operations of the War for this Year.[3] Congress have resolved that eight regiments of Militia to consist of 750 Men each forthwith be raised and sent into Canada 'till the first of December, to be raised in the Western part of Newhampshire one Regiment, 4 Massachusets, 2 Connecticut & one New York. I expect 25 thousand more men will be ordered to be raised for the same time for the defence of the Sea Coasts, from Newhampshire to Maryland inclusive. In short Sir, this will be the trying year, and if possible they must be hindered from getting any Foothold this Season; if that can be done, I think the day will be our own, and we be for ever delivered from our British Tyranny.

Yesterday one of the Continental vessels that was sent out for necessaries arrived here; she brought 7400 lbs of powder 149 Arms being all she could procure. The rest of her Cargo canvas &c. &c. she had like to have been taken by the *Liverpool* in this Bay, but two of the small continental vessels took her and a French schooner under their protection and the *Liverpool* did not think proper to engage them. Several French vessels from the West Indies have arrived here with Molasses, Coffee Linen &c. One of them was taken by a Man of War who examined all the Cargo and finding no Arms or Military Stores and not being willing to affront the French ordered her forthwith to proceed for France (where she pretended to be bound) having previously taken out the American Master & put him on board the Man of War; at night she shifted her course and came on here. I shall inclose a paper containing the Virginia and North Carolina Resolves concerning Independance. This province, New Jersey, and the Delaware Counties will soon take up Government, entirely under the people. New York and Maryland it is thought will soon follow. The constitution of Government that South Carolina has formed for themselves you have no doubt seen. Virginia, North Carolina & Georgia were forming their's when the last accounts left them.

This moment an express has arrived from Albany with the Copy of a Letter from General Sulivan Dated Ticonderoga May 27th. informing that it was reported there by a Man from Canada that Col. Bedel's regiment & an hundred men with Major Sherburn who were posted at a place called the Cedars above Montreal were attacked by the Soldiers from Niagara & Detroit with some French & Indians and were all cut off, but no particulars. Hope it will not prove so bad as reported; You will be likely to hear more before you receive this, if it is true.

By a St. Kitts Newspaper this moment recd., there is the address of the City of London to the King on American Affairs presented to him the 22nd of March & by his Answer we see he will have absolute submission or nothing: you will soon see it in the publick prints.[4] I am Sir, your friend and Servant.   Josiah Bartlett

FC (John Langdon Letter Book, Capt. J. G. M. Stone Private Collection, Annapolis, Md., 1976).

1. Not found.

2. Thomas Thompson (1739–1809) was a sea captain, builder, and merchant. A native of England, he came to Portsmouth about 1767, was active in its defense, and in 1776 supervised construction of the *Raleigh* of which he was appointed captain on 10 Oct. 1776. Foss, *Freemasonry*, 192–99, 499; NHSP, 7:632, 634, 673; "The Continental Frigate *Raleigh*," in NHGR, 2:177–87.

3. Washington was in Philadelphia from 23 May through 4 June. WGW,

5:78–97. Horatio Gates (1728–1806) had been commissioned a general in June 1775 and served to the end of the war. Patterson, *Horatio Gates*. Thomas Mifflin (1744–1800), a Philadelphia merchant and congressional delegate, had been appointed quartermaster-general of the army on 14 Aug. 1775. He was later governor of Pennsylvania and a supporter of the Federal Constitution.

4. The letter with the King's response appears in the *N.H. Gazette*, 22 June 1776.

FROM JOHN LANGDON

My Dear Sr.   Portsmo. 3d June 1776

Your esteemed favor of the 19th Ult. is now before me, it gives me pleasure to hear of your safe arrival, and health. The news from Quebeck is not so agreable, but by no means Disperits me, one moment, it ought rather to stimulate to noble actions. Just as I Began this letter, a Gentleman Arrived from Exeter and Reports, that by letter from Canada, of the Middle of may, says that our Reinforcements had got up, and Cut off the Advance guard of enemy, and had engaged the main body; (who were in persuit of our people) and Defeated them. Capt. Shackford has just got home from Halifax but has been four weeks from thence;[1] Says that no forces were arrived, the Officers and men were greatly Disperited, not the least intimation of going any where, abt two thousand saild the middle of April for Quebeck. Our Tories wondering abt with forlorn hope and down cast eyes. I am Just going to set off for Providence to see after guns, our ship is wait'g for them, and orders to ship men. I thank you for your intention of serve'g me in the Agency and shall in some measure depend upon it. But should such Deficulties Arrise as could not be got over, (which I can no way see) then I would recomend Capt. Supply Clap for Agent for Navey—and Mr. Joseph Whipple for Prizes.[2] I see the Deficulty of have'g any more then one Office other wise, if I should be appointed Agent and obliged to Stay here of Course, should be glad to Command this port while here for which I would ask no pay. You no my Ambition, for Millatary, and as I know of no Commission which our gentlemen would Complement me with; as they Choose rather to Confer honour and profit on those who have endeavor'd, to over set the government, rather then those who have ever, endeavoured to support it—however I shall do my duty as far as I know. I do not Expect to be honour'd in any way here nor Neither do I desire it now, as I would not Except any of their dirty sops, after every Dog had laped. Therefore shall depend on you and Brother Whipple for an Active Birth. Should I tarry at home and have a seat in the house I hope to have an oppertunity on the floor, to tell some folks their Villany[3]—I've been very, easey hitherto, but before I'll be Commanded by a Dam'd set of rascals who are put in office, and honest men left out I'll have a Rangle for it.

I have sent a letter to the Speaker Recommend'g Major Hacket for the Command of the Battalion, who is in my opinion the best officer in the Colony.[4] I've said nothing abt myself as I was in doubt abt my staying here, as Agent. I hope Major Hacket's name will come on, if it does pray give him the Command of the Battalion as I am sure you'll please all here and three Quarters of the Colony in general. I've mention'd his name to Colonal Whipple as Capt. of Marines, but should he get the Command or Second, it will suit him best. He has served the Continent in this ship, very much by doing the work so well, and give'g such Dispatch, he is young and Intreped, has served in the Army last war with great Reputation as an Officer.

Your letter to your Lady I forwarded by your Negro Boy (this day) who happen'd to be in Town—shall take Particular Care of any matters, you send to my hands. You and Brother Whipple will please to Communicate to each other any of my matters. Believe me to be with great Friendship Your's,   Jn Langdon

RC (NhHi: Langdon Papers).

1. Probably either Samuel (1728–1812) or Josiah (1747–1829) Shackford, brothers who were sea captains. Samuel was a selectman of Newington in 1776; Josiah was appointed third lieutenant of the *Raleigh* later in the year. Both were in Langdon's company of Light Horse Volunteers in the Rhode Island expedition of 1778. Bartlett, "Portsmouth Families"; *NHSP*, 8:257; 15:577; Mayo, *John Langdon*, 127.

2. Supply Clapp (1742–1811), a Portsmouth merchant, was a colonel in the militia, a member of the committee sent to Providence, R.I., in December 1776, agent victualler for the troops stationed at Piscataqua Harbor, and commissary of prisoners. In the 1790s he was the state commissary general. Clapp, *Clapp Memorial*, 21; *NHSP*, 8:763, 884, 891; 17:123–24, 446.

Joseph Whipple (1737–1816) was also a merchant of Portsmouth, a brother of William Whipple. Joseph represented the Coos district in the legislature, commanded the 25th regiment of militia in 1784, and was appointed customs officer

for the state in 1786. N.H.H.S. *Proceedings*, 2:289–320; Dodge, "Colonel Joseph Whipple," 20–31.

3. At the end of 1776 Langdon won election to the House of Representatives and served as speaker on its first day of the session, 18 Dec. 1776. *NHSP*, 8:428.

4. James Hackett (b. 1739), a shipbuilder of Exeter and Portsmouth, was commissioned first major of Col. Joshua Wingate's regiment of minutemen in September 1775. Hackett declined command of the Continental battalion then being raised, and Langdon employed him as master builder of the *Raleigh* in 1776 and of the *America* later. *Vital Records of Amesbury, Mass.*, 119; Potter, *Military History*, 1:350n; *NHSP*, 7:608; 8:141–42.

Joshua Wingate (1725–1796) of Dover had been raised to a colonelcy on 1 Sept. 1775. He commanded at Portsmouth that autumn, in the Canadian expedition of July 1776 and in the Rhode Island expedition of 1778. Wingate, *Family History*, 127–28; *NHSP*, 7:608; Potter, *Military History*, 1:274, 349.

FROM JOHN LANGDON

My Dear Sr.   Portsmo. June 3d. 1776

This will be handed you by Major Rogers who has been here for short time, in which I've had frequent Interviews with him and oppertunity of Conversing fully on matters, find him well inclined and ready to Serve his Country in this grand Struggle[1]—and as I wish his millitary abilities might be imployed for us, shall be much pleased if you'll speak to him on the Subject, and if any thing should turn up for his Advantage, and the real Service of the United Colonies, I've no doubt you'll do every thing in your power to Serve him and the Country. I am with great Respect yr. mo. obt Servt.   Jon. Langdon

RC (NhD). This is an entirely separate, and probably was the second, letter from Langdon to JB on this date.

1. Robert Rogers (1731–1795), a Rumford (now Concord) native, had led a Ranger unit on several valuable raids during the French and Indian War. He emerged as a romantic figure of that

war. With Langdon's letter Rogers travelled south. Washington arrested him at South Amboy on suspicion of duplicity with the enemy and sent him to Philadelphia under guard. His case was presented to Congress which decided on 6 July that he "be sent to New Hampshire, to be disposed of as the government of that state shall judge best." Rogers escaped to the British and led a unit at the battle of White Plains. He fled to England where he spent the rest of his life in obscurity. Washington to the President of Congress, 27 June 1776, *WGW*, 5:184–85; *JCC*, 5:503, 523.

TO NATHANIEL FOLSOM

Dear Sir   Philadelphia June 6th 1776

I have Enclosed to you a News paper Containing the adress of the City of London to the King and his answer by which we see what we have to Depend on from the ruling powers of Brittain.

The affair of Declaring these Colonies Independent States and absolved from all allegiance to the Crown of Brittain must soon be Decided whatever may be the opinion of the Delegates of Newhampshire on that matter. They think it their Duty to act agreable to the minds of their Constituents and in an affair of that Magnitude Desire the Explicit Directions of the Legislature of the Colony and that it may be forwarded to us as soon as possible.

Last monday we had an account that Col. Bedel with 300 or 400 men were Cut off at the Cedars above Montreal. We have Since had news that our people &c. got the advantage of the Enemy in the action and had Killed & taken a Considerable number. I believe there is nothing to be Depended on in Neither Report.

Two Privateers from this place have taken 3 Large Sugar ships with above 1000 Hogs'ds of Sugar &c. &c. &c. also Twenty four thousand Dollars in specie. If they are not retaken before they get in to Port it will be a fine Prize.

Please to give my best regards to the Council and assembly of Newhampshire & Believe me to be your friend & Humble servt.

Josiah Bartlett

Please to Convey my letter to Mrs. Bartlett.

RC (NN: Emmet Collection, No. 1541).

TO MARY BARTLETT

My Dear   Philadelphia June 10th 1776

Yours of the 23d of may I Recd the 8th Inst: and am glad to hear you are all well that tho Sally has been unwell She is better that Lieut Pearson is better: may Kind Providence preserve you all in health & safety till my return to you. I have had a very severe Cold the latter End of last week but am now much better. This is the Sixth letter I have wrote you from this City since my arrival my last was the 6th Inst: by Express to Exeter. I want to Know how Soon my letters by Newbury port get to you: I am Glad you find an oppertunity to send me a letter Every week. Your letters leave Newbury tuesday afternoon & I Receive them the next Saturday week.

Last thursday after Congress, I, with 5 or 6 other Delegates walked about a mile & half out of the City to see the Proprietors Gardens: there are a great many Curious trees, Bushes, Plants &c. Among the rest the alois[1] Plant is I think the most Curious. I Cannot Describe it as it is not like any thing I Ever Saw before. There are a number of Sweat & Sower orange trees, Lemmon trees, lime trees & Citron trees; the Same tree had some flowers, some Small & some ripe fruit at the Same time; the trees are about 8 or ten feet high Set in Boxes of Sand So that they Can be removed in Cold weather into a hot house, So that they grow & bear fruit all the year round. I Remember my Love to you all & Remain yours &c.

Josiah Bartlett

RC (Mr. Francis W. Bartlett, Kansas City, Mo., 1975).
  1. Aloe.

TO JOHN LANGDON

Dear Sir,   Philadelphia June 10th 1776

Your's of the 27th ulto is come to hand and am glad to hear you have had so good luck in building and launching the ship. I hope she will prove as good a ship as any of her bigness in the British Navy. Capt. Thompson is appointed to the command of her, the other officers are not yet appointed.[1] I hope the Captain will set about raising the men and that she will be fitted for sea as soon as possible.

I think with you that the brave Capt. Mugford and the men on board the privateers at Boston fought gallantly and did honor to the country;[2] but what shall we think of 500 of our men in Canada surrendering themselves prisoners to about the same number of the enemy. The accounts are very vague but thus much I believe is certain that almost the whole of Col. Bedel's regt and 100 men with Major Sherburne of Rhode Island are prisoners to the enemy and by what at present appears surprising surrendered without much resistance, when so large an army of our men were so near to assist them.

It seems as if our men in Canada were struck with a panic—what else could be the reason of their running away from Quebec and leaving their cannon and sick and every thing behind without firing one musket; in short I could never have believed that our men would be guilty of such conduct; however I hope and believe that when our army come to get settled and the officers and men reflect on what has passed, they will act with more spirit and retrieve their credit; the small pox among them is very frequent and very discouraging for which we must make proper allowance, but the conduct of the hardy sons of New Hampshire is truly mysterious.

You have no doubt heard of the two privateers from this place taking 3 large Jamaica ships very richly loaded, one of them is arrived here, the other two are said to be gone for New England: the cash amounting to 22400 dollars and the plate weighing 180 lb as near as I remember was taken on board the privateers and is safe arrived here.[3] The *Liverpool,* man of war lays at the capes of Deleware and has taken 2, or 3 vessels lately—one with dry goods. I want much to have our ships fitted to drive her off or take her.

I shall enclose you a paper containing the Bill of Rights drawn up by Virginia; you have seen the Virginia Resolves concerning Independence. I wish our Colony would give us Instructions in that head, for whatever may be our private opinions, instructions from the Colony either requiring, or only authorizing us to vote in favor of it, if we should think it for the best would carry great weight with it. The Congress has been so taken up with very important business that the affair of Agency has not been mentioned since my arrival—when it does shall not be wanting in seconding Col. Whipple.

By one of the enclosed papers you will see that the Assembly of this Province have given new Instructions to their Delegates.

11th By a letter just rec'd from Canada it appears that our men had neither provision nor ammunition and that was the cause of their surrendering.[4] I am Sir, your most humble Servant and what is more your sincere friend.   Josiah Bartlett

TR (DLC: Force Transcripts). Enclosures not found.

1. As recommended by the Marine Committee, Congress appointed Thomas Thompson on 6 June. *JCC*, 5:422.

2. James Mugford, of Marblehead, Mass., was captain of the *Franklin*, one of the naval vessels under general command of George Washington. Mugford died on 17 May while fending off a boarding party of British seamen in Boston harbor. Allen, *Naval History*, 1:74–77.

3. The prize vessels from Jamaica were *Lady Juliana*, *Reynolds*, and *Juno*.

NDAR, 5:429, 450–51.

4. JB was probably referring to Gen. John Sullivan's letter to John Hancock of 1 June, which arrived at Congress on the eleventh. Sullivan noted that provisions and gunpowder were in short supply and that the army was in a state of confusion. He did not, however, state directly that the surrender at the Cedars resulted from those conditions. Hammond, *Sullivan Papers*, 1:212–14; *JCC*, 5:431.

The following letter presents a mild expression of the anxiety JB and Whipple were feeling about New Hampshire's attitude toward independence. They had written on 28 May asking for instructions, and the time was drawing closer for making the decision. On 10 June the Continental Congress "resolved itself into a committee of the whole" to further consider resolutions concerning independence. This committee concluded that a smaller committee be appointed to prepare by 1 July— in case Congress should agree on independence—a declaration to the effect that "these United Colonies are, and of right ought to be, free and independent states; that they are absolved from all allegiance to the British Crown: and that all political connexion between them and the state of Great Britain is, and ought to be, totally dissolved." On the eleventh Congress chose Thomas Jefferson, John Adams, Benjamin Franklin, Roger Sherman, and Robert R. Livingston as the committee to prepare the declaration, JCC, 5:428–29, 431. In the meantime the New Hampshire General Court had already begun to prepare a formal statement of its position through a committee appointed on 11 June. As adopted on the fourteenth it asserted "that our Delegates at the Continental Congress should be Instructed, and they are hereby Instructed to join with the other Colonies in Declaring THE THIRTEEN UNITED COLONIES, A FREE & INDEPENDENT STATE." *A copy of the resolve accompanied a letter from Meshech Weare to JB and Whipple on 18 June; NHSP, 8:139, 149–50; MJB 876.*

TO MESHECH WEARE

Sir,   Philadelphia 11th June 1776

We some time ago signified our wish to know the sentiments of our Colony respecting Independence.[1] The Ques'n has been agitated in Congress, a Resolution pass'd Yesterday, to Chose a Committee to prepare & bring in a Declaration for that purpose, on the first of July, by which time it is expected that all the Delegates who have not already been instructed will receive ample Powers. As this is a Subject of the greatest importance, we beg we may be furnish'd with the Sentiments of our Constituents as we wish to Act agreeable to them let our own be what they may. We shall be in full expectation of an answer by the return of post. We have the Honour to be Your Most Obt Serts.

                                                        Josiah Bartlett
                                                        Wm: Whipple

RC (DLC: Peter Force Collection). In Whipple's hand; signed also by JB.
    1. See letter of 28 May.

FROM JOHN LANGDON

Dear Sir,   Portsmouth June 14th 1776

Your favour of the 3d Instant is now on the table I am very much Oblig'd by your being so particular, as I've much pleasure in Communicating part of your Letter to my and your friends. I dont wonder all the attention of Congress, is taken up in such important matters as must be now before them; am very glad Thompson is nominated, for the Command of our Ship: *but the Guns,* what shall we do for them;[1] my Spirits are little down upon that Head, as I find on going to Providence, that our Ship is the first by at least three Weeks or a Month of any on the Continent, tho' theres are what, you may *call* built, so as to Launch, yet they neither have Rudder, Ports, Channells done, besides many other matters, nor the *Mast* sorry to say it, Masts only are not half Compleated, our Ship all Painted, Carvd, work Compleated, Masts & Yards Compleated all in, and all the standing Rigging over head and Rattled down, all our Boats done, our Sails soon Compleated, except Light Sails, for which must have light Canvas, of which can get none. If the Guns had been on the Spot, and Orders to Enter Men, and Provide Provisions, the 1st day of June the Ship should have been ready to sail in all the Month, but when she'll go now, I know not, pray forward the Guns, and Orders for Hands, and to provide for provisions, &c. as soon as may be. Am Exceeding glad that such ample provisions is making for our defence, by raising such bodies of Men for the different departments, am clearly of Opinion with you, that should we ride out the Storm of this Season, our Ship will go safe to Land (You know our Ship is a good one) and our worse then infernal Enemies be disappointed in their diabolical designs. The arrival of Powder, and the French Vessells is good News; in short your kind favor is full of favourable, and useful Intelligence.

I most heartily Congratulate you, and Brother Whipple on the good News we have from Canada, I mean that of Arnold's having killed and taken 700 of them. We have had some commical Work in recommending Field Officers. Capt. Dame was first chose to Command & by Petition from the Officers from the Battery, was reconsidered and put out, very unfairly by the Petitioners. This Regiment under Colo: Gilman is to be kept up at the Colony Expence, and Colo: Hackett who is the best Man I know of Except Dame, in the Province: after Hackett was Nominated, he like a Gentleman offer'd to the Court to resign in favour of Dame, and take the second under him, but it was not granted, it now stands Colo: James Hackett Lieut: Colo: Tash, the other I know not. It would have been very happy for us to have had the advantage of Capt. Dames abilities, which are in my Opinion, equal to any on the Continent, and since the News of Foreigners being Employ'd he has been very high in his Opinion of the Injustice of the British Court.[2]

I some time ago recommended Doctor Jackson for Surgeon, of the Regiment, he is now the Surgeon of Colo. Gilmans Regiment, as that is the Case, I hope that Doctor Brackett will be appointed for the Continental Battalion as he most certainly deserves well of his Country; in our Govermental matters, he's done eminent Service for us.[3] This moment news that our People have attacked the Ships at Boston, and drove them out of the Harbour twenty Sail, including Transports. Push forward my good Friend we have nothing to fear, under the smiles of Providence. Inclos'd is a Letter from your Lady from who I receiv'd a Polite Note, in answer to one I wrote her, it came to hand too late for last Post. Your Friend and Hbl. Servant.   John Langdon

P.S. Put Brother Whipple in mind of Doctor Jno. Jackson for Surgeon of the Ship, inclos'd is List of Officers who I have spoke too for this Ship agreeable to his Letter.[4]

FC (John Langdon Letter Book, Capt. J. G. M. Stone Private Collection, Annapolis, Md., 1976).

1. As there was no furnace in New Hampshire capable of casting cannon for Langdon's frigate, he relied upon the Hope furnace at Scituate, R.I., owned by John and Nicholas Brown. When the Browns refused to treat Langdon with what he considered due respect, he refused to buy their cannon. It took almost another year to arm the *Raleigh.* Langdon's frustrated efforts are summarized

in Fowler, *Rebels*, 237–44, and can be followed in detail through sources printed in *NDAR*, 5; Cappon, *Atlas of Early American History*, 29, 105–06.

2. Theophilus Dame (c. 1724–1800) of Dover and Portsmouth was appointed a colonel on 8 June. David Gilman (b. 1735), a businessman, public official, and military officer from Pembroke, was commissioned a lieutenant colonel. Gilman petitioned the Assembly and wrote to John Dudley on the Committee of Safety impugning the character of Dame with the result that the vote was rescinded, and on 12 June Maj. James Hackett was made first officer, Maj. Thomas Tash (b. 1722) of Newfields, second officer, and Maj. David Copp, third officer. Hackett offered to serve under Dame, then accepted the appointment, and then resigned, on the thirteenth. But the House voted on the nineteenth to void its vote appointing Hackett, Tash, and Copp; and Isaac Wyman was appointed to replace

Hackett. *N.H. Gazette*, 15 Jan. 1800; Carter, *Pembroke*, 1:126; Fitts, *Newfields*, 655–56; *NHSP*, 8:137–38, 140–42, 155–56; Dudley Papers, NhHi; Potter, *Military History*, 1:287–88.

3. John Jackson (1745–1808), a physician of Portsmouth and cousin of Dr. Hall Jackson, signed as surgeon on the *Raleigh* in 1776. In 1782 he, with Drs. Hall Jackson and Ammi R. Cutter, opened a smallpox hospital on Henzell's Island in Portsmouth harbor. Joshua Brackett (1733–1802) was a Portsmouth physician and brother-in-law of William Whipple. Brackett graduated from Harvard in 1752, received an honorary medical degree in 1792, was a member of the Committee of Safety, and on 4 July 1776 was sworn in as a judge of the New Hampshire Admiralty Court. Shipton, *Harvard Graduates*, 13:197–201; Putnam, *Medical Society*, 15, 157–58.

4. Enclosure not found.

FROM NATHANIEL FOLSOM

Dear Sir   Exeter June 15th. 1776

I yesterday received yours of the 6th. instant together with the Philadelphia Papers inclosed for which I thank you. The requisition for Raising a Battalion for the Canada department wase immediately taken under Consideration by the General Court here. We have agreed to Raise the men with all Possible expedition.[1] I doubt not you will be pleased to hear that a prety General harmony in the Grand American Cause Prevails here—The vote for independency you will see is unanimous in both Houses. We have no particular accounts from Canada that Can be depended on further then you had when you Rote. The Counciel have this day voted a bounty of Forty Shillings in addition to 3£ the Price before given for all the Fire armes manufacterd in this Colony & deliverd to the Reciver General in one month Thirty Shillings for the 2d. month & 20 for the third. I forwarded your Letter to Mrs. Bartlet. Major Philbrock informs me She and the rest of your Family aire well. I wish you the divine blssing at the Congress. I doubt not if we remain firm & united we Shall under God disappoint the Sanguinary designs of ouer Enemies.

Pray Continue your Correspondence by Every oppertunety. My Compelements to Col. Whipple. I am your Friend & Humle Servant.

Nathl. Folsom

RC (NN:Emmet Collection, No. 456).

1. The General Court received John Hancock's letter of 4 June on the fourteenth advising of the congressional resolution that the state raise an additional regiment to go to Canada. The Assembly immediately established the regiment. *NHSP*, 8:145–56.

TO LEVI BARTLETT

My Dear Son   Philadelphia June 17th 1776

I Send this with my love to you and hope it will find you well as it leaves me. Your mother has wrote to me that She hears you are well and like being at School. I hope you will take Care to behave So as to have the good will of your Master & School Mates that I may have the pleasure to hear of your good behavior and that you make a wise improvement of your time to gain learning that the Cost I am at for you may not be in vain.

You have now an oppertunity to gain learning & to fit your self for whatever Station in life it may please God to place you. If you now neglect the prize put into your hands you will have Cause to repent it all your Days.

That you may remember that all favors & Blessings Come from the Supreme father of all, who is good to all, & his tender mercies are over all his works, and that God will take you under his holy protection is the ardent prayer of your affectionate father.   Josiah Bartlett

Give my Regards to Master Moody.[1]

RC (Mr. and Mrs. Rodney M. Wilson, Kingston, N.H., 1975).

1. Samuel Moody (1726–1795) of York, Maine, was master of Dummer Academy at Newbury, Mass., from its opening in 1763 until 1790. By 1778 the school was filled to capacity with sixty boys and turned away enough to fill Phillips Academy, Andover. Shipton, *Harvard Graduates*, 12:48–54; Cleaveland, *First Century of Dummer Academy*, 19–33.

TO JOHN LANGDON

Dear Sir,   Philadelphia June 17 1776

Your favor of the instant,[1] is come to hand and am sorry the news you mention from Quebeck is not true; things have taken an extraordinary turn in that country. The behavior of Col. Bedel and Major Butterfield[2] is very extraordinary: no doubt you will hear the particulars before this reaches you. Dr. Franklin Mr. Chase and Mr. Caryl are returned from Canada; their account of the behavior of our New England officers and soldiers touches me to the quick; by their account never men behaved so badly—some regiments not having more than 100 men, when it was expected there were six times that number; stealing and plundering arms, ammunition, military stores &c. and taking the battoes and running off: one man it is said stole six guns and to conceal them broke the stocks to pieces, cut up a tent to make a knapsack to carry off the barrels locks &c.—and all is said to be owing to the officers: unless our men behave better we shall lose all our former credit and be despised by the whole Continent. This is the account here; I pray God, it may not be so bad as is represented.

The greatest care must be taken to have good officers—the fate of America depends on it; however I make no doubt as soon as the present Commanders have time, they will get things in a better regulation and that some examples will be made to deter others from such conduct. Poor General Thomas[3] is dead and General Sullivan now commands in Canada; I expect soon General Gates will be ordered there.

As to Marine affairs brother Whipple will write you: a Board of War is now appointed consisting of Mr. J. Adams, Mr. Sherman, Col. Harrison, Mr. Wilson and E. Rutledge. I have taken every opportunity to mention to the members the affair of the agency and am surprised to find all of them agreeing that no member of Congress ought to be appointed to any post of profit under the Congress: so that as you are a Member, I am sure it will not go down, and I am by no means willing you should resign your seat here. As the affair of the ship will soon be finished and Col. Whipple will be for returning to his family, my opinion is that it will be best for you to come here as soon as you and Col. Whipple can agree on it and that the affair of the Agency be in the mean time left open—when you are here you will be better able to determine on several affairs.

The affair of a Confederation of the Colonies is now unanimously agreed on by all the members of all the Colonies: a Committee of one from each Colony are to draw up the articles of confederation or a Continental Constitution which when agreed on by the Congress will be sent to be confirmed by the Legislature of the several Colonies, as it is a very important business and some difficulties have arisen.[4] I fear it will take some time before it will be finally settled; the affair of voting whether by Colonies as at present or otherways is not decided and causes some warm disputes. The appointments of the officers of militia to be sent to Canada is with our Legislature and also the nomination of the field officers for the regt. stationed in our Colony so that unless any objection is made, their nomination will be confirmed. I hope the greatest care will be taken in the appointment to get bold, resolute, intrepid and experienced persons.

The affair of taking the sugar ships has so animated the people here that they are now fitting out 5 or 6 privateers more here.

I should take great pleasure in recommending some active berth for you but while you continue a member of Congress it will not take effect. If you are absolutely determined to resign and should do it I make no doubt some place agreeable to you might be found and in that case you must see that another is appointed in your stead to come here in about a month to supply Col. Whipple's place who is determined then to return. But it is my opinion you had better come here yourself at least once more. It is necessary however we should know your absolute determination as soon as possible.

Give my compliments to all enquiring friends. Major Patton Mr. Dean and Mrs. Susy[5] desire to be remembered to you. I am Sir your real friend.

Josiah Bartlett

TR (DLC: Force Transcripts).

1. JB was referring to Langdon's letter of 3 June.

2. Isaac Butterfield (1742–1801) of Westmoreland was first commissioned in

August 1775. Six months later he was assigned to Bedel's Canadian bound regiment. While Butterfield was in temporary command at the Cedars, on 19 May 1776, the British attacked his force, and he surrendered. Aldrich, "The Affair of the Cedars," 194–231; *NHSP*, 7:577. See above, headnote, p. 65.

3. John Thomas (1724–2 June 1776) of Kingston, Mass., was one of the first brigadier generals commissioned by Congress in June 1775. He was promoted to

major general in March 1776 and took over the American forces at Quebec on 1 May. Thomas died of smallpox.

4. JB was placed on the committee appointed on 12 June "to prepare and digest the form of a confederation to be entered into between these colonies." *JCC*, 5:433.

5. Probably Susannah Brackenbury, JB's landlady in Philadelphia. See MJB 738.

TO MARY BARTLETT

My Dear   Philadelphia June 24 1776

Your Letter of the 8th Inst:[1] inclosed in one of Polly's, & yours of the 10th Inst: inclosed in one of Major Philbricks[2] Came to hand Saturday the 22nd Inst: with the inclosed, and am happy to hear you & the family are well. Yours that you say you sent the 7th by the way of Portsmouth is not arrived; you may Depend that they Come the Quickest by the way of Newbury.

I am Glad to hear that the Sickness is abated with you; it is a pretty healthy time in this City at present, but as the hot weather has Come on for about a week & no rain the air seems to Stagnate, & if it should hold Dry, will I fear produce Sickness. I have for 2 or 3 Days past in the afternoon rode Back a mile or two & the very air of the Country seems reviving.

As to what you mention of the Skirmish of the men of war & the Gondaloes; it was Below the Boom Batteries &c. &c. made for the Defence of this City; they are not above 8 miles below the City, as being the most Convenient place to stop the Ships. I am not under the least fear of their being able to penetrate to this place, so you may make your self Quite Easy about me, on that account.

I am sorry to hear the frost has Done Damage with you: hope it has not Killed all the Beans &c. The Corn will Commonly grow again. How is the flax in General like to be; what are like to be the Crops of hay with you; how is the winter & Sumer Grain like to be &c.: Please to write me what is like to be the Success of the farming Business this year. Mowing English Grass was finished last week here.

As to news we have none Except the taking to 2 Scotch Company's of highlanders in the transports Coming to Boston which you will see the accounts of before this reaches you. The affair of the Newhampshire regiment at the Cedars in Canada, surrendering to the Enemy is a most Scandalous Business; Major Sherburne who went from Montreal with 110 men to reinforce Col. Bedel's Regiment at the Cedars, is now here & gives a very particular account of it.[3] The infamous Scandalous Behavior of some of the officers has brought Disgrace on the Province which will be very hard ever to wipe off.

I have been for about a week on a Committe of one member from Each Colony to form a Confederation or Charter of firm & Everlasting Union of all the united Colonies: It is a matter of the greatest Consequence & requires the greatest Care in forming it: when it is agreed to by the Committe, it will be laid before the Congress & when they have agreed to it, it will be sent to Each Colony to be by them ratified & Confirmed. May God grant us wisdom to form a happy Constitution, as the happiness of America to all future Generations Depend on it.[4]

I am in pretty good health Except something of a Cough that holds me Ever since the Cold I mentioned to you, but hope it will go off in a little time. Remember my love to all the Children particularly tell Polly I Recd hers, and hope she had a pleasant Jorney to Newbury & back & found her Brother well. I Suppose Levi will be at home by the time this reaches you as (if I am not mistaken) the vacation begins the first of July.

I hope Kind Providence will order all things for the best, and if Sometimes affairs turn out Contrary to our wishes, we must make our selves Easy & Contented, as we are not Certain what is for the best. I am Sincerely yours.   Josiah Bartlett

RC (NhHi).

1. Not printed; see MJB 880.
2. Neither the letter from Polly nor that from Philbrick has been found.
3. Henry Sherburne (1748–1824) of Newport, R.I., was a major in the 15th Continental Infantry in 1776 and was taken prisoner near the Cedars while leading a detachment to aid Bedel's regi-

ment. Later, Sherburne was promoted to colonel, served as treasurer of Rhode Island and as U.S. customs collector at Newport. *NEHGR*, 59:60; Heitman, *Historical Register*, 494.
4. A draft of the Articles in JB's hand and probably written in June (Nh) is on MJB 841.

FROM JOHN LANGDON

My Worthy Friend   Portsmouth 24th. June 1776

Your kind favor of the 10th I've Recd. am much obliged for your kind Congratulations, on our Launching our ship. We most Certainly have been highly favor'd Sons of fortune, in this matter, not one Accident haveing happen'd, thro' the whole, Building, geting masts in, and Rigg'g; our Topgallant mast are all on end, the Ship, Compleatly painted, ports all hawled up, makes a grand figure, and to my (and no doubt your) great Satisfaction, esteemed by every one who sees her as handsome, and as good a Ship as can be built in the Kingdom, (seasoning of timber excepted). The Discription you give of our Troops in Canada, is Truely to be lamented, there is some fatality attends us in that quarter, what has New York and Pennsylvania to answer for in this matter.

I like the Resolutions of Virginia well, they ever have been firm as Rocks, near Relations to the Yankees. Our Colony no doubt will be for independence, as I know of none who oppose it; Those who did, some time Since and had like to have over set the government (and would most Cetainly have done it, had it not been for few) have all been appointed to some office, either in the Civil, or Military Department, and those few who were worthy intirely left out; Strage Conduct this by which, the Houses have in great measure lost the Confidence of the people, it is much to be lamented to see the two houses Set'g at the Expence of one hundred or more, Dollars per Day expence, and the most that is done is puning, Laughing, appoint'g Officers one Day, Reconsider'g the next, not one Single Act yet passed of any importance. The Prizes lay here Seven months uncondemed, for want of an Act. The Privateers Determined not to Send in any more, as there's no law; abt. one thousand dollars of time taken up in the Debates to Recommend the Officers Choose'g Several Sets of men, of the best Character, and then Dismissing them, only by a petition of the Colonal and officers from our battaries, who wanted the posts themselves, its shock'g that those people who are the Servants of the Colony should have so much influence in the house to over set all their Proceed'gs, yet its the fact not one Single Commissary, Collector or place of profit, but what is Confer'd on a Member of one of the houses, Some hold three or four places, nothing done about our battalion on the Seas Coast. The Men kept up at the Colony expence, when they might as well be made Continental no Courts going on, no money come'g in; all going out, every thing growing valueable except money, that falling in its value, for want of being called in faster, to prevent emiting more.

All these things I tho't it my duty to mention to the Counsel and many of the house few days Since when at Exeter and told them the Confidence of the people, out of doors was going fast. And that their Acts and Resolves would have but little force, soon, unless more Spirited Conduct in appointing men who have influence, and who the people will follow, and not Suffer themselves to be turn'd abt. by their own Servants at pleasure. And in short to do the Necessary business of the Colony, instead of hearing Tory matters, bro't on by that honest man Jonathan Blanchard,[1] and Hilsborough party, and some other's little tales and Petitions; The great Necessity of going into Matters, of government as soon as possable, every one must See,—before the people's minds are too Much possess'd, with that levelling Spirit, and while Subordination to the Powers that Rules, (more especially as its' of the people themselves) is fresh in their minds. You may say because that I've been Disappointed myself, is the reason I complain, I wish it may be the only reason; but whether it's of myself or any other if its fact is it not hard, that there should not be no more honour, and gratitude, in those who are appointed Conservators of the peace and good order of the Colony, then to appoint those who are undeserving to places of Honour and profit, intirely obtained by the Risque, expence, and Laudable endeavours of those who Deserve well.

Should I be appointed Agent I shall Resign my seat in the house, if Desired by Congress.[2] Should be glad to know as soon as may be whether I am to Tarry here or not. Should there be any new Arrangement in the Navy and Flag officers Come in the way you may Remember me if you please, unless Some other, who is likely to do much better is in the way. I only mention this Suppose'g that Several flags may be appointed. You may beleive me to be your most hearty Friend with out flattery.

John Langdon

P.S. I have not heard from your Lady this week.

RC (MeHi: The John S. H. Fogg Autograph Collection).

1. Jonathan Blanchard (1738–1788) of Dunstable (now Nashua) represented Hillsborough County on the Executive Council and was on the committee to consider raising the battalion for the defense of Portsmouth. Blanchard served on the Committee of Safety, 1777–1778, as a delegate to the Continental Congress, 1783, 1784, 1787, and as a brigadier general of militia, 1784–1788. *NHSP*, 8:6, 141.

2. Langdon was appointed "agent of prizes for New Hampshire" by Congress on 25 June. *JCC*, 5:478.

FROM MARY BARTLETT

My Dear   Kingstown June 30th 1776

This morning I Recd your Seventh Letter[1] and am thankfull to hear you are in good health. I wish you Peace and Prosperity in all your lawfull undertakeing. I and the Rest of the family are by the favour of kind Providence in health. Sally is now Comfortably tho her Disorder which I mentioned in my Last Letter held her near ten Days. I have not had So much of the headach as usual but more of the Colich Pain.

As for farming business I Beleive Biley and Peter[2] maniges Pretty well. I gave Peter leave to go to Portsmouth as Peter Abbot and Ephraim[3] was their and he had a Great mind to Go. As for hay I belive it will be near or quite as Scarce with us as it was last year. Esqr. Hook[4] and Some others Say they Shall not cut so much as they did Last year. Inglish Corn Looks very well. If we have Rains I Hope it will turn out well. We had a fine Shower Last Sunday Evening. Indian Corn Some Backward But it Grows fast now; the weather very hot and Dry; the worms has eat Considerably of our Corn in the new ground; and Some other People Complain of the worms among their flax and Corn. Apples very Scarce I bilive there will not be much Cyder made this year. However I hope and trust we Shall be Provided for as we have Been in times Past Caried throw many trials and Difficulties Beyond Expectation.

I have Recd of Coll Nicholas Gilman[5] by Majr. Samuell Philbrick for your Service as Committy of Safty Six Pounds five Shillins Lawfull mony. The people in general amongst us Seem Cool and backward about listing and going into the war; they hear so much Bad news about the war at canaday.

Your letters Comes very well from newbury. I Recive one every Satturday for Some time Back. No funaral this week much more healthey than it was Some time Past.

I Belive Levi will be very glad with his Letter. He is very often Sending up word to know when I heard from you. I will Edeavour to Send him his letter the vacation being the tenth of July.

As for affairs at home I will Endeavour to take the Best Care I can. I Remain yours &c.

Mary Bartlett
Eight Letter

RC (NhHi). In Polly's hand; signed by Mary.

1. Fragments of JB's seventh letter, probably written on 17 June, remain in NhHi. See MJB 871.

2. Servants.

3. Peter and Ephraim Abbot were sons of Peter Abbot (d. 1774), who had been an innkeeper at Kingston. Kingston Vital Records, 63–64.

4. Jacob Hook (1724–1802) held property in Hawke (now Danville). Greeley, *Genealogy*, 73, 137.

5. Nicholas Gilman (1731–1783), an Exeter merchant, New Hampshire's receiver general (treasurer) from 1775 to 1782, also sat on the Committee of Safety and on the Executive Council, 1777–1783. He was the father of Nicholas and John Taylor Gilman. Gillman, *Searches*, 224–25. See also MJB 867.

TO NATHANIEL FOLSOM

Dear Sir   Philadelphia, July 1st 1776

Your favor of the 15th ulto is Come to hand. I am glad to hear that Harmony Subsists in our Colony in the Grand american Cause; we are now Come to the time, that requires harmony, togather with all the wisdom prudence, Courage, & resolution we are masters of, to ward off the Evils intended by our implacable Enemies. The utmost power of Brittain will be Exerted I believe in a short time; if the americans behave with their usual Spirit, I make no Doubt we Shall Defeat them, and fully Establish our freedom. But if they all behave as it is said Major Butterfield & his men Did in Canada to their Eternal Disgrace *Death*, nay what is tenfold worse, *unconditioned absolute Slavery*, will be our portion; But reason, faith, Enthusiasm or something tells me, this last Can never be.

I am Glad to hear our Colony has Continud the price of Salt petre for another year & that a powder mill is likely to be soon Erected and that you have given a Bounty for making fire arms; Quere whither offering 12 or 13 Dollars for Every good musket & Bayonet made in the Colony & Delivered within a year would not answer a very good purpose.

The giving a Bounty of twenty Dollars to the men for Canada will be a heavy Expence to the Colony, as I fear the Continent will not be willing to refund it; yet as it is absolutely necessary for the Defence of the Colony to Keep a Strong army at the lakes or in Canada, it may be prudent to give that Bounty if the men Could not be raised without, of which the Colony are the best Judges. But I am sorry to hear that the Colony have Determined to Keep up Col. Gilman's Regiment in the pay of the Colony. The Design of raising the Continental Regiment was for the relief of the Colony and that Portsmouth might be Defended at the Expence of the Continent, and I was in hopes those men we had there would be immediately put on the Continental Establishment (as has been Done in Several other Colonies) and others inlisted to make them up to a full Regiment; by that means the heavy Expence of maintaing those men would be Saved to the Colony: But if they are Kept in pay & another Regiment is raised beside; I fear when it is Known it will be thought to be more than is necessary, and possibly the Continental Regiment will be ordered or at least a Considerable part of it to some other place and the Colony reap no advantage by raising them. If it be necessary for the public safety I am willing to spare neither Cost nor pains; yet as almost Every Colony have raised men for their Defence at the Expence of the Continent, I should be sorry to loose the Benefit the Congress Designed us. I would not have you think by what I have wrote that I mean to Censure what you have Done; you may & no Doubt have good reason for it; But as things appear to me and as other Colonys have Done, I should not have thought best to Keep any men at portsmouth in the pay of the Colony—as I believe one full regiment will be Quite sufficient unless in Case of an attack when the Militia will be Called in.

The whole Congress are unanimous for forming a plan of Confederation of the Colonies, a Committe of one from Each Colony, have been upon it for about a fortnight at all oppertunities; last Saturday the Committe spent the whole Day on it, this Day after Congress we are to meet again when I Believe it will be fitted to lay before Congress. When the Congress will model it to their minds I Know not. Before it is in force it will be laid before all the Legislatures of the Colonies and Receive their Sanction. It is a Business of the greatest importance as the future happiness of america will Depend on it in a great measure; and you may Easily see the Difficulty to frame it so as to be agreable to the Delegates of all the Different Colonies & of the Colonial Legislatures also; for without the unanimous Consent of all it Cannot be Established.

May the Supreme Disposer of all Events overule this and all our affairs for the happiness & safety of America. Mr. Dickerson the Pensylvania farmer is one of the Committee.[1]

The Resolve of our Colony with regard to our Conduct in the affair of Independency Came to hand on Saturday, very seasonably, as that Question was agreable to order this Day taken up in a Committe of the whole House & every Colony fully represented; Thus much I Can inform you that it was agreed to in Committe & I make no Doubt but that by next post I shall be able to send you a formal Declaration of Independency Setting forth the reasons &c. By letters from General Lee we are informed that Genl Clinton with above 50 sail of ships &c. were before Charlestown South Carolina, and by an express from Genl Washington it appears that Genl Howe with near 100 sail is at sandy Hook so that we may soon Expect news of Consequence.[2] Genl Sullivan had retreated with our army as far as Nut Island. I hope sir you will Excuse the erasements and interlinings &c. &c. as I have not time to Copy or Correct this Long Epistle. Believe me to be your friend and Humble servant.

Josiah Bartlett

RC (PHi).

1. John Dickinson (1732–1808), a Penn-   sylvania delegate, had published *Letters*

from a Farmer in Pennsylvania to the Inhabitants of the British Colonies, pointing out the evils of British policies. Although he voted in Congress against the Declaration of Independence, he took up arms late in 1776 in defense of liberty. In 1776 he moved to Delaware, where he held several public offices.

2. An army under Gen. Henry Clinton and a fleet under Sir Peter Parker (1721–1811) attacked Gen. Charles Lee's force

at Charleston, S.C., on 28 June. Clinton's army became stranded on an island, naval cannon shot sank harmlessly into the wood and mud walls of the fort (later named Fort Moultrie), and American guns raked British vessels. Parker retrieved Clinton's army and sailed back to New York. Wallace, *Appeal to Arms*, 91–96; Nebenzahl and Higginbotham, *Atlas*, 55–60, 84; *DNB*, 43:265–66.

TO JOHN LANGDON

Dear Sir,   Philadelphia July 1st 1776

Yours of the 14th ulto is now before me. I am truly sorry that guns &c. for the ships cannot be got as soon as wanting, but so it happens— the Committee appointed for that purpose have not been able to procure them yet—as to naval affairs I must refer you to brother Whipple who continues of the Marine Committee alias *Board of Admiralty* and who will while here inform you from time to time what is to be done in your department as Agent for New Hampshire.[1]

I am sorry to hear our Colony have determined to keep up the provincial regiment at Portsmouth in the pay of the Colony, besides the Continental regiment. The design of raising that regt was to ease our Colony of that expense and I expected they would have been immediately put on the Continental establishment and our Colony eased of the burden. The cost of maintaining Col. Gilman's regt with the bounty given to the men going to Canada with our other expenses will be very great, and where we can save cost consistent with the public safety we ought to do it. In short in my opinion it will be no advantage to us, for when it is known that our harbour is defended by our own forces, it is very probable the Continental regt may be ordered some where else, which would not be the case if they were wanted as was expected for the Colony's defence. I have the highest opinion of Dr. Brackett but think he would not accept of the appointment of Surgeon to the Continental regt especially as it may possibly be ordered to some distant place and I fear he would take it as an affront to offer it to him. New Jersey have appointed a new set of Delegates consisting of five, among them is Dr. Witherspoon.[2]

The affair of Independency has been this day determined in a Committee of the whole House: by next post I expect you will receive a formal declaration with the reasons; the Declaration before Congress is, I think, a pretty good one—I hope it will not be spoiled by canvassing in Congress. Genl Lee by express informs us that 55 ships with Genl Clinton were before Charlestown, South Carolina: Genl Washington by express this day informs us that Genl Howe with near 100 sail were at Sandy Hook, so that we may soon expect serious work. Before this reaches you, you will hear that Genl. Sullivan has evacuated Canada and is at present at Isle Noix and I expect soon to hear he is at Crown Point:[3] the time is now at hand, when we shall see whether America has virtue enough to be free, or not.

Sir, you will excuse the erasements and many other defects in this scrawl as I have not time to copy or correct it. I am Sir your friend &c.

Josiah Bartlett

P.S. The transport with Highlanders that was taken by the *Cabot* and afterward retaken, is taken a second time by Capt. Barron and carried into Jamestown, Virginia.[4] She had 212 soldiers on board, being the whole of the soldiers in two transports taken by the *Cabot*: the other transport contained the officers of both and was retaken by the *Cerberus* man of war, and afterward taken again by the *Schuyler* and *Montgomery* & carried into New York.

TR (DLC: Force Transcripts).

1. Whipple had taken JB's place on the Marine Committee when JB returned home in March. Mevers, "Congress," 46.

2. John Witherspoon (1723–1794) was president of the College of New Jersey (now Princeton University) throughout the Revolution. He served several terms in Congress until 1782.

3. By Washington's order early in May, Sullivan led his troops from New York City up the Hudson to join Schuyler's forces. Sullivan found the northern army in a state of sickness and general disarray. On 7 June British forces defeated the Americans at the Battle of Three Rivers. Sullivan's army retreated southward to Isle-aux-Noix, Crown Point, and finally Fort Ticonderoga by early July. Wallace, *Appeal to Arms*, 85–86; Hammond, *Sullivan Papers*, 1:197–284.

4. Captains James and Richard Barron, brothers in the Virginia state navy, brought the transport *Oxford* into Williamsburg on 22 June. *NDAR*, 5:687.

FROM JOHN LANGDON

My dear Sir,   Portsmouth 1st July 1776

Your favor of the 17th ulto is now before me am very unhappy at the behaviour of our Men owing entirely to the Officers, which I've mentioned to our Assembly and Council, since Receiving your Letter, our Assembly will send to all the Towns, to apprehend all those Soldiers who have returnd; and send them off for the Army in Canada. I've taken the utmost pains to prevent their choosing *every thing* into Office whither fit or unfit, last Week went up before both Houses, to mention a matter, which shew them, the Necessity of appointing Men who know their Business. You no doubt know a certain Colo: David Gilman, who commands our Batterys here, he has several times refused the Civil Authority and says that if any of his Men commits any misdeameanour, he is only accountable before his Court tho' the act is Committed any where out of his Jurisdiction—a matter lately happen'd, which called on me to take it in hand. I waited on the two Houses, and desired to know whither the Civil or Military were to rule, for if the latter we must govern ourselves Accordingly and the longest Sword, would rule, however after saying much on the Necessity of having good Officers, that knew their Business, and that our all depended on't and the absolute Necessity of punishing any Officers that dare to Oppose, and did not assist the civil Government left it with them, and beleive will have good Effect.

I am much Obliged for your Friendship relative to the Agencey. I've wrote Brother Whipple fully on the matter and do hereby resign my seat in Congress, and shall do it to our Assembly when they meet if you think it Necessary, therefore there will be no barr to my being chosen Agent.[1] If Brother Whipple comes home immediately, and can take care of this Business for me whilst I come up, and then to have the appointment, of Agent, when I return home, which would be in few Weeks, this would suit me, but this I only mention by the by, as you have given me the hint, if the Congress will postpone the appointment of Agent, till I am there, and there should be no risque of my being disappointed, in the appointment, I would come up directly for few Weeks, and then return with the Agencey, but this you'll be Judge of, for if I should come up, must leave my Business not finished, and therefore must return soon. I am very happy at the near approach of an AMERICAN CONSTITUTION, for Heavens sake let their be an appeal to the Continental Assembly from every Goverment in every thing of moment, Relative to Govermental matters, for it some times happens, that a Majority of Assembly do great Mischiefe.

Our Assembly after much urging have done some thing in the way of passing Acts to put the Courts in motion for Condemning Prizes, and many others in those matters your Friend and humble Servant has endeavoured to do what lay in his Power, in getting the Wheels of Goverment to turn round.[2] I lately but quite unexpectedly had a Unanimous Vote of both Houses, sent appointing me Colo: of Infantry Co: under no other Command except General Officer, and this hapned after my having declined excepting any Commission, except what my Fellow Citizens could give me that of Captain. I shall not receive the Commissn unless my Company will engage to act as Light Infantry to the first Battalion. I shall remember with Gratitude your kind endeavour's to serve me, my kind Respects to Major Patten, Mr. Dean, and Mrs. Susey, And accept of the best Wishes of your Friend and humble Servant.   John Langdon

FC (John Langdon Letter Book, Capt. J. G. M. Stone Private Collection, Annapolis, Md., 1976).

1. There is no evidence that Langdon formally resigned his seat in Congress. Congress had made the appointment on 25 June, a fact Langdon could not have yet known. On 6 September the General Court recognized him as Continental agent with full powers to fit out New Hampshire's naval frigate. The frigate had received the name *Raleigh* by resolution of the Continental Congress on 6 June. *JCC*, 5:423.

2. On 3 July the General Court passed an act for erecting a court to try and condemn naval prizes and an act for establishing courts of law within the state. *Laws of N.H.*, 4:25–32, 34–36.

TO MARY BARTLETT   July 2nd 1776

I shall write here Some things that you or the Children may have a Curiosity to know altho of no great importance.

Soon after I Came here my horse got out of the Pasture and was not to be found for Some time but after some pains & trouble & 2 or 3 Dollars

Cost I recovered him again. Things are very Dear here I Bought a pair of shoes price 12 shillings 8 yards of linen Cloth for 2 shirts at Eleven shillings pr yard and not very fine neither making them 12 shillings 3 pr linen Stockings at 13 Shillings a pair 1 pair Cotton Do 12s:6d. 5 yards of Calico for a Gown this very hot weather at a Dollar pr yard. I believe I must get me a thin Coat but there is nothing to be had with giving an Extravagant price.

There is a great variety of Cherries here they are all sold by the pound. Common red Cherries at 5 pence the cheapest pr pound some at a shilling 18 pence and two shillings pr pound. Cucumbers about 10 Days ago sold for 18 pence a piece they begin to be plentier now. Last year apples are still to be sold in the Streets none under a Copper Some 2 & Some 3 Coppers apiece.

A few days ago I rode out about 6 miles to Germantown before Breakfast for Exercise. I went in to see the Brittish Museum So Called. It is a house Built on purpose to preserve all the natural Coriosities that Can be Collected from all parts of the world as Birds, beasts, fish shells, Snakes, plants & a great many other Curiosities. Among them there was a Shark a Crocodile a Cat fish, a Dog fish a sea porcupine a Creature Called a Hog in armour 2 ostrich's Eggs which were perfectly round & of the Colour of Ivory and I Guess would hold a pint & an half Each. There was a great many other Creature of a Strange make from any thing I Ever saw before & whose names I have forgot as I had but a little time there. Snakes Skins Stuft among them a Small Alligators Skin &c. &c. &c.

The Plumbs & fruits here much the Same as with you rasberries, mulberries, Black berries &c.

The prizes[1] I have here mentioned are not lawful money but Dollars 7s:6d apiece which is Pensylvania Currency.   J.B.

RC (NhHi). Forepart of letter missing. The date is at the end.
    1. JB meant to write "prices."

FROM PIERSE LONG

Dear Sir,   Portsmo. July 2d, 1776
    I Received your very agreeable favour of the 17th ult.[1] Am Truely sorry to be obliged to join you in Sentiment Respecting the officering our Troops, &c., especially those in Canada. At the same time, am Constrained to say the same Complaint is prevalent at this Metropolis. The unheard of attempts of the Commander of our forces here to Guide our General Court, are not to be paralleled, and the effect they have had supasses History. I'll endeavour to give you a sketch of our proceedings. Soon after we Received the permission from Congress to Raise a Battalion for our protection, we voted to nominate Theophilus Dame, Esqr. Collo., David Gilman Esqr. Lt. Collo., and James Hackett, Esqr. Major, which gave dissatisfaction to Collo. Gilman and the Troops now here only, (as every one else were exceedingly pleased.) Upon which Petitions were thrown into Court in abundance, one after another from that quar-

ter, which had the desired effect—for the appointment was reconsidered. And before we could proceed any further on that business, the order from you was Received to raise a Battalion for Canada, which we Emmediately went into, and as an Encouragment Voted a Bounty of 20 dollars per man and two months advance wages to each officer, and proceeded to the appointment of the different Commanders, the first of which is Confered on Collo. Wyman, the 2d. and Collo. Senter, the 3d. on Major Peabody, who I wish may do honour to themselves and the Colony.[2] I must at the same time (tho' disagreeable) advise you the men are hard to come at, and Returns are dayly making of the Ill success of the Captains in Raising them. I come by the desire of the Court now here, Encouraging those to List who are in the Colony service, though but few Incline, having Engaged at this time 60 only. If no better prospect of succeeding than now appears, I believe the Assembly will order them Draufted. You are not unacquainted with the Scarcity of men in this Colony, above half our number being in the Service already To Return to Collo. Gilman, (who I believe could do best at Home.) He still thinks he is Entitled to the Command of the forces to be stationed here, and believe he has a sufficiency of friends to get him nominated, and were I not Convinced it would give General uneasiness to this Town, I should cheerfully acquiesce in the appointment.

I hope the Behaviour of the British Pirates to the French, Dutch, and Spaniards, will beat up a Dust between them Powers. If so, I am convinced it will be an essential service to us. I am much obliged to you for the News paper you Inclosed, and in Return, please to accept of our Last. I wish it contained the disappointment of our Enemies in Every of their attempts.

The Powder we lent the Continental Army while before Boston, we are not able to get Back again, though we are much in want of that article, Especially as we now begin to think our frontier settlements are much Exposed. Some of our Court are gone home, who live that way, upon the Intelligence Received that our Army are Retreating out of Canada. I, for my part, am not Convinced of the Truth of the Report, nor shall be, till it comes better authenticated then it now is, as this we have got is by Deserters only.

The Rever'd Mr. J. Murry of Booth Bay is now here, who begs leave to present his most Respectful Complments to you, and prays your Interest in Congress for their Extending the Post to the County of Lincoln as per their Petition, in doing of which I should esteem a Peticur. favour.[3] We have just heard of the Vilanous Designs of our Enemies, in attempting to destroy our Magazine at New York. With the Council of War, it appears to me, that the perpetrators of so Hellish a plan ought Emmeadiately to Receive their just Demerits. We have a Report from Mistick that a design was formed of destroying that Likewise, but were happily descovered (tho' not taken) before their views were put into Execution. It has put us on our guard. The Watch is doubled that keeps our Magazine. I am afraid my Lengthey Letter will tire you. Major Philbrook informed me on Saturday Last, your family and friends were all well. I am with Real Esteem, Dr. Sir, Your most huml. Servt.   Pierse Long

P.S. My Motive for the Post Riding so far East, is because I am Certain they must be as anxious for news from their friends, as other people. And I am convinced of that People's Sincerity and Heartiness and our Glorious Struggles.   P. Long

Reprinted from *The Historical Magazine*, 8 (1863), 48–49.

1. Not found.

2. Isaac Wyman (1724–1792) of Keene, a lieutenant colonel in Stark's regiment at the Battle of Bunker Hill, was made a colonel on 19 June 1776. Joseph Senter (1723–1798) of Moultonborough and Plymouth was lieutenant colonel of Wyman's regiment, 1776–1778. Stephen Peabody (1742–1780), a farmer and town officer of Amherst, was adjutant in Poor's regiment at Winter Hill in 1775; major in Wyman's regiment in 1776; and lieutenant colonel in William Whipple's bri-

gade, 1778–1779. Heitman, *Historical Register*, 432, 489, 608; Griffin, *Keene*, 668–69; *NHSP*, 8:156; Stearns, *Plymouth*, 2:627–28; Secomb, *Amherst*, 721; Potter, *Military History*, 1:310.

3. The Reverend John Murray (1742–1793), a native of Ireland, came to the colonies in 1763 and was ordained in Philadelphia in 1765. He preached at the First Presbyterian Church in Boothbay, Maine, 1766–1779. Weis, *Colonial Clergy*, 148. See letter from Lincoln County, 18 April 1776.

The Declaration of Independence is dated 4 July 1776, although it was not signed by JB and his colleagues until 2 August. On 11 June Congress appointed a committee of five—Thomas Jefferson, John Adams, Benjamin Franklin, Roger Sherman, and Robert Livingston—to draft a declaration of independence in the event that Congress should decide upon it. The committee submitted a draft on 28 June. On 2 July Congress determined that the colonies were thereupon free and independent of Great Britain. Further debate ensued before Congress agreed on a draft of the written instrument, declaring independence on the relatively cool morning of 4 July. It was another month—until 2 August—before a good engrossed copy could be laid on the table for the signatures of delegates, some of whom had left Philadelphia since voting on it in July. See Boyd, Jefferson Papers, 1:413–33; and Smith, "Time and Temperature," 294–99.

*A Declaration by the Representatives of the United
States of America, In Congress Assembled*[1]

When in the Course of human events, it becomes necessary for one people to dissolve the political bands which have connected them with another, and to assume among the powers of the earth, the separate and equal station to which the Laws of Nature and of Nature's God entitle them, a decent respect to the opinions of mankind requires that they should declare the causes which impel them to the separation. We hold these truths to be self-evident, that all men are created equal, that they are endowed by their Creator with certain unalienable Rights, that among these are Life, Liberty and the pursuit of Happiness. That to secure these rights, Governments are instituted among Men, deriving their just powers from the consent of the governed, That whenever any Form of Government becomes destructive of these ends, it is the Right of the People to alter or to abolish it, and to institute new Government, laying its foundation on such principles and organizing its powers in such form, as to them shall seem most likely to effect their Safety and Happiness. Prudence, indeed, will dictate that Governments long established should not be changed for light and transient causes; and accordingly all experience hath shewn, that mankind are more disposed to suffer, while evils are sufferable, than to right themselves by abolishing the forms to which they are accustomed. But when a long train of abuses and usurpations, pursuing invariably the same Object evinces a design to reduce them under absolute Despotism, it is their right, it is their duty, to throw off such Government, and to provide new Guards for their future security. Such has been the patient sufferance of these Colonies; and such is now the necessity which constrains them to alter their former Systems of Government. The history of the present King of Great Britain is a history of repeated injuries and usurpations, all having in direct object the establishment of an absolute Tyranny over these States. To prove this, let Facts be submitted to a candid world. He has refused his Assent to Laws, the most wholesome and necessary for the public good. He has forbidden his Governors to pass Laws of immediate and pressing importance, unless suspended in their operation till his Assent should be obtained; and when so suspended, he has utterly neglected to attend to them. He has refused to pass other Laws for the accommodation of large districts of people, unless those people would relinquish the right of Representation in the Legislature, a right inestimable to them and formidable to tyrants only. He has called together legislative bodies at places unusual, uncomfortable, and distant from the depository of their public Records, for the sole purpose of fatiguing them into compliance with his measures. He has dissolved Representative Houses repeatedly, for opposing with manly firmness his invasions on the rights of the people. He has refused for a long time, after such dissolutions, to cause others to be elected; whereby the Legislative powers, incapable of Annihilation, have returned to the People at large for their exercise; the State remaining in the mean time exposed to all the dangers of invasion from without, and convulsions within. He has endeavoured to prevent the population of these States; for that purpose obstructing the Laws for Naturalization of Foreigners; refusing to pass others to encourage their migrations hither, and raising the conditions of new Appropriations of Lands. He has obstructed the Administration of Justice, by refusing his Assent to Laws for establishing Judiciary powers. He has made Judges dependent on his Will alone, for the tenure of their offices, and the amount and payment of their salaries. He has erected a multitude of New Offices, and sent hither swarms of Officers to harrass our people, and eat out their substance. He has kept among us, in times of peace, Standing Armies without the Consent of our legislatures. He has affected to render the Military independent of and superior to the Civil power. He has combined with others to subject us to a jurisdiction foreign to our constitution, and unacknowledged by our laws; giving his Assent to their Acts of pretended Legislation: For Quartering large bodies or armed troops among us: For protecting them, by a mock Trial, from punishment for any Murders which they should commit on the Inhabitants of these States: For cutting off our Trade with all parts of the world: For imposing Taxes on us without our Consent: For depriving us in many cases, of the benefits of Trial by Jury: For transporting us beyond Seas to be tried for pretended offences: For abolishing the free System of English Laws in a neighbouring Province, establishing therein an Arbitrary government, and enlarging its Boundaries so as to render it at once an example and fit instrument for introducing the same absolute rule into these Colonies: For taking away our Charters, abolishing our most valuable Laws, and altering fundamentally the Forms of our Governments: For suspending our own Legislatures, and declaring themselves invested with power to legislate for us in all cases whatsoever. He has abdicated Government here, by declaring us out of his Protection, and waging War against us. He has plundered our seas, ravaged our Coasts, burnt our towns, and destroyed the Lives of our people. He is at this time transporting large Armies of foreign Mercenaries to compleat the works of death, desolation and tyranny, already begun with circumstances of Cruelty & perfidy scarcely paralleled in the most barbarous ages, and totally unworthy the Head of a civilized nation. He has constrained our fellow Citizens taken Captive on the high Seas to bear Arms against their Country, to become the executioners of their friends and Brethren, or to fall themselves by their Hands. He has excited domestic insurrections amongst us, and has endeavoured to bring on the inhabitants of our frontiers, the merciless Indian Savages, whose known rule of warfare, is an undistinguished destruction of all ages, sexes and conditions. In every stage of these Oppressions, We have Petitioned for Redress in the most humble terms: Our repeated Petitions have been answered only by repeated injury. A Prince, whose character is thus marked by every act which may define a Tyrant, is unfit to be the ruler of a free people. Nor have We been wanting in attentions to our Brittish brethren. We have warned them from time to time of attempts by their legislature to extend an unwarrantable jurisdiction over us. We have reminded them of the circumstances of our emigration and settlement here. We have appealed to their native justice and magnanimity, and we have conjured them by the ties of our common kindred to disavow these usurpations, which, would inevitably interrupt our connections and correspondence. They too have been deaf to the voice of justice and of consanguinity. We must, therefore, acquiesce in the necessity, which denounces our Separation, and hold them, as we hold the rest of mankind, Enemies in War, in Peace Friends.

We, therefore, the Representatives of the united States of America, in General Congress, Assembled, appealing to the Supreme Judge of the world for the rectitude of our intentions, do, in the Name, and by Authority of the good People of these Colonies, solemnly publish and declare, That these United Colonies are, and of Right ought to be Free and Independent States; that they are Absolved from all Allegiance to the British Crown, and that all political connection between them and the State of Great Britain, is and ought to be totally dissolved; and that as Free and Independent States, they have full Power to levy War, conclude Peace, contract Alliances, establish Commerce, and to do all other Acts and Things which Independent States may of right do. And for the support of this Declaration, with a firm reliance on the protection of divine Providence, we mutually pledge to each other our Lives, our Fortunes and our sacred Honor.　John Hancock

Josiah Bartlett	Fras. Hopkinson	George Wythe
Wm: Whipple	John Hart	Richard Henry Lee
Saml Adams	Abra Clark	Th Jefferson
John Adams	Robt. Morris	Benja. Harrison
Robt Treat Paine	Benjamin Rush	Thos Nelson jr.
Elbridge Gerry	Benja. Franklin	Francis Lightfoot Lee
Step. Hopkins	John Morton	Carter Braxton
William Ellery	Geo Clymer	Wm Hooper
Roger Sherman	Jas. Smith	Joseph Hewes
Samel Huntington	Geo. Taylor	John Penn
Wm. Williams	James Wilson	Edward Rutledge
Oliver Wolcott	Geo. Ross	Thos Heyward Junr.
Matthew Thornton	Caesar Rodney	Thomas Lynch Junr.
Wm. Floyd	Geo Read	Arthur Middleton
Phil. Livingston	Tho M:Kean	Button Gwinnett
Frans. Lewis	Samuel Chase	Lyman Hall
Lewis Morris	Wm. Paca	Geo Walton
Richd. Stockton	Thos. Stone	
Jno Witherspoon	Charles Carroll of Carrollton	

MS (DNA: PCC).

1. When approved by New York on 19 July the title was changed to "The unanimous Declaration of the thirteen united States of America." The document now at the National Archives measures 29¾ by 24¼ inches.

TO MESHECH WEARE

Sir,　　　　　　　　　　　　　　　Philadelphia 9th. July 1776

Your highly Esteem'd favor of the 12 Ulto.[1] inclosing Instructions to join with the other Colonies in Declaring these United Colonies, Free & Independant States, came very Seasonably to hand. As we were so happy as to agree in sentiment with our Constituents it gave us the greater Pleasure to Concur with the Delagates of the other Colonies in the inclos'd Declaration, which was yesterday Publish'd in form in this City and is to be Publish'd at the Head of the Army at New-York next Thursday.[2]

A plan of Confederation is now forming, which when finished will be transmitted to each Colony for their aprobation.

Major Rogers (whose Conduct it seems was Suspicious) was taken up some time Since by order of General Washington and sent under Guard to this City. He Requested leave to go to England by way of the West Indies but Congress not thinking it proper, have directed him to be sent to New-Hampshire to be dispos'd of as the Authority there shall think Best.[3] We have the Honor to be with Great Respect Your Most obt Serts.

Josiah Bartlett
Wm: Whipple

RC (MH). In Whipple's hand; signed also by JB.

1. This was probably only the order to pay JB and Whipple for their congressional service. See MJB.

2. JB and Whipple had voted on 2 July in favor of independence and on 4 July to adopt the Declaration. *JCC,* 5:507, 510–15.

3. See John Langdon to JB, 3 June 1776 (second letter) and Weare to JB, 11 June 1776, n. 3.

FROM MARY BARTLETT

My Dear   Kingstown July 13th 1776

These Lines Leave me much better in health than when I wrote to you Last; the Sick headach I Mentioned Last week held me three Days & nights without Intermition; the Rest of the family are very well at this time; Levi Came home Last wednsday: he is very well & Likes the School very much. Our People met here for training & town meetings three Days this week to List men to go to Canada; & have Listed almost Enough. Old Mr. Proctor and old Willim Collins of this town & Several younger men have listed; they are to march next week I hear.

We have had plenty of rain about ten Days past & I Beleive hay will be vastly better than our fears Some time ago; English Corn I Beleive will be very Good; flax will be better than our fears were in times past; Indian Corn we Cannot tell what Crops we shall have yet, it grows very fast. People among us Dont mow yet as they think the grass grows faster now than it has this Summer before; they Say it is a quarter better now that it was a week or ten Days ago; apples will be Scarce with us this year.

I this morning Recd yours of the first Instant[1] and I hope you have Recovered your Health & got read of your Cough tho you Did not mention any thing about your health in your Last Letter. I advise you to Spare no Cost to make your Self Comfortable; I want your advice & assistance but must make myself Contented. I Beleive Biley & Peter manages your farming business very well. Peter is more Steady now than he was when you left him Before. I am under Some Difficulty to Send my Letters to the Post office; I wrote you last week & Sent it by Coll: Gale's Son;[2] he went Down to Dummers School Early a tuesday morning to bring up his Brother and Levi; & he forgot to leave the Letter in the Post office till he Came back; & then the Post had been gone half an hour, & I Suppose you will not Receive it the next week. I Shall write to you every week (by the leave of Divine Providence) if I have an oppertunity to Send them.

Major Philbrick Sent a Letter here to Send to you But it came two late to be Sent Last week: I Shall Inclose it in mine.[3] This is the tenth Letter I have Sent you. I Remain yours &c.   Mary Bartlett

P.S. I fear the Small Pox will Spread universilly as boston is Shut up with it & People flocking in for innoculation; the Select men of portsmouth have Petitiond to the Committy of Safty now Setting in Exeter; for leave to fix an innoculating hospital in their metropolis for the Small Pox and liberty is accordingly granted and the inhabitance of Exeter intend to Petition for the Same libirty.

The times Looks Dark and Gloomy upon the account of the wars. I belive this year will Decide the fate of america which way it will turn God only knows we must look to him for Direction & Protection; Job Said tho he Slay me yet will I trust in him. Mr. Thayr Gives his Regards to You.   M. B.

July 15th

We are all well.

RC (NhHi). In Polly's hand; signed by Mary.

1. Probably a reference to JB's letter of 2 July.

2. Probably James Gale (b. 1759) had gone for his brother, Jacob (b. 1764), who was a year younger than Levi Bartlett.

James and Jacob were sons of Col. Jacob Gale. Gale, "Gale Family Records," 16.

3. No letter of this approximate date from Samuel Philbrick has been found.

TO MARY BARTLETT

My Dear   Philadelphia, July 14th 1776

Yours of the 30th of June is Come to hand and I have had the pleasure of hearing from you & my other friends in New: Hampshire Every week Since I arrived here, but very possibly our letters may not be So regular to & from Each other as they have hitherto been; as the Brittish fleet & army at Staten Island & Hudson's River will no Doubt Endeavor to hinder the Communication between the Eastern and Southern Colonies which perhaps they may in some measure Effect.[1]

I am sorry to hear their is like to be a Scarcity of Hay and must leave it to you with proper advice to sell, fat or Exchange so many of my Cattle as you shall think proper and you will order all the Straw and fodder possible of Every Kind to be saved. Last Evening an Express arrived from General Washington with some accounts that required our being Called togather this Day (tho Sunday) to give some immediate orders:[2] I Expect Every Body will be very much Engaged for sometime to Come; some in taking Care of the harvest and many in opposing the several Brittish & German armies that are sent to Destroy & ravage the Country; But I hope & trust that the Supreme Disposer of all Events, who loveth Justice & hateth iniquity will Continue to favor our righteous Cause and that the wickedness of our Enemies will fall on their own heads.

I am glad to hear you & my family are well. I am so at this time & may we all Continue so till it shall please Providence to return me to you again in Due time.

I Can inform you that the greatest preparations are making to oppose the Powerful army that are now or will soon be near New York. I hope it will be Done Successfully however that Depends on Divine Providence whose ways are unsearchable by human beings. I shall Continue to write to you weekly unless I hear the Communication is stopped if it should for a short time I Doubt not it will soon be opened again.

By Polly & Lois letter[3] I was informed of the misfortune Mr. Wheeler &c. &c. &c. met with in their party of pleasure in the great pond and am glad it was no wórse; however this may show my Children the Dangers that are often run in Such gay amusements; Dangers at such times often little Known & less thought of. Please to inform Major Philbrick I Recd his letter but have not time to write to him this week. I am yours &c.

Josiah Bartlett

P.S. There is a report that General Clinton who was sent to attack Charlestown in South Carolina in Endeavoring to land was repulsed & Drove back to the ships & that he had lost some of his ships. I wish it may prove true tho at present we have no Certain account to be Depended on.

July 16th Closed, now well. We have lately had Considerable rains here So that there is no want. The 14th was a very wet rainy Day the whole of it. Remember me to the Children, and all friends.   J: B:

RC (MH).

1. On 4 July Congress heard from Washington that the British fleet, numbering 110 vessels, had arrived from Halifax, transporting Howe's army. Enemy forces arrived at New York through the summer in preparation for the Battle of Long Island, which occurred in August. *WGW*, 5:214–16; *JCC*, 5:516; Wallace, *Appeal to Arms*, 100–05.

2. Washington's letters to Congress of 11 and 12 July disclosed the immediate threat to New York. Of more pressing concern was the need for general supplies and ammunition for the flying camp—a highly mobile, strategic reserve unit of 10,000 men, which had been authorized by Congress in June but which failed to accomplish its purpose and ceased to exist in November. *WGW*, 5:251–55, 264–65; *JCC*, 5:558–59; Boatner, *Encyclopedia*, 371–72.

3. Not found.

TO JOHN LANGDON

My Dear Sir: Philadelphia, July 15 1776

Yours of the 1st instant is now before me, and I am obliged to you for your intelligence. The affair of the agency you have heard is settled, and in your favour, and I hope another Delegate will be appointed to attend Congress, as you have resigned.

The marine affairs I shall leave to brother Whipple, who will inform you from time to time what is to be done.

The Congress and people here are engaged in making preparation for the reception of the British fleet and army in the neighborhood of New-York. Lord Howe,[1] with the Germans, &c., is hourly expected. I pray God we may be able to give a good account of them. The Confederation is agreed to by the Committee, and is before Congress;[2] when they will finish it is uncertain. Two of the frigates here are launched. There is a report in town that General Clinton endeavoured to land his men at South-Carolina, and was repulsed with loss; I know not the particulars, and mention it only as a report. I hope you will excuse my not writing every week, as brother Whipple has written you everything of importance.

Major Rogers was taken up by order of General Washington, and having your letters of recommendation to us, the General ordered him to Congress to be examined; and though no absolute proof was made of his ill designs, his conduct appeared so very suspicious that he was ordered to be sent to New-Hampshire, to be disposed of by our Legislature; but before he was sent off, he found means to make his escape, and has not been retaken yet.

The Colony of New-York have fully acceded to the Declaration of Independence, so that it now has the sanction of the Thirteen United States.[3] The unparalleled conduct of our enemies have united the Colonies more firmly than ever.

The Convention of this Colony are to meet here this day, who will form a Constitution for the Colony, and take upon them its Government; in the mean time the Constitutions of Virginia and New-York are in this city.[4] I shall send them forward, and the Constitutions of the other Colonies as they are formed, as possibly something may be taken from them to amend our own. Please to give my best regards to all friends, and believe me to be your sincere friend, &c.   Josiah Bartlett

P.S. Colonel Roberdeau is appointed a Provincial Brigadier-General; Colonel Dickinson, Colonel McKean, and Colonel Cadwalader, are gone with their regiments to the Jerseys; twelve hundred Maryland Militia are hourly expected in this city to join the Army in the Jerseys; Colonel Miles, with one thousand Provincial riflemen, and with him our friend Major Patton, have joined the Army in New-Jersey; in short, Maryland and Pennsylvania are all in motion. This day an Artillery company of Militia, consisting of fifty-seven men, with two brass field-pieces, and every necessary accourtrement, marched for the same place. Mr. William Livingston, of New-Jersey, is appointed a Provincial Brigadier-General. Our friend, Mr. Deane, is appointed Captain of Marines to one of the frigates here. He desires to be remembered to you.   J. B.

Reprinted from Force, *American Archives*, 5th series, 1:348.

1. Admiral Sir Richard Howe (1726–1799) was commander-in-chief of the North American fleet, 1776–1778. He returned to active duty in 1782 and served as lord of the admiralty, 1783–1788. *DNB*, 28:92–101; Gruber, *Howe Brothers*.

2. The committee, including JB, presented its draft of the Articles of Confederation to Congress on 12 July. *JCC*, 5:546–56.

3. On 9 July New York's provincial congress resolved unanimously "That the reasons assigned by the Continental Congress for declaring the United Colonies free and independent States, are cogent and conclusive; and that while we lament the cruel necessity which has rendered that measure unavoidable, we approve the same, and will, at the risk of our lives and fortunes, join with the other Colonies in supporting it." Force, *American Archives*, 5th series, 1:1391.

4. Virginia adopted its constitution on 29 June. New York's Revolutionary constitution was held up by exigencies of war until April 1777. Wood, *Creation of the American Republic*, 133.

FROM JOHN LANGDON

My Friend   Portsmo: July 15th. 1776

Your favor of 1st July is now before me you perfectly Agree with me in Regard to keeping up the Regiment, under, Colonal Gilman, at the Colony expence, our Committee of Safety intend doing something in that matter (I think it most time). I do not allow myself (hardly) to think of the Expences, tho' I am very sensable, much might be saved, if men would act (pro bono) but, alas, we are not to expect this in our day— I've from time to time inform'd you of many, irregularities (in my opinion) in Colonial matters all can do, must, endeavour to mend.

I observe what you say of our mutual friend Bracket. He tho't, it would do, for him, otherwise should not have mentioned him—but suppose the Colony will appoint as the Director General of the Hospital—in my Opinion he's as well without. I was very happy to see that the Committee had voted Independance, hope it will be immediately Confirmed by Congress, *unanimously*. One of the the finest Compys we now have in the service begins to march this day, (abt Ninety) under Capt. Arnold[1] all Uniform'd in Shirts, with Gun, Bayonet, Blankets, and Tomehawk Compleat, this done, in one week in this Town, tho' front teer, exposed to ships of war. This Town has voted an inoculateing, hospital, expect soon to begin. Our Committee of Safety are sending of men to guard the frontiers; our men almost gone. Thank God we are like to have fine Crops, except hay that somewhat short. Corn never known to be so plenty this time of year. You must not expect to have any body in Mr. Whipples room till September when the Court meets, at which time I shall make a formal Resignation. Several french vessells from the West Indies have Arrived at Newburyport and Falmouth.[2] My kind Respects to all Friends, and let me subscribe myself your Friend.   John Langdon
Inclosed is letters to Brother Whipple which you'll open except one from his Lady which is marked and if he should have come away you'll inclose it Back, to me.

RC (NhD).

1. James Arnold signed the Association   in *NHSP*, 14:343–45.
Test in Portsmouth. His company, part   2. Reported in *N.H. Gazette*, 29 June
of Joshua Wingate's regiment, is listed   1776.

FROM MARY BARTLETT

My Dear   Kingstown July 20th 1776

This morning I Rec'd Yours of the 9th Instnt[1] and am thankfull to hear You are well. I hope your health will be Continued to you. I Should be glad to know if you think you Can Come home the beginning of the fall as you gave us Some Encouragement you hoped you Should be at home in September. We have not had our healths so well Since you left us this last time as we had when you left us before. I have been Poorly this ten Days Past. I am now better. Ezra was taken last monday in the afternoon (after we had Dated a letter to you that we were well) with the Canker and Scarlet fever. He has had a very high fever & broke out red all over till friday morning. He is now Some better. He has kept his bed from monday night till this morning.

The Rest of the family are very well at this time. Nothing Strange amonge us a General time of health. Mr. Thayer a Preaching with us Still he has not Givin his answer yet. Moses Sweat has kept School a month & now Mr. Secomb[2] has Engaged Polly to keep School a month & She is now a keeping upon the Plaine.

The men among us are very backward about going into the war they are not Contented with the Province bounty. Our men have had a town meeting & have voted to raise their bounty to fifty Dollars a man beside their wages. They are to begin their march to Day & meet at Esqr. Webster's at Chester. David Quimby of hawk is Captn., Jacob Webster first Lieut, John Eastman Second Lieut old Mr. Procter is gone Mr. Wheeler is a going.[3]

I wrote to you last week about the farming business. Our menfolks have Done hilling of indian corn and begin to mow Some of the thinest grass. We have not began to Reap yet—the weather wet and a fine growing time.

We have letters Brought into town from albany Dated about ten Days ago brought news that our Province men have all had the Small Pox and got almost well. They have had it very favourbly but two men have Died out of Capt. Tilton's Company vis John Peterson and one Whitcher Brother to Esqr. Whitcher.[4]

We hear of wars and tumults from one end of the Continent to the other; I Should be glad to Know if Your courage holds out yet about keeping & Defending america. I Remain Yours &c.   Mary Bartlett

RC (NhHi). In Polly's hand; signed by Mary. Sent "Free."

1. No letter to Mary of 9 July has been found.

2. Moses Swett (1754–1822) received an honorary degree from Harvard in 1790 and preached at the Congregational Church in Sanford, Maine. Stackpole, *Swett Genealogy*, 37. Simmons Secomb (c. 1740–1810) was a selectman of Kingston and county coroner. Abstract, Kingston Church Records, 18; *NHSP*, 8:24, 62, 247.

3. John Webster (1714–1784), a storekeeper of Chester, was also a selectman, representative to the General Court, and colonel of the Chester regiment in 1775. His regiment was to send fifty-five men to reinforce the army in Canada. Chase, *Chester*, 611; *NHSP*, 7:648; 8:186. David Quimby of Hawke (now Danville), lumber merchant, commanded the first company of Col. Joshua Wingate's regiment of 750 men. *NHSP*, 14:339–43. Jacob Webster (1745–1836), who had been a first lieutenant in the 2nd N.H. Regiment in 1775, reenlisted in June 1776 as first lieutenant under Capt. Quimby, marched through Vermont to Ticonderoga, served four months, and was discharged on account of sickness. Heitman, *Historical Register*, 578; N.H. Rev. Pension Recs., 57:156–58. John Eastman (1741–1804), cooper, was commissioned on 16 July 1776 as second lieutenant in Quimby's company and was stationed at Mt. Independence until December 1776. In 1778 he was a captain in the Rhode Island expedition and in 1780 was at West Point. Kingston Vital Records, MS, 68, NhHi; N.H. Rev. Pension Recs., 11:38–42. James Proctor and Abner Wheeler were in the Kingston militia. *NHSP*, 14:340, 342.

4. Philip Tilton (b. 1741), Kingston blacksmith, was commissioned a captain in the 2nd N.H. Regiment under Col.

Enoch Poor, 5 June 1775. He went to the northern army as part of General Sullivan's force in the spring of 1776. Tilton, *History*, vol. 1, no. 8, 240; N.H. Rev.

Pension Recs., 54:71–74.
   "Whitcher" probably refers to Isaac Witcher of Brentwood, born in Kingston, 1738. Whittier, *Descendants*, 31.

TO JOHN LANGDON

My Friend   Philadelphia July 22d 1776

By your's of the 6th inst I rec'd your genteel but just reprimand for not answering your letters and shall in future endeavor to give you the trouble of a line at least, every week without further excuse or ceremony.

By the enclosed paper you will see the account of General Clinton and Sir Peter Parker's defeat in South Carolina;[1] the Virginians have likewise drove Lord Dunmore from Gwin's Island with loss[2]—these are agreeable events after our repeated crises in Canada. Some of our Southern brethren seem much elated with their success—by all accounts the troops there behave with incomparable bravery—I am sorry I can't say the same of our troops in Canada. Some of the Southern gentlemen say America must be saved by the Southern not the Northern troops—however I hope it will yet appear that the New England Troops are not behind any in the Continent in point of bravery. The papers will inform you of the march of the militia of this State to New Jersey—three reg's are ordered from Virginia to the Jersies. I hope soon there will be an army there of 15 or 20,000 men besides those at New York. We must at all events prevent their getting possession of New York and Hudson's river which I believe is their principal view and by that way open a communication with Canada.

Lord Howe's proclamation has now convinced every body that no offers are to be made us but absolute submission.[3] I think it very happy for America that Britain has insisted on those terms for had she proposed a Treaty and offered some concessions there would have been danger of divisions or at least of our not acting with unanimity and spirit as I think will now be the case.

The convention here have taken on them the gov' of this Colony[4] and have appointed delegates for Congress, men who will forward and not hinder spirited measures—in short there is a far greater harmony in carrying on spirited measures in Congress than heretofore. The Conventions of even Maryland and New York seem now to be in earnest.

The confederation is now before a Committee of the whole, by reason of so much other business it goes on but slow: when it is laid before our Legislature brother Whipple expects to be at home and can inform them of some things they may want to be informed of, concerning it. Our Court I hear is to set again the first of September. With sincerity I am your friend.   Josiah Bartlett

P.S. I have omitted enclosing this day's paper as brother Whipple has sent one to you in his letter.

TR (DLC: Force Transcripts).

1. See JB to Folsom, 1 July 1776.
2. American gunners drove the Loyalist forces of Lord Dunmore off Gwynn's Island in Chesapeake Bay on 9 July.
3. Admiral Richard Howe's proclamation, issued on 20 June, is printed in

NHSP, 8:159.
4. The Pennsylvania Convention met on 15 July and adopted a constitution on 28 September. Force, *American Archives*, 5th series, 2:1–62.

FROM JOHN LANGDON

My Good Friend   Portsmouth, 28th. July 1776

Your favour of the 15th. is now before me, was happy to find that the Confederation of the Colonies, was like to take place soon, as I think it most Necessary step. It has always appeared to me to be good policy, hitherto not to interfere with the internal Poleice of any Colony, but the Matter is now very Different, as the whole Continent, have taken government. The Congress will no doubt Act as a legal body, and no doubt interfere in any Government that seems to go wrong. I observe what you say abt. Rogers am Sorry I gave any letters if they have been any means of his escape'g—his importun'g me for letters of introduction, to you and Brother Whipple made me give my letters at any rate, as I was senseable they would do him no good: even if he was well inclined, as his Charectar and person, was well known to most of the Members; I Certainly do not think him able, to do much damage, at any rate. I am much pleased at the hint you give of sending along the Constitution of the Several Colonies, as I think ours must ungo a Revision sooner or later as there's many things wrong.

I have been lately honoured with an appointmt to a Seat in our Inferiour Court along side of your honour; hope you'll be home by the time we set; should have most Certainly Declined, and was Determined, but Judge Weare and some others insisted upon it. It's quite out of my Road, don't know but shall be sick of it. Pray urge My Commission, as Agent that I might know what is my Department whither the whole business of the Continent (as well Prizes as Navy) or any thing else Comes under my Care, as its very Necessary I should know immediately. Want to know whether there should not be a Clark Allowed who should be Sworn, to the True performance of the Business—this would be Salutary thro' the Colonies, and prevent any Agent do'g wrong or unjust things. With my kind Respects to all Friends, you, have part of my best Wishes for your health and happiness. Your Friend and Servt.   Jno. Langdon

RC (NhD).

TO JOHN LANGDON

My Friend: Philadelphia, July 29, 1776

Yours of the 15th instant is now before me, and with you I lament the selfish disposition that is but too prevalent among almost all orders and degrees of men; even the Senate and Army are not entirely free. However, we must not expect perfection in human nature, but must endeavour to correct it in ourselves, and to point it out and oppose it in others.

The retreat of our Army to Ticonderoga has no doubt alarmed the western parts of our State, though I think there will be no great danger at present, as there is a very powerful Army there, who are now getting well of the small-pox, and will be soon ready for action, besides the numerous Militia who are marching to join that Army.

Our friend General Sullivan is disgusted at the appointment of General Gates to be a Major-General, and being sent to the Northern Army. By permission of the Generals Schuyler and Washington, he (General Sullivan) has left the Army, and is now here, and has petitioned Congress for leave to resign his commission. What will be done in the case I cannot say, but hope it will be settled without his dismission.

Brother Whipple is here yet, and will not set out for home till the Confederation is settled, which may possibly take a week or ten days' time, as there is a great deal of other business to be done in the mean time, and the sentiments of the members of Congress very different on many of the articles. I should be glad he might hear the whole of the debates here, and be present in our Colony when it is laid before our Legislature for their concurrence, to answer any questions and remarks that may be made upon it. It is a matter of the greatest importance, but the interests and opinions of the several members are so various that I see it will not be settled agreeable to my mind.

It is a very still time as to news here. The fleet and Armies at New-York and Staten-Island remain in *statu quo*. The Army in the Jerseys is increasing very fast, so that there will soon be a powerful body of men there.

July 31st.—I can now inform you that the affair with General Sullivan is settled, and he is to return to New-York, to be employed by General Washington in that department;[1] so hope you will not make many words about it. I am, sir, your friend and most obedient, humble servant.

Josiah Bartlett

P.S. By the enclosed you will see the resolves passed by Congress, and sent to Generals Howe[2] and Burgoyne, in consequence of the affair at the Cedars.

By letters yesterday from Virginia we are informed that Dunmore with his fleet has gone up Potomack River, has burnt some houses near the shores, and has endeavoured to burn more, but was hindered; that the Virginians had taken a tender with one of the most infamous Tories in the Province on board; the number of men and guns I have forgot. They have also taken a vessel from Dunmore, with linens, &c., said to be worth twenty thousand pounds sterling.

Reprinted from Force, *American Archives*, 5th series, 1:637.

1. Sullivan withdrew his petition on 29 July. See Whittemore, *John Sullivan*, 30–31.

2. William Howe (1729–1814), brother of Admiral Richard Howe, took command of the army at Boston from General Gage in October 1775. *DNB*, 28:102–05; Gruber, *Howe Brothers*.

FROM PIERSE LONG

D Sir   Portsmo: July 29th. 1776

I am extreamely obliged to you for the declaration Inclosed to me in yours of the 8h. Instant.[1] Its the Long looked fir come at Last. Youl please to pardon the Expression But had you Seen the General Satisfaction it gave when Read, Youd have thought with me that It could not come too Soon. I have the Satisfaction to Say That Joy appeared in the Countenances of the People, When it was per Order of the Committee published on the parade, by the High Sherriff. The Company of the Cols. Langdon & Sherburne, In Regimentals and under Arms, Added to the Solemnity: Three Huzzas With a God Save the free and Independant States of America, Ended the Declaration. Notwithstanding Three quarters of my Little Intrest, Is Lost by these Broils, I think the future happiness of America, which must Inevitible follow, will be more than Adaquate, Especially as we Shall then look back, And with Strict propriety Say The Opposition was Grounded on Strict Justice to ourselves and to posterity. I was at Exeter when it was published there,[2] But I think Our friends are more incumbred with those of perdition, Than we are in this town, Though I had almost forgot to have informed you, That a desconsolate appearance was Visible on the Countenances of Some Broken Counscellers and Scotchmen here. All our Troops are marched, to Join the Northern Army Who are a Compleat parcel of men, And I hope well officerd as we have taken Particular pains. But Still men will push in friends That are not Deserving. Our forts are almost Compleat. That on the Great Island is Equal to, if not Exceeds any in the Compass of my knowledge. When I Last Saw Major Philbrook, I made Enquiry after all your friends who were well. I this day saw Coll. Whipples Lady who was well. Being much in a hurry have not time to Copy this Scrawl. Youl please to Excuse Incorrectness. If its worth Reading you'l peruse it—If not, you'l Lay it aside. I am In haste D Sir—Your most huml Servt

Pierse Long

RC (Nh-Ar)
  1. Not found.
  2. See Nathaniel Folsom to JB, 14 Aug. 1776.

TO JOHN LANGDON

Sir   Philadelphia August 5th 1776

Since my last a vessel fitted out by the Secret Committee has arrived here from Marseilles in France which place she left the 8th of June. She has brought for the use of the American States 1000 good muskets, about ten tons of powder and about 40 tons of lead &c. &c. A small privateer from this City called the *Congress* has taken a vessel bound from the West Indies to Halifax and sent her safe into port beside a cargo of West India goods—there was found on board her 1078 Joes—672 guineas and some other gold coin. Capt. Barry in the *Lexington*, one of the Continental vessels has taken and sent in here a privateer of six carriage guns commanded by another of them infamous Goodrichs of Virginia. Capt. Weeks in the *Reprisal* another Continental vessel has taken and sent in a sloop bound from the West Indies to Liverpool—he has also taken a ship from Grenada to London which is not yet arrived—both loaded with West India goods.[1]

Since the Declaration of Independence your friend John Alsop has wrote to the Convention of New York to resign his seat in Congress and made some reflections on the Convention for their agreeing So unanimously to that declaration; the Convention in return voted cheerfully and unanimously to accept of his resignation with some severe and cutting reflections on him for his conduct, which were all sent to Congress.[2] I believe his boarding with our friend Wharton has been no advantage to him—possibly he was obliged to resign his seat as a previous condition to his taking full possession of the lady. As I had no letter from you last post (for I look on the cover to Col. Whipple's letters to be nothing) I hope you will consider this as bringing you one letter in debt or at least that it be put to my credit to make up former deficiencies, which will be but justice to Your most obedient.   Josiah Bartlett

P.S. August 6 Yesterday arrived here two prizes taken by Capt. Weeks— one the ship before mentioned, having on board it is said 500 hogsheads of sugar—the other a brig bound from the West Indies to Ireland taken since the ship and sloop—the particulars of her cargo I have not heard. This is the best way of supplying ourselves with necessaries since Britain will not suffer us to procure them by trade and I expect another year we shall be well supplied this way. Yours &c.   J.B.

TR (DLC: Force Transcripts).

1. See *NDAR*, 6:42–43, 63–64. John Barry (1745–1803), a shipmaster of Philadelphia, was one of the more successful officers of the Continental Navy. In 1794 the Congress put him in command of the *United States*. Lambert Wickes (c. 1735–1777) of Maryland took command of the *Reprisal* in April 1776. Following successful cruises in European waters, Wickes lost his life in a shipwreck. Clark, *Lambert Wickes*.

2. John Alsop (1724–1794), a delegate from New York, resigned on 16 July. *JCC*, 5:566.

FROM PIERSE LONG

Dear Sir,   Portsmo. August 5th. 1776

Your favour Inclosing a News paper, wherein is Contained the Account of the Battle at South Carolina & the particulars of Dunmores being Drove from Gwin's Island I Received, for which please to Accept of my thanks. Notwithstanding I wrote you Last Week, Yet when any thing New Arises I think am bound in duty to give it you. Last Saturday Evening Came to Town from Boothbay Capt. Hoply Yeaton, Who was Chief mate of the Ship *Polly* Capt. Lear of this place[1]—Bound from Antigua for London hav'g on board about four hundred hhds of Sugar. Was taken by Cap. White of Salam for a privateer Owned by Capt. Darby.[2] This Ship was one of the first fleet, Who Sailed from the West Indias The first of June. At the Same time White Took Six Others, One a Three decker from Barbadoes. He was Generous Enough to give the prisoners an Old prize for them to Go of in. Cap. Yeaton Says the Second fleet were to Sail the beginning of July & the Third the first of August. I sincerely wish our privateers may Catch the Chief part of them. He also says the Antigolians Continue to be much Enraged against us. I hope Hunger may soon Convince Them of Their Error as provisions are Very Scarce and Dear amongst them. They have no Idea of our privateers Crusing after those Ships to the Northward—But put them under Convoy to Clear them of the Islands Only As their fear is of the Americans, Who have been taken by them, Who they Suppose are at Statia And the foreign Leward Islands Waiting an Opportunity to Seize on those who are defenceless, as a Reparation for their Damages. We have Intelligence that Collo. Fenton has 20/pr. day allowed him in England for his Sufferings While here, And has had The offer of a Majority to Come out, But has Refused it being on his parole. God Grant Their Money may Soon be Exhausted—And then they will have Neither Money Nor Honour. I Long to hear of the Defeat of the British Troops and those in their pay at New York. I inclose you the Freemans Journal for your perusal—And inform you of the Health of your friends. I could wish for a Recommendation from Congress, Or your Own Advice To Our Assembly That a Sequestration may take place Upon the Estates of all those Rascals, Who are known Enemies, And are Gone from this place for Europe to plead against us, Or at Least to be out of the way, While we are all Exposing our Every thing thats Dear to Defend With our Own their Property. My Long Empty Epistle I am Afraid will tire your patience. You Please to Excuse Incorrectness—as I have not time to Copy. I am with Great Respect Dr. Sr Your mt huml. Servt.

Pierse Long

RC (NhD).

1. Hopley Yeaton (c. 1739–1812), a Portsmouth seaman, was appointed third lieutenant of the *Raleigh* in September. Later, in 1791, President Washington ap-pointed him to a captaincy in the revenue cutter service. Foss, *Freemasonry*, 161–68.

2. For an account of this capture see *NDAR*, 6:27.

TO JOHN LANGDON

Dear Sir,   August 11th 1776

Yours of the 28th ulto is come to hand and I congratulate you on your late appointment. Col. Whipple sets off to morrow morning for Portsmouth and takes with him your commission as Continental Agent and will be able to inform you every thing relative to it. He will be likely to make a little stop at New York and will go by the way of Providence and if possible procure the guns for your ship &c. which stops may prevent his being with you as soon as this may reach you, but will no doubt in a few days after. He takes with him Sixty thousand dollars for the account of New Hampshire.

By the public prints you will see there is a new emission of Brigadier Generals and four of the former Brigadiers promoted to Major Generals.[1] We find some difficulty to give satisfaction in the appointment of officers and on the whole it was thought the appointing the first Continental Colonel in the respective States to the rank of Brigadiers was the least liable to objections.

You have no doubt heard that Clinton and Cornwallis[2] since their defeat at South Carolina have joined General Howe—Governor Dunmore and his ragamuffins it is said have left Virginia and are supposed to be going to join General Howe. I think we may expect that some important event will soon take place at or near New York. God grant it may be favorable to the United American States.

August 13th Col. Whipple left us for New Hampshire yesterday 2 o'clock. I am your most obedient   Josiah Bartlett

TR (DLC: Force Transcripts).

1. On 9 August Congress promoted ten officers. *JCC*, 5:641.

2. Charles Cornwallis (1738–1805) came to America in command of seven infantry regiments as part of Clinton's expedition against Charleston, S.C. Wickwire, *Cornwallis*, 8, 80.

FROM NATHANIEL FOLSOM

Dear Sir   Exeter August 14th. 1776

I am now to acknowledge the rect. of your two agreeable Letters of the 1st. & 8th Ulto.[1] The Declaration is well receivd here, has been duely published &c.[2] As to myself and some of my particular Friends with whom I have the happiness to agree in almost every publick measure it was extremely agreeable—it will (I doubt not) have a happy tendency to unite us in the present glorious Struggle & by it many of the objections of wavering (tho' perhaps otherwise well disposed) persons are entirely answered. In short, as it is the first principle of every virtuous man to keep a Conscience void of offence towards God & man, it is the second thing he has in view to make it appear to the World. By the Declaration you make it evident to the World that you are neither ashamed to own the Cause of Liberty nor afraid to defend it, And I doubt not it will be defended even against the Ultimo Ratio Regis.

We have Letters from the Northern Army dated Mount Independence near Ticonderogue August 2d.—some of the Recruits had then arrived on the opposite side of the River, but had not gone over fearing the Small Pox. I suppose all the Troops from this State have arrived there before this—many of the Forces from the Massachusetts have already marched and the rest are to follow this Week. The men have been raised with the greatest difficulty for that department. The fear of taking the Small Pox has a much greater effect on our men than the fear of the Enemy. The Bounty here was fixed by the Court at Seven pounds Eighteen Shillings in Servile imitation of the Massachusetts, what is stranger still this did not Satisfy, several persons from the Massachusetts came over and offered our people an addition from Thirty to 45 dollars, and I am credibly informed that Sixty & Seventy Dollars have been given in that Colony in addition to the bounty fixed as aforesaid. I sincerely regret our enlisting Troops for such short periods; had the men at first been engaged for three Years or during the War, even with a generous bounty, immense Sums would have been saved (their present extraordinary pay being in general Spent in riot & extravagance) and a veteran Army formed.

I inclose you Ten of our Acts which passed last Sessions, these are all that are printed, and indeed all of any consequence which have passed excepted the Maritime Act, which is very long, and almost an exact Copy of that passed in the Massachusetts.[3]

I called at your house this day. Mrs. Bartlet is well, I informed her I should write you by this Post & offered to inclose a Letter, but She had not wrote. We had just entered on the affair of raising a Regiment for the defence of this Colony, agreeable to liberty granted by the Congress, when the requisition was received for raising one to join the Northern Army, before this was complete the demand for a second for the same purpose was recd—as soon as this business was finished. Orders were given out to the several Captains for raising the Regiment for our own defence. I suppose the men under Coll. Gilman will enlist without much difficulty, tho' even here we shall feel some of the effects of the illjudgd illtimed, monstruous Canada Bounty. The Field Officers will be nominated on the meeting of the Court (Septr. 5th.) and their names transmitted to Congress for approbation. We have compleated a Fort at Jerrys Point, for Twenty Guns (at present we Can supply it with only four) tis said to be as complete a piece of work as any erected in N. England.

Our Powder Mill is finished, and this day set to work in all its parts. We have but a small stock of Sulphur, if that can be procured I am in hopes Salt Petre will not be wanting to manufacture enough of that necessary article for our own defence. Necessity is the mother of invention. I am not over fond of Proverbs, but I confess this, tho' a very common one has lately often occurred to my mind. Who my dear Friend, among us, two Years ago thought of withstanding the Mighty Monarch of Britain aided by his Almighty (as he calls them & they call themselves) Parliament.

Please to present my best Respects to your worthy Colleage Mr. Whipple. I am Dr. Sir with the greatest esteem Your Obt huml. Servant.

Nathl. Folsom

RC (NhD). Enclosures not found.
1. Letter of 8 July not found.
2. Published as the last page of N.H.

Gazette, 20 July 1776.
3. See *Laws of N.H.*, 4:10–36.

TO WILLIAM WHIPPLE

Sir   Philadelphia August 18th 1776

Since you left this City the ship *Morris* is arrived from france, she has Brou't for the Congress above 100 Bolts of Sail Cloth which Cost above

3,000 pound Sterling. She has also Brou't for this Colony 53 tons of Lead & 15,000 lbs.[1] of Powder &c. A ship has also arrived from Lisbon which place she left the latter end of June. She has Brou't some necessaries for the Congress. The master Contradicts the report of the Portuguese Seizing american vessels and informs us of several of our vessels being at Libon when he left it and had free Liberty of trading. A french vessel from the west Indies & a Dutch vessel from St. Eustatia have arrived & have Brou't about 10,000 lbs. of powder.

I fear the Confederation will not be finished in time to be laid before our Assembly at their next setting; last week passed without Looking at it, other affairs have taken up the whole time, near two Days were taken up about Comodore Hopkins, and we had the pleasure to be, for the greatest part of that time, Entertained by the Eloquence of some of our southern Brethren, particularly that polite Speaker Middleton.[2]

The Congress at last found Hopkins Guilty of not paying proper attention to his orders and have ordered him to be Censured, thus Stands that affair at present.[3] The Report Concerning General Wooster is at length agreed to.[4] By Gen: Gates letters of the 7th Int: it appears that our affairs in that Department wear a much more favorable aspect than for some time past: 6 or 700 of our militia had arrived; Col. Bedel was Cashiered, Butterfield Cashiered & rendered incapable to hold a Commission under the Congress. I am sir your friend & Humble Servant.

Josiah Bartlett

P.S. August 20th Comodore Hopkins is ordered to his Command. Yesterday York's Brig arrived at Egg harbor from the west Indies 'tis Said she has Brou't 600 Stand of arms & ten tons of powder, this is the third voyage she has made since last winter for the Continent. A vessel has just arrived from Statia Dont hear what she has Brou't.   J: B:

RC (Ronald von Klaussen Private Collection, State of Florida, 1975).

1. JB used the apothecary symbol for pounds; see MJB 933.

2. Arthur Middleton (1742–1787), a delegate from South Carolina.

3. Esek Hopkins (1718–1802), a Rhode Island mariner, had been appointed commander-in-chief of the Continental Navy's first fleet in 1775. Instead of sailing to the southern colonies as Congress had ordered, Hopkins took his fleet to New Providence in the Bahamas. Upon his return he was called to Philadelphia. Congress considered his case during the summer, resolved on 16 August to censure

him for failing to carry out instructions, suspended his commission in March 1777, and dismissed him in January 1778. *JCC,* 5:662; Fowler, *Rebels,* 261, 277.

4. David Wooster (1711–1777) of Stratford, Ct., was commissioned a brigadier general in June 1775. He participated in the expedition against Quebec in 1775, becoming ranking commander upon the death of General Montgomery. Congress recalled Wooster on charges of being unfit for command and acquitted him on 17 August. He died defending Danbury, Ct. *JCC,* 5:664–65.

TO JOHN LANGDON

Dear Sir,   Philadelphia, August 19, 1776

Your favour of the 5th instant has come to hand, and am much pleased to hear of the success of the New-England privateers in capturing British ships. May they go on to distress the British trade, till they are taught wisdom by misfortune, since nothing else will effect it. I opened your letter to Colonel Whipple, agreeable to your order, in which I find you want information about the agency and marine affairs; but as Colonel Whipple will be able to satisfy you as to those matters, (who will be with you before this,) I shall say nothing about them.

Since Colonel Whipple left us the Ship *Morris* arrived here from Havre-de-Grace, in France. She has brought on Continental account above one hundred bolts of sail cloth, amounting to between fifty and sixty thousand yards. She has also brought for this Colony fifty-three tons of lead, and seven and a half tons of powder, &c., &c.

A ship has likewise arrived from Lisbon, with necessaries for the Continent, but cannot give the particulars. She left Lisbon the latter end of June, and left several other of our vessels there, who were permitted to trade freely, notwithstanding the report which lately prevailed, that the Portuguese had seized all American ships in their harbours.

One vessel from 'Statia, and one vessel from the French West-Indies, have also arrived, and have brought in about five tons of powder, &c. By a letter from 'Statia, dated 28th July, we are told that the Dutch have refused to renew the prohibition for sending out arms and ammunition; that the English have seized two of their ships, and sent them into England, under pretence of their supplying us with arms, &c.; that in consequence, the Dutch had ordered sixty ships of war to be fitted out, and to raise twenty thousand additional land forces, and had refused to lend England the Scotch regiments, as they had before agreed to. What dependence is to be placed in this intelligence, I can't certainly say, but believe some part of it, at least, is true, I hope all. By sundry letters, it appears that both the French and Dutch are very fond of our trade, and have sent and are sending to the West-Indies large quantities of arms, and every other article that we are like to want.

The insolence of the commanders of the British men-of-war in the West-Indies, is become intolerable. It seems that one of them some time since went into the harbour at 'Statia, and after waiting some days, attempted to take possession of some American vessels there, but was prevented by the Dutch. She then left the harbour, and the next day seized a ship bound from 'Statia to Amsterdam, and carried her into one of the English Islands, and there he detains her. This has so exasperated the Dutch, that the Governour of 'Statia has (it is said) ordered the Captains of the ports to fire on any English man-of-war that comes within reach of their guns. This looks like kicking up a dust. I am, your most obedient, humble servant.   Josiah Bartlett

P.S. August 20th.—Yesterday a vessel arrived at Egg-Harbour, that was sent to the West-Indies on the account of the Congress. It is said she has brought six hundred stand of arms and ten tons of powder. The particulars of the fire-ships attempting the men-of-war, and burning a tender, and of the men-of-war getting down by New-York, you will hear before this reaches you. Ut sup.   J. B.

Reprinted from Force, *American Archives*, 5th series, 1:1060.

FROM JOHN LANGDON

My Friend   Portsmo. August 19th. 1776

Your favo'r of 5th I've Recd. and most heartily Rejoice with you at the Success of our Arms, in taking so many prizes, they are continually coming in here. Capt. Brown in Small Sloop has Just Arrived here from Holland belonging to Colonal Sears of Newyork[1] and others she is Landed with Medecine, linning, & valuable Cargo. If the Committee had let me have the Guns for this Ship when they have been laying at Providence near two months and the ships there not ready to Receive them, we should no doubt have taken more prizes then would have paid for our whole fleet—however by some fatality or false Information we have been kept from them. Our people are entering on board privateers very fast so that we shall have few hands left for the Continent. All this for want of guns for our ship, the people do not like to enter without guns as they want to be out after prize money.

Ah My Friend Alsop is it so with you—it is two late for these gentlemen, to shew what they would be at. The burying is gone by who lost Mark Anthony the World. *Woman* or Lady—the Same thing. You say you had no letter from me the last post only the Cover to Col. Whipple's. Ah is this the way you hoped to get clear of former Deficiencies; this won't do my good Friend. I am very glad, Notwithstanding, you are oblige to take hold of Such oppertunities as these, to pay your debts (of letters). It plainly proves me not in the least Deficient, when you call a long letter of mine only Cover because one was Inclosed to Broth Whipple. No my old Friend, your best way is to leave it to my Generosity, and I will forgive those few omissions you have been Guilty of in not write'g every week. However, you promised you'd not forget me for the future, therefore, I pass it over and now shake hands in Friendship. I wish you every happiness with halth. Your old Friend   John Langdon
P.S. If any thing should Turn up abt. Admirals in the New appointments. If it comes in well and good.

RC (NhD).
1. Capt. Francis Brown had just arrived from Amsterdam and reported seeing a fleet of about thirty sail in the English Channel which he believed to be Admiral Howe's. *N.H. Gazette*, 24 Aug. 1776. Isaac Sears (1730–1786) owned several privateers during the Revolution.

FROM JOHN LANGDON

Dear Sir,   Portsmo. 26th Augt 1776

Inclos'd is a Letter to Mr. Hancock which you'll please deliver, it is to desire that he would inform me what my Department is, and whither that all the prizes don't come into my hands, since my Appointment. Pray send me my Commission under the Presidents hand, that I may be clear in what I do. Pray let this come by return of Post by all means—I've heard nothing from you, nor Colo. Whipple the last Week, his on the Road. No Guns nor any prospect of any. I wrote you on this day by Commodore Manly[1] to which I refer you. A Ship from the Bay of Hondurus, sent in here. I am Agent but cannot Act for want of Orders. I am your most Obl. Servt.   John Langdon

Remember you did not write me this last Week, to say you wrote me by Mr. Whipple wont do.

FC (John Langdon Letter Book, Capt. J. G. M. Stone Private Collection, Annapolis, Md., 1975). Enclosure not found.

1. John Manley (c. 1734–1793), a Boston mariner, became well respected for his exploits as a captain in George Washington's fleet in 1775–1776. Commissioned by Congress into the Continental Navy early in 1776, Manley commanded the *Hancock*.

TO WILLIAM WHIPPLE

Dear Sir,   Philadelphia August 27th 1776

Last week the articles of confederation were finished by the Committee of the whole House: they are again printed as now amended by the Committee and are delivered to the members in the same manner as before and are to undergo one operation through Congress more, before they are sent to the several States for confirmation[1]—what alterations will be made in them I know not but am afraid none for the better. This will occasion such a delay that there is no probability it will be sent in time to be laid before our Assembly before your return here, so I would not have you wait for it but return as soon as convenient.

The new articles of War have passed Congress:[2] the plan of a T--y of foreign alliance has passed in the Committee of the whole. By the leave of Lord Howe the famous Lord Drummond has by a flag to General Washington, proposed sundry articles as the basis of a negotiation, or conference (they are nearly the same as those proposed by Lord North—called Lord North's conciliatory propositions) and he requested leave of General Washington, for himself and one or two more to repair to this City, to propose those terms, which he had the impudence to say would have been accepted by the Colonies a few months ago. The General did not think proper to give him leave to come here, but in his answer told him, he should send the papers to the Congress and wait their answer: he severely reprimanded Lord Drummond for his officiousness in meddling with the business, but especially for his going to the army under General Howe, contrary to his parole of honor, which he gave when he was permitted to leave the Continent.[3]

I need not tell you the Congress have not accepted the proposed conference with his Lordship. Lord Howe has wrote an answer to Dr. Franklin's letter to him which you saw. It is full of professions of friendship for America, and of esteem and regard for the Doctor very polite but very artful.

By a letter from the Agent who was sent in the *Reprisal*, Capt. Weeks to Martinico, he informs us, that the Governor (or General as they call him) told him that he had lately received orders by a frigate from France to give all possible assistance and protection to the American vessels and that he was ordered to send out some ships of war to cruise round the Island for their defence, and that the Same orders had been sent to the other French Islands: he also told the Agent that if the American cruisers should bring any prizes into the ports of Martinico, he should not prevent their selling or disposing of them as they should think proper (This is in confidence).

We have just rec'd the account of the enemy landing on Long Island: by the General's account our men are in good spirits, seem firm and ready for action, from this and from some other circumstances, I hope I shall soon hear of the enemy's defeat and quitting the country, never more to return as enemies, which will give the greatest pleasure and satisfaction to your friend & hble Servt.   Josiah Barlett

p.s. Mr. Wm. Barril[4] is sick with a fever. Dr. Rush says he is very dangerous. Please to give my regards to our friend Col. Langdon as I have not time to write to him; tell him I have not recd his letter last week as usual. I have rec'd your's of the 20th[5] from Milford's. Yours ut sup: J.B.

TR (DLC: Force Transcripts).

1. See *JCC*, 5:674–89.

2. The revised Articles of War were not finally adopted until 20 September. *JCC*, 5:788–807.

3. Thomas, Lord Drummond (b. 1742) had come to America in 1768 and in 1776 made several proposals for achieving peace. See Washington to Drummond, 17 Aug. 1776, and Washington to Congress, 18 Aug. 1776, in *WGW*, 5:449–52; and Burnett, *Continental Congress*, 147–49.

4. William Barrell kept a store in Philadelphia where congressmen sometimes purchased food and drink. Burnett, *Letters*, 1:3.

5. Not found.

FROM MARY BARTLETT

My Dear   Kingstown August 29th 1776

Last Saturday I Recd yours of the 11th of august[1] & am very Glad to hear You was in Good Health, I hope you will Continue So. I and the Rest of the family are in Pretty Good Health. A very healthy time with us tho Some few families have the Scarlet fever & Canker yet. Esqr. Nathl Bacheldor's family[2] has most or all of them had it and they have Lost one child (Last week) a Little Boy about Six years old; the rest of their family are better.

Mr. Thayer Preaching with us yet, he has not given his answer. Polly is a keeping School yet. A very Still time about news. Prices of things have Been Extravagant—molasses four & Six Pence pr Gallon Sugar & Butter one Shilling LM pr Pound Each & new England Rum five shillins pr Gallon west India Seven & Six Pence pr Gallon Cotton wool four Shillins pr pound. Bohea tea ten Shillins pr pound & other things in Porpotion. Mens Days work Some three Shillins & Some four Shillins pr Day.

But I Believe things are now falling In their Prices. Brother Cooper was hear Last week from Portsmouth & Says that West Indie Goods are fell in their Prices Almost one half.

A very wet time for a month or Six weeks Past Except Lats week a good time to get in hay no rain; Some few People are Done; I hope we shall finish in a week or ten days. A heavy Cold Storm of wind & rain a monday & tuesday which Beat Down Considerable of the Indian Corn which very rank & high. Some they Say measured Eleven feet high; Indian corn is in the milk. I had no oppertunity to Send to you Last week either the Storm or Busy time hindred People's going to newbury. I have now an oppertunity to Send to the Post office & I Fear if I neglect this I Should not have another.

Mr. Lemuel Noyes[3] was hear & Said Levi was well yesterday.

You wrote that Coll: Whipple was a Comeing home But I have not Seen or heard from him yet. I am Yours &c. Mary Bartlett

RC (NhHi). In Polly's hand, signed by Mary.

1. Not found.

2. Nathaniel Batchelder (1726–1809) of East Kingston had a family of ten children. Pierce, *Batchelder, Batcheller Genealogy*, 145.

3. Lemuel Noyes (b. 1743) was from Newbury, Mass., the site of Dummer Academy, where Levi was attending school. Noyes, *Genealogical Record of Noyes*, 1:72.

TO JOHN LANGDON

My Friend: Philadelphia, September 1, 1776

I am now to acknowledge thy favours of the 7th[1] and 19th ult., which are come to hand, and ere this, you have received by Colonel Whipple, every necessary both for fitting out the ship and for your conduct as agent. Pray send her to sea as soon as possible, that she may be doing something to distress our enemies and assist our friends.

By the enclosed papers, you will see what is the news current here. The affairs at New-York seem at present to engross our chief attention. We have not had the particulars of the engagement last week on Long-Island, but believe it was very sharp and bloody. Generals Sullivan and Lord Sterling are prisoners to the enemy. I believe the enemy out-generalled our people, by decoying them out of their intrenchments, and then surrounding them; but before this reaches you, you will have later accounts from our Army, and more particulars than I can inform you.

September 2d.—This morning General Sullivan arrived here on his parole. He says he has a verbal message from Lord Howe to propose his being exchanged for General Prescott; and Lord Sterling for General McDonald. He also says that Lord Howe is desirous to converse with some of the members of Congress, not as such, (because he cannot acknowledge any such body,) but as private gentlemen, to see if they can't agree on some proposals for accommodation, and that he will meet them in any convenient place. These are verbal messages, and we have besides every reason to believe that Lord Howe has not, and cannot in the nature of things, have power to grant any terms that we can possibly accept; yet, as these reports are spread among the people by half Tories and those called *moderate men*, who (if it should be refused) would represent it that the Congress refused to hear his proposals, and would add ten thousand lies of their own, on purpose to disaffect the common people, especially at this very critical time. When I consider these things, I am at a loss what is best to be done; however, I hope we shall be directed to those measures that are best for the United States.[2] I am, sir, your most obedient.

Josiah Bartlett

P.S. Wm. Barrell is dead and buried.

Reprinted from Force, *American Archives*, 5th series, 2:105.

1. Not found.

2. During the Battle of Long Island on 27 August, John Sullivan and William Alexander (Lord Stirling) (1726–1783), a Continental brigadier general who had held the chief command in New York City since March of 1776, were captured.

Sullivan was talked into taking Howe's proposal to Congress, which sent three commissioners to meet Howe on Staten Island. The meeting produced only a stronger determination by Congress to pursue the war effort. Sullivan was exchanged in time to take part in the Battle of White Plains in October. Whittemore, *John Sullivan*, 38–39, 41–43; JCC, 5:730–31, 737–38, 765–66.

TO NATHANIEL FOLSOM

My Dear Sir,   Philadelphia, September 2, 1776

I have received yours of the 14th ultimo, with the acts of our Legislature enclosed, for which I thank you, as it gives me particular satisfaction to be informed of the situation of affairs in our own State. I am fully sensible of the great difficulties we labour under by the soldiers being enlisted for such short periods, and that it would have been much better had they at first received a good bounty, and been enlisted to serve during the war. But you may recollect the many, and, to appearance, almost insuperable difficulties that then lay in our way. No money, no magazines of provisions, no military stores, no government; in short, when I look back, and consider our situation about fifteen months ago, instead of wondering that we are in no better situation than at present, I am surprised we are in so good. Who of us at that time expected that the infatuation of Britain would have forced us to the state we are now in? As circumstances now are, I think we ought, by all means, to be provided with a well-disciplined army, to serve during the war, and that they ought to be raised as soon as possible.

I am glad to hear that our powder mill is ready to be set going. Pray take particular care that the powder is good. A considerable quantity made by one of the mills of this State appears not to have above half the force of good powder, and does not catch quick. The danger from bad powder in an engagement is so great that the Congress have ordered that no powder be sent to the army but such as has been well tried and approved by inspectors appointed for that purpose, and have recommended it to the several Legislatures to appoint inspectors to prove all the powder that is made or imported into their respective States. A copy I will enclose if I can procure one before the post sets off. I will also enclose the orders of Congress concerning wounded and maimed soldiers and seamen.[1]

The affairs at New-York seem at present almost wholly to engross our attention. We have not had the full of the particulars of the action of the 27th ultimo on Long-Island from the General; but by the best accounts we have obtained it appears that our people were decoyed and surrounded by the main body of the enemy, and obliged to fight their way through, or surrender prisoners. It appears there must have been some very great neglect, either in not sending out proper guards and parties to gain intelligence, or they not doing their duty. General Sullivan and Lord Sterling are prisoners, and I believe six hundred or seven hundred others. The consequence has been the evacuation of Long-Island and Governour's Island, of both which the enemy are now in possession—a very unfortunate beginning of the campaign there. However, it is not irreparable, and I hope it will make both officers and soldiers more careful to keep proper guards, and not suffer themselves to be taken by surprise any more.

After writing the above, General Sullivan came to my lodgings in this city, and, by his account, the affair at Long-Island was much as I had heard. He says he has two verbal messages from Lord Howe, which he is on his parole to come to Congress to propose. One is, the exchange of himself and Lord Sterling for Generals Prescott and McDonald; the other is, to propose a meeting of some of the members of Congress, (as private gentlemen, for he can't acknowledge any such body as Congress,) to see if they can't agree to some propositions for an accomodation without further bloodshed; and says he will meet at almost any place for the purpose. These are only verbal messages, and I can easily foresee great difficulties that may arise, let the Congress accept or refuse the proposed conference. What the Congress will do is at present uncertain; but hope they will be directed by the Supreme Disposer of all events to do in this, and every other affair before them, what will be most conducive to the safety and happiness of these American States. So wishes your friend and most obedient and humble servant.   Josiah Bartlett

Reprinted from Force, *American Archives*, 5th series, 2:118.

1. The recommendations for the welfare of maimed troops were determined on 26 August, those concerning inspectors of gunpowder on 2 September. *JCC*, 5: 702–05, 729.

FROM PIERSE LONG

Dr Sir,   Portsmo. Septembr 2d. 1776

I am now to acknowledge the Receipt of your favour of the 17th. Ulto.[1] I am Truely glad to hear of the Several Arrivals at Phila. &c. of Powder and Other Necessarys by which it Appears That we have friends abroad.

Though the worst of Tyrants our Late King Endeavoured to get Prohibited by those powers By which means he Imagined We Should become an Easy prey to his Bloody Mercenaries, To whom (if we conquer them which I do not doubt) I hope we Shall Show no mercy. As to Powder I am well perswaded That that Article will be made in Plenty. Our Mill has been to work this Week and I do assure you Its my opinion it Exceeds any Other on the Continent. It has only One Shaft, Which Carrys 44 pestles in Two Mortors. That Together with Every Necessary Required is Compleated And is capable of Turning Out at Least 24 or 2500 wt. per week—its also Supplyed with Salt petre and Sulpher Sufficient to make Near Two hundred Barrels of Powder. I am a Little Concerned What we Shall do for Sulpher, As that appears to me to be the Only Article we Shall want—Towards manufacturing any quantity. The day the Committee went up to View these works, pleasure Satt on there Countenances Especially when they had taken from the drying house Powder of 24 hours Old only And fired Balls at Least 60 yards which Sent the Balls Through a Hemlock Slat 4 Inches thick and quite Dry. And after it had passed Through, penetrated at Least 5 Inches into an Apple Tree—I mention this to acquaint you with the Strength thereof.[2] I hope the Account you give of the Dutch Armaments preparing will be Confirmed. But I am a Little fearfull it is not So, As there is now in this place a Sloop from Amsterdam, which Left it on or abt. 15 June and gives no Such Acct. Collo. Whipple Arrived in Town the Night before Last. I accompanied him from Exeter As he came through their to deliver Some Money. It is what is dayly wanted Though we were Careless enough Not to Request any, And are under Obligations to you and him for Requesting and Getting it for us. The Assembly Setts this week.[3] The Flower Ship is Condemned with her Cargo Three quarters of Which goes to this State, and 1/4 to the Captors. The Masts and Vessels that was made use of to Load Ships are also Condemned to this State.

If at any time I could be of Service to you or Congress in this place Should be glad of Commands. In the Intrim I am in Haste Dr Sir Your most Obd. hum. Serv.   Pierse Long

P.S. If their Should be any Books Printed with the Resolutions of Congress from time to time Should be glad you'd Inclose me One As also Two or Three of the Declarations of Independency, printed by Dunlap.[4] As Some friends here Could they get Such Would Glass and frame them, They being much pleased at Seeing mine you Sent me make So good an appearance. Now its Compleated—I do assure you I would not Exchange it for any other Ornament. Youl please to Excuse Interlineations and Erasements as I have not time to Copy.

RC (NhD).

1. Not found.

2. Samuel Hobart (1734–1798) of Hollis had contracted with the state to manufacture gunpowder and moved to Exeter, where he purchased a mill at Kings Falls.

The works were designed by Maj. Lemuel Cox (1736–1806), an "ingenious" mechanic from Boston, later famous for building bridges. The finished powder mill was inspected by the Committee of

Safety in August. There was a building for purifying and pulverizing the saltpeter on one side and "on the other a Room very curiously done for drying the Powder." A committee of the state received saltpeter made by individuals and delivered it to Hobart's mill from October 1776 to September 1778. Cox was in Exeter in October apparently to help run the mill. Worcester, *Hollis*, 212–13; Bell, *Exeter*, 328–29; *N.H. Gazette*, 24 Aug.

1776; State of N.H., "Account of Salt Petre," NhHi; Lemuel Cox to Robert Treat Paine, 8 Oct. 1776, R. T. Paine Collection, MHi. The Committee of Safety had advertised for someone to build a gunpowder mill in New Hampshire as early as May. *N.H. Gazette*, 22 May 1776.

3. The General Court met from 4 to 20 September. *NHSP*, 8:319–48.

4. John Dunlap (1747–1812), a Philadelphia printer.

TO WILLIAM WHIPPLE

Dear Sir: Philadelphia, September 3, 1776

By that time this reaches you I expect you will be near ready to set out on your return to this city. Make all convenient haste. The Congress is, at this time, very thin. Colonel Lee is arrived here, but several others have taken leave of absence, among them Mr. Jefferson and Mr. Haywood.[1] The unhappy affair of the 27th, on Long-Island, has occasioned the evacuation of our works there and on Governours's Island. Our people were ensnared and, what vexes me, in a very careless manner.

Yesterday General Sullivan arrived at my lodgings, being on his parole. He says he has a verbal message to Congress, to propose himself and Lord Sterling in exchange for Generals Prescott and McDonald. He also says that Lord Howe expressed himself very desirous of an accommodation with America, without any more bloodshed—that he was very willing to meet, at almost any place, a number of the members of Congress, (as private gentlemen, for he could not own any such body as Congress,) to try if they could make any proposals for an accommodation; that he said he had waited near two months longer in England than he should have otherwise done, to procure proper powers for a final accommodation, with which he said he was now vested, &c., and he allowed General Sullivan to come here to propose the aforesaid conference to Congress. What will be done in the affair by Congress I know not, but think there are difficulties on both sides. If the Congress should accept of the proposed conference, only on a verbal message, when at the same time Lord Howe declares he can consider them only as private gentlemen, especially when we are certain he can have no power to grant any terms we can possibly accept, this, I fear, will lessen the Congress in the eye of the publick, and perhaps at this time intimidate people when they see us catching hold of so slender a thread to bring about a settlement. On the other hand, General Sullivan's arrival from Lord Howe with proposals of an accommodation, with thirty falsehoods in addition, are now spread over this city, and will soon be over the Continent; and if we should refuse the conference, I fear the Tories, and *moderate men*, so called, will try to represent the Congress as obstinate, and so desirous of war and bloodshed that we would not so much as hear the proposals Lord Howe had to make, which they will represent (as they already do) to be highly advantageous for America,—even that he would consent that we should be independent provided we would grant some advantages as to trade. Such an idea, spread among the people, especially the soldiers, at this time, might be of the most fatal consequence. Whatever is done by Congress in the affair will, I hope, be ordered for the benefit of America.

William Barrell died on Sunday morning and was buried last evening. I am, sir, your friend and most obedient.   Josiah Bartlett

Reprinted from Force, *American Archives*, 5th series, 2:137.

1. Richard Henry Lee had arrived about 27 August. Thomas Jefferson left on 2 September and Thomas Heyward, Jr., of South Carolina took leave officially on the fourth. Burnett, *Letters*, 2:lxvii, lxx–lxxi.

TO MARY BARTLETT

My Dear   Philadelphia Septr 9th 1776

I had not the pleasure of Receiving a letter from you by last Saturdays Post as usual but hope by the next to hear you are all well.

I am sorry to inform you that I am in a poor State of health, & have been so, for more than a fortnight; I have a bad Cough and a slow fever with a poor appetite for food and something of a purging. I have been vomited & purged & am taking Sundry medicines, which I hope will procure me relief if it is agreable to the will of God: I have been able to attend the Congress Every Day, tho Sometimes I have been obliged to leave it before it Broke up. When the weather permits, I ride out 3 or 4 & sometimes five or six miles in a Day before or after Congress: I have Confined my self for food to hasty pudding (or as they Call it here mush) & milk for breakfast and Supper, & to Soop or fresh broth for Dinner, and shall omit nothing that I shall think likely to be serviceable to me: I think my asthma or Stuftness for breath is rather abated, and I hope (if it is for the best) I shall be able next post to inform you that I am better on all other accounts.

Last week General Sullivan Came here on his Parole with two messages from Lord Howe. One was for the Exchange of Genl. Sullivan & Genl Sterling, for Genl Prescot & Genl McDonald which we had taken from them; which the Congress have agreed to: the other message was to Desire that two or 3 of the Members of Congress as private Gentlemen would meet him at any time & place they should think fit to see if they Could agree on any proposals for puting an End to the war & Establishing peace between the two Countries: The Congress have appointed 3 members to meet him, not as private Gentlemen but as members of Congress, to Confer with him & Know what he has to offer us as terms of peace and by what authority. The members appointed are Dr. Franklin of this City Mr. John Adams of the Massachusetts Bay & Mr. Rutlidge of South Carolina.

Remember me to all friends in a particular manner to my Children and hope neither you nor they, will be too much Concerned on my account.

My Dear adieu: and when I write again I hope I shall be able to inform you I am better in health.   Josiah Bartlett

RC (NhD).

FROM MARY BARTLETT

My Dear   Kingstown Septembr 9th 1776

Last Saterday I Recd two Letters from you one Dated 19th of august[1] & the other august 26th and am thankfull to hear you are able to attend Congress tho you had an ill turn which Lasted you three or four Days. I hope you are well at this time: I and the Rest of the family are very well at Preasant, except Miriam. She had Been Poorly Some Days I hope no more than a Cold, and I hope that your and our healths may be Continued to us.

As for Coln. Whiple he has not been here nor Sent: Major Philbrick was here yesterday and Said he Saw Coln. Whipple at Exeter last week and he Said he had Some money for me which he left at Portsmouth, he forgot to bring it up. As for the farming Business you wrote you Should be glad to know about. Our men Folk are Some Belated about their work, so much wet weather for Six weeks every few Days Rain Except one week no Rain. I hired a man one week about hay. Help is So Scarce we Could not git one Days work about Reaping upon any account & none about mowing But what I Paid the money for. We have almost Done haying Biley Says he beleives we Shall have about sixteen Load when it is all in. Our English corn is not threshd yet only Some to Sow. But I Beleive it is no more than a midling crop. The Drought hurt our flax Some it is Something Short.

I Beleive it is not much Better than it was Last year. Indian Corn looks very well (except it is very much Blown Down in the Storm of last week). If the frost holds of ten Days or a fortnight Longer I Beleive it will be out of the way of the frost.

Apples Scarse; Plumbs in the garden Plenty. As for the Boards I heard nothing about them before you wrote about them. Old Mr. Proctor is gone into the war. He told me he would Leave orders with Jonathan[2] to Provide Boards & Lime, But I Beleive Lime is Scarce; I Sent word to Jonathan Proctor about the Boards & he Said he would endeavour to get them. Coll: Greeley has not Been at our house Since you Left home. I Saw him one Day at the meetinghouse Door. I asked him to come here at noon he Said he must go to Coll Stevens's. He Sets in Coll Stevens's Pew frequently on Sundays as there is no Preaching at the East Parish. I will Send word to Coll Greeley about the Boards.

I Do not write this by way of Complaint. I Beleive Biley & Peter has Done as well as can be expected & other People you Know will take Care of Self first.

Pray Do come home before Cold weather as you Know my Circumstances will be Difficult in the winter If I am alive.[3] In hast from yours &c. Mary Bartlett

P.S. The Bearer of this Letter is that Gentleman that carried on the works of the Powder mill at Exeter, that Ingenious Major Cox Late of Boston which the Exeter Paper gave an account of.[4]

Esqr. Hook gives his Respects to you. You will See the Death of Benoni Eaton in Leiut. Pearson's Letter.

RC (NhHi). In Polly's hand; signed by Mary. Docketed "Letters from Mrs. Bartlett to me at Congress."

1. Not found.

2. Jonathan Proctor (1751–1820) was a son of James Proctor of Kingston. Proctor, *Genealogy*, 23, 44.

3. Mary was pregnant with Hannah, born 13 Dec. 1776, died 17 April 1777. Kingston Vital Records, 68.

4. See Pierse Long's letter of 2 Sept. 1776.

TO WILLIAM WHIPPLE

Dear Sir,   Philadelphia Sept 10th [1776][1]

The proposal of Lord Howe for the exchange of Generals Sullivan and Lord Sterling for Prescot and McDonald is accepted by the Congress: we have also agreed to send three of our members, not as private gentlemen but as a Committee of our body, to meet Lord Howe to know of him whether he has any terms of peace to propose, and what they are &c. &c.—whether Lord Howe will meet them as a Committee of Congress is uncertain. The gentlemen appointed are Dr. Franklin, Mr. Adams and Mr. Rutlidge—the two former had the unanimous vote of Congress and at the first vote there was a tye between Col. R. H. Lee and Mr. Rutlidge, but as Mr. Lee had opposed the measure, he declined being voted for, as he said he could not accept; the votes then were for Stogden[2] and Rutlidge and the latter carried it. Nothing has since been done about the confederation as the Congress is pretty thin[3] and hurried with other business.

I am sorry to hear you did not arrive at Boston till the 20th ult. as I fear you will not return here so soon as I could wish and what makes me more anxious for your speedy return is my ill state of health which has hindered my constant attendance at Congress. I have for above a fortnight been troubled with a very severe cough and asthma and with a slow fever if not a hectic and though I have attended the Congress every day, I have been often obliged to leave it long before it rose. I am loath that our Colony should be unrepresented and therefore hope you will return as speedily as possible. There is a report from the Board of War now before Congress for putting our army on a more respectable footing than at present: the Substance is that 84 regiments should be enlisted to serve during the war and to give as an encouragement 100 acres of land, and dollars bounty to be proportioned to such State, who are to take care that it's quota is raised. The proportion Set to our Colony is four regiments which is too much and shall try to get it altered if I am able to attend Congress when it comes on. This plan perhaps may be somewhat altered but will I am pretty sure be adopted in the main.[4] Quere— whether as this is like to be the case it is best for our State to do any thing at present about raising the regt ordered in the Spring for our own defence, and whether petitioning Congress to take into their pay our Colonial troops will not be best considering all circumstances. You'll excuse me as I am hardly able to write. I am your friend &c. &c.

Josiah Bartlett

TR (DLC: Force Transcripts).

1. On the copy the year is in parentheses followed by a question mark. Contents leave no doubt that this was written in 1776.

2. Delegate Richard Stockton of New Jersey.

3. The records reveal that only thirty-two congressmen, including the three who were in New York meeting with Howe, were officially attending on this day. Congress was "thin" indeed. Burnett, *Letters*, 2:xxxix–lxxiii.

4. When adopted on 16 September the plan called upon New Hampshire to furnish three battalions. The bounty was twenty dollars. *JCC*, 5:762–63.

FROM WILLIAM WHIPPLE

My Dear Sir,   Portsmo. 10th Septr. 1776

I had the Pleasure of receiving your favor of the 27th Ulto & heartily rejoice that your great affairs are in such forwardness. I am much pleased at Genl. Washingtons treatment of Lord Drummond, we have had various reports about his Lordships propositions, they turn out much as I expected. The accots we have from York are very Unfavorable. I hope when we get the perticulars our affairs there will appear better then from the present appearences they seem to threaten.

I think I wrote you in my last that Mr. Langdon was gone to Providence. He is not yet return'd from thence. I hope he will be able to get the Guns on some terms or other.[1] The *Milford* Frigate is now Cruizing on the Coast & takes every thing that attempts to pass, she has with her, several small arm'd vessels. If Mr. Langdon gets the Guns & can obtain leave to send the *Raleigh* out as soon as ready & orders are forwarded also for one of the ships at Newbury I make no doubt they will give a good accot of those Piratical Rascals that infest our Coast. I think Mr. Langdon will get the Guns in that case the *Raleigh* will be ready for sea before orders can arrive here provided they have not left Philadelphia before this reaches you. There is about 60 men on Board. The officers are very uneasy to be at sea one of the Lieutenants has already left her to Command a Privateer at Boston where very great encouragement is given, which I fear will make it difficult to get the ships man'd. I hope the Rank of the Officers is settled, & the Commissions on the way here. As I before observed one of the Lieuts has quited the ship viz: John Whealright who was Appointed second Lieut. Please to nominate in his stead, Hopley Yeaton, who will make full as good an officer. I wish he may be immediately appointed & his Commission sent him.[2] I wish more attention was paid to Naval affairs, a great number of Prizes have been retaken which its probable would not have been the case if proper attention had been given to the Naval Department in season.

I spent two days last weak in Exeter. Our Genl Court goes on much in the old way spending much time about trifles, however they have done some business pass'd an act to prohibit the Exportation of Lumber till the 20th of November[3] & have chosen a Committee to prepare a Bill for the punishment of treason. I am not able to determine who will be our colleague. Genl Folsom is gone to have the small Pox some think to prepare for Philadelphia. I wish we may get Walker 'tho I fear he will not be prevail'd on to except.[4]

I find Congress are like to have some business by appeals from the Maritime Courts, the Case of the Brig: *Elizabeth* (which I suppose has reached you by this time) is a very Extraordinary one. I hear a ship of Mr. Sheafs[5] is Condemn'd at Providence. She was bound from the West Indies to London. His property was transferr'd to protect her from the British ships, another ship belonging to Capt. Lear[6] of this town is under the same circumstances, but not yet tryed. She is at Salem. I have not yet determin'd when to set out, & shall be glad to have your opinion whether it will be best for our colleague to go with me or follow some time after me.

I have seen the Powder mill at Exeter. It is the best I have seen. The man that contriv'd it has discover'd great ingenuity, I have desir'd him to furnish me with a plan of it which I shall take with me. I dare say it will be much approv'd of. Please to present my Regards to all those who you know I Esteem & be assured that I am Your Sincere Friend &c.

Wm: Whipple

RC (NhD).

1. On Langdon's troubles obtaining cannon see Langdon to JB, 14 June 1776, n. 1.

2. John Wheelwright, son of Jeremiah Wheelwright, had been appointed on 15 July at a wage of $20 per month. Yeaton was appointed on 28 September. Odiorne, *Genealogy*, 41; NHGR, 2:180–81.

3. The lumber act passed on 12 September. *Laws of N.H.*, 4:37–39.

4. On the twelfth the General Court appointed Matthew Thornton to Congress. Timothy Walker, Jr. (1737–1822) was a Concord merchant and member of the House of Representatives. He sat on the Committee of Safety, 1776–1777, served as an associate justice of the Court of Common Pleas, and was chief justice of the state, 1804–1809. In 1777, 1778, 1782, and 1785 he was chosen to represent the state in Congress, but he never attended. NHSP, 8:333; Shipton, *Harvard Graduates*, 14:107–11. Walker's early manuscript diaries are bound with those of his father, Rev. Timothy Walker, at NhHi.

5. Jacob Sheafe (1715–1791) and his son Jacob, Jr. (1745–1829) were Portsmouth merchants. Brewster, *Rambles*, 2nd ser., 129–32.

6. Tobias Lear (c. 1736–1781), a Portsmouth shipmaster, was the father of the Tobias Lear who was George Washington's secretary. Brewster, *Rambles*, 1st ser., 268; NHGR, 1:18.

TO WILLIAM WHIPPLE

Dear Sir: Philadelphia, September 14, 1776

I have not received a line from you since yours of the 20th ultimo,[1] from Milford. I have wrote to you every week since you left this City, which I hope are come safe to your hand, but shall not write you after this as I expect you will be on your return here by the time you receive this, or soon after. I hope our Legislature has appointed another Delegate to return with you, that I may return home immediately on your arrival, and try whether a change of air will be serviceable to my health, which is very much altered since you left me, though I am now rather better than I was last week. I shall be under some difficulty about procuring a horse and waiter to attend me on my return, unless you and your colleague will agree to deliver up one of yours to me for that purpose on your arrival, and keep but one to wait on you both here. If you shall not agree to that, I have wrote to Mrs. Bartlett to procure (if she can) a man and horse, and send with you here to accompany me back, as I think it will be much cheaper and better than to hire here. Pray inform Mrs. Bartlett of your determination, that she may know what to do.

Last Wednesday our Committee met Lord Howe on Staten-Island, where they ate and drank together. He treated them with great civility and politeness; and after about three hours' conversation, they took their leave of each other. His Lordship's conversation was full of his friendship for America—particularly the town of Boston, for their respect to the memory of his brother. He said that the ravaging and destroying America would give him great pain and uneasiness. Dr. Franklin replied that we should take proper, and he hoped effectual, care to prevent his Lordship's feelings on that account. On the whole all the terms he had to propose were, that we first of all lay down our arms and return to our allegiance; and then, he said, the King and Parliament would consider the acts we formerly complained of, and if they judged it proper would alter or amend them. They told him that General Sullivan said, that his Lordship in conversation told him that the King and Parliament would give up the right of taxation and of intermeddling with the internal police of the Colonies, and desired to know what authority he had to say it. Lord Howe replied, that General Sullivan must certainly have misunderstood him, as he had no right to say any such thing, nor did he believe the Parliament would give up those claims. The Committee are about to publish the whole affair, which I hope will stop the mouths of the weak and credulous, who have had great hopes of peace from the supposed great powers entrusted with Lord Howe as a Commissioner for that purpose.

Captain Wickes, in the *Reprisal*, is returned from Martinico, which he left the 26th ultimo; he has brought four or five hundred muskets, some powder, &c., &c. The affair of the *Reprisal* and the *Shark* man-of-war in the harbour of St. Pierre, in Martinico, occasioned the British Admiral Young[2] to send to the French General, informing him that the Captain of the *Shark* would have taken the Pirate ship commanded by Captain Wickes if it had not been for the French Forts protecting him, and he, in the name of his Britannick Majesty, demanded that she should be forthwith seized and delivered up into his hands, or otherwise his protecting, not only the trading ships of Rebels, but their ships-of-war, would be deemed a breach of the peace between the two nations, and that on his refusal he should immediately send a man-of-war to acquaint his Britannick Majesty of the circumstances, &c., &c.

The French General, in answer, told Admiral Young that he had been misinformed concerning the affair; that the Forts did not interfere, but that the *Shark*, after engaging the American vessel for some time, thought proper to quit her and sheer off, and that the Forts did not fire on the *Shark* till after she had quitted the *Reprisal*, and was attempting, as they suspected, to seize an unarmed vessel that was then within reach of their cannon; that Captain Wickes had put himself under his Most Christian Majesty's protection, and that he should not deliver him up, or suffer him to be injured while there; that if the Admiral had been well acquainted with him (the General) he would never have made such a demand of him; that he should immediately send an account of the affair to the King, his master, to whom alone he was answerable for his conduct, &c., &c. This is the substance as near as I can remember. I have seen authentick copies of both.

The affair of the Confederation rests at present. The Committee of the Whole have agreed that ninety regiments shall be inlisted for five years, if not sooner discharged by Congress. The affair of bounty is not yet settled; the proposal of giving lands as a part of the bounty has boggled us; however, it will be got over in a few days, I believe, and sent forward. The great difficulty of raising men for so long a period, made me think it my duty to prevent more being required of our State than their just proportion by numbers; and by producing the return of our number of inhabitants, I have got the proportion to be fixed at three instead of four regiments for our State, to be raised and completed for that term.

Mr. Wythe is come to Congress.

My very poor state of health makes it uncertain whether I may not be obliged to leave Congress before your return. If it should happen so, I should be very glad to meet you on the road, and would therefore propose your coming the upper road to Hartford, if you can conveniently. I am, sir, your friend and most humble servant.   Josiah Bartlett

Reprinted from Force, *American Archives*, 5th series, 2:323–24.

1. Not found.

2. James Young (d. 1789) entered the Royal Navy in 1737, was appointed commander in chief of the Leeward Islands station in 1775, and was promoted to admiral in 1778. *DNB*, 63:376.

FROM WILLIAM WHIPPLE

My Dear Sir,   Portsmouth 15th Septr 1776

Being Extreamly anxious to know how matters are going on, I was much disapointed by not receiving a letter from you last post. The accots: we have from N. York are very imperfect & Confus'd, tho' it seems to be Settled that our Troops have quitted Long Island, the Consequence I fear will be, that they must also Evacuate York. I have had a hint that Congress have directed Genl: Washington not to destroy that City if he shod be obliged to leave it; is this right? Why shod we be so careful to furnish the Enemy with convenient Winter Quarters? It appears to me that the consequence will be that the States will be put to the Expence of five, if not ten times, the value of that Cursed City which ought to have been destroyed long ago.

A Letter from the President requiring more men from this state to reinforce the Army came to hand Yesterday just after the adjournment of the Genl: Court, however as many of the Members had not gone off, they Collected & came to a Resolution to raise 1000 men, orders were accordingly sent to the Colonels of the Melitia immediately to draught their respective proportions, & I hope they will in a few days be on their march.[1]

Col. Thornton is Elected our Colleague. He has not given his answer but I am in no doubt he will accept. In that case I Suppose we shall set off togeather about the 10th Octor.

In my last I inform'd you that Mr. Langdon was gone to Providence to get Guns, not doubting he wod Succeed, but he is return'd much disapointed, has been most shamefully trifled with by the Naval Committee (as they Call themselves). It seems this Committee Consists of twelve men five or six of whom are Owners of the furness. They (the Naval Committee) agreed that Mr. L-- shod have the guns that they had provided for one of the ships under their direction on condition that he wod Contract with the owners of the Furness to replace them—this he consented to but when he come to talk with these Gentln they declined Contracting with him as agent but if he wod contract in his private Charecter they wod furnish him with the Guns at £100 Lawl Moy pr Ton half the Money to be paid on signing the Contract & Intrest for the remainder till paid. Mr. Langdon looking on these Proposals as a great Indignity offer'd Congress & as a gross insult to him, quited them, & damns them for a set of ————. I really think the conduct of these Gentn is very extraordinary. Mr. Langdon has taken great pains to furnish them with Masts & they gave him encouragement that they wod furnish him with Guns but when they had got the masts they care but little about the other part of the bargin. I dont know what Money these Gentn have had towards Building the Ships but I think as they are so scrupulous of the Honour of Congress their accots. ought to be settled before they have any more Money. I don't see how this ship is to go to sea this winter unless guns are sent from Phila:, or a possitive order from the Merine Committee for some of those guns at Providence which will be leying there all winter useless unless order'd for some other ship as it is impossible both those ships shod be man'd this Year.

It seems there are many Complaints about the Maritime Courts. The Court here has acquited a vessel that ought to be condemn'd, & other Courts condemned vessels that ought to be acquited. Mr. Sheaf has had a ship condemn'd at Providence as British Property, she was bound from the West Indies for London. His property was transfer'd to prevent her being seized by British ships. I really think his case hard he intends to petition Congress. Another ship belonging to Capt. Lear of this town under the same Circumstances is to be tryed, at Salem to morrow. If this ship shod be condemned the Owners of her will also apply to Congress so it's probable you'll have business enough of this sort on your hands.

Your family were well yesterday as I was informed by Major Philbrook by whom I sent the money. I suppose Mr. J. Adams is by this time on his way home. If he is still with you Present my Regards to him. I am Sincerely Yours. Wm: Whipple

RC (PHi).

1. Hancock's letter of 3 September is printed in NHSP, 8:361–62.

TO JOHN LANGDON

Dear Sir: Philadelphia, September 16 1776

I have not had the pleasure of receiving but one letter from New-Hampshire for some time. I fear there is some stoppage in the post, and that my friends in New-Hampshire find it as difficult to get letters from this place as I from them.[1]

The Congress have passed a new order concerning the posts, which will, I hope, put them in a better situation. Yours by Captain Roche I have just received,[2] and if it is in my power to serve him, will do it, depending on your recommendation; but at present know of no place open for him.

The Secret Committee are in want of proper goods to export to an European market, such as potash, dry fish, beeswax, &c., &c.; and they have desired me to write home to New-Hampshire to know whether any quantity sufficient to load a vessel or two can be procured; if so, they would give somebody a contract for that purpose. Please to make inquiry, and to inform me if such things can be procured and sent from our State. It will be an advantage both to the publick and to individuals. I have wrote to some others to make the same inquiry.

As to news we have nothing very material here, and must beg leave to refer you to my letter to Colonel Whipple for what I have to send. I suppose you have formally resigned your seat in Congress, and another is appointed in your stead. Pray send them forward with all expedition, as my ill state of health will, I fear, prevent my attending Congress till they arrive here. I am, sir, your sincere friend and humble servant.

Josiah Bartlett

Reprinted from Force, *American Archives*, 5th series, 2:350.

1. See also JB to Mary, 16 Sept. 1776, MJB 973.

2. See Langdon to JB, 13 Aug. 1776, MJB 930. John Roche, a captain in the West Indian trade, was in Philadelphia when Congress hired him to supervise construction of the second naval vessel to be built in New Hampshire, later named *Ranger*. Roche expected to be named captain, but lost the command to John Paul Jones. Fowler, *Rebels*, 263–65. See also JB to Langdon, 23 Sept. 1776.

TO MARY BARTLETT

My Dear   [Philadelphia] Septembr 17th 1776

I sent you a letter yesterday by the Post but as I have Recd none from you for sometime I Suspect the post is interrupted and that you receive none from me. So I Now write you a line by this Express to let you Know that I remain in a poor State of health Tho I hope rather better Especially my Cough. I have a fit of a slow fever Every afternoon & night.

I hope our Colony have appointed another Delegate to Come with Col: Whipple and that they will be here as soon as possible and that I shall be able to attend Congress till their return here. On their return here I shall immediately (if able & nothing Extraordinary hinder) set out on my re-turn home and should be glad if you Could hire a Good Strong horse and man & send with Col. Whipple to attend me back unless Col. Whipple & the other Delegate shall Consent to let me have one of their Servants & horses to Come back with me on their arrival here. I have wrote to Col. Whipple to Desire he would inform you whither I may Depend on one of their men & horses to Come back with me or not that you may Know what to Do about hireing one to send to me.

I hope I am rather better on most accounts, I have never omitted being at Congress Every Day tho I am often obliged to leave it before it ad-journs. My appetite for light food is better & my Cough & asthma is much better if it Does but hold my fever & Sweats Continue bad tho I sometimes hope not Quite so bad as they have been. I want to hear from you. The last letter I Recd was yours of the 19th of last month. My Dear farewell & I hope I shall hold growing better and soon hear from you & my family that they are well.

                                    Josiah Bartlett

September 23d 1776

As I was Disappointed in sending the foregoing as I Expected I Can now inform you I have Recd two letters from you Since writing that on the other side viz yours of the 29th August and 9th Inst: and am very glad to hear you are all well. As to my self I am Stronger and I think bet-ter than I have been tho neither my Cough nor fever has left me. When my fever and Sweating increases my Cough abates and when the fever abates my Cough increases. However on the whole I hope I am getting the better of them both. I Eat no meat but my appetite for light food is much better & it sets better on my Stomach. I ride Every Day when the weather is fair and find it Dont tyre me So much as it Did ten Days ago. If I think it Consistent with my Safety I shall tarry here till my Col-leagues return But hope they will be here So that I may return before the Cold weather Sets in as I fear my health will not be Sufficient for under-taking such a jorney in Cold bad weather.

I would by all means have the Plaistering finished that was omitted before the winter sets in. You will be very uncomfortable unless it is Done and I would have you Employ Capt. Calef or Esqr. Hook to get a Hogs-head of lime immediately and look out for a Mason & let it be Plaistered by the last of October if possible. I hope I shall be at home by that time. However I would by no means have it omitted to be Done this fall Even Tho the Expence should be a little Extraordinary.

Tell Polly & Lois that Goods here are higher I believe than they are with you and believe I shall find Great Difficulty to get my Self & my own Cloathing &c. home. However if I recover my health & tarry till Col: Whipple arrives I will then look round & Consider what is best to be Done as to what they request.

RC (NhHi).

TO JOHN LANGDON

Dear Sir: Philadelphia, September 23, 1776

Yours, by Captain Manly, I have received, and should have been glad of affording him any assistance in my power, but unluckily they (the Marine Committee) commonly meet in the evening, when I am not able to attend them on account of my health. The latter end of last week Captain Roche called on me, and told me Captain Manly was taken very sick. I have not heard from him since, so hope he is better.

I hope Colonel Whipple and your successor as a Delegate are now setting off for this city to relieve me. I am very anxious to have them here, as some very important affairs are before the Congress, and my health will not permit my constant attendance; and I am loth to be absent, as you know the voice of a single Colony is often very important. I shall not write to Colonel Whipple, as I think he must be on his journey before this reaches you.

I am sorry our affairs at New-York have succeeded so badly. We want a regular, well-disciplined army, and more experienced Generals. A regular standing army we must have, at all events, against another year. You will see the plan the Congress has laid for effecting it. The conduct of some of the New-England soldiers this year has afforded me great pain, though I believe some of the disaffected this way have represented their conduct worse than it deserved, yet the affair at the Cedars, and of some at New-York, are not to be excused.

I have this moment received Colonel Whipple's letter of the 10th instant, wherein he recommends Hopley Yeaton for a Lieutenant of your ship, in the room of Mr. Wheelright, and some other marine affairs, which I shall lay before the Marine Committee, and try to procure the orders he mentions, though at present I cannot meet with them in the evening, as I am at present troubled with a fever-fit every evening; however, I will do the best I can in the affair. Colonel Whipple informs me the Colony had not then appointed another Delegate in your stead. I hope the Colonel has set off without him, and the other may be appointed and follow after as soon as convenient.

I hope you will soon have the *Raleigh* fit for sea.[1] I will try to procure orders for her and one of the Newbury ships to take the *Millford* frigate, which it seems is a great plague to the Northern States. Prepare her as soon as possible for the business. I am, dear sir, your sincere friend.

Josiah Bartlett

Reprinted from Force, *American Archives*, 5th series, 2:459–60.
1. The *Raleigh* did not get to sea until August 1777. *NHGR*, 2:178.

FROM WILLIAM WHIPPLE

Dear Sir   Portsmouth 23d Sepr 1776

Your favor of the 3d inst did not come to hand until the 20th owing I suppose to some interuption in the passage of the post thro' New York.

Our Genl: Court have Issued precepts to call a new House on the 21st Decr: & have adjourn'd to the first week in Novr.[1] It is Currently reported that Congress have appointed a Committee to confer with Lord Howe & by what you write I fear it is true, what purpose can this Conference answer? I can conceive of none, unless it be to cause divisions among us, Amuse the Army & Give the Enemy an opportunity of takeing some Capital advantage, this no doubt is what his Lordship has in view; He tels you he is vested with ample Powers to accomodate matters, but cannot Treat with Congress, who can he treat with. I believe I may answer for him that he will treat with any body that will apply to him for Pardon. I must confess it grieves that that body who are intrusted with the Liberties of this extended Continent shod be led by such Phantoms, nothing that they can do will in my Opinion lessen them more in the Eyes of the Public I therefore wish it may not be true.

Three men who were taken in Canada with Genl: Thompson pass'd thro' this town Yesterday. They made their escape in July were some time among the French inhabitants by whom they were very kindly Treated, they came by Arnolds rout to Kenebec. It was reported, before they left the French settlements (which was about a month ago) that Genl: Thompson had sail'd for New-York.

A transport was sent in here yesterday by a small Privateer belonging to Newbury. She was bound to St. Vincent in the West Indies with seven others for Soldiers. She has on board 20 Chaldron Coals & 6 months Provisions for 100 men.

I heard from Your family last friday they were then well. I shall set out in about 12 days but suppose must go over Dobs's ferry as its Probable the Enemy have possession of York at least that's the report here. I am very Respectfully Yours.   Wm: Whipple

I this moment hear that a vessel is off this Harbour Bound to Newbury 29 days from Martinique. She sail'd from thence in Company with the *Reprisal*.

RC (MH).
1. The General Court adjourned on 20 September "to the last Wednesday of November," but had to meet in special session for three days in mid-October. *NHSP*, 8:347–57.

TO [JOHN LANGDON]

Dear Sir: Philadelphia, Sept. 30th, 1776

Last Saturday I rec'd yours of the 19th inst.,[1] and am very sorry for your bad success in procuring guns for the frigate; you say you have mentioned the affair to the President, & I hope some order will be taken about it, but what I know not. I have not been able to attend either the Marine or Secret Committee for some time past and Congress but little. It is now five weeks since I have been troubled with a severe cough, slow fever, Profuse Sweats & loss of appetite, Except for light food. By the advice of my friends & Physicians I design to leave this City in a few days & try to move homewards, in hopes a change of air, moderate exercise & a recess from business may assist in restoring my health. Mr. Hancock has offered me a seat in his carriage, which I shall accept, as it is impossible for me to return on horse back in my present state of health. I rec'd Col. Whipple's letter of the 15th, where he informed me he expects to set out for this place about the 10th of October. I hope he will set out before that time, when he comes to be informed by my letters of my bad state of health & the necessity there is of a Delegate here; there is no news here more than you will see in the Public prints. I am your friend,

                                              Josiah Bartlett

P.S. My horse is just now lamed by a kick of another horse, which I fear will hinder my return at present.   J. B.

Reprinted from *Letters by Josiah Bartlett*, 45.
   1. No letter of the 19th has been found.

TO MARY BARTLETT

My Dear   Philadelphia Octobr 7th 1776

I was Disappointed of Seting out last week for New hampshire as I Expected which I hope is all for the best as I now think I am really geting better and hope in a little time I shall have more Strength to undertake Such a Jorney. Three or 4 Days last week I thought I was almost well. My fever & Sweats intirely left me & my Cough and soreness in my breast was almost gone and my appetite good Enough; for 2 or 3 nights past I have had some of my Sweats but hope they will leave me again in a little time, my appetite now Craves more than my stomach is able to Digest and am obliged to be very Careful not to eat too much. I Believe I shall try to wait till My Colleagues arrival before I set out for home as it will be very Disagreable to me to leave our State unrepresented in Congress and by Col. Whipples letter of the 23d ulto. I think I may Expect him here in about 12 or 14 Days from this time when if I am able as I hope & Expect I shall be I Shall with pleasure Set out for Kingstown where I hope I shall arrive Safe & find you all well.

I have not had the pleasure of receiving any letter from you since yours of the 13th ulto but Col: Whipple in his letter of the 23d informed me my family were well the friday before so I suppose that the reason I had no letter from you last post was because you had no oppertunity to send one to the Post office.

As to news we have none here at present. The inclosed papers Especially the form of Government of Pensylvania take Care not to lose but lay up safe. Remember me to the Children & all friends and be asured I remain sincerely yours   Josiah Bartlett

RC (NhHi). Enclosures not found.

TO JOHN LANGDON

Dear Sir   Philadelphia, Octobr 7th 1776

As I have not been able for some time to attend the Marine Committe I last Saturday took the liberty to show Mr. Morrice your letters Concerning the Conduct of the Providence Committe about Guns and soon found Mr. Hancock thro the multiplicity of Business had not laid the affair before the Marine Committe. Mr. Morrice resented their Conduct extremely and Desired liberty to lay the letter before Congress but as I was uncertain but some bad Effect might arise from laying it before the whole Congress I Declined it. He then Desired liberty to lay it before the Marine Committe to which I Consented.[1] He said he would Do his utmost that your ship should have them Guns at Providence and without paying that Enormous price for them. I am in hopes them guns will be ordered for your ship & one of their's ordered to wait till guns Can be sent from here where they are Contracted for at 35 & 40 pound this money pr tun.

I Believe (inter nos) your letters to the President Concerning marine affairs have not been laid before the Committe nor much attention been paid them. The great & important Business in which he is Constantly Employed and the almost immense numbers of letters which he is Constantly receiving on the most interesting subjects makes it impossible for him to attend to them all and lesser matters must be neglected. I sincerely wish he did not belong to the Marine Committe but would Confine himself to the affairs of Congress which is Business abundantly sufficient to Employ the time of any one human being.

I was Disappointed of seting out last week as I Expected and as I am in hopes I am some better than I have been I Believe I shall try to tarry here till Col: Whipples arrival which I think I may Expect in 12 or 14 Days from this time according to his letter of the 23d ulto.

As for news we have none at this time. How long we shall be without any I Can't Say as by the last accounts from Ticonderoga they were Dayly looking for Burgoine up the lake and it seems Genl Howe is preparing to attack our Camp at Harleam. God grant we may have better fortune than we had at the attack on Long Island. The Enemy are now in Possession of Stratton Island, Long Island, Governor's Island, the City of New york & Powles's hook. I pray God they have now reached their

Ultimatum and that from this time their power may Decline.[2] I am your very hearty friend.   Josiah Bartlett

RC (PHi).

1. Langdon's letter of 14 September precipitated one from the Marine Committee to the R.I. Frigate Committee on 9 October directing them to send cannon to Langdon. In a letter to Langdon of the same date the Marine Committee noted that JB, not Robert Morris, had presented Langdon's letter. Langdon finally obtained guns for the *Raleigh* from various local sources. Paullin, *Out-Letters*, 1:21–23, 25–26.

2. To follow the movements of American and British forces in New York during September and October see Wallace, *Appeal to Arms*, 111–23.

TO JOHN LANGDON

Dear Sir: Philadelphia, October 15th, 1776

As I rec'd no letter from Col. Whipple or you last week, I am in hopes he is on the road here and will bring your letter with him. I wait with some impatience for his return, as it is very hard for one Delegate to constantly attend Congress and the several Committees where one Delegate is appointed from each state, especially if unwell, as has been my case for some time past; however I am now much better, and hope to be able to ride home in a short time on horse back.

Yesterday the Committee appointed to hear the appeal from the Maritime Court in Newhampshire concerning the *Elisabeth* made their report, which was accepted;[1] they have reversed the sentence of our Court and have ordered a Salvage of one tenth part to be paid by the Claimants as she did not come under the order of Congress of Novemb'r & Decemb'r last. Afterwards the Congress by a vote gave up to the said claimants their share of the said tenth, so that they will have but one twentieth part to pay, beside the Costs.

The same Committee have had Mr. Sheafe's Petition under their consideration but have made no report. By what I have conversed with them I believe they will not think themselves authorized to do anything in that affair as there is no appeal from the Court to the Congress, & the opposite party not present to be heard in the case and nothing but the Petition without anything more before them, they all say the case appears to be hard but know not how to remedy it without more proofs than they have at present and without the opposite party being heard and the case brought properly before them.

Before this reaches you, you will see the several orders of the Marine Committee about Guns for your Ship and the reason of those orders. The Rank of the Captains are settled.[2] Capt. Thompson is the Sixth, Capt. Manly is uneasy at his being the 3d and has Desired leave to Resign, whither his resignation will be accepted or his rank altered I am uncertain. Capts. Manly & Roche are got pretty hearty again as to their health. As to news you will see what is passing here by the inclosed paper. By letters from France of the 3rd of August we have some favorable advices. In haste my friend adieu.   Josiah Bartlett

Reprinted from *Letters by Josiah Bartlett*, 46–47.
1. See JCC, 5:751, 835, 848; 6:870–73.
2. On 10 October Congress settled on the rank of twenty-four captains in the Continental Navy. JCC, 6:861.

TO JOHN LANGDON

Dear Sir: Philadelphia, October 19th, 1776

This will be handed you by Capt. Roche who has at length finished his business here and got orders for you to build another ship as you will see by the letter from the Marine Committee to you. After I wrote you last tuesday I rec'd yours of the 30th ulto. and desired the Clerk of the Secret & Marine Committee to take out from the books the sums of money you have rec'd of each of those Committees, the sum you have rec'd of the Secret Committee is Twenty Five Thousand Dollars but the Clerk was to engaged he could not give me the other account this time, will try to send it you next week. I mentioned in the Marine Committee that you were Desirous to know whither you were to allow any passengers or Seamen on board any of the prizes their adventures or private property more than the wages to the seamen agreeable to the resolve of Congress; they informed me they had not given any orders about it, and that it was not in their power to give any orders Different from the Resolves of Congress, yet it seemed to be the desire of the Committee that such Passengers & Seamen as behaved themselves Decently should be dealt well by and not striped of everything that might be taken from them by the Rules of War.

As for news I have none at present to Communicate, we have had no certain accounts from our Camp at Harlem since the 13th, there are some flying accounts but Capt. Roche as he passes that way will be able to give you a true account of our affair there.

A great number of foreigners, especially French Officers, are Daily almost arriving here & requesting to be employed in our Army, many of whom are well recommended.[1]

Col. Whipple is not arrived here yet I shall look for him every day now till I see him when I shall return home and after your example enjoy the pleasure of residing in my own Country in future. Remember me to all freinds and be assured that I am your affectionate friend. Josiah Bartlett

P.S. I am in much better health than I was for four or five weeks.

Reprinted from *Letters by Josiah Bartlett*, 48–49.
1. As a member of the committee to examine qualifications of candidates for military office, JB was greatly concerned with the influx of French officers seeking employment. JCC, 3:416; 6:1066–67; Higginbotham, *War of Independence*, 214–16.

FROM WILLIAM WHIPPLE

My Dear Sir, Phila 8th: Novr: 1776

Our Colleage arriv'd the 3d inst.[1] He cross'd the River several miles above Dobb's ferry by which means I suppose you Miss'd him. He complains much of the Roads & I believe justly. He was Inoculated yesterday, but attends Congress. Nothing meterial has happen'd since your departure, some private Letters from Genl Lee of yesterdays date are very incouraging. If you pass'd through the Army, you must be sensible of the want of Cloathing & as you know what was done in Congress respecting that matter no doubt you'll use your influence to draw the attention of the Executive Power of Our state to that Subject.

I find the Genl. Court of the Massachusetts have increas'd the pay of their Soldiers & have sent a Committee to Camp to inlist the men, but Genl: Washington wod not consent to their giving out Orders till the matter was layed before Congress. One of the Gentn arriv'd Yesterday. What will be done in the affair I know not, we really have a Choice of Difficulties which I am in no doubt we shall get over but the thing is to make advantages of those difficulies. The Massachets: have increas'd the pay of their Soldiers to 10 Dols: pr Month for the new army. If that shod be come into, the charge of the Army will be so great that it will discourage many & undoubtedly will cause some heart burnings in a certain Assembly; on the other hand, if the matter has taken air among the Soldiers & shod not be agree'd to there is great danger that we shall have no Army. This affair is referr'd to a Committee who I suppose will report tomorrow. Shall be able to give you a more perticular accot: of the matter in my next,[2]—in the mean time I hope every measure is & will be taken to raise our Proportion & as many more as possible.

I shod have speculated this side down but have a most violent headake which has increased within a few Minutes, to such a degree that it deprives me of the power of thinking. Must therefore bid you Adieu Yours &c. W. Whipple

9th Just receiv'd advice that the Enemy had retreated from Crown point & expect an express every hour that will give the perticulars. Genl: Howe has suddenly remov'd from White Plains it is conjectur'd with a design to cross the North River. 4,000 of our army have cross'd above him ready to attack him on this side.[3]

RC (NhD).

1. Matthew Thornton presented his credentials to Congress on 4 November. *JCC*, 6:920. Whipple had arrived on 24 October to relieve JB who left on the 26th.

2. See Whipple's letter of 16 Nov. 1776.

3. Under Sir Guy Carleton's leadership the British Army on Lake Champlain left Crown Point on 4 November in order to shorten its line of communication for the winter. In New York Gen. William Howe turned his army away from White Plains, captured Fort Washington, and pursued the Continental Army into New Jersey. Higginbotham, *War of Independence*, 162; Nebenzahl and Higginbotham, *Atlas*, 86.

TO JOHN LANGDON

Dear Sir   Kingstown Novembr 11th 1776

I arrived here last Saturday much better in health than I was for sometime past; The letter from the Chairman of the Secret Committee will inform you that the proposal of shipping Masts &c. was quite agreable: I intend as soon as I am a little rested to ride to Portsmouth to see you. The Marine Committe have wrote to Governor Trumbull requesting him to send the Guns that were prepared for the frigate in Connecticut to you, for your ship which I hope he will Comply with.[1] In haste I Remain as formerly your friend & most Obedient,   Josiah Bartlett

RC (MH).
  1. The Marine Committee's letter, 25   1:45–46.
Oct. 1776, is in Paullin, *Out-Letters,*

FROM WILLIAM WHIPPLE

My Dear Sir,   Philadelphia 16th Novr: 1776
  The Sudden & freequent movments of the Armies renders it impossible to give a just accot of their Situation. Howe has Retreated from White Plains, by the last accot was encamped on the Bank of the River blow Dobbs's ferry & by the disposition of his army it is judged intends making a desent on New-Jersey, in order to counteract him, part of Genl Washington Army (about 4 or 5000) have cross'd the River above him & are now on this side ready to receive him. They are continually Skirmishing in small parties, in which we always have the advantage. By some accots from deserters it is conjectured by some that a large detachment say 10,000 will go to South Carolina. I wish it may be true let them divide if they dare, a fleet of about 100 sail left Sandy Hook last Wednsday supposed to be bound for Europe.
  A Committee from the Massachusetts Genl Court arrived at the Camp about a fortnight ago to Commission the Officers &c. As that Genl Court had raised the pay of their Soldiers 20/ Per month. The Genl: choose the Matter should be layed before Congress before they proceeded to business accordingly one of Committee came here. This affair has perplext congress exceedingly, all the Southern states think the Incouragement to the Soldiers much too great before & if this committee are permitted to follow their Instructions the pay of the whole army must be rais'd. This by no means could be consented to, Congress have therefore revoked their Resolution for Inlisting the army during the war, & recommend the inlistment for three Years only, as You'll see by the Resolution transmited by the President. I Heartily wish this may have the desired effect, I really think they (the Massachusetts) were very wrong in raising the Monthly pay. If they supposed the encouragement given by Congress insufficient why coul[1] they not have increased the Bounty, or have persued some measure, that would not have effected the whole Army. This affair has caus'd more perplexity & uneasiness than any thing that has happened in my time.
  One vessel has arrived here from France since Your departure with arms & amunition only, several others will soon follow her, with such articles as are at this time more wanted. Harrison is arrived from Virginia, there has been a new Election in Delaware McKean, & Rodney, are left out & the Farmer[2] is elected instead of one of them, but he has not yet taken his seat. Our Colleague is as well as can be expected, the operation of the small pox has kept him two days from Congress. I hope he

will be able to attend in a few days. Please to present my most Respectful Regards to Col: Weare, Docr: Thompson, the Gnl: &c. &c. &c. I will trouble either of them with a letter when ever they'll give me an opportunity. I want very much to hear from you, perticularly as to your health, tho' I am in no doubt the Northern air & a *sight of Your Family* will do great things. I hear a great number of Torys are sent into our state from that of New-York. I hope proper care will be taken of them, as well as those in and of our state.[3] What think you of transporting them? This I wod like exceedingly, but then I'm puzle'd for a place bad Enough to send them to. Scotland indeed might do, but the difficulty is, how to keep them there, but to be serious, I think some very spirited Measure must be speedily taken with those people & I know of none that will answer the purpose so effactually as clearing the United states of them by some means or other. I can think of but two ways of effecting this, that is death or transportation, & Humanity inclines me to the latter indeed we had better send them to the Enemys army then let them continue among us. On the whole I dont Know but this wod be a good peice of policy, to send not only the avowed Torys but all those who are not active in their Countrys Cause with their Families, to Lord Howe, and let him make the most of them.

I have run on to a much greater length then I expected to, when I took up my pen by which means I shall loose the benefit of a Sermon, this forenoon, which I shod charge to your accot if I thought you could possibly reap any benift from this lenghey Scrawl but as that cannot be the case, I must put up with the loss & bid you Adieu assureing you that I am very Sincerly Yours   Wm Whipple

RC (InU).
1. Could.
2. John Dickinson.
3. Several documents relative to the New York Tories who were sent to

Exeter are printed in *NHSP*, 8:379–81, 390, 393–95; see also Upton, *Revolutionary New Hampshire*, 123.

TO WILLIAM WHIPPLE

My Dear Sir: Kingstown, Novemb'r 25th, 1776.

I arrived here the 9th Inst: after a very agreeable Jorney and better in health than when I left you, and am now (Dei Gratia) in a comfortable state of health, as I hope this will find you & your worthy colleague: as to news of the movements of the armies at New York they are so various and contradictory that I hardly know anything that is to be depended on since I left you. However I think it cannot be long before the Campaign must be closed & the armies retire to winter quarters; the report of the Day is, that the Brittish army has crossed over Hudsons river into the Jerseys but wither true or not is very uncertain here.

By accounts from the Northern army it appears that Gen. Carlton & his army are returned into Canada & so there is an end of the Campain there.[1] Major ----- is come with a request from Gen. Gates that the Regiment Stationed at Portsmouth may be sent to him & Col. Poor's[2] Regiment who have undergone the fatigue of the Campain be sent home to Recruit, but as the Officers are not Commissioned and there is no order of Congress or of General Washington for their removal I know not what will be done about it. The men seem very loth to be sent to the Northward as there are very Grevious Complaints of the Soldiers suffering not only by sickness & a total want of medicines but for Provisions and Cloathing and that by the Exorbitant prices of the necessaries sold by the sutlers they have been obliged to expend the whole of their wages to prevent them from starving. I really fear we shall be unable to procure an army for that Department unless effectual care is taken to have them better supplied & cheaper than they have been the year past. I really think an enquiry ought to be made how it Happened that the sick soldiers could not have any medicines from the Physicians of any kind, when I know large quantities have been sent there:[3] and I could wish persons were appointed to supply the army as sutlers with things at the prime cost and any necessary expense of dealing them out, &c., be paid by the publick.

The Convention of New York have sent our State a present of above 200 tories to be taken care of by us, some of them to be confined in close gaol, others to be confined to certain limits on their Parole.

The extravant rise of things especially merchants goods has raised a great clamor in the country and has given a handle to some restless persons in the County of Hillsborough to call a Convention of the Committees of the several Towns to meet at Dracut the 26th inst. to redress this & some other greviances. I am informed they have had one meeting, & have now sent to the greatest part of the Towns in this State & to a great number in the Massachusetts and expect a very grand meeting, what will be the consequence I know not but am much afraid of some bad effects and am very sorry that the infamous conduct of some traders who pretend to be great sons of liberty should give any just grounds of complaints to the people.

I hope soon to receive a letter from you and hope you will inform me of every interesting particular that you are at liberty to communicate both foreign and domestic. I suppose the *Reprisal* has sailed & I hope got clear off the Coast. Has Pennsylvania settled Government & how? Has Maryland formed a Constitution?[4] I am very anxious to know how things go on; here all is doubt & uncertainty.

Please to give my best regards to Col. Thornton & his Lady who I hope are safe arrived, & will remember me to Miss Susy, Capt. Dean, Mr. Boyle, &c. I am with great esteem your affectionate friend and Humble Servt.   Josiah Bartlett

Reprinted from *Letters by Josiah Bartlett*, 57–60.

1. Guy Carleton (1724–1808), first Lord Dorchester, was governor-general of Quebec. He led British forces on Lake Champlain through the Battle of Valcour Island in 1776 to Crown Point. To maintain communications the British moved back to Montreal for the winter. Carleton sailed to England in 1778, and returned

in 1782 to take command at New York, where he supervised the evacuation of British troops following confirmation of the peace treaty. *DNB*, 9:93–95.

2. Enoch Poor (1736–1780) took command of New Hampshire's 2nd Regiment in May 1775. In the spring of 1776 Washington had sent his regiment to the northern army in New York. Poor served with

valor until his death from a fever. Thompson, "Enoch Poor," 48.

3. The medicine had reached the troops in early November. See Jonathan Blanchard to Meshech Weare, 9 Nov. 1776, in *NHSP*, 8:391.

4. Maryland adopted its constitution on 9 November. Wood, *Creation*, 133.

TO WILLIAM WHIPPLE

My Dear Sir: Kingstown, Decembr 2d 1776

I am to acknowledge the Receipt of yours of the 8th ulto. and want to hear the Determination of Congress about increasing the soldiers wages. Our Court has voted to give our men the same wages that the Massachusetts gave, and knowing that they had voted ten dollars per month our Committee that went to appoint the officers, have given orders & have enlisted a number of men on those terms, so that it will be impossible now to raise them on any lower terms; they have appointed officers for but two Regiments, viz., Starks[1] & Poors. General Ward[2] gave orders to Col. Long to march his Regiment from Portsm'o to Ticonderoga, but I understand the men say they inlisted on the encouragement given by their officers that they should not be called away out of the Province, and many of them I am informed refuse absolutely to march, many necessaries are wanting for them before they can go which will take some time to procure, and they have not Rec'd any pay except one months wages from this State.

General Washington has requested a thousand more men from this State to be inlisted till the first of March, the General Court which began their sitting last Thursday has it now under consideration and will I believe comply with his request, had we rec'd his letter seasonable we should have sent to our men that are with the army & I believe could have prevailed upon them to have tarried for that time, but by some mischance his letter tho dated the 6th ulto. did not arrive till the latter end of last week.[3]

We have for some time had very disagreeable news from the army, the Tories here say the Regulars drive our army before them like a parcel of sheep, that they have driven them 40 or 50 miles with the greatest precipitation, and by our late accounts we have that the Enemy are in possession of the Forts Washington & Lee and some say with all their artillery, stores, &c., between 2 & 3000 men taken prisoners, but we have no certain accounts only common fame, and I hope it will not prove quite so bad as is reported tho I am pretty certain things wear a pretty unfavorable aspect in that Quarter, but whither from cowardice, treachery or want of experience I am not certain tho I would hope the latter. These things raises the heads of the Tories and very much depresses the spirits of the friends of Liberty. If you have any good news to inform us of pray send it along as soon as possible to chear our Drooping Spirits.

Give my best Regards to Col. Thornton who by this time I hope has got well thro the small pox. I wish you health & happiness & am your friend.   Josiah Bartlett

P.S. The weather here has been this fall & is now remarkably fine and pleasant.

5th. The General Court has voted to send 500 men agreeable to Gen. Washington's request to be immediately raised & sent, & to send & try to raise 500 more out of our militia at N. York. They have also voted to supply Col. Long's regiment with necessaries for their march but I fear they will not be prevailed on to move soon, if at all. We have had a confirmation of the loss of the forts Washington & Lee. Agreeable to the request of Congress we have purchased a considerable quantity of shoes, stockings, mittens, hats, shirts, &c., &c., and many more are agreed for, and have wrote to Congress for money to pay for them agreeable to order. Twenty thousand dollars are requested for the purpose, and I hope you & your Colleague will use your endeavors to see it is sent forward soon, as our treasury is almost empty & I am loth we should make more paper money at this time. Not having an oppertunity of sending this letter I am now arrived at the 6th and we are now told that General Howe is marched with 20,000 men for Philadelphia, and by a letter from Rhode Island we are informed that a large fleet of the Enemy have arrived there, but the news here is so various & contradictory that we know not what to believe, Tho lately the Bad news has turned out to be true & the good false; the Spirits of the people here seem much Depressed with our Repeated losses & I fear in the army too; unless something turns up more favorable I Dread the Consequence, I hope the Congress act with more Spirit than they have done lately or else I am assured they will lose much of their former influence. Pray use your influence to keep up a consistency in their Conduct, the want of it is much complained of (this inter nos).   J. B.

Reprinted from *Letters by Josiah Bartlett*, 60–63.

1. John Stark (1728–1822) of Londonderry saw service with Rogers' Rangers during the French and Indian War. With Enoch Poor and James Reed he was one of the original New Hampshire colonels in the Continental Army. His regiment, like Poor's, went to Fort Ticonderoga in the spring of 1776. He resigned in March 1777, but reentered active duty for the Battle of Bennington and remained in the service until 1783.

2. Artemas Ward (1727–1800) of Shrewsbury, Mass., served in the Continental Army from 1775 to 1777. At this time he was temporarily in charge of strengthening defenses around Boston.

3. The General Court convened on 27 November with JB on the Council. JB was part of a committee to consider Washington's request, and on the fourth the Court voted to send one thousand equipped men to the army. *NHSP*, 8:397, 401–03.

TO WILLIAM WHIPPLE

My Dear Sir   Kingstown Decembr [c. 15] 1776

Your favor of the 16th Ulto I Recd a few Days Since for which I thank you, but the resolve of Congress Disapproving of the increase of the

Soldiers Monthly pay which accompanied it, has thrown this State into the greatest perplexity: Before my return our Legislature after the Example of the Massachusetts had voted to give the Soldiers £3 pr month & had sent a Committe to Ti:—to Commission the officers for 2 Regiments & Set them to inlisting the men, which they performed & returned home & Brought Recommendations of some officers for the other Regiment, and the Begining of this month our Court Appointed the field officers of the third Regiment (Major Scammel to be Chief Colonel)[1] and were preparing to Set forward the inlisting here on the Same Conditions as speedyly as possible, when to our great Surprize we Recd the Said Resolve of Congress which at once Struck all Dead, for Every member well Knew it would be vain & Idle to the last Degree now, to send our Recruiting officers to inlist men at forty shillings pr month: I Could heartily wish our State had taken Some other way (by a yearly bounty) to have made up the Same value to them without increasing their monthly pay, this I told Several of the Members soon after my return, but as matters now Stand we must give £3 pr month or have no men; The perplexity was so great that the Court Dessolved last friday without Coming to any resolution about it;[2] The new House are to meet the 18th when I hope Something will be Done.

I am very loth to go on to raise men Contrary to the Resolves of Congress which has hitherto been held here as Sacred yet I think the Salvation of the Country Depends (under God) on an army; and if we Can't raise it as we would, we must Do it as we Can. Beside Sixty shillings now is by no means Equal to what forty was at the Commencement of the war and that the soldiers know by Dear Experience as many of our men who were unwell have been obliged to Expend the whole of their wages to get a few necessaries, by the Extravagant Demands of Sutlers &c. &c. I have had very grevious Complaints of their want of Every thing but bread & fresh meat without Sauce vegatables of any Kind. This I mention that Some Care may be taken to have the army there better Supplied another year as I am perswaded many lives have been lost by that means beside the Descouragement to the recruiting service.

We have had no Certain accounts of our affairs in the army since the loss of the forts washington & Lee. The reports that seem most Credited at present are, that part of Howes army are gone by water to Rhode Island, and that *He* with the greatest part are marching southward for Philadelphia and was got as far a Brunswick.

The Tories here seem much Elated & say our army have lost all their Cannon & field pieces and are so Dispiritd that they Dare not oppose their march and that great numbers of americans Joyn the Enemy's army on their march &c. &c. I hope things are not so bad as they report, Tho I fear our affairs at present wear a very unfavorable aspect. I think (my friend) we have been too negligent in procuring foreign assistance, while G: Brittain not Contented with all her own forces togather with her tools & Dependants here, she has been hireing foreign Mercenaries & Courting all the powers in Europe to assist her against us: and unless we have some speedy foreign assistance, I fear we run a great hazzard by the unequal Conflict: I wish the Congress would take into Consideration the powers given to the foreign Ambassadors and greatly Enlarge them; as Speedy assistance both by land & sea is in my opinion absolutely necessary to our safety both to keep up the spirits of our own people & prevent many of the americans from Deserting the Cause thro fear. We ought by no means to Stand hesitating & Bogling about terms at this time when our all is at Stake but take Assistance on Such terms as we can have it tho it may not perhaps be on so good terms as we Could wish.

We have raised 500 men to be under the Command of Col. David Gilman to reinforce the army till the first of march agreable to General Wasingtons request: I hope they will march in a few Days. The raising men for such short periods is a most Expensive & ruinous method but must be followed till another sort of army can be procured. The unbounded avarice of the merchants Especially some who have made large fortunes by privateering has given universal uneasiness here: perhaps there is now in the Country as large a quantity of some sorts of west India goods as there was Commonly at any one time before the war yet the merchants have Engrossed it and there is now as great a Scarcity as was ever Known, rum is sold by Hogshead at 10/ & 10s:6d pr gallon and hardly to be got for that Sugar none to be bought. What will be the Consequence of these things and where it will End God Knows but fear it augers ill to our affairs unless speedily remedied.

I have wrote you a long Scrawl full of ill tidings & Complaints, perhaps you will think I am Spleeny & melancholly, but you may be assured I am not, and send you this because I have no better news to send you & in hopes that you at the Congress Knowing our Disorders may prescribe proper Remedies for their Cure. Please to give my best regards to Col. Thornton and accept the Same your self from him who is without flattery your Sincere friend & Humble Servt.   Josiah Bartlett

FC (InU). Docketed: "Bartlett to Whipple, Copy, Decembr 1776." The exact date is conjectured from the contents.

1. See *NHSP*, 8:355. Alexander Scammell (1747–1781) of Durham served as a major until being commissioned a colonel on 10 Dec. 1776. He continued in active service until taken prisoner in September 1781.

2. The General Court dissolved on 13 December. *NHSP*, 8:419.

The following letter was written from Baltimore. Fearing British invasion, Congress had voted on 12 December to leave Philadelphia and reconvene at Baltimore on the 20th. JCC, 6:1027–28; Burnett, Continental Congress, *232.*

FROM WILLIAM WHIPPLE

My Dear Sir,   Baltimore 23 Decr: 1776
    The many Misfortunes that have attended the American arms since you

left Phila have undoubtedly reach'd you, the loss of fort Washington has been the Source of all these misfortunes, as the Success of the Enemy there gave them incouragement to persue victory, so it struck our troops with a panic that spred through the Country, & this unluckely happen'd at the time when the inlistment of the greatest part of the Army expired. However the People of Pensilvania are now turning out with spirit. Great numbers have already join'd Genl Washington. The people of Maryland are also turning out, the Jersey Men are by this time fully convinced of their errors, for the Ravages committed by the Enemy in their way through that state is really shocking to Humanity. They spared neither Age nor sex whig nor tory the Brutal vengence of an abandon'd Soldiry was exercis'd on all with out distinction. Thus we see what is to be expected from those worse then savages, but if they shod gain footing in New England we are to expect, if possible, greater cruelties then New Jersey has experienced. The whole vengence of the most abandon'd of the Human Race will be exercis'd on that Country it therefore behoves us with the utmost assiduity to raise a sufficient force to oppose them. I have not heard a word from New Hampshire for more than a month past, but I hope the new leavies are nearly compleated. I expect there will be another Regiment required of our state as the prevailing opinion is that the Army must be augmented on the new establishment.

Congress adjourn'd from Phila. the 11th inst: & meet here the 20 are now doing business with more spirit then they have for some time past.[1] I hope the air of this place which is much purer then that of Phila. will brace up the weak nerves, I think it already has that affect.

The *Sachem* is ariv'd at Phila. with about 1000 stand of arms & a considerable quantity of Blankets & other woolens. A letter from Mr. D-- of 1st Octor gives very incouraging accot.[2] I wish to communicate them to you, but am not at Liberty. The British Court are trying every act in their power with every Court in Europe but can not get any Satisfaction from Fr. or S.-- to use the words of a Correspondent, "a Genl: war in Europe seems unavoidable."

The Fortress at Ticonderoga is left exceedingly weak & the time that the few troops that are there is nearly expir'd so that if that place is not very soon reinforc'd there is great danger of loosing it. No time shod be lost in geting a sufficient Garrison at that important post.

How does taxing go on? Do you raise much money in that way? The People certainly were never so well able to pay a large tax as at this time. Who shall we get for a Brigadier Genl:. I wish Genl: Folsom wod take the Commission. Genl: Lee I suppose you have heard is taken. This a loss to us but I hope not so great a loss as People in general immagine.[3]

Before I conclude this I wod just remind you that I have not receiv'd a line from you since you left Phila: Wishing that I may soon have that Pleasure for the present bid you Adieu & am with great Respect Your Most Hum. Servt. Wm: Whipple

RC (NhD).
1. Congress actually adjourned on the 12th. *JCC,* 6:1025.

2. Silas Deane reported that he had a supply of goods which he expected to ship to America by mid-October. Prospects also looked good for a French loan to the colonies on favorable terms. Deane to the Committee of Secret Correspondence, in Wharton, *Diplomatic Corre-*

spondence, 2:153–57.

3. Gen. Charles Lee was captured at a tavern in Basking Ridge, N.J., on 12 December. John Sullivan took command of Lee's troops. Wallace, *Appeal to Arms,* 126.

FROM WILLIAM WHIPPLE

My Dear Sir,   Baltimore 31st. Decr. 1776

Your favor of the 25 ultimo came to hand yesterday. I rejoice that you have recovered your health. The clouds have thickened exceedingly this way since you left Philadelphia, but they now begin to disperse. The Enclosed[1] will inform you of a successful Enterprise at *Trenton,* and if our troops follow their flow, as is their intention, I am in no doubt the Enemy will be obliged to leave *Jersey;* which will end the campaign gloriously on our part. A number of light horse, without their riders, was taken at Trenton, not mentioned in the Generals letter—and a considerable number of prisoners brought in since the inclosed returns. There was about 2500 crossed the river with *General Washington,* one division was commanded by *Sullivan* the other by *Greene.* They were composed of those Troops that came from the northward, some with *Lee* and others with *Gates.* This event will have a very good effect, it puts new life into the Pennsylvanians and will add greatly to our strength from *Jersey,* that people who have been treated with such brutality by the British troops will be inspired with revenge, so that the advantage the Enemy have gained in the Country will, eventually, operate against them. Hence the wise disposer of all things directs human affairs.

The *Andro Doria* is arrived at Philadelphia with a very valuable cargo. On her passage from the West Indies she fell in with a British sloop of War, which after an obstinate engagement struck to the American flag. The prize is not arrived.[2]

By a circular letter from the President you'll see the General is vested with almost dictatorial Power. This measure was thought absolutely necessary for the Salvation of America. There is also measures taken (which I hope will be effectual) to prevent the abuses suffered by the soldiers last campaign. I am in no doubt that the grievances so justly complained of in every department will be redressed so far as is possible, and the causes of them removed.

Col. Poor is recommended by the General for a Brigadier—as there will soon be a considerable addition to the list of general officers its probable that Gentleman will be promoted. I heartily wish some method could be adopted to bring Gen. Fulsom into the field, but how this can be effected I dont know. I hope proper measures are taken to complete the new bodies—for Heaven sake and for the sake of every thing thats valuable on Earth dont act 'till this business is done. The soldiers may be assured that the Causes of their complaints will be removed—its of the last importance that the garrison at Ticonderoga should immediately be reinforced.

If the proposed Army (which is to be increased to 110 battallions) should be completed, I am not in the least doubt that the enemies of America will be completely vanquished next campaign. The Tyrant will undoubtedly summon Earth and Hell to his assistance to carry his infernal plans into execution. He has made another application to the Court of Russia, but there is just reason to believe he has been unsuccessful. Every artifice has been used to make the Court of France believe that an accomodation would take place but Congress have instructed their commissioners to assure that and other European Courts that they are determined to support the Independence of the American States. Affairs in France wear a very favourable aspect.

Gen. Gates arrived here a few days ago very sick, but is recovering. Business goes on briskly. More has been done in one week here than was done in two months in Philadelphia.

A perfect restoration of health, and that every happiness may be yours, is the Sincere wish of your affectionate friend and Humb. St.

Wm: Whipple

Jany 2d Seizing the oppertunity this has designed I have the pleasure to congratulate you on the arrival of the two Brigs, *Lexington* and *Friendship* at this place. The former was taken as she was going into Delaware by the *Pearl* Frigate of 32 guns, who took out all her officers and put on board 7 or 8 men, but the weather being so bad they could not change the crews—the *honest* tars took possession of her and brought her safe into this port. The vessels have both very valuable cargoes on board. Your. W: W:

TR (OCHi). Docketed: "Correctly copied from the original in the possession of Joseph B. Boyd."

1. Enclosure not found. The Battle of Trenton took place at dawn on 26 December. Wallace, *Appeal to Arms*, 129–31.

2. On the arrival of the *Andrew Doria* see Robert Morris to John Hancock, 23 Dec. 1776, in *NDAR*, 7:574.

FROM WILLIAM WHIPPLE

My Dear Sir,   Baltimore 13th Jany 1777

Since my last we have had accots of many Skirmishes in Jersey in which our Troops have been Victorious. We lost about 20 men at Princetown on the 3d inst among which was some Brave Officers. I don't recollect their names except Coll: Hazets of Delaware & Major Morris of the Phila Milia. Genl: Mercer was said to be among the slain, but it seems he was only wounded & like to do well.[1] He had 5 Bayonet wounds. About 100 of the Enemy were kill'd in this action & 3 to 400 taken. We have kill'd & taken more then 2000 since Chrismas. Our loss since that time does not exceed 40. The last accots from the Genl: was the 7th inst.[2] He was then at Morris town & the Enemy no where to the westward of

Brunswick; I am inclin'd to think that the Humain Mr. Howe is sick of his Winter Campaign, & I fear will escape with the Remains of his Army into York. The Ravages committed by the Enemy have had a most excellent effect on the people of Jersey. The Melitia now turn out with great spirit & Harrass the Ravagers of their Country on every quarter. I fancy the Tyrant of Britain has been Premature in confering the Dignity of Knighthood on his Humane Dispenser of Pardons.[3] His Popeship seems to be in a fair way to loose all his Laurells. The Hessian Officers complain much, that they shod be distinguish'd as Plunderers, when, they say, the British Troops Plunder more then they do. I believe the truth is, they both endeavour to excel in what they know will recommend them to their Commanders in chief.

I am really at a loss to account for my not receiving any intelligence from N. Hampshire. I am as great a stranger to what is doing in that state as to what's doing in the moon. How goes on your recruiting service? What officers have you for the new Army? It is of the last importance that the new Levvies shod be Compleated without loss of time, the greater our exertions the sooner we shall put an end to this destructive war.

Business goes on with spirit since we have got out of the Putrid Air of the Sodom of America. Several Prizes have lately arrived here. The Delaware is again Clear of the Enemies ships, I suppose they were call'd in for the protection of York, for it seems the Present inhabitants of that City were exceedingly alarmed at our late Success.

I shall set out for home in about a fortnight unless I am reelected in that case I shall have no objection to continuing here till the season will admit of traveling with more comfort then at present. We have various reports from Rhoad Island but no authentic advises.

My Colleague[4] is well & desires his Compliments to you. We agree very well in sentiments, but, *Inter Nos*, N. H. is oftener div--d then she used to be. My Regards to all Friends & be assured that I am with every Sentiment to Esteem Your Friend &c.   Wm: Whipple

RC (NhD).

1. In all, thirty-three American officers and men were killed and about forty were wounded in this campaign. Among the officers slain were Col. John Haslet, Surgeon Anthony Morris, Jr., and Brig. Gen. Hugh Mercer, who died on 12 January from wounds. Peckham, *Toll of Inde-* pendence, 27, 29.

2. Printed in *WGW*, 6:477–78.

3. For his victory at Long Island William Howe was knighted as Companion of the Bath by George III. Wallace, *Appeal to Arms*, 133.

4. Matthew Thornton.

TO WILLIAM WHIPPLE

My Dear Sir   Exeter, January 15th 1777

Last Saturday I rec'd yours of the 23d ulto after a long interruption of our correspondence; the communication being of late interrupted, I have not wrote you so often as I designed—I have wrote you 3 or 4 times since my return none of which I understand you have rec'd. I have rec'd three only from you. I should have wrote you by Squire Betton[1] but was at that time at Providence, one of the Committee of the New England States to see about an army for the defence of Rhode Island, and to lay a plan to prevent the amazing depreciation of the paper money—what was transacted there you will be informed of, before this reaches you, as the several States were requested to transmit to Congress a copy of what was done.[2]

I am fully sensible of the difficulties attending the setting prices to any thing, much more to every thing, but unless something was done so as the soldier might be ascertained of what he could purchase for his forty shillings, no more would enlist, nor could we with reason expect it: what will be the effect of establishing prices I know not, however it must be tried: We have had many and great difficulties in raising the Continental army, the different plans laid by the Massachusetts which our people think we must adopt, has much retarded the business. We have now in conformity to them, offered a bounty from this State of twenty pounds in addition to the Continental encouragement and to hire money at six per cent to pay the bounty—I have used my utmost endeavors to reduce the interest but hitherto in vain: we seem now in earnest and I hope we shall get our quota in a little time. Esquire Betton will inform you of the situation of affairs here. I was at Providence when I was appointed a member of Congress for this year, otherwise I should have refused as my health though much better than when I left Philadelphia is too weak to bear another Summer in Philadelphia and Baltimore I suppose is still worse—Somebody must be appointed in my stead, but the Court is at present so engaged that they will not attend to it I believe till next setting.[3] The late successes of the regulars have much elated the Tories and depressed the spirits of others, and before the news of our success at Trenton our affairs here wore a very gloomy aspect—that affair has altered them much for the better. I hope the Congress will leave nothing unattempted to procure foreign assistance, for without it, it will be in vain for us to expect to defeat the whole power of Britain and all her allies assisted by a great number of internal enemies among us, which injure us more than 4 times their number in General Howe's army. Quere—whether it would not be advisable to order that every man that will not join heartily in the defence of the country should be sent with their families to General Howe and there taste the sweets of the Govt they desire to be under. The County of Grafton by the influence of Dartmouth College have refused to send members to the Council, or Assembly and of consequence to be subject to the Laws of this State; they have printed a piece wherein they lay it down as a rule that every town whether they consist of 5, or of 5000 have each an equal right to an equal number of representatives; the House and Council have appointed a Committee to repair to that County and try to settle difficulties—Col. Weare Esquire Giles, Mr. Wentworth and your humble servant are ordered on that service.[4] I hope money will be sent forward as we are obliged to advance the money for the Continental as well as Provincial bounty.

We have had great difficulty with Col. Long's regiment—General Ward ordered them to march to Ticonderoga—the field officers were not commissioned nor had they received any pay from the Continent and on application to the paymaster at Boston, he said he had no money and could not pay them—the soldiers are very uneasy and say they expected not to be sent from Portsmouth, are not provided with clothes for so tedious a winter's march in this cold climate. In order that nothing may be wanting in our power to get them off, we have payed their wages which has much exhausted our Treasury—I am still doubtful whether they will march. We have sent to all the recruiting parties for the Continental army to march their men as fast as possible in small parties to Ticonderoga agreeable to order of Congress, but am afraid there are but a few that will be ready to march soon, however all will be done that can be. The post since the last regulation of Congress is almost entirely stopt; what is the reason? it ought to be enquired into by Congress,—I fear some bad designs have been the cause.

We have various reports of the situation of affairs in the Jersies since that of the 26th but no certain advices. Oh that the Supreme Disposer would grant success to our arms and defeat forever the designs of our inveterate enemies. Give my regards to Col. Thornton and accept the same yourself from him who is your sincere friend & humble Servt.

Josiah Bartlett.

TR (DLC: Force Transcripts).

1. James Betton (1728–1803), a farmer of Windham, was a justice of the peace, town officer, and representative to the General Court. On 26 December he was sent as an agent to the Continental Congress to bring back a large amount of money granted to the state for carrying on the war. Correspondence bearing on his mission as well as an itinerary of his journey are printed in Morrison, *Windham*, 337–45. See also *NHSP*, 8:439, 532.

2. With Nathaniel Folsom and Supply Clapp, JB participated in a New England convention on economic matters between 25 Dec. 1776 and 2 Jan. 1777. The manuscript of the proceedings (NhHi) is on

MJB 1058, and is printed in NHHS, *Collections*, 9:245–71. See also *NHSP*, 8:431, 434.

3. JB, Whipple, and Thornton were appointed delegates on 24 December. The Court adjourned on 18 January. By the time it reconvened on 12 March, JB had begged to resign the appointment. See his letter of March 1777, *NHSP*, 8:437, 469, 503.

4. See *NHSP*, 8:450, 463. Benjamin Giles (c. 1717–1787) was a mill owner in Newport. A leading citizen in the western part of the state, he represented six towns in the legislature. Wheeler, *Newport*, 396–97.

FROM WILLIAM WHIPPLE

My Dear Sir   Baltimore 7th Feby 1777

I have receiv'd Your favor of 2d Dec. but not 'till the 26th Jany. What occasions this delay in the posts I know not, but suppose the fault must lay with the Post Master Genl:[1] he has lately had a Rap, which I hope will have a good effect. I am sorry there is such Backwardness in Col. Longs Regiment to March, but its what I always feared. I hope the new army will soon be rais'd, for this Method of Calling out the Militia to march such a distance, is the most ruinous plan that ever was invented. I am sorry you want any thing to keep up Your Spirits, I shod think the Glorious Cause in which we are ingag'd is sufficient for that purpose. The prospect of laying a foundation of Liberty & Happiness for Posterity & securing an Asilum for all who wish to injoy those Blessings is an object in my opinion sufficient to raise the mind above every misfortune. The loss of Forts Washington, & Lee, is not I hope to be imputed to Treachery, or Cowardice, but rather to want of Experience this defect time will supply, & the enormous ravages commited by the Enemy wherever they have pass'd will teach the people wisdom, & inspire them to Noble Deeds.

The Principle objects of attention is, to raise & supply the army, & prevent the Depreciation of the Currency, the last is the most difficult, but I hope not impracticable. The proceedings of your Convention at Providence, has been transmited to Congress by Gov: Trumbull & in general highly approv'd of, but the recommendation to issue money on interest universaly Condemn'd. I hope there will be no need of Issuing any, but if that cannot be avoided, I sincerely wish the evil may not be accumulated by adding interest. I cod wish N.H. had follow'd the example of her neighbouring sister states, in laying a large tax, that is certainly one of the wisest steps that can be taken. Nothing in my Opinion can tend more to establish the Curcy & the People never can be better able to pay a tax then at Present. I hope a recommendation will soon go to the several states to sink the money emited by them as soon as possible.

There is more unanimity in Congress then ever, the *little* Southern jealosies have almost subsided, & the Dickinsonian Politics are Banish'd. J. Adams & Lovell are arriv'd from Massacts an exceeding good representation from Virginia, a new member from N. Carolina, (one Mr. Burke) who I think is the Best man I have seen from that Country.[2] Business goes on smoothly within doors & I am told the recruiting service goes on Briskly without. By Private letters from Spain of 17th novr there seems to be no doubt of a general war in Europe, on the whole I think affairs wear a *favorable* aspect, tho' we have heard nothing from our Commissioners but are in daily expectation of very pleasing Intelligence from them. France, Spain, & Prussia, its probable are meditating some grand plan. I believe we may as well ceede Hanover to Prussia, & give Great Britain to France; what think you of this scheme?

I suppose you have seen the British Tyrants speech, but least it may have escap'd you I inclose it.[3] I dont know how it may strike your fancy, but it pleases me much. He now thinks the Contest Arduous & notwithstanding the assurances of amity from the several Courts of Europe he thinks it necessary to take care of himself. I fancy the wrech begins to see his danger.

Authentic accots of the Cruelties exercised by the Enemy in New

Jersey are collecting & will soon be Published. We are now sending off about 600 men to suppress a Tory faction in two of the Counties of this state on the Eastern shore. This business I expect will soon be effected when the troops are to march on to join Genl Washington. Three men of war now lay in Chesepeak Bay who have taken several vessels one in perticular outward bound, with a load of Tobaca for the Public accot.

It is a long time since I receiv'd a line from N.H. the latest was by Mr. Betten which were dated in Dec. It gives me great pain that Mr. Betten shod be so long detain'd, but there was no possibility of avoiding it, the Treasury being almost empty, & the most pressing demands from all Quarters, so that we have been in a perplex'd Scituation, but have now got pretty well over those Difficulties, there being only one demand of consequence now on the Treasury. I wish the accots may be sent forward and a requisition for more money as soon as possible, so that the money may be forwarded when an opportunity offers. I have given it as my opinion to the President that he advance 400 Dollars to Mr. Betten and charge it to the state of N.H. and he (Mr. Betten) to be accountable to the state for that sum, the whole of his expences will then be a fair charge against the Continent.

When do you think of coming this way again! I shall not be able to stand it above three Months longer, & Col: Thornton seems determin'd to return home in may, so I hope you'll get a good Colleague and relieve us the begining of may at farthest. If you'll give me timely notice of Your Coming, I'll meet you half way. I already find the want of exercise notwithstanding I have had a ride of 100 miles within two months. This place is so intolerable muddy there is no such thing as walking, & I have really no time to ride.

Please to give best respects to Docr: Thompson, I am half a letter in debt to him, but fear I shall not be able to pay him, by this coneyence, but shall very soon, as I love to be punctual in paying Debts, especialy of this sort. I wish he & some others of my Friends wod increase my obligations in this way. While I am on this subject I must beg leave to remind you, that I have not heard so often from you as I cod wish, but flatter myself when you recollect how anxious you used to be to know how affairs were going on at home, that you will not be unmindful of me—in the mean time be assured I am with real esteem Yor Sincere Friend & Humle Sert.   Wm. Whipple

RC (MdBJ).

1. The postmaster general was Richard Bache (1737–1811) who had been appointed on 7 Nov. 1776 in the place of his father-in-law, Benjamin Franklin. Rich, *History of the Post Office*, 49.

2. James Lovell (1737–1814) served until 1782, Thomas Burke (1747–1783) until 1781.

3. Enclosure not found. JB's copy may have been the one reprinted in *N.H. Gazette*, 25 February. The speech, delivered to both houses of Parliament on 7 Nov. 1776, hailed the success of British operations at New York as "so important, as to give the strongest hopes of the most decisive good consequences." The King sought to obtain Parliament's support for the campaign of 1777 which was expected to be arduous and expensive.

FROM WILLIAM WHIPPLE

My Dear Sir,   Baltimore 22d Feby 1777

I have receiv'd Your favor of the 15 Ult. The intolerable delays &
uncertainty to the Post has prevented my writing so often as I should
otherwise have done, but I hope an effectual remedy will spedely be
apply'd to this evil when our correspondence will meet with less interruption. I am sorry your Health will not admit of Your returning to Congress. My Colleage seems determin'd on taking his departure in may, at
which time I am very desireous of returning also, in short no pecuniary
advantage wod. induce me to tarry even to the end of that month. I
therefore hope to have leave to go home the begining of may.

After repeated requisitions of Genl: Washington, Congress have made
a number of Genl Officers. The Genls: Proposal is, that there shod be a
Major Genl: to every three Brigades and a Brigadier to every three Regiments. He also proposed three Lieut. Genls: but this I believe will not be
speedily comply'd with, as its the general opinion in Congress that the
Senior Major Genl: may answer the purpose for the present. Five are
added to the list of Major Genls: and ten to the list of Brigadiers. Among
the latter is Col: Poor who was strongly recommended by Genl: Gates
as well as by the Commander in chief. This will make a vacancy in your
late arangment which I hope will be well fill'd. I only wish the real merit
may influence the choice.

I am fearful that sending men off in small Parties will be injurious to
the recruiting service, as sending part of a company will backward the
inlistment to compleat it. I hope proper care will be taken to send good
Surgeons as much depends on them—Morgan & Stringer are both dis-
plac'd, & the Medical Department will be put on a very differant footing
from what it was last Campaign.[1] You are sensible of the necessity of a
reformation perticularly in that department & I hope great care will be
taken in the appointment of Regimental Surgeons. I also hope proper
measure will be persue'd by each state to furnish their respective Soldiers
with cloathing for notwithstanding every method that can be taken by
Congress, there will be but a scanty supply unless the different states pay
perticular attention to their own men.

Inclos'd is a copy of a letter from Genl: Lee which gave me no small
uneasiness when I first heard of it least some might think it expedient to
comply with the request, but to my great joy when it came before Congress
there did not appear one advocate for the measure, it evidently appearing
to be a scheme of those incendiaries (the two Howe's) to amuse, & slaken
our measures, but they are disapointed! Lee at the same time wrote to
Genl: Washington desiring him to send one of his aids de camp to him &
his dogs which I suppose the Genl: has comply'd with.[2] Soon after Lee
was taken Genl: W.-- was directed to offer six Field officers for him, that
being the price of a Major Genl: and at the same time to assure Howe
that the treatment that Lee receiv'd shod be exactly retaliated on them,
which promise I hope will be religiously adhear'd to!

Nothing meterial has lately happen'd in the Army. We hear frequently of small Skirmishes in which we always have the advantage. The Enemy are closly confin'd to Brunswick & are put to great difficulties for forage &c. but our army is not strong enough to attack them, the Southern troops are daily joining the Army, & all that have not had the small Pox are inoculated in their way. I cod wish that measure were adopted with the Eastern troops I think it might be done without loosing much time.

We are still anxiously expecting Intelligence from Europe. The *Randolph* is at last gone to sea & the *Delaware* I expect will soon follow her. The *Virginia* is nearly ready also but I hear nothing of the Frigates at the Northward.

Congress have determin'd to adjourn to Phila. next Tuesday so you may expect my next will be from that place. In the mean time be assured that I am with great Respect Your very affect. Friend & Humle Sevt.

Wm: Whipple

RC (NhD).

1. Dr. John Morgan (1735–1789), founder of the University of Pennsylvania Medical School, had been made director of the Continental medical service in October 1775. Congress degraded him a year later and dismissed him in January 1777. Dr. Samuel Stringer (c. 1734–1817), of Albany, N.Y., was appointed chief medical officer of the northern army in September 1775. He was dismissed with Morgan in January 1777. Bell, *John Morgan*; *JCC*, 2:249; 7:24. Congress managed its medical business through a Medical Committee.

2. Enclosure not found. Lee's letters are referred to in *JCC*, 7:134, 140.

TO THE GENERAL COURT

March 1777

I Beg Leave to return my Sincere Thanks to the State of Newhampshire for the Unmerited Honor they have Done me in Repeatedly appointing me one of their Delegates to the Continental Congress and Tho' I am fully sensible that I am not Equal to the important trust, yet Since it is their pleasure I should Cheerfully Endeavor to serve them in that Capacity to the utmost of my abilities; would my health permit; But past Experience has Convinced me that my Constitution is not sufficient to undergo the fatigues of that aduous Business in the Summer season in that Hot & Sultry Climate and must therefore Beg Leave to Resign my Said appointment or to be Excused from attending Congress the Ensuing Summer and that another may be Chosen in my Stead which will much oblige their most Obedient Humble Servant.   Josiah Bartlett

Draft signed (MeHi: The John S. H. Fogg Autograph Collection). The General Court had reappointed JB on 23 Dec. 1776. *NHSP*, 8:437.

TO [WILLIAM WHIPPLE]

My Dear Sir,   Exeter March 1st 1777

I am just returned from the County of Grafton where I have been with Col. Weare and Mr. Wentworth for 4 weeks trying to settle the dificulties about govt there, but without the success I wished for: the towns near

Hanover and under the influence of the College, seem obstinately determined to rule this State or to keep every thing in confusion.[1] Col. Bedel since his return from Philadelphia seems very busy & officious with the malcontents—he was appointed Chairman of the Committees in that part of the State who call themselves a Convention—nothing will content them, but a dissolution of all govt here and that in future every town in the State should have an equal number of Representatives, though some have more than an hundred times as many inhabitants as others. The New Hampshire grants so called have declared themselves a separate State and have sent men to Congress to get it confirmed, who I suppose will be with you before this comes to hand, and will no doubt cause you much trouble.[2] I think it a very wrong time to enter on these disputes—Col. Bayley[3] was appointed one of the men to wait on the Congress, but by what he told us I believe he will not accept of the appointment. I hear Col. Bedel and some others are trying to get a regiment raised to be stationed on Connecticut river on the Western parts of the State by order of Congress and it is said for Col. Bedel to have the command of them. If such a regt should be raised I believe his appointment to the command would be very disagreeable to this State. It is currently reported here, that the sentence of the Court Martial against Col. Bedel is disannulled by Congress and he employed to gain intelligence from Canada and that he has taken measures for that purpose: I sincerely wish we may receive more advantage from his correspondence with Canada than our enemies. We have met with many and very great difficulties in raising the Continental regiment and notwithstanding the enormous bounty given I fear they are not much more than half full and of those who are enlisted but very few have sufficient arms nor do I know how they will be supplied, as all the good arms almost have been sent into the army—some have been lost or spoiled and most of the rest sold or disposed of by the soldiers there rather than be at the trouble to bring them home however every thing will be done that can be to supply them. We are now procuring large quantities of rum, sugar &c. &c. and sending them to Ti-- for the supply of our men this summer—if the sledding holds I hope we shall soon have a large quantity there.

I want much to hear how affairs go on in the Courts of F., and S. and whether we are to expect any foreign assistance or must still encounter the whole power of Britain and all her allies.

The account of the State Lottery is very much approved of here and if tickets were sent they would sell very fast.[4] I hope Esquire Betton will bring a quantity when he returns. Please to inform me whether the Congress will continue at Baltimore for the summer and if it should remove, to what place it is most likely. Your's of the 31st of Decr is the last I have rec'd from you—I hope you will write to me every opportunity—I should have wrote to you oftener but as you will perceive I have not had opportunity being great part of the time since my return absent, and not in the way of sending to you. We have been obliged to strike off 40,000 pounds L. M. in large treasury notes of 5 & 10 pounds, to carry six per cent interest,[5] to pay off the State bounty to the soldiers as the making more money without interest would be fatal to the credit of the whole.

As to clothing and arms for our men I think it is absolutely impossible for this state to supply them and I think very reasonable that we should have some of these that are brought in by the Congress to supply our troops and that they may have an equal advantage from them with the Southern troops. There are great complaints from the soldiers that the Southern troops are much better clothed and taken care of than our's and that the cloths sent by Congress was chiefly delivered to them, which gave great uneasiness—I hope proper care will be taken of this matter. Give my best regards to Col. Thornton and to all friends and believe me to be Sincerely yours. J.B.

TR (DLC: Force Transcripts).

1. Meshech Weare and John Wentworth, Jr., had been appointed on 3 January; JB was added on the fourteenth. *NHSP*, 8:450, 463. The difficulties arose from the plan for representation of the western towns in the General Court and remained unresolved into the 1780s. See Daniell, *Experiment*, 145–63.

2. The petition from the towns constituting the New Hampshire Grants, dated 15 Jan. 1777, reached Congress on 8 April. On 30 June Congress dismissed the case as being out of its jurisdiction. *JCC*, 7:239; 8:509–10.

3. Jacob Bayley (1728–1815) of Newbury, Vt. took a prominent role in military and civic affairs of his state. He was a brigadier general in 1777. Bayley. *Account of the Bailey-Bayley Family*, 12–52.

4. Congress operated a lottery from time to time during the war, never realizing much income therefrom. On 14 Feb. 1777 it authorized the Board of Treasury to send first class tickets to the states. Burnett, *Continental Congress*, 379; *JCC*, 7:119.

5. See *NHSP*, 8:465–66.

TO WILLIAM WHIPPLE

My Dear Sir,   Exeter March 15th 1777

Esquire Betton who arrived here safe the 7th inst delivered me yours of the 7th ulto for which I thank you and am very sorry my letters are so long getting to you. Mr. Betton I understand met with no great difficulty in his return. The people here are much disappointed in his not bringing any lottery tickets; they would sell here very fast; I hope a considerable number of them will be sent here speedily otherwise I believe our House of Assembly will be for setting up a lottery for this particular State, so great is the itch of the people to become adventurers.

The General Court is now sitting and I hope next week to inform you who will be appointed to relieve you and your Colleague a spell this summer as I shall resign my seat.[1] General Washington has ordered our three regts to march to Ti---: Some have marched already—Very few have enlisted since I wrote you last; the men waiting to have the regiments filled by a draft when they expect an additional bounty from private persons—the Massachusetts have taken that measure and our State must do the Same—I expect it will be done next week.

By some intercepted letters from Govr Wentworth, John Cochran &c. to some persons in this State dated January 17th and 23d they say that

G. B. has engaged 20,000 Russians 12,000 Wertemburgers &c. and expect to be in this State either in peace or war this summer and have advised their friends to move their best effects from Portsmouth as they say there will be destruction of property without any reserve. They seem to be very much pleased with the expectations of success and say that the Southern Provinces are all about to lay down their arms and submit— however I hope there is not much credit to be given to their information. I can't yet believe that F and S and Prussia &c. will lay still and see G. Britain employ Russians, Hessians and the Lord knows who to subdue us—I hope we shall soon hear better tidings from Europe.

There are many Continental Bills passing, which are suspected of being counterfeit and we find much difficulty in detecting them for want of the proof sheets of each emission being sent to our Treasury agreeable to the order of Congress. I am desired to write to you and request that they may be sent forward: I believe that many that are suspected are only from the alterations made in the different emissions. Give my best regards to Col. Thornton and accept the same for yourself from your Sincere friend.   Josiah Bartlett

We have sent 28 loads of Suttler's Stores to Ti--- for our soldiers:—pray remember to send forward Some Lottery Tickets and the proof sheets of money.

The weather here is now very warm and Spring-like. Pray inform me whether the Southern States hold firm—whether N. Carolina has taken up govt—whether Pennsylvania is like to unite in a form of govt and what—has Maryland taken up govt.

My health though better than when I left Philadelphia will not permit my attending Congress this summer—hope Col. Walker and Mr. Wentworth[2] will be sent to your relief—am not certain as several others are talked of.

May the Supreme Ruler direct your counsils with wisdom, may our enemies be defeated in their villainous designs, may success and victory attend the American arms and may the United States of America soon be the happiest, most flourishing and most virtuous people on this globe. Such are the earnest desires and first wishes of.   J.B.

This moment rec'd yours of the 16th ulto with a copy of Lee's letter[3] to Congress for which I thank you. I confess I am not competent at this distance to determine concerning (the) prudence of Congress in not sending a Committee to New York agreeable to his request. However at present I can see no disadvantage that would be likely to accrue had that measure been taken and I fear such determined resolutions not to hold any conferences concerning peace with G.B. will be apt to disaffect many people when publicly known, as people in general seem almost tired of the war. If you had sent possibly something might have turned up much to our advantage at least it would convince both Whigs and Tories that we were desirous of peace on reasonable terms and cleared the Congress of the aspersion cast on them by our enemies that they are averse to peace so that they may keep the whole power in their own hands—These are my hasty thoughts on the matter. I am &c.   J.B.

TR (DLC: Force Transcripts).
1. See JB's letter of March 1777.
2. John Wentworth, Jr. (1745–1787), an attorney of Dover, represented New Hampshire in Congress during part of

1778. Burnett, *Letters*, 3:lv.
3. No letter of 16 Feb. 1777 has been found; but Whipple inclosed Lee's letter in his to JB of 22 February.

TO LEVI BARTLETT

Dear Son   Kingstown March 23d 1777

I am glad to hear by your letter of the 21st Inst:[1] that you are well Excepting a Cold: hope you are better of it now: I and your mother, and all the family are Comfortable Except the Babe which is not very well.[2] I Designed to have seen you before now but have been so Engaged I Could not, and as the vacation is so near, it is not likely I shall see you till you Come home: I will try to send for you the 10th of next month when I understand the vacation begins. I Dont know whither I Can procure a Virgil for you before you Come home if you Know of any to be sold you may Engage it & I will send the money by you when you return: The vacation is so near your mother will not send you any more Cloathing till you return home. If you Can purchase two Quire of writing paper and bring with you I shall be glad, however you need not put yourself to much trouble about it if you Can't Easily procure it. I hope I shall have the pleasure at your Return to find you have made proper improvements in your learning, if so I shall not regret the Cost. I am your affectionate father.   Josiah Bartlett
Mrs. Noyes is much better.

RC (PHi).
1. Not found.
2. Hannah, the "Babe," was born on

13 Dec. 1776 and died 17 Apr. 1777.

TO WILLIAM WHIPPLE

My Dear Sir,   Kingstown March 26th 1777

Your favor of the 22d ulto is the last I have rec'd from you—My health not permitting my attending Congress I have resigned my seat and the State have chosen Col. Walker and Mr. King delegates to relieve you and Col. Thornton. Mr. King I believe will not accept so we shall have another to appoint in his stead. As those that will be sent will be new members, I believe it will be best for one of them to set out as soon as may be to relieve one of you and the other of you to tarry a month, or two till he gets acquainted with the business and then the other to join him. This seems to be the opinion of the Court and I hope it will not be disagreeable to you as I think it will be for the public good.

Col. Poor's advancement has caused Col. Stark to resign, so we have now two regiments destitute of chief Colonels:[1] The difficulty of filling those vacancies any other way than by advancing the other officers is so great that I believe that method will be adopted though all of them may not be quite so agreeable—General Washington has recommended that method.

We have proportioned the three regiments to the several towns and hope it will not be long before they are filled up, though many who would be very willing to serve for one year look on the enlistment for 3 years as selling themselves for slavery for life. The utter impossibility of our arming our troops has induced the State by General Sullivan's advice (who is now in this State) to apply to Col. Langdon to have them supplied out of the Continental arms lately arrived at Portsmouth in the French ship which I believe he will comply with—some of our men have marched for Ti-- and more will soon follow.

By this time I suppose you have rec'd the packet that came in the French ship to Portsmouth and know pretty near the situation of affairs in Europe and what we have to hope and what to fear from the quarter; —reports here are so very various and uncertain that I know not what credit to give to any of them. I am very anxious to know the contents of Dr. F's letters and if it is permitted hope you will inform me the substance of what they contain. If G.B. is to hire (as the late Govr Wentworth in one of his lately intercepted letters says) 20,000 Russians, 12,000 Wertemburgers &c., &c., and we have no assistance we must expect a trying time of it this summer—However I can't yet believe that will be the case and the late supplies from France look very favorable. I cant help being very desirous to hear how affairs go on as it appears to me that the fate of America, if not of Britain and of millions of both of the present and future inhabitants of both countries hang suspended on the transactions and occurrences of the present year. May the Sovereign Disposer order all things for the best good and happiness of America and may peace harmony and independence soon succeed our present calamities.

The General Court is now sitting and doing business much as usual.[2] I have used my endeavors to have a large tax laid on this year but before that is done they have ordered a new inventory of the polls and estates to be taken in order for a new proportion; this will be attended with some difficulties as it will be taken differently from the former method by including the value of all the unimproved lands and every other species of estate and the County of Grafton and part of Cheshire are so disaffected that I believe they will take no notice of the order. Those people are determined to legislate for the whole State or set up a State by themselves. A certain D:D: and a certain late attorney from Connecticut assisted by the Hero of the Cedars seem determined to put every thing into confusion: what their designs are time will discover, but I hope to prevent their taking effect.

Col. Nicholas Gilman is appointed Commissioner of the Continental Loan Office—if a 1000 of the Lottery Tickets were sent him I believe he could soon take the money for them. I believe they would do more towards enlisting the soldiers than double their value in money. I believe if we had the tickets before the soldiers go off they would purchase a thousand at least as they have money very plenty by the extravagant bounties given them and it would be no real damage to most of them to part with it in that way. I hear you have raised the interest of the money borrowed by the Loan Offices to 6 pr ct which I think will procure the money.

You see I have wrote a long scrawl containg but little intelligence—however it is such as I have to communicate—I wish it better for your sake. One advantage I expect to receive (as you promise to be punctual in making returns) that as you reside at the seat of intelligence your answers will be much more interesting and convey to me more important news than it is possible for me to communicate to you. I am with great esteem & respect your friend and most obt humble servt.   J. Bartlett

p.s. Exeter 29th To my great surprise both Walker and King have resigned nor can they be prevailed on to retract, so that I am as much at a loss who will be sent as ever.[3] I hope to be able next week to inform you what is done farther—as the House will rise I expect the last of the week it must be settled before they rise. Give my regards to Col. Thornton. I am ut supra.   J.B.

TR (DLC: Force Transcripts).

1. Stark's resignation was received on 22 March. On 1 April the General Court voted that Joseph Cilley replace Stark and Theophilus Dame replace Poor. When Dame declined the next day, the legislature appointed Nathan Hale. *NHSP*, 8:518, 527–29.

2. The legislature met from 12 March to 12 April. *NHSP*, 8:503.

3. Neither Timothy Walker, Jr., nor George King attended Congress. Nathaniel Folsom and George Frost received appointments on 1 April. *NHSP*, 8:528.

TO WILLIAM WHIPPLE

My Dear Sir,   Exeter March [April] 5th 1777[1]

I have not had the pleasure of a line from you since yours of the 22d of February hope you will not forget to write me every week or fortnight at farthest.

I have but just time to inform you that the Court have appointed Genl. Folsom & George Frost Esq.[2] our Delegates for Congress to relieve you and your Colleague. Frost has accepted & the General will not refuse. One of them I expect will set out in about a fortnight, or 3 weeks to relieve one of you and the other in about 5 or 6 weeks after to relieve the other. We have lately had several pieces of news not very agreeable —the affair at Peekskill and the account of about 25 of our men killed and taken at Lake George by the Indians are among them.

Col. Cilly[3] is appointed to the command of Stark's Regt. and Col. Hale[4] to the command of Poor's. About 300 men marched yesterday from Exeter to Ti-- well armed with the French Arms. The Court continues setting. I have nothing new to write. Give my regards to Col.

Thornton and don't forget to write as often as possible. I am with great respect your sincere friend and humble servant.   Josiah Bartlett

TR (DLC: Force Transcripts).

1. JB intended to write April. See Whipple's letter of 23 April.

2. George Frost (1720–1796) of Durham served as a delegate until April 1779. *NEHGR*, 104:245.

3. Joseph Cilley (1734–1799), an attorney of Nottingham, received the appointment on 1 April. He later was promoted to major general of the militia, held a seat in the state senate, and served as a justice of the peace for Rockingham County. *NHSP*, 8:527. Cilley's manuscript returns for the 1st N.H. Regiment, 1778–1780, are in NhHi.

4. Nathan Hale (1743–1780), a merchant of Rindge, was appointed on 2 April. He had served in regiments of the militia and regular army. He was taken prisoner in July 1777 and died while under guard at New Utrecht on Long Island. Stearns, *Rindge*, 148–56; Heitman, *Historical Register*, 267.

FROM WILLIAM WHIPPLE

My Dear Sir,   Philadelphia 7th Apl 1777

Your favor of the 15th Ulto came to hand Yesterday. I hope Mr: Bettens arrival will hasten the recruiting service, its high time the Troops were in the field. For Heavens sake hurry them on, tho' I hope they will all have march'd before this reaches you. Genl: Gates sets out to day to take the Command of the Northern Army.[1]

One of the Lottery managers is gone Eastward & I hope has Tickets enough to satisfy the thirst for Gaming for I shod be exceeding sorry to hear our state had set up a Lottery.

I find Gov. Wentworths letter has made no great impression on your mind nor can it on any one that knows him. In my last I gave you the state of matters in Europe so far as I could collect them from the latest and Best accounts from thence, by which there is very little probability, of Britain geting such an army from Russia &c. as he tels of.

The Southern States are at least as firm as ever. N. Carolina has form'd their Government & Chosen Karswell, Govr, Maryland has also form'd a Govt: & placed Tho. Johnson in the Chair,[2] who has pass'd a Campaign in Jersey, and its said is now as firm as a Rock. The opposition to Govt: here daily declines & they now go on tolerably well. N. York I expect will give an Infinity of trouble, a long letter was laid this morning before Congress from that Convention respecting the N. Hampshire Grants, a deputation is also arriv'd from the Green Mountain Boys, but their matters are not yet laid before Congress. I sho'd not much care if the Devil had them all.

What advantage could have arisen from a compliance with Genl: Lee's Request?[3] Genl Howe certainly wod not agree to the conference unless he Expected to reap some advantage by it. He surely wod not permit an interview that cod possibly opperate to his disadvantage. If he has powers to treat with America as Independent States, the door is always open for him, we know very well he has no new powers, nor nothing to offer but Pardon or submission. At the same time that we cod receive no possible Benefit by complying with the Request, the Enemy wod profit much by it. A Packet wod be immediately despatch'd, & all the Courts in Europe amus'd with our negociations & the strongest assurances given that peace wod soon take place in America. This was the use made of the Conference last faul by which means the stores that are now arriving, have been delay'd at least 4 months. The incidious designs were so very evident that there was not a single advocate for the measure.

By intelligence receiv'd by deserters & others the Enemy seem to be prepereing to put themselves in motion, which way they will bend their course is a matter of great speculation. Some suppose this City is their object others think they will make a decent on the Eastern shore of Virginia & Maryland while others are of opinion that they will persue their original plan up Hudsons River. For my own part I think they are very much puzels for if they divide the small force they have ruin awaits them.

I am very glad I am like to be reliev'd & hope it will be by the Gentn you mention since you are determin'd not to spend another Summer in Phila. I hope they will be here by the middle of may.

Please to present my Respects to all Friends & be assured you have the best wishes of Your very affectn Friend & Humle Sert.   Wm: Whipple

RC (NhD).

1. Congress appointed Gates to the command on 25 March. *JCC*, 7:202.

2. Richard Caswell (1729–1789) was a delegate to the Continental Congress, 1774–1776, and governor of North Carolina, 1776–1780. Thomas Johnson (1732–1819), a delegate from Maryland, served as governor of his state from March 1777 to November 1779.

3. Although Whipple does not mention enclosing Gen. Charles Lee's letter to John Hancock of 4 Feb. 1777, a copy of it, in Whipple's hand, exists with this letter to JB in NhD. Lee requested that two or three congressmen come to New York to confer with Gen. Sir William Howe in regard to peace terms. Lee had been Howe's prisoner since December.

TO WILLIAM WHIPPLE

My Dear Sir,   Kingstown April 21st 1777

Your's of the 1st inst[1] by Capt. Wentworth is come to hand and am very glad to be informed of the favorable accounts rec'd from Europe and thank you for communicating them to me. I have for some time been very sensible of the difficulties and dangers from such a flood of paper Bills and believe we shall lay on a pretty considerable tax the present year; the Legislature seem sensible of the necessity of it and in order to its being laid equally have ordered a new proportion to be made among the several towns this Spring. We have lately discovered a most diabolical scheme to ruin the paper currency by counterfeiting it—vast quantities of the Massachusetts Bills and ours that are now passing are counterfeit and so neatly done that it is extremely difficult to discover the difference. We are but newly acquainted with the scheme and have not made all the discoveries we hoped for, but by what appears at present, it is a Tory plan and one of the most infernal that was ever hatched—there are great numbers of people bound together by the most solemn oaths and imprecations to stand by each other and to destroy the persons who betray them; besides ruining the paper currency it seems their design is, this Spring to spread the small pox through the country—R. Fowle, Benjn. Whiting and some others[2] in the State are certainly concerned and we have reason to think most of the Tories in New England are in the plan. Last Thursday by agreement Massachusetts and this State seized on a considerable number who are now confined—hope we shall make further discoveries and defeat the plan—no trouble, pains, or danger will be spared for that purpose.

In my last I informed you of the appointment of General Folsom and George Frost to be delegates to relieve you. Folsom contrary to all expectation has declined accepting; Frost told me he expected to set out sometime this week, so he may possibly be with you before you receive this. The Court has adjourned to the 4th of June and none can be appointed to relieve you till then—I suppose Col. Thornton will return on Frost's arrival. The raising the army for three years is (as I always expected) attended with extreme difficulties but we are exerting every nerve to surmount them. I hope there is three quarters of them raised, and near two thirds of them marched for Ti - -. We want to raise men for our own defence and for the assistance of Rhode Island, but dare not for fear of putting a full stop to raising the Continental regiments, for nobody will enlist for 3 years, if he has an opportunity to engage for one only.

Since you have raised the interest, I believe the Loan Office goes on here pretty well. Col. Gilman who is the Commissioner lately told me he wanted to send for more certificates. I believe he lately answered an order for fifty thousand dollars drawn on him by your President; however, he has or will soon inform the Board of Treasury of the state of his office.

Since so much money has been found to be counterfeit people begin to be scrupulous of the Continental Bills, and are looking out for marks, but by reason we have no standard of the former emissions we are not able to detect them, if there are any, and I have some reason to suspect there are some and that they came from New York. I wish you would procure proof sheets of every emission, and send them forward to be kept in the Treasury of this State for that purpose agreeable to a former order of Congress: this I formerly mentioned in one of my former letters, but know not whether you have rec'd it; it would be a good opportunity to send it by Col. Thornton when he returns.

If you know what was the business, General Lee wanted to communicate to Congress when he requested some members to be sent to him, please to inform me if proper.

We seem to have many difficulties to encounter both from our open and secret enemies within and without who are meditating our destruction by fraud and deceit as well as open violence; however I trust that by the assistance of that power who loves justice and hates iniquity and oppression, the United States will rise superior to all their Machiavillian plots and schemes and will be soon happy and prosperous, blessed with peace, health and plenty. That you and I may live to see that happy day is the sincere wish of him who is with great esteem and respect your very affectionate and humble servant.   Josiah Bartlett

April 22d. I have just rec'd the good news of the arrival of another French ship, the particulars you will receive as soon or sooner than this.   J.B.

TR (DLC: Force Transcripts).

1. Not found.

2. Robert Luist Fowle (d. 1802) published the *New Hampshire Gazette* in partnership with his uncle Daniel Fowle from 1764 until he removed to Exeter in 1773. Robert Fowle was suspected of counterfeiting bills of credit which he printed for the state and was arrested on 15 April 1777. He turned state's evidence while out on bail, escaped and fled first to Ticonderoga and then to Canada. He joined former Gov. John Wentworth's Volunteers in New York, and in December 1781 sailed to England. He received a pension from the British government to compensate for the loss of property confiscated by New Hampshire. After the war Fowle returned to Exeter. Bell, *Exeter*, 301–03; NHSP, 8:545, 558–59, 668; N.H. *Laws*, 4:177–80, 191–93; N.H. Loyalists Transcripts, 2:657–703. The warrant for Fowle's arrest is in Misc. MSS., 17A-11, NhHi.

Benjamin Whiting (d. 1779) was sheriff of Hillsborough County when accused of being a Loyalist by the county congress in 1775. His case was dismissed by the state for insufficient evidence. Suspected of passing counterfeit money in April 1777, he fled from New Hampshire and served as lieutenant in Gov. Wentworth's Volunteers until his death on Long Island. He was proscribed and his estate confiscated by New Hampshire. N.H. Loyalists Transcripts, 5:2536–53; NEHGR, 9:306; NHSP, 8:82, 156, 546; N.H. *Laws*, 4:177–80, 191–93. The "others" included Joshua Atherton, Jonathan Clark, Silas Hedges, John and Stephen Holland, Josiah Moody, Richard Cutts Shannon, John Shephard, John Shephard, Jr., Leonard Whiting, Obadiah Williams, and John Wilkins, all arrested in April of 1777. Warrants for their arrests are included on MJB 1152–53, 1155, 1161–64, and at the end of roll 2.

FROM WILLIAM WHIPPLE

My Dear Sir   Philadelphia 23d Apl 1777

Your two favors one of 26th march & the other 5th *march* which I suppose shod be *april* came to hand Yesterday. I find You have hard work to Persuade gentn to serve their Country, what can be the meaning of this? Do Gentn still think it Hazardous to appear in a Charecter that will render them obnoxious to the British Tyrant & his infernal Tools? Or are they afraid their Private interest will suffer? The day Perhaps is not far off when some of those Gentn: who now are so loath to step forth, will be making interest for a seat in Congress, they may be gratified for what I care, and let those who are now Laboring in the vineyard enjoy the Blessings of Domestic Happiness, with the Pleasing Reflections, that will result from a Consciousness of having lent their aid when their Country most wanted it—however it seems you have at last found two Gentn: who will come, & I wish they may set out as soon as possible. Col: Thornton intends to leave this place in about ten days & I wish to follow him before the weather is too warm.

The last accot: from Our Commissioners wase under the 6th Febry. They then had not heard of our successes in Jersey but I imagine our dispatches must have reach'd them soon after.[1]

The accots then Circulating all over Europe were such as were most agreeable to the British Court and really stager'd some of Our Friends but notwithstanding this our Commisrs: had establish'd a Bank in France, & one of them had set out for Spain[2] another was to go in a short time for Holland. There did not appear to be the least probability of Britains geting any assistance from Russia the most they expected to reinfore their Army in America with is 10,000 but the Court of France say they cannot send near that number. There is every appearance of a general war in Europe & it is my opinion that Hostilities are commenc'd by this time. The Opposition to the Measures of administration in England increases, which will help to Confound their Councils,—we daily Expect to have more perticular accots. Our Commissrs say they did not chuse to write so perticularly by Merchant ships as there had been some instances of carelessness in masters that had been taken who suffer'd the letters to fall into the Enemies hands.

Our army is daily increasing and by the accots receiv'd by Spies & deserters that of the Enemy is daily weakening so that I think our prospects are tolerably good. I shall write you more fully in a few days in the mean time beg leave to assure you that I am very Sincerely Yours.

Wm: Whipple

RC (NhD).

1. The letter of 6 February from Commissioners Benjamin Franklin, Silas Deane, and Arthur Lee is printed in Wharton, *Diplomatic Correspondence*, 2:261–65. The commissioners did not learn of the battles in New Jersey until late March. See Franklin to Lee, 21 March 1777, ibid., 296.

2. Arthur Lee.

TO JONATHAN CHASE[1]

State of New Hampr } In Committee of Safety

May 1st. 1777

Whereas it has been represented that many Towns in this State notwithstanding their unwearied endeavors and offers of large Bounties have not yet been able to procure their full quotas of Men for the Continental Service—Therefore at this critical season to the end that the Men to compleat the Battalions may immediately March—The Committee are of Opinion that such delinquent Towns may fill up their number at present with Men inlisted for eight Months, or a Year as they see fit provided they will be careful to provide others to take their places when the times are out of those Men they now send. No Continental or State Bounty can be advanced to any but such as inlist for the War or three Years as the Votes of Congress and the General Court of this State forbid it. The travel Money will be paid when they pass Muster.

This resolve was passed at the desire of several Towns.

Josiah Bartlett Chairn[2]

P.S. Coll. Chase. The Enemies Army is moving on all quarters—for Heavens sake! for your Countrys sake! & for your own sake! exert your self in getting your Men & sending them forward without a Moments loss of time.   J: Bartlett

RC (N). In clerk's hand; signed by JB.

1. Jonathan Chase (1732–1800) of Cornish had held command of the territorial regiment since August 1776. He was made a brigadier general on President Langdon's staff in 1788. Child, *Cornish*, 1:287–89; *NHSP*, 7:584. See also Cornish Bicentennial Commission, *Gen-*

eral Jonathan Chase: His Papers.

2. The resolve was passed by the Committee of Safety on 1 May. JB acted as chairman of the Committee when Meshech Weare was unable to attend. Bouton, "Committee of Safety," 93; *NHSP*, 8:536.

TO SEVERAL MILITIA COLONELS[1]

State of New Hampshire.   In Committee of Safety
Sir,   May 3d. 1777

By Repeated expresses we are Assured our Enemies are moving on all Quarters, and unless Sudden Reinforcements are Thrown into Ticonderoga, that Important Post will be lost, and all your part of the Country laid open to the Merciless Rage of our Vindictive Enemies. The Supineness, and Careless Temper that has but too much appeared thro' the Country of late will be our Ruin unless Imediate Exertions be made to save our Country.

The Massachusetts have ordered for the Militia in the County of Berkshire to March to Albany, and 1500 of Hampshire to Ticonderoga. I Entreat you by all thats Sacred to raise as many of your Militia as possible and March them to Ticonderoga, & Reflect a Moment on Such a Scene as this. Supose your House in Flames, your wife, your Daughters Ravished your Sons, your Neighbours Weltering in their Blood, and the appearance of a few Moments bringing you to the same Fate. Consider these things I say, tell them to your Militia, and Surely you may tell them with the greatest Probability unless they, together with the Country in General awake from the Sleep they are now in. Yet if the Country will now Exert themselves like men of Spirit & Resolution, I firmly believe, that God who has hitherto saved the Americans, will now Assist their Endeavours and a few Struggles more fix their Liberties on a Solid Basis.

The Strongest Assurances are Received from France that few or no Troops will arrive this year to Reinforce our Enemies. Almost all Europe our Friends & preparing to Assist us. Shall we then remain Idle and Suffer that diminished Army which we kept from getting so Little ground last year to proceed with Rapidity this. By order of the Committee I am your H. St.   Josiah Bartlett Chairn

P.S. Inclosed I send you a Resolve[2] passed for filling up the Continental army for 8 months—passed before the late News yet desire you would proceed therein so as to be in the best manner you can.

RC (Nh-Ar). In clerk's hand; signed by JB. Docketed: "Copy of orders to Several Colonels on Connecticut River May 1777."

1. As JB noted in his letter to Jeremiah   Powell, also of 3 May, addressees were

colonels of Cheshire County: Enoch Hale of Rindge, Jonathan Chase of Cornish, Samuel Ashley of Winchester, and Benjamin Bellows of Walpole. Notice probably went also to Col. Israel Morey of Orford in Grafton County.

2. Enclosure not found.

TO JEREMIAH POWELL[1]

State of }   In Committee of Safety
New Hampr }   May 3d. 1777

Yours of the first Inst was received last Evening by the Express. Orders are going off this Morning to the Several Cols. of the Militia in the County of Cheshire to march Imediately with all the Militia that can possibly be Spared to Ticonderoga. Efforts are making to fill up with speed our Continental Battallions, for Eight Months, or one year, which Method we had Adopted before the Receipt of your Resolution. I am Sorry to say that a great degree of Backwardness in engaging in the Army (Especially for as long as Three years) appears in this State. But I hope the Manoeves of the Enemy will now Rouse our Country from the Lethargy which has so much Seized it of late. Be Assured that this Committee (in recess of the General Court) will exert every thing in their power for the weal of their Country. In behalf of the Committee I am Sir with great Regard your very Huml. Sevt.   Josiah Bartlett Chairn.

RC (Nh-Ar). In clerk's hand; signed by JB.

   1. Powell was president of the Massachusetts Council.

TO WILLIAM WHIPPLE

My Dear Sir,   Kingstown May 9th 1777

By this time I expect Mr. Frost is with you and has informed you of the situation of our affairs when he left us. We have since made considerable discoveries of the designs of the Tories—large quantities of the Bills of this State, Massachusetts, Connecticut, Rhode Island, and of the Continent are counterfeited and passed among us. Gold and silver we have certain proof is also counterfeited by these infernal vermin, so that there is at present a great stagnation of the currency and I fear least a total stop will soon take place. Many circumstances concur to make us think, we shall soon be attacked by the British Troops, and that numbers from among ourselves will join them and that they have for some time been preparing for that purpose stores of provisions &c. to a considerable amount, purchased by counterfeit money. The spirit of the people is much abated and we find the greatest difficulty to fill the Continental regiments, though no cost nor pains have been spared to effect it. We have now ordered the remainder to fill those battalions to be raised for 8 months, or a year and others to be sent to supply their places before their times are out. We have ordered a view of arms of the Militia and alarm lists through the State, and it appears not more than half of them are well armed, if so many, owing to so many of our best arms being sent off from time to time with the men into the armies, very few of which have been returned—lead and flints not to be procured, and though large quantities have arrived at Portsmouth for the use of the Continent, yet we can procure none without an order of Congress. In this situation of our affairs, and as the general good of all the States is the wish and design of the Congress, I would earnestly entreat you to apply to that body for the loan of a few of the brass field pieces for our protection, and if it can be done that some of the small arms, lead and flints may be left in some safe place in this State to be used here in case of an attack. I would also desire that care may be taken that our troops in the service of the Continent may have a proper share of the clothing procured by Congress, as it is impossible for us to clothe them with any thing besides shoes, stockings hats and perhaps some other small articles. Col. Langdon and many others have desired me to write you on this business and I expect the Committee of Safety will write you by the next post on the same subject as they have the matter much at heart.[1] We have taken up a considerable number of persons on suspicion of their being concerned in counterfeiting the Bills of credit and several are committed to gaol: several others, against whom we have positive proof of their being concerned in that black business have absconded and I suppose gone off to the enemy. Col. Holland against whom we have clear proof has escaped out of gaol and notwithstanding our outmost vigilance has I fear got to the enemy.[2]

The designs of our enemies to destroy our military stores has induced the Committee to propose to Col. Langdon immediately to remove the Continental stores from Portsmouth;[3] the powder belonging to this State is now removing from Exeter—Such large quantities so near the sea will be a great temptation to the enemy to attempt their destruction and the destruction of the town, by a sudden attack, as we have no doubt of their being acquainted with the circumstances and by means of their shipping can soon and easily send a number of men for that purpose, if nothing more.

My dear friend, things here at this time appear very dark and gloomy, but you may depend on it, that we shall do all in our power to extricate our affairs from their present difficulties, and past experience of relief in such difficulties makes me still hope that Providence will work out our deliverance and that we shall still see good days according to the days wherein we have seen evil, which is the ardent wish of him who is with great esteem your affectionate friend and humble servt.   Josiah Bartlett

TR (DLC: Force Transcripts).

1. The letter was written on 10 May. *NHSP,* 8:561–62.

2. Stephen Holland (born in Ireland c. 1733) served as an officer in the British army, retired in 1762, and settled in Londonderry, N.H. He became prominent as a merchant, tavern keeper, public official, and colonel in the militia. He operated secretly as a Loyalist and was finally arrested for counterfeiting in April 1777. He escaped, was recaptured in Boston, and was returned to Exeter on 11 June. In May 1778 he was convicted of high treason. He escaped again, joined the Prince of Wales American Volunteers in Rhode Island, and after the war returned to Ireland where he was living in 1797. He was recompensed by the British gov-

ernment for the loss of his large land holdings confiscated by New Hampshire. Scott, "Colonel Stephen Holland," 15–27; N.H. Loyalists Transcripts, 2:777–989; *NHSP*, 8:507–08, 546, 582, 675–77, 703,

732. See also *Laws of N.H.*, 4:177–80, 191–93.

3. Dated 3 May, the letter to Langdon is printed in *NHSP*, 8:553–54.

FROM WILLIAM WHIPPLE

My Dear Sir   Philadelphia, 19 May 1777

My last was by Mr: Champney since which I have not had the Pleasure of any of Yours. Mr. Frost arriv'd the 15th inst by his Credentials I find I am superceeded, he tells me that was not the intention of the Court.[1] I also find by Your letters that it was there wish that I might tarry some time after Mr. Frosts arrival which I shall do, if I can with propriety, tho I wish to be on my way home before the weather is uncomfortably warm.

A ship arriv'd a few days ago from Nants. She brings letters of the 20th march but no dispatches of very great importance, those are expected by a Packet which was to sail in two or three days. Perhaps she is already arriv'd, at some distant port. This ship is landing her Cargo at Cinnapuckcen[2] several of Enemies ships being still, in Delaware Bay. Her cargo consists of Arms & Cloathing. The *Reprisal* has carried into France five Prizes since the two she took on her passage from hence one of them a Packet from Falmouth for Lisbon. Capt. Weeks writes, he is cleaning his ship at Orient & has wrote to the Commissioners for leave to come home so he may be soon expected.

By a letter from Dr: Lee dated at Burgos in spain (he being on his way to Madrid) large Quantities of Cloathing are prepareing in that Kingdom for this Country. Some are already sent to the Havanna this is done without application. He also says the King of Portugal is dead & that a large body of Spainish Troops are marching to the Frontiers of Portugal.[3]

I shall set out in about a fortnight perhaps I may write you, once more before I leave this. If any thing happens worth Communicating I certainly shall,—in the mean time I am very sincerely Yours   Wm: Whipple Mr: Frost desires his Compliments.

RC (N).

1. Frost's credentials are printed in *JCC*, 7:365.

2. Kenepuchen, south of Delaware Bay, in the Cedar Islands off the Maryland coast. Nebenzahl and Higginbotham, *Atlas*, 15.

3. Arthur Lee (1740–1792) was a Vir-

ginia delegate to Congress, 1781–1784. In 1776 Congress appointed him one of its commissioners to France with Franklin and Deane. Lee's letter of 8 March is printed in Wharton, *Diplomatic Correspondence*, 2:280.

FROM WILLIAM WHIPPLE

My Dear Sir,   Philadelphia 28th May 1777

Your favor of the 9th inst came to hand Yesterday, I am extreamly sorry you shod be under the necessaty of filling up the Regiments with eight & twelve months men as it appears to me there will always be a difficulty in replacing them. I can conceive of no reason for an abatement in the spirits of the People unless it is that those miscreants who are aiming at the distruction of their Country, are not treated with that just severity which their Crimes deserve. What purpose will it answer to fill the Goals? These Villains have all friends, & while they remain with you 'tho they are in Goal they will be raising their parties, whereas if they are under Ground or out of the Country they will soon be forgot. The necessaty of the Case will surely justify the most severe & decicive measures. I am always for persueing lenitive measures, when such will answer the purpose, but experience has tought us others must be adopted.

I am fully sencible of the necessaty you are under of a supply of Military stores & shall do every thing in My power to obtain them.

I wish to know what Concurrent circomstances leeds you to apprehend a speedy attackt. The Enemy certainly have no troops to spare from N. York, nor can they have a considerable reinforcement from Europe, very soon, however there is no doubt its best to be prepared at all points for which purpose the most Vigorous exertions shod be use'd. It will by no means do to dispond because a few scatering Clouds pass between us & the sun, proper Exertion will soon dispel them. We shod never suffer Gloomy reflections to incombra the path, but look forward to the Glorious prize, with a determination to obtain it, and all those difficulties that a Gloomy mind wod deem insupportable will be meer mushrooms, as we get over difficulties no doubt new one will start up, but Pacience, & Vigorous perseverance will surmount them all. I wish I had some good news to send you to Cheer you up, however I hope to bring you some shortly as I shall leave this so soon as I can get some necessary matters settle'd in Naval department which (to my Grief) is not on so respectable a footing as I coud wish.

Our army is daily increasing. There is a report that a Lieut Col Walcot was kill'd on the retreat of the Enemy from Denbury, & that Govr, alias Major Genl: *Tryon* who commanded that notable Expedition, is dead of the wounds he receiv'd there.[1]

I shod send you some new papers but have none by me & as the post hour is arriv'd have not time to send for any must therefore bid you Adieu after assur'g you that I am Sincerely Your Friend &c.

Wm: Whipple

RC (NhD).

1. British Col. William Tryon led 2,000 troops and Loyalists on a raid in Connecticut from Westport through Danbury to Ridgefield on 25–27 April destroying army stores and burning houses. Peckham, *Toll of Independence*, 33. Whipple's American reference is probably to Oliver Wolcott (1726–1797), one of Connecticut's delegates to Congress who was also a leader of the Connecticut militia. Cash, "Oliver Wolcott," 43–69. Both Tryon and Wolcott lived to fight again.

FROM GEORGE FROST

Dear Sir   Philadelphia July 7th 1777

I Rec'd your favour of the 14th. Ulto.[1] Inclos'g a coppy of a letter from our Cols. at Ticonda. and laid it before Congress who gave orders for a Supploy of Cloathing to be forwarded with all dispatch to Ticonderoga for the trups there;[2] I should have backed the aforesaid letter by laying yours also before congress but could not without dishonour to my selfe not to say with som Reflection on My Worthy frind Col. Bartlet (as the Manner of his addres was to Col. Whipple and in his absence to Geo: Frost thereby treeting me as a spare Topmast) for I trust it was not out of any disregard.

You say the State is about to make Application to Congress for Money to redeam our paper bills. I wish I could give you any incoragement of Succes. The Treasure here is so low that it takes all the money for the Armey. I wrote you in my last Col. Whipple Rec'd an Order on the loan office for 100,000 Dollars. If you are in Cash at Sd. office perhaps you may git a further Order on it. I am sorry for the distress you seem to be in on Account of our Money being Counterfited, I hope the State wont be wanting in Duty to themselves in not haveing a proper Spirit to Inflict a proper punishment on those (without Distintion) who are the Authers of so heanious a crime of Countifiting our money. I shall give you som parragrts. of a letter from a gentleman of Distintion in Spain (You'l see it was not Intended it Should be made public) dated March 18th. 1777.[3] As for an Immediate declaration in your favour they say this is not the moment & for reasons which if I might venture to Commit them on this paper I think you woud deem satisfactory. The same reason render an explicet acknoligement of your Independency & a treaty of Alliance With You inadmissible at present but am desired to assure you of their taking a sincere & Zealous part in the Establishment of your liberties which they will promote in every way consistant with their own Situation. I cannot help thinking that the postponing a treaty is happy for us since our present situation would raise demands and perhaps enforce Concessions of which we might sorely Repent hereafter. I am sensible that in Consequence we shall be obliged to make greater exertions & to serch Deeper for resources within our selves but this must in the end be highly benificial to a young People. It was in this manner the Roman Republic was so deeply rooted and then the liberty which are hardly earned will be highly prized & long preserved. I mentioned in my last that the Germans intended to be sent the latter end of this month thro Holland were to Consist of seven thousand recruits but from the Best Accounts I can git they will neither be so forward nor so numerous as was intended, to retard them the more I have proposed to the Commissioners at paris to Remostrate with the States General against granting them a passage which is to expediate their embarkation, & I have written to Holland to have the Account of the Captivity of their Countrymen and the refusel to Exchange them, settle a Cartel distributed among the troops in german before they Embark. If they are not very beasts indeed this will rouse a spirit of Indignation against their Buyers & sellers. You'l please to give my Best Respects to the Honoble. Counsel and Remain Sr. Your Most Obt. Humble Servt.   Geo: Frost

RC (PHi). Addressed by Frost "To the Honobl. Josiah Bartlet Esqr."

1. Not found.

2. No letter from the colonels at Ticonderoga to New Hampshire of this general date has been found; but a letter from the Committee of Safety to the congressional delegation on 10 May 1777 emphasized the need for clothing and supplies at the fort. Congress ordered clothing and arms for the northern department on 5 July. *NHSP*, 8:561–62; *JCC*, 8:535.

3. Arthur Lee to the Committee of Secret Correspondence, 18 Mar. 1777, in Wharton, *Diplomatic Correspondence*, 2:292–96.

FROM GEORGE FROST

Dear Sir   Philadelphia July 12th. 1777

In my last I wrote you some parragrafts of a letter from Spain. The post went so sudden I had not time to finish it and would now continu. them.

We are Assured by Both France and Spain that such a Disposition of their fleets & forces will be made as ought to perswade England that she cannot Sustain the war against you as she has planned. Your Wisdom will direct you how far to trust to those assurances or their expected consequences when our stake is so presious that the most ardent & Unremitting exertions cannot be too great, not that I suspect the sincerity of those Assurances but the effects they are to produce.[1] From Germaney they have little more to hope to Raise Recrutes. To Russia alone they may apply if the Cloud that is rasing from Constantinople should blow over without which it is Impossable they should have any aid from thence, but if this should happen, it will be our endeavour & I hope we shall succead in rasing the Opposition of Other European powers to that measure. I mean to propose on my Return to Paris the sounding both the Emperour & the King of Prussia (to which Courts we (the Congress) have sent Commissioners to announce our Independency and Settle a treaty of frindship and Commerce)[2] on this subject. The one wishes to promote the port of Ostend the other of Einden & by those we may perhaps work them up to our wishes. It is upon this View of things that I found My hopes of the next Campaign being the last struggle of any Importtance the Enemy can make against us. The Dutch on whom Britian so much depend withold their money as far as they can find Spanish paper to rest it in. The degree of their alarm from France & Spain may be seen from the Embodying of the Militia & their Expences.[3] I belive their divisions at home are Apparent from the suspensions of the Habus Corpus Act which will proberly realize their apprehensions of Domistic troubles. The measure of their inequity is now full when they have put the liberty of every Subject in the power of the most merciless & Unprincipled Tyrent that every disgraced a throne.[4] The state of Europe is such as to render it morally certain that a war in Europe will relive you from extraordinary exertions befor a year has passed away, for you'l see the desine of this letter from our frind in Spain was not to be maid public but I have taken the liberty to send such part as I thought would be agreeable to you and the rest of my good frinds at Court to know. After all that the Courts of France & Spain have said our security and welfare is within our selves with the Blessing of our Good and Gracious God on the means he has put in our power which I trust you and every lover of his Country will exert to the Utmost of his power and if we support our Independency this year the Day will be our owne.

How has quited the Jerseys and is gone to New York but where he is going is Uncertain (he found it Impractable to penatrate througe the Jerseys to Phila.). Some says to New England others suppose he is going Up the North River or to the Southern States. On the whole it is soposed he dont know what to do himselfe at present[5] and it is said by some that came out from New York lately that the first in Command of the Hessions is much disgusted and has gone home. I fear things dont go well with our Armey at Ticonderoga, but we are in good spirits here. Am Sir Your Most Obt. Humble Sert.   Geo: Frost

p.s. After you and my good frinds at Court (to whom please to present my sincear Regards) have read the papers please to let my Frind Esqr. Thomson have 'm that my frinds at Durham may see them.

RC (NhD).

1. At this point Frost paraphrases the next half paragraph, picking up his direct quoting at "To Russia alone . . . ." Wharton, *Diplomatic Correspondence*, 2:294.

2. The parenthetical comments are Frost's.

3. At this point Frost begins to paraphrase again.

4. This ends Frost's attention to the letter.

5. The British plan for 1777 called for Howe to recapture Philadelphia in time to sail back up the Hudson or North River to join with Burgoyne's army moving south from Lake Champlain. Howe was delayed in securing Philadelphia, and Burgoyne was defeated at Saratoga in October. See Wallace, *Appeal to Arms*, 134–57.

FROM NATHANIEL FOLSOM

Sir   Philadelphia agust 5th: 1777

I arrived here in good Health the 20th: of July. On my joining the Congress I found them worried with Petitions from a great Number of French Gentlemen for Commissions to Serve in our army and Continnue to Plague us to this day.

Saterday Mr. Bass[1] Came to Congress from Portsmouth and brought Letters from ouer agents in france up to the 26th. of may, by which we are informd that ouer Effaires bair a feavourable aspect all over Europe, that a fund is Estabelishing in france and Spaine Suffishant to Support the Cradit & Pay the intrest of ouer Continental money—and that if we Can hold ouer owne this year a war will most Sertainly take Place before the Comemencement of annother: and we aire further informd by them that it is the opinion of the ministers of the Last menshoned Corts that they Can be at Present of more Servise to us then thay Could be if thay wase to Declare war against Briton. The Loss of Ticonderoga hes given grate unEasyness: Generall Schyler and Sant Caire aire orderd to head

Qurters in order for an inquirey into thaire Conduckt:[2] the other Generals that Sat in Councel arre to Stay at thaire Departments till General Washington thinks thay Can be Recald without hurting the Service: General Gates is orderd to take the Comemand in the northen Department. Congress have Past a Resolve that Newhampshier, Massachusetts, Conneticut, new jersey and new york & Pennsylvania Raise & march as many of the militia to Serve in the northen Department till the fifteenth of november as General Gates Shall think Suffishent for the Defence of that Part of the Cuntrey.[3] You will See by the Paper Inclosed that the Enemys fleet have been hovering abought the Capes of the Delleware amounteing to 228 Saile Till fryday Last & have Since Disapeaird. It is Prity generely thought thay aire bound up the north River or to Rhode island: General Washington is incampt at Garmantown with abought foure Thousend troops but I believe will in a Day or two march towards the north River. I am with Respect your Humle. Servent.

Nathel: Folsom

RC (NhD). Franked: "On Publick Service."

1. Probably Joseph Bass (1744–1822), an upholsterer of Portsmouth, who served as a military paymaster during the war and later was a customs officer. Foss, *Freemasonry*, 388; *NHSP*, 14, 339. The letters may have arrived in a French ship which was in Portsmouth Harbor for the fourth of July celebration. *N.H. Gazette*, 12 July 1777.

2. Arthur St. Clair (1736–1818) was a major general who had been sent to defend Fort Ticonderoga. This recall resulted in a court martial which exonerated him. St. Clair later served as governor of the Northwest Territory. *JCC*, 8:590, 596.

3. The resolution is printed in *JCC*, 8:614.

FROM GEORGE FROST

Dear Sir,   Philadelphia Augst. 19th. 1777

I Rec'd yours of the 25th Ulto.[1] (it came to hand after the post was gone). You say the Appointment of Genl. Schoyler to the Command at the Northward gave great uneasiness to New Hampshire and I'l add to many other States also and that very Justly. The Deligate from the Eastern States told Congress that the People in those States had no confidence in Sd. Genl., but the Influence of said man and the Deligates of New York (Dewane & Duer[2] in my opinion is no better then their Genl.) had more wait in Congress at that time then all the Deligates from the Eastern States and obtained a majority of one Vote in his favour. They now see the Ill Consequence of that Appointmt and have order'd Genl. Gates to Supersead him in that Command and sopose he is at that post if well before this time. Schoyler and St. Clear is order'd to head quarters in order for tryerl. I hope you'l furnish the Court of Inquir'y with all the proofs Relating to the Situation that post was in and in what manner the troops was furnished. Schoyler & St. Clear writes to Congress and Says most of the troops was old men, Boys, & negroes and unfit for garison duty and their Armes very bad & but one baginet to ten men, that many

of the Officers mutinous and a disgrace to an Armey that he (Schoyler) wants power from Congress to suspend them. Thanks be to praise they are suspended themselves. I Rejoice to here that our brave Countrimen are marching with Spirit & Viger to opose their Enemi—may the God of Armies go forth with'm. Our Commissioners at the Courts of France and Spain have Established a loan for the payment of the Interest that is or may arrise on our money Issued by congress which we may draw from time to time on Sd. Commissrs at Paris at the Rate of five livers money of France for every Dollar which will we trust give our Loan office certificates as great if not greater Credit in Europe then the Bank notes of Great Britain. As they carrey larger Interest and Incorage every monied man with us to put his money in sd. office as they may be here to Receive the Interest in Dollars as aforesaid and that there Courts have particuler strong Reasons for keeping out of the war as long as they can, besides the general one that on both sides the nation attacking losses the Claim which when attacked it has for aid from its Allies and we have these advantages in their keeping out of the War that they are better able to afford us private assistance that by holding them selves in Rediness to invade Britain they keep more of her forces at home and that they leave to our Armed Vessels the Whole harvest of Prizes made upon her Commerce. The Commisioners have purchas'd 80,000 muskets a number of pistols &c. at second hand that if but one half arives safe they will be cheep. All Europ is for us. The Articles of Confederation and the Seperate Constiutions of the several States are published in france which affords abundance of Speculation to the Politicions of Europ and it is a very general opinion that if we succeed in establishing our liberties we shall as soon as peace is restored receive an immence addition of numbers and welth from Europe. Those who love liberty give general joy and our Cause is Esteamed the cause of all mankind. Glorious is it for the Mericans to be called by providence to this post of Honour, Cursed and Detested will every one be that deserts or betrays it. The Congress is about setling the mode for drawing bills for the Interest of our money and it should be made publick that we now have a fund in france for the payment of the Interest on our bills of Credit which knolidge coming to the public will conduce them to put their money in to the loan Office thereby we sopose may have a sufficient to carrey on the war without emiting any more bills. Am with much Esteam Sr. your most Obt. Sert.   Geo: Frost
P.S. Inclosed you have a Copey of a letter from Genl. Lincoln to Genl. Schoyler.[3]

RC (MeHi: The John S. H. Fogg Autograph Collection). Franked.
    1. Not found.
    2. James Duane (1733–1797) and William Duer (1747–1799).
    3. The enclosure, Gen. Benjamin Lincoln to Gen. Philip Schuyler, 8 Aug. 1777, is in NhD. The letter, written from Bennington, deals with Gen. John Stark's attitude. Stark had just arrived at the army camp and was voicing contempt of Congress for having passed over his promotion in preferment of others. Schuyler forwarded the letter to Congress. This enclosure is included on the microfilm of the Papers of Josiah Bartlett at Dartmouth College in its proper chronological place.

THE COMMITTEE OF SAFETY TO JB AND NATHANIEL PEABODY[1]

In Committee of Safety

Gent.   augt. the 23. 1777

You are Appointed, and Desired Immediately to Repair to Bennington, and do Every thing in your power to assist the Sick and wounded men of General Starks Brigade of Melitia of this State, and to Consult with and advise General Stark with Respect to any further operations, and to procure an Exact Account of the late action of Genl. Starks with the Brittish Troops.[2] And you are Empowered to do and Transact any matters and things with Respect to Said Brigade that you may think necessary.

Draft (Nh-Ar). Docketed: "Orders to Col. Josiah Bartlett & Col. Nathl. Peabody. Aug. 23, 1777."

1. Nathaniel Peabody (1741–1823), a physician of Atkinson, was commissioned a justice of the peace in 1771 and later served as a member of the Committee of Safety and a delegate to the Continental Congress, 1779–1780. He was adjutant general of the militia and major general, 1793–1798.

2. American forces under Gens. John Stark and Seth Warner defeated British troops of Cols. Frederick Baum and Heinrich von Breymann in two engagements near Bennington, Vt., on 16 August. Wal-

lace, *Appeal to Arms*, 156–57. Stark described the events in a letter to the Committee of Safety, 18 August, which is printed in *NHSP*, 8:670–71. He sent it express by Josiah Crosby, who probably reached Exeter on the twenty-third, in time for the Committee to order JB and Peabody to Bennington. The order was the last recorded business of the Committee on that day. On the twenty-fifth the Committee voted to reimburse Crosby for bringing the letter. Bouton, "Committee of Safety," 113.

FROM GEORGE FROST

Dear Sir,   Philadelphia Sept. 8th 1777

I Rec'd your favr. wrote in Kingstown Augst.[1] wherein you say you were just returned from Springfield and the result of the Commissioners from the several States laid before Congress which we have Rec'd but have not as yet acted on it.[2] The Avarice Venality and disipation prevaling among all Ranks here in this quarter and Increasing more & more in the Eastern States I fear it will be Impractable to addop the measures Recomended by your Committee, altho I think with you that it is Very alarming and fear it will be attended with Very ill Consequences. As to the support of the Credit of our money I can conceive of but two ways— first our Commisons. in France & Spain has procured for us a loan to pay the Interest of all the money we shall borrow by our loan office certificates at the rate of five livers France for every Dollar Interest which we sopose will give great incorragement to the monied men to lend the United States. The Other is that all the States go Immediately into large Taxation by which means we shall be able to pay our Armey &c. but If those two Measures should fail and we are obliged to Emit more money (which I hope that wont be the case) it will sink it very low indeed. As to the Northern affair, they have been Very Alarming but at present through the Goodness of God I trust they are at present very favourable. You'l see more perticuler by the news papers and that Congress has adopted measures for Inquirng in that Affair. We Could have wished Borgoyne had pushed his armey lower down then he has that we might have marched an Armey in his Rear as well to attack him in the front, we hope however that our brave Starke will be able to perform the former wile Genl. Gates attacks their front.

Genl. Howes armey is some weare nigh Caskeen bridge, and Genl. Washington head quarters at Wilmington whose Advance parties has had several scermishes (as they are Called). According to fortain of war sometimes they gitt the better and sometimes we have the better of them. We Dayli Expect to here of a General Battle. I have not seen the map you mentiond but am Informed by Good Judges its a pore one. I'l make further Inqy. and see it. If I think it will answer your Expectation will send it you by first good oppetunity (we have been greatly perplex'd with a number of french officers. Some Came over under Extrodary Contracts by Mr. Deane and others to seek Rank & Service in our Armey. No less then five or six Majr. Generals, Briga. Genls. Cols. &c. &c. to have plas'd them all we must have superseeded nigh half of our Officers. Trust we shall send'm for the greater part Back to France). I should be glad to be informed wether our Troops has Rec'd their clowes as we are Informed Clothing at the Northen Armey is scarce. You'l see by the papers Inclos'd what Situation we are in with regard to some princpel quakers &c. I fear we shall meet with a great Deale of trouble with them. Am Sr. with great Esteam Your most Obt. Humble Sert.

Geo: Frost

RC (MiU-C). Franked.

1. Not found.

2. Between 30 July and 6 August JB and Nathaniel Peabody attended a conference at Springfield concerning the calling in of paper currency and prevention of depreciation and counterfeiting. Massachusetts, Rhode Island, Connecticut, and New York also sent delegates. *NHSP*, 8:629–30, 690–91. The convention resolved to recommend to their state legislatures that they repeal price fixing laws and redeem outstanding fiat money. Upton, *Revolutionary New Hampshire*, 160.

TO ABRAHAM FRENCH

State of }   Kingstown Sept 10th 1777
Newhampshire }   To Capt. Abraham French

Pursuant to orders from the Committe of Safety & from Congress for a part of our militia to march for the Defence of the western frontiers &c.—you are Required to Draft or otherwise to Engage the one Sixth part of the men in your Company not already in the war including the alarm list that are fit to bear arms and able to march & perform their Duty to march to Bennington and to be under the Command of General Starks or Such other General officer as shall have the Command thereabout to Serve until the last Day of November next unless sooner Discharged. The officers to have the Same pay as those in the Continental army and the soldiers fifteen Dollars pr month and one month's pay advanced.

Every man to Equip himself with a good gun and Cartouch Box & a Bayonet if possible.

You are to make Return of your having so Done as soon as possible.
Josiah Bartlett Colonel

The Commission officers of Kingstown East Kingstown Hawke & Sandown & Newtown are to meet at the widow Abbots in Kingstown friday next at 4 of the Clock afternoon to agree on officers to take the Command of one Company. Please to notify as many of them as you have oppertunity.

Septembr 16th 1777[1]

Pursuant to the within I have Drafted one Sixth part of my Company all of whom have passed muster Except John Calfe Junr who has not appeard to pass muster.   Abraham French Capt.

MS (NhHi).
   1. On reverse of JB's order, written by JB, signed by French. The order, issued by the Committee of Safety on 6 September   ber, went also to Cols. Wentworth, Evans, Moulton, Gilman, Bartlett, and McClary. Bouton, "Committee of Safety," 115.

TO WILLIAM WHIPPLE

My Dear Sir   Kingstown September 22nd 1777

The Time for which our militia under General Starks was raised being nearly Expired, the Committe of Safety have raised one Sixth part of the Six lower Regiments and they are now on their March to reinforce the army in the Grants, and they are Directed to put themselves under the Command of the Continental General nearest Bennington, unless Gen: Starks will tarry & take the Command of them, and in that case Gen: Starks is Directed to be under the Command of Such Continental Genl. By the Conversation I had with him at Benington and letters he has sent the State I fear he will not tarry. I am much Surprized to hear the uneasiness Expressd by the Congress at the orders given him, by this state; I think it must certainly be owing to their not Knowing our Situation at that time. The Enemy appeared to be moving down to our frontiers and no men to oppose them but the militia & Col: Warners Regiment not Exceeding 150 men, and it was impossible to raise the militia to be under the Command of Genls in whom they had no Confidence, and who might immediately Call them to the Southward & leave their wives & families a prey to the Enemy; and had Genl Starks gone to Stillwater agreable to orders; there would have been none to oppose Col. Baum in Carrying Genl. Burgoines orders into Execution: No State wishes more Earnestly to Keep up the union than Newhampshire, but surely Every State has a right to raise their militia for their own Defence against the Common Enemy and to put them under such Command as they shall think proper without giving Just cause of uneasiness to the Congress. As to the State giving such orders to Genl Starks, because he had not the rank he thought himself entitled to, (which seems to be intimated) I Can assure you is without foundation and I believe never Entered the mind of any of the Committe of Safety who gave the orders: however I hope by this time the Congress are Convinced of the upright intentions of the State and the propriety of their Conduct.

Capt. Thornton of Thornton in this State was taken prisoner at Bennington in the Enemys lines and is now in Exeter Gaol.[1]

I have no news to write you; by the accounts from the Northward & Southward we are hourly in Expectation of receiving very important news: I pray God it may be good & Such as will serve to relieve us from many of our Difficulties.

The Genearal Court is now Seting at Portsmouth and have under Consideration the report of the Committe at Springfield which I believe will be agreed to. I hope the Congress will take some measures to keep up the Credit of the Currency or otherways I fear it will soon loose all Credit to the utter ruin of the best of Causes.

FC (NhD). Docketed by JB: "Bartlett to Whipple Copy, Septr 22nd 1777."

1. Captain Matthew Thornton of Thornton was a nephew of Dr. Matthew Thornton of Londonderry, member of the Continental Congress. Captain Thornton was a member of the Provincial Congress in 1775, then served under Col. Timothy Bedel in the Canada expedition of 1776. Thornton defected to the British and on 16 Aug. 1777 was captured within the breastworks during the Battle of Bennington and imprisoned at Exeter. He petitioned for liberty in December 1777 and again in December 1778; was tried for treason in 1779; and was acquitted. He then left for New Brunswick. See a sketch of the Thornton family in NHHS *Proceedings*, 3:97–107; NHSP, 7:455; 8:700–01. His petition of 1777 and trial papers are at NhHi, his petition of 1778 at Nh-Ar.

TO LEVI BARTLETT

My Dear Son   Kingstown Septembr 22nd 1777

I Returned from Bennington the 10th Inst: after a pretty fatigueing Jorney: after looking after the Sick & wounded at Bennington and viewing the ground where the Battle was, I went to Hudsons River to See the army under General Gates at Half moon, and saw Peter Abbot, Mr. Samuel Sweat & most of the men that went from this Town.[1]

I am pretty well at this time as are your Mamma & Sisters & Brothers, who all remember their Love to you. I hope you are well & that you take proper care to improve the advantage you now enjoy to procure learning: Tell Jacob Gale[2] his father Sets out this Day to Join the army at Bennington to tarry till the last of November if wanting. I would have you write up as soon as you have oppertunity.

I am now tending the General Court at Portsmouth which I Expect will last some weeks.[3] I am your affectionate father.   Josiah Bartlett

It has been something sickly among Children several have Died, but it is now [illegible] healthy: Your mamma sends you a Boot Buckle by Lemuel Knight the bearer.

Since writing the aforegoing I Recd yours of the 18th.[4] I fear I shall not be able to procure you a Virgil before vacation however I shall try: you need not buy any paper for me as I am not at present in want.

I am just going to Portsmouth. If your Mamma can, she will send you an ink pot, if she does not you must try to buy one. I have this moment heard our army has gained a great victory over the Enemy at the northward, but have not heard the particulars or whither it is to be Depended on, if it is true you will hear more of it before you Receive this letter. Yours ut supra.   J. B:

September 23d We are all well to Day—your father has Just Set out for Portsmouth. Coll. Gale & Cap. Currier Calld hear on their way to Bennington this morning, Esqr. Bachelder Set out yesterday. Give my Compliments to miss Judith Noyes. I am your Loving Sister.   Mary Bartlett

RC (The Philip H. and A. S. W. Rosenbach Foundation). The manuscript is mottled. The postscript dated 23 September is in Polly's hand.

1. According to a letter of 3 September from General Gates to the President of Congress, JB and Nathaniel Peabody left army headquarters on the fourth. PCC, Item 154, p. 250. The two physicians settled their accounts for the journey with the Committee of Safety on the twelfth. Bouton, "Committee of Safety," 117.

2. Jacob Gale (b. 1764) was a son of

Jacob Gale of East Kingston who was lieutenant colonel of JB's regiment. Gale, *Gale Family*, 205; NHSP, 14:475, 478.

3. This session of the General Court ran from 17 to 27 September. NHSP, 8:681–99. This marked the first time the constitutional General Court met in Portsmouth.

4. Not found.

FROM GEORGE FROST

Sir   York Town Jany 31st. 1778

I wrote to the Honoble Presedent on the 24th Instent and Inclosed him a warrant of the 23d. from the Treasurer, on Esqr. Gilman for 50,000 Dollars. Hope it will come safe to hand & be duly hond. but if there should not be money in the Office to pay the same, you'l be kind enough to Inform me as soon as possable, that we may contrive some other way for a supploy. Should have been glad to have done it before, but could not perswade the Treasure board to joine in a Report sooner. A Committe of Congress (Genl. Folsom is one) is at Camp to setle measures for the next Campaign hope it will be a more successful one here than the last.[1] What was the cause, or to whom to lay the Charge I know not that the Enemy should make such parade in and out Philada., when our Continental Armey was nigh double to that of the Enemy. It is said that a Council of Officers in the Armey has proposed to Genl. Washington to nominate 6 Leut. Genls. said Leut. Genls. to nominate 12 Majr. Genls. and the Majr. Genls. to nominate 54 Briga. Genls. It is also said that the said Officers propose that all the solders shall take an oath of fidelity to their Officers. It is also proposed that all Officers in the Armey to be setled on half pay that may not be in actual service on Conclusion of the War, and that all Officer's Widows shall have a pension dureing their widowhood. We have some Advocates in Congress for the pension. Your prudence will sergest how far to Communicate this Intelligence. Shoud be glad to have your and our best friend's Oppinon on the matter. Inclosed You have sundry Resolves of Congress which came from the press after I had sealed mine to the hond. Presedent. We have had lately arrived in North Carolina, 129 bales of Woolings & linnens for the use of the Continent or States which came from France by the way of the West Indies. Have no public letters the Vessel (under French Coullers) was borded by an English friget was obliged to distroy her English papers for fear of being taken. A paragraft of a letter from a Merchant in London in August to a Genl Officer in New York, writes that both public & privet Credit is Greatly sunk, that Bankruptures are frequent, and that they would be more so if they were not supported by the bank, that subscriptions in the new loan which proposes 5 prct to the lenders goes on slowly and that the Dutch Refuse to subscribe anything, that bills are already sold at considerable discount 2 & ⅜ prct and that everything there depended on the present Campaign being decisive. As they are disapointed in this I hope they will be disapointed in all their future plans is the Hartey prayer of your most Obt. humble Sert.   Geo. Frost

RC (NN: Emmet Collection, No. 459).

1. Folsom, Francis Dana, Joseph Reed, John Harvie and Robert Morris were appointed on 10 and 12 January to visit army headquarters on behalf of Congress. *JCC*, 10:39–41. The committee's mission is discussed in Burnett, *Continental Congress*, 298–316.

From Frost's letters it is evident that JB had not ceased to correspond with Congress, though his letters for late 1777 and early 1778 are missing. As a member of the Council, JB was occupied by the General Court meeting in Exeter from 11 February to 14 March 1778, and on the last date the Court appointed him and John Wentworth, Jr., as delegates to Congress. NHSP, 8:766–86. In addition, JB's responsibilities continued at home, as a justice on the Court of Common Pleas in Rockingham County, as a physician, and as commander of the 7th militia regiment.

TO GEORGE FROST AND NATHANIEL FOLSOM

Gentlemen   Exeter March 14th: 1778

It was expected that delegates would have gone from hence to relieve you the first of this month having been appointed in Febry last, but several unforeseen difficulties have Arisen that prevented it hitherto.[1]

The subscriber, and John Wentworth Junr. Esqr. of Dover are now Appointed, and have Signified their Acceptance to the Court and expect to begin their Journey by the Middle of April, which is as soon as we can possibly get ready.[2]

Inclosed, is a vote of the General Assembly Empowering and desireing you to Tarry at Congress until other Delegates arrive, which I make no doubt but you will comply with.[3]

By order of the Court I transmit you a Resolve of our Legislative body for agreeing to the Articles of Confederation perpetual union &c.[4] These Articles were printed & dispersed throughout the State and most of the representatives were Instructed thereon by their Constituents. When it was taken under Consideration Several Articles were opposed perticularly the eighth, yet after much time spent thereon the whole was agreed to and the Delegates ordered to ratify it in behalf of the State, as you will see by the sd Resolve, yet, I am to desire you if that Matter should be taken up by Congress while you tarry, not to let the Tenor of your Instructions be known until you find that the Other States agree thereto. The Confederation is lookt upon by this State as a Matter of so much Importance, and the Difficulties naturally Attending such an Union by so many States Differing in so many Circumstances rather induced the Council & Assembly to comply therewith, than an Opinion of the perfectness of the Articles agreed to by Congress—Provided that the value of all Lands & Buildings on the Continent is as Equitable a mode to proportion the Taxes or Quota of Tax that each State pays as any other. Yet we are of opinion very great obstacles are in the way of ascertaining the true Value of such Lands & Bildings throughout the States. If any of the other States should move for an Alteration in sd Eighth Article it is Expected you will join in the Motion, but if the Other States are all agreed, you will produce the Resolve & agree likewise. By order of the Council and Assemble I am &c.   J. Bartlet. President p. T.

FC (Nh-Ar: Weare Papers). In a hand other than JB's.

1. Apparently JB meant that the election had been prevented, for there is no record of elections prior to 10 March when John Wentworth, Jr., and William Whipple were elected. *NHSP*, 8:780.

2. JB was elected on the twelfth. On the thirteenth he asked to be excused, but the House negatived his plea and confirmed his selection on the fourteenth. Ibid., 782–83.

3. Enclosure missing, but see the vote in ibid., 781.

4. The resolve of 5 March is printed in ibid., 778. JB had held the chair, and had undoubtedly directed the proceedings, while the General Court met as a committee of the whole to discuss the Articles on 24 February. Ibid., 773–74.

The Articles of Confederation were facing opposition in Congress owing to the existence of such problems as representation, the basis of taxation, and the disposition of western lands claimed by several states. These issues are discussed in Jensen, *Articles*, especially pages 140–60.

TO MARY BARTLETT

My Dear   York Town May the 21st 1778

I arrived here this morning by the favor of Providence in good health, and hope this will find you & the rest of the family so. I wrote you a line the 17th[1] from Bethlehem in this State which was the first oppertunity I had to write to you. I found great Difficulty on the road procuring hay &c. for our horses. Except that, & a great Cold I had for near a week soon after I set out, we have had a pretty agreable Jorney: Saturday the 9th I Crossed Connecticut River at Springfield, the 13th I Crossed Hudsons River at fish Kills, Sunday 17th I Crossed Deleware River at Eastown, and this morning Crossed the Susquehannah River, about a mile & half wide, at 11 miles Distance from this place. Mr. Wentworth & his waiter were innoculated at fish Kills and rode with us till last tuesday when begining to have the Simptoms, I left them at Reading about 46 miles from this place. I am in hopes they will have the Small pox favorable & will Come here in a few days. I find this Town much Crowded, am in hopes I shall procure good Lodgings in a few Days, at present put up at a Tavern. Our Publick affairs wear a very favorable aspect. General Washington thinks the Brittish army is about to quit Philadelphia. If so tis likely the Congress will adjourn there or to some other place nearer the Sea. Charles Chace[2] is well. Remember me to my Children & all friends. Hope I shall hear that Rhoda is better & all things go on well with you.

The Lottery is Drawing, but can get no account at present of your tickets, the highest prize was Drawn to the United States being a ticket unsold & taken to the risk of the Publick. Next week tis probable I can inform you of your luck.

22nd I am now well and Sincerely yours &c.

Josiah Bartlett

24th I Send this by the post and least it should fail I shall write in a few Days by a man who is going to Boston.   J: B:

RC (NhHi).

1. Not found. The date that JB left Kingston has not been determined. The last regular entry in his daybook for this period is 4 May, so that, according to the contents of this letter, he left between 4 and 8 May. "Daybook," NhHi, MJB 5037. He presented his credentials to Congress on 21 May. *JCC*, 11:519–20.

2. Charles Chace (1755–1842) was a hatter in Kingston and accompanied JB to Congress as a personal aide, as had Gideon George in 1775. Boardman, *Robert Calef*, 56.

TO MESHECH WEARE

Hond Sir   York Town May the 27th 1778

I arrived here the 21st Inst: in the morning. Mr. Wentworth & his waiter were Innoculated at Fish Kills the 13th, and rode with me to Reading about 46 miles from this place, where by the advice of Genl Gates, they tarried till they should get thro' the Disorder: Mr. Wentworth began to have the Symptoms about 20 miles before he arrived there: I have not heard from him since I left them the 19th.

I think it my Duty to inform you that the President of Congress thinks himself neglected in not receiving answers to his letters. He Desired to know of me whither our *Governor* had Receivd any letter from him for Eight months past: that he had Recd no answer to any of his for that time, tho he had taken particular Care to Send Duplicates as often as he trusted them to the Common posts. I Endeavoured to Excuse the matter as well as I Could, by telling him that some of his letters were little more

than Covers to acts & Resolves of Congress which were supposed to require no other answer than a Compliance with their Directions: That I
Believed some answers had been sent since that time, which by reason of
the irregularity of the post were not come to hand. He said that Every
letter that he wrote by order of Congress, Deserved an answer, at least
so far as to let it be Known that it was received; that the way to Know
whither any letter miscarried, was to keep up a constant Correspondence
and note the last letter sent; that it would be but a small matter on the
Receipt of Every letter to inform of its being Receivd, if nothing more;
and when any thing was Done in Consequence of any order of Congress
to let it be known &c. &c. &c.

The Confederacy is not yet Ratified, North Carolina being unrepresented & two or three of the other States not having impowered their
Delegates to Confirm it: It is the opinion here that it will be Universally
agreed to.

I have nothing new to inform you of, more than you will see in the
Public papers. I am with the greatest Respect Sir your most obediant
Humble Servant   Josiah Bartlett

RC (MHi).

FROM SAMUEL PHILBRICK   Dated at Kingstown may the 29th
Sir   1778
I take this opertunity to write to you: hoping that you had as pleasant
a Jorney as the Length of way would admit of: and that you are now in a
Good State of helth; and will always be Directed by unering wisdom to
Act and Do that which will be for Your Greatest Honour: & for the
Peace & wellfare of this State in Perticular: and for the Peace & well be-
ing of the whole in General. I would Inform Your Honour that the Gen-
eral Court mett agreeable to the adjournment on the 20th Instant: but
Could not Proceed to buisness untill fryday afternoon the members of
Counsel not attending—on fryday afternoon the Honble. Counsel and
House Confer'd togather on the nessesary business and made Report, to
Choose one Person to Send to the Contnental Army to Recive and Deliver
the Suplys Sent from this State by the Board of War; and to account for
the Same; also to Chuse one Person to go on with the Continental accounts: (and Mr. Noah Emery[1] was Choosen to Recive the Suplys for
the Army but he Refused upon which the Court voted to Leave the
appointment of both Said offices to the Committe of Safty)[2] the Committe on further Conferance Reported to Choose a Committe of Safty
and to adjourn on Saturday at one a Clock to the Second wensday in
august: and to Do no more buizness than Could be Compleated by that
time—accordingly thay Choose a Committe of Safety Passed Some Small
Rools and Some accounts &c.—& also passed an act in addition to the
act to Enable the Constables or Colectors to Colect nonresident Proprietors taxes: (the Conduct of the Constables & Colectors were Greatly

Complaned of) and for a Remedy in this act the Constables or Colectors are to make out a Compleat List of all the nonresident's tax (the town and State tax) in Seperate Colums: Certifyed by the Selectment & Send it to John Taylor Gilman[3] who is appinted to Recive Said List: and he is to Aadvertize the Same three weeks Sucsessively in the Hamps. Paper that if the Sd nonresidents do not Pay their tax to him (or the Constable or Colector of Said town) within Eight weeks with five pr Sent for his trouble in Reciving: & also the Cost of the Advertizeing: then So much of their Land will be advertized to be Sold as will Pay Said tax and all Charges—(and the Said John Taylor Gilman or his Sucsesor in ofice at the End of Said Eight weeks is to Return the List he Recived of Said Constables or Colector Certifying who has Paid their tax to him and who has not Paid: with the money that he Recived that belongs to Said town agreeable to Said List: and the State Tax he is to Pay into the Hands of the Treasurer & take his Recipt)—and the Constables or Colectors of the Several towns are to Advertize the Delinquant nonresident's Lands three weeks in one of the Hampshire Papers and also Post it up in the town where the Lands Lay: and in the two next adjacent towns: that So much of their Lands will be Sold at the End of Said three weeks as will Pay Said tax and all Charges—and theay are to Sell & to Give deeds according to the former act &c. thus I have Given you Some account of what Passed at the Session of the Court: and we adjourned accordingly to the twelveth of august.

I would Inform you that one Great Reason of our adjourning So Soon the Small pox has Broke out at one of the Kimbals aboute half a mile South of the Road that Leads to Exeter and the town has Given Leave to Inoculate & it is Said that there is upwards of two Hundred Inoculated in three or four Houses in that neighbourhood among which is Coll N: Gilman Coll Hobart & wife Mr. Odiorne Dea'n Brooks Coll S: Folsom &c. &c. I have nothing More that Comes to my mind only the Court Gave out an order by way of Resolve to the Sherif of this County to put the Select men of Londonderry in Possession of Coll Holand's Lands & tenement: (his wife and accomplices having bid Defiance to the Court the Laws or any authority in this State) further Saying the Coll would Soon Return with more Honour then Ever and Set his foot on the neck of his Enemys &c. Miss Bartlett and the Rest of your famely are well we have not had any Person Broke out with the Small Pox Sence You Left the Town. The Season has been very Dry untill with in five or Six Days. We have been favored with Rain by Showers and now we have the old may Storms Returned as has been Common in other years. I hope You will bare with me in writing So much I being unable to do much worke and in a Poore State of helth but I hope a mending. I Shall Imbrace Every opertunity to write to your Honour; and Give Some Short Scetch of what Passes in the State according to my Knoledge. This from Your Verry Humble Servant. Samuel Philbrick
p:s: Pray Give my Greatest Compliments to Esq. Wintworth.

RC (NhD).

1. Noah Emery (1725–1788) was a merchant and attorney of Exeter who later in 1778 became and remained a member and clerk of the General Court. Emery served also as clerk of court for Rockingham County. Stevens, *Noah Emery.*

2. Joseph Leigh of Portsmouth was appointed receiver of supplies in place of Emery on 2 June. Leigh became a shipmaster after the Revolution. Bouton, "Committee of Safety," 153; Brewster, *Rambles,* 2nd ser., 150.

3. John Taylor Gilman (1753–1828) of Exeter was assisting his father, Nicholas Gilman, who was state treasurer. John served in the House of Representatives, 1779–1781; as a delegate to the Continental Congress, 1782–1783; as state treasurer after his father's death in 1783; and as governor, 1794–1805 and 1813–1816. In later years he was also a treasurer and trustee of Phillips Exeter Academy. Gilman, *Searches,* 225–28; Gilman is not mentioned by name in the act. *Laws of N.H.,* 4:163–64.

TO JOHN LANGDON

My Dear Sir,   York Town June 1st 1778

Before you receive this, I suppose you will have rec'd the Order of Congress for going on with your ship, which is to be changed to a two decker and to carry 56 guns—viz 28 of 24 lbs & 28 of 18 lbs.[1]

Mr. Wentworth was innoculated at Fishkill rode to Reading where he remained a week, is now here & attended Congress the day before yesterday.

As to news I have nothing material to write you—the substance of the treaty with France you know. The Ship which arrived from Spain only brought a duplicate of that Treaty. Spain will not accede to the treaty till the arrival of her West India fleet, unless drove to it by England. It is then expected she will act as openly as France. Our Ambassadors inform us Spain and Portugal have settled their disputes & Portugal has acceded to the family compact. The extract of a letter in the enclosed paper dated February 28th 1778 is from Mr. Lee one of our Commissioners.

The Common opinion in the army is that the enemy are about to leave Philadelphia, while some suspect it to be only a political manoeuvre to draw our army into a disadvantageous situation and to attack them. The Tories are stealing out of the City and taking the Oaths to the State. We have no further account of the famous British Commissioners who are to restore peace to America. I believe before this time they are satisfied they will effect nothing unless they enlarge the powers given by their late act of Parliament. One of our Ambassadors tells us the British Ministry publicly gave out that they have sent half a million of guineas to pave the way to a reconcilliation and that Lord North informed Count Maurepas that he was sure of a majority of Congress. To such vile shifts are they drove to prevent foreign powers from assisting or acknowledging us: but all will be in vain. Give my best regards to General Whipple and remember me to all friends. I shall hope to hear from you as often as convenient. I am your friend and most obt Servant.   Josiah Bartlett

TR (DLC: Force Transcripts).

1. The ship was the *America,* originally planned as a seventy-four gun ship-of-the-line. Congress' order of 29 May was sent in a letter from the Marine Committee to Langdon on the thirtieth. *JCC,* 11:555; Paullin, *Out-Letters,* 1:248–49.

FROM WILLIAM WHIPPLE

My Dear Sir,   Portsmouth, 1st June, 1778

I hope this will find you safe arrived at York after an agreeable journey, or perhaps it may follow you to Philadelphia, for I cannot suppose the enemy will long be in possession of that city; we have a rumor that they are preparing to leave it: if that is the case I hope our army are in a condition at least to give them a kick, though I should be much better pleased to hear they were stopp'd with all their effects. That would be a grand stroke, but L fear there is not a sufficient spirit of enterprise in our army to make the attempt; however, I shall be satisfied if we can get entirely rid of the barbarians in the course of this campaign. I find they are making little incursions and attacking defenceless places in the neighborhood of Rhode Island, but these I take to be the last struggles of expiring tyranny—however, I could wish we had a sufficient body of soldiers there to prevent the ravages, which I doubt not would be the case, were it not for the infamous spirit of privateering that so generally pervades at this time. I understand that about one hundred and fifty men from this state have joined general Sullivan, not one hundred from Massachusetts, none from Connecticut—on the whole, he has about five hundred men with him, a grand army for a major general's command.[1]

Since I have mentioned privateering I must beg leave to observe something further on that subject. I wish some method could be adopted to abate the rage for that business, which appears to me the most baneful to society of any that ever a civilized people were engaged in. The officers that command these vessels are generally the most profligate fellows that are to be met with, and if by chance a man of fair moral character engages in the business, he very soon degenerates and falls into all the vices of his associates.

The passion for this business daily increases; there is no less than six privateers now in this port belonging to Massachusetts, besides three or four fitting out here; three have at least sailed from here this spring that came from other places to fill up their complement of men, and I have heard of great numbers that have sailed from the neighboring ports, besides those that have called here: in short the sea is swarming with these —I had almost said freebooters—indeed they are but little better. I am very apprehensive that unless some measure can be adopted to check the voracity of these people, they will exceedingly disgrace the American flag, and how this is to be done I know not, unless a total stop is put to the business. This I think ought to be done immediately, for besides preventing the mischief that will certainly happen if you do not stop them, I know of no way else to get your public ships manned; for give what encouragement you will, those who are concerned in privateering will find means to prevent men from engaging in the public service. Your ships of war must lay by the walls, or perhaps some of them may get half manned —if they do not go to sea in that conditions the officer is blamed, and if they do he is sure to be disgraced. Under these circumstances can it be expected that an officer of reputation would choose to serve the public? I heartily wish to see the American navy respectable, but I do not expect it until privateering is discouraged and the business of the navy put wholly into the hands of men whose private business does not militate with that of the public. I hope to hear from you soon, and as often as your leisure will admit of it.

I have no news to tell you: the convention meets next week at Concord.[2] I shall take care to inform you of what passes then; in the meantime wish to be informed of what is doing in the grand councils of America so far as may be consistently communicated. I should be glad to know the characters of any new members that have joined congress since I left it. I expect you will have to contend with British commissioners, and perhaps with British gold. If I could be as sure of the firmness of every individual as I am of some, I should be perfectly easy about negociations.

Please present my best respects to your colleague, also to Messrs. Lovell, Adams, Gerry, Ellery, colonel Lee, and Mr. Robert Morris, if he is with you, and accept for yourself the best wishes of your Very affectionate friend and faithful humble servant.   Wm: Whipple

Reprinted from *The American Pioneer*, 2 (1843), 20–21.

1. In March Sullivan was given command of the Continental troops in Rhode Island. *WGW*, 11:57–58; Whittemore, *John Sullivan*, 84.

2. In February the General Court had called for a convention to form a permanent plan of state government. Delegates elected in the spring met in Concord on

10 June 1778. The state papers list JB and Samuel Philbrick as delegates from Kingston. Perhaps JB had allowed himself to be elected before he decided to accept appointment to the Continental Congress. *NHSP*, 9:834–37, 852; Daniell, *Experiment*, 168–70.

FROM MARY BARTLETT

My Dear   Kingstown June 4th 1778

I have heard no news from you Since you Left us; I hope you will not forget to write to me, a few lines at Lest that I may know of your wellfare. I hope and trust you are in health and have had a Plesant Journey & have met with no Difficulty—we are all through mercy in a Comfortable State of health tho Some of us have bad Colds. Rhoda is better in health than when you left us. I have heard from Levi a few Days ago, he was well then. We have a long Cold N:E: Storm for ten Days past which is not over yet. It was Clear two nights and frosts which Did some Damage among Beans Pompion's and Corn But not So hard as to kill them all. A General time of health. A School with us but no preaching Mr. Thayer has been gone three weeks to his mother's.

An accident happened at andover Last tuesday. The Drying Powder house Blew up with three men in it which were all kill'd in an Instant.[1]

I hear the Enemy is Expected this way from Philadelphia. Major Philbrick is Choosen to Go to the Convention at Concord. No new with us—the times much as Usal. The Children all Remembers their Duty to you and wants to hear from you—I hope I Shall hear from you in a few Days. This is the fourth time I have wrote to you. From yours &c. &c.

Mary Bartlett

RC (NhHi). In Polly's hand.

1. The explosion in the mill of Samuel Phillips, Jr., killed three men and caused a brief suspension of operations. Fuess, *Andover,* 176.

TO MARY BARTLETT

My Dear   York Town June 7th 1778

Last wednesday the 3d Instant I Recd yours of the 16th of may am very glad to hear you are well & that Rhoda is rather better. I am in good health as is Charles Chace Mr. Wentworth & his man. We have procured Lodgings at a German House about a Quarter of a mile from the Court house where the Congress sets: his name is Andrew Hoffman. Their manner of Cooking their victuals is very Different from the English manner, tho they Do what they can to accomodate us; they understand but little English, just Enough to be understood.

I have wrote to you several times the last Dated the first Instant some of which I hope you have Recd before now.

Yesterday Congress Receivd letters from Lord Howe & Genl Clinton informing us that they were two of the Commissioners appointed by Parliament to Settle the Dispute with America.[1] But as it appears by the act of Parliament which they sent us they are not authorised to acknowledge our Independence I Suspect a peace will not soon take place Tho I believe that the fighting Business is Chiefly over. I have wrote Major Philbrick more fully about it.

I informed my Children in my last that they had not Drawn any of the large prizes in the lottery. I cannot now tell them whither they have Drawn any of the smaller prizes for I have not been able to get a sight of the list but make no Doubt I shall be able to Do it in my next.

I hope you & my family are Still in health & that affairs go on well. Remember me to Mr. Thurston Dr. Gale Mr. Thayer Capt. Calef & all friends. I am yours &c.   Josiah Bartlett

RC (NhHi).

1. The other commissioners were Frederick Howard (1748–1825) who had become the fifth Earl of Carlisle in 1758 and was treasurer of the household and member of the privy council; William Eden (1744–1814), an attorney, member of Parliament, and intimate friend of Howard; and George Johnstone (1730–1787) who had early distinguished himself in naval service, had served as governor of West Florida, 1763–1767, and was a member of Parliament. *DNB,* 28:14–17; 16:362–64; 30:75–77. For the story of Congress' reaction to the Carlisle Commission see Burnett, *Continental Congress,* 335–38, and Higginbotham, *War of Independence,* 240–41.

TO NATHANIEL FOLSOM

Dear Sir   York Town June 12th 1778

I arrived here the 21st ulto, & was obliged to put up at Stake's Tavern for several Days before I Could procure other Lodgings. I now put up at one Hoffmans on the west Side of the Bridge quite at the west end of the Town at a German House, where I am obliged to be a German in most Respects. We have been in hopes ever Since I arrived here that we should soon get back to Philadelphia, But the accounts from thence are so various & Contradictory and the arrival of the Brittish Commisrs At that place makes the Enemys Design of Removal Some what Problematical. If they mean to Evacuate the place, I Expect it will soon be Effected, as Genl Washington has Removed our army towards the City. The latter End of may Genl Clinton & Lord Howe sent the late famous acts of the Brittish Parliament to G. Washington and Requested leave to send out a person to him, which He Refused & informed them that if what they had to Communicate to him was what came under the military Department, He Desired it might be sent him in writing, but if it was of any other nature their applications ought to be made to Congress; the Begining of this month they sent the Same acts in a letter signed by Ld. Howe & G. Clinton Directed to the President of Congress Signifying their being authentick Copies & saying they wished they might have the Desired Effect. The Congress Directed the President to inform them that when the King of England was seriously inclined to put an end to the Cruel and unprovoked war he had waged against the United States they would readily Concur in all proper measures Consistent with the Rights of Independant Nations, the Intrest of their Constituents & the Sacred Regard they owed to Treaties. The 9th Instant Genl Clinton sent a letter to G. Washington informing him of the arrival of the Earl of Carlisle, Mr. Eden & Governor Johnstonce the Commisrs and Requesting him to grant passports to Dr. Ferguson their Secretary[1] to repair the next morning with letters to Congress; G. Washington Refused the passports till he Recd the order of Congress on that matter. The Congress have not yet Determined on it. I believe he will not be permitted to Come to Congress But G. Washington ordered to Receive the letters at the line & send them to us. A French Ship of 50 Guns is arrived at Virginia with Cloathing &c. &c.

The Congress have not yet Ratified the Confederation, two or 3 of the States not having Signified their assent. I Expect it will not be long before it will be Confirmed. The Indians & some Tories have Committed Depradations on the western parts of this State & virginia, measure are taking to Chastize them I hope Effectually. Give my sincere regards to the Council of Safety & accept the Same your self from him who is your sincere friend and Humble Servt.   Josiah Bartlett

RC (PHi).

1. Henry Hugh Ferguson (b. 1747) was the husband of Elizabeth Graeme Ferguson (1737–1801) of Philadelphia. Ferguson, a Scotchman, had gone to England and Scotland on business in 1775 and did not return until 1777. Washington refused to permit Ferguson to visit his wife's estate but allowed her to see him in his capacity as British commissary of prisoners. For Ferguson's role in the peace commission's proceedings his property was confiscated though Mrs. Ferguson was allowed to hold her property and died in Philadelphia.

FROM SAMUEL PHILBRICK

Dear Sir   Kingstown June 17th 1778

I have taken this opertunity of Giving You the Earlyest Information; of what the Convention of this State, have done Relitive to forming a Plan of Goverment and I Should be verry Glad if Your Honour would make Such Remarks on any or all the votes, as You in your Wisdom Shall think ought to be altered: and favour me with the Same before the Convention meets again to Receive the form or Plan of Goverment from the Committe.[1] We have nothing that is new worthy of notice turned up among us Sence You Left the State (more then what I have hinted in the other Letter and this). I Saw two of Your Daughters a day or two Past; and theay Informed me You were Safe arrived to Congress: and that You had not wrote anything that was Remarkable in Your Letter. We have many flying Reports amongst us at this time but accounts vary So much we no not what to beleve: Some Say that Philadelphia is Burnt by the Enemy: and others Report that the Commissioners are Come with full Authority to Settle a Peace with Amaraca: and that theay are willing to acknoledge us Independant: &c. but we Cannot beleve Either of the Said Reports: (the first we hope is not true)—and the Last wants Confermation.

Sir I hope You will over Look the many Impertinent hints & observations that I have made—and that these Lines will find You in a Good State of helth & Possesed of that (Firmness of Mind) with which You have Ever distinguished Your Self: doing Honour to this State; and Promoting the Peace and happiness of the whole United States. So no more at Presant but I Remain Your Most obedeant and Verry Humble Servant

Samuel Philbrick

RC (NhD). Noted with address: "from New Hampshire."

1. Philbrick enclosed his own two-page summary of the constitutional convention of 10 June (MS: NhD). It is reproduced in MJB 1355 and is printed in Colby, *Manual of the Constitution*, 78–79.

TO WILLIAM WHIPPLE

My Dear Sir,   York Town June 20th 1778

I congratulate you on our army's being in possession of Philadelphia.[1] We rec'd the intelligence this morning by express from General Washington; the particulars of which important event and the circumstances and movements of the armies in consequence, I expect you will receive before this reaches you, and I believe we shall soon take leave of this dirty place and remove Congress to some place where we may be better accomodated. I make no doubt you have heard of the arrival of his Brittanic Majesty's Commissioners, and of their letters being sent to Congress; I now enclose you a paper which will inform you of all the transactions of Congress relative to that affair which will I hope give full satisfaction to every honest American.

I have the pleasure to inform you that every member of Congress was firm and steady, never to make peace, but, on the principles of absolute

Independence. I am sorry that the answer was deferred some days on account of the zeal of some members for sealing the letters up and sending the letters back without reading, in consequence of some harsh expressions against the King of France; however it was overruled as you will see and a more proper method in my opinion taken. What will be their next steps, time only can discover. In the packet to Congress were enclosed a great number of letters to the separate members—some from Governor Johnstone to such of the members as he was acquainted with; and others from other persons in England who had any acquaintance with them. The enclosed from Robert Trail[2] came directed to you as a Delegate of Congress which was opened and I now enclose it to you.

As to Marine affairs, Congress are very sensible some very essential alterations are necessary and seem determined to attend to it, as soon as the Confederation and some other very important matters are finished. I wish I could inform you that I thought it would soon happen, but the multitude of business that is daily crowding upon us, and the time it sometimes takes to determine on some not very important matters makes me fear it will not take place so soon as I could wish. Besides the want of men in Congress acquainted sufficiently with Marine affairs is another great difficulty and causes that Committee to be filled with some persons like myself, unacquainted with the business they are ordered to superintend.

"I heartily wish (with you) to see the American Navy respectable, and hope it will be put wholly into the hands of men whose private business does not militate with the public;"[3] but I cannot be fully of your opinion that it would be for the public service to put an entire stop to privateering, as I think experience has shewn that privateers have done more towards distressing the trade of our enemies and furnishing these States with necessaries, than Continental ships of the same force, and that is in my opinion the greatest advantage we can at present expect from our Navy: for at this early period *we* cannot expect to have a Navy sufficient to cope with the British. However I am quite convinced that it might with proper management be in a much better situation than at present and should be happy to see it soon take place.[4]

The Congress is at this time pretty full. I know not whether you are acquainted with the President, Mr. Laurens: I think him a very sensible, judicious man, acquainted with the world and makes an excellant President.[5] Mr. Drayton, the Chief Judge of So. Carolina is a sensible judicious man, a good speaker, firmly attached to Independence and not given to the chicane common to lawyers. Mr. R. Morris from New York is an eternal speaker, and for artifice a *Duane* and for brass equal to any body I am acquainted with. Mr. Adams from Virginia is a member: he informs me that he was innoculated with you at Elizabeth Town and desires to be remembered to you.[6] On the whole I think we have a pretty good Congress and if we have nothing more to fear from British arms and policy than from their gold, I think you may make yourself perfectly easy as is your sincere friend & most obt. servt. J.B.

Mr. Wentworth desires to be remembered to you.

TR (DLC: Force Transcripts). Enclosures not found. The letter is from York, Pa., often written "York Town" by JB and other delegates, and not to be confused with York-town, Va.

1. British forces departed Philadelphia between 8 and 18 June and headed for New York City under the command of Gen. Sir Henry Clinton. American forces immediately moved into Philadelphia, the Congress followed later. Wallace, *Appeal to Arms*, 184.

2. Robert Traill had been a merchant and comptroller of customs at Portsmouth prior to the Revolution and had married a sister of William Whipple. He took sides as a Loyalist, was with former Governor Wentworth on Long Island in 1777, and was proscribed in November 1778. Brighton, *They Came to Fish*, 2:83; *NHSP*, 8:659; *Laws of N.H.*, 4:177–80.

3. JB was partly quoting, partly para-phrasing, a statement in Whipple's letter of 1 June.

4. For more on naval affairs see Morgan, *Maritime Dimensions*.

5. Henry Laurens of South Carolina had been elected president of Congress on 1 Nov. 1777.

6. William Henry Drayton served in Congress from March 1778 to August 1779; Thomas Adams, from April 1778 to April 1779.

FROM JOHN LANGDON
Dear Sir,

Portsmouth, New-Hampsre
June 20th. 1778

Your esteemed favour of the 1st Inst. I rec'd last Night inclosing your Letter, which I've forwarded, also the News paper, for which, I thank you. I have not received any Orders for going on with the Ship therefore they must have miscarried, if they were sent on. Should Orders come without a supply of money it will be impossible for me to carry them into execution. To order the Board at Boston to supply me with money will by no means be so well as for me to have it directly here, for if it goes to Boston, of course their own wants must be first supplied & if any left it will come to me, therefore if anything fails it must be at this Port for want of proper supplies. Give me but an equal chance here, and if the Shipping is not as soon dispatched & as well equip't from this place & with as little expence as any other Port then the fault will be here. I could wish that yards were once established, at the most proper places, thousands might be saved, in my Opinion.

I wrote you in my last Letter to desire the Marine Committee to forward on the amount of the several sums of money I've received of them, as I intend closing my Accots. with the Board at Boston. Pray see this done immediately if you please & that the Board at Boston have full Power to settle my Accots. with the Marine Committee.[1]

We have Just heard of the arrival of the Commissioners at New-York should this be true, please to make short work with them by their acceeding to our Independance, withdrawing their Fleets & Armies & then trade will take it's course; numbers of Cruisers are in our Bay, we have Just heard of the loss of the Ship *Portsmouth*. We met in Convention at Concord at the time appointed & after several Days Debate chose a Commee. to draw a Plan or form of Government, who are to meet at the same place the 7th: July for that purpose.[2]

The Legislative is to consist of two Branches, Assembly & Council, every hundred Families to send one Representative, those Towns under, to couple, the rest of the State in proportion, each Town to pay their Own; many other matters were concluded on, but as the whole will undergo a Revision it's not worth mentioning.

I've not time to give you the particular Arguments of Esquire G——s & some other *great* men as you must easily conceive of them. My kind Congratulations wait on Mr. Wentworth on his Recovery from the small Pox. I am verry Respectfully Your Obliged Friend & Hum. Serv.

John Langdon

RC (PPAmP: The Sol Feinstone Collection of the American Revolution).

1. The "Board at Boston" was the Navy Board of the Eastern Department, established by Congress in the spring of 1777 as an administrative arm of the Marine Committee. James Warren, William Vernon, and John Deshon served as the original set of commissioners of the board which had its headquarters in Bos-ton. See Fowler, *Rebels*, 74–77, and Mevers, "Congress," 85–94. A similar naval board had been set up previously for the Middle Department.

2. For names of other members of the committee see Philbrick's enclosure with 17 June 1778, MJB 1355.

TO MARY BARTLETT

My Dear   York Town June 21st 1778

I have Recd your letter of the 28th of may and it gives me great pleasure to hear you & the rest of the family are in a Comfortable State of health and that Rhoda gains Strength.

I am well & by the favor of Providence I have had my health Ever Since I arrived here hope it will be continued to us all. The weather and air here is Clearer & I believe more wholesome than at Philadelphia.

Last Thursday the 18th inst: our army took possession of Philadelphia, we had the account of it by Express from Genl Washington yesterday morning;[1] I Expect you will have the particulars before you Receive this more fully than I can at present inform you.

This Town is not large Enough to accomodate the multitude of people that have constantly Business with Congress. This lays us under great Difficulties and raises the price of Every thing to an Enormous heighth. Beside the Disagreeable manner in which these people Cook their victuals, and the Sluttish manner of washing our linnen in Cold water only, which has already almost ruined mine, makes me willing to quit this place, Tho I believe it to be a healthy place. To get rid of these & many other Difficulties and to be nearer the army which is Removed Northward, I Believe Congress will soon Remove to some other place, I Expect to the City of Philadelphia; and by the time this reaches you, it is probable we shall be packing up for that purpose.

The Brittish Commisrs have Sent letters with their proposals to Congress and we have given them our answer. All the transactions you will see in the inclosed paper: I think a very short time now, will Determine whither the Enemy will Remove their armies and make peace or whither they will try the fate of another Campain.

Remember my love to all my Children & send Levi word that I am well; I am glad to hear that our mens Business goes on well. The Weather here has been very seasonable, not over hot, & rather wet than Dry: I want to Know how hay is likely to be with us; how the English Corn is like to be; whither the worms Destroy the Indian Corn; how the flax is like to turn out &c. &c. Remember me to David Sanborn and tell him I feel pretty Easy about my farming affairs as long as I know he has the Care of it. Remember me to Mr. Thurston Dr. Gale Capt. Calef Mr. Thayer &c. &c. &c.

I have not failed to write to you as often as once a week since I Came to this place and shall Continue to write to you: Your letters Come pretty regularly to me & hope mine will Do the same to you. This letter will go in one to major Philbrick[2] by an Express Sent by the President to Exeter & sets off this day: I am yours. J. Bartlett
Tell Peter if he Behaves well he may Depend on my promise.

RC (NhHi).

1. Washington's letter of 20 June to Congress is printed in *WGW*, 12:97–98.

2. No letter from JB to Philbrick for this period has been found.

TO MARY BARTLETT

My Dear   York Town June 28th 1778

Yesterday Congress adjourned from this place to meet in Philadelphia on thursday the 2nd of July next: The President & many of the members are gone, and by tomorrow noon Scarcely any English person will be left in this Town, as the original Setlers here are German & talk that Language. I Expect to set out in a few Days so that the next letter you Receive from me will likely be Dated in Philadelphia; I have not had any letter from you Since yours Dated the 28th of May; hope you have Recd mine regularly as I have wrote you almost Every week, my last was the 21st Inst Enclosed in one to major Philbrick and went by Express. I am in health & have been as well Since I have been here as I am Commonly or rather better. I hope the air of Philadelphia will suit me as well, tho I had rather not have moved there Quite so soon, till the City had been more thoroughly Cleansed: Charles Chace is well. Mr. Wentworth is not well which will hinder me from going to Philadelphia for Some Days at least otherways I should set off to morrow morning.

The Enemy left the City the 18th and the last account we have of them, they were not half the way to Amboy & our army very near them, so that it seems probable a Battle will soon take place between the two armies:[1] God Grant it may prove Decisive in favor of America. As the armies are about 100 miles nearer you than I am, it is probable before you Receive this you will have later accounts from them than I Can send you. Many of the German Troops have Deserted from the Enemy Since they left Philadelphia.

We happened to have Sight of the Ecclipse of the sun last Wednesday; it was So Cloudy all Monday & Tuesday, & Wednesday till about 8 of the Clock in the morning that the Sun did not once appear, afterwards the Clouds broke so that we had a pretty good Sight of it. It was much the largest Ecclipse I Ever Saw, It was all Covered Except a very Small rim at the Nortwest, Smaller than the bright part of the moon when she first appears after the Change. The weather here now is very hot & have been so for 3 Days past.

June 29th   I am sorry to inform you Mr. Wentworth is very Sick with a fever & Billious vomiting and Purging, and has been Confined for above a week. He is *not* willing his friends should be informed of his Sickness which is I fear attended with great Danger. Remember me to all friends and particularly, Remember my Love to all my Children and my sincere affection to your self; yours   Josiah Bartlett

RC (NhHi). Franked.

1. The Battle of Monmouth, N.J., between the main British army under Clinton and the Continental Army under Washington was in fact taking place on the twenty-eighth, while JB wrote. See Wallace, *Appeal to Arms*, 187–90.

FROM WILLIAM WHIPPLE

My Dear Sir   Portsmouth, June 29, 1778

I have sometime expected to be favored with a line from you, but have not yet been so happy, though by other hands I have had the pleasure to hear of your arrival. I hope by this time your colleague has happily passed through the small-pox—please present my best regards to him; I could wish to be informed of his health, how he likes his present employment, &c., &c. by his own hand.

Common fame says the British commissioners are arrived: if, as I suppose, you have had a message from them before this time, it would give me great pleasure to know how they or their message are received, though I doubt not they will be treated with a firmness and dignity becoming an American congress.

I wish I had something new or entertaining to give, but I have not; we have not even had any prizes lately arrived, but several of our privateers have been taken, and the jails at Halifax are full of American prisoners, where they are treated as usual, some compelled to go on board their ships, others starved to death in prison. By the last accounts, between four and five hundred were there treated in the most inhuman manner by those barbarians, who still laugh at our threats of retaliation, and well they may when our officers suffer themselves to be insulted in the grossest manner by prisoners; general Phillips' letter to general Heath, is an instance of their insufferable impudence—but I must quit this subject, for I find the recollection of those matters will soon put me out of all temper.

I find it is determined to go on with the ships that were originally designed for 74's, on a plan that is proposed by Mr. Landais. This plan I have been informed of, and am much surprised that the committee should adopt it, for sure I am those ships never will be got to sea with two tiers of guns. I cannot conceive what arguments Mr. Landais could use to persuade the committee that a ship with fifty-six twenty-four and eighteen pounders, to two decks, will fight as good a battle as a seventy-four that carries fifty-six, fifty-two and eighteen pounders, besides her quarter-deckers. The fifty-six gun ship is under the same disadvantage of fighting her heaviest guns between decks, that a seventy-four is; her lower guns will be as near the water, within a small trifle, as the seventy-four's.[1] But she is to cost much less, that is true; she will cost as much less as fifty-six guns will cost less than seventy-four, and that, I am sure, is all the difference in cost. But then, again, she will require fewer men; that I also agree to: she will not require as many men by one hundred as a seventy-four. She is also to sail much faster, as she will swim two or three inches lighter; it is probable she may sail a trifle faster, but there can be no material difference in their sailing. I understand that Mr. Landais is appointed a captain in the American navy—perhaps he is to command one of these ships—I must allow that a two-decker will have much genteeler accomodations for officers than a ship that carries only one tier of guns; and experience has taught us, that our officers, both by land and sea, are fond of being gently accomodated; perhaps this consideration may, in some measure, have influenced Mr. Landais' opinion in favor of two-deckers; otherwise, if he is really acquainted with maritime matters and the peculiar circumstances of America, I think he would give the preference to such ships as I sometime ago proposed to Mr. Ellery; which was to turn those ships that were designed for seventy-fours, into frigates that might mount thirty-two thirty-two pounders on the gun deck, and fourteen twelve's on the quarter-deck and forecastle. They will carry their heavy guns between three and four feet higher than Mr. Landais' fifty-six gunship will carry her lower tier, consquently will be able to fight them as long as any two decker can fight her upper tier, and will have an inconceivable advantage in fighting those heavy guns on an upper deck. They would swim more than a foot lighter than the fifty-six gun-ship, and would have much less top hamper; consequently, would sail much faster, and cost much less, and would not require so many men by one-fourth.

If it is not too late, I could wish the experiment might be made with one of them. I have not heard whether Mr. Morris is returned to congress or not; if he is, and should think worth while to consider my plan, I flatter myself he would not disapprove it, for I know him to be a very good judge of those affairs. But, perhaps, it is too late to make any alteration in the plan, I must therefore leave it to your discretion to take any notice of what I say on the subject or not; but I must take liberty to predict that those two-deckers will never go to sea; and I believe I may venture to say, that the frigates that are in Boston will never get to sea till a stop is put to privateering. As to our state affairs I must refer you to those of your correspondents who are on the stage of action, as they can much better inform you than is in my power.

Please present my most respectful compliments to those gentlemen who you know I esteem, and accept for yourself the best wishes of your very affectionate friend and Most obedient humble servant.   Wm: Whipple

Reprinted from *The American Pioneer*, 2 (1843), 72–74.

1. Congress was in a receptive mood when the young Frenchman, Captain Pierre Landais (c. 1731–1820), proposed to reduce the size of the *America*, then being built at John Langdon's yard in Portsmouth. The Marine Committee later ordered Langdon to revert to the original plan. Construction was slow for lack of funds. In 1782 the ship was launched, only to be given by Congress to France. Landais remained in American naval service until 1781. Fowler, *Rebels*, 248–52.

FROM MESHECH WEARE

State of   ⎫   In Committee of Safety for said
New Hampshire ⎬   State at Exeter July 3d. 1778
Gentlemen   ⎭

Many Cogent reasons have determined the Minds of the legislative Authority of this State, against further Emissions of money, and to sink the mony already Emitted, which together with the frequent demands for money, & large Sums already advanc'd, on account of the United States, has so far exhausted our Treasury[1]—That we are under the disagreeable Necessity of Requesting your assistance in applying to Congress for a Grant of Two hundred Thousand Dollars, or such other Sum of money as may be adjudgd Expedient and such as to this State as Soon as Such Grant may be Obtain'd. By Order of the Committee.

M Weare Chairman

RC (DNA:PCC, 64). In a clerk's hand, signed by Weare. Addressed to JB and John Wentworth. Enclosed in letter of same date from Weare to JB. See p. 421 and JB's acknowledgment, 20 July 1778.

1. On 5 Mar. 1778 the General Court authorized the treasurer to issue £40,000 in treasury notes. This issue brought the total of state notes in circulation to over £150,000. New Hampshire issued no more circulating bills. This state money, combined with Continental currency circulating in the state, served to hasten the depreciation of all currency. Upton, *Revolutionary New Hampshire*, 141–42; *NHSP*, 8:779–80.

According to a table of depreciation enacted by the General Court in 1781, the value of paper money by April 1779 had decreased to the point that £1,104 of paper money were required to equal £1 of silver. *Laws of N.H.*, 4:420.

On 9 July 1778 JB signed the Articles of Confederation, thus becoming the only practicing physician to sign both the Declaration of Independence and the Articles. The engrossed copy of the Articles is in MJB, 1378, and is printed in Jensen, Articles, 263–70. Also signing on this date were delegates from Massachusetts, Rhode Island, Connecticut, New York, Pennsylvania, Virginia, and South Carolina. Delegates from New Jersey, Delaware, and Maryland lacked authorization to sign, and North Carolina and Georgia were unrepresented. JCC, 11:677. JB had been assigned to the committee charged with drafting the Articles in June of 1776, had copied the early draft in his own hand (MJB 841), and was instrumental in obtaining its acceptance by the New Hampshire General Court. Page, "Josiah Bartlett and the Federation."

FROM MARY BARTLETT

My Dear   Kingstown, July 10, 1778.

I and the rest of the family are thro Devine providence in good health att this time except Rhoda and she is Comfortable her Countenance Looks better and she has some better appetite to her food, and she is able to do some light work. I hope this will find you in good health:[1] we hear there has been a general Battel in the Jersies, and our armie Drove the enemy some miles with Considerable Loss, and 1200 of the enemy *Dessarted* the next Day and Came to our army. I wish it may be true.[2] The People among us highly approve of the Conduct the Congress Gave the Commissioners in not accepting their offers. A healthy time among us. The small pox att exeter goes harder with the second class that was inoculated than it did with the first. I hear several has died with it, and it spreads. A man came out of the hospital that belongs to Brentwood and all his family has taken it of him. The weather with us is extremely hot & Dry. Rain is very much wanted. Grass Drys very fast, English Corn & Flax begins to turn yellow, Indian Corn looks very green and grows fast. Every thing among us Rises in the prices Six Dollars for a Gallon of New England Rum shugar five shillings a pound veal 1s. a pound: Indian Corn five Dollars a Bushel & Rye Six or Seven Dollars a Bushel. Your Rates is 24£:4s:2d:2q. The Revd Mr. Thayer & Dr. Gale Return their compliments to you. The Children all Remembers their Duty to you. From Yours &c.   Mary Bartlett

TR (NhHi). Copied in 1937 by Miss Hannah Bartlett Rollins of Dover from another copy made in 1901.

1. The same day JB wrote a brief letter to Mary saying that he was in good health (NhHi). Not printed. See MJB 1384.

2. On 28 July the *New-Hampshire Gazette* reprinted an account of the Battle of Monmouth written by George Washington for Congress and originally printed in the *Pennsylvania Packet.*

TO MESHECH WEARE

Hond. Sir   Philadelphia July 11th 1778

This is Just to inform you that a French Squadron of 12 ships of the Line & 4 frigates under the Command of vice admiral Count De Estang is arrived off the Capes of Deleware[1] & finding the Brittish Fleet & army had Escaped from this City Sailed last Thursday morning for New York, with orders to Cooperate with us for the Destruction of the Brittish fleet & army in america. They have taken the *Rose* frigate, Sunk a 30 Gun Ship, taken several prizes & run aground & taken the *Roebuck* in the Capes of Deleware: Monsier Girard Ambassador & Plenipotintiary from the Court of France Came in the fleet,[2] has sent to Congress to notify his arrival and He is Expected in this City tomorrow, Mr. Deane is with him. An officer from the admiral is now here to procure fresh provisions (for which they will pay the Hard money). There are so many Landmen & mariners on Board that they Can land four Thousand Troops on occasion. In order if Possible to put an End to the Brittish Fleet & army before the arrival of Succors the Congress have authorised Genl Washington to Call on any or all the States he may think proper from New Jersey to Newhampshire Inclusive for the assistance of militia & voluntiers.[3] If he should Call on our State I hope they will Exert themselves to the utmost & at once put a final End to the power & hopes of our Enemies in America.

Mr. Wentworth had a fever at York Town was pretty bad. I tarried with him 4 Days after the Congress adjourned left him better Thursday the 2nd Instant have not heard from him Since. Hope he will be here the beginning of the week. I am Sir with great Respect your most obedient Servant   Josiah Bartlett

I would not have you Consider this as a publick letter as I write in the greatest haste as tis 10 at night & the Express Setting off. Cannot correct much less Copy it.   J: B:

RC (MHi). Franked.

1. Charles Hector Estaing (1729–1794), Comte d'Estaing, a successful career officer in the French army and navy, was given command of the fleet sent to aid the Americans. He damaged Admiral Byron's British fleet in the West Indies in 1779, but thereafter lost favor with the court. Comte d'Estaing regained favor in 1783, supported the King at the opening of the French Revolution, and was guillotined. Boatner, *Encyclopedia*, 349–50.

2. Conrad Alexandre Gérard remained as the French minister to Congress until October 1779, when the Chevalier Anne C. de la Luzerne replaced him. Burnett, *Continental Congress*, 346–49, 439.

3. See resolution in *JCC*, 11:684.

FROM WILLIAM WHIPPLE

My Dear Sir   Portsmouth, 12th July, 1778

Your much esteemed favor of the 20th ultimo, is now before me. The evacuation of Philadelphia is an event I had been some weeks expecting to hear of. I hope (with you) that congress may find some place more commodious than where you now are; but I think, were I with you, I should not wish to go to Philadelphia till the hot weather was over, nor then if a better place could be found; which, in my opinion, is not difficult. But that is a matter not for me to judge of, nor is it of much importance where they set, so long as they continue to act with that firmness which is so conspicuous in their conduct towards the British commissioners, a conduct that must do them eternal honor. No transaction of congress ever gave more general satisfaction in this quarter.

We had yesterday some imperfect account of a battle fought on the 28th ultimo, in which it is said the enemy left three hundred on the field, and our army took one hundred prisoners; our loss not ascertained. This victory does not satisfy the *most* sanguine amongst us; others (with whom I place myself,) think this, with *better*, will do. I hope we shall have a particular account of all the movements, &c.[1]

As I am happy in agreeing with you in opinion, in general, I should be exceedingly glad if there was a coincidence in our sentiments respecting privateering. I agree with you that the privateers have much distressed the trade of our enemies; but, had there been no privateers, is it not probable there would have been a much larger number of public ships than has been fitted out, which might have distressed the enemy nearly as much, and furnished these states with necessaries on much better terms than they have been supplied by privateers? However, I will not contend with you about the advantages or disadvantages that have been the consequences of that business; all I wish to convince you of is, that it is *now* attended with the most pernicious consequences; which there would be no need of my undertaking, if you were only to pass three months in this or any other town where the spirit for privateering rages with such violence as it does here. No kind of business can so effectually introduce luxury, extravagance, and every kind of dissipation that tend to the destruction of the *morals* of a people. Those who are actually engaged in it, soon lose every idea of right and wrong; and for want of an opportunity of gratifying their insatiable avarice with the property of the enemies of their country, will, without the least compunction, seize that of her friends. Thus far I am sure you would agree with me had you the opportunity, before mentioned, of making your observations. But perhaps you may say, these are evils attendant on this business to society in general. I will allow that to be the case, but then it must be allowed they will operate with more violence in this country, in its present unsettled state, than in a country where all the powers of government can be vigorously exercised; but besides these, there are many other mischiefs that attend this business peculiar to these states in our present circumstances. Some of the towns in this state have been obliged to give four hundred dollars bounty, per man, for men to serve three or four months at Rhode Island, exclusive of that allowed by the state. This is wholly owing to privateering. The farmers cannot hire a laborer for less than thirty or forty dollars per month, and, in the neighborhood of this town, three and four dollars per day, and very difficult to be had at that; this naturally raises the price of provisions—Indian corn is not to be purchased under six dollars per bushel. There is at this time *five* privateers fitting out here, which I suppose, will take four hundred men; these must principally be countrymen, for the seamen are chiefly gone and most of them are in Halifax jail; besides all this, you may depend, no public ship will ever be manned while there is a privateer fitting out. The reason is plain—those people who have the most influence with seamen think it their interest to discourage the public service, because by that they advance their own interest, viz. privateering. In order to do this effectually, every officer in the public service, (I mean the navy,) is treated with general contempt: a man of any feeling cannot bear this; he therefore, to avoid these indignities, quits the service, and is immediately courted and caressed to go a privateering. By this means, all the officers that are worth employing will quit the service, and you'll have the navy, (if you think it worth while to keep up that show) officered by *tinkers, shoemakers* and *horsejockeys*; no gentleman worth employing will accept a commission. This, you may depend upon, will soon be the case, unless privateering is discouraged and the business of the marine, in this department, more attended to and conducted with more regularity. In short, it would be much better to set fire to the ships now in port than to pretend to fit them for sea, for as matters now are, (if I am rightly informed, and my authority is very good,) the public are at an amazing expense to procure men for privates; for if they, the public ships, get two men one day they are sure to lose four the next, who take care to carry off with them the advanced pay, &c.

I think I have given you a long chapter on privateering, much longer than I intended when I began. I have said the more on the subject, as it is the last time I shall trouble you with my sentiments of that business; and as I have got to the end of my sheet, I will conclude the long scrawl with my best wishes for your health and happiness, and with the fullest assurances that I am Yours, very affectionately, Wm: Whipple

Reprinted from *The American Pioneer*, 2 (1843), 74–76.

1. In the Battle of Monmouth the British lost more than 450 (killed, wounded, and missing); American losses numbered over 360. Peckham, *Toll of Independence*, 52.

TO JOHN LANGDON[1]

Dear Sir   Philadelphia July 13th 1778

I this day rec'd your favor of the 20th ulto. The account of the money you rec'd of the Marine Committee I procured and was enclosed in Mr. Wentworth's letter to you of the 20th ult. which I hope you have rec'd. Your letter to the Marine Committee of the 20th ulto came by today's post and will be considered as soon as opportunity permits: the removal of Congress to this City has greatly retarded business. We have not yet procured proper offices for our several Boards and Committees—hope in a few days we shall be better accomodated and attend with more alacrity to business. The Congress meets in the College Hall, as the State House was left by the enemy in a most filthy and sordid situation, as were many of the public and private buildings in the City. Some of the genteel houses were used for stables and holes cut in the parlor floors and their dung shovelled into the cellars. The country Northward of the City for several miles is one common waste, the houses burnt, the fruit trees and others cut down and carried off, fences carried away, gardens and orchards destroyed—Mr. Dickenson's and Mr. Morris' fine seats all demolished—in short I could hardly find the great roads that used to pass that way. The enemy built a strong abattue with the fruit and other trees from the Delaware to Skuylkill and at about 40 or 50 rods distance along the abattue a quadrangular fort for cannon and a number of redoubts for small arms; the same on the several eminences along the Skuylkill against the City.

Mr. Wentworth was taken sick the 21st ulto, with a fever and a bilious vomiting and purging which lasted him near ten days and hindered me from leaving York Town till the 2d inst. when I left him better—have not heard from him since—hope to see him here in a few days.

The confederation was signed last week[1] by the delegates of the New England States, New York, Pennsylvania, Virginia and South Carolina; North Carolina have sent their ratification of it, but had no delegates in Congress to sign it. This day a delegate is arrived from Georgia who says he is authorized to sign it in behalf of that State. New Jersey, Delaware and Maryland have objected to it and not authorized their delegates as yet to sign it. Congress have wrote to them and I have reason to think they will accede to it.

In forming a plan of Govt for our State, I hope particular care will be taken to form a proper Executive Body to see the Laws carried into execution; our present plan is more deficient in that, than in any thing else. When I came to Congress the President asked me if our Govt had rec'd any letters from him for eight months past, and seemed very uneasy that he had rec'd no answers to his letters; I excused the matter as well as I could—but really Sir, is it to be expected that our very worthy president (who by the way is only paid by the day as other members, a small sum not sufficient to half maintain himself) should be at the trouble to receive, file, copy and answer from time to time all such public letters without any compensation; to do it properly he ought to be allowed a Clerk for the purpose and receive something handsome for his own time. No State in the Union is without some such executive officer or body and I am persuaded no State can long exist with any tolerable degree of order and dignity without it. Some supreme executive power must be somewhere lodged separate from the legislature, no matter by what name it is called, whether Governor, President of the Council, or Executive Council; but such a power there must be to act, when the Legislature is separate and cannot act, otherwise there is at such times a partial dissolution of the Govt. Beside the impropriety and danger many States think there is in the Legislative and Executive being lodged in the same body, Such a sort of Executive as the Governor of Connecticut is possessed of, I should think would answer the purpose very well.

The occasion of my writing the above is owing to a paragraph of a letter I received from Major Philbrick wherein he informs me the Convention voted that the Supreme Executive should not be wholly separate from the Legislative.

As to news here I beg leave to refer you to my letter of this date to General Whipple[2] and request you to inform him of such parts of this as you may think worth communicating. I am with respect your friend & humble servt.   Josiah Bartlett

Pray did Mr. Paine, Woodward and the others on Connecticut (River) join you in Convention?[3] How did they like what was done? Will they join in forming a plan of Govt &c. &c.

TR (DLC: Force Transcripts).

1. On Thursday, 9 July. *JCC*, 11:677.
2. Not found.
3. Elisha Payne (1731–1807), an attorney of Cardigan (now Orange), was a justice of the Court of Common Pleas for Grafton County and a trustee of Dartmouth College. Bezaleel Woodward (1745–1804) was a professor at Dartmouth College and a son-in-law of President Eleazar Wheelock. Both men sup- ported the attempt of sixteen towns east of the Connecticut River to join Vermont. Those towns did not send representatives to the constitutional convention held at Concord on 10 June 1778. Bell, *Bench and Bar*, 557–58; Walton, *Vermont Records*, 1:275–78; Dexter, *Biographical Sketches of Yale Graduates*, 3:89–92; Chase, *Dartmouth*, 447–76; *NHSP*, 9:833–37; 10:288 n.

TO MARY BARTLETT

My Dear   Philadelphia July 14th 1778

I had not the pleasure of Receiving any letter from you by yesterdays Post, shall Expect one by the next. It give pleasure to hear from my family more Especially to hear they are well. By the favor of Heaven I have had my health as well since I Came from Home as I had it for some time & I think rather better than usual. Hope it will be Continued if for the best. God Grant you & the Rest of my family may Enjoy an Equal share of Health of Body & peace & Contentment of mind.

We have had some Exceeding Hot weather here it is now a little Cooler. We are troubled with one of the Plagues of Egypt which the Enemy left here when they Evacuated this place, I mean Swarms of flies. They are much lessened since Cleansing the place of the Filth & Dung &c. &c. Tho they are Still very troublesome. I wrote you the 6th Inst soon after I Came here & a Line with Mr. Thurston's the 11th[1] by Express which I hope will Come safe to your hand. On Sunday about two o'Clock Mr. Girard the French Ambassador made a Publick Entry into the City from Chester 15 miles Down the River where the ships Stopt for want of wind to bring them up. He was attended by three members of Congress who were ordered to Conduct him to Lodgings here. 13 Cannon were fired when He Dismounted at his Lodgings. I was introduced to him the Same Day at the Presidents Lodgings about an hour after his arrival where he Came to pay his Respects to our President. He is a pretty Large man not very fat about 50 years old as I guess speaks English tollerably well for a french man, was Richly but Decently Dressed, Behaved with Ease & Dignity without any of the foppish airs of your low bred french men. He has the Sole power of ordering the Count de Estaing the french admiral with his squadron as he pleases.

The Names of the french Line of Battle ships in the Squadron are, the *Languedock* 90 guns *Tonant* 80, *Caesar* 74, *Zele* 74, *Hector* 74, *Pro-*

tector 74, *Marselles* 74 *Guerrier* 74, *Fantesque* 64, *Province* 64, *Valliant* 64 *Sagittaire* 50 guns.

RC (NhHi). Incomplete manuscript.
   1. No letter of the 11th to Thurston has been found.

FROM MESHECH WEARE

Sr.   Exeter July 18th. 1778

On the 4th Instant[1] I wrote you by the Post And in my letter inclosed a Request of the Committee to you to Apply to Congress for a Grant of some money to be Sent to this State As the demands on Our treasury are so great that it is frequently exhausted. I wish to hear from you by the first Oppertunity whether you have Receiv'd my letter, As I have sent Several letters by the Post to the President which I find by his last letter to me he had not Receivd, which is very unluckey for me who am so much in arrears in answering his letters: but hope he may have receivd them before now Or I shall scarce know what apology to make to him. I hope also you have Receivd the letter I wrote you. I congratulate you on the victory Obtaind by Genl. Washington over the enemy on the 28th June. Genl. Clinton has as yet got nothing to boast of. I have nothing very material to Acquaint you with from hence except the proceedings in the County of Grafton. A Number of towns have joynd themselves to Vermont and have been receiv'd by them as part of their State And they are Appointing officers, Courts, &c. which is like to make the utmost confusion and trouble among the People there & in this State And will probably give some trouble to Congress before the matter is Setled.[2] I Suppose the General Court of this State when they meet in Augt next will think it necessary to enquire into the Affair get a full state of facts and take such Measures As may be tho't Advisable. I shall endeavour As far as I can from time to time to give you such information as I can Obtain Respecting that or any Other Matter.

Please to give my Compliments to Mr. Wentworth. I would Have wrote to him but it is so difficult for me to write, that I hope he will excuse it but will not on that Account Omit writeing to me As there may be Oppertunity. I Am with great Esteem and Regard yr. Obet. Humle. Sert.   Meshech Weare

RC (NN: Emmet Collection, No. 104)
   1. See Weare's letter of 3 July.   2. See Weare's letter of 19 August.

TO MESHECH WEARE

Hond Sir   Philadelphia July 20th 1778

I have Received your favor of the 3d Inst: This Day with the order of the Committee of Safety to Mr. Wentworth & my Self to apply to Congress for Two Hundred Thousand Dollars in behalf of our State, and will take the Earliest oppertunity to lay the Same before Congress.[1]

The Enormous Sums of money it takes to Supply the army & navy at the present advanced price things, and the great Desire of Congress to avoid as much as possible the Emission of more bills of Credit, will I fear retard the Business, and perhaps lessen the Sum granted, But I shall use my best Endeavors that the Requisition may be Complied with.

The former Commissions and instructions for armed vessels being Judged very Defective, the Congress some time ago appointed a Committe to make a new Draft & lay it before the Congress for their approbation, but by reason of the multiplicity of Business, it has not yet been Done. As soon as any are printed, I will Endeavor to send some forward to our State.

I am sorry to inform you, that Mr. Wentworth is not yet arrived here from York Town; He was taken Sick about the 20th of June with a fever & a Bilious vomiting & purging, Remained bad about ten Days, and occasioned my tarrying with him till the 2nd Inst: when I left him better; and was in hopes to have seen him here before this time, But I was Just now informed by Secratary Tompson's Lady who left York Town last Wednesday, That a few days after I left him, He had a Relapse, but was again better before she left the place.

The Confederation is agreed to by all the States, Except New Jersey, Deleware & Maryland, and I have Signed it in Behalf of our State, but as the Power to Ratify was Given to the *Delegates* in Congress, I have Some Doubt (as have some others) whither my Signing it is a Sufficicient Ratification notwithstanding our appointment authorizes us severally to Represent the State in Congress and if Mr. Wentworth should not be able to Come here soon & Sign it, I Earnestly Request the State to give some order about it.

As I am informed that the Legislature of our State is to meet the Begining of next month & Desire their attention to the appointment of Delegates to meet in the new Congress that is to be Convened the first monday in November, agreable to the Confederation: and I would Beg leave to Remind them, that after that time no State Can be Represented by less than two Delegates at a time in Congress, so that if two Delegates only are sent, and Sickness or any other misfortune should prevent the attendance of one of them in Congress, (as has unhapily been the Case most of the time Since my arrival) the State will have no vote.

Your answer to several letters sent by the President of Congress to our State has been Receivd & read,[2] and I am glad to be informed by you that in future all Such letters will Receive an answer as soon as may be after their Receipt.

I am sensible Sir, that the present Plan for the government of our State is, in nothing more Defective than in the want of a proper Executive power whose Duty it should be to Receive & answer all letters sent to the State, and see its good Laws Carried into Execution: Ours is the only State in the union (I Believe) who are Destitute of Such a power and I sincerely hope our Convention will take proper Care of that very necessary & important article, in their Plan for the future government of the

State. I am with the greatest Esteem & Respect your most obedient servant   Josiah Bartlett

RC (MHi). Draft (PHC: Charles Roberts Autograph Letters Collection).

1. In the draft JB wrote "and use my best Endeavors that the Requisition may be Complied with" which he crossed through in favor of "to lay the Same before Congress." He does employ the earlier phrase to close the second para-

graph, but only after qualifying the possibility of obtaining the cash.

2. Weare wrote to Laurens on 4 July 1778, acknowledging his debt of letters. PCC, Item 64.

TO WILLIAM WHIPPLE

My Dear Sir,   Philadelphia July 27th. 1778

Your's of the 12th instant is just rec'd and am glad to hear that our conduct to the British Commissioners has given general satisfaction. By their last letter they seem to threaten us with an appeal to the people at large: I hope and believe they will gain no great advantage by that measure.

I am fully sensible of the force of your arguments against privateering and if some proper methods were taken to restrain it to proper bounds, I make no doubt the public would be much benefitted by such restrictions; but (for want of a competent knowledge of those affairs I make no doubt) I am not quite satisfied that a total prohibition would be serviceable. The Congress have some time since determined as soon as possible to take up the Marine affairs and make some very essential alterations in it and also the affair of our money which seems to be going to confusion by the enormous rise of every thing, but when it will be done *God knows*. The almost innumerable letters and business that daily crowd upon Congress for want of regular Boards, properly appointed and filled, and the time it takes in such large Assemblies, to transact business, keeps us forever behind hand in our affairs and I am sorry to say that sometimes matters of very small importance waste a good deal of precious time, by the long and repeated speeches and chicanery of gentlemen who will not wholly throw off the lawyer even in Congress.

Till we get into better regulations as to our Marine affairs, I am persuaded no class of men are so much wanted in Congress as men acquainted with that business, for though Navy Boards are established, yet there is a constant appeal to the Marine Committee of Congress, who I am sure are at this time inadequate to the business. I hope our State will have wisdom enough to appoint you to relieve me here in the fall and that you will have virtue enough still to forego your own private interest for the public good and will accept of their appointment and without flattery I really think you would be very serviceable to the public here, especially in the Marine Department. If I knew you would not attend Congress I should be glad you might be appointed one of the Navy Board at Boston, for I am sure that Board does not attend sufficiently to the business.

Mons: Girard has not yet had the ceremony of an audience but believe it will take place some day this week: the ceremonials are agreed on by Congress and the House nearly cleansed and fitted up. The *Minister* seems urgent to have it as soon as may be.

The French fleet are gone to Rhode Island and you will hear of their operations sooner than we, the Admiral seems very desirous of doing something to effect and was greatly mortified when he found there was not water sufficient for his large ships to go up to New York. I have nothing to write you in the new's way—have sent you a paper or two by which you will see what is stirring here.

Please to inform Col. Langdon I rec'd a letter for Mr. Wentworth, which by the superscription I believe came from him and shall keep it till Mr. Wentworth arrives here which I hope will be the latter end of this & beginning of next week.

Remember me to Col. Langdon, Mr. King, Mr. Gain's, Col. Wentworth and all friends and believe me to be your sincere friend.

J. Bartlett

As this is erased, blotted and huddled together in a shameful manner please to destroy it as soon as read for I have not time to write it over.

TR (DLC: Force Transcripts).

FROM JOHN LANGDON

Dear Sir   Portsmouth August 1 1778

Your favor of the 13th Ulto have just received, and am much obliged by your kind Intelligence: The Acco. of Money came to hand in Mr. Wentworth's Letter which exactly corresponds with my Books. No doubt the removal of Congress to Philadelphia must have retarded the Business very much. The conduct of the British has been truely systematical the whole Voyage thro'; I shall not pretend to describe their dirty Behaviour, only say, it is poor Spite.

I am very glad that Mr. Wentworth is like to do well, hope he is with you e'er this; his Father was with me just as I received your Letter and was much satisfied with your Kindness. For Mercy's sake do all you can to compleat the Confederation, for on this depends every Thing; it gives me Pleasure that it's so forward; when it's compleated, some bold Stroke must be made at our Currency, as all Business is at present draged along in a most miserable manner while our Circulating Medium is so fluctuating, and this might be done (in my opinion) without so much dificulty as some are ready to think: suppose one half to be taken out of Circulation by Continental Security at 4 Per Cent to the Holders or their Heirs, the other half would be much better for the purpose intended, than the whole therefore it would not hurt the Money Holders, and surely those who have no Money would not complain.

I am exactly of Opinion with you respecting our form of Government, it's impossible to give dispatch, or keep up any Dignity in Government without some supreme executive Power, and to have one Branch of the Legislature to execute those Laws, which they themselves have made is an Absurdity, for in that case there would be no need of the other Branch, as no Laws could be passed but what they saw fit to Execute.

I am amazed that I have no Orders respecting the French Ship the *Duchesse of Grammont* as she lays here at great Expence to somebody; it's three Weeks since I Recd a Letter from the Board of War, in which they mention the Commercial Committee[1] having received my Letter of the 5th of June respecting the Cargo and no doubt all the Letters that came by that ship were received at the same time—perhaps Orders have been sent and the Letters have miscarried: in such important Matters, Duplicates should come, to prevent Miscarriage, pray think of this Immediately.

The Schooner *Amity* Packet, Capn. Palmer is taken and carried into New York;[2] I've waited on the Navy Board at Boston with the Marine Committee Accot which contains every thing but the 74 Gun Ship, and it seems satisfactory—shall close the whole as soon as I get out the Navy Boards Accots. as the Ballance of the Marine Committee's Accots. will be carried to that. I intend to furnish you with the Cost of the *Raleigh* and *Ranger* soon, and hope the other Continental Ships will turn out as good, as well equipt, and as Cheap; which I doubt; to say nothing of the Places where some are built; the Risque of getting out of such places to the Continent is worth 20 Per Cent. These things must be overhawled, and put on a better footing, many Thousands are lost by their continuing in the present Situation. If I could get Time would wait on the Marine Committee at Philadelphia to talk over some of these matters and State the Facts; and then on a proper survey of the Ports by Persons appointed by Congress for that purpose, they will know the best places for Navy Yards.

We are going to send two Vessels to Maryland or Virginia for Flour, Corn &c. part of which I shall want for the use of the Continent, therefore I hope no Embargo will hinder them as we can't do without. I shall take Liberty to draw on the Commercial Committee for the purpose, as I am in advance for them. I shall inform you futher on this Matter.

I most heartily Congratulate you and my good Friend your Colleague on the prospect of our public Affairs. Pray don't forget to write me (one of you) every Week, and enclose a Paper at my Expense. I have been much out of Town otherwise I should have wrote oftener. Nothing material to inform you of, only preparing for Rhode Island Expedition.[3] I am very Respectfully your Mo. Obt. Servant   John Langdon
My very kind Respects to Mr. Wentworth. I expect to Set out for Rhode Island in two days from this, mondy 3d. Aut.

RC (MiU-C).

1. The Commercial Committee or Committee of Commerce of the Continental Congress had been created in July of 1777 to replace the Secret Committee and the Committee of Secret Correspondence. The Committee of Commerce functioned as an executive department responsible for the importation of powder and munitions. *JCC*, 8:533; Burnett, *Continental Congress*, 119.

2. Probably Thomas Palmer, who had commanded the armed schooner *Enterprise* from Portsmouth in 1776. Potter, *Military History*, 1:367; NHSP, 17:323–

24; *NDAR*, 7:430–31.

3. In August of 1778 Langdon led a company of forty-six cavalry (outfitted partly out of his own pocket) with the New Hampshire force under Gen. William Whipple against the British at Newport, R.I. Mayo, *John Langdon*, 172; *NHSP*, 15:577–79.

TO MESHECH WEARE

Hond Sir   Philadelphia August 4th 1778

Your favor of the 18th July is Just Recd and must beg leave to Refer you to a letter I wrote (previous to the Receipt of yours) to Colo. Nicholas Gilman[1] Giving him an account of what is Done in Consequence of the application for money for the use of our State. Money Cannot be sent from this place at present nor will it be Easy to procure an order for money till the Difficulties I mention in my letter to him is Cleared up by Letters from our State as is therein mentioned; afterwards Drafts on the Loan office or on our own Treasury as part of the money to be raised for Continental use as has been Done on the Treasurer of Connecticut & Massachusetts Bay. If such Drafts would answer please to inform me.

I am sorry to hear that the Condesending measures used by the State to the Inhabitants of some part of the County of Grafton has not been attended with any salutary Effect. The Hampshire Grants by Receiving & Countenancing them, have fell into the Snare laid for them by New York, to prevent the State of New Hampshire from intresting themselves in favor of said Grants. Some transactions of Vermont in Banishing some of their Inhabitants has been loudly Complained of by the state of New York and the men stopt from being sent to the Enemy according to the order of Vermont. This & some other Complaints will be likely to bring those affairs before Congress who must finally settle those Disputes as soon as our other affairs give a little oppertunity.

I have nothing material to Communicate to you. The French Minister is to Receive audience of Congress on thursday next. The Success of the affairs from Rhode Island will be likely heard before the Recept of this.

Mr. Wentworth is not arrived here from York Town nor have I heard from him for some time. I hope the State will take Care at their next session to appoint Delegates to Relieve us in the fall. In haste I am Sir with great Respect your Most obedient Servant   Josiah Bartlett

Please to Consider this as a private letter as it is wrote in a hurry.

RC (MHi). Franked.

1. Letter to Gilman not found.

FROM MESHECH WEARE

Sr   Hampton falls Augt. 8, 1778

I this day receivd your favor of the 20th. ulto. Am glad to hear that you have receivd my letter inclosing the Order of the Committee for Applying to Congress for a grant in favor of this State. I was much afraid my letters had miscarried, as by the last letter I receivd from the President, I perceivd he had not then receivd either of the letters I had wrote to him. If Congress can be prevaild on to make a grant, the earlier it can be Obtaind And forwarded the better, As Our treasury is so often empty, that on any emergency we are put to great difficulty. We had a requisition to send men to Rhode Island for the reduction of that place, we had not money in the treasury so much As to pay their travil Money, And were Obliged to Apply to the Select men of the several towns to advanse Money, to be repaid when Money came into the treasury.[1] However men have turn'd Out Spiritedly, And I hope that enterprise will be crowned with success.

I Am very sensible of the necessity of an Executive branch in the legislature, but Am greatly afraid we shall never Obtain it. The convention in general, seem to have a Strange prepossession Against it, every thing must be done by the two branches, And no superiority of One more than Another, And I am greatly Surprised to find Mr. Livermore[2] Strenuous for this Measure, the consequense will be that the business never will be done. I should have tho't what we have Already experienced sufficient to convince Any one of the necessity of such a branch, there is no one whose business it is, one more than Another, to lay any matters before the general Court, And move for a determination on them or to return Any Answers what is done or why it is not done. Letters are laid before the general court and read, and some things are taken up and Acted on, Others forgot, & no persons Appointed to return Any Answers about them: I have never suppos'd that it belonged to me without perticular direction, to do Any of these thial gs, but that I should be tho't Assuming if I did: but Surely there ought to be some one, whose proper business it should be. But there seems to be a Strange fear that such an One would soon grow up to be a *Governor*.[3] But I understand you have had more perticular information from Other hands, of what was done at Convention than I have time to give.

You will see by the inclosed copies[4] of a letter I have receiv'd from Mr. Estabrook,[5] And the Resolve of the State of Vermont, to what a length matters are now carried in that quarter; which I fear will Occasion very great confusion, and trouble. I understand in those towns that have joyn'd, the vote was carried by a bare Majority, And great warmth prevails Among them, And bad consequenses are Apprehended. I expect Our General Court which is to meet next week will think it An Object worthy their Attention,[6] And that some remonstrance will be made Against their proceedings.[7] For what Endless Confusion Contentions Uncertainty of property and Villanies of every Kind do such proceedings lead to, And all this bro't About by a few evil designing Men, to Agrandise themselves, And that they might hold possessions, which they feard to submitt to a fair and legal decision. You are well Acquainted Sir with the whole proceedings respecting this Matter, And well know that these Revolters have not the least foundation for Complaint, nor the shadow of An Argument to Support them. Surely Congress will never Justify such proceedings so far As to Acknowledge them As a Sister State, And then what will become of them? They must have a high Opinion of themselves, if they think they can live Independent of all the world And Altho (As I suppose) they have such an Opinion of themselves they may find themselves Mistaken. But you will have an Opportunity it is likely to find something of the mind of the members of Congress respecting Such proceedings which I should be very glad to know.

I am Sorry for Mr. Wentworth's Sickness, but hope he may have so Recoverd, as to be able to Assist in Congress by this time. What you write respecting Ratifying the Confederation, & Choosing Delegates, I shall lay before the General Court. I Am with much Respect yr. Obt. Humle. Sert.   M Weare

RC (MH). Draft (MHi).

1. Sullivan's letter to Weare of 24 July 1778, requesting troops for the Rhode Island campaign, is printed in Hammond, *Sullivan Papers*, 2:105. The actions of the Committee of Safety, of which Weare was chairman, are recorded in Bouton, "Committee of Safety," 161–63.

2. Samuel Livermore (1732–1803) of Portsmouth was New Hampshire's attorney general during the Revolution. Later he sat in the U.S. Congress and as chief justice of the N.H. Superior Court.

3. At this point in his draft Weare had written and crossed out "notwithstanding Annual Election or Any limitation on his power."

4. Enclosures not found. See Weare to JB, 19 Aug. 1778.

5. In the draft: "who Stiles himself chairman of a Convention of Comms."

6. The General Court met at Exeter on 12 August. *NHSP*, 8:787.

7. A line in the draft is crossed out so heavily that it is unreadable.

TO MARY BARTLETT

My Dear   Philadelphia August 18th 1778

I hope this will find you & the Rest of my family well, Tho I have not had the pleasure of Receiving any letter from you the two last Posts. Charles Chace is got So much better as to walk abroad. Mr. Wentworth is here but not able to attend Congress.

I am in a Comfortable State of Health. The weather here is very wet & Disagreable. On Tuesday the 11th Inst: we had a severe Northeast Storm of rain, and it has Continued Rainy the greatest part of the time Since and Still Continues. If they have the Same weather at Rhode Island, it will be very bad for our army there.[1] We have Recd no account from that place Since Gen: Sullivans letter of the 10th Inst giving an account of his being landed on the Island and the french Fleet leaving him, to Engage the Brittish Fleet.[2] We are anxious to hear the Event.

I have nothing further of importance to Communicate to you. Hope you will write to me as often as you Can with Conveniency.

I am at a loss to account for your letters Coming so irregularly, hope mine Come to you more Steadily. The last letter I have Recd from you is Dated the 17th of July. Remember my Love & affection to all my Children and accept the same yourself from yours sincerely   Josiah Bartlett

RC (NhHi). Franked.

1. The same storm had prevented fighting between the fleets off Newport. The British fleet sailed back to New York; the French fleet went on to Boston, taking with it the troops originally ordered to aid Sullivan's expedition. Wallace, *Ap-*

peal to Arms, 193–94.

2. Sullivan's letter of 10 August to President Henry Laurens was optimistic: "Congress may Rest assured that I Shall Endeavor to Surmount Every Difficulty & Effect the Design of the Enterprize with as much Expedition as possible. I have the pleasure to Inform Congress that great numbers of volunteers have Joined me." Hammond, *Sullivan Papers*, 2:191–92. Congress received Sullivan's letter on Saturday, 15 August. *JCC*, 11:801.

TO JOHN LANGDON

My Dear Sir,   Philadelphia August 18th 1778

Your favor of the 2d inst[1] is come to hand and I have communicated to the Commercial Committee what you wrote me concerning the French Ship *Duchess of Grammont* and find they have rec'd your letter to them on that subject. I have urged their immediately taking up the matter and sending you directions as soon as possible.[2] I am sorry to say our Treasury, Marine & Commercial Affairs are in a very bad Situation owing to their being conducted by members of Congress who can spare but little of their time to transact them, and are so constantly changing that before they get acquainted with the business they leave Congress and new members totally ignorant of the past transactions are appointed in their stead. This gives me great uneasiness and I wish I could see any prospect of a speedy remedy, but the multiplicity of business that is daily crowding on Congress and the time it takes to transact matters in so large an Assembly filled with lawyers and other gentlemen who love to talk as much as they will not allow me to hope that our affairs will be very soon properly arranged.

As to your loading vessels with provisions in Maryland &c., while the Embargo lasts you are sensible it cannot be done without an Order of the Congress for that special purpose which I fear will be hard to procure at present unless the French squadron shall be so successful as to block up the enemy's ships of war and prevent the danger of it's falling into their hands.

August 18—Mr. Wentworth has signed the confederation and is still here but in such a state as not to be of any service to himself or the public and I fear there is but little hope of his getting well while he tarries here. I believe it would be for the best (if he could be persuaded to think so) for him to set out immediately for home and another delegate for our state to come forward as soon as possible. I hope you have appointed delegates[3] to relieve us early in November when the confederation takes place,[4] as I shall be unwilling to tarry any longer if I should be able to stay so long; please to take particular care that others may be sent forward seasonable.

All the talk here is about Rhode Island and the French fleet, of which you know more than I, so shall say nothing about it, wish it may prove fortunate. I am Sir, your friend and humble servant.   Josiah Bartlett

TR (DLC: Force Transcripts).

1. JB meant the 1st.   2. Not until 6 Oct. 1778 did Congress

order money for Langdon to pay for loading the vessel. *JCC*, 12:985–86.

3. On this date the General Court was choosing JB, William Whipple, John Wentworth, Jr., and George Frost to be delegates to Congress for the year beginning 1 Nov. 1778. *NHSP*, 8:790.

4. Actually, the Articles of Confederation did not go into effect until March of 1781. Jensen, *Articles*, 238.

TO WILLIAM WHIPPLE

Dear Sir,   Philadelphia August 18th 1778

Your favor of the 2d inst I rec'd yesterday and perceive you intend for Rhode Island and I suppose you are now in the vicinity of that place. Rhode Island and the French and English fleets at present engross all the conversation here. I wish we may have a pleasing account from them— as for foreign intelligence we have none later than the 3d of June which has been published in the newspapers. The faces in Philadelphia were much altered but the Whigs are returning fast, so that it begins to look more natural. Our old landlady is the same as usual and remains in the same house when the true sons of America went off at the approach of General Howe and left her house. She was soon after supplied with British officers for boarders and as soon as they left her, her house was filled up again with Whigs, so that when I came here I could not be supplied with lodgings at her house.

The majority of the Quakers remain the same dark, hidden designing hypocrites as formerly—however as the laws of this State are very strict against all persons who do not take the Oath of allegiance to the State and abjuration of the King of England, not allowing of their buying or selling, receiving debts and in short nearly outlawing them. The Quakers many and I believe most of them are coming in with a sanctified phiz and taking the oath or affirmation, for if you touch their worldly interest you touch their conscience and their best beloved deity.

While affairs remain as they are at present I believe it will be difficult to obtain from Congress a permission to load vessels with provisions for New Hampshire, least they should supply the enemy instead of the inhabitants of New Hampshire. I am very sorry to hear bread is so scarce with you and am persuaded it is not owing to the natural scarcity but to other causes among which the fluctuating state of our money is the principal. The Congress are this day to take up that matter and try to provide a remedy. But the affair is so embarassed, I have but little faith, and fear we shall not be able to effect much, during the war such amazing sums being necessary for the supply of the Army and Navy.

Mr. Wentworth is in town but does not attend public business.

Mr. Deane has been called in before Congress to give an account of our affairs in Europe and of his conduct there—this has taken up some time and is not yet finished.[1]

The letter to Judge Brackett was handed to me while sitting in Congress by one of the members, it seems to me by Mr. Hudson of South Carolina, who is now at Boston, but I am not certain.[2] When I took it I asked I recollect from whence it came and the member said it was handed to him and could give me no account about it. I am your affectionate friend   Josiah Bartlett

TR (DLC: Force Transcripts).

1. Silas Deane had been recalled from Europe late in 1777, had arrived on the same ship with Gérard, and had testified on 15 and 17 August as Congress debated several charges against him resulting from his conduct as commissioner to France: his unrestrained promises of military commissions to Frenchmen; his overindulgence in commercial ventures; the possible misapplication of public funds; and the unresolved question of whether French supplies furnished secretly through Beaumarchais were to be a charge against the United States or a gift of the French government. The debate continued into 1779 and left stains on both the reputation of Congress and the character of Deane. Burnett, *Continental Congress*, 360–69.

2. Richard Hutson (1748–1795) represented South Carolina in Congress during 1778.

Beginning in the summer of 1778 the controversy among New Hampshire, New York, and Vermont about jurisdiction over the territory in sixteen towns of New Hampshire east of the Connecticut River but west of the original grants to John Mason, absorbed much of the time and energy of the Continental Congress as well as of state governments. Questions of legal jurisdiction over the towns had become increasingly more important following New Hampshire's adoption of a constitution in January 1776 and Congress's declaration of independence that July. The New Hampshire towns disavowed the authority of the state and requested union with Vermont. Following almost another decade of political turmoil, the towns returned to the jurisdiction of New Hampshire in 1784. The complex controversy, which has received a variety of labels from historians, is well treated in both Daniell, Experiment in Republicanism, 145–62, and Upton, Revolutionary New Hampshire, 188–98. Many of the original documents relating to the New Hampshire side of the matter are in a collection known as "Vermont Controversy" at the New Hampshire State Archives, and others are scattered elsewhere. Many are printed in NHSP, 10:199–500; Slade, Vermont State Papers, 89–137; and Walton, Records of Vermont, 1:405–41.

JB had already been instrumental in attempts to placate the Grafton County towns. His participation in continuing efforts to resolve the controversy is revealed in his correspondence.

FROM MESHECH WEARE

Gentlemen   Exeter, August 19 1778

By order of the Council & Assembly of this State, I am to inform you, that the pretended State of Vermont, not content with the Limits of the New Hampshire Grants, (so called) on the Western side of Connecticut River, have extended their pretended jurisdiction over the River, and taken into Union, (as they phrase it) sixteen Towns upon the Eastern side of Connecticut River, part of this State, and who can have no more pretence for their defection, then any other Towns in the State, the Circumstances of which you are well acquainted with, and great pains are taking to perswade other Towns to follow their Example.

Inclosed I send you the Copy of a Letter from Mr. Estabrook, who stiles himself Chairman of the Committees, from several Towns &c., also the Copy of a Resolve of the said nominal State of Vermont, on which you will make your own Comments.[1] By the best information I have from that County, nearly one half of the People in the revolted Towns, are averse to the proceedings of the Majority; who threaten to confiscate their Estates if they don't join with them, and I am very much afraid the Affair will end in the shedding of Blood.

Justices of the Peace have been appointed & sworn into Office, in their Towns, under the protended Authority of said Vermont, & Persons sent to represent them there.

I must not omit to let you know, that Colonel Timothy Bedel, who has received great Sums of Money from Congress, or their Generals; under the pretence of keeping some Companies last Winter, & now a Regiment for the defence of that northern Frontier, or to be in readiness for marching into Canada, (tho very little Service has been done as I am inform'd) by the influence of the Money and his Command, has occasioned a great Share of the disorders in those Towns. Tis wished by the more sober solid People in that Quarter, he could be removed to some other Command, if he must be kept in pay & employed.

I am directed to desire you on receipt, of this, to advice with some of the Members of Congress on this Affair, & proceed as you may judge expedient, also advising as aforesaid, to endeavor to obtain the Aid of Congress, if you think they can with propriety take up the Matter: Indeed unless Congress interfere, (whose Admonitions I believe will be obeyed) I know not what consequences will follow, its very probable the Sword will decide it, as the Minority in those Towns, are claiming protection from this State, and they think themselves bound by every tie, to afford it, And you know every condescending Measure that could be invented has been Tried from the begining of the Scism and rejected.

I doubt not of your Application & Efforts in this Matter which if effective will exceedingly serve the State & probably prevent numberless Calamities to the People. I am with much respect & esteem Gentlemen Your most obedient humble Servant

M Weare
President of the
Council of New Hampshire

P.S. I inclose Copy of a vote appointing each of you Delegates to serve in Congress in November next and shall be glad you'll inform me as soon as you can of its being agreable to you.[2]

RC (DNA:PCC, 40). In clerk's hand; signed by Weare. TR (MH). In JB's hand. Enclosures not found.

1. Nehemiah Estabrook (1715–1787) of Lebanon had written to Weare on 25 June 1778. Estabrook probably enclosed two resolves of the Vermont General As-

sembly with his letter: that of 18 Mar. 1778 accepting the proposals of the New Hampshire towns and ordering that they be laid before Vermont citizens for their consideration; and that of 11 June voting to accept union with the towns. Estabrook, *Genealogy*, 22; *NHSP*, 10:277–78; Slade, *Vermont State Papers*, 259, 271.

2. See JB to Langdon, 18 Aug. 1778, n. 2.

FROM MARY BARTLETT

My Dear   Kingstown August 21st 1778

Last Sunday I Recd two Letters from you Dated the 20 & 27 of July & by them I find you are in a good state of health, and Publick affairs wear a good aspect. I hope the war will be att an end in a Short time, pray Do not make your self uneasy about us at home we are all of us in a Comfortably state of health. The Chlidren are all very well; My Constitution is not very Strong and am often unwell. I am very Sorry you meet with so great a Disapointment in not hearing from us in so Long a time as you mentioned in yours of the 20 of July; I have taken particular Care to Send to you every week Since you Left us but one and then I gave the Reasons in my next. I make no Dought but you have recd it Long before this time with Some inclosed in it for Charles Chace, in that I wrote more fully, and Lest you have not had it I'll tell you the reason why you had not one the first week. I Sent one to exeter a Saterday morning our Constable Called att exeter Saterday evening to See if there was any for me, by Mistake he took the Same a brought it back ten of the Clock att night and it was two Late for me to Send again that week; there Shall nothing be wanting on my part to Convey Letters to you every week while you tarry att the Congress. I have very often Sent them to exeter by Major Philbrick and when I had no oppertunity that way I have with pleasure Sent to exeter on purpose to Carry them that you might not be Disapointed. I hope in a Short time there will be an end to these written Convayences by Seing you att home; in the mean time I hope the Care of kind providence will be over us in all our lawfull undertakings. People are very busy to and from Rhode Island and many minds what is become of the french fleet, and are very anxious to know how affairs will end among the rest. Colln. Baker of Dover[1] was hear this week to enquire after Mr. Wentworth. I told him what you wrote about him; he Said he beleive Mrs. Wentworth had but one Letter from him since he Left them and that was Dated in June. They heard he had been Sick and was better. They Did not hear of that ill turn you mentioned he had; he did not Say but Mrs. Wentworths family was well. Among them that is gone on Newport is Colln. Peabody, Colln. Gale, Capt. Calef, &c.&c. and all the Vollenters that went from this way is Gone on with their horses. The Weather with us warm and pleasent fine weather for indian Corn it fills very fast. Our men folks are preparing to Sow the winter Rye. David Sanborn is very Steady and mannages your affairs very well.[2] A School with us and our Littel Boys attends Constantly. I beleive Levi is well though I have not heard from him Since I wrote to you Last about him.

p.s. I beleive your Letters are all Come Safe to me as I have had as many

as one a week tho they Comes two and three att a time. I have had the perusall of Major Philbricks Letters you mentioned; and I thank you for the News Papers you sent me. This from yours &c.   Mary Bartlett
The Children Remembers there Duty to you.

RC (NhHi). In Miriam's hand. Noted with address: "Prov Free."

1. Probably Otis Baker (c. 1726–1801) of Dover who was active in public affairs and was often referred to as "Col. Baker." Dover Historical Society, *Collections*, I, 203; *NHSP*, 8:28, 78.

2. David Sanborn (1753–1817) was a neighbor and an occasional employee of JB. Sanborn, *Genealogy*, 129, 192.

TO MARY BARTLETT

My Dear   Philadelphia 24th August 1778
    This Day your two letters of the 24th & the 31st of July[1] were brought me by the Eastern Post, and am very happy to hear you were all well & that Rhoda in particular had in a great Measure Recovered her health; I am glad to hear of rains being sent, after the sharp Drought you mention, hope they will be Continued so as to Revive the Languishing fruits of the ground Especially the Indian Corn, a Scarcity of which would be very Destressing in Newhampshire, Tho but of little consequence here. I am sorry to hear there is like to be a Scarcity of Cider, as I sensibly feel the want of it here, where there is always a Scarcity or rather where they never use much of it, and what is made is very inferior to the New England Cider; If I am not likely to make any I hope you will purchase a few barrels if you Can Convenienly at the proper time of making, as I should be glad of a little (after so long fasting from it) when I return home.
    I wrote you last friday by Mr. Wentworth, who Set out that Day for his own Home for the Recovery of his health, he was not able to attend business here and his health grew rather worse than better. Charles Chace is better but so poorly that I have sent him out of the City into the Country ten or a Dozen miles for 2 or 3 weeks for the Recovery of his health, So that I am here at present without Colleague or waiter but in a pretty good State of health, hope it will Continue, as I have used Every precaution I thought would Contribute to my health: The weather was very wet, with a Disagreable muggy heat for near a fortnight, but is now Cleard up Cool & pleasant & much more agreable. The very irregular Manner in which I Receive your letters, sometimes 2 or 3 at once & then missing 2 or 3 weeks without receiving any, makes me Suspect that the Post has left off riding to Exeter as usual: Does my letters Come to you in the Same irregular manner.
    I have no news of importance to write you, Rhode Island & the French Fleet are the great objects from which we Expect the first news of Consequence.
    As I have no great news to write you, I will fill my letters with Smaller matters: This State have made a law for Confiscating all the Estates real & personal of those Inhabitants who Joined the Enemy, and are Seizing & Selling them for the use of the State: and no person is allowed to Sell

or buy or recover any Debt, make a will or transact any business, who Does not take an oath of allegiance to the State & an abjuration of the King of England before a Certain Day. Monsr. Gerard the French ambassador has given all the members of Congress an invitation to Dine with him to morrow being the Birth Day of his most Christian Majesty the french King: The ambassador has paid visits in form to all the Delegates; he began with Newhampshire and paid me the first visit about ten Days ago.

Board & Every thing here is very Dear, I give 20 Dollars pr week for my own Board, that is only my victuals and Lodging; my Drink & washing I pay for Beside, horse keeping in proportion, wine 16 Dollars pr Gallon &c. &c. &c._Now for fashions; when the Congress first moved into the City, they found the Tory Ladies who tarried with the Regulars, wearing the most Enormous High head Dresses after the manner of the Mistresses & wh - - - s of the Brittish officers; and at the anniversary of Independance they appeared in public Dressed in that way. To mortify them, Some gentlemen purchased the most Extravagant high head Dress that Could be got and Dressed an old Negro wench with it, she appeared likewise in public, and was paraded about the City by the mob. She made a most shocking appearance, to the no Small Mortification of the Tories and Diversion of the other Citizens; The head Dresses are now Shortning & I hope the Ladies heads will Soon be of a proper Size & in proportion to the other parts of their Bodies.

The little bobed Hats for the men are growing fast out of fashion, the mode now is large round brims & Cocked nearly 3 Square, no hats are now made in any other mode here. So much for fashions, for the Satisfaction of my Children. Remember my love to them and to all Enquiring friends. Yours   Josiah Bartlett

RC (NhHi). Franked.
    1. Mary's letter of 31 July commented on the rain. Not printed. See MJB, 1412.

FROM SAMUEL PHILBRICK
Hond Sir   Kingstown august 26th 1778
    Your Kind favour of the 28th of July[1] I Recived the 15th Instant—and I am Greatly abliged to you for your advise to me in regard to my relaxt State of Helth; with the many other Kindnesses I have Recived from you—and I hope that I am Some better in helth at this time then I was when I wrote to you Last—hoping these will find you in Good helth.

    I Laid your Letter before the Council & Asembly and theay appeared much pleased with your proceedings in Congress Relitive to the Requition made by the Committe of Safty of this State for money—but Some of the members Seem to be much puzzled with the Information you Gave; that their were no persons appointed yet for Settling the Continental accounts nor rules laid down for that purpose: by reason of a letter Mr. Emerson Sent home from the State of Connecticut;[2] in which he Informed that the

Committe on Said accounts; had almost Gon through the accounts of that State: & were in hopes to Get Leave to Come to Boston; to Settle the accounts of this State; and the Massachusetts &c. We have not got our accounts Redy for Setlement: but I hope theay will be redy verry Soon— neither is their any person appointed to Go forward with Said accounts &c.[3] The General Court meet the 12 Instant and Sett but part of two weeks: but few of the members attending; & did but verry little business of Great Importance; Excepting Choosing Dilagates for Congress: who are as followeth: the Honble Josiah Bartlett John Wintworth Esqr. Genl. Whipple & Genl. Folsom: Either two to have full Power to Represent this State in Congress.

Also passed a resolve that the Superiour Court Should Sett at Keen at the next term—and wrote a Letter to the Seperates on the Grants and to those on the East Side of the River: whome theay have Recived into their Union &c. &c. The General Court of this State adjourned to the Last wensday in october: at which Session I Expect that three weeks will be taken up with pettions that are now on file. The Committe of Safty are the Same that were appointed the Session before Excepting two viz Esqr. Loverell & Colo. McClary who were appointed in Lue of Colo. Peabody & Colo. Moony—Peabody being with the volunteers at Rodeisland.[4]

We have been favoured for Some time with much Rain: and Exceeding warm weather: but the wind togather with the Rain has hurt our Indian Corn verry much—people are Generally helthy with us: Mis Bartlett and the Rest of Your famely are well. Colo. Gale is Gone to Rode Island— and I fear by the best accounts that I Can Get that our Army will meet with much dificulty at that place: but I heartyly wish them Sucsess—we Passed a vote that the Board of war Shall forward all nessesarys to our troops at Rode Island [Cloathing Execpted] as theay Shall find it nessaserry for their Comfort &c. I have nothing that is of Importance to write at this time more then I have hinted at—as Saith Esq. Giles who for reasons unknown Did not attend with the Committe that was Chosen he being one of them: to form our new Constitution—neither Did he attend at this Session of the General Court. So no more at Presant but I Remain Your Sincear friend and Verry Humble Servant   Samuel Philbrick

RC (NhD). Franked: "Free N. H."

1. Not found.

2. Moses Emerson (1717–1779) of Durham had served as commissary for the army in 1775. In 1778 he was appointed commissioner of accounts for the eastern district with his office at Hartford, Conn. Emerson died in Philadelphia while on business with Congress. Shipton, *Harvard Graduates*, 10:166–68.

3. The congressional commissioners of accounts for the northern department in 1778 were John Welles, Eleazer Wales, and Edward Chinn. The record is unclear whether New Hampshire designated anyone to keep these particular accounts. Since Nicholas Gilman remained state treasurer and Thomas Odiorne was appointed in December to keep the state's accounts with individuals, it is likely one or both maintained Continental accounts. *JCC*, 10:114; 11:613; 12:1078; *NHSP*, 8:816.

4. Jonathan Lovewell (1713–1792) of Dunstable (now Nashua) and John McClary (1719–1801) of Epsom served on the Committee of Safety in 1777 and

1778, as did Hercules Mooney (d. 1800)
of Lee from 28 May to 26 Aug. 1778 and
5 Jan. to 7 Apr. 1779. Fox, *Dunstable*,

191–92; Stearns, *Genealogical*, 2:524–25,
910–11; *NHSP*, 8:792. See also Bouton,
"Committee of Safety," for 1777–1779.

FROM MARY BARTLETT

My Dear   Kingstown August 28 1778

Yesterday I Had the pleasure of Receiving a Letter from you, Dated august 4th. I am very thankfull to hear you are well. I wish you may Continue So; we Viz this family all of us are in very good health except Miriam & Sally are within these few days been troubled with a Colick pain are now better; Rhoda I think is heartyer than Miriam: I am very Sorry to hear that Charles Chace was Sick I hope he is well before this time. Also that Mr. Wentworth had not joined the Congress. I hope he has recovered his health and is able to Assist you before this time. You have had the ill fortune to be left alone a great part of your time & each time you have been to the Congress; it is Likely you have heard there is four Delagates appointed in this State to attend Congress, Viz General Folsom, of exeter and Coll Whipple, of portsmouth & your Self & Mr. Wentworth. I do advise you to write in very pressing terms to the Committe of Safty or the Delagates or where you think proper (as the General Court is adjourned to the Last of october) to have the other members prepare & set out as soon as possible to releve you as I think you will be glad to quit the business by the time they arrive; this is my judgment; but you must do as you think best: tho you are appointed for another year I do not think you will be willing to tarry over the winter as Mr. Wentworth, and Charles Chace, has been sick.

I beleive it is very discoureging to you, tho there has been three very hot Days this week it is now Cooler and very Comfortably and very pleasant weather to ripepen the fruit of the earth which is some thing backward; indian Corn Looks very well, if the frosts holds of there will be good Crops, Corn, hay, I believe will be plenty; Potatoes, & beans, & Pompions, and Such things will not be so plenty; we have had innumarable Sight of Devouring insects among us this year such as bugs, & Grass hoppers, they Come even into our bed Chambers.

David Samborn says our farming business goes on middling well: they have sown the winter Rye & got in all the hay without much wet upon it. When I heard from Levi was the Last of july. He was well and Sayd he had not Learnt any french and he did not know when he should.

As to your Letters I beleive I have recd all of them in Course by the Dates tho they Come very Scattering Sometimes one two and three att a time. I will take Particular Care when I recive Letters from you to mention them in mine to you.

I have wrote to you every week since you Left home but one and then I gave my reasons for it in my next which you have Recd att Last as you mentiond.

As to publick news I Shall say nothing about them what people Say one day they Contridict the next. I acknowledge my Letters are very imperfect. A general time of health your Relations were all well last week. I have two brothers gone to Rode Island viz Joseph & Matthias Bartlett.[1] This from yours &c.   Mary Bartlett

RC (NhHi). In Rhoda's hand.
1. Joseph (b. 1726) was the second and Mathias (b. 1742) was the fourth son of
Deacon Joseph Bartlett of Newton. "Bartlett Genealogy," 6.

FROM BENJAMIN THURSTON
Honble Sir,   Kingston Aug'st 28th. 1778
   I with pleasure received your favor of July 8th[1] & am much obliged, for your narration of facts & circumstances relative to the conduct of the british Army when at & about Philadelphia. Tho' such depredations must inspire every generous mind & well wisher to the rights of mankind with resentment, and a Spirit of retalliation, yet I am not much surprised to find such devastations marking the footsteps of an army, appearing in arms, not for right, & lawful dominion, but from contracted mercenary views of private emolument, from revenge, pride or the like. Minds capable of being actuated by motives of this nature in matters so important as are now depending, are capable of almost any enormity. This is a truth abundantly demonstrated by the devastations & inhumanity which have accompanyed the marches, & victories which our common enemy have at any time accomplished. But, both reason and analogy seem to demonstrate the period to be at hand, when america shall no more see or hear of the devastations of lawless power, when the wheel of providence will give this extensive but now injured country the superiority in the scale of national power to their enemies, that they may reverse the tables, & teach them the folly of british policy by administering a lesson of retalliation. May you & I honble Sr live to see this happy time when America may thus make reprisals, & support the dignity of her independancy. The time is hastning. American valour & policy have fixd her almost secure on the broad bases of liberty, which is supported by & helps to support every sinew of our common wealth government, & consequently which we hope the shocks of eropean tyranny will never injurously reach. By late accounts it seems british administration, have never for many centuries, been so hampered by unwise policy. The hostile attempts of some & the recognition of our independency by other States in Europe, together with the almost entirely ineffectual endeavors to subjugate the States, are an eventual demonstration of this. America seem now to be just upon giving the last blow to british tyranny on this side the atlantick. The state of the british army at the south, by accounts is hazzardous; & their forces at Rode Island are now besieged, & in probability must acknowledge our superiour power. Our army last Thursday under the Command of General Sullivan consisted of about twelve thousand; They are in high Spirits. There are eighteen gone upon this expedition from this place; & it is observable, that almost all those who are gone from this part of the States are the best of men, men of intrest, & capable of enduring the fatigues of

the Camp. One french Ship of war being much damaged has put into Boston to refit; the remainder of the fleet are got into rode Island. Other facts of a publick nature I might mention, but Congress receiving the first intelligence in things important, I trust I can give you no publick information. I have with much satisfaction perused those penslyvanian papers you transmitted to your family, Should be happy in seeing more of the same kind. The season of the year with us, has been, & now is excessive hot; tho mostly healthy, & plentiful in produce. The fruits in general remaining ungathered & ripening, wear a favourable aspect; however I would not forget to observe there are but few apples, growing, & will be but little Syder. I Should acknowlege it as a favor to receive, & should read letters from you with great pleasure, by every opportunity. From your most sincere friend & humble Servt.   Benja. Thurston.

N.B. The honble Legisture of this State have elected four members to sit in general Congress the ensuing Year, viz The Honble Josiah Bartlet, John Wentworth, Nathl Fulsome[2] & Willm Whipple Esqrs.

RC (NhD).
   1. Not found.   Frost on 20 August. *NHSP*, 8:792.
   2. Folsom was selected in place of

FROM WILLIAM WHIPPLE

My Dear Sir: Portsmouth, 7th Sept., 1778

Your favors of the 20 & 27 July and 18th Augt. were put into my hands on my arrival last evening from Rhoad Island. A particular account of that expedition, together with the causes of its failure, you undoubtedly have had before this time. I shall therefore content myself with telling you that about twelve hundred Volunteers turned out from N. Hampshire on the occation, and had matters been so circumstanced that they could have been called to immediate action, it's very probable wod. have been essentially serviceable; but those people who engaged in the service for an uncertain time generally fix a time in their own minds, and when that time is expired, it is as much impossible to keep them even half an hour, as it is to alter the course of the Sun. This was the case with the New Hampshire Volunteers. After being on the island a fortnight they began to be tired, and of course to go off, so that by the day of action scare a man was left of those I was sent to command, notwithstanding I used every method I could devise to retain them only three days. However, I wod. not have you suppose that this desertion was peculiar to the N. H. volunteers, for those from the other States acted the same part, so that by the day of the action we had not so many men as the Enemy could bring against us. This circumstance with others, that no doubt are before Congress, will, I flatter myself fully justify the army in quitting the Island, especially as the retreat was effected without any loss on our part. A particular return of our loss in the action of the 29th no doubt has been forwarded by Genl Sullivan. Our loss was really very small, considering the severity of the action, and every one present must allow that no men could behave better than the whole of our army. However, the Expedition has failed, & those who are not by Contract obliged to continue in the field are returned to their respective homes, waiting the next call.

I find by the newspapers that the French Minister has had the audience you mentioned, and I think it wod. have been full as well not to have given the world so perticular an accot. of settings, risings & bowings, &c. &c. &c. The publication of such trifling circumstances can answer no valuable purpose.

I am very sensible Congress must be very hard drove, but I can conceive of no business that demands attention more than Currency and the Marine affairs. Unless something is done to give stability to the currency, your navy will sink to nothing, and the army will soon become clamorous.

I have nothing new to give you. The French fleet are at Boston, refitting, but the part they will act when fitted for sea, time only can determine. People in general this way are much disappointed with their past conduct, but I hope their future will be more agreable. We have a report that Byron[1] is arrived with a fleet at York. If this is true, and no Fleet from France to support the Count D'Estaing, I think he must be in a bad situation. By next Post I may be able to give you some accot. of *our* State affairs—in the mean time be assured that I am, very sincerely Yours,

Wm: Whipple

My respects to Mr. Lovell. I shall write him by next post.

Reprinted from *The Historical Magazine*, 6 (March 1862), 76.

1. John Byron (1723–1786), second son of William, fourth Lord Byron, entered naval service in 1746 and was appointed vice-admiral on 29 Jan. 1778. He had command of the North American station with specific instructions to intercept the French fleet of d'Estaing. Byron held the command until October 1779. *DNB*, 8:161–63.

TO MESHECH WEARE

Hond Sir   Philadelphia Septr 8th 1778

I have Received your favors of the 8th & 19th ulto and must inform you that I can see no prospect at present of my being able to procure money to be advanced & sent to our State by Congress and for the reasons I mentioned to you & to Colo. Nicholas Gilman in my letters of the 3d & 4th of last month; when I Receive answers to those letters I shall Conduct my self in that matter according to your Directions; The Delegates of Massachusetts Bay took an order on their own Treasury for 300,000 Dollars to be advanced to them out of the money they were to raise for the use of the Continent, but as I was Doubtful whither a Similar order on our Treasury would answer your end, I Did not move for it, as I make no Doubt you will make use of the money raised by taxes in our State if necessary for the public service.[1]

I have Communicated to several of the N:E: Delegates what Relates to some of the Towns of our State Joining themselves to the State of Vermont (as they are pleased to Call themselves). My present opinion is, that it will be best to lay the matter before Congress for their Direction, but I shall Consider more of it, & take further advice before I proceed. Those Delegates to whom I have Communicated the affair, seem surprised at the ungenerous and impolitic Conduct of vermont, and I have reason to Believe they will find few or none in Congress that will Justify their Conduct or Espouse their Cause.

I have Recd a Copy of the appointment of Delegates to attend Congress the first of November next, and I must beg leave inform you that I can by no means attend Congress after the last of october next: By reason of Mr. Wentworth's Sickness I have not Recd the least assistance from him, and am obliged to attend so Closely to public business *without* any interval of Relaxation, that it will be necessary for my Constitution of body & mind to be relieved then, if I am able to hold out till that time. I hope Sir you will give Mr. Whipple & Frost notice & that they will be here seasonable as the State will not be Represented after that time till they arrive.

Mr. Wentworth left this place the 21st ulto. and is by this time I hope nearly arrived home. I am Sir with great Respect your most Obedient Servant   Josiah Bartlett

RC (Nh-Ar: Weare Papers). Draft (NhD). Though substantially the same in content, the draft differs considerably in wording from the RC. The draft is reproduced on MJB 1466.

1. The General Court had levied a tax of £80,000 on 4 Mar. 1778, £60,000 of which was to cover a requisition from Congress. *NHSP*, 8:778–79.

TO WILLIAM WHIPPLE

Dear Sir,   Philadelphia Sept 12th. 1778

By the last post I had the pleasure to receive a copy of the Vote of the General Court appointing you a delegate to Congress and I hope that no private considerations of any nature will prevent your acceptance and that you will have as great a hand in making peace and confirming our Independence as you had in carrying on the War and declaring our total separation from Britain; as it is very probable negotiations for peace will be carried on the ensuing winter, I sincerely wish you may be present in Congress when they are under consideration. I could wish you and your colleague would be here the latter end of next month that I might have a day or two with you before I set out for home, which I shall do the 1st of November, as I can by no means tarry over the winter and every day after that time will make the journey more and more disagreeable and my tarrying longer will be of no service, as being alone, I cannot represent the State after that time; I shall therefore think myself at liberty and that it will be best for me to return at that time whether you are arrived here or not.

Please as soon as you receive this to send me an answer that you have accepted and that you will be here by the latter end of next month.

The enclosed paper will inform you what the British Commissioners have been sending to Congress and that we have not thought proper to make them any other answer than the Resolve concerning releasing the convention prisoners. The letter to them signed W. H. D. was wrote I suppose by Chief Justice Drayton member from So. Carolina as were the former letters under that signature. We are at a loss to guess at the future designs of the enemy. Some think they are about to leave these States others that they will make an attack on New England in order if they are strong enough by sea to destroy the French fleet—whatever their designs are I think a few days will discover.

I am much chagrined at the disappointment in the Rhode Island Expedition and I dare say you were equally so, especially if you was on the Island as I suspect you was by your last letter to me in which you informed me you designed to set out in a day or two if your health permitted. I am with respect your friend and servt.   Josiah Barlett

TR (DLC: Force Transcripts).

FROM WILLIAM WHIPPLE

My Dear Sir,   Portsmouth Sepr 13th 1778

Since my last I am inform'd that Mr: Wentworth has returned home in a bad state of health, & that your ill health will not permit you tarry long after him, however as the weather is growing cool I hope you will be able to tarry till you are releaved, who you will be releav'd by, is impossible for me to say at present. I receiv'd a letter yesterday from the Committee informing me that I was appointed at the last session of the Genl Court, & requiring an answer, which they shall have in a day or two, tho' I have not yet fully determin'd what my answer will be, but at present am inclined to think it will be in the Negative. It certainly will be unless I can have assurance of better treatment then I have heretofore receiv'd. Could I be made sensible that I could be essentially serviceable to my Country I think I cod with pleasure forego many private advantages, but no consideration can be a sufficient inducement to me to submit to abuse from that very Body who I am sacrifising my interest to serve, that I have been treated very scurrilously you are a witness.[1] Such treatment in future I am determined to guard against, I shall therefore wait on the Committee tomorrow or next day. A conference with them will determine me the result you shall have by the first opporty.

The Count D'Estaing is fitting his fleet at Boston from whence they are obliged to send here for all their Masts & timbers. A considerable quantity have been sent round, & more going. I suppose by the time this Fleet is ready for sea it will be time for them to go to the West Indies so we can expect no great good from them. We are told Byron is arrived at Sandy hook but there is no accot of his being followed by a Brest Fleet.

This you will receive by Major Gardner who has business with the Clothier Genl:. As you are acquainted with this Gentn he needs no farther introduction from me.[2] You no doubt will render him any services he may need, to him I must beg leave to refer you for any perticulars this way, &

by his return I hope to be furnished with such occurrences as you may suppose will afford any Gratification to Your very affectionate Friend & Most Huml. Sert. Wm: Whipple

RC (MeHi: The John S. H. Fogg Autograph Collection).

1. See letters between JB and Whipple of 11 March 1778. MJB, 1305, 1307.

2. William Gardner (1751–1833), a Portsmouth merchant, was a deputy clothier to the Continental Army. Reimbursement for a recent purchase of clothing was among his items of business with Continental Clothier General James

Mease. Gardner served as state treasurer, 1789–1791, and then as Commissioner of Loans for the U.S. in New Hampshire. *NHSP*, 21:800–01; *JCC*, 11:845–46; 12: 982; Brewster, *Rambles*, 1st ser., 307–11. See also Potter, *Military History*, 1:351, and Bouton, "Committee of Safety," 120, 140.

FROM NICHOLAS GILMAN

Dear Sir   Exeter September 14th. 1778

I receiv'd yours of the 3d Ultio. and wrote you Immediately after the receipt of it,[1] but fearing my letter Should not come Safe to your hand, I now write You by Colo. Folsom, who waits on Congress for the Purpose of receiving some money if it can be obtained.

The President has Wrote the Honble. Congress respecting our Continental accounts. I had not the Particuler Knowledge of what was wrote but am Certain this State is Very Considerably in advance for the united States.[2]

In addition to all our other Charges we have at least 1400 men to pay who were Called for by General Sullivan (pursuant to General Washingtons order) for the Expedition against Newport, besides 300 men which we have there, for nine months. We have now a Call from General Sullivan for more men (which if we furnish) will make a further demand for money[3]—If Congress does not Supply us with a Sum I fear we Shall be unable Either to Supply our Continental troops, or furnish the Quota of melitia that is required, or even pay those who have Served us.

Our continental Soldiers were almost naked last winter and Destitute of most the Comforts of life as you well may remember, which moved the Court to appoint a Board of War in order to have them the better Supplied which Board has receiv'd out of the Treasury for that purpose only Since their appointment £41,000. When I Transmitted my last Loan office account To the Honourable Board of Treasury I wrote them that I was paying the warrants in favour of this State as fast as I receiv'd the money into the office, and the Reason why I did not Charge them in account was that I could not pay them for want of money in the office. They will See by my Account Herewith Transmitted them, how the matter Stands Respecting the Loan office.

I have lodged the Account which you Sent me of Moneys receiv'd from Congress with the Committee of Safety and find it to be right.

I have lately heard your good family are all well. I Heartily wish you Health, and Every assistance, and Blessing in your Important, and arduous Employment, and am with the Most perfect Esteem & respect.—Sir Your Most Obedit. & Very Huml. Servant   Nich. Gilman

RC (NhD). Marked with address: "Per Colo. Folsom."

1. Neither letter found.

2. Weare's letter of 18 September pointed out that Congress owed £72,230 in credit to New Hampshire. PCC, Item 64. See Philbrick to JB, 26 Aug. 1778.

3. Gilman was referring to Sullivan's letter of 26 August which requested rein-

forcements as "absolutely necessary" for the continuance of his siege of Newport. By mid-September Sullivan's army had taken up winter quarters in Providence, and his needs were no longer so pressing. Hammond, *Sullivan Papers*, 2:267–69.

FROM SAMUEL PHILBRICK

Kind Sir   Kingstown Sept. 19th 1778

I Recived Your favour of the 11th ulto[1] and find my Self Greatly Indebted to You; for the Repeated favours; You have Shewn me: and were it in my Power to Return You the Like; I Should be Greatly Pleased. We have but Little news with us Since General Sullivan Left Rode Island: only that the British Troops are preparing for Somthing of Importance; Some Say to Come to Boston to take the French fleet: but I hope theay will be Disappointed; the French having thrown up Strong workes on the Islands; to defend them Selves: and I under Stand that Every preparation is making that is thought nessaserry to Defend the harbour &c. The Committe of Safty hath appinted Colo. Samll Folsom to go to Congress with the foot of our Continental accounts:[2] and if You Can obtain a Grant of money for this State: he is to Bring it: our Situation for the want of money at this time is verry bad; for if the Enemy Should make a decent on Boston or any other State; we Could not raise any men for want of money: and we have demands Comming in Every day & the Treasurer Cannot Answer them—but I need not mention these things as you will have a better account by the Letters Sent by Colo. Folsom then I can give you.

I would Inform You that the nessesarys of Life are much dearer then theay were when you went away; but we have had a fine Season for the Indian Corn; and I beleve there will be a Large Crop which will Releve many destressed ones.

Mr. Wintworth Got home Last week—and we Indevering to Get General Whipple to Go to Congress Imeadeatly; and I hope that Esq. Frost will Go also with the General—for I fear that your patience will be worn out attending alone: but I hope you will be blesed with Helth; and be Enable'd to Do that which will be for the Good of the United States; and for this State in Perticular, and Return to Your famely and friends again with Honour; and be Recived by all with the Greatest Respect. It is with much haste I have wrote these Lines; and I hope You will Excuse me for bad Language &c. So no more at Presant but I Remain Your Friend and Verry Humble Servant   Samll Philbrick

RC (NhD).

1. Not found.

2. On 19 September the Committee of Safety voted £100 to cover Folsom's ex-

penses to Philadelphia. Bouton, "Committee of Safety," 166.

TO JOHN LANGDON

Dear Sir   Philadelphia Septr 21st. 1778

Your favor of the 5th inst[1] is now before me. We have had all the particulars of the Rhode Island expedition transmitted to us by General Sullivan and have rec'd a letter or rather a folio book from Count d'Estaing in justification of his conduct.[2] I make no doubt he acted what he thought for the best and had it not been for the unlucky storm which it was impossible for him to foresee, it is very probable that it might have been for the best: nor do I think him so much to blame for going to Boston with his shattered fleet when he knew Admiral Byron's fleet might be hourly expected which joined to Lord Howe's fleet and all the troops at New York ready to be sent immediately to assist them might endanger the total destruction of the whole French squadron. I hope great care will be taken not to throw too much blame on the French, and raise a misunderstanding between us and them in this early period of the Alliance, than which nothing could give our enemies greater pleasure. The Rhode Island expedition though not successful, yet brought no disgrace on our arms, nor have the enemy any great cause of boasting.

Our commercial, marine and treasury affairs are in a very bad situation and will never be otherwise while they are managed by Committees of Congress who are many of them unacquainted with the business and are continually changing and by that time they begin to be acquainted with the business they quit, others come in who know nothing that has been done; thus we go on from time to time to the great loss of the public.

But you will ask why don't you put those affairs into other hands to be conducted who may give their whole time to business. There are several reasons—first we have not time to make the proper arrangements and form proper systems for conducting the business; above six weeks ago we ordered that Tuesdays, Thursdays and Saturdays in every week should be set apart for arranging the Treasury Board and for the affair of finance and nothing is yet compleated; so much business is dailey crowding on Congress, and so much time taken up in doing business in so large a body of men a great number of whom are lawyers and who think proper to make a long speech or two on every question however trifling &c. &c. &c. &c. that I fear it will be a long time before proper systems will be formed and when that is done I fear we shall be as much put to it, to find *proper men* to fill those important departments who will lay by all their own business and attend wholly to the public for years together and perhaps for life; they ought to be men of the first character for probity integrity and attention to business, but such men can always find employment in a more private life, more to their ease and advantage.

Generals Whipple and Folsom I am informed are appointed to represent our State after the first of November. I hope they will be here by the last of October as I shall be glad to see them before I set out for home.

By accounts from the West Indies (which is credited here) we are told that France declared War against Britain the 8th of July and that it was proclaimed in Martinico the 15th of August. I am Sir your friend and most obedient Servant   Josiah Bartlett

TR (DLC: Force Transcripts).
    1. Not found.
    2. Sullivan's letter of 31 August was received on 7 September. D'Estaing's, dated 26 August, reached Congress on 9

September. *JCC,* 12:884, 892; PCC, 160, 164; Hammond, *Sullivan Papers,* 2:280– 86.

TO MESHECH WEARE

Hond Sir   Philadelphia Septr 26th 1778
    Soon after I Recd your letter of 19th ulto with the Inclosures Relative to a number of Towns on the Eastern Side of Connecticut River Joining themselves to & being Recd by the Nominal State of Vermont I Communicated the Matter to the New England Delegates & to Some others all of whom seemed much Surprised at their Conduct. After some time for Consideration they advised me to lay the Letter & papers before Congress and Request their advice in the matter which I accordingly Did and had the satisfaction to find that Every person who spoke on the Subject severely Condemned the Conduct of the Revolted Towns & of Vermont; what was proper to be done was all the Difficulty.[1] After some little time Spent as it appeared to be a matter of Consequence the Congress Resolved that on friday the 18th Inst; the Congress would go into a Committe of the whole House to take into Consideration the Said letter & papers. The Delegates of New York moved that Sundry letters & papers from their state, which had been presented and some others that they had further to lay before Congress Relative to the Conduct of Said Vermont might be taken into Consideration at the Same time and tho it was opposed by some members as a Distinct & seperate matter it was Nevertheless agreed to. On the 18th matters of a very pressing nature laying before Congress the affair was ordered to be postponed. On the 19th Colo. Ethan Allen Came to this City from Said Vermont and understanding in what Situation the affair was and that their Conduct with Regard to the Said Towns was universally Condemned He Earnestly Requested me not to press Congress to take up the matter till he had an oppertunity to Return to Vermont & lay the matter before their Assembly who are to meet the 9th of October and he Says he is perswaded they will Resind their vote for Receiving those Towns and Disclaim any pretensions to the East Side of Connecticut River. He informs me the vote was past by a Small majority soon after his Return home from his Long Captivity and that agreable to a promise he made me when I see him in the Jersies as I went to Congress and he was returning home he had opposed the Measure and

that if Vermont Does not Rescind the vote He with a very Considerable number who he is Sure will Join him will petition Congress against it and that he will himself present the petition to Congress and will use Every other means in his power to procure Newhampshire Redress against So unjust and impolitic a measure. He has also promised that he will immediately write to you & inform you what the Assembly shall Do in the matter whither they Rescind it or not and will also write to our Delegates here or Come himself in Case their Assembly Does not Renounce their Connection with those Towns. According to his Desire and the Desire of a number of the Delegates here, who think it much best to have it Settled in that way at this Critical time I have agreed not move for its being taken up by Congress till I hear further from him or Rceive further orders from our State. If Vermont Should Renounce any Connections with those Towns I Could wish our State would Continue Still to use Every proper Condscending & Lenient measure to unite them firmly with us, as those Broils in the States are very injurious to the Common Cause and Keep up the Spirits of our Enemies who get intelligence of Every thing of that Kind.

One of the New York Delegates has informed me that they have wrote to their State advising them Either to Send a Committe to our Assembly or to Request our State to appoint a Committe to meet with one from their to Consult & agree on measures to be Jointly taken by the two States Relative Vermont.[2] But as the Claim of New York to the whole of Vermont in my opinion is not better founded than the Claim of New Hampshire to the same and as the Decision of the Question to whom it properly Belongs will probably at this time be attended with very important Consequences and as our present Dispute Concerning the Towns on the East Side of the River is of a very Different Nature from the other & will probably soon be Setled to our Satisfaction I humbly beg leave to submit it to your Consideration whither it will be advisable for our State to be hasty in Entring into any agreement with New York on the subject at least till you Know what the Conduct of Vermont will be relative to those Towns.

I believe it is the Desire of the major part of the members of Congress (if possible) to keep of the final Decision of the old Dispute Concerning the New Hampshire Grants to Some future time when it may be Setled without any Danger to the Common Cause.[3] I have the Honor to be with great Respect your most obednt Humble Servt.   J. B.

P.S. As I Cannot Represent the State in Congress after the first of November and can by no means tarry over the winter I shall Consider my self at liberty to set out for home the begining of the month of Novr: whither other Delegates have arrived or not.   J: B:

FC (VtHi). Docketed by JB: "Copy of a Letter to the President Weare Septr 26th 1778." Changes made in the draft may be read on MJB 1785.

1. JB laid the matter before Congress on 16 September. *JCC*, 12:916–17.

2. See Gouverneur Morris to the Governor of New York (George Clinton), 27 Sept. 1778, in Burnett, *Letters*, 3:428.

3. Morris noted that "The Temper of

Congress in this Business from what passed lately, seems to be if possible to keep matters quiet untill the Enemy leave us, when the Forces of the whole Conti-nent may be turned to reduce them if refractory to the Resolutions of that Body." Ibid.

FROM MARY AND LOIS BARTLETT

Honord father   Kingstown September 26th 1778

We were very Impatient to hear from you as we had not heard Since by Mr. Wentworth (and Did not Know but you were Sick) till Last night to our Great Joy we Received yours of the 24th and 31st of august which Inform us you were well then, & that you Intend to Set out for home the Last of October or the first of November. We are all very well, and hope this will find you Enjoying the Same Blessing. Pretty Healthy in this Parish Tho it is Sickly in Some places round us with the Dissentary; Mr. Hook of Hawk Lost a Child with it Last week, & the Revd Mr. Cotton of Sandown[1] has it very Bad; it has Prevailed So in Some places as to Sweep of whole families—Aunt Ruth Bartlett Calld hear Last Sunday & Said She Left Judith very Sick with the Dissentary and was a going to See Mrs. Gorden who was Sick with the Same Disorder.[2]

The Disappointment of our troops at Rhode Island or Something Else has Causd an amazing Rise of West India Goods Sugar at Eight Shillings a pound, & other things in proportion; and the farmer is as bad as the merchant, for Indian Corn is Seven Dollars pr Bushel, ordanary Beef one & Six pence pr Pound, Cyder 20 or 30 Dollars pr Barrel, Butter none under four & in Some places Seven Shillins pr Pound; in Short they that Live Between the farmer and merchant Come Poorly off.

Mother wrote a Letter to you & Sent to Exeter Last Thursday which I Suppose you will have with this. I have Done keeping School—no School on the Plain Except a Singing School two Evenings in a week, which Miriam Rhoda and Josiah attends. I thank you for taking So much thought of us as to write any thing for our amusement.

General Folsome has Declined going to Congress and we are to hear to Day where Coll Whipple Excepts or not—it is talked Some as tho Mr. Thurston will be chose a member of Congress next Choice.

I persieve by the news paper you Sent that Lord North Begins to open his eyes & Come to his Senses. I hope we Shall Soon have Peace and plenty & every one Set under his own vine and fig tree & none to make us afraid; is the [   ] of your afectionate Children

Mary Bartlett
Lois Bartlett

RC (NhHi). In Polly's hand; signed also by Lois. Part of page two is missing.

1. Josiah Cotton (1703–1780), a Congregationalist and a graduate of Harvard in 1722, preached in Providence, R.I., 1728–1741, Woburn, Mass., 1747–1756, and Sandown, N.H., 1759–1780. Shipton, *Harvard Graduates*, 7:50–56.

2. Ruth Currier Bartlett (b. 1720) was the wife of JB's brother Stephen (1717–1769). Judith (b. 1744) and Miriam Bartlett Gordon (b. 1749) were two of their nine children. Currier, *Genealogy*, 147; "Bartlett Genealogy," 11.

TO MESHECH WEARE

Sir   Philadelphia October 6th 1778

By the vote of the Legislature of our State of the 19th of August last, I find it will Require two Delegates to Represent the State after the first of November next, the reason of which I Suppose was that they Expected (as I Did) that the Confederation would be Ratified by all the States so as to take place at that time. But as neither Jersey Deleware nor Maryland have yet agreed to it, and as we have been informed within a few Days that the Legislature of Maryland is adjourned to December, it is now Certain it Cannot take place so soon as was Expected and there is a probability at least that it may not take place for a Considerable time to Come; I would therefore Earnestly Recommend it to the General Court as Soon as they meet, to pass a vote authorising any One of their Delegates to Represent the State in Congress until the Confederation is Ratified by all the States; and that the vote may be forwarded to your Delegates here as Soon as possible. The utillity (if not necessity) of Such a vote is so obvious that I need not say any thing in favor of it, and only Request that it may be Attended to.[1]

Your Letter to the President of the Congress of the 18th of September, was handed me by Colo. Samuel Folsom who arrived here the 4th Inst: and was yesterday Read in Congress. I have obtained a Grant for the State of One Hundred & fifty Thousand Dollars to be Sent you out of the Treasury here, also an order on the Loan office in New Hampshire for fifty Thousand Dollars and am in hopes I shall procure the money so as to Dispatch Colo. Folsom in a few Days.[2]

Your letter to me by Col: Folsom I have also Receivd.

You will find in the inclosed news paper an additional act of Congress Relative to wounded & Disabled officers & soldiers.[3] I am sir with the greatest Respect your most obedient Servant   Josiah Bartlett

RC (Nh-Ar: Weare Papers). Draft (NhExP).

1. The requirement was altered on 31 October. *NHSP*, 8:798.

2. See *JCC*, 12:981–82.

3. Enclosure not found.

TO MARY BARTLETT

My Dear   Philadelphia October 10th 1778

This will be sent to you by Colo. Folsom by whom I Recd yours of the 19th ulto. I wrote you the 5th Inst: by the post but it is likely you may receive this before that Comes to your hand for I find my letters to you by the post are near a month old When you Receive them for the most part. I Believe I shall set out for home the first week in next month and hope to see you by the 20th But if General Whipple should Come here alone I may be Detained here till the 15th or 20th of the month but I am Determined to Return home as soon as I Can with propriety after the month of November Comes in.

The weather here is now uncommonly warm for the season but it is not likely it will hold So long. I am in pretty good health, Charles Chace is well & is at work at his trade and talks he is willing to tarry here over the winter. I make no Doubt you will take Care to order some wood to be procured for you by Carting before winter sets in, and if necessary hire David Sanborn to tarry with you till my Return in order to prepare for winter.

It is very probable I shall not write to you more than twice more from this City.

I have no news to send you. Remember me to all Enquiring friends & particularly to David Sanborn. Remember my Love to all the Children and accept the Same your Self from yours   Josiah Bartlett

I have sent a small pamphlet by Colo. Folsom.

RC (NhHi).

FROM WILLIAM WHIPPLE

My Dear Sir   Portsmouth, 13th Octo. 1778

In my last I told you I had some thoughts of taking a seat in Congress. I have since come to a determination to set out about the 20th inst and hope to be with you by the first of nov:; if any thing shd happen to prevent my joining you so soon as I expect, I hope you will not leave Philadelphia so soon as you talk of, a week or two will make no great difference in the traveling. I do not understand that I am to have any company as those Gentn who were chosen to go with me have all declined. The Genl: Court sets in about two weeks when I suppose some body will be chosen. I must intreat you not to leave Philadelphia till I arrive and am with great sincerity Yours,   Wm: Whipple

RC (NNPM).

FROM NICHOLAS GILMAN

Sir,

In Committee of Safety,
Exeter, October 16th, 1778

You will receive this by General Whipple, who is appointed to represent this State in Congress for the year. The Committee are Informed that you have Expressed your Intention to leave Congress the last of this month. You will find by the Vote of the Council and Assembly of this State, you were chosen to Represent this State for one year after the first day of November next; and as our State cannot have a vote in Congress with a less Number than two members, it is Earnestly Desired (if you cannot tarry longer) that you will be so Kind as to tarry untill Esqr. Frost shall arrive, which will probably be in a fortnight after General Whipple.

There has been many Complaints from our officers in the Continental Armey, that our Soldiers there are not Cloathed according to the Resolution of Congress, (and) that they have used every argument to Quiet them, for long time past. And lately there is a Petition and Remonstrance from the field officers of the three Battalions belonging to this State, shewing that the men are Quite Impatient, and even tax them with falsehood, for their promises that they should soon receive their Cloathing; that Desertions had become frequent on that account, and that it would be Impossible for them to keep the men in Camp unless immediate attention was paid to Cloathing them according to promise. In consequence of which, the Authority of this State gave an order on the Continental agent to Deliver 1200 Suits of the Continental Cloathing which was in Store at Portsmouth, to our Board of War, to be by them forwarded to Camp for the use of our Troops, on which the Agent exhibited a resolve of Congress, of May last, forbiding him to Deliver any Cloathing or other Stores, Imported on account of the United States, to the Authority of any State without the Special Order of Congress for that purpose. You are sensible that it is out of the power of this State to Cloath their men, and that there is a great Deficiency some where. More than 20,000 Suits of Cloaths has been laying at Portsmouth for a considerable time past, and it is generally said there is plenty of Cloathing now in Different Stores for the whole Army.[1] If that is really the case it's a great pitty that they should not be forwarded to Camp. Doubt not but you will use your Influence in forwarding that matter. On behalf of the Committee, I am, Sir, Your most Obedt Huml. Servt.   Nichs. Gilman, Chan. P.T.

Reprinted from *The Historical Magazine*, 7 (February 1863), 50–51. Noted with address: "Favoured by Genl. Whipple."

1. The matter of clothing had come before the Committee of Safety on 1 and 9 October. Congress had resolved on 28 May 1778 to suspend all further purchases of clothing until the clothier general and his agents settled their accounts with the Board of Treasury. This was likely the principal reason for deputy Clothier William Gardner's journey to Philadelphia in September. See Whipple to JB, 13 Sept. 1778, n. 2; *JCC*, 11:545; Bouton, "Committee of Safety," 167–68.

TO JOHN LANGDON

Dear Sir   Philadelphia October 27th 1778

In Reading the Several letters & other Publications of the Brittish Commissrs, you will observe that they are Constantly Endeavouring to make people on both Sides the water, Believe, That Congress Have Exceeded their powers in Rejecting their (the Commsioners) offers of Reconcilliation & Entering into an alliance with France; and that in both of these instances the Congress had acted Contrary to the Sentiments of their Constituents. Whether they are really Deceived by the Tory accounts they Receive from the Several States, Or whither they mean to Deceive others, I am not Certain; But of this *I am* Certain, that so long as Brittain has the Smallest hope Remaining of these States Submitting again to her Domination, she will never Recognize our Independance & Consequently the war must Continue. It is therefore our interest to Convince Brittain & Every Body else, that the French alliance and the Rejection of the Brittish Commisrs offers of Reconcilliation are universally approved of by these States: For this purpose I should think it would be proper for the legis-

latures of the Several States in this Union (as of their own motion without the advice of Congress) to pass Resolves Signifying their approbation
of Those measures: And in order effectually to Cut off all their pretences
for applying to individual States or persons, To Resolve that the Congress
of the united States are solely vested with power on our part for Contracting foreign alliances, for making & Conducting war & for Restoring
peace, and that They & They only have full power for making peace with
Brittain on the principles of our absolute Independance & not other wise;
and that These States Repose Entire Confidence in them for those purposes.

If the several States would carefully Draw up & unanimously pass Such
Resolves, publish them to the world in the public newspapers and send
attested Copies to their Delegates in Congress to be made use of as occasion might Require, I am persuaded that it would effectually cut off all
the hopes our Enemies may Still Entertain of their being able to Devide &
flatter us into Submission. And as they are now Convinced that they are
not able to Conquer us by force, I Doubt not Such Resolves would greatly
facillitate their acknowledging our Independance and offering us reasonable terms of peace.

I Believe Such Resolves will be passed by several of the Legislatures,
and as our assembly will likely be seting when you Receive this, I thought
proper just to *Hint* the matter to you for your Consideration.[1] In the Enclosed papers you will find the Remarks of Common Sense on the Com-
misionrs Manifesto, also a Geneuine petition of the Refugees in New
York to the Commisrs. The petition appears so ridiculous that I should
not have believed it Geneuine had we not had the best proof of its authen-
ticity.

You have heard I Doubt not that Mr. Simpson has the Command of
the *Ranger* & that she togather with the *Boston* & *Providence* may be
hourly Expected at Boston.[2]

As my power of Representing the State will Expire next Saturday, I expect to set out for Newhampshire the Begining of next week and hope
proper Care will be taken to Keep up a Representation here I am sir with
great Respect your most obedient servant.   Josiah Bartlett

RC (Nh-Ar: Weare Papers).

1. On 17 November the General Court, meeting as a committee of the whole, agreed "That a Resolve be Passed by the General Assembly of this State signifying that they highly approve of the conduct of the American Congress in rejecting the offers of the Commissioners from the King of Great Britain; and also their conduct in making Warr or Peace, and in making alliances with any Nation or Nations, as Congress shall see fit." *NHSP*, 8:803.

2. Thomas Simpson (c. 1728–1784), a Portsmouth sea captain, was also Lang-

don's brother-in-law. He was appointed first lieutenant of the *Ranger* in 1777 and was made captain of the ship in July 1778 at Brest. The *Ranger*, in company with *Boston* and *Providence*, left Brest on 21 August and arrived in Portsmouth on 16 October. The latter ships sailed for Boston on 22 October. Bartlett, "Portsmouth Families"; Morison, *Jones*, 107, 167–70; Log of the *Ranger*, 18 Aug. 1778–2 Mar. 1779, printed in Jewell, "A Curious Relic," 64–68, 100, 129, 244, 340, 407.

JB also wrote to Mary on 27 October signifying his intention to leave Philadelphia "this Day week," or Tuesday, 3 November. MJB 1538. He apparently got away as intended, for Whipple, in a letter to Weare of 24 November, notes his arrival in Philadelphia on the fourth, a day after JB had departed. Burnett, Letters, 3:507. Whipple took JB's place as New Hampshire's sole representative in Congress until George Frost joined him. JB arrived home on 16 November (JB to Whipple, 9 Dec. 1778).

FROM WILLIAM WHIPPLE

Dear Sir   Philadelphia 30th Nov. 1778

I have not receiv'd a line from New Hampshire since my arrival here. Mr. Frost who arriv'd the 25th Inst. brot with him an act empowering one Delegate to represent the State.[1] Had it been sent some time before the State would not have been so long unrepresented and his coming rendered the act less necessary. I wish to be inform'd what number of the journals of Congress have been sent to the state & whether any indexs have been sent to the first Volume.

The Treaties of alliance &c. with France are printed. I sent one Book to the President last week, & shall send one to you by the first convenient opportunity.[2]

Nothing material has happen'd since Your departure—the business of finance goes on very slowly however some of the principal Questions have pass'd the Committee of the whole which leads me to hope we shall make a considerable progress in this important business in a few days.

A report prevails that there was an action between the French fleet & admiral Kepels the 3 & 4 Octor and that the former had greatly the advantage.[3] This accot comes different ways but still I think it wants confermation.

Col. Allen[4] is here. He tells me the Green Mountain assembly have renounced the 16 towns and wrote to New Hampshire on the subject. Young Whealock is also here but I have not seen him—he seems to avoid me.[5] I shall write fully on this subject shortly.

Pray let me hear from you as often as possible if I am to judge of the future by past proceedings I must expect no intelligence but through the channel of private Correspondents. I am with great sincerity Yours,

Wm: Whipple

Reprinted from *The American Pioneer*, 2 (1843), 168–69.

1. Whipple had left home before the General Court acted on 31 October. *NHSP*, 8:798.

2. Several printings were issued in 1778. See Evans, *American Bibliography*, Nos. 16,145–16,148.

3. Vice Admiral Augustus Lord Keppel was given command of the British Channel fleet in 1778, despite his not having commanded at sea for fifteen years. Hig-

ginbotham, *War of Independence*, 145.

4. Ethan Allen was in Philadelphia to win congressional friends for Vermont. Pell, *Ethan Allen*, 156–57.

5. John Wheelock (1754–1817), a son of Eleazar Wheelock, had served as lieutenant colonel of Col. Timothy Bedel's Continental Army regiment. On 28 Nov. 1778 Wheelock brought a "Representation of the Assembly of Vermont" to

Congress. He followed his father in the presidency of Dartmouth College. Potter,

Military History, 1:330, 351; *JCC,* 12: 1174n.

TO WILLIAM WHIPPLE

My Dear Sir   Kingston 9th December 1778

I have this minute Recd your favor of the 17th Ulto[1] and am sorry to find N:H: then unrepresented; I arrived here the 16th Novr and attended the G. Court the next Day, and was informed that the order for one Delegate to Represent the State was passed and sent forward to you the last Day of october. There is some fatality in the post offices, several of the most important Public letters sent to & from me, have Miscarried while private letters have Come safe. In particular some important letters Relative to the Vermont Disputes have never Come to hand which gives reason to Suspect foul play somewhere. I have mentioned the matter to Mr. Hazzard[2] who is here & he has promised to Enquire about it & particularly for a letter of mine to the President Weare Dated 26th of september[3] Containing important intelligence Relative to that Dispute: any important letters had best be sent by Expresses to Boston if possible.

As to Public news I have none to send you: The Genl. Court Dissolved last Saturday was Seven,[4] and a new one will meet the 16th Instant. To morrow is to be observed as a State Thanksgiving.

Michael Wentworth is arrived here from France.[5] The Court in the last session passed an act to forbid the Return of the Refugees who have left this State; also an act appointing persons to take possession of the Estates real & personal of several of the most notorious of them. If you Can procure & send me the Laws of Pensylvania Relative to the Refugees & their Estates I shall take it as a favor, as our Court Design to pass some other laws on that subject.

I am very Desirous to be informed what will be Done by Congress about the finances; we seem to be runing to Destruction unless some speedy Remedy is adopted. Large taxes no Doubt will be one method, but that alone will not answer while the war Continues. The Quantity of money must be lessened or it will soon be good for nothing & Every thing fall into Confusion.

What has been Done about G: Lee, Schuyler & Sinclair.

A Certain man who Calls his name Bradman and Says he Belonged to Shrewsbury in New Jersey and was taken by the Enemy & Carried to Hallifax is about here keeping a Singing School and travelling from one Town to another and by his Conduct has rendered himself Suspicious to some persons. I wish you would Enquire of the Jersy Delegates if they Know him, & what is his Character. He says he had a son brought up at the Jersy College. If so Dr. Witherspoon can give you his Character. He seems to have no Desire of Returning to new Jersy. Please to write me as often as possible. I am sir with great Respect your most obedint servant & sincere friend   Josiah Bartlett

RC (NhHi). Docketed: "Receivd 12th Jany 1779."

1. Not found.

2. Ebenezer Hazard (1744–1817) of Philadelphia was surveyor-general of the post office, 1777–1782, and postmaster general, 1782–1789. On 22 Dec. 1778 the N.H. legislature voted to request him to have a post office established at Exeter. *NHSP*, 8:815.

3. Apparently the letter was found; see above.

4. The Court was dissolved on Saturday, 28 November. *NHSP*, 8:809.

5. Michael Wentworth (d. 1795) was born in England, became a colonel in the British army, retired, and came to Portsmouth in 1767, where he married the widow of Gov. Benning Wentworth. They lived at Little Harbor. He was not named in the acts passed in November 1778 proscribing Loyalists and confiscating their estates. Wentworth, *Genealogy*, 1:290–91; Brewster, *Rambles*, 1st ser., 105; *Laws of N.H.*, 4:177–80, 191–93.

FROM WILLIAM WHIPPLE

My Dear Sir   Philadelphia 14th Decr 1778

Since you left Congress Messrs: Jay, & Deane have taken their seats. The first mentioned Gentn was last Thursday put into the Chair on the resignation of that very worthy Gentn you left in it. I have so high an opinion of Mr: Laurens that I must confess I exceedingly regreted his leaving the Chair. However I hope it is again well filled. Mr: Jay is a Gentn of acknowledged abilities and great application. I have therefore no doubt the Business will be well conducted so far as it respects the President.[1]

The Business of finance is in considerable forwardness, I hope in a few days more the present System will be finished by Congress, & doubt not the States will do their part with alacrity. The Tax will be very considerable perhaps 15 or 18,000,000. This seems a large sum, but when we consider the immense sum in Circulation I cannot think it will be difficult to raise provided it is justly proportioned.

Mr: Wheelock has been here with a number of applications among which is one for the Indian School. This is not yet determined, another that Bedels Regiment might be keept up, this produced an order that the Regiment should be immediately Disbanded.[2] He also brought a letter from a Joseph Marsh,[3] a copy of which I have inclosed to Col: Weare. Mr. Wheelock was here some time before I saw him & from some circumstances I thought he avoided me, but a day or two ago he favoured me with a visit the principal design of which was to perswade me that his Father was not concerned in the intended revolt of those towns on the River, however he did not fully satisfy on that head.

The Enemy have been up Hudsons River with 50 transports, burnt a few huts near Kings Ferry & returned, it is supposed they expected to find a quantity of provisions there, but they were disapointed. By the last accots from York they still seem to be preparing to go off but the season is so far advanced I cannot think they will go till towards Spring—our Army is going into Winter Quarters.

I have much to say to you about some late publications but time will not permit me at present. I must therefore bid you Adieu. Yours very sincerely   Wm: Whipple

P.S. I was a little surprised at a letter from the Council of New-Hampshire recommending Mr: Temple to Congress. I cannot recollect any Gentn of that Board who have had an opportunity of being thoroughly acquainted with that Gentlemans Charecter. Surely his having formerly been Leiut Govr: of New Hampshire can be no recommendation. There are many anecdotes of him (some of which are well authenticated) that renders Mr. Temples Charecter at least problematical, indeed in Some Gentlemens minds they amount to a conviction of his being a tool of the British Court.[4] More of this hereafter. Yours &c.   W W

RC (PHi).

1. Henry Laurens (1724–1792) of South Carolina was president of Congress from 1 Nov. 1777 to 9 Dec. 1778. John Jay (1745–1829) of New York succeeded Laurens and served until 28 Sept. 1779.

2. On 27 November Congress ordered that Bedel's regiment be disbanded and that Wheelock's petition be referred to the Board of Treasury. Wheelock was finally granted $925 to cover expenses incurred in supporting Indian youths of the Caghnawaga tribe. *JCC*, 12: 1166, 1230.

3. Joseph Marsh (1726–1811) of Hartford, Vt., had won election as lieutenant governor of Vermont in March of 1778. As chairman of a convention of the New Hampshire Grants, Marsh wrote a letter to the president of Congress on 23 Oct.

1778 covering a plan to settle the controversy with New Hampshire. Marsh's letter denied that Ethan Allen had authority to talk with Congress about the controversy. *NHSP*, 10:289–90.

4. John Temple (1731–1798) had been surveyor general of customs for the northern colonies and lieutenant governor of New Hampshire. In England at the beginning of the Revolution, he was permitted to accompany the peace commissioners to America in 1778. For this service the Crown rewarded him with a baronetcy and appointed him British consul general in New York. Charles W. Akers, "New Hampshire's 'Honorary' Lieutenant Governor," 79–99; *NEHGR*, 10:75, 76.

TO WILLIAM WHIPPLE

Dear Sir,   Exeter December 24th 1778

My last to you was dated the 10th inst acknowledging the receipt of yours of the 17th ulto—since which I have seen your's of the 24th ulto to the President,[1] and am very sorry to find N. H. then unrepresented notwithstanding the order for one delegate to represent the State was sent off the last of October.

The General Court is now sitting, but expect they will adjourn this week to sometime the latter end of Feby or beginning of March.[2] The Members of Council for Rockingham the same as last year. Woodberry Langdon is appointed for Portsmouth in the room of Mr. Cutts. Genl Folsom for Exeter instead of Mr. Odiorne—Mr. S. Livermore and Judge Blodget are members of the Assembly and a great number of other changes.[3]

The disaffected towns in the County of Grafton have not appointed members for our Assembly as we expected, but since they were disowned by Vermont are trying to form another separate State by taking in the towns East of the mountains on the West side of Connecticut river under the name of New Connecticut; in short some persons there seem determined to make all the trouble and mischief possible. The Hero of the Cedars[4] (it is said) makes use of his Continental Commission to give him influence in disturbing this State. I could wish enquiry was made by whose authority he was appointed and what service he and his men have done the year past.

The State of our money is every day more and more alarming and unless some measures are speedily adopted I dread the consequence. Nothing of greater importance than the finances can possibly (it appears to me) demand the speedy and serious attention of Congress.

A Committee of which Mr. Drayton was Chairman was ordered to get the whole of the transactions relative to the British Commissrs &c. printed in a pamphlet; when it is done, shall take it as a favor if you would procure and send me one of them.

Please to give the enclosed plan of Govt to Mr. Drayton, as he earnestly requested me to send him one.[5]

Judge Weare remains President of the Council and our friend J. Langdon Speaker of the Assembly. As to foreign news there is none stirring. Give my regards to your colleague and to all friends and accept of the best wishes of one who is your sincere friend & obt Servt.   J. B.

The Legislature being determined to pass some laws for confiscating the estates of persons who have fled to the enemy, I desire you to procure and send me the several Acts of Pennsylvania and any other State relative to that matter that you can procure.

TR (DLC: Force Transcripts).

1. Whipple's letter to Weare is in Weare Papers, Nh-Ar.

2. The Court met from 16 to 26 December; adjourned to 10 Mar. 1779. *NHSP*, 8:815, 822.

3. Woodbury Langdon (1738–1805), a Portsmouth merchant, was John Langdon's brother. He had been in London on business from autumn of 1775 to summer of 1777. In 1779 he was elected to the Congress. Mayo, *John Langdon*, 157.

Thomas Odiorne (1733–1819), an Exeter shopkeeper, was first chosen a representative in December 1776. He was a member of the Committee of Safety, 1777–1778. On 23 Dec. 1778 he was appointed agent of the state to keep its accounts with individuals. Bell, *Exeter*, genealogical section, 33; *NHSP*, 8:428, 458, 737, 792, 816.

Samuel Blodget (1724–1807) of Goffstown was a merchant, a manufacturer of potash and pearl-ash, and a builder of the Amoskeag canal at Manchester. He was a justice of the Inferior Court of Hillsborough County. *NHSP*, 8:820.

4. Col. Timothy Bedel.

5. Enclosure not found.

The following letter and succeeding correspondence between JB and William Whipple during early 1779 centers largely on the congressional plan of 2 Jan. 1779 to call in monetary notes emitted by congressional acts of 20 May 1777 and 11 April 1778. The money had been easily counterfeited and many fraudulent bills were in circulation. The 1779 resolve allowed the bills to be paid into the treasury as payment for taxes or to be exchanged for loan certificates. Congress hoped, as did JB, that most people would pay their taxes with the bills, which could then be physically destroyed. In fact, it becomes obvious that JB had hoped that Congress would allow the bills to be used only for the payment of taxes. The alter-native—exchanging the bills for certificates—would increase their face value (though the treasury would continue to destroy the bills), hence continue to feed the fires of inflation.

FROM WILLIAM WHIPPLE

My Dear Sir,   Philadelphia 3d of Jany 1779

Yesterday put a finishing stroke to the plan of finance, that was under consideration before my arrival & I suppose long before your departure. I heartily wish it may have the desired effect—by accots receiv'd from every quarter Our paper Currency is in a most miserable situation but I hope the remidies now applied will be something more than palliatives, indeed I have not the least doubt of it if the states will exert their powers to put in execution the recommendations.[1] I flatter myself that New H. will not be deficient in that respect. Taxation is the only means to effect a cure & every state will find great advantage in taxing as high as possible while money is plenty. Connecticut (who never looses sight of her own interest) raised £800,000 last year by Tax, which was collected in five or six different payments. This I think was a wise measure, & I wish it may be adopted by the State whose interest I have most at heart. There are but few men but will pay £25 pr Qtr: with more cheerfulness then £100 per year in one payment. The two Emission which are to be paid in by the first of June amount to 41,500,000 but this is to be redeem'd partly by Loan Certificates or new money which the artificers are now preparing the Machines for. It is said this new money can not be Counterfieted. I suppose it is meant not so easily counterfieted as that now in circulation, no doubt the Gentn of the Treasury have exerted their inventive faculties to guard against the ingenuity of villains, but it must be left to time to determine their success.

Having got pretty well over finance (at least for the present) the next standing Job, (I suppose) will be Foreign Affairs. This business I expect will produce much altercation and that not without a due proportion of warmth. Our Friend who left Congress the day you did is still absent, but some late publications in the news papers will bring him back sooner then he intended. He is expected very soon, all his eloquence will be used in support of his Friend & the Friends of Mr. D - - will equally exert themselves. For my part I shod be very willing to consign Mr. D - - over to Common Sence, & never hear his name mention'd again.[2]

Congress is fuller then I ever knew it at this time of year, all the States are represented. I wish I could say they were Confederated, but our Fro-ward Sister M - - & her little Crooked Neighbour still stand out.[3]

No late accots from Europe, the last advices from New York, say, they are in great want of Bread, & that 20 sail of outward Bound transports, were lately drove on shore by the Ice, most of which (its said) will be lost.

There has been no post in from the Eastward for three weeks (the last letters I receiv'd from N. Hampshire were dated in Novr:). This I imagine is owing in some measure to the badness of the Roads. I have never seen so much snow in Philadelphia as within ten days past, the River is compleatly shut up. The prises of every thing here, has doubled, since you left this City.

The inclos'd letter was delivered to me some days ago in the shattered condition that I inclose it, and which I trust you will find it.[4] It does not appear to me to have been opened but thouroughly worn in somebodies pocket. In hopes of hearing from you soon I am Most sincerely Your very Affectionate Friend &c.   Wm: Whipple

RC (NhD).

1. On 2 January Congress called on the states to pay their quotas of the sinking fund due up to the end of 1778. *JCC*, 13:21–23.

2. This refers to the controversy within Congress centering on Silas Deane. See

Burnett, *Continental Congress*, 360–69.

3. Delaware ratified the Articles of Confederation in February, but Maryland held out until March 1781. Jensen, *Articles of Confederation*, 197, 238.

4. Enclosure not found.

TO WILLIAM WHIPPLE

Dear Sir,   Exeter January 20th 1779

This I expect will be handed you by Mr. Emerson who is to set out in a few days for Philadelphia. The letters by post are very slow in passing the last I have rec'd from you was dated 30th Novr. As to news I have none to write, at least that is good. The amazing depreciation of money threatens us with ruin—every thing has risen near double since you left this State and continues rising Our Continental Officers are laying their complaints before the State and requesting that their wages may be made good by us: what is Congress about since I left it—I expected long before this time to have heard of some measures adopted to appreciate our money, unless something is soon done God knows what will be the consequence. It appears to me that nothing of equal importance can possibly come before you.

By the newspapers I find our foreign affairs are again under your consideration. I am much surprised at Mr. Dean's address to the public; it made a great noise here for a little while. The answer and remarks of *common Sense* has quitted the minds of the people and in some measure turned the suspicion on Mr. Dean.

The Resolve of Congress of 29th December about masts and spars has been rec'd by the Committee and proper orders given for the purpose.[1] I want much to know what is doing the other side of the water and whether we are likely soon to have peace. Though I have no great fear of the power of our foreign enemies, yet under our present circumstances especially on account of our money nothing but peace will (I fear) save us from destruction unless Congress can speedily adopt some measures to satisfy the army and put our money on a better footing.

January 24th. Since writing the above I have rec'd your favor of the

14th of December and am glad to hear that Col. Bedel's regt is disbanded and that the affair of finance is almost concluded; wish it may be such as will relieve us from our present fears and distresses. We have discovered several sums of counterfeit continental bills and so well done that they are scarcely distinguishable from the true, and from several circumstances I have reason to think that large quantities of it are now in circulation. There has nothing new turned up relative to the revolted towns, nor any propositions been made the State for an accomodation, but all things remain as they were. Private intelligence from New York says that the Commissioners before they left that place, told the refugees that garrisons would be left at New York and Rhode Island the ensuing summer sufficient to keep those places and that their forces would be chiefly employed in the West Indies against the French this year, which would oblige them to make peace; that before next summer is out our money would be destroyed and it would be impossible for us to raise a new army after next fall, when the time for which the army is raised will expire—that then they should return with all their force and should make an easy conquest of the country. This I have reason to think is the talk among the refugees, whether it be true, or false that the Commissioners said any thing of the kind, you are as good a judge as I am. The same intelligence says that Congress are striking off Bills of 100 dollars and that they are preparing to counterfeit them in New York, and that they, the counterfeit bills will soon be out. Whether such Bills are ordered to be made by Congress you can tell. If so I make no doubt of the other part of the story as to their counterfeiting them is true likewise.

I thank you for the newspapers, by which I see more of the publications relative to Mr. Dean. I am with respect your friend and most obedient   Josiah Bartlett

Mr. Emerson not going so soon as was expected, this is sent by the Post: please to write me by every opportunity. Just as I am sealing this, a person from Newbury says they have heard there, that Congress have cried down one or two of the emissions of our money—if so I suppose it part of the system of finance.

TR (DLC: Force Transcripts)
1. The resolve recommended that New Hampshire and Massachusetts prevent masts and spars in their harbors from falling into British hands. *JCC*, 12:1259–60.

TO WILLIAM WHIPPLE

My Dear Sir,   Kingstown Jany 28th 1779

Since I wrote to you last week I have seen a Boston newspaper and in it the Resolve of Congress of the 2d inst for ascertaining the time for redeeming our paper currency and for calling in the emissions of May 20th 1777 and April 11th 1778:[1] the stopping those emissions makes a considerable stir, every man looking over his money to see how much he has of it, and by what I have heard the greater part of the circulating Bills among us are of that sort: several persons have applied to Col. Gilman to put them into the Loan Office, but as he has rec'd no order relative to it, he is not willing to receive them at present. I hope he will soon receive proper instructions, otherwise those that apply will raise a clamor. The news of the great tax to be raised this year is a subject of much conversation, but as every body are convinced of the necessity of lessening the circulating bills and of the advantage of paying them in, when they can be procured for a small value, I hope and believe the Resolve will be cheerfully complied with by every body but the Tories and Monopolizers. They, I expect, will make as much noise as they can. I should be glad to know what sums were emitted of those dates, so as to be able to tell how much the circulating medium will be lessened. I hope few or none of them will be exchanged for other bills.

I am very sorry to find such heats have arisen in Philadelphia on Mr. Dean's account. This gives our enemies great pleasure to find the Whigs at sword's drawing among themselves. I wish, I sincerely wish a speedy stop may be put to those disputes, or that they may be managed with more temper and candor for the good of the common cause: Mr. Dean's conduct appears to me exceeding imprudent especially for a man in his character—what could be his design in his publications—surely he could not expect by them to convince Congress of his fitness to be employed as a foreign Ambassador, nor could he expect by it to oblige them to pass over all his former transactions without further enquiry. I should be glad to know whether there can be any body in Congress that can justify his late conduct.

Pray is the Lottery drawing; if so please to let us have as soon as you can, a list of the prizes. If Congress have adopted any other measures for appreciating the currency or for giving satisfaction to the army on that account, please to inform me, we have various reports here about the dissatisfaction of the army &c. &c. but know nothing for certain. I want much to hear what the British Parliament are doing; for whether we are to have peace or war the ensuing summer, will depend on the measures they adopt this winter: I heartily wish for peace with the establishment of our Independence and if Britain acts wisely, she will immediately give up her claim to the United States, and offer us peace and unless she can find means to embroil Europe in a general war, & engage some other power against France, I think she will do it this winter. I am your sincere friend

Josiah Bartlett

The General Court is to set the 10th of March when it is likely they will take into consideration the contents of your letter of the 14th of December to the President relative to the New Hampshire grants. The last letter I have rec'd from you was dated 14th December—hope you will take every opportunity to inform me what is passing in Congress—the letters by the post are long on the road before they arrive and I think there is some great defect either in the postmasters or postriders, or both. Please to give my regards to your colleague.

1. *Josiah Bartlett House, Kingston, N.H., 1774 and later.*
Photograph by Bryant F. Tolles, Jr.

Photographs by Bill Finney unless otherwise credited.

2. *Watch said to have belonged to Bartlett and to have been hanging on a finial of the clock saved from the first Bartlett house which burned in February 1774. Courtesy of Mr. and Mrs. Rodney M. Wilson, Kingston, N.H.*

3. *Queen Anne table said to have belonged to Mary and Josiah Bartlett and saved when the house burned. Courtesy of Mr. and Mrs. Rodney M. Wilson, Kingston, N.H.*

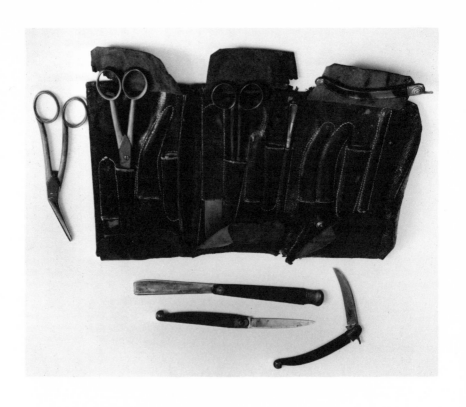

4. Pocket medical case, circa 1770, which belonged to Bartlett. Courtesy of Mr. and Mrs. Rodney M. Wilson, Kingston, N.H.

5. *Leather breeches traditionally worn by Bartlett on journeys to Philadelphia in 1776 and 1778. Courtesy of Mr. and Mrs. Rodney M. Wilson, Kingston, N.H.*

6. Example of Bartlett's handwriting at age 60. His signature had not varied. Courtesy of J. Duane Squires, New London, N.H.

TR (DLC: Force Transcripts).
1. See *JCC*, 13:21–22.

TO WILLIAM WHIPPLE

My Dear Sir,   Exeter Feby 6 1779

Since my last to you I have rec'd your favor of the 3d ulto for which I thank you: the two emissions of bills that are cried down by Congress are coming fast into the Loan Office here, and I hope but few people will desire to have them exchanged for other bills—nobody yet seems to desire it. The measure of immediately stopping their circulation is attended with as few difficulties as we could reasonably expect. A dispute has arisen whether they are not still a lawful tender in this State by virtue of our laws and yesterday a cause was tried in the Court of Common Pleas in this town, the merits of which turned on the validity of a tender made of this money since it was known to be cried down by Congress to discharge an obligation for money. The Court were divided in their opinions, but the Jury gave against it's being a legal tender.

As to news it is the stillest time I have known for some time, and our internal affairs remain in statu-quo. The operation of the late measures on the prices of things is yet unknown, but think it must lower them something at least, but there will be no radical cure till we have a peace and our expenses lessened. Whether we are to have peace or war the present year, is determined by the British Court ere this, and I feel very desirous to know; in short I long for the time when wars shall cease from the ends of the earth, and mankind be taught to cease from desolating the world and murdering their brethren to gratify the ambition of tyrants, the vilest and meanest of the whole human race. Such is the disposition of your sincere friend   Josiah Bartlett

TR (DLC: Force Transcripts).

FROM WILLIAM WHIPPLE

My Dear Sir,   Philadelphia 7th Feby 1779

I thank you for the information contained in your favor of 24th Decr: last which is the last letter I have receiv'd from you. Col. Beadle's Regiment is dismiss'd. I need not inform you of the difficulty of procuring a just enquiry into the conduct of an Officer at a distance from the Army, this I suppose occasion'd the act of Congress impowering the executive authority of the several States for that purpose. I wish it was done by N. H. in this instance. I have no doubt there has been great abuses commited in that Country, & I know of no power so competent to investigate the true state of matters there as the executive authority of the State.

The plan of finance has reached you I suppose some time ago. You'll observe the Quota of N. H. is not so high in proportion as last year. I procured this abatement not because I thought the sum more then the state would be able to raise but because you might be more at liberty to act your discretion, however I hope you will raise a much larger sum, as you will be allow'd interest for all you raise above your just proportion, & there can be no better time to collect money then when it is plenty. I hope some other method will be devised to help our Currency. What is already done can be nothing more than mere palliatives.

The transactions relative to the British Commission &c. are not yet finished. I shall do myself the pleasure of sending them to you as soon as they come from the press.

I have inquired of the Jersey Gentn respecting the man you mention, and they know of no such person. I think it very probable he is an imposture and ought at least to be well watched.[1] The speech of the Foolish Tyrant of Britain will shew that his mettle is much lowered, it must be very humiliating to ask the Mediation of Spain & meet with a refusal.

It is reported, but not from so good authority as I cod wish that Spain has a fleet of 44 sails of the line besides Frigates &c. in Cadiz Bay, & are speedily to be join'd by 10 more from Ferool & Cathergena. If this shod be true they certainly are meditating some important stroke.

The success of the Enemy to the Southward will give them Spirits. They have got possession of Georgia & our Friends from Carolina are not free from apprehension that Charlestown is in danger. The People from N. Carolina & Virginia are marching to the assistance of their Neighbours with great spirit and I hope will frustrate their (the Enemies) designs.

John D - - n is chosen to represent Delaware in C - - but has not yet taken his seat,[2] that State hath acceded to the Confederacy. There now only remains Maryland who you know has seldom done any thing with a good Grace. She has always been a froward hussey. It is a misfortune that such differences shod take place between our Commissioners but it is not to be wondered at that the watchfulness of A. L. shod draw on him the enmity of those who are utter strangers to the feelings of Patriotism that influences that Gentns Conduct. However, I need not trouble you with my opinion of those Characters, you are well acquainted with them, I well remember your opinion of a certain Person (now in this City) early in 76 before his departure from America. It wod have been fortunate for this Country if others had entertain'd the same opinion of them then that you did, but he was then, as he now is, supported by charecters who will never suffer Martyrdom for the cause of Virtue.

Europe is now full of negotiations which it may be expected will reach America in the spring, when probably we may be entertained with a new set of proposals from Britain, tho' I can hardly think her vain enough to entertain even an Idea of any thing short of Independence even that, my judgment, ought not to satisfy us, unless she will quit all pretensions to Canada & Nova Scocia. As for the Floridas I think we may consent to divide that Country with Spain if she will furnish us with funds to sink our paper money. Whatever may be the result of negotiations we must prepare for another vigorous Campaign for which purpose I hope every exertion will be used to recruit the Army. New Hampshire I am confident will not be backward in this respect.

Please to present my Respects to all Friends in your circle, I have been weekly expecting to be favoured with a line from some of them. Col: Peabody promis'd me he would write to me, & I did expect D. Thompson & Genl Folsom wod have done me that Honour. You know the rule that You & I settled is that he that stays at home should commence the correspondence. I am very sincerely Yours &c. &c.   W W

If I was accustued to make apologies this scrawl wod need one.

RC (NhD).

    1. See JB to Whipple, 9 Dec. 1778.

    2. John Dickinson, who had previously represented Pennsylvania, had been elect-

ed from Delaware on 18 January and took his seat in Congress on 23 April. Burnett, *Letters*, 4:l.

FROM WILLIAM WHIPPLE

My Dear Sir,   Philadelphia 18th Feby 1779

Your two favors of the 9th & 20th Jany came to hand Yesterday. I do not wonder at your uneasiness on accot: of the situation of the Currcy: I hope what has been done by Congress will have some tendency to re-establish the credit of it, however something more must be done, & I trust very shortly will. I am sorry to find Your mind in so gloomy a situation, "You fear, nothing but peace will save us from destruction." There my Friend are sentiments calculated for the merideon of Pensylvania. Peace to be sure is desireable but in my Opinion a secondary Object. War with all its horrors is preferable to an inglorious peace. I hope we shall never consent to such a peace as will involve posterity in greater evils then we have suffered. I have no doubt but there is vertue enough in the Army to undergo the fatigues of one more campaign. They must be sensible that everything that can be is done for their comfort, & I will undertake to say that the strictest justice will be done them when it is in the power of their Country to do them that justice.

I have heard nothing of Genl. Sullivans calling for the Militia he has never intimated any such intentions to Congress nor can I have the least conseption what they can be wanted for at this time.

The design of the publication you mention I believe was to conceal the Villany of the publishers. I need say nothing to you of the Charecters he endeavours to blacken you know them to be some of the best that this contest has brought on the stage. The Charecter he chiefly aims at, America is certainly under very great obligations to. To him we are indebted for every peice of good information we have received from Europe since the commencement of the dispute with Britain. I am well satisfied the publisher wod give all his smugled wealth to recall that performance but it is too late. He has 'tho' without intention given the key by which his base designs will be discovered & I hope public justice will be done.

There can be no dependence on the intelligence you get from York that part respecting the 100 Dollar Bills certainly is not true.

By the last accots from Europe American affairs have a much better aspect there then here the perticulars I have not Liberty at present to communicate but I flatter myself I shall e'er long have it in my power to give you such intelligence as will dispel those Glooms that at present seem to pervade your mind. But I hope every faculty will be exercised to have a very respectable army in the field. If that is effected I have not a doubt but we shall (under the smiles of Heaven & assisted by our allies) Humble to the dust the proudest nation in the world have peace on our own terms & make America the seat of Happiness; that these Glorious events may speedily take place—God of his infinite Mercy Grant Amen. Yours Most sincerely   Wm: Whipple

RC (NhD).

TO WILLIAM WHIPPLE

My Dear Sir,   Exeter Feby 20th 1779
    Your favor No. 3 of the 13th ulto[1] is come to hand and shall in future number my letters to you; this I think is the sixth I have sent you since I came home.
    The Resolve of Congress for calling in the two emissions will have a very salutary effect unless a great number of the holders of those bills should carry them in to be exchanged for others, which I begin to suspect will be the case; if it should, the good effect of the Resolve will be frustrated in a great degree.[2] I must confess I was sorry to see the liberty given to exchange them for other Bills. Many people who when they first heard of the Resolve, seemed determined to take certificates of interest, now finding money begin to be in demand by stopping the circulation of so large a number of the bills and that there is liberty given to exchange them (which by the way was not mentioned in public at first) are now for exchanging them. I shall be much obliged to you if you will procure and send me the Laws of Pennsylvania relative to the refugees and their estates, and the laws of any other of the States that you may be able to procure relative to that matter.[3] The present Legislature seem determined to sell the estates real and personal of the Absentees forthwith and have appointed a Committee to draw up an Act in the recess of the Court to be laid before them at their next sitting for that purpose, and Mr. Livermore who is one of that Committee is now in town on that business. I am very desirous of seeing what has been done by the other States and the methods they have taken, in so intricate and delicate a business before we proceed, as I have not the vanity to think that this State is fittest to take the lead in the affair.
    I take notice of your sentiments relative to some persons *at this time* trying to make themselves popular and getting into public business, and think we have much to fear from them, as such late conversions are seldom to be depended on, and I wish some of them may not designedly introduce themselves to important stations to defeat our Independence and that there may be a collusion between some of them and our enemies. I may possibly be too suspicious, but think the utmost care ought to be taken to guard against it. I hope the States will take proper care to entrust

their important business in the hands of those only who have, who may be depended on and who have stood firm in our greatest difficulties.

But popular applause you know is often easily gained or lost, and such persons will often very artfully fall in with any popular opinion and appear very zealous on purpose to carry their points. I have nothing new to write—believe me to be your sincere friend   Josiah Bartlett

P.S. Is Col. Ethan Allen at Philadelphia—what is his business. We have nothing new relative to Vermont but our disaffected towns seem determined not to join us and to put the State to all the trouble in their power: the towns on both sides of the river are determined to belong to the same State, either Vermont, New Connecticut and New Hampshire. I hope when the Court meets, some measure will be adopted relative to that affair, but what it will be is uncertain. Please to let me hear from you as often as is convenient to you. I shall write you often whether I have any thing worth communicating or not; at least to let you know that I have nothing to write you. Ut supra.   J.B.

Give my regards to your Colleague.

TR (DLC: Force Transcripts).

1. Not found.

2. As part of its financial action on 2 January, Congress had called in bills emitted on 29 May 1777 and 11 April 1778. The bills were receivable for debts and taxes due to the Continental treasury or could be exchanged for loan certificates. *JCC*, 13:21–22.

3. In reply to JB's several requests for the Pennsylvania statutes Whipple finally sent them on 3 July 1779. See MJB 1650.

FROM WILLIAM WHIPPLE

My Dear Sir,   Philadelphia 7th March 1779

Your favor of the 6th Feby came to hand the 3d inst. I am happy to find the calling in so considerable a sum is attended with so little inconveniency, this circumstance leads me to hope you will be able to raise a much larger sum by Tax then is recommended for the Current Year. It is needless for me to point out the great advantage it will be to the state to Tax as high as the People can possibly bear, it is so evident that every one must see it. I have never yet heard whether the Continental Tax for the last Year has been Collected. If it has I think Congress ought to have been made acquainted with it. I wonder much that a Court of Law should be in doubt whether a Resolution of Congress can superceed the Law of a *Sovereign* State however I hope in time N. H. as well as the other States will feel the importance of Sovereignty.

A report prevails to day that Genl Lincoln has had an action with the Enemy in Georgia & gain'd considerable advantage.[1] We have also an accot: which is said to be brot: by a vessel to Alexandria from France that two Frigates had taken 20 sail of British Transport with 1600 soldiers on board bound from Ireland to America & carried them into Port L'Orient. If these Stories are true Perhaps a confirmation of them may arrive before I close this.

You seem very desirous for peace; in that I most heartily concur with you, But in order to obtain such a peace as will establish happiness in America, we ought to make the most Strenuous exertions for war. We ought to be United in Council & Formidable in the Field. I hope this will be the case, and that this Campaign will put an end to the cruel ravages so distressing to every humane heart.

How are you like to go on with Your constitution? I suppose while you were here you collected all those that have been formed by the different states. I have seen several, but there is none pleases me so well as that proposed by the Convention of the County of Essex.[2] I think that with a few alterations wod be a most excellent form of Government. I wish N. H. may agree on one so well calculated for the Happiness of the People. I am with real Esteem & Respect Your sincere Friend & very Huml. Sert.   Wm Whipple

I have inclosed a paper contag Govr: Johnstons Speech in Parliament to Col: Weare.[3] An American answer is in the press.

RC (PHi).

1. Whipple was referring to the victories of Col. Andrew Pickens at Kettle Creek in Georgia on 3 February and of Gen. John Ashe at Augusta, Ga. Triumph was temporary, for on 3 March Ashe's forces were mauled by a British regiment under Col. Mark Prevost. Wallace, *Appeal to Arms*, 205.

Benjamin Lincoln (1733–1810) of Hingham, Mass. had been in the Continental service since February 1777 and head of the army in the southern department since September 1778. He was captured in May 1779 at Charleston, was exchanged and took part in the Battle of Yorktown, served as secretary at war, 1781–1783, led

the militia to suppress Shays's Rebellion in 1787, and was collector of the port of Boston, 1789–1809.

2. Whipple was referring to the Essex Result, a document written by Theophilus Parsons of Newburyport, Mass., in 1778 in reaction to the proposed Massachusetts constitution. The Essex convention at Ipswich had recommended an independent executive and legislative representation proportionate to the population. Several New Hampshire lawmakers held the document's concepts in high esteem. Daniell, *Experiment*, 170, 172.

3. Whipple and Frost wrote to Weare on this date. Weare Papers, Nh-Ar.

TO WILLIAM WHIPPLE

My Dear Friend   Exeter 13th March 1779

Your favor of the 7th ulto I have rec'd and is the last from you that is come to hand.

The General Court met here the 10th inst. and is now sitting and entering on business; they have agreed to a Tax Bill for the current year of 250,000 for the Continent and State[1]—nothing more of importance has yet been transacted—shall try to inform you from time to time of the most material business that shall be done this session. Some conversation has passed relative to claiming Vermont, but am uncertain at present whether any thing will be done about it at this time.

We have reports here which are credited, that Congress have rec'd very interesting and agreeable intelligence from Spain: Common Fame says, Alliance, Ships of War and money are offered you, and on the most liberal terms; if it be true this is very agreeable news, but if the pride of the British Tyrant would permit him to offer us peace with Independence &c.

it would be more agreeable to me; in short I grow perfectly weary of the war; it is enough to make one sick of human nature to think mankind should be such fools, as to distress, wound maim, kill and destroy one another for no other reason but to gratify the will and pleasure of Tyrants, who will take care to keep in a whole skin themselves.

Capt. Nathl. Giddinge of this town who lately returned from New York where he was a prisoner on parole,[2] when the British forces set out to attack Elizabeth Town and saw them at their return informs us that they made a very shocking appearance when they came back, mired up to their middles—that he saw about 40 wounded men taken out of their boats on the wharf where he was and two that died of their wounds on their passage—that from their conversation it appeared that they had been very soundly drubbed, but being on parole he was not at liberty to make any inquiries—he heard an officer of Admiral's ship say there was 70 men wounded belonging to their ship. We have not had the American account of the affair.[3]

I have seen the charges of the Executive Council of Pennsylvania against G: Arnold and am very sorry for the differences and disputes that arise among us—this gives the enemy more courage than almost any thing else. Some reports are circulating here to G: Arnold's disadvantage, which I hope will not prove true.[4]

I hope you will inform me of every interesting matter that you are at liberty to divulge from time to time as I have nothing more at heart at present than the welfare and happiness of the United States.

I want much to hear that G: Lincoln has driven the British forces from Georgia. I am my dear Sir your sincere friend &c.   Josiah Bartlett

TR (DLC: Force Transcripts).

1. The act passed on 19 March. *NHSP*, 8:823.

2. Nathaniel Giddinge (b. 1744) had been allowed by the General Court in December of 1778 to sail the schooner *Hermit* to one of the southern states for provisions. Bell, *Exeter*, genealogical section, 14–15; *NEHGR*, 23:50, 53; *NHSP*, 8:816.

3. The men seen by Giddinge were re-turning from the battle at Elizabethtown, N.J., in which a British force of 2500 under Lt. Col. Thomas Stirling attacked Gen. William Maxwell's command. Peckham, *Toll of Independence*, 58.

4. Gen. Benedict Arnold (1741–1801) was in command of the American military force in Philadelphia. See Wallace, *Traitorous Hero*.

TO THE GENERAL COURT

March the 16th 1779

To the Honourable the Council and House of Representatives of the State of Newhampshire

The Subscriber, having been honoured for Some time past, with the Command of the Seventh Regiment of Militia in this State, and at the Same time Employed in other public Services of a Different nature, and being of opinion that there is an impropriety in the Same persons acting in a Civil & Military Character at the Same time,[1] & being very Desrous[2] to be Discharged from his Military office, Begs Leave, and Does hereby Resign his Command of Said Regiment, and hopes his Resignation will be acceptable to your Honors. I am with the greatest respect your most obedient & very humble Servant   Josiah Bartlett

In Council March 16th. 1779 The foregoing Resignation of Colo. Josiah Bartlett being read and Considered—Voted that the same be Received and Accepted. Sent down for Concurrence.   E. Thompson Secy

In the House of Representatives March 18th: 1779—The above Vote of Council was read and concurred.

John Dudley
Speaker pro temp.

RC (MeHi: The John S. H. Fogg Autograph Collection). Docketed: "Colo. Bartletts resignation as Coll. of the 7th Regt. of Militia."

    1. JB may have been anticipating adoption of the plan of government that was submitted to New Hampshire citizens in 1779, the twenty-seventh article of which prohibited simultaneous holding of civil and military commissions. The 1779 constitution was rejected. *NHSP*, 9:841–42.

    2. Desirous.

TO WILLIAM WHIPPLE

My Dear Sir,   Exeter 20th of March 1779.

    Your kind favor of the 18th ulto is come to hand, and am glad to hear that our affairs have a much better aspect in Europe than here. There are sundry reports circulating here concerning a Spanish alliance and the loan of a quantity of specie; if specie is to be had, I am of opinion it would be best to procure enough to pay the wages of the army &c. this present year —that will prevent disputes with the army about depreciation, which otherwise we shall be engaged in; will give time to call in and burn some of the circulating bills, and help to appreciate the remainder. The Resolve of Congress for stopping the two emissions has not had so good an effect as I expected; when the news first arrived it stopped for a short time the rise of every article, and many things fell and were sold for considerable less than before, but within 3 or 4 weeks they began to rise again and are now higher than ever and no prospects of a stop. Two things have contributed, in my opinion, to lessen the effect of that measure; one that the Loan Office certificates in the present depreciated state of our money, answer in any considerable payments instead of money, and the other is, that very large quantities of those emissions will be carried into exchange for other bills; but let the cause be what it will, it is certain money is not bettered by it as I had reason to expect. Indian corn is now sold for 15 dollars per bushel, hay from thirty to forty pounds per ton and other things almost in the same proportion.

    Generals Poor and Starks, Col Cilley and several other of our Continental Officers are now here with a petition to the General Court, to have the wages of our regiments in the Continental Army made good according to contract, that is to make up the depreciation, which they say is 15 for one; the Court are desirous of doing as much for them as they are able at this time and promising them that at the close of the war, they will see that their wages are made good to them; but that it appears will not satisfy them.

What they, the Court, do I will endeavor to inform you in my next. Is any thing likely to be done by Congress to satisfy their loud complaints: if not difficulties I fear will arise. Perhaps you will say I am in the dumps and always looking on the dull and melancholy side; but you are mistaken—I think it is proper the delegates at Congress should be informed of the situation of affairs, with all their difficulties and dangers, as they are viewed by their constituents, that they may conduct themselves accordingly and provide proper remedies if in their power and you must expect while at Congress to hear from me all the difficulties that seem to threaten us, especially such as I think it may be in the power of Congress to remove. Were I to talk or write to you in a different situation, I should do it in a different manner; for I really view our present political situation with all its difficulties, vastly preferable to what they were a year or two ago. This I write once for all as a preface to all the gloomy and melancholy letters you may expect to receive from me if things dont go on right.

I hope next week to inform you who will be appointed delegates to relieve either you and your colleague if you should be desirous of returning before November next, Mr. Wentworth and your humble servant having resigned their seats.

There is a Spanish vessel into Portsmouth; what she has brought &c. &c. you will no doubt before this reaches you, have a better account of, than I am able to give you.

This State is under some difficulties on account of the Flag of Truce that was stopped at Portsmouth by order of Congress. The men are making loud complaints and request to be released or considered as prisoners of war & exchanged. We have applied to Congress for directions on the subject, but can get no answer, and no doubt they have forgot all about it before this time. Our people complain that something is not done about it, as none of the prisoners of our State are suffered to be exchanged by the enemy till the flag is discharged. Please to see that some orders are given about it. Yours with sincerity   J. Bartlett

TR (DLC: Force Transcripts).

FROM WILLIAM WHIPPLE

My Dear Sir   Philadelphia 28th March 1779

Some days ago I hastily acknowledged the receipt of your favor of the 20th Ulto.[1] I am fully of your opinion, & was at the time that the good effects of calling in the two Emissions will be in a great measure marred by Exchanging them, but you know the best Political systems are often destroy'd by one stroke of bad Policy.

I believe I sent you some time ago News papers containing the Laws you mention respecting the Estates of *Refugees* (as you call them. You'll pardon the criticism, but I never liked the word as applid to those People nor can I like the Epithet used by the Massachusetts assembly viz *Ab-*

sentees. Those people have either fled from justice or deserted the Cause of their Country & therefore I think are more properly to be called *Fugitives* or by some other epithet more descriptive of their true Charecters.) You say you have not the vanity to think N. H. the fitest State to take the lead in this business; I will not pretend to say, who ought to take the lead, but every state should judge of their own circumstances, and pass such Laws as the scituation of their affairs require.

Great dangers may arrise from placing too great confidence in men who are not Heartily attached to the Independence of America such charecters shod be watched with the most jealous Eye, but there are another set of people that we are to apprehend great danger from; I mean those who entertain principles repugnant to Republicanism; such undoubtedly there are in every part of the World & it will be happy for N. H. if such charecters do not insinuate themselves into Your councils & by their baleful influence weaken the foundation of that noble fabric (which I suppose you are about to erect) & render it unworthy the acceptance of the Goddess to whom it ought to be dedicated. That Heaven may guard my Country against the influence of such false Patriots is the most fervent wish of Your very affecte Friend and most Humle Sert.   W W

29th Your favor of the 27th Feby is just come to hand. The Report of the dispatches with proposals of peace &c. is without the least foundation, this is only a Tory Tale calculated to put people off their guard & slaken their exertions in the insuing Campaign. I believe I informed you in some of my former letters that the last accots from Europe Breathed nothing but War. Tho' I do not believe they would persue the plan were it not for the unhappy scituation of our Currency & the Flattering accots they have had of our dissensions, these circumstances have encouraged them to try another Campaign; but I hope notwithstanding the many difficulties we have to encouter we have still virtue enough left to withstand their utmost efforts. Indeed I have not a doubt but we shall succeed but still every exertion is necessary to recruit, & put the Army on a respectable footing.

Mr: Frost intends to leave me in about a fortnight. I wish to know who is to take is place, also when I may expect to be relieved. My anxiety, for the determination of some important matters will induce me to tarry as long as my constitution will bear this Climate, but I do not think is possible for me to tarry longer than may.

The last accots from S. Carolina were favorable. A recommendation is gone thither for raising some regiments of Blacks. This will I suppose lay a foundation for the emancipation of those poor wreches in that Country, & I hope be the means of dispensing the Blessings of freedom to all the Human Race in America.[2] Adieu Yours &c.   W W

RC (NhD). Marked above salutation: "No 11."

1. Brief letter of 23 March asking JB's opinion about levying an additional tax. Not printed, see MJB 1600.

2. The resolution called for South Carolina and Georgia to raise three thousand black troops. *JCC*, 13:387–88. Tradition holds that Whipple emancipated his own black body servant, Prince Whipple, during the war in recognition of his services. Kaplan, *Black Presence*, 44–46.

TO WILLIAM WHIPPLE

My Dear Sir,   Exeter April 3d. 1779

Your two favors of the 28th Feby and 7th March are come to hand.
The Continental tax for last year was laid, but the very great expenses
the Board of War are at in supplying the Continental soldiers (which last
year ammounted to above 70,000 pounds L.M.) together with the additional wages and to bounties to the soldiers stationed at Rhode Island,
and the volunteers there and a thousand other expenses that are daily arising &c. &c., has taken away the whole and left us in debt. There is some
of the money taken out of circulation, in the Treasury which I hope will
be sent in part of the tax (perhaps one half of it) if it is possible to go on
without exchanging it for current bills. The Order of Congress of the 10th
ulto for filling up our Continental regiments, is now before the Court,[1]
and they determined to endeavor to comply with the requisition, which
will take about 600 men, very large bounties must be given or no man will
be procured, and I much doubt whether a sufficient number can be procured at any price to enlist during the war, if there is to be an active campaign expect we must fill them up for a short term.

There is a very earnest request from Rhode Island for 300 men to be
sent for their defence as have been done for the last two years, on which
nothing is yet determined. The plan of Govt or new Constitution is not
yet complete: the Convention last October after voting the outlines of it
appointed a Committee to draw it up and adjourned to the beginning of
June next. I have seen the plan they propose to lay in and find it is the
present plan, very little altered. I like many things in the Essex plan but
fear it will be difficult to make any very material alterations from the
present modes. Many people seem to be afraid to trust the Supreme Executive Power out of the hands of the Legislature for fear they should in
time grow to be as arbitrary as a *Governor*. I think it will be some considerable time before we shall have a new government established.[2] I
send you enclosed the Resolve of the General Court for quieting the
minds of our officers and soldiers by which you will see what vast sums
we are obliged to expend as a State; in short unless you were to attend the
General Court you can have no adequate idea of our expenses that must
be provided for by the State.

This State have offered a bounty of three hundred dollars in addition
to the 200 Continental bounty, to every man that enlists in our Continental regiments during the war.[3]

The General Court is expected to adjourn to day, till about the middle
of June next. We have as usual spent a great deal of time about petitions
and Mr. Allen from the nominal State of Vermont has been here with a
petition to us to settle a line between N. H. and Vermont. General Bailey
and Mr. Phelps have been with us as agents for a Convention of a number of Towns on both sides of Connecticut River, requesting us to lay
claim to the whole of the grants west of Connecticut river.[4] A good deal
of time has been spent on it and is now left for consideration to the next
session of this Court. Col. Ashly and Col. Joshua Wentworth have been

chosen delegates and have refused and a number of others have refused when nominated, which has prevented their being appointed. Mr. Woodbury Langdon was chosen by the House last evening, which I expect will be concurred this morning.[5] Yours most sincerely   J. B.

P.S. Mr. Langdon's appointment as a delegate is concurred and he has accepted.   J. B.

TR (DLC: Force Transcripts).

1. The General Court met from 11 March to 3 April. *NHSP*, 8:822–26.

2. The constitution submitted in 1779 was rejected. For the next two years advocates of state constitutional reform were silent. Daniell, *Experiment*, 169–70. The 1779 constitution is printed in *NHSP*, 9:834–42.

3. See resolutions of 31 March. *NHSP*, 8:825.

4. Davenport Phelps (1755–1813), a 1775 graduate of Dartmouth, was a grandson of Eleazer Wheelock. On 17 Mar. 1779 Jacob Bailey and Phelps brought the General Court a proposal for uniting the New Hampshire Grants with New Hampshire. A legislative committee chaired by JB recommended that New Hampshire exercise jurisdiction over the towns only as far as the western bank of the Connecticut River until Congress settled the dispute. Chase, *Dartmouth*, 75–

76, 477–78; *NHSP*, 10:336–38; Walton, *Vermont Records*, 1:432–35.

5. Samuel Ashley (1720–1792) of Winchester served as a colonel in the militia, justice of the Court of Common Pleas for Cheshire County, and member of the Council and of the Committee of Safety, and was chosen a delegate to the Continental Congress on 24 March. When he declined, Nathaniel Peabody was appointed. Potter, *Military History*, 1:305; Waite, *Claremont*, 392; *NHSP*, 8:808, 821, 824.

Joshua Wentworth (1742–1809), Portsmouth merchant, was a colonel in the militia, member of the board of war, and later councilor and state senator. He was appointed a delegate on 1 April. Woodbury Langdon was chosen on 3 April. Wentworth, *Genealogy*, 1:559–60; Brewster, *Rambles*, 1st ser., 116–18; *NHSP*, 8:816, 125–26.

TO WILLIAM WHIPPLE

My Dear Sir,   Kingston April 24th 1779

Your favor of the 23d of March[1] is come to hand. I am very sensible of the difficulties on account of the depreciation of the paper bills, and that emitting more for carrying on the war will add to the depreciation, if not entirely ruin them. That heavy taxes are necessary, and I am sorry we did not begin earlier, but the present situation of our affairs is such that I fear whether we shall be able to raise for the use of the Continent more than what is already called for, beside our other taxes. The Continental tax will be but a little more than a third part of the taxes that will be to be raised this year. The Continental tax of this State is 150,000 pounds—the State tax 100,000 pounds and before the Court rose, they agreed that 100,000 pounds more must be raised for supplying the State this year which will be laid on at their next meeting. The Board of War expended in supplies for our soldiers in the Continental Army last year 74,000 pounds, and if they are supplied in the same manner this year, it will take at least double that sum, and I fear much more; then there is the money to be paid our officers in part towards making up depreciation will be a considerable sum; 500 dollars bounty to be paid to 600 men to be enlisted to fill up our Continental regiments will be a heavy charge, if they are raised agreeable to the vote of the Court, and if not raised in that way, they must be drafted or procured in some other way perhaps as burdensome, beside the Towns are obliged to supply the families of the soldiers at the stipulated prices, which amounts to a great sum in many towns, and the other State charges are by no means small. There is this year a considerable County Tax; add to them the Taxes in the several towns for the poor, schools, ministers, highways &c. &c., and you will be satisfied that the Taxes will be as high this year as the people will bear wthout grumbling. I have consulted with the President and the Committee of Safety, and they think another Continental Tax this year will be attended with great difficulties.

This State have not paid their last year's continental tax, the bounties and pay of the volunteers to Rhode Island with a number of other unforseen charges swallowed up all the money raised for the Continent as well as for the State. There is perhaps 60 or 70,000 dollars of the money that is out of circulation now in the Treasury, which I hope will be sent forward as part of our last year's Tax.

I see by the Boston newspapers that a packet is arrived from France with dispatches for Congress, and the people here seem anxious to know their contents. The success of the Continental frigates gives the people a pleasure to balance their uneasiness at their laying so long idle at Boston.

The letters in the newspaper you sent me, said to be wrote by Carter Braxton, I believe to be genuine as they are the exact picture I had formed of him in my mind, while at Congress with him.[2] I wish he had half the honor and honesty that I am persuaded the Lees are possessed of.

What I have wrote concerning taxation is what appears to me will be the sentiments of the people at large in this State, which I judge of by their representatives in the Assembly. My own sentiments are, that some method must be taken to stop the depreciation, or we are ruined, and if no other and better method can be adopted for that purpose, I should be willing to sell one half of my moveable estate to redeem so much of the money as to appreciate the remainder—but the reigns of Govt are so weak and the people at large so ignorant of the consequences of the depreciation that I am persuaded it will not bear at this time; another year I should hope that instead of six millions, twenty millions may be raised or perhaps more if the Tax raised this year goes down well. I am with respect your friend &c.   Josiah Bartlett

TR (DLC: Force Transcripts).

1. Not printed, see MJB 1600.

2. Carter Braxton (1736–1797) represented Virginia from August 1775 to August 1776, from 1777 to 1783, and in 1785.

TO WILLIAM WHIPPLE

My Dear Sir,   Kingstown May 19th 1779.

Your favor of the 27th of April is come to hand, and am very glad to hear you are willing to tarry some time longer. Col. Peabody I expect will be the bearer of this: the other delegate I suppose will not set out till you give notice of your being about to return: if your health will permit, I should be glad you would tarry out the year.

I hope you will introduce the new delegate to the firmest Whigs and prevent his being taken in by artful men of a different character before he is acquainted with them.

We have had a requisition from General Gates for 300 men to be raised for the defence of the State of Rhode Island, as we have done every year since the British troops took possession of part of that State; but as the General Court passed no order for their being raised, the Committee of Safety don't think themselves authorized to do it till the Court sits, which will be the 16th of June, nor do I see how it will be possible to raise them for want of money. Our Treasury is quite empty (except of the money taken out of circulation and not enough of that belonging to the State to pay our last year Continental Tax). We have hired all that we can possible procure to pay the extra wages to the Rhode Island men last year, to pay the Officers in the army agreeable to a Resolve I sent you, to pay bounties to soldiers to enlist in the Continental Army and other charges.

I am very desirous to know the contents of the packet from France and hope by the next post to receive the account of it from you.

The great scarcity of corn has induced the farmers here, to exert themselves to raise as much this year as possible, I believe that there is at least one third part more planted and sowed this Spring, than in common years. The season at present looks promising—the trees are in full bloom and look finely.

As to any thing you may be desirous of knowing as to the situation of affairs here I must refer you to Col. Peabody and subscribe myself your sincere friend   Josiah Bartlett

22d. Several circumstances concur to convince me that there are Agents in many places employed by the Enemy to destroy the credit of our currency by raising the prices of every thing to the most astonishing degree and I have some reason to think they will try when we are in confusion about our money to add the Province of Maine to Nova Scotia—for particulars enquire of Col. Peabody. Yours   J. B.

TR (DLC: Force Transcripts).

FROM WILLIAM WHIPPLE

My Dear Sir,   Philadelphia the 21st May 1779

My last I think was the 11th inst[1] since which I have not been favored with any of Yours. I have been some time in expectation of a Colleague to supply the place of Mr: Frost, who I suppose must have been at home some weeks.[2] My Task is really arduous, but my anxiety to see a determination of some important matters now under consideration prevents my pressing a speedy relief.

The State of the currency is truely deplorable, but not so alarming in my judgment as the failure of public Virtue. The former may possibly be assisted by human means, but we must depend on him who alone can control the hearts of men to establish the latter.

We are now about trying once more what can be done to save the sinking credit of the money. The prevailing Opinion is that nothing will do but (I was going to say) *excessive* Taxes, but I will soften the epithet & adopt the words *very high*. If a sufficiency can be raised by Taxes to support the war, further emissions will be unnecessary. This is part of the plan now under consideration, a consequent Resolution past this day to raise 45,000,000 to be paid in by the 1st of Jany.[3] I must suspend giving you my Opinion of this measure for the present. Let it suffice to say there was a great Majority in favor of the question, & but a small Majority against the Question for 60,000,000. This is a bold Political Stroke, and I hope will be carried into effect, as to all appearance nothing else can save us from destruction. The People in this part of the country are every where clamerous for heavy Taxes, the greatest difficulty appears to me is, the levying it on the proper persons. If the whole sum could be drawn from those speculating miscreants, who have been sucking the Blood of their country, it would be a most happy circumstance, and I hope the assessors will be particularly attentive to those people. He who increases in wealth at such times as the present, must be an enemy to his Country, be his pretentions what they may. If the Connecticut mode of collecting Taxes, was adobted the business would be much facilitated; In that State five or six Taxes are collected in a Year by that means they collect very large sums without produceing the least uneasiness among the people. If the people are duely impress'd with the advantages they will derive from paying in their money while it is at the present low state they certainly will do it with chearfulness. Spirited measures with the Property of the fugitives, as well as with the persons of the resident enemies, to the Revolution, would in my humble Opinion have an exceeding good effect, at this particular Crisis.

The Enemy seem determined to carry on a predatory war agreeable to the threats held up in the British Commissioners Proclamation last Summer. Their Conduct in Virginia is an evidence of this, for the particulars I must beg leave to refer you to the new papers. Time only can inform us of the events of the present Campaign, but this we may be assured of, that nothing is so likely to give us success as vigorous & decisive measures both in Council & in the Field.

A Mr: Hamilton Gov of Detroit is taken prisoner (by Major Clark of Virginia) with his Garrison at a post he held on the Ohio, this vipers nest has been exceedingly troublesome to our frontiers. Whether our troubles in that quarter will be soon ended, depends on the success of the expedition into that Country under the Command of Genl Sullivan.[4]

Whether we shall have any naval assistance from our ally (depends in my judgment) on the Chapter of accidents but this is not the Opinion of many others; but Mum!

I want every State in the Union to feel the importance of Sovereignty,

& I wish the United States were fully sensible of their importance among the powers of the Earth; we should then under Heaven depend on our own strength & banish from among us every Idea of servility, which now like the Tares among the wheat, prevents the growth of that virtuous republican pride so essential to the happiness of America.

You have several times mention'd to me the Flagg that was detained by order of Congress & as I know the importunity of the people must be very troublesome I heartily wish Congress could be prevailed on to decide on that matter but from various causes nothing has yet been done 'tho several reports have been made & recommitted. On the whole I think it will be best for the executive authority of the State to act their own judgment in that matter.

Mr. Emerson of Durham who was a Commissioner of accots: died here last week of the small pox after three or four days illness. I shall get what information I can of his affairs here, for the satisfaction of his Family, with whom I most heartily sympathise. I am very sincerely Your Friend & Huml. Sert.   Wm: Whipple

RC (MB).

1. Not found.
2. Frost had left Congress in mid-April.
3. New Hampshire's share was $1,500,000. Before the end of 1779 Congress had recalled $95,000,000 in old money. *JCC*, 14:626; Ferguson, *Power of the Purse*, 34.
4. With a force of approximately 170 Americans and Frenchmen, Col. George Rogers Clark had captured British Col. Henry Hamilton, commandant of Detroit, at Vincennes on 25 February. To follow through, Washington assigned Sullivan to lead an expedition against the Six Nations. Wallace, *Appeal to Arms*, 200–03; Peckham, *Toll of Independence*, 58; Whittemore, *John Sullivan*, 115–18.

TO WILLIAM WHIPPLE

My Dear Sir,   Exeter May 29, 1779

Your favor of the 10th Inst[1] is come to hand and must confess myself greatly surprised to hear that you have had no public dispatches since the beginning of December. I had not the least doubt that the packet in to Boston was sent for that purpose and that in consequence of it you were now taking measures. Since I wrote you last, I find our paper currency expiring: what will be the consequence God knows, I have long foreseen and dreaded the event.

Where is General Washington and his army. The enemy are sending their forces to the West Indies, Georgia, South Carolina &c., and leave but few to garrison Rhode Island and New York—yet they are alert and continually making depredations upon our people with little or no loss, while our army to all appearance are either dead or so fast asleep that they cannot be waked; where is the spirit that actuated us in the beginning—Gone Alas! I fear forever. Perhaps I am more gloomy than there is any occasion for—I wish it may be so, but at present our affairs appear to me to wear a very melancholy aspect.

What is become of the lottery—is it finished drawing or is it postponed.

I have a great deal more to say, but want both time and words to express my sensations except one only that I am your very sincere friend

Josiah Bartlett

TR (DLC: Force Transcripts).
  1. Not found.

TO WILLIAM WHIPPLE

My Dear Sir,   Exeter 19th of June 1779.

Your favor of the 24th ulto[1] inclosing one of the 21st is come to hand —we have likewise rec'd the Vote of Congress for raising 45 millions of dollars: this is truly a bold stroke. I wish it may be a good one, if nothing else will answer, we must try it, and leave the event to Providence; if people could be brought to see their own interest, I am sure they would pay it cheerfully, but many people can never be persuaded that any thing is for their interest that takes money from them. The General Court met here last Thursday and have *that* affair, and the filling the Continental regiments, and raising a regiment for the defence of Rhode Island now under consideration; what shall be done, I will endeavor to inform you in my next. Many people seem much dissatisfied with the Tax, yet I think I can perceive that the talk of it, has given a little more life to the Currency.

The Convention at Concord agreed on the enclosed plan of Govt for this State, two of which you will please to present with my regards, to Col Peabody, who I suppose is with you before this time.[2] The County of Grafton who were disaffected, took no notice of the Convention nor of any of the Orders from this State and consequently pay no Continental or State Tax.

The avarious disposition of the people, and the supineness and inactivity of our armies, are truly alarming, while the enemy seem more active and enterprising than usual. I wish our difficulties may rouse the Continent from their lethargy (which has been the case formerly) otherwise we have much to fear. The idle hopes of peace, of new and powerful allies, of some secret and important good news rec'd by Congress which have been circulated in the public papers, have greatly contributed to this lethargy; people began to think all our troubles were at an end, and they had nothing to do but to take the advantage of approaching good fortune, and each one lay up an estate for himself, and now to find themselves disappointed of their expectations creates a very great uneasiness.

Among all our difficulties and disagreeable prospects, we have one prospect that is very agreeable: I mean the present appearance of a good crop of all the fruits of the ground. I believe there never was at this season a more fruitful appearance universally, in this part of the Country; God grant it may continue prosperous to the end of the year.

Your letter to the President enclosing the Resolves of Congress of the

1st and 2d inst, for a Committee to repair to the New Hampshire Grants is just rec'd and sent to the Assembly;[3] what they do relative to that business I will inform in my next. Ira Allen Esq., brother to the Colonel is now here with letters from the legislature of Vermont, soliciting the settlement of the boundary line between New Hampshire and Vermont.

The flag that was stopped by order of the Congress has been discharged about 10 or 12 days and is gone: after your letter of the beginning of April came to hand informing that Congress was likely to give some orders in the matter,[4] the Committee of Safety countermanded the Orders for her discharge till hearing nothing farther, after repeated Solicitations, they sent her off as above mentioned.

I am very sorry to hear of the death of Mr. Emerson, an honest worthy man. Adieu my Dear Sir, and believe me to be your sincere friend

Josiah Bartlett

Pray what is become of the Continental Lottery which began drawing last winter.

TR (DLC: Force Transcripts).

1. Only an extract of Whipple's letter of 24 May has been found. *The Collector*, 58 (August-September 1945), Item N 2660.

2. Enclosure not found. See JB to Whipple, 3 Apr. 1779, n. 2.

3. On 2 June Congress chose a committee of five—Oliver Ellsworth, Pierpont Edwards, John Witherspoon, Samuel Atlee, and Jesse Root—to visit the towns in the New Hampshire Grants with the intent "to promote an amicable settlement of all differences, and prevent divisions and animosities so prejudicial to the United States." *JCC*, 13:674–76.

4. On 23 April the Committee of Safety had ordered the sheriff of Rockingham County "to put in readiness for Sailing the Flag that Came from N. york, detained last fall by order of the Genl Assembly, now in his Custody in order for their returne again." Bouton, "Committee of Safety," 184–85.

FROM WILLIAM WHIPPLE

My Dear Sir   Philadelphia 20th June 1779

You may well think it strange that we are so long without intelligence from Europe a circumstance that I cannot acct for unless we may suppose there has been many miscarriages.

Your distress on account of the Currency is not to be wondered at, it is really an object of great concern & demands the most serious and diligent attention three days in the week are devoted to that business & I hope a bill will soon make its appearance that will dispel the gloom that now overspreads the countenances of America Friends. You ask where Genl W and his army is. I can only answer that they are in the Neighborhood of Hudsons River: the movements of the Enemy on that River and of our army in consequence, you undoubtedly have a history of, before this time. It is surprising that we have no authentic intelligence from S Carolina since the 5th May, when undoubtedly very important events have taken place there, since that date, the reports (which are many) all agree that a general action has happened & that we have gained a complete victory the particulars are hourly expected perhaps I may have the satisfaction of inclosing them in this letter.

I believe the drawing of the lottery is nearly finished but my attention has been so much engaged in other matters that I have not thot lately of making inquiry. I suppose the General Assembly are now sitting & I hope something will be done respecting the Grants. New York are continually pressing to have that business drawn to a conclusion, and insists that there shall not be a seperate state, but will acquiesce in any other mode of settling the dispute. I think it of importance that N H shod lay in her claim and send some person here well informed, to support the claim. Shod that country be added to N Y she will be a powerful and I am apprehensive a troublesome neighbor. I know you must have important business before you, but this is an object of such magnitude as in my humble opinion demands the earliest attention. I have been for a long time daily expecting a colleague but am still without one; you are not acquainted with the disadvantages I must necessarily labor under for want of assistance. When I left home it was my intention to return in May but as I am determined never to turn my back upon difficulties I have no objection to continue here till those we have now to encounter are conquered but must confess I think it hard that I cannot have the aid of a Colleague—both the Lee's have taken leave of Congress, the *Dominion* now makes a very indifferent figure, but I understand there are some appointments which (when they arrive) will place that State in a more respectable point of light. It is not an agreeable thing to see a state divided, that has never yet been the case with N H, but will it not be the case when the two last chosen gentlemen appear together? Unanimity is ever desirable in public councils but never more necessary than at the present day, besides the disadvantages to the public it must be very disagreeable to any Gentn to be opposed to his Colleague in office. I think these considerations ought to have some influence in the choice of public characters.

22d Colo Peabody arrived last evening. I find by him that I am not mistaken in my conjecture respecting him and his intended Colleague, cannot something be done to prevent the evils that may be the consequence of a division of sentiment.

I am happy to hear you have such promising prospects of a plentiful Harvest, from all accounts there never was so great an appearance of plenty in this country as the present season affords. Will not these distinguished marks of the favour of Heaven dispel our Glooms and animate us to cooperate in the promotion of our Country, happiness & in that way show our gratitude to divine Beneficence.

The *Boston* & *Confederacy* have sent in here a ship of 24 guns and 95 men, a private cruising ship & it is reported this morn'g they have taken the *Delaware* & destroy'd another ship of war but this wants confirmation. I hope shortly to have it in my power to give you such information as will tend to dispel the clouds that seem at present to interrupt your happiness, in the mean time be assured that I am, Your very sincere Friend & Obedt. W.W.

Reprinted from *The Historical Magazine*, 14 (November 1868), 215–16.

TO WILLIAM WHIPPLE

My Dear Sir,   Exeter June 25th. 1779

The General Court have passed a Tax Bill to raise their quota of the 45 millions agreeable to the vote of Congress and I have reason to think it will be raised with less difficulty than I feared. Every body seems now fully satisfied that some strenuous exertions must be made, or our Currency is at an end. The Court has ordered the address of Congress to be printed in hand bills and dispersed through the State, and to be read in the meeting houses immediately after services and in the first town meeting in every town after they receive them and I am in hopes it will have a good effect.[1] You will have seen the Boston Resolves relative to prices before this reaches you.[2] Newburyport and other towns are adopting similar measures. The Court has ordered every town to procure their men to fill up the Continental regiments by enlistment for the war or for 12 months by draught or otherwise, on penalty of being fined by the Court at the discretion for every man deficient. They have ordered a regiment of 300 men to be raised for the defence of Rhode Island, in the same manner for six months from the time they arrive at Providence, and I believe great exertions will be made to raise them; but the great difficulty of raising men at this busy season of the year, when more hands are wanting, than are to be procured to secure the fruits of the earth, which are at this time remarkably promising, the great price which is given for labor, and the depreciated state of the currency, together with the great expense of men by the war and gone on board privateers, will make the raising them very difficult if not impracticable—however I hope the most of them will be raised.[3] The Court have voted to lay in a claim to the New Hampshire Grants west of Connecticut river but to acquiesce in the determination of Congress, if they shall think proper to acknowledge them as an Independent State. I expect a Committee will be appointed to wait on the Committee of Congress that are to repair to the grants agreeable to the Resolve of Congress of the 1st inst. that you transmitted to the President of this State.[4] We have had some very imperfect accounts of the defeat of the British troops at Charlestown S. C.—expect soon to hear more particulars;[5] this defeat will (I have reason to hope) be attended with very beneficial consequences at this critical time. The enemy it seems are landed and fortifying at Penobscot, which I suppose is the beginning of a plan to annex the Provinces of Maine to Nova Scotia, which I am apt to think they have adopted. The General Court seem determined to rise to morrow: the price of Indian corn has fell to 20 dollars per bushel or less, owing principally I suppose to the fine prospects of a plentiful harvest. The General Court have reduced their wages to five dollars per day about half their expenses, in order to set an example to their constituents.[6] I am with great respect your friend and servant.   Josiah Bartlett

TR (DLC: Force Transcripts).

1. The General Court ordered the dispersal of the proclamation on 18 June, and voted on the 26th to raise £450,000 in taxes. *NHSP*, 8:827–31; *Laws of N.H.*, 4:215–16.

2. The Boston Resolves intended to fix prices on certain necessities as a deterrent to rampant inflation. The resolves, a product of a meeting of Boston citizens on 25 May, were printed in the *N.H. Gazette*, 15 June 1779.

3. The order passed on 23 June. *NHSP*, 8:829–30.

4. On the following day the Court elected Ebenezer Thompson to journey to the New Hampshire Grants and wait on the committee expected there from the Continental Congress. *NHSP*, 8:831; JB to Whipple, 19 June 1779, n. 3. Whipple had sent the congressional resolutions to Weare on 4 June. Burnett, *Letters*, 4:249.

5. Rather than defeating the British at Charleston in May of 1779, the Americans, by virtue of strong defenses around the city, delayed its capture by the British for a year. Wallace, *Appeal to Arms*, 205–06.

6. *NHSP*, 8:831.

The General Court closed a session on 26 June and immediately the government of the state fell to the direction of the Committee of Safety, on which JB was the second ranking member in 1779. During the summer the committee faced several serious situations in addition to its concerns about inflation and depreciation of currency. An Indian attack on the upper Coos provoked a petition asking the committee for assistance in the form of military protection. Immediately the committee sent twenty-four militiamen with pay, bounty, and provisions to protect the region until 1 October.

On another front, the committee, having been asked secretly to cooperate in the Continental expedition against the expected British landing in Penobscot Bay, ordered a ship fitted out with provisions and sailors and sent to join the fleet forming at Boston. The expedition (which has been called America's largest amphibious undertaking prior to Gen. Winfield Scott's landing at Vera Cruz in 1847) suffered from numerous delays, querulousness over command, and lack of secretiveness, but sailed in July. It became trapped in the bay, was destroyed by the British, and resulted in one of the more dismal American failures of the war. This and other failures damped the high hopes held by JB, Whipple, and other Americans as is evident in their correspondence. See Fowler, Rebels Under Sail, 111–18.

TO WILLIAM WHIPPLE

My Dear Sir,   Kingstown July 10th. 1779

I have not rec'd a letter from you since yours of the 27th of May:[1] I have some suspicion it is owing to the posts being obstructed by the enemy in Hudson's river.

Sundry newspapers from New York and Newport which I have lately seen, assert that France is seeking for peace with England and have offered, through the Spanish Ambassador to renounce all connections with America; the Tories and suspicious characters have had the same story here for some time past. Please to inform me whether you have any reason to think there is any foundation for such reports. The French I believe have been rather unlucky since the war: the loss of Pondicherry will be considerably felt, but I should hope not discourage them to such a degree as to sue for so inglorious a peace. As to news there is none passing at present; the Indians the week before last came into the upper Co'os and captivated some people—a small scout is ordered up for their protection.[2] The expedition to Penobscot, I suppose, has, or will soon sail— the *Hampden* is fitted out at the charge of this State to join in the affair.[3] I have some apprehensions least some of the large British ships should arrive at Penobscot before our fleet get there and disappoint our hopes.

The true state of affairs at the Southward remain still uncertain, nor can I account for it's remaining so long in suspence: I wish it may prove to be as fortunate as we were led to believe from the first reports.

Mr. Secretary Thompson who was sent to Vermont to wait on the Committee of Congress,[4] is returned without seeing them; it seems they came two at a time and went off without seeing each other, nor did they give the people who intended to wait on them time sufficient for that purpose—they were all gone previous to Mr. Thompson's arrival, nor could I learn that any of the people East of the river had an opportunity to see them.

I want to receive a long letter from you giving me an account of the true state of our affairs at Foreign Courts; what are the prospects of Congress concerning peace or new alliances &c. Please to give me all the information of the situation of our affairs and the important matters that are (or ought to be) under the consideration of Congress—by letter if you continue at Congress; if you return soon, I hope to receive the information *viva voce*. I am with sincere regard your most obt servt.

Josiah Bartlett

TR (DLC: Force Transcripts).

1. Not found.

2. On 3 July the Committee of Safety received a petition from Coos asking for assistance and ordered a party of twenty-four militiamen to patrol the region until 1 October. Bouton, "Committee of Safety," 192–93.

3. On 30 June the committee voted to equip the *Hampden*, belonging to John Langdon. Ibid., 192.

4. See Whipple to JB, 19 June 1779, n. 2.

FROM NATHANIEL PEABODY

Dear Sir   Philadelphia 13th. July 1779

I Gratefuly acknowledge the Rect. of Your favours of the 19th. ulto[1] —with proposals for a form of Government in that State. I have also had the pleasure of reading Yours of the 25th. ulto. to General Whipple and am exceedingly pleased with Sundry matters of information Contain'd in those letters—(some of which I shall beg leave to write more fully upon hereafter).

I think the State have Conducted prudently with respect to the New Hampr. Grants—part of the Committee Sent by Congress to investigate the Grievances, and Designs of the People on those Grants, have lately return'd to this place, Their report not yet made known to Congress—Suppose I shall be able to give it you in my Next. Col. Ethan Allen and Mr. Fay[2] have lately been in this City whereby they missed of being present at the Conferrance at Bennington. I inclose You, a hand bill, seting forth the Conduct of the People on Said Grants[3]—upon which the late Complaints from New york against them were founded—Also Several Newspapers. In my last to his Honr. Mr. President Weare I sent Sundry papers, & handbills hope they will arrive Safe.

I am happy to hear the State have so readily Complyd with the indispensably Necessary Resolves of Congress respecting a Tax, for their proportion, of the 45,000,000 Dollars, at this Critical Situation of our Finances; And for raising Their Quota of Troops, as the most Vigorous exertions in the People, at this time is absolutely Necessary to appreciate our Currency, recruit, & support our diminished Army; for without this it would be the height of presumption to expect a Short & Successful War, or a happy & honorable Peace. But my Dear Sir, when I take a retrospective View of those truly Patriotic Characters which at first adornd the Councils of These United States And laid a foundation for a Vast Empire, An Asylum for Civil, and Religious *Liberty* whose Generous breath Glowing with an ardour becoming free born Americans, Vanquished every idea incompatable with industry, frugality, Virtue, and the Union, freedom, & happiness of their Native Country, And at the Same time reflect how the Scene is now Changed, when I see Banquiting, Pageantry, Luxury, dissipation and unhappy disputes & divisions, Spoken against and detested by every honest republican, Standing, or making rapid progress, where it ought not, I am filld with Solemn Surprize and naturally Conclude those Aspects portend Some dire Event, unless averted by a Speedy refformation!! But must dismiss the Subject for this time. Should I attempt to write you relative to the Situation & movements of our Army, apprehend it would by no means reach you till after the Several News papers will have made Such Circumstances Public.

I think I may venture to Conclude that Genl. Whipple will tarry here a few months longer unless it Should be more Convenient for a New Member to Come forward and Supply his place in Congress. This is to you but not to the world. Hope you will write me as often as you Conveniently Can and Stimulate others to the like kind office.

Youl please to present my Compliments to His Honr the President & the Rest of the Honl. Committe—and be kind enough to inform me in your next who they are.[4] I am Dear Sir with unfeigned Esteem & Respect Your most Obedient And Very Humbl. Servt.   Nathl Peabody

P.S. Please to forward the inclosed Letter to Mrs. Peabody. By Desire of a young man I inclose one Letter also to Chase.

RC (MHi). Peabody wrote "N.2" above the salutation. Enclosures not found.

1. Not found.

2. Jonas Fay (1737–1818), a physician of Bennington, Vt., was representing Vermont's claim to congressional recognition.

3. A proclamation signed by Thomas Chittenden as governor and Jonas Fay as secretary was issued on 3 June 1779. Evans, *American Bibliography*, No. 16652. Burnett suggests that this was the handbill that Peabody sent. Burnett, *Letters*, 4:314, n. 3.

4. There is no indication that the membership of the Committee of Safety differed from those appointed on 1 April 1779: Meshech Weare, JB, Ebenezer Thompson, John McClary, John Dudley, Nathaniel Folsom, George Gains, Josiah Moulton, and Samuel Hobart. *NHSP*, 8:825.

TO WILLIAM WHIPPLE

My Dear Friend   Kingstown July 24th 1779

Since I wrote you last I have rec'd yours of the 20th ulto also yours of the 3d inst[1] per Capt. Martin. I am very glad you will consent to tarry some time longer at Congress, as you must be better acquainted with the present situation of our public affairs than it is possible for a stranger to be. Mr. Langdon was to have set out the beginning of this week for Congress on a supposition that you was on the return; but your letter of the 20th came to me while the Committee of Safety was sitting; I read to them what you wrote about tarrying longer—they were highly pleased with it, and wrote to Mr. Langdon that you would consent to tarry some time longer and would notify the Committee some time before you left Congress, that another delegate might be sent to supply your place and the Committee desired him not to proceed till further orders.

I find by the papers that terms for a negotiation instead of being a profound Cabinet secret, are discussed in the public papers: Americanus I suppose to be G. M.[2] of N. Y. who used to sign *the American*. I am very sensible of the present unhappy situation of our public affairs and ardently long for peace—but had rather risk the continuance of the war than give up our right to the fishery. It appears to me to be of the greatest consequence to all the United States, for without it where is our nursery for seamen, and without seamen we can never be respectable by sea and of consequence of but little weight with the powers of Europe; beside the vast advantage of the fishery in trade equal almost to the Mines of Mexico.

Several of the N. H. men in the Continental service have been disabled from service in the marching regiments by wounds or otherways—some have been discharged with recommendations for allowance, others have been sent to join the Corps of Invalids at Boston, and as the forts at Portsmouth are in want of men to garrison them and many of those are sufficient for that purpose, would it not be advisable for them to be sent there, and if so, will it not be necessary that an order be sent to the officer commanding the Invalids in Boston to send them there and if those who are now in this State who are are now on the list of Pensioners should be ordered there by the State will it not be considered by Congress as a release of the pension they have allowed them. Please to inform me your sentiments on the subject and if necessary procure an order for their being sent to there from Boston.

The Committee are extremely desirous you should tarry at Congress as long as possible and have ordered me to signify the same to you. They are very sensible of the fatigues and hardships that you must necessarily be under by so long a stay there, but think your tarrying at this time will be an essential service to this State and perhaps to the Continent. The Committee intended to have wrote you this week on the subject of your tarrying as long as possible at Congress, but urgent business have so taken up their time that it cannot be done by this post and hope you will consider this request as coming from them.

We are now raising men for the forts at Portsmouth as we are apprehensive the enemy may pay us one of their burning visits.

Please to inform Col. Peabody I have rec'd his letter by Capt. Martin and will write him by the next post. I am with great respect your sincere friend &c.   Josiah Bartlett

As I write in haste you will excuse this hasty scrawl.

TR (DLC: Force Transcripts).

1. Not printed, see MJB 1650.

2. Gouverneur Morris (1752–1816) of Morrisania, N.Y., who served in Congress during 1778–1779, wrote a series of articles on Continental finances for the *Pennsylvania Packet* in 1780 which he signed "An American."

FROM WILLIAM WHIPPLE

My Dear Sir   Philadelphia 3d Augt 1779

I wrote you pr last post when I believe I acknowledged the receipt of yours of the 10th July. I am sorry Mr: Secy Thompson did not see the Committee of Congress at Vermont however I hope every measure will be taken to support N. Hampshires Claim to that Territory. N. Y. has been very quiet about that matter ever since the return of the Committee but this Calm will not last long. You are too well acquainted with the arts & insidious designs of certain men, to need their charecters from me. If the Claim of New Hampshire is not supported that Country will assuredly be annex'd to N. Y. which I am sure must be attended with disagreeable consequences not only to N. H. but other Eastern States. I intended to have wrote you largely on this subject but having been several times interupted & my head crowded with a thousand other matters, I am under a necessaty of defering it for the present.

Our accots. from the West Indies are by no means unpleasent. I will give them to you so far as my recollection serves me from hearing Mr. Bingms Letter read which came to hand yesterday.[1]

Count De Estaing with 25 ships of the line & 11 Frigates sail'd from Martinica the 28th June for Granada.

Admiral Byron being inform of the Capture of St. Vincents on his arrival at St. Lucia in the Evening of the 30th sail'd the 1st of July in the morning with 18 ships of the line & 3 Frigates in order to retake it being then ignorant of the Expedition against Granada. He appeard before St. Vincent & demanded a surrender but a deputation of the principal inhabitants informing him of the Resolution of the Caribs to carry devastation through the Island if an attack should be made & beseaching him to leave them to their destiny; & at the same time he being inform'd of the critical scituation of Granada abandon'd his project & directed his Course for that Island which it is not improbable might have surrender'd before his arrival as the french fleet had four days start of him.

Byron took 2000 Troops with him from St. Lucia whos Baggage were on board the transports & were destined for this Continent—from these circumstances there is the highest probability that an action has happened indeed reports will have it so, but I hope I shall not wear the Charge of Infidelity for not giving into reports too readily however I will agree with the multitude so far as to allow that appearences are very favorable.

Please to inform me whether the journals of Congress which I directed to Col: Gilman are come to hand; I shod also be glad to know if you ever received the "Observations on the American Revolution" which I sent to you in Feby or march.[2] I sent at the same time a number to be distributed but have never heard if any of them came to hand. I most Heartily wish your Penobscot Expedition may succeed nor can I see any thing against but the delays that have taken place in preparing which may give the Enemy opportunity to get reinforcements. Should it succeed I can see no difficulty in crossing the Bay immediately & takeing possession of Nova Scocia. This would be so glorious an acquisition that it wod surely be worth Hazarding much for. Pray let me know if such a plan is in contemplation. Col: Peabody informs me he has inclos'd the latest News papers.

By the conclusion of Your last letter you seem to expect me home shortly; I have stay'd much longer then I intended, or perhaps then is desired by my Constituents. If the latter shod be the case a very short notice will be sufficient for my departure from this place. I am extreamly anxious for the determination of some important questions which ought to have been decided many months ago. This & some other matters which I shall communicate to you when I may have the pleasure of a tete-a-tete conversation, on some future day will accot for my continuing so long here; & since the summer is so far spent I think to take the pleasent part of autumn to travel in unless it shod be otherwise order'd by the authority which placed me here & who's orders I shall always be happy in Obeying. I am my Dear Sir most Respectfully Yours   Wm Whipple

RC (NhD).
1. William Bingham (1752–1804) of   Philadelphia served four years as Conti-

nental agent at Martinique.

2. *Observations on the American Revolution*. Published According to a Resolution of Congress, by their Committee, For the Consideration of Those who are Desirous of Comparing the Conduct of the Opposed Parties, and the Several Consequences which have Grown from it. (Philadelphia: Printed by Styner and Cist, in Second-Street, MDCCLXXIX). 122 pages. Drawn up by Gouverneur Morris. Evans, *American Bibliography*, No. 16625.

TO WILLIAM WHIPPLE

Dear Sir,   Kingstown August 4th 1779.

Your favor of the 12th ulto is come to hand and thank you for the enclosed newspapers: although I am very sorry to find that the most important secrets of Congress are become the subjects of newspaper's altercation, yet since it is so, I am glad of the opportunity of seeing those publications: I fear those publications will prove of infinite disservice to these States—what will the enemy, nay what will our friends and allies think when they see the disputes and animosities that subsist in Congress? and that that Body has not the prudence to *conceal* the most important secrets even that of the terms to be insisted on in a negotiation for peace: will not our enemies think they have nothing to fear, and our friends and allies nothing to hope, from such (I had almost said a despicable) body of men: and is there not reason to fear some others in these States may think them unworthy of the Supreme Power and be willing to put it into other hands who they may think will use it better? But I forbear, your own ideas I make no doubt will furnish you with some melancholly reflections on this account.

The affair of South Carolina, as you observe, fall infinitely short of what was reported, and I am under some apprehensions whether some of the Southern States will not fall under the power of Britain; if so, it will put off peace (the object of our wishes) to some distance, unless they should be given up in the settlement, for I apprehend Britain will not consent to give them back if she can hold them; is it not therefore of the utmost importance that a sufficient force should be sent this fall to dislodge them before winter, when I hope some negotiations for a peace will take place? and cannot such a force be collected from Virginia and some other of the Southern States who are the least subject to diseases, on account of the climate? The fall and winter I should think the most proper time for campaigns in that country; if it is possible to rid that part of the country from those ravagers, I should think no time should be lost in effecting it; but what is to be expected from so trifling and divided a body as the newspapers represent ———— to be.

7th By the Boston newspapers I find an account of the arrival of a French frigate with a new Minister Plenipotentiary and that Mr. J. Adams is returned in her;[1] I now expect Congress will have a particular account of the situation of affairs in Europe and what assistance of money or shipping is to be expected this campaign and what force the enemy are likely to send against us. I almost wish myself in Congress for a few days to hear what intelligence he brings. We have at present no certain news from Penobscot since the 29th ulto, when our people had landed, taken 2 batteries &c. We hourly expect further intelligence which I expect you will receive before this reaches you. The fore part of this letter was wrote immediately on reading the papers from Philadelphia in great haste and perhaps with too much freedom; but I know you will easily pardon the quick sensibility I feel at any thing that reflects dishonor on the Supreme Power of these States, or endangers their happiness, especially from one who you know is your and our country's most sincere friend and devoted servant

Josiah Bartlett

The Resolve of Congress for borrowing 20 millions is come to hand: the General Court not being likely to sit till after the time limited was expired, the Committee appointed the members of the Court to endeavor to procure loans and sent each member a handbill including the Resolve and a recommendation to them for that purpose;[2] but I fear we cannot expect much from the people of this State; few of them are possessed of much cash, and the high prices of every thing require a man to have 20 times as much as formerly for common pocket expenses—nor do I think there is at present too great a quantity of money, if the prices continue as at present and people were under no fear of a further depreciation. What made money appear to be plentier than it really was, was owing to every man's pushing it off, as soon after he rec'd it as possible for fear of its depreciating in his hand, which will not be the case when that fear is removed. In short the greatest part of our people will be hard put to it to procure money sufficient to pay their taxes, Continental, State and Town; in some towns the Taxes to raise Town bounties for the soldiers and supply the soldier's families nearly or quite equal the Continental Tax. Yours

J. B.

TR (DLC: Force Transcripts).

1. After more than a year in France (he had sailed from America in February 1778), John Adams returned to Boston on board the *Sensible* with the Chevalier de La Luzerne in August 1779. Butterfield, *Diary of John Adams*, 2:273, 363, 400; Smith, *John Adams*, 1:429–35.

2. As part of its attempt to decrease the currency in circulation Congress resolved on 29 June to call in $20,000,000 as a loan to the United States at 6 percent interest. The N.H. Committee of Safety sent the printed resolve to every town. *JCC*, 14:783–85; Bouton, "Committee of Safety," 198.

TO WILLIAM WHIPPLE

Dear Sir,   Kingstown August 21st 1779.

I have rec'd your favor of the 27th ulto and thank you for the information you give of the situation of foreign affairs by the latest intelligence you had then received. You have now had later and I suppose very authentic information, since you wrote by Mr. Adams who has been with you no doubt.[1]

I am of your opinion that we ought not to put too much dependence on foreign alliances, but on Heaven and our own exertions; yet in the present situation of our affairs, the loss of our allies on the one hand, or the gaining of new and powerful ones on the other would no doubt be attended with very important consequences to us on many accounts. I have no doubt that our Cause is as just as any the Israelites were ever engaged in, and I am sorry to find that like them we are a crooked and perverse generation, longing for the fineries and follies of those Egyptian task masters from whom we have so lately freed ourselves and were willing to return to slavery in order to enjoy them, and though I believe the Country will be finally delivered from War and Slavery, I wish we may not travel in the wilderness in which we are at present, till this present generation are gone off the stage and a more virtuous one have arisen in it's stead. I hope our present situation will not continue forty years as their's did, and trust there are some Calebs and Joshuas among us who will live to see the promised peace and rest, and that you, my dear friend, will be one of them.

The expedition to Penobscot not being planned with that secrecy and prudence that it ought to have been, has miscarried. Some of our little fleet are lost, and I am in great concern for the remainder of them. The *Hampden* which was engaged by this State it is said is taken.[2] The Eastern parts I am afraid will suffer much, if not fall into the enemy's possession; their main design this campaign I believe was to take and keep possession of the two extremities of these states, and so by degrees to reduce the whole to their obedience. I hope some effectual means will be taken to disappoint them.

Exeter, August 21st P. M. Have just rec'd yours of the 3d inst and am to inform you that we have reason to think we have lost the greatest part of our fleet that went to Penobscot though we have no certain information of it; you will no doubt hear the particulars of that unhappy affair before this reaches you. The Journals of Congress which you sent to Col. Gilman are rec'd. The observations on the American Revolution which you write you sent in Feby or March have not come to hand, nor have I seen one of them. I shall write you farther soon—I am glad to hear you are willing to tarry till Fall, though I want much to have the pleasure of a private conversation with you. I am with sincere regard and respect your most assured friend &c.   Josiah Bartlett

TR (DLC: Force Transcripts).

1. Adams did not go to Philadelphia on his return, but he wrote Congress of his return and asked that his accounts be settled. Smith, *John Adams*, 1:436.

2. The Committee of Safety eventually had to reimburse the owners of the *Hampden*. Bouton, "Committee of Safety," 204, 248. See also JB to Peabody, 26 Feb. 1780.

As the following letter discloses, Woodbury Langdon arrived in Philadelphia on 3 September. He stayed there only until mid-November. To help cover his expenses, Langdon had been advanced £1,000 by the Committee of Safety as early as 29 May. Bouton, "Committee of Safety," 189.

FROM NATHANIEL PEABODY

My Dear Sir   Philad. Sept. 7h. 1779

Your kind favour of the 21 ulto[1] inclosing one from Mrs. Peabody I have duly recd and am extreamly oblig'd by the *Care* you have taken in forwarding Letters to & from me. I inclose you Several papers, & extracts by which you will have some information &c.[2]

The Spanish Ambasador left the British Court the 18th. of June last and went immediately to france. The British Court have Sent out two Emissaries to seduce these States from their Alliance with France. I should forward a long Copy of Mr. J. A—ms report upon important matters of Public Concernment, made, officially, Since his return[3]—but you will soon have it by Genl Whipple who Sets off for home in Consequence of Mr. L—d—n's[4] arival here the 3d instant—A Circumstance, to me not a little Extraordinary. Genl Whipple had been Strongly urged, by order of the Supreme Authority of the State to tarry here as long as he Possibly Could—upon which Ocasion I had the honr. to add my most Ardent wishes for his Compliance. And notwithstanding his long absence from his family, & Domestic affairs, he willing to Serve his distressed Country and Gratify the Good People of the State—Consented to Tarry till one month after he should advise the State of his design to leave Congress—which intention was made Known to the Committee who approved thereof, and Gave the Necessary orders to Mr. L—don —of all which Mr. Whipple was fully advised.

If this New menouver is by order of authority, I leave you to Judge what impressions it must Necessarily make upon the mind of a Gentlman of Mr. Whipples Sensibility—but if it is in violation of Such orders You will Judge of the Designs of the Violation—And of the Measures necessary to be taken upon the insult. Congress have resolved that the Emissions of Bills of Credit, of the united[5] Shall at no time Exceed Two hundred million of Dollars, and that they will Stop as far Short of that Sum as the Exertions of the Several States Shall enable them.[6] A particular account of the Several Emisions, is making out, determin'g the Sum Now in Circulation—which I Shall Transmit you. I have the Honr. to be with the highest Esteem Your most obedt. Huml. Servt.   Nathl Peabody

N.B. Youl please to keep the Contents of this Letter intirely from the Connections of Mr. W. L—d–n &c. I know I am Safe.

RC (NhD). Marked "No. 7" above salutation. Franked.

1. Not found.

2. Enclosures (NhD) are copies of John Adams' letters of 27 Feb. and 1 March 1779 from Passy which are printed in Wharton, *Diplomatic Correspondence*, 3: 69–72.

3. Adams' report to Congress, in which he outlined the diplomatic position of each European state, is printed in Wharton, *Diplomatic Correspondence*, 3:278–86.

4. Woodbury Langdon.

5. Peabody must have meant to write "united States."

6. The resolution was made on 3 September. *JCC*, 15:1019.

TO NATHANIEL PEABODY

My Dear Sir

Hartford, Connecticut
October 20th 1779

I am now here with Colo. Joshua Wentworth from our State waiting for the arrival of Committes from the other New England States and New York to take into Consideration the Land Embargoes that are now in force in most of them, and other matters to be adopted by those States for appreciating our Currency; If I should not have time before I leave this place to inform you of the measures that shall be recommended, you will soon see them in Congress, where no Doubt they will be immediately sent.[1] Genl Whipple was not arrived home the 14th when Colo. Wentworth left Portsmo. Tho I was informed by a man from Philadelphia who I met on the road here, that he left Congress the latter End of September. We are very anxious to hear from the french fleet and various Rumors & Reports have Spread round the Country of his Success at Georgia and arrival at Sandy Hook; which I begin to fear will turn out like Lincoln's affair at Charlestown S: C:; No Certain accounts of him are received here since his arrival at Georgia. God send him Prosperity and Success Equal to our most Sanguine wishes.

The General Court is to meet at Exeter this Day and I Suppose they will immediately attend to the Choice of Delegates and send the Choice forward as soon as possible.

I have seen Dr. Hedges[2] in this Town and he Desires me to inform you that he was now seting off for the Eastward.

21st Mr. Cushing has informed me that G. Whipple was at Boston the 15th Inst:

I have seen the order of Congress of the 6th & 7th Inst: for raising fifteen million Dollars monthly,[3] and Sincerely wish it were possible to be Carried into Effect, but from my present Idea of the matter I think it not possible to be Carried into Execution in N. H., and I fear that the order will Throw the Assembly into great Confusion on many accounts, first they will not Consent to lay a new tax till there is a new proportion. Throw[4] the State as you are sensible the present proportion is very much Complained of, and the making a new proportion will be a work of sometime; next, assessments to be Collected monthly will be attended with insuperable Difficulties on the wild lands in the State &c. &c. However I am very sensible of the advantage that will arise from Taxing as heavily as the people will bear and if I return before the matter is Determined by our Court I shall do all in my power to Encourage the matter. I Expect to know before I return what Connecticut does in the affair and perhaps their Determinations will have Some Effect on our Court. I am yours Sincerely   Josiah Bartlett

RC (N). Docketed by Peabody: "Recd Novr. 2d—returned a Small note only."

1. JB and Wentworth had been ap-   pointed on the 8th by the Committee of

Safety. A letter from the Massachusetts Council proposed that delegates from Massachusetts, New Hampshire, Rhode Island, Connecticut, and New York meet on 20 October "to agree upon a Method for keeping up a free & general intercourse in trade, &c., upon principles correspondent with the public good, and Effectually to distroy the practices of those people who prey upon their Country, and to consult and agree on any other measures that then & there may be thought necessary for the Welfare of the united States. . . ." On 26 November the Committee ordered payment of £178:12 to JB in settlement of accounts for atten-

dance at Hartford. Bouton, "Committee of Safety," 206, 210. A copy of the convention proceedings (PCC, Item 33) reached Congress on 10 November and was acted upon on the 19th. *JCC*, 15: 1254, 1291.

2. Silas Hedges of Dunbarton had been suspected of counterfeiting in 1777. Redeemed, he was mentioned by JB again. *NHSP*, 8:546, 694, 734; Hedges to JB, 5 Oct. 1777, MJB 1251; JB to Peabody, 4 Nov. 1779.

3. See Peabody to JB, 18 October, MJB 1693.

4. JB probably meant "throughout."

TO NATHANIEL PEABODY

My Dear Sir   Exeter November 4th 1779

While at Hartford (from whence I returned the 2nd Inst.) I Recd your favor of the 12th ulto[1] and since my return I Recd yours of the latter End of September & 5th of October and in those letters I Recd the Copies of G. Burgoines private Letters to the Secretary of State, Sundry pamphlets of the Journals of Congress with News papers &c. &c. for which I am much obliged to you. The General Court have been siting about a fortnight, have Resolved to lay in our Claims to the Newhampshire Grants west of Connecticut River, and appointed Mr. S. Livermore in Conjunction with our Delegates in Congress to appear &c. assert and prosecute our Right and an Act is now Drafting to impower Congress to take up the matter agreable to their Resolves for that purpose.[2]

A vote has passed empowering you & Mr. Woobry Langdon to Represent this state in Congress till Relieved or Recalled a Copy of which I suppose will be sent by the president. Gen: Whipple & Genl Folsom are appointed Delegates but whither either of them will accept is at present uncertain, I Believe Genl Folsom will accept and perhaps Mr. Whipple may be prevailed on to attend next Spring if necessary.

Col: Samuel Folsom & Col: Moses Nichols are appointed to Repair to the Army & Endeavor to Reinlist our soldiers During the war whose times are near Expiring.[3] The G: Court seem to be of opinion that no more taxes can be raised by this State till there is a new proportion among the several Towns, and are about sending out precepts for that purpose: The Requisition of Congress for our proportion of 15 millions monthly has not yet been acted upon, but from what I can at present learn am in hopes it will be raised Tho not so soon as is Desired.

The Result of our meeting at Hartford will Come to Congress before this reaches you, Please to inform me what are the Setiments of Congress Relative to the measures proposed & whither there is a probability of the several States Coming into those measures. I well know the Difficulties of Regulations of prices, but unless Something is soon Done to Stop the

Depreciation of the Currency it will soon Cease to be a Circulating Medium and the Distress & Dangers that will follow are obvious to Every man of common sense; and what better measure can be taken to keep off so Dangerous a Situation? Taxes alone we find by fatal Experience will not, and if the Taxes are Collected and the money will not purchase the necessaries for the army what will it avail. If anything better can be adopted than we have proposed I shall Chearfully agree to it, if not is it not best to try Regulations once more on the proposed plan till the opperation Expected from those large Taxes begin to take Effect? If that alone will Relieve us, the Regulations will of Course be at an End when people cannot get so much for their articles as the Stipulated prices.

The Committe of Safety in the last Recess of the General Court had Recd information That some persons in this State & the State of the Massachusetts, were Concerned in Carrying on a Correspondence with the Enemy by means of a Salt works near Cape Cod, and that one to two of the Refugees were in this State secreted that Came out that way. The Committe ordered Robert Smith to take up Sundry suspected persons and Enjoined our selves to secresy. The matter however got to the Ears of the parties and such proof was made that it was Conveyed to them by Col: S: H—t who you know has lately been of that Committee that the others of the Committe ordered him not to meet with us till the matter was Cleared up or the Seting of the General Court. The Court Since their Seting have taken up the matter and after a full hearing and the Evidinces on both Sides produced, the Assembly have Expelled him their House, as I am informed, nem: con:[4]

We have for Sometime had various Rumors of the Success of the French fleet to the Southward but no Certain intelligence to be Depended on. The Enemy's Leaving Rhode Island and the Forts up the North River shew their apprehensions. There is a Report here that the Brittish Troops have left Penobscot, and from Several Circumstances I apt to believe it true, Tho there is no certain accounts Come to hand. I am Respectfully yours   J: Bartlett[5]

Novr 6th Mr. Jesse Johnson[6] & Dr. Hedges are in Town and were last Evening with the President, Mr. Dudly & myself &c.

RC (NN: Emmet Collection, No. 452).

1. Not printed, See MJB 1692.

2. See *NHSP*, 8:834; and *Laws of N.H.*, 4:233–36.

3. The several appointments mentioned are printed in *NHSP*, 8:832–34.

4. As a "special sheriff" of Rockingham County, Robert Smith (1735–1795) of Londonderry apparently carried out specific assignments such as this one for the Committee of Safety. Smith was often assigned to confiscate and hold in trust estates of fugitive Loyalists during the period from 1777 to 1783. [Leonard and Smith], *Genealogy of William Smith*, 6–7;

MJB 2037; *NHSP*, 10:456–57. See also references to Smith in Bouton, "Committee of Safety."

Samuel Hobart (1734–1798) operated a powder mill in Exeter and was a member of both the House of Representatives and the Committee of Safety in 1779. During October the committee investigated complaints that Hobart had revealed important secrets to the enemy, and the House expelled him. The charge may have been groundless, for in 1785 he was settling his accounts with the state. After the war he lived in Kingston. Hurd, *Hillsborough*

County, 452; Bouton, "Committee of
Safety," 206, 213; *Laws of N.H.*, 5:195;
NHSP, 18:756–57.

5. Peabody's acknowledgment, 30 November, is in MJB, 1718.

6. Probably Jesse Johnson (c. 1732–

1800) of Hampstead. He was then establishing a home in Enfield. His son, Jesse
Johnson, Jr. (1762–1816), later supported
the Federal Constitution in the 1788 state
convention. Noyes, *Hampstead*, 390–91.

TO NATHANIEL PEABODY

Dear Sir   Exeter December 18th 1779

Your Last favor that is Come to hand is Dated the 16th of Novr:[1] and
that only a Cover to some News papers &c. This I Esteem as a favor, but
if your More important Business & your other Correspondencies would
give time for you to write me more fully of the Situation of affairs it
would be much more agreable. General Folsom will no Doubt be with
you long before this reaches you and give you a particular account of
affairs here; The new General Court met here the 15th and have formed;
The members of the Council for Rockingham the Same as last year
Except Coll: Thornton in the room of Col. Walker who was omitted at
his own Request. The County of Strafford the Same as last year; from
the other three Counties we have no Returns, but have heard that Mr.
Abbot and Timothy Farrer Esqr. are appointed for Hillsborough. Col.
Hunt & Col. Enoch Hale for Cheshire in the room of Colls. Ashley &
Bellows and Deacon Worster for Grafton in stead of Col. Johnson. There
are a great many new faces in the House of Representatives whither the
Changes are for the better or worse time will Discover. Capt. Samll Gilman is not Reappointed nor are Col. Tash & Esqr. Blodget, Mr. Livermore is appointed by Holderness &c. Col. Langdon is speaker & Mr.
Emery Clerk. The President, Secretary, & Treasurer the same as last year
and things at present appear pretty easy, how long it will last is uncertain.[2]

The Committe that was sent to the army to reinlist the men have Returned with but little Success. The Complaints of the army are very great
for want of necessary Cloathing and other things and on account of the
Depreciation of the money. How we shall Satisfy them or do them Justice
I know not, but suppose Something will be attempted by the Court before they adjourn, which I Expect will be the latter end of next week for
about 3 weeks, Then to meet and finish the necessary Business. Nothing
is yet said about Mr. L——e's being appointed Member of Congress,[3]
that perhaps may bring us into the situation we were at the Dissolution
of the late House, which no Doubt you will be informed of by your Colleague. Capt. Gile, Capt. Calfe & Esqr. Ladd are reelected.[4]

We hoped and Expected that some of the Towns in the County of
Grafton that had refused to send Members to the assembly would this
year have sent, but I Cannot hear of one Towns Choosing Except those
few that sent last year.

I should have wrote you something more particular of the situation of
affairs here on account of the Depreciation &c. &c. &c. &c. but Expect

you will be fully acquainted of all our Circumstances by G. Folsom. Please to give my sincere Regards to the General and be asured that I Still am your and his sincere friend   Josiah Bartlett

RC (PHC: Charles Roberts Autograph Letters Collection).

1. Not found.
2. Members of the General Court are listed in *NHSP*, 8:839–41.
3. Samuel Livermore was elected to Congress on 1 Jan. 1780. *NHSP*, 8:845.

4. The reelection of Ezekial Gile of Plaistow and Atkinson, John Calfe of Hampstead, and Timothy Ladd of Salem were of special interest to Peabody, who was from Atkinson.

FROM NATHANIEL PEABODY

My Dear Sir   Philada. Feby 8th. 1780

Your Obliging favour of the 27h[1] of Decr. Came to hand last evening And you may Depend upon my investigating the matters you refer to without loss of time, and shall advise you of the true State of Facts so far as I shall be able to obtain them.

Mr. Livermore arived here last Saturday, in good time as the Vermont affair is soon to Come on before Congress. Vermont refuse to refer the Decision of the Matters in dispute to be determined in the mode prescribed by the Resolves of Congress. What operation that will have in the premises is uncertain—there Agents, are here with Powers to support their Independance and Enter into the Union. But not being Clothed with a weding Garment Can they be received, or even heard by Congress.

Agents are here from the Inhabitants on both Sides of Connecticut River, who seem to be in favour of the State of New Hampr. which is not a Disagreable Circumstance in our favour.

Congress are about to Call upon the several States, to fill up their Battallions in the Continental Army and to furnish their respective Quotas of Supplies for the army, and no time ought to be Lost to accomplish so important an undertaking, as much will Depend upon the Exertions of the People, in preparing for the next Campaign. A prospect of pursuing the war with Success, or Negociating a *peace* to advantage Demand the same Noble Exertions on our part. The Quota of men to be Compleated by N. Hampr. will be about *1200* men in all.

We have nothing recent from Europe except some friendly Communications made by the Minister of France, respecting the Intentions of the Christian & Catholic Kings in Cooperating with us the Ensuing Campaign.

Our finances still remain in a Deranged Situation which Greatly Embarrasses every public proceeding.

Bills of Exchange meet with a Dull Market—and we Can promise our selves but Little from the Sale.

I Should be extreemly well pleased to hear how you proceed in the State of N. Hampr. with respect to Public affairs.

But hope to be at home very early in the Spring and beg your influence that a member may be sent on to relieve me as soon as Possible or Else the State will be left with but one member in Congress. I am Dear Sir Your Sincere Friend most obedt. & very Humble Servt.   Nath Peabody

RC (PHC: Charles Roberts Autograph Letters Collection). Marked by Peabody: "No 22."
   1. Peabody probably meant 25th.

TO NATHANIEL PEABODY
Dear Sir   Exeter February 26th 1780
   By some means or other our Correspondance has lately been much interrupted, The last of your favors that have Come to hand was Dated the 24th Decembr, nor have I been able to write you so often as formerly on account of the Difficulty of Conveying my letters to the post office.
   The General Court began their session the 9th Instant and are now seting. They have not yet got thro the Act for proportioning the several Towns, nor have they voted the Sums of money to be raised for the State & Continent the Current year but will be Done before they rise.
   The people at Co'os have been alarmed by intelligence that the Indians that were Drove in, by G: Sullivan Design to pay them a visit from Canada this winter, and have petitioned the state for help, in Consequence of which 100 Men have been ordered to be Drafted from the Cols. Stickney, Kellys & David Websters Regiments & sent to their assistance.[1]
   I much fear we shall not be able to pay any of the last part of the Tax laid the year past for the use of the Continent. The amout of our Expences are Enormous; last summer the loss of the *Hampden* was about £100,000. The Board of Warr have Received large Sums for Supply'g necessaries for the army, and have laid an Estimate of four Hundred Thousand pounds more that are immediately wanted for that purpose, half of which sum they have had an order for this week. The Rolls for Col. Mooney's Regiment for the Defence of Rhode Island which have been passed this week amounts to upward of 26 thousand pounds. Beside near 40,000 Dollars which were advanced them as bounty & travel money before they marched.[2]
   Every officer & soldier in the Contl army who are at home Receive money in part toward Depreciation viz a Col., four Thousand Dollars, Lt. Col. 3,200, major 2600, Capt. 2000, Lt. 1400, Ensign 1100, surgeon 3200, surgeons mate 2000 Do, Each non Commision officer 500 & Each private 400: We have already advanced I belive about 40,000 pounds for Bounties to reinlist the Continental Troops. These with an innumberable other Sums which we are paying will I fear make it impossible to pay much of what was raised last year for the use of the Contint to the order of Congress. I hope the Court will be more liberal in Taxing this year than they were last.
   I wrote you the latter End of Decr, and the presidt wrote the Treasury Board relative to a mistake in the Treasury Books of the Sum of 200,000 Dollars which was Charged to this State in July 1778, I hope you have

been able to Clear up that Matter as I am well Assured it must be a mistake. You request me to send you Copies of the acts & Laws passed since you left us, but as Mr. Emery is now procuring a new set of all the laws of the state to be printed in their order & the late laws on that account not being yet printed, it is not in my power at present to Comply with your request, will Endeavor to do it as soon as I am able.[3] The Deplorable Situation of our money almost raises the Hyp:[4] it Depreciates as fast as Ever, with us the Exchange is Recconed from 40 to 50 for one & some things to 100, where it will end God knows and what will be the Event. I Believe I informed you in my last of the mode adopted for setling the Depreciation with the army.

I have nothing to write you in the news way, please when you write, to inform of all the news and the Situation of affairs as far as is proper.

I want to hear what is Done with Vermont, the Determination of Congress about taking up the affair at present is no doubt settled before this. A late Publication of Vermont on the Dispute no Doubt you have seen if they are not suffered to be a State by themselves I Dread the Consequence but I hope prudence will Guide your Counsels. Adieu

J: Bartlett

P.S. Gen: Sullivan has Recovered his health in a great measure. Last week he waited on the Court and the President by order, Congratulated him on the Recovery of his health, the successes of his last Campain and gave him the thanks of the State for his past services. The adress with the Genls answer I may have an oppertunity to send you next week. Give my sincere Regards to Genl Folsom.[5]   J: Bartlett

RC (PHi).

1. Thomas Stickney (1729–1809) of Concord, Moses Kelly (1739–1826) of Goffstown, and David Webster (1738–1824) of Plymouth were colonels of the 11th, 9th, and 12th regiments of N.H. militia. NHGR, 1:449; Kelly, *Genealogical Account of John Kelly*, 28–29; Stearns, *Plymouth*, 1:392–405; Potter, *Military History*, 1:321, 346, 352.

2. JB wrote this sentence in the margin of the manuscript with an indication that it fit in at this point.

3. In November of 1779 the House appropriated funds for printing state laws, and in October of 1780 the General Court issued instructions to clerk Noah

Emery on how to distribute the volumes. Stevens, *Noah Emery*; NHSP, 8:836, 876; Bell, *Bench and Bar*, 342.

4. An eighteenth-century abbreviation referring to a headache.

5. Sullivan led an expedition against the Six Nations in western Pennsylvania and New York between July and October of 1779. Upon completion of the expedition Sullivan submitted his resignation to Congress and returned to his home in Durham. Whittemore, *John Sullivan*, 132–52. The address of the General Court and Sullivan's answer are printed in Hammond, *Sullivan Papers*, 3:181–83.

TO NATHANIEL FOLSOM

My Dear Sir   Exeter March 11th 1780

Tho you have not favored me with a line since your arrival at Congress,[1] that has Come to hand; Yet I make no Doubt you will be pleased to hear from time to time how our public affairs are Carried on, and it will give me Equal pleasure to receive similar information from you.

At the first session of the present General Court we had a more Disagreeable session than the last of the late house when you were present, and on the Same Account. A Certain Gentleman[2] who was Displeased with the members of the Comtte of Safety last summer, for Desiring his Brother not to proceed to Congress, took Every means in his power to injure them, finding fault with Every thing they Did, and taking advantage of the new members to insinuate things much to the Disadvantage of many of the Comtte, and Carried matters so far that the Court Reduced the Comtte to five,[3] and took from them almost all the powers they formerly had, not allowing them to settle any Accounts or Draw on the Treasurer for money on any account whatever; and many Constables & other Coming in the Recess and finding they Could not get their accounts settled as usual, without making another Jorney have raised a great Clamor against the Court: The first session lasted to the first Day of Janry and then adjourned to the 9th Febry, at which time they met and have hitherto had a very peaceable, quiet session. The Speaker has not yet attended this session; We are in hopes to rise next week, having got the most material Business in a good way. The Proportion between the Towns is made. We have agreed to raise Thirty Six hundred Thousand Dollars for the use of the Continent, to be paid into our Treasury at 3 Equal payments viz the first of June, august & october, and we have voted to rase just as much more for the State for the Current year, to be paid the first of June, october & Janry;[4] I hope the State Tax, if it Can be Collected will Discharge our Expences and allow us to pay part or all our last year Contl. Tax, as we have been obliged to make use of the money raised for that purpose, to pay the Rhode Island Soldiers, to pay Continental and State Bounties to inlist Soldiers, to find Cloathing for them and Provisions while here, to pay Depreciation to the officers & soldiers agreable to our promise to them &c. &c. &c.

I want to hear what you have Done about Vermont, hope you will not proceed so hastily as to produce Bloodshed. The green mountain Boys have high spirits, and if things are Drove rashly it is my opinion, it will be attended with fatal Consequences, Especially if they should be ordered to N:Y:. What news from Europe? will the war Continue or is there a probability of peace? I think by the time you Receive this you will have such intelligence as will satisfy you about it. Please to write me often & give me all the intelligence you Can. We have had but little news of any kind this winter. The severity of the season has prevented arrivals by land or water as usual. I hear that a Packet was brought in the flagg from Hallifax, Directed to the Honble Henry Lawrens Esqr. President of Congress, on his Brittannic Majesty's Service, and franked. This has Caused some speculation at Portsmo. It will be Received before you see this, should be glad to know from whom it Came & Contents if proper. Adieu my Dear General and Believe me to be your sincere friend &c.   Josiah Bartlett
Please to inform my friend Col. Peabody I have Received no letter from him since his of the 24th of December, perhaps he has forgot me, please to Remember me to him.[5]

RC (PHi).

1. Folsom presented his credentials on 30 Dec. 1779 and attended until 15 Sept. 1780. Burnett, *Letters*, 4:liv; 5:lviii.

2. John Langdon, who was Speaker of the House. *NHSP*, 8:841.

3. The Committee appointed by the legislature on 1 January consisted of Meshech Weare, Ebenezer Thompson, Josiah Moulton, John Dudley and George Gaines. Gaines (1736–1809) was a selectman of Portsmouth for thirty years, a representative to the General Court, and

state commissary. Brewster, *Rambles*, 1st ser., 134–35.

On 18 March the General Court restored JB and John Calfe to the newly appointed Committee of seven members and reassigned some of the Committee's authority. *NHSP*, 8:845, 854.

4. The act was passed on 15 March. *Laws of N.H.*, 4:254–62.

5. Peabody wrote a short letter on 17 March. MJB, 1764.

FROM NATHANIEL FOLSOM

Dear Sr.   Philadelphia Apriel 17th. 1780

I Rec'd your feavour of the 11th. of March tusday last which wase Very Exceptable as I am allways well Pleased to here how our public affairs go on—but lament that what wase Done with the best Intentions to Serve the Public by those who from the begining have been faithfull frinds to the glorious opposition made against tyranny should be by misconstruction false Representation be the means of Insureing the Public as well as Individuels, but we must go on and do our Duty and Prepair our backs to bare any thing theay will Please to lay on us—but ingrattiude and to be wounded in the house of our frinds is a trial we neede Peatience to bare up under—but the testimony of a good Conscience in doing our Duty faithfully will be our best Support. On our arrival at this Place the Deprishation of the Currancy wase so Rapped the inhanced Price of all the nesesareys of life wase so grate that it Seemed imposable to go on a month longer with our Public affairs—which drove us to Preportion the Subsistace of the army on the Several States—and to new Ragulate and Establish the Currency—Since which money appresheats. Our Produce is falling and our Public affairs ware a more favourable aspect.[1]

As to Vermont there wase Several Violent attempts by the Delegates of newyork and newhampshier to bring the matter before Congress but without the least apperence of Success.

We Produced our Credenshalls the acts of the lagislatuer impowering Congress to do every thing they had requiered of us.

Seting forth at the same time the grate Expence the State had been at by Complying with there Request but all to no Purpose I wase informed by individuals that what had been done on that affair wase Done by Coaxing and driveing.

Therefore I have no Expectation of any Settlement till after the war is over if I Can believe the Present members. But all this is but my Private Judgement and I wood not have it made Public.

Mr. Livermore left this Place the 8th Instant who will give you a more Peticuler account to hom I wood Refer you. The accounts we have from Europe from our good frind & ally by way of his minister here, and by our agents in france are that we aught at all Events to make a Vigorous Campain this Summer that the haughtyness of the Cort of Britton will not allow them yet to acknowlege the Independence of these States that if they find they have any Ships to Spaire after makeing there own flagg triumphant in the Chaniel we may Depend on Sume in the Course of the Camppaine. I hope Genll. Whipple will be hurred on and that I may be Releved Soone.

The Massechuces have made applecation to Congress by there Delegats to Know whether they wood Pay for the Cost of the Expedishon to Penopscot and to allow them to keep back Part of this years tax on that account the latter wase Complied with.[2] We had Newhampshier Put to the trial with them but faild. The members thought it wase time enough when the State made application.

Remember me to all my old frinds and believe to be as much Conserned for the Public as ever. I am with Sincer Respect your Very Humle. Servent. Nathl. Folsom

RC (NhD).

1. Congress had ceased printing paper money by order of 3 September 1779, but depreciation continued at a disheartening rate. Lacking a means of readily producing cash, Congress shifted much of the financial responsibility for the war to the individual states. Finally, on 18 Mar. 1780 Congress revalued "old" Continental money at 40 to 1 of specie. The states were to retrieve the old bills through taxes over thirteen months and return them to Congress which would then issue new bills for every twenty old bills retrieved. Both the states and Congress would guarantee the new money. The amount of new money in circulation would then stabilize and its value remain constant. New Hampshire's was the only congressional delegation divided on the finance vote of 18 Mar. 1780: Peabody opposed it; Folsom voted in its favor. It passed, with the southern states in opposition. *JCC*, 16:262–67; Ferguson, *Power of the Purse*, 46–52; Nettels, *Emergence of a National Economy*, 29–30.

2. Massachusetts applied on 22 March. On 8 April Congress agreed to allow Massachusetts two million dollars toward dislodging the British from Penobscot. *JCC*, 16:276–77, 340–42.

TO NATHANIEL FOLSOM

My Dear Sir   Kingstown May 13th 1780

Your favor of the 17th ulto is Come to hand and am glad to hear that money with you has grown better since the Resolve of Congress of the 18th of March. With us it is the reverse paper bills will not buy more than half or at most two thirds as much as before that Resolve Came to hand and many people will not take them on any account whatever. The Resolve of Congress of Febry last for proportioning the supplies for the army and that of the 18th of March about the money arrived here near togather after the Gen. Assembly had adjourned to the first wednesday of June. The importance of the Subjects obliged the Comtte of Safety to Call the Court togather the 19th ulto who sat that week and the week following. The Act that was passed Relative to the money is sent forward to Congress and will no Doubt Come to hand before you Receive this; They passed also an order to the Courts of law in this State Directing them in making up Judgments, to Consider the value of the money at the time the Debt was Contracted and to allow the Depreciation agreable to a table of Depreciation Calculated for setling with our soldiers which Extended to the first of Janry last, and from that time to Consider the money at 40 for one till further orders. This was Done only for the present necesity, when the Court meets on the 7th of June that matter will be taken up more at large.[1]

The matter of procuring supplies for the army was taken into Consideration and voted to Comply with the resolve of Congress as far possible, the Beef Can be procured after there is time for fating it by grass, at present there is none to be procured if Called for, the mode of geting the beef is put off till the next session when I hope the new money will be out and more valued than the present or else I fear it will be impossible to procure it any other way than taking it by force. The inclosed resolve was passed to prevent the articles we were to supply being Carried out of the state. These land Embargoes I greatly Dislike, but the State of Massachusetts are Continnually laying them on Every occasion. This was past in our own Defence as that State on Receiving the Resolve of Congress immediately prohibited any of the articles they were to procure being sent out of that State, and no Embargo being laid here. Their Sharpers it is said Came to Portsmo. & bought all the rum & molasses they Could procure and were buying up the beef Cattle in order to raise the price knowing it must be had by the States for the army. The rum proportioned to this State I fear we shall not be able to procure as the Massachusetts Embargo prevents our procuring it from that State and there is no probability that so much will be Brought in to Portsmo. this year, the Trade of that Town is almost ruined. I am informed by Gentlemen of Credit at Portsmo. that out of Twenty Six sail of vessels which saild from Portsmo. this year there is Certain accounts of the loss of seventeen, and several of the others not yet arrived & uncertain as yet what will be their fate.

Mr. Livermore Returned while the Court was Setting. He informed a comtte of the whole, of a Partition Treaty between our Delegates & those of N. York for a Devision of Vermont, by what I can learn it is Disagreable to the Majority of both Houses, however it is only my opinion, nothing was acted on it.[2] Mr. Whipple Declines going to Congress and nobody Else is appointed, but Expect the next session Somebody will be Chosen to Relieve you if you request it. I feel much Concerned for the fate of Charlestown S: C: and our army & navy there wish it may turn out better than my fears.[3] I am Dear Sir your sincere friend and most obedt Servant

Josiah Bartlett

Please to give the inclosed letter to Colo. Peabody if present and Communicate to him the substance of what I have wrote of the affairs of this state.[4] J.B:

RC (NHi). Enclosure not found.

1. The resolve of February concerning supplies for the army is printed in *JCC*, 16:143–45. Copies of the resolve, and that of 18 March on finance, reached the Committee of Safety on 31 March. Bouton, "Committee of Safety," 214. On 29

April the General Court passed acts to comply with the financial resolve of March and to prevent the transportation of cattle, beef, rum, and molasses out of New Hampshire. *Laws of N.H.*, 4:289–91; NHSP, 8:855–59.

2. It appears that nothing had been determined by Congress on the matter by the time Livermore left. See *JCC*, 16:222, 273; 17:448–53.

3. Gen. Benjamin Lincoln's force withstood a British siege of Charleston until 12 May, when the army of 5,500 surrendered. Wallace, *Appeal to Arms*, 210.

4. Letter not found.

The N.H. General Court, with JB on the Executive Council, met from 7 to 18 June 1780. NHSP, 8:860–68. In accordance with resolves of the Continental Congress and a report over JB's signature, the Court acted to raise six hundred men for the eighteen regiments of state militia. On 22 June the Committee of Safety appointed JB to muster and pay the troops assigned to rendezvous at Kingston, which included the regiments of Cols. Wentworth, Moulton, Evans, Gilman, Gale, John Webster, Gregg, Badger, and McClary. To pay these troops JB was allowed $110,000. Bouton, "Committee of Safety," 219–20. Accordingly, on 28 June President Meshech Weare formally notified JB of the appointment (not printed, see MJB 1792). The force was to muster on 12 July and serve until the end of 1780.

FROM JOSEPH BADGER[1]

Sir   Gilmantown, July the 21st 1780

I have some very troublesome men in my Regiment who are always doing Everything in their power to discourage men from Enlisting in the service and the officers have seen fit to draught some of them, and they have Deserted. Now I would wish to know the pleasure of the Committee of Safety what I shall Do with those men in Case they Can be found after the soldiers are all marched. If those men should Escape without Punishment I shall find it very Difficult if not Impossible Ever to Raise my Quota of men again. I beg youd be kind Enough to Comunicate this to the Committee of safety and should take it as a Great favour if I might have some order from that Honble Body how to proceed. I am Sr. with Great Respect Yr Honrs most obt. Huml. sert.   Joseph Badger

RC (Nh-Ar: Weare Papers).

1. Joseph Badger (1722–1803) of Gilmanton had served as colonel and mustermaster of the militia in his region before being appointed brigadier general on 27 June 1780. He served on the Council and then as probate judge for Strafford County, 1784–1797. In 1788 he at first opposed, then voted for, ratification of the Federal Constitution. "Memoir of the Hon. Joseph Badger."

FROM NATHANIEL FOLSOM

Sr.   Philadelphia agust. 14th. 1780

I Recd. your letter of the 13th. of may the 10th of June and should have answered it before now but I have Several Reasons to offer by way of Excuse.

One is I have bin alone ever since abought the 20th of April and have not bin absent one hour when Congress were setting since my arrival at this Place. The other is the wather hase bin so hot that when out of Congress we have full imploymant to find air anough to breathe in. The last is you Seemed to be so angery at the Resolution of the 18th march relative to finance—that I thought I wood let you Cool a little before I Rote again.

When I left newhampshire the Exchange was abought twenty for one and on my arrival at this Place I found it Sixty and before the 18th. of march it wase allmost an hundred for one on an average. And had it not bin for that Resolution of Congress which Seemed to make you so uneasy by the midle of may it wood not have Purchest any one thing in the market. This is not my opinion only but allmost every member of Congress. And as you Did not go So far as to say you thought the exchange as fixt was to high or to low, or that it aught or aught not to be fixt at all Puts it out of my Power to give you sattisfaction on this Subject.

I suppose you will expect I Should say something abought our Public affairs in general as they appear to us who are on the Spot where information of every kind is most likely to be had—much Very much my good frind is depending in my opinion on this Camppain—as the exertions of the Several States are Very grate. Unless Some important Blow is Struck or something Decissive is Done—I am affraid of the effect it may have on the People at large if cald upon for the like exertions another year and the disadvantages we may be laid under if a negotiation for a Peace shood take Place is obvious.

I can informe you our Gennerals spirits and expectations are Riseing —and allso that we expect every day to hear of the arrival of the 2d. Division of Ships of War from France on which depends in my opinion all our offensive opperations.

Yesterday I heard Coll. Peabody was unwell at Morristown. I Shall Set out for home on the 20th. of September at farthest if I shood live so long and am able and Shall expect Somebody to Relieve me by that time or the State will be unrepresented.[1]

The intense hot wather we have had here for a long time Past and Constant Confinement hase brought me somewhat low a Ride to the northward I hope will be of Service to me. Be So good as to informe President Weare that there hase bin no Publication of the Prises drawn in the last lottery as yet as soone as there is any I will forward it to him. Sr. I am with Respect your Most Obt. Humll. Servent   Nathll. Folsom

RC (NN: Emmet Collection, No. 340).

1. On 21 September Peabody noted that   1811.
Folsom was on his way home. See MJB,

Nathaniel Peabody soon followed Folsom back to New Hampshire, leaving the state represented in Congress solely by John Sullivan who had accepted the appointment during the summer. JB's correspondence with

Congress ceased, so far as is extant, until John Taylor Gilman went to Philadelphia in July 1782. JB became even more active in state affairs as a justice of the Court of Common Pleas of Rockingham County and as a member of the Council and the Committee of Safety where his influence was second only to that of Meshech Weare who was aged and failing in health. Many committee reports appeared before the General Court over JB's signature. See MJB and NHSP, 8. When Weare was unable to preside over meetings and perform duties of the Committee of Safety, JB took on those responsibilities. Hence JB signed many of the Committee's letters.

The Committee was faced with maintaining the state's defenses even though the thrust of the war effort had shifted to the southern states. Also, New Hampshire authorities were responsible for maintaining authority in the recalcitrant towns in western New Hampshire. The Continental Congress had been unable to determine whether to create a separate state of Vermont or to decide who held jurisdiction over the Connecticut River valley towns. During 1781 disaffection increased in western New Hampshire as thirty-six towns in Cheshire and Grafton counties joined the Vermont Assembly. For a while the territory lived under two sets of authority. Finally, in January 1782, both Vermont and New Hampshire prepared to call up militia to restore order. The New Hampshire General Court issued a proclamation of rebellion and gave all citizens in the western towns opportunity to recognize the Connecticut River as New Hampshire's western boundary. The Vermont Assembly, caught up in charges of negotiating with the British, dissolved its union with New Hampshire's towns and established the eastern boundary of Vermont at the Connecticut River. The Vermont Controversy was thus settled technically although many citizens in western New Hampshire remained perplexed and sullen, and Vermont was not admitted to the Union until 1790. Upton. Revolutionary New Hampshire, 194–98.

TO FRANCIS BLOOD[1]   In Committee of Safety
Sir,   Exeter Mar 9th. 1781

You are desired to furnish Gen. Nichols at Amherst and Colo. Ellis[2] at Keen with such quantities of Beef or Pork, Meal or Flour as may be necessary to supply the Troops now raising in the Western part of the State with Rations while at the places of Rendezvous and when they march to carry them to the next issuing Commissary agreeably to a Vote of the Genl. Court—& you are to receive such quantities of Meal or Flour from any Town or Towns as may be necessary for the above mentioned supplies and to assure such Town or Towns that the Value of such supplies of Meal and Flour will be deducted out of the proportion of Beef, or paid for in Money as the General Court may Determine & you are to give your Rects. to the Towns accordingly.

(Signd) Josiah Bartlett
Coll. P.T.

TR (NhHi).

1. Francis Blood (1736–1814) served Temple as a town officer, a representative to the General Court, and a justice of the Court of Common Pleas. Military service led to his appointment as collector general of beef, by an act of the General Court in January 1781. *History of Temple*, 634–38; *Laws of N.H.*, 4:356.

2. Moses Nichols (1740–1790), a phy-

sician of Amherst, was appointed colonel of the 8th militia regiment on 5 Dec. 1776 and was a brigadier general in 1781. Potter, *Military History*, 1:344.

Timothy Ellis (1724–1817) of Keene was a major in Nichols' militia regiment, rose to colonel, and resigned in 1783. Griffin, *Keene*, 593; Potter, *Military History*, 1:323.

FROM ROGER SHERMAN[1]

Sir   Philadelphia July 31. 1781

Enclosed is a copy of an act of the General Court of the Massachusetts, respecting the State of Vermont, the matter has been debated for Several days past in Congress, on a report of a Committee, to whom was referred a Letter from the President of your State. The Committee reported as their opinion, "that copies of the Act of Massachusetts be Sent to the States of New Hamshire and New York and that the expediency of passing Similar acts be referred to them. And in case they relinquish their Claims of Jurisdiction over the Grants on the west Side of Connecticut River Bounded, East by Said River, North by Latitude forty five degrees, West by Lake Champlain and the west lines of Several Townships Granted by the Governor of New Hamshire, to the North west corner of Massachusetts; and South by the North line of Massachusetts; Congress will Guaranty the Lands & Jurisdiction belonging to the Said States respectively lying without the Said limits, against all claims & Encroachments of the people within those limits." What will be ultimately done in Congress is uncertain some Gentlemen are for declaring Vermont an Independent State, others for explicitly recommending to the States aforesaid to relinquish their claims of Jurisdiction, others, only for referring it to their consideration as reported by the Committee, and some few are against doing any thing that will tend to make a new State.[2] I am of opinion that a speedy, & Amicable Settlement of the controversy would conduce very much to the peace & welfare of the United States, And that it will be difficult if not impracticable to reduce the people on the east side of the River to Obedience to the Government of New Hamshire until the other dispute is Settled, that the longer it remains unsettled, the more difficult it will be to remedy the evils, but if the States of New Hamshire & New York would follow the example of Massachusetts, respecting the Grants on the west of Connecticut River, without waiting for a recommendation of Congress, the whole controversy would be quieted, very much to the advantage and Satisfaction of the United States, and that the Inhabitants of New Hamshire and New York living without the limits of the disputed territory would return to their Allegiance. The British Ministry esteem it an object of great importance to them, to engage the people of Vermont in their Interest, and have accordingly Instructed Gen. Clinton & Gen.

Haldiman[3] to use their best endeavours for that end. And tho' I dont think the people have any inclination to come under the British Yoke, or to do any thing injurious to this Country, yet if left in their present Situation, they may be led to take Steps very prejudicial to the United States. I think it very unlikely, that Congress can attend to the Settlement of the dispute by a Judicial decision, during the War, for though the parties were heard last fall respecting their claims, yet it cannot now be determined upon the right, without a new hearing, because there are many new Members that were not then present.

I am credibly Informed that a great Majority of the members of the Legislature of the State of New York at their last winter session were willing to relinquish their claims of Jurisdiction over that district, and that they Should be admitted to be a Seperate State, but the Governor for some reasons prevented an act passing at that time. We have no news remarkable here. Paper currency is very much at an end, Some of the new Bills are bought & sold, but Silver and Gold are the only currency—the prices of Commodities are much fallen, many articles are as low, as before the war. I send you two of the last news papers. And am with Great Esteem & Regard Your humble Servant,   Roger Sherman

P.S. Since writing the foregoing Congress have recommitted the report. New York delagates arrived to day—They are instructed to move for a decision of the affair of Vermont.

RC (PHi). Draft (MHi). Enclosure not found.

1. Roger Sherman was a congressional delegate from Connecticut.

2. The Massachusetts act, dated 8 Mar. 1781, agreed to recognize Vermont's claims according to any determination by Congress on the problem. Walton, *Vermont Records*, 2:199. Sherman was chairman of the five-member committee which had been appointed on 9 July specifically to consider Weare's letter of 20 June. Submitted to Congress on 20 July, the committee's report received consideration on the 24th, 28th, and 31st. Congress appointed a new committee on the 31st, of which Sherman was a member. After further consideration, Congress made resolves on 7, 20, and 21 August which guaranteed New Hampshire, Massachusetts, and New York jurisdiction over lands that had been in question. *JCC*, 20:732, 770–71; 21:787, 812, 818, 836–39, 886–88, 892–93.

3. British General Sir Frederick Haldimand (1718–1791) was at this time commander-in-chief of British forces in Canada.

TO SAMUEL HUNT[1]

Sir,

In Committee of Safety
Exeter Septr 27th: 1781

Inclosed is a Copy of a Letter from Majr Genrl. Heath—in Consequence of which we have ordered the Militia raised by this State commanded by Colo. Runnels to Rendezvous at Charlestown as soon as possible.[2] You will see by said Letter that the Genrl thinks proper that the Issuing Commissary in this State should be ordered to Serve them with provisions—but the Committee not knowing who is issuing Commissary, nor the Situation of the Continental Stores at Charlestown are desirous if there is any person appointed that you would inform him of the matter, if not, that you would undertake the issuing said provision—in case you cannot—that you would appoint some proper person to do it. If there is no Continental Stores you will please to call on Francis Blood Esqr. for supplies of Beef and Bread from time to time as you may stand in need of as we have wrote to him to furnish you with supplies for that purpose.

As you are Deputy Quarter master we Expect you will do all in your power to furnish Officers & men with Barracks, fuel, & cooking utensils.[3] By order of the Committee   Josiah Bartlett Chairman

P.S. As these men are raised at the Expence of the United States you will receipt for any provisions &c., which you may receive from Esqr. Blood in the Same manner you have done for the Beef Cattle, & issue any salted Beef or any other provision or Stores which you may have belonging to the United States that may be necessary for them.

If there is not any Ammunition belonging to the United States which these men may Obtain, you will See that they are furnished from the Stores belonging to this State and call on any person or persons who may have charge of the same for that purpose. Please to write as soon as possible.   J: Bartlett Chairmn

RC (MA). TR (DLC: Force Transcripts).

1. Samuel Hunt (1734–1799) of Charlestown had held several local and state offices and was keeper of military stores at Fort No. 4, Charlestown. Saunderson, *Charlestown*, 164–66, 432–40; NHSP, 7:577.

2. William Heath (1737–1814) of Roxbury, Mass., served in the Continental Army as a major general from 1776 to the end of the war. In 1781 he commanded the army on the lower Hudson in New York. The enclosed copy of Heath's letter has not been found, but the original, dated 17 September, is in Weare Papers, Nh-Ar. Heath had informed the Committee of Safety that a British force under Col. Barry St. Leger was moving southward from Canada toward Fort Ticonderoga. In reaction, the Committee wrote to Cols. Daniel Reynolds (MJB, 1937) and Francis Blood (MJB, 1939) directing Reynolds to march his men from Springfield to Charlestown and desiring Blood to issue beef and provisions as needed by Hunt.

Daniel Reynolds (1742–1795), a carpenter of Londonderry, held public office before and during the Revolution, and led troops at the Battle of Bennington. In 1781 he raised a Continental regiment of which he was colonel. Runnels, *Genealogy*, 8, 16–17; Potter, *Military History*, 1:363–64.

Also on this date the Committee of Safety sent orders to militia and military leaders in the state that they should be prepared for defense in case of British attack. MJB, 1942.

3. Apparently Hunt carried out the order. With the TR there is a receipt for supplies dated 23 Nov. 1781: "Recd. of Colo. Hunt Commissr. of Issue at Charlestown on acct of the within Returns Nine hundd. Sixty nine pounds Bread & ten & half pounds Candles— fourteen Rations for four Days reduced out of Capt Heads & Woodman's Companies—Josiah Flagg Cr. Mastr."

TO MESHECH WEARE   In Committee of Safety
Dear Sir   Exeter Septr. 28th 1781

Inclosed you have a Copy of Majr. General Heath's Letter in Consequence of which we Sent an Express (Early yesterday morning) to Springfield & have ordered Collo. Runnels with the men Under his Command to repair Immediately to Charlestown in this State. We have directed that those Men who have not already Marched from hence should Immediately March to Charlestown by the nearest Rout—have wrote to Collo. Hunt respecting Supplies, & to Francis Blood Esqr. to receive Bread from the Towns in lieu of Beef & to Supply him with Beef and Bread in Case their is not Continental Stores Sufficient there.

We shall write to General Heath & request that the Regiment may remain within this State or parts Adjacent for the defence thereof—have given further Instructions to Collo. Runnels (in Case no Continental Genl. Officer is in that department) to receive orders from any General Officer of this State. We Inclose you One of the Resolutions of Congress & the order of the Committee Annexed, which we have Sent out to the Several Towns in the Counties of Cheshire and Grafton.[1]

It is the Unanimous Opinion of the Committee that you would send an Officer to Charlestown & take out of Goal there one Smith[2] belonging to Hindsdale said to be Apprehended & Confined there in an Illegal manner—and have him before you and if so Confined as to us Represented, discharge him or take such further Order thereon as you shall think best.

We have received a Letter from Congress this day informing that five States were Unrepresented there, & requesting that we may be represented there as they were at the Eve of great Events. We Submitt to you the propriety of your writeing to Governor Chittenden[3] relative to the Situation of Affairs in the Western parts of this State. We are your most Obedt. Servts.

> Josiah Bartlett
> in behalf of Comtte

RC (MHi). In clerk's hand; signed by JB. Enclosure not found.

1. The enclosure was the congressional resolution of 7 August guaranteeing New Hampshire its original claims in the event Congress should recognize Vermont's independence. *JCC*, 21:839; Bouton, "Committee of Safety," 268.

2. Probably Joseph Smith, "a Soldier claimed by Boscawen, Plaistow, Ply-

mouth & Wentworth." The case was determined on 5 October. Bouton, "Committee of Safety," 267, 269.

3. Thomas Chittenden (1730–1797) served as governor of Vermont from 1778 to 1797 with the exception of 1789–1790.

TO WILLIAM HEATH
Sir,

In Committee of Safety
Exeter Septr 29th 1781

Your letter of the 17th instant directed to the President of this State was received the 25th Instant, the President being absent, the Committee have taken the same under consideration.

The accounts we have lately received From the western parts of this State, serve to confirm us in the sentiments held forth in your letter, that the enemy will probably attempt to make inroads on the Settlements at Connecticut river. Some part of our militia had marched previous to the receipt of your letter and had orders to rendezvous at Springfield but the great difficulties subsisting in the western part of this State on account of the dispute of Vermont, in addition to the probability of the enemy's movements that way, induced the Committee to order that those men who had set out for Springfield should be immediately marched to Charlestown, and that those who had not marched, should be sent thither by the nearest rout.

We are doubtful whether the Continental Stores there are sufficient for the men, and have given orders for the supplying them from the provisions which we were to raise by order of Congress the present year. We have given orders to the Commandant of the Regiment to report to you his name, rank & the number of militia with him agreeably to your letter.

The greater part of the Towns in two Counties of this State east of Connecticut river, deny the Jurisdiction of the State & have joined the State of Vermont (so called) and notwithstanding the late Resolutions of Congress still persist in joining Vermont.

The difficulties are so many and great in those parts, that the Committee are of opinion, it is absolutely necessary the men should remain in that quarter. If they should be ordered to the Southward the march will be long & the term of their Enlistment being short, will expire before they can do much Service. If you should be of opinion that they may remain there and no Continental Officer should be in that quarter to give them orders, Bridier Genl. Bellows (of this State's militia, who lives in Walpole)[1] will be near, & will give the necessary Orders in case of Alarms &c. I am, with due respect Your most Obedient Servt.

Josiah Bartlett Chairmn

RC (MHi). In clerk's hand; signed by JB.

1. Benjamin Bellows (1740–1802) held many public offices but had declined to attend the Continental Congress when elected to it in January 1781. He led a militia regiment from 1775, was com-missioned a brigadier general in 1781, and later rose to major general. Potter, *Military History*, 1:304–07; NHSP, 7:577; 8:884; 21:782–83.

FROM IRA ALLEN[1]

Sir,   Exeter Decm. 29th. 1781

As it appears on all sides that Both New Hamshire & Vermont are willing to submit to Congress the settlement of the Dispute Between the Respective States and as the Legislature of Vermont are not Possessed of the Act or Acts of New Hampshire refering them matters to Congress have to Request a Copy of Said Act or Acts Together with a Copy of the Resolution of the Legislature on the Proposals of the Legislature of Vermont in October last—That I may lay them before the Legislature of Vermont at their session in Jany. next thereby to facilitate a settlement at Congress. I am Sir, with due Respect your Humble servt.   Ira Allen

RC (Nh-Ar).

1. Ira Allen (1751–1814), a brother of Ethan, was one of the more influential leaders in Vermont. As a member of Vermont's Council, he had represented the state's claims to Congress earlier in 1781. Allen and Roger Enos announced their arrival in Exeter and their intention of attending the General Court in a letter of 21 December, also addressed to JB. MJB, 2040.

TO TITUS SALTER[1]   In Committee of Safety
Sir   Exeter Feby 2d. 1782
   Whereas there is great reason to apprehend that the Enemy have a design to destroy the Ship now building at Portsmouth for the use of the United States—You are hereby required to keep a strong Guard at the Great Island and constantly in readiness with a good Boat to go on Board & Examine all Vessels & small Craft of every kind that may Enter the Harbour & you are to cause such examination to be made as shall be sufficiently satisfactory.   Josiah Bartlett Chn

FC (Nh-Ar: Committee of Safety Letter Book). Printed in *NHSP*, 10:577.

   1. Titus Salter (1722–1798), ship captain and merchant of Portsmouth, commanded Fort Washington there at the beginning of the Revolution and again at its close. The ship referred to in the letter was the *America*. Emery, *The Salters*, 34–39; *NHSP*, 8:119–20, 955; Preble, *United States Navy-Yard*, 15–18.

Through the first half of 1782, JB remained exceedingly busy in his positions of a judge, councilor, and chairman of the Committee of Safety, a position he was filling more regularly because of Meshech Weare's frequent absences. A number of short letters over JB's signature went out in April to militia officers, dealing chiefly with provisioning and paying the troops who remained in service of the state and Continent. The surrender of Cornwallis at Yorktown in October 1781 completed the last major campaign of the war. Smaller engagements continued to occur (though none is recorded in Vermont, New Hampshire, Massachusetts, or Rhode Island) until April 1783, making it necessary to keep up defenses. Peckham, Toll of Independence, *92–99. In January 1782 the General Court elected John Taylor Gilman to Congress. Gilman took his seat on 20 June as one of the two state delegates required by the Articles of Confederation, which had taken effect on 1 March 1781. Active with his father, Nicholas, in managing the financial affairs of New Hampshire during the Revolution, Gilman had worked closely with JB on several occasions.*

FROM JOHN TAYLOR GILMAN
Sir   Philadelphia July 9th: 1782
   I take this Opporty to write you by Mr. Smith of Boston. The United States being informed by Doctr. Franklin's Letters, that France did not hold themselves obliged to pay any more Bills for Interest due on the Loan Office Certificates and that they would be protested if drawn, a Committee was appointed to Consider of this Subject & report to Congress, the Substance of which report was that no more Bills Should be drawn for payments of Interest. While this Report was under Consideration a Memorial was presented Signed by some of the Citizens requesting that Congress would postpone their Determination on this Subject untill they could have a Meeting of the Holders of Loan Office Certificates.[1] You will see by the News Paper what the Citizens have done. Some are

for appropriating the five per Cent Impost for the purpose of paying the Interest on the whole Loans, others for funding those Loans which were made prior to the first of March 1778, and that this Interest shall be first discharged, but How can Congress appropriate a fund which is not yet granted to them. What will take place I cannot say. We have no late News from Europe. Their are Several reports in this City respecting Two Actions at the Southward in both which it is Said Our Troops were successfull, but nothing to be Depended on. It remains uncertain whether there has been any actions or not.

In my Letter of the 26th Ultimo. to the Honble. the President, I urged that the State Should be represented here, perhaps it may be thought by some, that I say too much on this Subject but I am Confident if such persons were here they would alter their Sentiments. The Vote of One State in Thirteen is of some Importance. There are many things absolutely necessary to be Reformed, notwithstanding all our reformation plans we are now paying a large Number of Civil & Military Officers who are doing us no Service—figure to your self Sir the pay and Subsistance of at least Thirty Field Officers, Eighty Captains & 160 subalterns besides a Number of General & Staff Officers (all belonging to one State) who have not private Soldiers Enough to give each Officer a Servant, & in other States their are Regiments fully Officered who perhaps have not Ten Private soldiers belonging to them—and these States will perhaps have almost as large Accounts against the united States as some others who keep up a good proportion of Soldiers by reason of their almost numerous Officers. I would not be understood as Endeavoring to prevent N. H. from raising Soldiers, but I must repeat that I think a Vote here (though very Expensive) should be an Object of the first Consideration Both as it may be of Service to the Genl. Interest of all the States and the particular Interest of New Hampshire, but as I think I have discharged my Duty in this respect I shall Endeavour when I write the State in future to find some other subject.

The Delegates from Carolinas & Georgia have Money advanced them out of the public Treasury agreeably to a Resolution of Congress passed about One year agone, those who have Families here are to have 200 Dollars per month, those who have not, 150 Dollars per month, to bear their Expences which is to be Charged to their respective States. There are five from South Carolina & Three from Georgia now present.

A large Committee are appointed, to report some plan for lessening our Expences, but what they will be able to do I cannott Say. The post Sets out from this place on Wednesdays I Suppose my Letters do not reach Exeter untill the Friday Fortnight after Sending them. Perhaps this may reach you by the Same Post as my Letter to the President of the 3d. Instant[2] as Mr. Smith will carry it directly to Boston. I want to hear what has been done at the late Session of the Genl. Court, the Titles of the public Acts with some general Sketches of the most material Business would be very pleasing. One Letter from Collo. Langdon, One from Genl. Whipple & One from Genl. Bellows is all I have received from

New Hampshire Since I left there, I Expected Several by yesterdays post, but was disappointed.

Great preparations are making by the minister of France to Celebrate the birth of the Dauphin, on Monday next, it is expected it will be the most Brilliant affair ever known in America. You will not Consider this as an Official Letter, but Communicate the Same so far as you may think proper.

I should be glad if I had some agreeable News to Communicate to you, but have not any thing Important. Make my Compliments to the Gentlemen of the Committee of Safety & inform Esqr. Dudley[3] that it is my Opinion he must alter his Opinion respecting our having Peace this year, though every Appearance Seems to Indicate a Very Inactive Campaign. I am with much Esteem & Respect Your Hum. Servt.

John Taylor Gilman

P.S. As I have not time to write my Hon'd Father by this Post your Communicatg this to him will be Esteemed a favour.

RC (MeHi: The John S. H. Fogg Autograph Collection).

1. Burnett believed that the memorial was a letter from Blair McClenachan, John Ewing, and others read in Congress on 3 July. Burnett, *Letters*, 6:381 n.

2. In Weare Papers, Nh-Ar.

3. John Dudley (1725–1805) engaged in agriculture and lumbering in Raymond.

Like JB, Dudley was a justice of the peace. During the Revolution Dudley sat in the legislature and on the Committee of Safety. He was a justice on the Court of Common Pleas and then on the Superior Court, 1784–1797. *NHSP*, 21:794–98; Bell, *Bench and Bar*, 39–41.

FROM JOHN TAYLOR GILMAN

Dear Sir   Philada Augst. 5th. 1782.

The Letter which you did me the favour to write on the 5th. Ultimo.[1] I receiv'd on the 22d. What will be done respectg Vermont affairs I cannot Say, I Suppose under present Circumstances it would not be possible to have any thing determined in Congress respecting them. I am well informed that one Reason given (in private by some Gentlemen from the Southward) why they would not make them a Seperate State is because it would be adding One more to the Votes of the Eastern States, which they Say they will not do untill they can add one to the Southern likewise. I need not Comment on this. I am Sensible while the Vermont business remains undetermined N. H. will be in an Unhappy Situation. I am Informed by the New York Delegates that their State has lately (in Consequence of repeated Applications) granted a Number of Commissions to people in the County of Cumberland which I think Joins on the River. A Member of Congress from New Engld. with whom I am Intimately acquainted, this day Shew me Copy of a letter which he was going to Send to a Gentn of high rank in the State to which he belonged & in answer to One he had recd. Urging that Vermont might be made a Seperate State, in which he Says, "I am fully Convinced of the Justice & policy of making them a Seperate State, but it is as likely that Great Britain will Cede Scotland to the United States as that the present Congress will make

Vermont an Independant State." I wish N. H. may not be again Duped In this affair. I Enclose you a list of Officers &c. by which you will See how great a Number of Officers some States have, who have but few privates[2]—and yet in some Instances those States who have so few men have (not long Since) made a large number of Officers to fill up Vacancies. There is now a Resolution of Congress against Issueing new Commissions.[3] Please to keep the Inclosed list in some measure Secret (I do not mean from the Commte.) but would not wish to have it made too public.

It is Evident that our Minister at the Court of Madrid has recd. dishonourable & Fallacious Treatment from that Court.[4] Congress have this affair now under Consideration what will be done I cannott Say but when I consider the Conduct of that Court & the Terms heretofore assented to on our part as the Basis of Treaty I really wish a Treaty with them may not take place, but from some Information (later than Mr. Jay's tho' not official) it is probable they have altered their Conduct & perhaps have before this Concluded a Treaty. It seems to be agreed that Spain have decided Intentions of obtaining Gibralter and that they wish the present War may Continue. The Subject of former Instructions to our Commissrs respecting a Treaty of peace &c. will I Imagine be taken up in a few Days. It is Important but what can be done where so much has been undone I cannot Say.

In my letter to you of the 9th. Ultimo. I wrote something respecting Loan Office Certificates, this business is in the Same Situation it was when I then wrote you. I will Venture to Say to you one thing, which is if N. H. does not adopt a System of Policy for her Self she will probably be left in the Rear. I am Sorry to Say that it is my Opinion their is not a probability of the accounts between the Several States being adjusted for a long time. I find it is very Expensive living here, beef has been frequently sold for 16d. per pound, butter at 3/—Though these articles are much higher than things in general yet almost Every article is Dear. I Shall want some money by the first of September but know not how I am to be furnished, if you will Inform me I Shall be thereby obliged. Their is Eleven States now Represented in Congress & would be 12 but one of the Delegates of Maryland went home a few Days ago, it is Expected he will return Immediately. Thus have I almost filled up my paper & I am afraid you will think unprofitably. I Should be glad to give you more of facts & less of Opinions, but for want of the one I adopt the Other. I Shall be glad to hear from you frequently. I am with much Esteem your Hum. Servt.

J. T. Gilman

P.S. As I write you freely, if you find any part of this or any other of my Letters which ought to be kept Secret you will undoubtedly keep it as Such.

RC (NhD).

1. Not found.
2. Enclosure at NhD.
3. Resolution of 11 July. *JCC*, 22:382.

4. Jay's letter is printed in Wharton, *Diplomatic Correspondence*, 5:336–77. Congress received the letter on 2 August

and resolved on further instructions to Jay on the 7th. *JCC*, 22:428, 455–56. Jay had arrived in June to begin formal peace negotiations. By October, Jay had a draft of a preliminary treaty ready to present to Britain and France.

FROM JOHN TAYLOR GILMAN

Dear Sir   Philada. Septr. 11th. 1782

Your obliging Letter of the 17th. Ulto.[1] I received the 2d. Instt. I observe your Sentiments respecting peace, and those of our Friend. I have been so much of an Unbeliever in this matter, that I can scarcely expect my sentiments to have Weight, yet I am sure your acquaintance with me is such that you will not think I have any Aversion to an Honorable peace, but on the Contrary that I should rejoice most Sincerely at such an Event, and my greatest anxiety is that the prospect appears to me so distant.

You will see by the News-Papers accounts of the late Change in the British Ministry.[2] What will be the Consequence time must Determine.

I am Still of Opinion that the Enemy have Hopes of making a Seperate Peace with us, but if this is the Case they must be Disappointed. Our Independence and the Alliance with France must go Hand in Hand. Believe it may be depended on that abt. 1500 Troops have lately sailed from New-York, said to be for Hallifax, what their next destination may be I cannot Say, perhaps a Plundering Expedition.[3]

A Resolution has lately passed respecting Interest on Loan-Office Certificates which suppose you will see by the time this reaches you.[4] Genl. Washington has removed Head-Quarters to Verplank's Point. The French Army from the Southward Marched through this City a few Days Since are now in the Jerseys. Twelve States are now represented in Congress.[5]

It was Expected that Rhode-Island would have passed the Impost Act but their Assembly broke up a few Days Since without doing it. Nothing Done or likely to be done respecting Vermont affairs, or the Western Lands.

It is so long since we had any account from our Ministers In Europe that whether they are Dead or living I cannot Say. I have wrote in several of my Letters respectg Money, hope it will not be many Days before I receive some. I shall be glad to hear from you frequently. Please to make my Compliments to my Friends with you—and believe me to be with much Esteem Your most Hum. Servt.   John Taylor Gilman

RC (Morristown National Historical Park, Morristown, N.J.).

1. Not found.

2. The influence of Lord North's ministry with Parliament declined after 1780, and in February of 1782 the House of Commons voted to renounce all attempts to regain America. North, Germain, and Sandwich resigned and were replaced by opposition forces led by Rockingham and Shelburne. Higginbotham, *War of Inde-*

pendence, 422.

3. During the two years between the last major battle of the war, Yorktown, in October 1781, and the signing of the peace treaty in Paris, in September 1783, the British army in America concentrated on holding the port cities while the American army determined to contain them there. The British evacuated

Charleston in July 1782 and Savannah that December. Sir Guy Carleton took command of the troops in New York City from Clinton in 1783 and managed the withdrawal from that port as soon as he learned of the signing of the treaty. Wallace, *Appeal to Arms*, 264–70.

4. Having determined that no more cash was available from European loans to back up loan office certificates then being issued by states as the principal fi-nancial vehicle in America, Congress resolved that Superintendent of Finance Robert Morris order the states to stop issuing bills of exchange for interest accrued on loan office certificates. See *JCC*, 23:554–55.

5. New Hampshire alone lacked the required minimum of two delegates for representation, as Phillips White did not arrive until 4 November.

FROM JOHN TAYLOR GILMAN

Dear Sir   Philada. Septr. 17th. 1782.

After I had wrote my Letters of the 11th. Instt. official accounts from Holland as late as 13th. July were received by the Arrival of a Vessell in this Harbour. I just noted this in my Letter to the Honble. the President of the State & Mentioned that those accounts were very agreeable Especially in some particulars which I was not *then* at Liberty to Mention. This Vessell is One of Three which was Loaded in Holland with Cloathing &c. on account of these United States, which was purchased & Expected would have been brought here some Considerable time past, but was delayed by Vile Mismanagement, are informed that another of these Vessels is Arrived at Boston by which Suppose you have the accounts of the United Provinces acceding to our Independence, if you have not you will see them by the News-Papers; The particular Circumstance which I had reference to in my Note in the President's Letter is the Negociation of a Loan in Holland. Mr. Adams informs that he has Opened a Loan for 5,000,000 Guilders (Equal to about 1,875,000 Dollars) this Loan is going forward as fast as can be Expected, about one fourth part of the Money was ready when these accounts came away; This will be of great service to us & I doubt not but it will be better managed than some Loans have heretofore been.

I think our Enemies must have given up all Hopes of making a Seperate Peace with Holland, but believe they have some Expectations that the Empress of Russia will Interfere in their favour. Their is some probability that they will Evacuate New-York this fall, but this is altogether Uncertain. It is the general Opinion that the Commanders at New York are not yet Informed of the Intentions of the British Ministry in this particular. If they Should leave that place it is probable they will send a Considerable force into Canada in order to Extend the Boundaries of that Government Agreeably to the Quebec Bill, and that they will Maintain as much Territory to the Eastward as possible, prosecute the War against our Allies with their Utmost Vigour, & Endeavour by their Emissaries to make a Seperate Peace with us, but this is Conjecture, for my Own part I am at a loss to know whether their withdrawing their Troops with those Views would be of any advantage to us; but if they should meet with any Considerable Loss in the Naval Way before the Close of the

Year, they may be Lead to think Seriously of a Genl. Peace the Coming Winter.

You have undoubtedly seen the Resolutions for Reducing Officers in our Army, and those other Resolutions respecting Interest on Loan Office Certificates.[1]

Congress have agreed to call on the several States for 1,200,000 Dollars to pay the Interest of Domestic Debts, the plan is not yet Compleated but it is Intended that Bills be Drawn on the Several States for their proportions of this sum and that the Holders of public securities within Each State shall be Intitled to payment out of the Monies raised in such State before any others are paid, perhaps this Tax will not be agreeable to the Ideas of some, but what can be done better; the Resolution to prevent Drawing Bills was absolutely Necessary at the time it passed, as we did not then know of any funds on which we had a Right to Draw, and it is in my Opinion Ill policy to pay the Interest of Domestic Debts by foreign Loans.

I suppose you have the Resolutions of N. York (passed some time Since) with respect to Holding a Convention for the purpose of Considering the Articles of Confederation &c. That those Articles are Deficient and Imperfect in some degree must be allowed, but the Query is whether their is any, the least probability that a Convention would make any material alterations for the better, which would probably be agreed to by the Several States; I Suppose our Legislature will be adjourned before this reaches you, I Should Imagine that they have not come to any determination on this matter. You will observe by the Resolutions for Reducing the Officers &c. that they are to retire agreeable to former Resolutions which gave Half pay, perhaps this will not be agreeable to our Legislature, but their was no other alternative, they would have been Continued drawing whole Pay, Subsistance &c. if this had not been done. The saving which will be made by this Reduction is Calculated at about 700,000 Dollars P. Annum.

In Two of my Letters to the Honble. the President of the State I wrote respecting Depreciation &c. due to the Army for the years 1780 & 81. I have not had any thing in Answer therefore Conclude my Suggestions on that Subject were not agreeable, but as I then thought, and Still think it to be an affair worthy the Serious attention of the State, I considered it as my Duty to mention it.

In a Letter from Portsmouth of the 31st. Ulto. which I Receiv'd P. last post is a Paragraph to this purport after mentioning the time at which the Genl. Court was to meet my Honble. Correspondant adds "I hope we Shall then Send you a Colleague provided we can find a proper one but as disagreeable as your Situation is at present I Should think it would be more so to have a Colleague to divide with." I Should not have taken so particular Notice of this Paragraph but I have had several other Letters from different Persons in which are Expressions somewhat to the Same purport; I am not Sensible of any particular Circumstance between me &

either of the Gentlemen now in the Delegation, or between me & any One who I think is likely to be appointed that would probably Occasion Division of Sentiment in public affairs; but if it should be most agreeable that Two Delegates should Immediately come on, I hope no Sentiment of Delicacy or any other Consideration as it may personally respect me will prevent them for a Day, for Should Two Delegates arrive here before the time for which I was appointed Expires, I Shall be happy to See the State have a Vote here & Shall Immediately Retire with more pleasure than I came on.[2]

The general Tenor of my Letters will Evince with what Unreservedness I write you, but I Should be happy to give you, & through you my other Friends, more particular information on the Subject of our public affairs if the Conveyance was Safe.

The Division & Distraction in the Councils of our Enemy, the wretched State of their Finances, together with the United Efforts of those who are now Opposing them, will I hope Compel them to think Seriously of a general Peace before another Campaign. The war has now been carried on for more than Seven years & they can furnish themselves with Seventy times Seven Reasons if so many are necessary to Convince their Cruel Obstinacy that they never can obtain their first object, Viz our Dependance on them. That Peace may be Speedily Established on an Honourable & permanent Basis, from which may flow Happiness to Society & much Felicity to Individuals, is the most Ardent wish of One who though he has Contributed but little to the Common Cause of his Country, yet has the happiness on the most Serious reflection to Consider that his *Mite* has been always ready at his Country's call. I am with Sincere Esteem Your Obedt. Servt.   John Taylor Gilman

P.S. Please to make my Compliments to my Friends with you. I need not Repeat my desires to have Letters from you frequently, hope in your next you will write me freely & fully.

RC (NhD).

1. The resolves for reducing the number of officers passed on 7 August. *JCC*, 22:451–53. Resolutions respecting interest on loan office certificates passed on 4, 10, 18, and 28 September and on 10 October. *JCC*, 23:545–47, 564–71, 586–91, 624–26, 642–45.

2. Woodbury Langdon, Samuel Livermore, Timothy Walker, and Gilman had been appointed in December 1781 and January 1782 to serve until November 1782. In September 1782 Gilman and Phillips White were elected to one-year terms beginning 1 November. Gilman served alone from May 1782 until joined by White on 4 November. *NHSP*, 8:923, 929, 950.

FROM JOHN TAYLOR GILMAN

Sir   Philada. Octr. 23d. 1782.

I have received your's of the 5th. Instt.[1] you ask my Sentiments respecting a Settlement with the officers for rations &c. I have received a Letter from Lieut. Blanchard[2] in which he informs me that he does not doubt but the wishes of the Officers in that matter will be Complied with, and Requesting me to Transmit him some Resolutions of Congress which I Shall do if there are Such.

My Letters to the Honble. the President, which I had reference to in my Letter to you of the 17th. Ulto. were of July 17th. and Augst. 5th.[3] which by his Letters I am Informed he received, and as Lt. Blanchard writes me that the State have Concluded to finish those Settlements, it is unnecessary for me to Say any thing further on that Subject. Indeed I then wrote my Sentiments fully.

As to Rations I don't know of any Resolutions by which the matter is Submitted to the Several States for Settlement. It is my Opinion that the State ought not to make any Settlement, or pay any Monies to be Charged the United States, without seeing Resolutions of Congress authorizing them so to do, unless in Cases of Necessity.

It is an Opinion which Many Persons have, that the accounts between the Several States never will be adjusted. I have lately heard some Members of Congress give their Sentiments fully to that purpose, and it is my Opinion that the Conduct of some of the States are much Influenced by those Ideas. That it will be much for the Interest of some States not to have a Settlement made is Obvious; and with such Ideas, should a Settlement at some very distant period, take place, will it not be very difficult to obtain allowance for Charges which are not Authorized by Congress. I am an advocate for the accounts being Settled between the Several States, (not on the principle that very great advantage would Accrue to the State of N. H. in particular from Such Settlement, as I know the Opinion of some is, but because) Common Justice Demands it and I think the public safety will require it, but if such settlement was to take place to-morrow why Should N. H. take on herself more of the Debt than is required by Resolutions of Congress. I wish both the Soldiers & Citizens belonging to N. H. and to whom the United States are Indebted, to be provided for, but (when the Necessity of the Case does not require the Contrary) Resolutions authorizing payment should be first had. Notwithstanding the Complaints which have been made by some of the N. H. Officers, it is my Opinion that no State in the Union has made Settlements with their Troops on more Liberal principles than N. H. has, and that their is but few, if any, of the States whose public Securities are of more Value than those of N. H. were when I left there, and I presume the Liquidateing Act has been pursued, which I think is so well Calculated as to Increase their Value.[4]

Perhaps it may be worth while to look into the Resolutions of Congress of Feby 29th. April 10th. Augst. 8th. & 12th. 1780. respecting Depreciation &c.

The Subject of Continental Currency has been taken up, but no Conlusion made. Is it not very Extraordinary that States who have it not, say to those who have more than their proportion; you grasped after it, you had no right to Collect more than was *required of you by the Resolutions of Congress*. In that Case their would have been Enough left for us to Collect, it had a Currency with us at the rate of 1,000 for One. You have Collected it, you must make the most of it, take little or nothing for it &c. &c. &c.

I will Just ask your Attention to some Sentences in the Financiers Letter of July 29th. It is (as Congress have it) in the 3d. Page of the 4th. Sheet, and on the Subject of Borrowing Money from the Dutch.[5] I think the Sentiments there may Serve to Corroborate some of my Ideas in this Letter.

I do Assure you Sir that the Subject of this Letter gives me pain. I Should have been much better pleased to have made the Representation Verbally, but as I am favoured with an Oppty to Send it by a private Conveyance to Boston hope it will go Safe. On the one hand these are Subjects which persons in my Situation should Handle with Caution and on the other I think it my Duty while in public service to give such Information as may prevent the State from being too much Injured. I have marked this as private [   ] to be as much so as is Consistant with the good of the [   ] at any rate I know it will be Safe with you, and wo[   ] you make Such Use of it as you think proper.

I have not a Single Article of News to give you. I would answer your Letter more fully, but the Gentleman by whom this goes to Boston is just going. I am with much Esteem Your Obedt. Servt.   John Taylor Gilman

RC (NhD). Franked. Marked "(Private)." The blanks are the result of a hole in the manuscript.

1. Not found.

2. Lt. James Blanchard (b. 1742) of Dunstable served with Col. Alexander Scammel's 3rd N.H. Regiment from 1776 to 1781, first as quartermaster, then as paymaster. Heitman, *Historical Register*, 107. In his letter to Meshech Weare of 17 July Gilman noted that Blanchard had been with him for some days on behalf of officers and men of the New Hampshire Line "to see if a Settlement for their Wages and Subsistance Money could be made here." Burnett, *Letters*, 6:385–86 (original in Weare Papers, Nh-Ar).

3. Printed in Burnett, *Letters*, 6:412–13.

4. On 16 Jan. 1782 the General Court passed a liquidating act allowing holders to state securities to bring them in to be redeemed according to their current value as established by the table of depreciation enacted on 1 Sept. 1780. As Richard Upton has pointed out, the liquidation act in no way penalized current holders, but hurt only those who had held on to the securities for a period and then had been forced to sell them below par value shortly before the liquidation act took effect. *Laws of N.H.*, 4:439–41; Upton, *Revolutionary New Hampshire*, 147.

5. See Morris' letter in Wharton, *Diplomatic Correspondence*, 5:619–34, specifically 622–23, for comments on borrowing from the Dutch.

TO EBENEZER FRYE[1]   In Committee of Safety
Sir,   Exeter, 25 October 1782

The time for raising and mustering Soldiers for the State being expired —your continuance in this State as Muster Master is no longer necessary.

Josiah Bartlett Chairman

FC (Nh-Ar: Committee of Safety Letter Book). Printed in *NHSP*, 10:601.

1. Ebenezer Frye (1745–1828) of Pembroke had served as a captain in the 1st New Hampshire (5th Continental) Regiment since 1775. N.H. Revolutionary Pension Records, 13:277–78; Barker, *Frye Genealogy*, 56.

TO ISAAC WILLIAMS[1]

Sir   Exeter, 22 November 1782

You will issue Provisions to the Recruits now raising in this State in such quantities and at such times as may be requested by Major Caleb Robinson who is appointed Muster Master at this place,[2] he certifying that such person or persons are Recruits.[3]

You will not issue provisions on Account of this State to any other persons without Special Order therefor from the General Court or this Comtee.   Josiah Bartlett Chairmn

FC (Nh-Ar: Committee of Safety Letter Book). Printed in *NHSP*, 10:602.

1. Isaac Williams (c. 1738–1819), Deacon of the Congregational Church in Exeter, was issuing commissary for the army. See Bouton, "Committee of Safety," 254, 300; and Folsom, "Cemetery Inscriptions," 41.

2. Caleb Robinson (1746–1799) of Exeter, who had served since 1776, was breveted to the rank of major in 1782. *NHSP*, 8:955; Heitman, *Historical Register*, 470; Cleveland, *Genealogy*, 1:823.

3. Towns delinquent in recruiting men for military service had been granted an extension to 1 Jan. 1783 by the General Court on 21 November. *NHSP*, 8:955.

FROM PHILLIPS WHITE[1]

Sir   Philadelphia Decr, 4 1782

Agreeable to your desire I now set down to write your Honr, a few lines, but have nothing new of consequence. Mr. Gilman, wrote to the Hon'le President, on the affair of Vermont, the Day before I arrived here, sence which I gave a few hints respecting the same.[2] It appears that something should be done soon, it looks likely to me, that the final Decision will greatly depend on the inclination of New Hampshire & New York, for which reason it is highly necessary that we have instructions—if nothing was done on the Subject the last Session of the Genll Court, I hope there will be something done, the begining of the next. The Deligates from N. York appear to be very earnest to have a final determination. The Members from said State at present are Mr. Floyd, and Mr. Hambleton,[3] who we think are more cordial than some others have been &c.

No official account from the southward, people are in doubt respecting the evacuation of Charleston.[4]

We hear that Murrimitism, prevails among you, and that several worthy members of the Genl. Court are concerted. If so, doubtless they can give a reason of their hope. We remain with sincere respect Sir your Humle Servt.   P. White

P.S. I would not have you think that I am covetous, by my sending only half a sheet, the reason of my doing it, is on account of a complaint that the members incumber the mail, with large Letters, &c. &c. There has been an attempt to prevent private Letters going post free—however I shall run the venture to inclose a Newspaper this once as it will be coverd in one. Mr. Gilman will send to the Honle. President.

RC (NhD). Franked.

1. Phillips White (1729–1811) of South Hampton was a delegate to the Continental Congress from 4 Nov. 1782 to May 1783. He served as a member of the General Court, 1775–1782, as probate judge for Rockingham County, 1776–1790, and later as a member of the Council, 1792–1794.

2. Gilman had written to Meshech

Weare on 29 October and 20 November, White on 6 November. Burnett, *Letters*, 6:526–27, 535, 546.

3. William Floyd and Alexander Hamilton.

4. The British evacuated Charleston on 14 December. Wallace, *Appeal to Arms*, 264.

FROM JOHN TAYLOR GILMAN

Dear Sir   (Private) Philada. Jany 9th. 1783

It is so long a time since I had the pleasure of a Line from you, that I Scarcely know whether you wish to hear from me however I shall Hazard a few Lines. Your last Letter was dated Octr. 5th.

You will see by my Letter to the Honble. the President what has been done respecting Contl. Money;[1] as I think their is not any the least prospect of any thing being done to good purpose at present I Imagine the Delegates of Massachusetts will not move the Subject again very soon, and I shall not unless I hear from the State on the Subject. I have seen the Resolve of the Genl. Court for Compleating their Battalions in Consequence of the Application of Genl. Washington.[2] This was a plan agreed on by him & the Secretary at War. It was altogether unknown by Congress (Except some Individual Members) untill about the 25th. of December. I had been Informed of it by a Letter from the Army but not in time to write to the State previous to the November session. Otherwise I Should have hazarded my Sentiments on that Subject in Contradiction to the Application. The Arangement of the 7th. of August ought to have taken place in the N. H. Line. Congress were Informed a few Days Since (about the 27th. December) that application had been made, and that New Hamp. had agreed to raise their Troops, which was the principal Argument made use of for Suspending the Arangment which Resolution I Inclose you.[3] I am for General Arrangements & requisitions. I by no means wish to see the State of New Hampshire backward in Complying with the General Requisitions of Congress, But in this Case, I think in the first place that it is not probable we shall want more men, and in the Second if we did they ought to be raised from those States who are much more delinquent than New Hampshire. The State of Pennsylvania have perhaps four times the Number of Inhabitants and as to Extent of Territory & wealth I cannot Say in what proportion they are to us but you can Judge, and you will see by this Resolution that, that State propose to Compleat Three Battalions to N. H.'s Two—but I need not add, your having recourse to the List of the Army which I Sent you some time Since[4] will shew you the numbers of Each State's Troops. The State of Rhode

Island (you are Undoubtedly informed) have Unanimously rejected the plan of an Impost, Virginia have repealed their Act and at present I See no prospect of Congress having any Funds on which to Secure their Creditors. The Securities are many & they have been sold at great Discount, in this place.

The Conduct of some States seems to be such as tho' they Expected each State would be obliged to settle with their own Citizens. For my own part I hope the Confederation will be Strengthened and that we shall Continue United for a long time to Come, but if other States make Use of Such Policy, will it not be necessary for N. H. to do so too. Perhaps I write too freely on this Subject, but when I hear some persons say our Accounts will not be adjusted (between each State) and the Arguments of others on the Subject of Continental Currency I think it my Duty to mention the matter.

The Subject of obtaining the Value of Lands and Buildings in Each State to ascertain the proportion of public Expences agreable to Confederation has been taken up, a Report is now under Consideration for Carrying that Article into Effect. It seems to be a general Opinion that the Value cannot be Ascertained with any degree of Accuracy—if it could, would it be Equal? It is said (from the Circumstances of the War) that if it would have been Equal when Confederation was proposed it would now be very Unequal; my Own Opinion is that it never was nor will be Equal unless some other Tax (such as an Impost) or others which might be devised should go along with it. If we find so great difficulty in Ascertaining the proportion of Each Town & Parish, what may we Expect between State & State. My Opinion is that the Quota of each State will not be Determined agreeable to the Mode of Confederation and that unless the States can be Induced to grant some kind of Taxes as Imposts &c. that each One will have to pay the debts due to their own Citizens & how our foreign debt will be paid I cannot Say.

But enough on this Subject, perhaps my fears have out run my reason.

We are Daily Expecting some further accounts from our Commissrs in Europe by which we shall be able better to determine whether we may Expect Peace soon or not. For my Own part I cannot but hope we shall have Peace before the time for Opening another Campaign, but the Instability of our Enemy's Councils are such that we cannot depend on it untill we know the Articles are Signed.

Hope the State have Appointed Delegates to Relieve us the beginning of April.

Nothing further done respecting Vermont. Please to make my Compliments to my Friends with you. I am Your most Hum. Servt.

John Taylor Gilman

P.S. Mr. Jefferson of Virginia who was appointed one of our Commissrs. for making Peace is Just Setting out for Europe.[5]

RC (NhD).

1. Gilman to Meshech Weare, 9 Jan. 1783, noted that Congress had been un- able to settle on a rate of exchange for Continental money and that all states

were delinquent in collecting it except New Hampshire, Massachusetts, and Rhode Island. Burnett, *Letters*, 7:10–11.

2. The Court acted on 23 Nov. 1782 to hasten recruitment. *NHSP*, 8:956. See JB to Isaac Williams, 22 Nov. 1782.

3. The enclosed resolution of 31 Dec. 1782 suspended the resolutions of 7 August for reducing the number of army officers so far as they related to New Hampshire, Rhode Island, and New Jersey. *JCC*, 23:837.

4. See Gilman to JB, 5 Aug. 1782.

5. Jefferson received his commission on 8 Jan. 1783 and left Philadelphia on 26 January. Boyd, *Papers of Jefferson*, 6:2, 213–15.

FROM PHILLIPS WHITE

Sir   Philadelphia Janry 9th 1783

I have not been favour'd with a line from you. I want to hear how Publick affairs go on in New Hampshire, (the Eastern mail did not come in this week). We have no official account of the Evacuation of Charleston, but have no reason to doubt of the truth of it as Published in the inclosed Newspaper.

The affair of Continantal Bills now remaining in the hands of individuals &c. was debated yesterday in Congress. It was put to vote to sink them at 40 for one, and at 75, both negatived. The members from those States that have more than their Quota did not wish to have it tried at a lower rate, some of the Southward members mention'd a much lower rate. There were more that voted for 40 than for 75, it was on the principle of policy, that rate being what it was set at march 18th, 1780.

I perceive that the State of New Hampshire have been trying to raise more men for the Army which I am sorry for, as they have already more in the Army than their proportion with most of the other States, and as Congress is at a loss to know what measures to take to Quiet the minds of those already on Duty not only of New Hampshire line but all the other. There is a Committee here from the Northern Army who have presented a memorial &c. to Congress, of their grieveances. Both officers & soldiers are uneasy for want of present pay, & of the uncertenty of future pay, the officers of half pay in perticular.[1]

Mr. Morris informed me that he had appointed Mr. Stephen Gorham of Boston Commissioner of Continantal Accounts for the State of New Hampshire. Doubtless there will be no objection, to the appointment, he is a person of integrity & ability has been employed in Committee for three years past on Continantal & other Publick accounts.[2] I remain your Honours most Humble Servt.   P White

RC (NN: Emmet Collection, No. 487).

1. The members of the committee from army headquarters at Newburgh, N.Y., were Maj. Gen. Alexander McDougall, Lt. Col. John Brooks, and Col. Mattias Ogden. Their petition asked for an advance on back pay, a commitment by Congress to pay the remainder due, and settlement on the promise of half pay for life to the officers. Jensen, *The New Nation*, 36, 72.

2. Stephen Gorham (1747–1826), a Boston merchant, was a brother of Nathaniel Gorham (1738–1796), a Massachusetts delegate to Congress. The General Court approved Stephen's appointment in February. *NEHGR*, 7:252; Meshech Weare to Robert Morris, 7 Mar. 1783, in *NHSP*, 10:607.

FROM JOHN TAYLOR GILMAN

Sir   Philada. Jany. 16th. 83.

On the 15th. Instt. I received your favor of the 28th. Ultimo.[1] Their was no Mail from New England last week, the Mail of this week (tho' it usually comes in on Monday mornings) did not arrive untill yesterday. Mr. White received your Letter of the 23d.[2] P. same.

Am sorry to find that the Honble Court have not made any order on the Subject of Vermont affairs. Some time past I was Induced to think, this business would have been settled Speedily, but that prospect has almost Vanished. It has been repeatedly debated and might now be taken up again if their was any prospect of any thing being done towards a Conclusion of it.

You mention the Subject of Depreciation &c. I have no Copy of my Letter to you of the 9th. Instt. but think I Mentioned, that a Commtee. of Officers from the Army was here; the Subject of those Settlements, Half-Pay &c. is now under Consideration.

As to the Frigate you Mention she Run on Shore in a Storm, Cut away her Masts &c. which were lost, but is got off, & now here.

Yesterday Dispatches were received from Genl. Greene respecting the Evacuation of Charlestown. The Enemy left it very Quietly in Consequence of an Agreement that they should not be Molested on their Retiring; the Southern States are Once more freed from the Enemy. I wish they would be so wise as to Quit New-York & Penobscot immediately, they have Traversed our Country, (almost every [   ] of it) but their present possessions are [   ].

As to a General Peace I have wrote my Sentiments P. Genl. Whipple and it Unnecessary to repeat them.

Genl. Whipple spent several Days here.[3] I conversed with him very freely on the Subject of Vermont & several other matters. He informed me, that if the next meeting of the Assembly should be at Exeter, that he would go there for the purpose of giving such information as he had obtained here respecting our affairs and to him I must beg leave to Refer you. Have now under Consideration a Mode for Ascertaining the Quota's of each State agreeably to the articles of Confederation.

Our Letter of the 11th. Ultimo.[4] mentioned our desire that Delegates might be appointed to relieve us the beginning of April. Am not Informed whether any Appointments have been made, if not hope it will be done early next session which (by your Letter) appears probable will be in February tho' I am not Informed to what time the Assembly did adjourn.[5] Another part of that Letter was on the Supply of Money which hope will be seasonably provided.

By the Paper I see their is a very great proportion of New Members in the Assembly. Wish it may prove to be for the Interest of the State.

I wrote you a Letter on the 23d. Octr. but have not been informed whether it reached you.

What is done respecting the new Constitution?[6] What is doing with the Confiscating Act?[7] Who are Members of the Commtee of Safety?

Have no Official Accounts from Europe of later date than I have Mentioned in former Letters. Please to make my Compliments to my Friends with you. Am with much Esteem Your Obedt. Servt.

John Taylor Gilman

P.S. Mr. White desires his Compliments to you.

RC (NhD). Bracketed spaces are the result of a tear in the manuscript.

1. Not found.
2. Not found.
3. William Whipple was financial receiver for New Hampshire, 1782–1784, and was probably in Philadelphia on that business.
4. Gilman and White to Meshech Weare, 11 Dec. 1782, *NHSP*, 10:495–96.
5. During its session from 12 February to 1 March the General Court appointed Nathaniel Folsom, Abiel Foster, JB, Ebenezer Thompson, and Jonathan Blanchard as delegates to Congress. Only

Foster accepted. He began attending in July. *NHSP*, 8:964–72.
6. On 28 February the Court resolved "that the present form of Government be continued in its full force until the tenth day of June 1784, notwithstanding a general pacification should take place in the mean time." *NHSP*, 8:970.
7. In February the Court authorized probate judges to liquidate the sums paid into the treasury by trustees of confiscated estates. *Laws of N.H.*, 4:504–05.

TO BENJAMIN RUSH[1]

Sir

Kingstown Janury 25th 1783

I Some time Since Saw a pamphlet wrote by one Martin if I mistake not, who Says he has found out a *Certain* Remedy for Cancers, Schirrous & Shrophalous Tumors[2] and Tho' I have no very good opinion of Nostrums & quack medicines in general; yet at the Same time I think it not improbable, that Some more efficatious medicines than has hitherto been known, may hereafter be found out, for the relief of those unhappy persons who suffer by those dreadful Diseases.

Mr. Martin mentions Dr. Rush of Philada. as having Seen the good effects of his medicines and reccomending persons afflicted with Such Disorders to his Care: and as I had the pleasure of an acquaintance with you when we were Members of Congress, and think I can Depend on your Judgment I have taken the liberty of troubling you with an account of the Circumstances of a young woman, a Daughter of mine who is troubled I fear with a Disorder of that kind, and to Request the favor of you to inform me, whither you are Sufficiently acquainted with Mr. Martin's Practice to reccomend his medicines? What is the manner of their opperation and whither in your opinion they may be used with Safety and whither they will probably be Servicable in the Case of my Daughter.

She is a young married woman, naturally of a Delicate Tender Constitution: in the month of May last was Delivered of her first Child:[3] about Two months before her Delivery, she Discovered a Small hard Tumor on the Side of her Throat under her right Ear, without any pain or Soreness, and the Color the Same as the other flesh; Sometime after, other Small indurated Glands were perceived near the former, but Chiefly on the Back part towards the Spine of the neck, which have Since increased So as almost to form one body with that first mentioned; a number of other

Small indurated glands have been perceived in Several other parts of that Side of the neck, Some of which have by Degrees lessened & Disappeared, while others have made Their appearance in Different places on that Side of the neck: Sometimes the large Tumors have Stood at a Stay or rather Decreased for Two or Three weeks togather: at other times they have increased fast, for a like Space of Time; The Tumors at this time may be Distinguished one from the other, and appear not to be round but of an irregular form; That part where it first began, now feels (she Says) Tender & Disagreably when handled. After Delivery she was Sick with a slow fever much resembling a Hectic for 2 or 3 months: one of her Breasts inflamed and Came to an imperfect Suppuration, but is now well & she Suckles her Child. Her health is also pretty well Restored: she has taken pretty freely of the Bark, but no mercurials of any kind as the State of her health was Supposed not to admit of it: A mercurial Plaister has been kept on the Tumors.

This I Expect will be handed you by Mr. Gilman one of our Delegates in Congress, and Beg that your answer may be given him who will Convey it me, and if you should advise to the use of Martin's, nostrum will if he Conveniently Can procure & Send it to me—any advice you may think proper to send me will be Esteemed a favor to your Most obedient Servnt.

Josiah Bartlett

RC (PPL). Draft (Nh).

1. Benjamin Rush (1745–1813) of Philadelphia was, with JB, one of the physicians who signed the Declaration of Independence. See Butterfield, "Benjamin Rush," 18–42.

2. Hugh Martin, *A Narrative of a Discovery of a Sovereign Specific, for the Cure of Cancers* (Philadelphia: Printed by Robert Aitken, 1782), 15 pp. [reprinted 1784]. Evans, *American Bibliography*, Nos. 17,582, 18,574. Martin was a physician of Virginia who had served as a

surgeon's mate in the Continental Army from 1778 to 1781. Heitman, *Historical Register*, 381.

3. JB was writing about his daughter Miriam (b. 1758) who married Joseph Calef of Kingston on 28 June 1781 and gave birth to her first child, Josiah, on 21 May 1782. She was delivered of a daughter on 20 May 1784, and died, perhaps in childbirth, on 27 Aug. 1785. Boardman, *Robert Calef*, 76.

FROM BENJAMIN RUSH

Sir,   Philada: Feby: 23. 1783.

I was made very happy in an Opportunity of complying with the request of a gentleman with whom the dangers of our country produced a connection equally honourable & agreeable in Congress in the year 1776.[1]

I have a high opinion of Dr. Martin's medicine in the cure of cancerous tumors & ulcers, but it is only when they are *local* diseases. Scrophulous[2] tumors being generally connected with a Scrophulous diathesis of the whole System have in several instances eluded the power of his remedy. Upon shewing him your letter he said he had no doubt but your daughter's case was within the reach of his medicine—but added that it would be necessary for him to see her & attend her to render his medicine effectual. This would be to expose her to great & unnecessary trouble & expence, for as his medicine consists of nothing but a vegetable caustic, you may obtain in your fields or woods a dozen vegetable substances that will answer the same purpose. I have known the powder of poke root, as also the powder of the white Hellebore root, & even the berries of the Night Shade produce the same salutary effects with Dr. Martin's medicine. All these vegetable caustics have these two Advantages over the mineral Caustics. They corrode, or rather seperate *morbid* flesh *only*, and they never defeat their own operation by producing a scar. If you are satisfied that your daughter's habit is not Scrophulous, I think you may try either of the above caustics with the same prospect of Success, as you could Dr. Martin's powder. The external surface of the sores must first be a little excoriated, or the vegetable caustics will not produce the necessary inflammation or Seperation in them.

I have lately seen a pamphlet published in England by a Mr. Justamond in which great effects are ascribed to a lotion applied freely to the part of a Solution of green vitriol in water in Scrophulous tumors. The flores martiales were given at the same time internally. A Swedish Physician (whose name I have forgotten) has lately published some remarkable cases of cures of Scrophulous tumors being performed by the Hemlock given internally & applied in cataplasms to the diseased parts.

I think I have seen bad effects from the application of mercurial medicines to Scrophulous tumors in the neck. The tumors were removed it is true, but a consumption followed. I have seen the best effects from a drain being opened upon or near the affected parts—an issue obtained by a caustic of any kind will answer this purpose.

The bark should be continued in large doses. Salt water should be drank in the summer season—and when this cannot be obtained, I have often substituted with great Advantage a teaspoonful of common Salt every morning.

Gentle exercise, & the cold bath should not be omitted—the last remedy to be used if the other remedies fail.

With sincere wishes that the information contained in this letter may prove useful to your daughter, I am Sir with great respect Your most Obedient humble Servant   Benjn Rush

RC (NhD).
   1. See JB's letter of 25 Jan. 1783.   2. Scrofulous, or diseased.

TO SAMUEL CHASE[1]   In Committee of Safety
Sir,   Exeter March 13 1783
   You are hereby authorized & requested to rent out for one year from the first day of this instant March, the lands of Absentees & Subjects of Great Britain which you were authorized to rent out the last year. You will make the best terms you can for the use of this State and make Return of your Doings to the General Court or Committee of Safety as soon as may be.   Josiah Bartlett Chn

FC (Nh-Ar: Committee of Safety Letter Book). Printed in *NHSP*, 10:607–08.

1. Samuel Chase (1739–1816) of Litchfield had served in the state legislature and the militia during the Revolution. On 12 Apr. 1781 the Committee of Safety appointed him as agent of confiscated Loyalist property in Hillsborough County, a position he filled for several years. Stearns, *Genealogical*, 4:1597.

TO MESHECH WEARE

In Committee of Safety

Sir,   Exeter June 27th. 1783

Inclosed you have a Vote of the General Assembly in which it is desired that Mr. Nathanael Gilman of Exeter be recommended to Congress as a proper person for a Loan Officer in this State.[1] And it is the Opinion of this Committee that at the Same time you inform of the Above recommendation Congress be informed of the proceedings of the General Assembly, respecting paying the Interest (or issuing certificates for the Same) on the Loan office Certificates issued in this State, agreable to the Inclosed Resolve of the 28th of February last and Request that the Loan Officer may be Instructed to comply with the said Resolve of Court,[2] and after Liquidating said Loan Office Certificates to give other Certificates for their Value in Specie or such other order Respecting the Same as they may think proper; the Necessity of our adopting that mode of paying the Interest on Loan Office Certificates you are well acquainted with & will please to write what you think proper on the Occasion.

Josiah Bartlett Chairman

RC (MHi). In clerk's hand; signed by JB.

1. The vote on 20 June recommended Nathaniel Gilman, Jr. (1759–1817), of Exeter who was a son of Nicholas Gilman and a brother of John Taylor Gilman. Nicholas, who had been Continental Loan Officer, had died in 1783. This appointment was to fill that office. Nathaniel later held office as state senator, representative, and treasurer. Gilman, *Searches*, 230–31; *NHSP*, 8:983.

2. The resolve is printed in *NHSP*, 8:970–71.

FROM ABIEL FOSTER[1]

Sir,   Princeton August 23d. 1783.

I arrived here on the 27th. Ultimo:, after a very uncomfortable Journey in a most severe heat, from the ill effects of which I am now recovered to a good State of health, and have been able to attend Congress every day, one only excepted. The Representation from the States is small, there being seldom more than eight present, & often not more than seven. I have taken the liberty to write to the Honble. President, and to suggest the propriety of furnishing a representation from New Hampshire, in case Mr. Langdon declines to come on, sooner than the time to which the General Court stands adjourned &, this I have done not only from my own Opinion on the subject, but from the general Opinion of the other Deligates, who conceive it, at this time, very important to have a full representation.[2]

The question for returning to Philadelphia, has been several times debated, and at length Negatived; notwithstanding that the Executive of

Pensylvania, has, thro' the Deligates of that State, expressed its wish for the return of Congress to its former Seat. No assurances have been given of protection should there be any occasion for it in future. I therefore presume, you will be of opinion Congress could not with propriety return, under these circumstances. The General Assembly of Pensylvania is now sitting, whither it will cast any censure on the Executive, or give any assurances to Congress of aid & protection against insult in future, time only can discover: should this step be taken, yet the difficulties which have heretofore attended all attempts to remove from Philadelphia, may possibly recurr so forceably, as to prevent a return to that City.[3] I hope in the course of next week, Congress will determine on the application from New Hampshire, relative to the Loan Office Certificates. In the present week I have omitted to call for the report, as I was satisfied the States present, would not have determined it agreeable to the wishes of my constituents.

This day his Excellency General Washington arrived here from the Northward, he will tarry some time, & then proposes to retire to his Plantation in Virginia. Sir Guy Carleton hath given information to Congress, that he has received orders for the final evacuation of New York, but hath said nothing respecting evacuating the other posts within the United States, however that may possibly be also in his instruction.

I enclose the last Philadelphia Paper, and beg the favor that you will send me any thing which may be interesting especially whatever may enable me to serve the interests of that State I have the Honr. to represent.

There seems little hope that the late recommendation of Congress with respect to impost, will be adopted by Rhode Island, perhaps not as it stands, by some other of the States:[4] the consequence will be unhappy to public credit, and induce a necessity of other expedients, if indeed they can be devised, for providing for the public Debt. I am Sir with great respect & esteem your very humble & most obedient Servant.

Abiel Foster

RC (NhD).

1. Abiel Foster (1735–1806) of Canterbury had graduated from Harvard in 1756. He preached at the First Congregational Church of Canterbury from 1761 to 1779 and served in Congress 1783–1785, 1789–1791, 1795–1803. Shipton, *Harvard Graduates*, 14:15–19.

2. Foster had written to Weare on 11 August. Burnett, *Letters*, 7:257. Foster was New Hampshire's sole representative making New Hampshire technically unrepresented.

3. Congress had left Philadelphia in June following harassment from soldiers of Pennsylvania regiments. When the Pennsylvania government failed to assure the safety of congressmen, President Elias Boudinot called for removal to Princeton where Congress could be protected by some of Washington's troops. Burnett, *Continental Congress*, 576–79.

4. The impost act of 1781 would have allowed Congress to levy an impost of 5 percent on all goods imported into the United States as a means of paying the war debt. The act was offered as an amendment to the Articles of Confederation requiring that it be ratified by all thirteen states. New Hampshire ratified on 6 Apr. 1781. By November 1782 all states had ratified the impost except Rhode Island which never did so. The "late recommendation" was that the individual states invest Congress with the power to levy import duties on goods brought into their boundaries. This was

resolved on 18 Apr. 1783. *NHSP*, 8:898; 24:257–61.
Jensen, *The New Nation*, 58, 63–67; *JCC*,

FROM JOHN TAYLOR GILMAN
Treasury Office
New Hampshire   Exeter Novr. 14th. 1783
   Received of the Honble. Josiah Bartlett Esqr. and Capt. Josiah Gilman
(Two of the Committee appointed to Settle the late Treasurer's Ac-
counts) one Hundred & Three Thousand and Sixty Dollars in Bills of
the New Emission Emitted by this State, for which sum I am Account-
able to the State
                                       Per J. T. Gilman Treasr.

103,060 Dollars

FC (Nh-Ar). See also MJB, 2350, 2355, 2364 relating to the committee to settle
accounts.

TO THOMAS MIFFLIN[1]
Sir,   Exeter January 31, 1784
   I have the honor to enclose to your Excellency a Copy of an Act of this
State for granting to the United States in Congress assembled, certain Im-
posts and Duties upon foreign Goods imported into this State, and for the
purpose of paying the Principal and Interest of the Debt contracted in the
prosecution of the late War with Great Britain.[2]
   I have the honor to be, with the highest Respect, Your Excellencys
Most Obedt. Humble Servt.   Josiah Bartlett President P. T.

RC (DNA: PCC, 64). In a clerk's hand; signed by JB. Marked with address: "(public
Service)." Docketed: "Read 1 March." Enclosure not found.
   1. Mifflin was president of Congress   Court on 2 Jan. 1784 passed an act grant-
from 3 Nov. 1783 to 3 Nov. 1784.   ing to Congress certain imposts and
   2. In compliance with Congress's rec-   duties on foreign goods imported into the
ommendation in April 1783, the General   state. *Laws of N.H.*, 4:537–39.

FROM ABIEL FOSTER
Sir,   Annapolis 21st. Febry. 1784.
   I was this day favoured with yours of the twenty third of Janury. last[1]
informing me of my reappointment to serve as a Delegate in Congress for
which I was the more obliged as I began to feel my self very disagreably
situated neither having any thing to do here or any means to enable me to
return to N. Hampshire.
   In my official Letter to the President you will see my determination
with regard to my appointment;[2] I am sorry to find by your Letter that
that Honble. Gentleman who hath presided in the State during the trying
Scenes of the late war with so much reputation, is so indisposed as to be

unable to attend the duties of his Station, and sincerely wish the returning Spring may so far restore him that he may be able to aid in the public counsels.

In one of my late Letters I requested some information from the Honble. the President relative to public affairs. Should his indisposition render him unable to gratify me I must beg the same favors from you, and shall thankfully acknowlege them.

I find by a New Hampshire Paper that the Legislature have passed the impost Act.[3] Jersey, Pennsyvania, Delaware, Maryland & Virginia have done the same. Conneticut is at present in too great a pet with the Commutation to comply, but possibly may in time agree to it. Rhode Island, if I can judge from the sentiments of its Delegates here, will be slow in this business; but I do not wholly dispair even of that State. From the Carolinas and Georgia I have heard nothing on which I can ground an opinion.

I think Congress will adjourn the last of April or early in May. If a Committee of the States should be left sitting that duty will fall to Mr. Blanchard & I shall return to New Hampshire; but it is much talked of to leave no Committee.

I have lost no time in Congress for the want of my appointment, the indisposition of two Delegates having prevented an House from the time I went out till I was able to re-enter. I shall by much obliged by any communications which you may favor me with. And am with great respect and esteem Sir your very humble & most obedient Servant   Abiel Foster
P.S. I intended copying this, but the want of time prevents me, hope you will exuse the erasements & inaccuracies.   A. F.

RC (NN: Emmet Collection, No. 458).
  1. Not found.
  2. Foster awaited Blanchard's arrival "with great impatience." Foster to Weare,

3 Feb. 1784, Burnett, *Letters*, 7:436.
  3. See JB to Thomas Mifflin, 31 Jan. 1784.

FROM JONATHAN BLANCHARD

Sir   Annapolis March 5th. 1784

I do my self the honour to put under Cover, for your perusal, an Extract of a Law pass'd in Jersey, for establishing a Revenue &c.[1] You will find in that Act, a Succedaneum[2] for hard money, which we seem not to have. That only the amount of one years interest is to be emitted in paper.

Several States have fully complied others complying; Virginia has pass'd the impost Act, and 'tis said, that Rhode Island is coming too. That it is probable, and I flatter my self with a General Agreement in this Matter. If the impost will discharge the foreign interest, of wch. I believe there is no doubt, the sale of Lands, may Collect our Domestic Securities.

The State of Massachusetts have remonstrated to Congress, on the Subject of Commutation. The Eastern Delegates used every effort to Obtain Liberty, for their states to settle with their own line of the Army but Congress from a sence of the Officers having received their Securities, that good faith should be preserv'd, and the very disagreeable consequences of a Repeal, have not, nor are likely (in my Opinion) to resind.

I deliverd your Official letter to the Presendent of Congress enclosing our impost Act[3] and in my Letter to our President I omitted mentioning of it.

A Packet from France arriv'd here Yesterday & bro't despatches for Congress. The Letters from Dr. Franklin are on the Subject of Commercial Treaties with the several powers in Europe. The papers are all committed and as soon as I can come at them I shall forward such Extracts as fully to inform you of every Matter on this head.

Congress have in contemplation an adjournment & Recess, after about 10 Weeks–without leaving a Comtee. In that case I shall instantly repair to New-Hampr., & be careful to avoid Public expence. The Comtee. on the Civil list, have reported since my Attendance, & reduced the pay of their servants to a very great amount.[4]

My health is much improv'd since I left N. H. I should be happy to receive every communication necessary in my Department. My Colleague, desires to be kindly rememberd to you. I have the honour to be, Sir, Your Most hble Servt.   Jona. Blanchard

RC (NhD).

1. The enclosed act is included on M JB 2414.

2. Substitute.

3. JB's letter of 31 January was read in Congress on 1 March. *JCC*, 26:110.

4. *Ibid.*, 125–27.

FROM JONATHAN BLANCHARD

Sir   Annapolis 20th of April 1784

I wish it were in my power to Give you an Agreeable Account of our debates in Congress—but very little has been done since the present year Commenced.

Permit me to Suggest the Utility of an impost for the use of our State if that measure is not already Adopted.

It remains a matter of great doubt whether all the States in the Union will come into the recommendation of April 1783—Even so far as the impost.[1] The States this way have agreed to a private impost, by which means they have raised very large sums. And it gives me no small pain to find so large a balance in the Public Account against New-Hampshire. I am Greatly at a loss to know how she can remit the amount, or even her proportion of the interest of the foreign debt. I think she cannot.

The Southern Gentry prefer extravagance to Oeconomy and seem to take a pleasure in Granting monies which they cannot Command and were it not for the New-England Delegates the Lord only knows to what length Congress would run. I conceive it therefore very much to our purpose to keep up a Representation.

If a pritty full Delegation is on the Ground in Novr. annually it is supposed that the Necessary business of these States may be compleated in the Space of three Months and I think under this view some of our best hands may afford to come, and if they *Snarl some times*, at Others an Agreeable Amusement will take place.

As to an adjournment it is not as yet agreed to & a Comtee of the States are not appointed & until these matters are Generally discuss'd I can give no Opinion. Out door talk is an adjournmt on the 26th. of May &a Note has fix'd it at Trenton.

Mr. Foster is well but Wishes to return to his family. I hope he may be prevaild on to tarry so long as just to save the rising of the assembly the 2d. Week in June.

No news & time will not permit to Say more than that I am Sir Your Most humble Servt.   Jona. Blanchard

RC (NhD).
1. See Abiel Foster to JB, 23 Aug. 1783.

FROM ABIEL FOSTER

Sir   Annapolis 1st. May 1784

I was favoured with yours of the 11th. April,[1] yesterday; for which I am much obliged. I am happy to find the legislature are turning their attention to a revenue from trade. Mr. Blanchard & myself were on the point of suggesting that measure to our State, as we conceived the sums necessary for the support of public credit, could not be raised in the usual mode of taxation, & found that similar steps had been adopted by all the comerial[2] States. A recommendation is forwarded to the respective States with a view to counteract the police of Britain to injure our carrying trade, I wish it may be complied with by the states, and convince Her that America is too wise to be sported with, and can act in such Union as to defeat entirely her injurous attempts.[3]

Your observation on the Journal is very just. During the winter little business has been compleated from the want of a representation; when barely seven States were present, a single dissenting Voice, from most of the States, prevented the completion of any matter for which that number was necessary, and the same fate frequently attended the business of nine States, when only that number attended; and besides, the enemy were not at our Gates to stimulate Union & dispatch. However, many matters difficult in their nature, & of great consequence in their effects, have been digested in Committees, which I hope will soon be finished, to the satisfaction of the public. It has also been a painful circumstance to the attending Members to be unable to proceed in necessary measures, & provide for the public exigencies, from the want of more States on the Floor. Congress have agreed to meet in November at Trenton in Jersey.[4] A Grand Committee are now sitting on a Memorial from Massachusetts on the subjects of old Continental Money, an allowance for the Penobscott expedition, and for extra bounties for Soldiers. What will be the issue of this application remains uncertain. New York are likewise calling on Congress to decide the controversy of Vermont, this is in the hands of a Committee.

The Quota of New Hampr. to the 8 Million dollars, we were sensible was too large, & had been objected to by the State;[5] this was at the same time, the case with most of the eastern States. The Delegates from those States were desirous to have altered, but as Congress were not possessed of the returns necessary to fix the equal proportion, they judged an attempt to take up the matter on new grounds would be impracticable and therefore consented to let the Quota stand and be credited at a future day. I am Sir with great respect and esteem your very humble Servant.

Abiel Foster

RC (NhD).

1. Not found.

2. Commercial.

3. On 30 Apr. 1784 Congress debated the issue of restricting imports and resolved to recommend that the states invest Congress with power to prohibit imports in vessels other than those of the United States or of powers with which it had commercial treaties. *JCC*, 26:317–

22.

4. See ibid., 295–96.

5. The congressional table of requisitions and payments shows that New Hampshire had been apportioned $373,598, of which $3,000 was paid by 31 Dec. 1783, leaving $183,799 due immediately to meet the debt of half the eight million. Ibid., 309.

JB, having been appointed to the state Superior Court on 14 Nov. 1782, was kept busy on its circuit to the five counties. He had been instrumental in securing voter approval of a new constitutional government for New Hampshire in October of 1783. Governmental operations slowed during the waning months of 1783 and into 1784 until the new government took effect that June. Most business was carried on through the Committee of Safety, of which JB became permanent chairman late in 1783. He continued to send out brief official notices for the committee, and his influence continued to grow within the state. When the house of representatives and the newly-constituted senate met in Concord on 2 June 1784, JB had charge of swearing in all the members. On 4 June the house voted "That the Hon. Josiah Bartlett, Esq; be requested to tarry in this place for a few days to assist in the qualification of such Senators and members of the House of Representatives, as are not already qualified." The senate readily concurred. NHSP, 20:39–40, 62, 64. The Constitution of 1783 made no provision for a governor; but rather provided the position of president of the legislature. The election by the people gave the position to Meshech Weare who remained the leading public figure of the state until his death in January 1786. Weare thus holds title to being New Hampshire's first post-Revolution chief executive, although JB, who was in office when constitutional revisions went into effect in 1792, retains the claim as the state's first titular "governor."

FROM JONATHAN BLANCHARD

Sir   Annapolis June 6th: 1784

Since my last I have not been favd. with a line from you.

Congress are now Adjournd to meet at Trenton on the 30th. of Octr. next. The Comtee. of the States to remain here, if they do not *desert*, but some are taking French *leave*, I shall tarry so long as any propect remains of doing business, and when that is over, I shall return to N. Hampr.¹

The Public Affairs are in better Situation I apprehend, than at any earlier period since the War. Many important matters have been Agreed on, within two or three months past.

Mr. Morris's bills on the agents in Holland are paid. The Troops at West point to be discharged, & militia Calld from Connecticut, N. York N. Jersey & Pennsylvania to Garrison the Frontier posts. The Massa. has put in a Claim, to Lands Claimd by N. York, & praying for a federal Court to decide; Notice is Orderd to N. York;² so much for Massa. Politicks. No determination respecting Vermont, some of the Southern Delegates Declare Openly, that they will not consent to her being admitted into the Union, for it will give a ballance to the Eastern *Scale*, which Eastern *Scale* has been pritty formidable for two months past, and been Generally able to Carry a Good, and to defeat, a bad Question.

Mr. Foster set out yesterday I expect that he will very soon call & see you.

The Department of finance is put into Comn. I send you a Copy of the ordinance for perusal,³ I hope it will meet the Approbation of the Legislature. Money matters must be attended to, & Great power being lodgd in the hands of one man, may prove a Dangerous Engine. I am Sir Your Most hble Servt.   Jona. Blanchard

RC (PHi).

1. Blanchard had been put on the Committee of the States on 29 May to transact business during the Congress recess. Congress adjourned on 3 June. *JCC*, 27: 477, 557.

2. The notice to New York is ibid., 547–50.

3. The copy of the ordnance of 28 May 1784, in Blanchard's hand, is in NhD.

TO NATHANIEL PEABODY   Kingstown April 13th 1785
Sir   Wednesday 5 oClock A:M:

I am very unhappy in Disappointing you and the other Gentlemen yesterday and should be glad if I Could wait on you this Day but as I have tried and find that there is no possibility of riding a much less way, that I was obliged to leave one horse at Exeter finding it impossible to ride home, and on Monday I tried to Ride in hopes to get part of the way to Hampstead, So as not to Disappoint you yesterday, but got plunged and thrown from my horse and obliged to Return.¹ I am Sure it is impossible to ride at this time to Hampstead from this place, and my health will not permit me to attempt travelling on foot so far. Give my Regards to the Gentlemen attending and believe me to be your & their friend and most obedt Servant   Josiah Bartlett

P.S. I am very unwell, perhaps owing to my walking from Exeter on foot Saturday last

RC (NhHi).

1. JB was probably trying to get to Hampstead for the town meeting held on 12 April. Hampstead was attempting to obtain representation on the General Court and had adjourned its meeting in March until 12 April in order that the matter could be more thoroughly discussed. Hampstead Town Records, Nh.

FROM EZRA BARTLETT

Dear Sir   June 22nd. 1786

In compliance to your command, I here give you an account of my studies since I have been to the Phillips Exeter Academy: I have lernt through Erasmus once, Eutropius once, castalio once part through, Latin Grammar twice, through Greek Grammar once, the greek Testament to the second of Corinthians once, half through Ovid once, 963 Lines in Vergil, Lernt proside twice, made 19 Chapters of Latin, Wrote 1 Book of Coppies: thus I have given a brief account of my studies.

I have been to Portsmouth since I was at home. I like it very well; I heard that my little cousin was unwell & should be glad to hear from her, but I expect to go home on Saturday next, I suppose you will not have an Opportunity before. I am better in health than when I was at home last, I like the academy very well. You said you did not think the greek Language would be of much service to me, but as the Preceptor thought it would & my class-mates study it I have taken his advice & do study it: you said if the French language was taught in town that it would help me to learn it but it is not taught.

For news I hear that It is reported in Exeter that Col. Peabody was at Concord, & that they had not seen him after he first came, his servant & horses are in Concord. It is supposed that he hath made away with himself.

P.S. I forgot to mention in my letter, that the Preceptor requires two letters every week from the English scholars & one from the Latin Students. I Remain you Dutiful Son.   Ezra Bartlett

TR (NhHi). From a copy typewritten in 1937.

TO CLERK OF THE PROPRIETORS OF PERRYSTOWN[1]

Sir,   Kingston, Dec. 22, 1786

You doubtless remember that before the late war the Masonian Proprietors made a demand of the proprietors of Perrystown of a sum of money to be paid to prevent the said town from being declared forfeited, and re-granted, (i.e., to other petitioners,) and that the Perrystown proprietors agreed to pay a considerable sum to the Masonians, and voted a tax to raise the money,—and that Major Bartlett[2] and myself, by order of the proprietors, gave security for the same. That security still lays (as I am informed) uncancelled. What has been done with the money raised by said tax, I know not, but think it is time that the Proprietary affairs should be settled, and *that* security taken up by some means or other, for I am not willing to have it lay any longer against me.[3]

I should think it best that a meeting of the proprietors should be called as soon as conveniently may be, to call the former Collectors to account for the moneys that they have received and agree upon some method of settling with the Masonians.

Perhaps there may be some other business which I am unacquainted with that may be necessary to be acted on by the proprietors at said meeting.

As I am informed that you are Clerk of the proprietors, I would request that a meeting may be called for the above purpose, and any other that you may think necessary, as soon as may be, and I will endeavor to attend the meeting and use my efforts to have the affairs settled.

I have frequently mentioned this affair to Esq. Samuel White,[4] and he gave me reason to expect that a meeting would be called, but I have not heard of any, and I am not easy to have it lay so any longer. I am, Sir, your friend etc. etc.   Josiah Bartlett

Reprinted from Worthen, *Sutton*, 1:22–23.

1. John Knight (c. 1750–1813), town clerk of Atkinson, was also clerk of the proprietors of Perrystown (now Sutton). Russell, "Town Officers of Atkinson"; Worthen, *Sutton*, 1:27–29.

2. Enoch Bartlett. See Worthen *Sutton*, 1:24.

3. See several documents showing JB's involvement with Perrystown in MJB, 406, 499, 1931, 2512.

4. Samuel White (1734–1801) of Haverhill, Mass., owned land in Perrystown, was moderator of the proprietors' meeting in 1764, and was added to a committee consisting of JB, Enoch Bartlett, and Timothy Ladd to obtain a new grant of the town in 1772. *Vital Records of Haverhill, Mass.*, 1:312; 2:329, 492; Worthen, *Sutton*, 1:16, 21.

TO JOSEPH BARTLETT[1]

Dear Sir   Kingstown February 22nd 1787

I am very Sorry to hear of your bad State of health and hope that before this time you are geting better: I have had no certain information what your disorder is, but by what I hear, Suppose it to be a Colic of the billious kind, and that after you had got Some better you have had relapses. To be taken down again after geting better and of so tedious & painful a disorder, is very apt too much to discourage the patient, which is frequently rather a hindrance to a Speedy recovery. That disorder is perhaps as painful & tedious to be borne as any perhaps that mankind are aflicted with, but is Seldom fatal, and when it is so, it commonly, if not always is, in the early Stages of it. Patience, Courage and a proper resignation to providence is not only a Duty, but is a good means towards a speedy recovery.

Tho' I make no doubt you have had very good advise in the physical way, yet I know some good physicians are very Sparing of anodines in that Disorder, which, when the pain is Severe, I look on as one of the best of medicines, and that the disorder may be much sooner Cured by so free a use of them as to take off the Spasms that always attend, than without them, and Especially anodine glisters which assists the Discharge by taking off the Spasms from the lower part of the intestines which obstructed the Discharge, beside the great advantage from the quiet & Ease they afford. To prevent relapses which are very apt to happen when the intestines are much weakened with the disorder, you are sensible that food of the easiest digestion is necessary, and great care to be taken not to take Cold & to keep up perspiration, for which purpose I have frequently found great advantage by the patient wearing a flannel or Baize shirt next his skin or the whole trunk of the body wrapped in wollen under the shirt.

I Sincerely hope and Believe from what I have heard of your disease, that you will recover your health and usefullness again, which is the Sincere Desire and wish of your hearty friend   Josiah Bartlett

RC (Salisbury Historical Society, Salisbury, N.H.).

1. Joseph Bartlett (1751–1800), a nephew of JB, was the first physician to settle in Salisbury. Born in Amesbury, Mass., he studied medicine with JB in Kingston and set up a practice in Salisbury about 1771. Dearborn, *Salibury*, 397–98; Bartlett, *Genealogical*, 43–45.

Between May and September 1787 the constitutional convention met in Philadelphia with John Langdon and Nicholas Gilman attending for New Hampshire. The Constitution was then sent to individual state conventions called explicitly to consider its ratification. In December 1787 the New Hampshire legislature resolved to submit the Constitution to a convention of delegates elected by the people, and ordered four hundred copies printed for distribution. NHSP, 21:151–52. The convention assembled at the courthouse in Exeter on 13 Feb. 1788. JB, representing Kingston, was immediately called upon to be temporary chairman. Elections the next day voted John Sullivan to be president. When it became obvious that a majority of the convention opposed the Constitution, its friends secured an adjournment on 21 February and scheduled the next meeting for 18 June in Concord. There, with JB in the van for ratification, the document was accepted on 21 June 1788 by a majority of ten votes. Its proponents had proposed twelve amendments, partly to satisfy opponents, and duly sent these to Congress with the announcement of ratification. New Hampshire was the ninth state to ratify, thus assuring the Constitution's adoption. Walker, History of the New Hampshire Convention; *Oliver,* "Keystone of the Federal Arch."

TO JOHN LANGDON

Sir   December the 27th 1788

I have received a letter from the Secretary[1] informing me that the Legislature at their last Session at Concord did me the honor to appoint me a Senator to the Congress of the United States and requested an answer at their next now present Session.[2]

In answer to which I must inform your Excellency[3] and the Legislature, that I am Sorry to find that the circumstances of my family and my own precarious State of Health will not permit me to accept of the appointment, as I am convinced that I Should not be able to give that punctual attendance that the importance of the Business requires: I have and shall ever retain a Gratefull Sense of the honor and Confidence reposed in me by the Legislature in their appointing me to a trust so honourable & important and nothing but the want of Health in my Self and family would induce me to decline the Business, as I now do. With Sentiments of esteem I am your Excellency's most obedient and very humble Servant

Josiah Bartlett

RC (MeHi: The John S. H. Fogg Autograph Collection).
1. Letter not found.
2. The Senate and House concurred in JB's appointment on 12 November. The legislature adjourned on 13 November and reconvened on 25 December. *NHSP,* 21:340, 359, 366.
3. Langdon had been elected state president in March 1788.

FROM JOHN PICKERING

Dear Sir,   Portsmouth 7th. March 1789

I have laid before a very full meeting of the Bar, the situation of your Son & your desire to have him study Law with me—Upon which, the Gentlemen were *unanimously* of opinion that, the time he had been studying under my direction, could not be considered as any part of the Five years required by the general rule;[1] and upon that condition only, would consent that he should be received into the office. I think the determination rigid, but do not conceive myself at liberty to depart from it. With sentiments of esteem & friendship I am Your very hble Servt.

John Pickering

RC (Nh).
1. Members of the New Hampshire Bar held their first recorded meeting in Concord in June 1788. As part of its regulations established at this meeting, the Bar Association stated that a candidate for the Bar must have a college degree and three years of apprenticeship or five years of study in the office of a practicing attorney of a superior court. It is uncertain which of JB's sons had applied. "Records of the Bar," 3.

TO RHODA TRUE

Dear Daughter   Kingstown July 14, 1789

I am sorry to inform you that your mother was taken Suddenly ill this morning and remains so at this time. I am very much afraid her disorder will prove mortal. I should be glad if you would come down as soon as you can and if my fears should be verified, Should be exceeding glad if you Could tarry with us some time as you know your Sister Lois's Situation and nobody but Sally to take care of things! Your sister Greely is here, but her circumstances will not permit her to tarry. Your mother's disorder is of the apoplectic kind.[1] In haste from your Loving Father

Josiah Bartlett

TR (NhHi). From a copy by Miss Hannah Bartlett Rollins of Dover.

1. Mary died later in the day. Lois, who never married, was apparently ill; Sarah was sixteen. Mary Bartlett Greeley (Polly) had two young chidren at home and was pregnant with Josiah Greeley, born 23 Aug. 1789. Her husband may have been ill, for he died on 3 Dec. 1789. Greeley, *Genealogy*, 99.

FROM JOSIAH BARTLETT, JR.

Hond. Sir   Andover August 15th 1789

Having an oppertunity to write by Dr. Shepard,[1] I embrace it. After enquireing of the health of you & the rest of the family, would acquaint you that I am well. Mrs. Kittredge has been unwell of a slow fever but is now about house.[2] It is quite healthy no acute disorder except some complaining with Symptoms of a Slow-nervous fever. I was at Londonderry last monday saw Dr: Moss.[3] He tell me that the measles are prevalent & of a bad kind, putrid, tho' none have died. Have given the pile Cupro Armentto a Mr. Page of sickley weak habit with the desired effect gr. 1/ss to a pill. I wish you'd send by the first Conveinency. I am Hond. Sir your Dutiful Son   Josiah Bartlett Junr

RC (NhD).

1. Samuel Shepard (1739–1815) of Brentwood was a physician and an ordained Baptist minister. Sprague, *Annals*, 6:135–36.

2. Susannah (Osgood) Kittredge (1754–1840) was the wife of Dr. Thomas Kittredge (1746–1818) of Andover, a Massachusetts legislator and a councilor of the Massachusetts Medical Society, under whom JB's sons Levi and Josiah, Jr., studied medicine. Jackson, *Physicians of Essex County*, 68; Kittredge, *Kittredge Family*, 29–35.

3. Moody Morse (1740–1830), a physician of Salem, moved to Londonderry in 1790 and practiced there until 1816. Parker, *Londonderry*, 356.

TO [THE GENERAL COURT]

Gentlemen   Exeter September 17th 1789

Agreably to your request, to be informed of the reason why the Superior Court did not Sit in the County of Grafton last term;[1] would observe, that the Court at present consists of but three Judges and that the absence of Either of them prevents all proceedings: That the Honble Judge Langdon[2] informed us that he Could not attend at Plymouth last Term and that in Consequence of that information we thought it our duty to adjourn that Court to prevent the Suits and actions in that County from falling Through. We are Gentn your Humble Servants

                                                           Josiah Bartlett
                                                           John Dudley

RC (Nh-Ar). In JB's hand; signed also by Dudley.

1. The Superior Court should have met at Plymouth in Grafton County on 26 May 1789. *Laws of N.H.*, 5:45.

2. Woodbury Langdon had been appointed in February of 1786 to fill the vacancy caused by William Whipple's death on 28 Nov. 1785. *NHSP*, 20:301. Langdon was impeached for his failure to attend court in Grafton County. Daniell, *Experiment*, 225–26.

The year ended with John Sullivan serving as president of New Hampshire and JB in his eighth year on the Superior Court. Samuel Livermore resigned as chief justice during 1789. The governor and council considered ten men, including JB, for the position, and chose JB in January of 1790. JB held the chief justiceship for only six months, until he replaced Sullivan as president that June.

FROM JEREMY BELKNAP [1]

Worthy Sir   Boston March 6 1790
    May I beg the favour of you to deliver the inclosed & to assist me by your influence in procuring me information agreeably to the tenor of the request in the printed Letter, which I am endeavoreing to circulate thro' the State of New Hampshire.
    As you have long been in public Life I flatter myself that from a Correspondence with you I shall be able to obtain some knowledge on other points beside those which are here stated. I could wish you would recollect & give me a summary acct of the altercation between N. Hampshire & Vermont about Government which took place somewhere about the year 1778 & so to 1780 or 81.[2]
    Having sent these Letters abroad, I hope to pick up some gleanings of information. As your Office calls you into all parts of the State I should be obliged by your recommending an attention to the subject, to such Persons as you may think qualified & disposed to aid the Cause. I am Sir with much Respect Yr Obed. Servt.   Jeremy Belknap
I have left the Letters for the other Parishes in Kingston blank. I wish you to direct them to such Persons as you please.

[Enclosure]
The Subscriber, being engaged in continuing the *History of New Hampshire*, and intending to give a topographical description of the Country, and a particular account of every occurence, which may deserve the publick notice, takes this method of applying to the Ministers and other Gentlemen of note, in the State, and begs the favour of them to collect and transmit to him, such information as can be obtained on the following heads.
1. The time when each township was granted; whether there were any interfering grants; when and how accommodations were made; when the settlement began; whether it was interrupted, and by what means.
2. The sufferings of the people by French and Indians wars; the number and names of the killed, wounded and captived; their treatment by the enemy; their death or redemption, with particular dates.
3. The names of the several Ministers of every denomination; the time of each one's settlement, death or removal, and age.
4. Singular instances of Longevity and Fecundity; and such observations on the diseases, deaths and ages of the Inhabitants, as may elucidate the influence of the climate on the human body.

5. Observations on the weather; on mountains, rivers, lakes, falls, caverns, minerals, stones, fossils, pigments, medicinal and poisonous vegetables, and any other natural productions.

6. A particular account of any monuments or relics of the ancient Indians.

7. Observations on soil, cultivation, fertility, and particularly on the several kinds of grass, grain, fruits, and esculent vegetables which have been cultivated, with and without success.

8. An account of the manufactures and fisheries.

9. The number of persons lost out of each town by means of the late war.

10. Whether schools are kept, and whether supported privately or publickly.

And generally any other matter worthy of historical notice. Your attention, Sir, to these *desiderata* is humbly requested; your answer will be gratefully received and it is wished that it may be sent, free of expense, by the first of *October* next, to Your Humble Servant,   Jeremy Belknap
Summer Street, Boston
March 1, 1790

RC (NhD). Addressed to JB as chief justice.

1. Jeremy Belknap (1744–1798) was a Congregational minister at Dover, 1766–1786, and then at the Federal Street Church in Boston, 1787–1798. He published a *History of New Hampshire*, 3 vols. (Philadelphia and Boston, 1784–1792). Kirsch, "Jeremy Belknap."

2. JB answered on 25 Feb. 1791.

TO SEVERAL BARTLETT CHILDREN

Tuesday morning 9 o'Clock
Dear Children   Charlstown No. 4 May 18th 1790

As I was very unwell when I left home, I Send this, by the post to inform you that I am in pretty good health, I was something tired the first day in riding to Amherst, but have now got pretty well. Judge Langdon is not arrived and if he does not come (as I suspect he will not) the Court here will be short.[1] At Amherst one Michal Keif an Irishman was Convicted on two indictments of dispersing incendiary threatning letters and of Burning Mr. Atherton's Barn with Cattle & hay in it & was sentenced to set on the Gallows with a rope round his neck to be whipped 30 stripes & imprisoned Six months. He was sentanced on fryday morning and at noon when a Can Knife was handed in with his dinner he cut his own throat and died instantly.[2] I hope this will find you all well. I am your affectionate father.   Josiah Bartlett

RC (From photograph of original in NhHi; original not found).

1. As chief justice JB was riding circuit for the Superior Court. Amherst was the seat of the spring session for Hillsborough County, Charlestown (Fort Number Four), for Cheshire County. *Laws of N.H.*, 5:45.

2. Keiff was suspected also of having kindled the fire that consumed Charleston in 1775 and the fire that burned the courthouse in 1788. Secomb, *Amherst*, 347–50.

FROM NATHANIEL PEABODY

Sir   Concord June 7th. 1790

Being appointed by the Legislature a Committee to make arrangements for the reception of your Excellency, we beg leave to inform you, that the Senate and House of Representatives attended by a corps of Infantry will receive your Excely at the ferry and attend you to Lodgings, which the committee have provided for your Excelcy at Colo. Greens.

With sentiments of esteem, I have The honr to be, your Excelcys most obedt & very Hul Sevt

> Nathl Peabody by order
> of the Committee

RC (Nh). Noted with address: "Per Express." JB had been elected President of the Senate on the 5th.

FROM THOMAS JEFFERSON [1]

Sir   New York June 8, 1790

I have the honor to send you herein inclosed, two copies duly authenticated, of the Act for the encouragement of learning, by securing the copies of Maps, Charts and Books to the authors and proprietors of such copies, during the times therein mentioned; Also of the Act for finally adjusting, and satisfying the claims of Frederic William de Steuben;[2] Also of the Act for giving effect to an Act, intituled, "An Act to establish the Judicial Courts of the United States," within the State of North Carolina; Also of the Act supplemental to the Act for establishing the Salaries of the Executive officers of Government, with their Assistants and Clerks; and of being with sentiments of the most perfect respect, Your Excellency's Most Obedient & most humble servant.

> Th: Jefferson

RC (MB). In clerk's hand; signed by Jefferson, though probably a few days after the 8th, as Jefferson accompanied President Washington on a fishing trip between 7 and 9 June. Boyd, *Papers of Jefferson*, 16:2.

1. Jefferson had accepted the position of secretary of state on 14 Feb. 1790. By sending these copies, he was complying with a congressional resolution of 5 June 1789 directing that two copies of every law be transmitted to each state chief executive within ten days after its passage. *Annals*, 1:419–20.

2. Friedrich Wilhelm (Baron von) Steuben (1730–1794), a Prussian soldier, had come to America in 1777 (arriving in Portsmouth on 1 December) to volunteer his services to the Continental Army. His success in training and disciplining American troops led Congress to commission him as inspector general with the rank of major general. He had asked for remuneration only if the war was successful, and on 28 May 1790 Congress passed a bill to grant him $2,500 annually. *Annals*, 2:1621. See also Palmer, *General von Steuben*.

The preceding letter, addressed to "The President of New Hampshire," would have gone to JB, for on Saturday, 5 June 1790, he was elected president of the state. In the general election he had received the third highest number of popular votes (1,676), but none of his principal ri-

vals—John Pickering, Joshua Wentworth, Nathaniel Peabody—had received the required majority of the 7,762 votes cast. Therefore, when the General Court convened on 2 June, the House of Representatives took these four candidates as a slate from which it chose Pickering and Bartlett for the Senate's consideration. The Senate selected JB. He accepted and took the oath at 9:30 A.M. on the eighth. The journal of the House for 9 June records that, following a number of other matters of business, "The Secretary [Joseph Pearson of Exeter, Secretary of State] came down with the following message from his Execellency the President." NHSP, 22:8,9, 11, 41–45, 50, 52–54.

TO THE GENERAL COURT

[9 June 1790]

Gentlemen of the honourable Senate and Gentlemen of the Honourable House of Representatives

Though it would have been highly improper and unbecoming in me to have sought the Honbl. Office in which you have been pleased to place me, yet I could not think it my duty to decline the appointment.

I have so often in times past experienced the candour & indulgence of my fellow Citizens that I cannot now entertain the smallest doubt but that I shall have every Assistance in your power to bestow while I attempt to discharge the duties of an honourable, but arduous employment. If the most faithful attachment to the Interest of the State, & the most diligent & constant application to the duties of my Office can in any measure compensate for the want of greater abilities, my fellow Citizens & you Gentlemen shall have no cause to complain of having misplaced that Confidence which you have in this appointment reposed in me.

I congratulate you Gentlemen & my fellow Citizens at large on the present prosperous State of our affairs. A retrospective view of the Scenes through which we have lately passed would Serve to give the most lively contrast to our present Situation and future prospects.

Through the partiality of my fellow Citizens I have been called in various Stations & employments to manifest my love and attachment to my Country in times of danger & distress and the best part of my life has been spent in support of a cause which it hath pleased divine Providence to crown with success. That our Country is now free and that we have now the means of attaining all the blessings & advantages resulting from a free & equal Government we are under Heaven indebted to the valour & patriotism of our Citizens as yet unparralleled in the Annals of History. And it is peculiarly grateful to me in the evening of my days to be called by *such* Citizens to the chief seat in Government.

The public letters received since the last Session & many other papers being still in the hands of my Predecessor in office[1] and through a close attention to the business of another department from which I have been Suddenly & unexpectedly called it is not in my power to be as particular as I could wish in pointing out to you the many & important concerns which demand your immediate attention. You will permit me however to observe in general that on the promotion of agriculture the encouragement of the manufactures of our own Country and the practice of the Virtues of economy & frugality and above all a strict adherence to our engagements both public and private must essentially depend our happiness & prosperity.

A revision of the laws & Statutes practised upon in this State I have long considered as a matter of the highest importance & am happy to learn that this object has already engaged the attention of the Legislature. I hope nothing will be wanting on your part to bring this business to a close as soon as conveniently it can be done.

You will judge of the propriety of taking the necessary measures at this Session for electing the Representatives to Congress.

I Shall take care to lay before you the public papers as they come to hand. I need not recommend to you Gentlemen dispatch in conducting the public business nor need I say how necessary unanimity is for that purpose—from the Characters of the respectable Gentlemen who compose both Houses I am led to form the most flattering presages from your joint deliberations and you may be assured Gentlemen that nothing shall be wanting on my part to promote the welfare happiness & prosperity of our common Country.

Given at the Council Chamber at Concord the 9th day of June Anno Domini 1790.   Josiah Bartlett

MS (NhHi). Signed by JB. The journal copy (Nh-Ar) differs only in that ampersands are generally spelled out.

1. John Sullivan was president 1786–1788 and 1789–1790.

FROM THE GENERAL COURT

The Committee on the Presidents Message to both Houses report the following answer.

May it please your Excellency   June 12. 1790

The Senate & House of Representatives beg leave to congratulate your Excellency & the State, on the auspicious event of your being placed in the chair of Government. After having so long enjoyed the confidence of the public in the many important stations your Excellency has heretofore filled, we are peculiarly happy to find you still so attentive to the calls of your Country, as to quit an honorable and lucrative office, to enter on the arduous duties of first Magistrate of this State. From your intimate knowledge of the interests of the public, & your long tried attachment to the rights of Men, we form the most flattering presages, that under your administration the Government will be prosperous & the people happy. Having spent the best part of a valuable life in the service of the public, & risked both life & property in its cause, we rejoice that the people yet mindful of such obligation, have given you the highest testiment of their gratitude, in their power to bestow. A view of the Dangers we have passed, contrasted with the happiness we now enjoy, affords the most agreable sensations, & pleasingly reminds us of your Excellency's ardent Exertions to warding off those dangers, & conducting us to our present situation. We are happy to find that the encouragement of the agriculture & manufactures of our Country has attracted yr. Excellency's attention, we are deeply sensible of their importance, & altho' they now languish under the oppression of antient prejudices, we hope, by suitable rewards to the industrious & enterprising, no longer to be indebted to foreign climes for articles that may be better raised & manufactured among us.

An adherance to engagements as well private as public, we consider on the palladium of our honor & happiness, & the flourishing State of our Country, with its increasing resources we presume will soon free us from the imputation of violated faith. We are pleased to find that the revision of the Laws meets your Excellencys approbation, & are happy in assuring you that we hope soon to have this important object compleated.

All communication from your Excellency we shall receive with pleasure, & chearfully join in every measure to promote the general Good. That you may long live & enjoy the benedictions of a grateful People, & at some very distant Period be called to inherit the rewards of the Christian & the Patriot is our fervent Prayer.

Oliver Peabody, for the Committee

State of New Hampshire
In the house of Representatives June 11th, 1790.
The foregoing answer being read and considered voted that it be received and accepted.

Sent up for Concurrance
Thos. Bartlett Speaker.
In Senate June 12th. 1790 read & unanimously concurred.
J. Pearson Secy.[1]

MS (Nh-Ar).

1. Oliver Peabody (1753–1831), an Exeter attorney, served a very brief term in the 1790 Senate before being appointed judge of probate for Rockingham County in 1790. He was a state senator, 1793–1796, and state treasurer, 1795–1804, and served as the state's agent with the New Hampshire Bank in December 1792. Bell, *Bench and Bar*, 560–61; *NHSP*, 22:1 n., 621.

Thomas Bartlett (1745–1805) of Nottingham had sat on the Committee of Safety and had been a militia officer during the Revolution. As a member of the General Court he was Speaker of the House from September 1787 until 1791. Stearns, *Genealogical*, 1:159–60.

Joseph Pearson (1737–1823) taught school in Exeter and Concord after having graduated from Harvard in 1758. During the war the General Court put him on a committee to sign paper money and in 1783 began to assign him to various specific posts. He served as secretary of state from 1786 to 1804. Shipton, *Harvard Graduates*, 14:306–07.

TO LEVI BARTLETT
Dear Son   Concord June 14th 1790
This is Just to inform you that I am well, that it Seems to be the de-

sign of the Court to rise the latter end of this week and I wish you would Send Peter Abbot up, so as to be here on friday Evening to return with me. I expect to return on Saturday but if the Court shall Sit longer I shall keep him here till my return.[1] I hope this will find you & the rest of the family well. Yours &c.   Josiah Bartlett

RC (J. Duane Squires, PhD., New London, N.H., 1975).
   1. The legislature, meeting in Concord, adjourned on Saturday, 19 June, after   having resolved to meet again on 5 Jan. 1791. *NHSP*, 22:31.

FROM WILLIAM GARDNER [1]

Sir   June 16th, 1790
   I take the liberty to inform your Excellency that the large Iron Chest which contains the money belonging to the public is the property of Colo. James Sheafe,[2] of whom I borrowed the same on condition to return it when call'd for. This day I received information that he must have it immediately—therefore request your Excellency will please to make it known to the honorable Court that another Chest may be procured in lieu thereof[3]—otherwise the money will be insecure to the State & a source of much disquietude to Your Excellency's Most Obedt. Hl. Servt.
                              Wm. Gardner, Treasr.

RC (Nh-Ar).
   1. Gardner was state treasurer from 7 Jan. 1789 to June 1791. *NHSP*, 21:251; 22:211.
   2. James Sheafe (1755–1829), a Portsmouth merchant, was a son of Jacob Sheafe. Between 1788 and 1802 James served successively in both houses of the state legislature and in both houses of the   U.S. Congress.
   3. On the 18th the House appointed a committee to investigate the true ownership of the chest and to report at the next session. Until then, the Court instructed Gardner to keep the chest. *NHSP*, 22:28, 88.

FROM [LEVI BARTLETT]

Dear Sir   Kingston June 18th 1790
   You'll recieve this from Abbot who I sent off this morning early.
   You wrote you expected to return on Saturday. The People have enquired & are Desirous of showing their respects by making a small excursion to escort you into Town if they could know which way & on what Day you will return. If they don't hear any further from you they will meet you on the Deerfield road on Saturday. Am in hopes we shall be a little better ppd. than before for them. The Family are all as Well as Usual.

Draft (NhD). Docketed: "Copy to his Ex. June 18th 1790."

The First Federal Congress met in three sessions—4 Mar. 1789 to 29 Sept. 1789, 4 Jan. 1790 to 12 Aug. 1790, and 6 Dec. 1790 to 3 Mar. 1791—with New Hampshire represented in the Senate by John Langdon and Paine Wingate and in the House of Representatives by Abiel Foster,

Nicholas Gilman, and Samuel Livermore. One of the early orders of business for Congress was the settling of financial accounts between the states and the Federal Government. John Taylor Gilman, who was familiar with state finances and who became state treasurer in 1791, had evidently gone to New York City, where Congress was meeting to investigate the progress that had been made toward settling accounts.

FROM JOHN TAYLOR GILMAN

Sir   New York June 26th 1790

Addresses, Congratulations &c. to Men who are placed in high Stations, are so common, that I should not presume to Say any thing on the Subject, did I not flatter myself that your knowledge of me, will Induce the fullest belief of the truth of my Assertion, when I Inform your Excellency that I am highly gratified with your being placed in the Office of Chief Magistrate in the State of New Hampshire; and that it is my most Sincere wish, that your Presidency may be Easy, pleasant and Advantageous to yourself, as I am Confident it will be to the Honor and true Interest of the State.

Congress have had a long session already, yet I think it is most probable they will not rise until some time in August—though some are of Opinion the session will end in few days.

The business which has been compleated is small when compared with the time—and it is now Extremely difficult to form an Opinion whether any thing of Consequence will be done respecting the public debts this Session. The Assumption of State debts and the Temporary & Permanent residence of Congress are Subjects which seem to interfere in almost every Important Question respecting Funding the debt. The house are near Equally divided respecting the Assumption and the parties, each Charge other, with bargaining for Residence, Assumption &c. You will probably have heard that the Bill providing further ways & means, which has been a long time before the House, was lost, on the Question for Engrossing for the Third reading. A Committee is appointed to report other ways & means, but I cannot conceive what they will find less Exceptionable, than the Bill which was rejected. The fact is, most of those who are for assumption, seem determined that funds shall not be provided for Contl. debts, unless the State debts are provided for at Same time, add to these Such are against funding the debts at any rate, & those who may have Objections to the ways & means, thinking better might be found, and it appears most probable that the debt will not be properly provided for this session, unless the State debts are assumed; but I Confess, I am Quite at loss in this business, and have seldom been so much puzzled to Conjecture what is likely to place.

The funding Bill, as it is termed, is postponed in the Senate. They have altered it materially from what it passed in the House. The Several alternatives are struck out—proposed to Loan at four Per Cent without any other allowance for reduction of Interest. All that relates to Lands

Struck out—permanent provision to be made for Subscribers to new Loan. Non Subscribers to have four Per Cent paid & Indorsed—the provision Temporary.[1]

The particular business in which I am, is in a disagreeable situation, owing to the Confused State of the Transactions, & the manner in which many of the States have made out their accounts; such a Jumble of papers were (perhaps) never seen before—many are full in the Opinion they will never be Settled.

As the time Limited by the old Congress is nearly Expired, a New Bill has passed the House (& is now before the Senate) for prolonging the time for Three Years further, adding Two more Commissrs—Enlarging the powers &c. This Bill allows a further time for States to Exhibit Claims, seems to make Charges for General, or particular defence Equally allowable & that the Quotas of States shall be fixed by their present numbers. What will be the End I cannot Say, but the business is very disagreeable to me, and to be Absent from my Family makes it much more so.

Have no further Accounts respecting war between Britain & Spain, than has been published in the papers. Some Say Spain is not in Condition to war—others that they would not have given Such provocation unless they had Assurance of being Assisted by other powers.

I shall be Extremely sorry if Congress should rise without providing for the debt; but I fear it will be the Case. Many seem free to Vote away the Monies in almost any other way, rather than pay debts. The Galleries of the House being open many of the Speeches are for them, & for the Press; Indeed the House is overdone with long Speeches—which very seldom tends to throw light on the Subject.

As I am near the End of my paper and it is probable you will have Letters from the Members here, who can give you better Information, I Close taking the liberty to Subscribe, with due respect Your Excellency's most Obedient Servt.   J T. Gilman

RC (MB).

1. Gilman was referring to Secretary of Treasury Alexander Hamilton's proposals for liquidating the national debt. Hamilton's plans for funding the international debt and for assumption of domestic state debts by the federal government were adopted in August 1790. There are several excellent discussions of Hamilton's program; see especially Nettels, *Emergence of a National Economy,* 109–29.

FROM JOHN WHEELOCK

Sir   Dartmouth College July 1st. 1790

I emprove the first convenient opportunity in behalf of the members of the Board of Trustees of this College[1] to express our happiness, that the voice of a free people has placed your Excellency at the head of this republic. As citizens we rejoice at the indowments, which providence has bestowed on you to discharge your trust in the first department of government.

From the spirit & intent of our Charter, and as conceived of by a vote of the Board, you have as President of the State a right to act in all matters as a Trustee of this Institution. We ask the favour of your friendly patronage: and have the utmost confidence in that love to mankind, that prudent zeal for the good of this State and for the increase of useful knowledge in it, which has marked the career of your public life till this time.

The annual meeting of the Trustees will be on the fourth tuesday in Augt. the day preceeding our Commencement: And, it would give us singular pleasure, could you find it consistent with your important concerns, to honour the Board with your presence.

By an act of the Legislature the honourable Council with your Excellency are incorporated with the Board for the inspection & controul of all property, which has and may be given by the State to the Seminary.[2] There are matters, which will come before them: and measures of any kind, that you and they may in your wisdom advise or propose, the members of the Board in this quarter will at all times pay the most respectful attention to. In sentiments of the greatest respect and esteem I am in behalf of the Trustees, Sir! Your Excellency's most obedient & very humble servant,   John Wheelock

RC (NhD). Addressed to JB as president of the state and trustee of Dartmouth.

1. Wheelock succeeded his father as president of Dartmouth in 1779. Chase, *Dartmouth*, 564.

2. The act had been passed in February 1789. *Laws of N.H.*, 5:396–97.

FROM WILLIAM GARDNER

Sir,   Exeter August 9th. 1790

The inclosed Letter I have just received from the Honble Mr. Wingate informing of the Bill for funding the National Debt—having passed both Houses of Congress—which embraces the Assumption of 21½ millions of Dollars of the State Debts. As he wishes your Excellency to be made acquainted with its contents—have accordingly inclosed the same.[1] Being much engaged in business prevents doing myself the honor of waiting on you in person. I am very Respectfully Sir Your most Obedt. & very Huml. servt.   Wm. Gardner

RC (NhD).

1. Wingate's letter to Gardner of 29 July (NhD) is in MJB, 2667.

FROM WILLIAM PAGE[1]

Sir,   Charlestown Augt. 20th. 1790

I was so unfortunate as not to be able to send by Leml. Holms Esq.[2] for money to pay the Expence of the Committee &c. attending on the tryal of Judge Langdon, altho I made a Journey to his house, he was gone a few hours before I arived. I suppose however it will make no difference as your Excellency doubtless took the advice of the Council on the subject of drawing on the Treasury. I am not able to send an account of the expences not having received all the Accounts, but if your Excellency will be so good as to direct the Treasurer pay me fifty dollars for the above purpose the bearer Mr. Silsby will receipt it, and I will be answerable for the same.[3] I am Sir in hast your Excellency's Most obet Sert.   W. Page

RC (NhD).

1. William Page (1749–1810), a physician of Charlestown, was a member of the General Court from 1788 to 1792. On 18 June 1790 he was appointed with Edward St. Loe Livermore and Jeremiah Smith to draw up articles of impeachment against Superior Court justice Woodbury Langdon. Saunderson, *Charlestown*, 498–99; NHSP, 22:89–91, 93.

2. Lemuel Holmes of Surry had been a representative to the General Court and was a member of the Council, 1790–1794. Kingsbury, *Surry*, 693–94.

3. At its next session, on 11 Feb. 1791, the General Court voted to pay Page and the committee £30.17.0 "for expences &c

on the prosecution of Wy Langdon Esq." who was under impeachment for failing to attend sessions of the Superior Court in Grafton County. Langdon was never tried. He resigned his judgeship and obtained a federal appointment as commissioner for settling accounts between the United States and individual states. Daniell, *Experiment*, 225; NHSP, 22:128, 256, 278.

Ozias Silsby (1761–1833), a post-rider, had graduated from Dartmouth in 1785 and lived in Chester. Chapman, *Dartmouth*, 38–39; Silsby, "Silsby—Silsbee Genealogy," 1:34–35, 90–91; NHSP, 18:818.

FROM JOHN WHEELOCK

Sir,   Hanover Augt. 30th. 1790

Please to accept my thanks for your favour of the 28th ult:.[1] The Board of Trustees are gratefully impressed with a sense of your wisely directed attention for the happiness of mankind, the prosperity of this State, and the interests of useful literature in this Seminary.

Will your Excellency permit me to communicate what is given me in charge from them; that influenced by an exalted opinion of your merit, and as a faint testimony of their respect for the same, the Corporation have conferred the Second honours of the University. We shall be happy, Sir, if this instance should be favoured with your acceptance.

The rev'd Profr. Smith,[2] if it can be consistent, proposes to wait on you, and deliver this letter. He will be able to give any information of particulars among us. In sentiments of most exalted respect, I am Sir, Your Excellency's very obedt. & humble servt.   John Wheelock

RC (NhD). Noted with address: "hon'd by rev'd Profr Smith."

1. Not found.

2. John Smith (1752–1809) was the chaplain of Dartmouth College, profes-

sor of learned languages, and a trustee. Chase, *Dartmouth*, 614, 630–31; Sprague, *Annals*, 2:90–92.

FROM REUBEN AND RHODA TRUE[1]

Hond. Sr.   Salisbury, 19 October 1790

This morning just before sunrise our Child departed this life. I would be very glad if one or both my brothers could come up to the Funeral. We shall Bury it on Thirsday. Your Dutiful Children.

Reuben True
Rhoda True

RC (NhHi).

1. Reuben True (1761–1826), a native of Hawke (now Danville), moved to Salisbury shortly after he married Rhoda Bartlett, JB's daughter, on 22 Feb. 1789. The couple had two children, Levi and Josiah. The letter refers to the death of Levi. *NHGR*, 3:133; Hammond, "Gravestone Inscriptions," 18; Dearborn, *Salisbury*, 139–40, 174, 220–21.

FROM JOHN TRUMBULL[1]

Sir   Boston, 8 November 1790

I have taken the Liberty to enclose to your Excellency a paper from which you will learn the nature of an undertaking in which I am engaged and in which I have occasion for the Portraits of many of the great characters of our Country. Your Excellency was a member of that Congress who pass'd the Declaration of Independence, and laid the foundations of a new Empire:—the conspicuous characters in which you have since acted, unite with this circumstance to render me desirous of possessing your Portrait to be introduced on this occasion.

I propose to be at Exeter on the 20th inst, where if your Excellency would make it convenient to give me a meeting of a few hours, you will very highly oblige Sir Your Excellency's most obedient Servant.

Jn. Trumbull

TR (Mr. S. Bartlett Howard Private Collection, San Mateo, Calif., 1975). Docketed: "Copy of the copy of the original letter found among the papers of Dr. Ezra Bartlett his son." Enclosure not found.

1. John Trumbull (1756–1843) was a military officer and one of the foremost artists of the American Revolution. Following the war he spent a number of years in London, returning in 1789 to undertake, among other works, his portrait of the signers of the Declaration. See Jaffe, *John Trumbull*.

The pencil sketch drawn by Trumbull at this meeting is in the collections of the New Hampshire Historical Society (see frontispiece of this volume). In September 1823 Trumbull reported to Ezra Bartlett that the sketch had been carefully preserved and that he could paint copies "as good as I would have made originally," for $100 apiece (NhHi). Not until 1836 did the family order a painting from Trumbull. The bill, dated New York, 30 Nov. 1836, shows the price of $100 plus $17.52 for a frame and packing case (Mr. S. Bartlett Howard, San Mateo, Calif., 1975). A portrait of JB in the possession of Mr. John Bartlett of Aurora, Ill., is thought to be Trumbull's original. Copies are known to be at the New Hampshire Historical Society, at Dartmouth College in Hanover, at the New Hampshire State House, Concord, at the home of Mr. and Mrs. Rodney M. Wilson in Kingston, and at Independence National Historical Park in Philadelphia.

FROM PAINE WINGATE[1]

Sir   Philadelphia[2] Dec. 18. 1790

I have enclosed several news-papers which contain all the material intelligence which my present situation affords. We have no late foreign news. The doings of Congress have not yet been considerable; altho' we made a Senate on the first day of meeting, and the members of both houses are very generally present. The communications from the President, and the replys of the two houses will be seen in the news-papers herewith transmitted.

The expedition against the Indians north west of the Ohio has, in my opinion, been unfortunate.[3] The official accounts hitherto received have been very imperfect, containing little more than the general orders & the return of the killed & wounded. It appears that we have lost 183 men and it is said that most of the wounded fell into the enemy's hands and were barbarously murdered, which is not unlikely considering the small number of wounded returned. The expence of the expedition, as laid before Congress, is estimated at one hundred thousand dollars; and there is too much reason to apprehend that further military opperations will be necessary before peace can be established with those hostile tribes. The national credit is however considerably rising in the public opinion. It is said (I cannot say with how much truth) that the 6 pr Cent funded debt has been sold in Holland as high as 124 pr. Cent., and since the President's speech the securities in general have risen here, as will be seen by the last prices current published.

It seems to be the hope & expectation of most of the members, that Congress will rise on or before the 3d of March next. I have the honor to be your Excellencys most obedient & humble Servant   Paine Wingate

RC (MH).

1. Paine Wingate (1739–1838) was a clergyman and public official of Stratham. He served in the Continental Congress, 1787–1788, and in the U.S. Senate, 1789–1793. See Wingate, *Paine Wingate.*

2. On 31 May 1790 the house had voted to hold the next session of Con-gress in Philadelphia instead of New York. The Senate concurred. *Annals,* 2:1626.

3. In October 1790 the northern Indians routed a small army under Gen. Josiah Harmer at the Maumee River. Kohn, *Eagle and Sword,* 105–08.

FROM JOHN WHEELOCK

Sir!   Dartmouth College Decr. 20th. 1790

I take the liberty of informing your Excellency that a great part of the members of our Seminary have expressed a desire to turn their diversions and amusements into another chanel: and, instead of spending their leasure hours at usual play, they wish to employ them in learning the military exercise. They would, likewise, esteem it, as a very great favour, if the Legislature could consistently grant them the use of a number of arms, should there be any belonging to the State, and not appropriated, the Arms to be receipted for, and to be returned, without damage, on demand.

Considering such a sort of exercise as manly; as not interfering with the hours of study; as being of some service towards an easy deportment; and as one qualification to their usefulness in the cause of their Country, should there be occasion, I informed them, that I would communicate their desire to you; and that I did not doubt, but your Excellency and the others of the legislature would cheerfully do any thing, that might be consistent, and for their good.

The matter, Sir, is proposed for your judgment; and if the plan should be approved of, I beg the favour, unitedly with the officers, and solicited by the members, that your Excellency and the honourable Legislature would, if consistent, grant to the Students of the College the use of stands of Arms with accoutrements, we engaging that they shall be returned in good order, whenever called for.[1]

The Honle Mr. Freeman[2] is so obliging as to attend to the preceeding matter; and will be able to give any information concerning the same. I am, with most affectionate respect, Sir! Your Excellency's very obedient & humble servant.   Jn Wheelock

RC (NhD). Note with address: "hon'd by honl. J. Freeman Esq."

1. In January 1791 the legislature agreed to send 130 stand of arms in return for a £300 bond from Wheelock to guarantee preservation of the weapons. *NHSP*, 22:100, 149.

2. Jonathan Freeman (1745–1808) of Hanover was a state senator and member of the Executive Council in 1790. He was a treasurer and then for many years a trustee of Dartmouth. From 1795 to 1799 he sat in the U.S. Congress.

The General Court met at Concord between 5 January and 18 February 1791. Since the adjournment of its first session on 19 June 1790, JB had been kept active in Council meetings at Kingston and Exeter in July, August, and October. Following this current session of the Court, the Council met in March and May before reconvening in Concord for the June legislative session. NHSP, 22:258–73.

TO THE GENERAL COURT

Concord January 5th. 1791

Gentlemen of the Senate and Gentlemen of the House of Representatives

It is with peculiar satisfaction I again meet you in Session when the rapid progress of Agriculture and manufactures and the flourishing state of commerce wear so favourable an aspect and when the great national affairs that concern the United states in General which formerly occupied a considerable part of the time and attention of the state Legislatures having by the adoption of the General Government devolved on the national Legislature has afforded us a favourable opportunity to attend with more deliberation to those matters that principally concern the interest of this state in particular, and this being the Season of the year when this Legislature can most conveniently attend to the affairs of the public, you will permit me to suggest for your consideration such matters as appear to me to require your attention the present session.

The Secretary will lay before you such public papers as I have received since your last meeting among which you will observe an Act of Congress past the fourth of August last entitled "an Act making provision for the debt of the United states" which will I apprehend require your early attention.[1]

The proposal of ceeding the light house in this State which was under your consideration the last Session will probably be resumed at this time and determined in such manner as you shall think will be most for the Interest of the state and the expences we have been at in Supporting the light since the 15th of August 1789 adjusted in order that the money may be received agreably to the Acts of Congress.[2]

The Act for raising a Revenue in this state by Excise I would recommend to your consideration, whether as our affairs are now circumstanced the continuing it longer will be beneficial to the public you will determine, and if you should think proper to continue the excise in whole or in part whether a different mode of collecting it might not be adopted with advantage.[3]

A revision of the Laws and Statutes practised upon in this state and adopting them to our present situation is a matter greatly to be desired, that the people at large may know what are the Laws that are now in force, and if your Committee who were appointed for that purpose are ready to report I should hope the business will be properly attended to the present Session.

The advantage of good roads to keep up a free and easy communication through the state and proper encouragement to post riders to carry dispatches and intelligence through the different parts of it is so great that it is worthy your consideration whether the expence that will accrue will not be greatly overbalanced by the advantages that may rationally be expected from it in giving the citizens a better opportunity of being with the public affairs of the state and more effectually uniting and cementing them in one common interest.

I have seen with some concern, considerable part of the time of the Legislature frequently taken up in hearing and determining on private petitions to the hindrance of public business, expence to the parties and the state and loss to the Individuals who compose the Legislature and I would recommend it to your consideration whether in many cases some other mode might not be adopted for granting relief that would do equal justice to the parties at less expence to the state and them.

Gentlemen of the House of Representatives

The settlement of the Treasurers accounts, making provision for the Supply of the Treasury and granting proper allowances to the public officers being matters that are usually transacted at this Season of the year will not I suppose pass unnoticed.

Gentlemen of the Senate and Gentlemen of the House of Representatives

Laws to encourage agriculture and Manufactures, Regulations that will tend to excite a Spirit of Industry and frugality, proper attention to the education of the rising generation who are soon to come on the the stage of Action to instruct them in the principles of knowledge and literature to implant in their minds the seeds of virtue and morality of benevolence and patriotism and the love of justice will I conceive tend greatly to promote the happiness and prosperity of the community, which are the great objects to which our care and deliberations ought to be directed and Gentlemen you may rely on my hearty assistance and cooperation in every measure that will conduce to the welfare of my fellow citizens.

Josiah Bartlett

FC (Nh-Ar: Journal of the House of Representatives); Draft (Nh). Delivered in the General Court on 6 January.

1. The Assumption Act. See Gilman to JB, 26 June 1790, n. 1.

2. On 22 July 1790 Congress acted to continue to pay all operating costs of lighthouses along the U.S. coast until 1 July 1791, to give each state time in which to cede the lighthouses and property to the federal government. On 14 Feb. 1791 the General Court acted to cede one and three-quarter acres of land with the lighthouse and fort on New Castle to the United States. The fortification that had been Fort William and Mary was to be renamed Fort Constitution. *Annals*, 2:2241; *Laws of N.H.*, 5:685–86. See also JB to George Washington, 24 Feb. 1791.

3. Acts imposing the excise on spirituous liquors, clocks, coaches, phaetons, and other wheel carriages were repealed by an act of 18 Jan. 1791. *Laws of N.H.*, 5:556–57.

FROM JOHN LANGDON[1]

Sr.   Philadelphia Jany, 7th. 1791

The Acts of Congress as they are passed from time to time, are no doubt Transmitted by the President of the United States to the Legislature of New Hampshire; the Proceedings of Congress in General are published in most of the Newspapers throughout the Union; the frequent Communications from our Members of Congress are therefore less necessary—but as the Legislature of our State will be in Session at the Receipt of this it may be of use to inform your Excellency and Both Houses, of Several Bills which are now before Congress, one for a Duty on Imported Spirits, and that which is Distilled, within the States, or rather a general Excise, another for the Establishment of a National Bank; the first of these will no doubt affect the Excise of New Hampshire and perhaps make it Necessary to Repeal our Law. The excise Law of all the States (except New Hampshire) are Repeald as I am informed.[2]

It is very generally Agreed that there must be a National Bank, the general principals of which are Contain in the Inclosed Bill, which may undergo some Alteration, tho' I dare say the Principals will be preserved. The great Utility of Bank Bills which will be Recd. in all the States, for imposts, Excises &c. will easily be perceived; to go into a particular detail of the many Advantages Ariseing from a Bank, in which the general government will be the greatest Stock holders, would far exceed the limits of a letter, and perhaps would be improper. If this Act for Establishing a Bank should pass this Session of Congress (which I have no doubt but it will) I would beg leave to submit it to the Wisdom of our

Legislature, whether it would not be greatly to our advantage if the State should become Stock holders. If my memory serves me there is now in the Treasury of New Hampshire, between thirty and forty thousand Dollars of Continental debt, also from Twenty to Thirty Thousand dollars in specie, these with any little Addition that might be made from Monies that may Come into the Treasury from outstanding Taxes; would make a handsome Stock to be subscribed to the Bank the Dividend of which would be paid, half yearly; and would in all probability Yeild from Eight to Nine pr Cent pr Annum Advantage. The Original stock would always be at the disposal of the State and would undoubtedly sell for specie at par, at any time when our government should think proper to part with it; and in all probability it would soon sell above par, the State therefore can run no Risque of Looseing.

In my opinion it would be a happy Circumstance, if, the general Government—the several states and Individual Citizens of the United States, could hold the principal part or the whole of the stock of this Bank rather than let foreigners step in and Reap the Advantage. Should the Bank in this City conclude to place their Capital in the National Bank the whole subscriptions would be soon Compleated, as three quarters of it is to be in the funded debt of the Union; It is of great importance to our state, that we endeavour by every means in our power to bring back from the Seat of General Government as much money as we can; the State being stock holders in the Bank will assist in this Business. This together with the Interest paid to our Citizens by the general government, and some other Advantages which may Turn up in the Course of the proceedings of Congress, would Counterballance the Monies Raised by Impost and excises and sent out of the State.[3]

I Trust your Excellency and the Honbl. Legislature will not think me impertinent If I take the liberty of Indulge'g a hope that the light House at Newcastle will be Ceded to the United States dureing the present session, and Indeed I could wish that the point of land, where the old fort stood, could be also Ceded, as a Battery might be placed there to protect our harbour, and Commerce at the Expence of the Union, which would be of Advantage to the State, and no Possable danger can Arise from it.[4]

If these hints Sr. should be tho't of any importance they will be attended to in the Course of the session, if not they will be passed over. I am senseable I shall be Excused for the liberty I have taken, as it proceeds from the sincere desire I have to serve my State. I have the Honour to be very Respectfully your Excellencys Most Hbl. Servt.

John Langdon

RC (Nh-Ar). Enclosure not found.

1. Langdon served as a U.S. Senator from 4 Mar. 1789 to 3 Mar. 1801.

2. See JB to General Court, 5 Jan. 1791, n. 3.

3. The Bank of the United States was proposed in 1790 by Alexander Hamilton and chartered by act of Congress on 25 Feb. 1791. Hammond, *Banks*, 114–18. See correspondence among JB, John Taylor Gilman, and Tench Coxe of 28 and 30 June and 9 July 1791.

4. See JB to General Court, 5 Jan. 1791, n. 2.

FROM ALEXANDER HAMILTON   Treasury Department
Sir   January 14. 1791

It is necessary to the adjustment of the public accounts, that the officers of the Treasury should be informed what sums in final settlement certificates were paid over to the several states by the agents for settling the accounts of their respective lines in the late army. The statements of those agents are the only documents on the subject of which the United States are possessed, and it will be readily perceived that they ought not to be accepted as satisfactory vouchers. I am therefore obliged to request the favor of your directing a return of the sum received by your state to be made out as expeditiously as may be convenient, and transmitted to this office.[1] I have the honor to be very respectfully Sir Your most obedt. servant

Alexander Hamilton
Secy of the Treasy

RC (MiU-C). In a clerk's hand; signed and franked by Hamilton.
1. On 17 Feb. 1791 the General Court agreed that JB should comply with Ha- milton's request. *NHSP*, 22:137.

TO LEVI BARTLETT
Dear Son   Concord Janry 15th 1791

I Recd yours of the 8th instant[1] hope Lois is comfortable again & that you and the rest of my family & your Sister Greely are well, Should be glad to hear from you by Col. Eastman.[2] I got up well and Remain so, am well accommodated here. I heard from your sister True this week that she was well, have not seen Mr. True yet. Business in the Court way goes on as usual, a good deal of business.

Expect to Count the votes for federal Representatives to day.[3] Judge Langdon we hear is appointed by Congress a Commissioner to settle accounts in the room of John Taylor Gilman who resigned. Mr. Gardner the Treasurer is appointed Loan Officer by Congress. Have nothing more new. Your affectionate father   Josiah Bartlett

RC (Mr. and Mrs. Rodney M. Wilson, Kingston, N.H., 1975).
1. Not found.
2. John Eastman was Kingston's representative to the General Court. *NHSP*, 22:38.
3. The voters elected Jeremiah Smith (4,422) and Nicholas Gilman (2,802) over John Samuel Sherburne (1,877) and Abiel Foster (1,338). Ibid., 265.

TO NICHOLAS GILMAN[1]
Dear Sir   Concord January 17th 1791

I Congratulate you on your reappointt. as member of Congress for this State. A Certificate is made out and forwared with this which I hope will come Safe to hand, Mr. Smith[2] is the other person appointed. The General Court is now Setting here are upon a revision of the Laws which will take a considerable time. Have nothing material to communicate to you. I have receivd your favor of the 9th ulto.[3] inclosing a news paper, wish you to inform me as often as Convenient of the transactions of Congress. And am Sir your friend &c. &c.   Josiah Bartlett

RC (ICHi). Stamped "Free."

1. Nicholas Gilman (1755–1814) was a son of Revolutionary state treasurer Nicholas Gilman and a brother of John Taylor Gilman. Nicholas was in Philadelphia in Congress where he had represented New Hampshire since March 1789. He continued in the U.S. House until 1797 and later served in the U.S. Senate, 1795–1811.

2. Jeremiah Smith (1759–1842), a Peterborough attorney, was a member of the state legislature, 1788–1791, and of the U.S. Congress, 1791–1797. Later he was chief justice of the N.H. Superior Court and governor, 1809–1810. Morison, *Life of the Hon. Jeremiah Smith, LL.D.*

3. RC (NhD). Not printed, see MJB, 2714.

FROM PAINE WINGATE

Sir   Philadelphia Jan. 26. 1791

I have not written to you but once since I came here, because I thought I had nothing interesting enough to communicate to you. Perhaps the same reason might opperate for my not writing now. Congress have compleated but little business in the present session. The Senate have passed a bill for a national bank, which is now before the house of Representatives and that house have at last got thrô the excise bill, so as to have it engrossed for a third reading. These two bills have met with considerable obstructions and delays; but I conclude they will pass in some shape or other before the end of the session. They are considered as the only indispensably necessary bills, and other matters, which cannot conveniently be dispatched before the third of next March, will I expect be postponed for the next session. A joynt committee of both houses have unanimously reported that it will be expedient for Congress then to rise. The Secretary at war[1] has reported as his opinion that there will be occasion for another expedition against the western Indians and that three thousand men will be necessary for the purpose, thô we have been told that the object of the former expedition has been accomplished. The expences attendant on our indian affairs, and the western country, are very unfortunate for our revenue. What congress will do is yet doubtful; any further measures of a hostile nature will be agreed to with reluctance, if at all. The former expedition was undertaken by the direction of the President under the general power he had of ordering the regular troops & of calling out the militia for the defence and protection of the frontiers. No doubt he was perswaded that this was the most adviseable mode of accomplishing this purpose, thô the event has not been correspondent with his wishes.

We have had a host of private petitioners before Congress, who if they were all to be gratifyed would nearly swallow up the whole revenue, but I believe the approaching adjournment will leave most, if not all of them, as they were. Several of the southern states appear by late accounts, to be much out of humour with some proceedings of Congress, especially for the assumption. There seems to be a spirit of discontent & jealously arising, and some speeches of the Southern members on the Excise bill are extremely calculated to excite & increase those jealousies. They are mighty averse to paying a duty on whisky; and one would be ready to suppose from their representation that the great burden of taxes would come out of them; whereas their indian affairs, their western country, & their other expences of government will nearly absorb all their proportion of taxes, & the States East of Virginia will have to bear the chief burden of the national debt. This is a mortifying consideration and will in its tendency be the ground of discord & jealousy between the Northern & Southern States. Necessity at present however must prove a bond of union, and I hope that at some future period our sentiments & our interests thrô the several states will better harmonise.

I will enclose some news papers which will contain the intelligence of the day. The atorney general[2] has reported a judicial system somewhat different from the present, which is not expected to be taken up by Congress in this session & it is too voluminous to enclose well in a letter, else I should transmit it. That with several other papers I must reserve for your inspection until I shall return. I have the honour to be with great respect and esteem your Excellency's most obedient & humble Servant,

Paine Wingate

RC (NhD).

1. Henry Knox (1750–1806) was secretary of war from 1785 to 1794. *BDEB*, 200.

2. Edmund Jennings Randolph (1753–

1813) was Washington's attorney general from February 1790 to January 1794. *BDEB*, 272.

TO LEVI BARTLETT

Dear Son   Concord January 29th 1791

I Received yours[1] by Colo. Eastman am glad to hear my family are comfortable. I have enjoyed a pretty good state of health since I have been here. Mr. True & Rhoda were here last week on friday, went home on Saturday were pretty well. As to what you write about Major Morrill[2] &c. I have heard nothing about it here, and believe there is nothing in it. I am so much engaged I have not time to write much, Think the Court will not rise till the latter end of the week after next if then. Think I shall not return till the Court rises. Yours affectionately   Josiah Bartlett

RC (Published by permission of Lincoln Savings and Loan Association, Los Angeles, Calif. On permanent public display at Independence Hall, Knott's Berry Farm, Buena Park, Calif., 1976).

1. Not found.

2. Oliver Morrill (b. 1734) of Epping was commissioned a major of the 4th

militia regiment in May 1790. *NHSP*, 21:753; Smith, *Morrill Kindred*, 2:15–16.

TO LEVI BARTLETT

Dear Son   Concord Febry 4th 1791

This is Just to inform you and my family that I am well and hope it

will find you and them so. I have nothing new to write you. We are very much engaged in business, the members of Court talk of rising the latter end of next week. I Something doubt it, think we Shall the week after next. Yours[1] by Colo. Eastman I Received am glad to hear you were well. This I Expect will be handed you by Judge White.[2] In haste from your affectionate Parent   Josiah Bartlett
Wrote in a hurry by Candle light this Morning.

RC (OClWHi).

1. Not found.

2. Phillips White had been a probate judge, and was currently sitting on the Executive Council.

FROM NICHOLAS GILMAN

Sir   Philadelphia 6th February 1791

I am honored with your very obliging favor of the 17th January and beg your Excellency to accept my sincere thanks for your kind congratulation on my reappointment.

The business now before Congress is a bill for the establishment of a national Bank and an Excise Bill—the former has past the Senate & the latter the House—the subjects being highly important have called forth much debate which will probably result in Laws to carry both into Effect. Of the excise on Spirits it is proposed to make it payable as near the fountain head as possible in order that it may operate equally on the rich & the poor and be less expensive and less odious in collection than has been experienced under some of the State regulations.

As it is the intention of Congress to rise by the third of March the report of the Attorney General on the Judiciary System and some other matters of less importance will lay over untill next Session which I suppose will commence in November or December.

Among the concerns of the present day nothing seems more important than that which respects the defence of the Western frontiers. The late expensive & unfortunate expedition against the Indians in that Country which seems to have been badly conducted under the command of Genl. Harmar[1] has tended only to irritate and combine the Indians West of the Ohio against our settlers in that Country. By recent accounts it appears that they have destroyed several of our settlements and filled the whole Country with dreadful apprehensions which send forth their deep toned crise to the Government for aid & protection. This I fear will prove an expensive Job for such is their present distress that a considerable expence in order to afford them relief seems inevitable. It is perhaps a misfortune that we have any connexion with that Country—I fear it will prove so in the end but we are now so involved that under present circumstances there seem to be no retreat and no consolation in a pecuniary view but that which arises from a distant hope that the sales of those lands may in time repay the treasury.

I beg your Excellency to accept my best wishes for your personal health

& Happiness and that you will believe me to be with great Exteem and attachment Sir Your very Obedient and Humble Servant,   Ns: Gilman

RC (NhD).

1. Josiah Harmar (1753–1813) of Philadelphia had commanded American troops since October 1776. After the war he led several expeditions against Indians of the northwest territory, that of October 1790 proving less than successful. Harmar was relieved of command and resigned in January 1792.

FROM PAINE WINGATE

Sir   Philadelphia Feb. 21. 1791

I have the honour of receiving your favour of the 28th ultimo,[1] and thank you for the information given, which was the first we had received here, of the choice of our federal Representatives. I shall always be happy to receive such information and advices from you, as you shall be pleased to give; especially such as relate to the state of affairs in New-Hampshire, which may be proper & conducive to the welfare of that State that I should be acquainted with.

We are now approaching to the close of the present session of Congress which will not afford time for the exchange of further communications. Much of the business contemplated to be done must be postponed until the next session, but no great injury is apprehended to result from it. The Law for a national bank has been for a week before the President for his approbation. Some begin to scruple whether he will sign it, and it is said that the price of public securities has fallen in consequence of such an apprehension. The Excise bill is nearly thrô both houses of Congress. The house of Representatives have agreed to most of the amendments made by the Senate, which it is conceived will remove many of the odious parts of the bill as it was first proposed; and I think it likely that this day the Senate will concur with the house in the other amendments. By the bill as it now stands the Intrest will be paid only by the Importers & distillers, and the retailers & other dealers in ardent spirits will have nothing to do in the business, which will save much embarrassment & expence in the collection. There is to be a supervisor of this part of the revenue in each State, who is to have the superindance of such inspectors as the President shall think necessary to appoint. The bill is too complicated to give a more particular account of it at this time. It has been violently opposed by some, chiefly from the South, and mischievous consequences are predicted to result from it; but since the assumption has taken place, if the Excise is an evil, I believe it is a necessary one. I shall think that this country, under its present weight of debt & increasing expences, is very fortunate, if we can get along without additional taxes. In my last letter I mentioned something about our Indian affairs. I will now enclose a bill which has passed the Senate as an amendment to a bill from the other house, by which you will see the great expence we are incurring by the increase of our military establishment. For my part I think it is a greater expence than was necessary, especially that which relates to the increase of the standing troops. The ostensible reason of garronsoning our out posts is not, in my opinion, the only motive with some for the increase of this establishment. It was however carryed by a majority of the Senate of 15 to 7.

The President has lately received some communications from a Gentleman he employed to find what was the disposition & sentiments of the British Court respecting the western posts & a commercial treaty with them, &c. Mr. Pitt & the Duke of Leeds both professed a wish that Great Britain & we might be on friendly terms & that the late treaty of peace might be fulfilld, but complained that their merchants had not been enabled to recover their debts &c., and it seems from the purport of the conferences which passed that we are not to expect that at present those posts will be given up.

I do not know that this information is given to the Senate as of a secret nature, but as it is not published here, perhaps it ought not to be communicated general & probably some further proceedings may be had in the train of negotiation. Indeed I do not consider my letters as official and therefore suppose they are not communicated.

Vermont is to be in the Union after the 4th of March next & to have two Representatives. Kentucky is to be in after next June twelve month to have the like number, and laws have passed for those purposes without opposition. I was in hopes that Congress would no more be interrupted or agitated with disputes about the place of residence for some years, but the President has proposd in a message, that the district of ten miles square should be somewhat altered. This question will in some measure try the sentiments of Congress whether they will do any thing that shall look like approving of the Potomac to be the place of permanent residence. The Presidents heart is no doubt much set on this place & there is as little doubt but that a majority of Congress are decidedly against it. The question therefore is a very disagreeable one to decide, & it will try the feelings of some of the Courtiers pretty much. The question is postponed until next friday & what will be the result I am in doubt, because I am uncertain who will prefer acting their private sentiments to every other consideration.

So far as I can judge near one third of the Representatives in the next congress will be new members. Only three new members are yet elected for the Senate, & Pennsylvania have not yet come to a choice. It is doubtful whether the old number there will be reelected or not.

Colo. David Humphries[2] formerly an Aid to the President is nominated for a minister resident at Lisbon.

I have the honour to be with the highest sentiments of respect and esteem your Excellency's most obedient & humble servant

Paine Wingate

RC (MB).

1. Not found.

2. David Humphreys (1752–1818), an intimate of Washington, had been chosen as special secret agent to London, Lisbon, and Madrid in 1790 to obtain information for the government.

TO GEORGE WASHINGTON

Sir, Exter February 24th. 1791.

I have the Honor herewith to enclose and transmit your Excellency an Authenticated Copy of "An Act ceding to the United States of America one Acre and three quarters of an Acre of land with the Fort and Light House thereon situate in New Castle."[1] I am with the highest Sentiments of Esteem and Respect Sir, Your Excellency's Most obedient and most Humble Servant, (Signed) Josiah Bartlett

TR (DNA:RG 46). In a clerk's hand. Attested by Tobias Lear, Washington's secretary. Enclosed with a letter of the 26th signed by Washington transmitting this and several other acts to Congress. See MJB, 2790.

1. See JB to General Court, 5 Jan. 1791, n. 2.

TO JEREMY BELKNAP

Revd Sir Kingstown February 25th 1791

Some time the begining of April last just before our Spring Circuit commenced, I received your favor of the 6th of March 1790 and was much pleased to find you intended to continue the history of Newhampshire. The papers that were inclosed I sent to the persons to whom they were directed Such as were not directed I gave to Such persons as I thought most likely to give you proper information and I fully determined as Soon as the Circuit was over to collect and send you every information in my power that I should think would be useful to you in the business more especially the altercation in this State relative to Vermont. But at that time being unexpectdly called to other Business and the latter part of Summer and fall my ill State of health Scarcely permitted me to give proper attention to the necessary business of the public, put it quite out of my power notwithstanding my inclination to comply with your request.

Tho these circumstances has prevented me from giving Such information as would other wise have been in my power yet I would hope no disadvantage will arise, as you have had a Correspondance with many Gentlemen of Character & abilities in the State who I doubt not have given you every information that would have been in my power to have given and that the work will suffer no detriment on that account. The people of this State in general, and the most respectable in particular are highly pleased that You have undertaken the further History of Newhampshire; the Specimen given in the former volume has contributed to raise their Expectations that it will be properly done; The Legislature at their late Session seemed pleased that you had proceeded in the Business and as a token of their approbation have voted you the Sum of Fifty pounds to be paid out of the Treasury as a present.[1] Myself and some others could have wished the Sum greater, but you are not unacquainted that the Legislature of this State in all their public grants have acted on a frugal plan, many times perhaps too much so, nor has all the members a proper Sense of the usefullness & importance of Such a work nor of the labor and Expence of Compiling it. Such as it is I ask your acceptance of it and if you will empower any person to receive it, an order on the Treasury will be made out and the money paid on sight. I am with much respect your most obedt Servant   Josiah Bartlett

RC (From photograph in NhHi of original. Original not found).

1. The General Court acted on 17 February. Perhaps the person most responsible for the success of Belknap's applica-tion was Dr. Joshua Brackett. Shipton, *Harvard Graduates*, 13:200; *NHSP*, 22: 136, 239.

TO WILLIAM WILLIAMS

Dear Sir   Kingstown March 21st 1791

I have received your favor of the 28th Ulto.[1] and am very sorry to be informed that Esqr. Wendell[2] has not Settled his affair with you; as to his circumstances for paying the demand, I know nothing but that they are nearly the Same as when you wrote me formerly on that Subject, I fancy not better. I am Sorry to Say he (I believe) never pretends to pay a debt so long as fair words & promises will answer, but when other means are made use of, he makes out to Settle it. When I received your letter Some years Since inclosing his promise with power to prosecute it with power of Substitution, I gave them to John Pickering Esqr. then attorney at Law, Since appointed Chief Justice of our Superior Court, and desired him to use Every lawful means to procure the debt without Suing it. After passing one Court and finding nothing but excuses and fair words, I ordered a Suit to be brought. When the time of trial came he proposed to pay a Sum of money as I remember about 25 dollars and leave in Pledge public Securities much more than Sufficient to pay the debt, provided I would consent that the action Should be continued to the next term without taking Judgment at that time, which I agreed to and the money & Securities were deposited with Mr. Pickering and the cause continued. Some considerable time after I Enquired of Mr. Pickering how the matter Stood & whither Mr. Wendel had paid the money, when he informed me that Mr. Wendel had brought him an order from you, to drop the action and had taken back the money and Securities from him. As you had ordered the Attorney to drop the action, and had given me no further instructions in the matter, I concluded that you did not consider me as having any thing further to do in the affair; And do not re-collect that I have enquird or heard any further about it. Since I have received your last letter, I am Suspicious Mr. Wendel did not inform you of the true State of the matter and that he imposed on your Humanity and benevolence to drop the action after I had Secured the debt, perhaps I was negligent in not giving you information how the matter Stood to prevent your being imposed on, but the difficulty and trouble and some cost that attended writing to you and my other engagements I must plead as an Excuse; Since I receivd your last letter I have wrote to Judge Pic-kering[3] to know if he has kept Mr. Wendel's promisory letter to you Safe, Expect to hear from him in a few days.

As to the Town of Fairfield in this State, I can give you but little information, as it is not commonly known by that name here, but by the name of Peeling. In looking over the Records of Charters I find it was Granted on September 1763 by the name of Peeling to people in and about Dover in this State, That in December 1771 it was regranted by Governor Wentworth by the name of Fairfield to people mostly of Connecticut among which are the names you mention;[4] I understand there are few if any Setlers in the Town, if any are on, whither they pretend to hold under the first or Second grant cannot inform you. I believe the Town is but indifferent, very mountainous and broken, no doubt there is some good Land in it. Governor Wentwoths regranting Lands has caused great Confusion in this State, when they will be Settled I know not; Three or four years Since the Legislature made a Law impowering the Superior Court of this State to hear and Determine those disputes and to determine what Towns had forfeited their Charters by neglect or otherwise to the State and giving the said Court a power of Chancery in many Cases, but by reason of Some defects in the Law, it has not as yet been practised upon.

I heartily Thank you for your good opinion of me and kind Congratulations on my late appointment and Sincerely wish & hope that for the short time I have to Continue on the Stage of action, no future Conduct of mine will give you just cause to lessen your good opinion of me.

I am Sorry to inform you that our late friend General Folsom died Sometime in May last after about ten days Sickness with a fever that came on with the infleuenza (as it is Called) which was then raging in these parts. I am Sir with great Esteem and Respect your most obedient Servant   Josiah Bartlett[5]

RC (CtHi). Addressed to "Col. Wm. Williams, Lebanon, Conecticut."

1. Not found. William Williams (1731–1811) of Lebanon, Conn., had served in the Continental Congress, 1776–1778 and 1783–1784, where, with JB, he had signed the Declaration of Independence and assisted in framing the Articles of Confederation. He probably owned property in New Hampshire through Wendell who was a major proprietor of lands.

2. John Wendell (1731–1808), a Portsmouth attorney, had graduated from Harvard College in 1750. His early financial successes were tempered by losses following the Revolution. Shipton, *Harvard Graduates*, 12:592–97. See MJB, 3232.

3. JB's letter to Pickering not found. The letters which JB gave to Pickering about the case are referred to in Pickering to JB, 7 May 1791, MJB, 2813.

4. In 1840 the town's name was changed to Woodstock. *NHSP*, 25:643.

5. JB and Williams continued to correspond on the matter. In a letter of 12 Mar. 1792 Williams noted that Wendell's "many fair words and promises to me in near 20 Letters, perfectly justifie your Character of him in yr favr of 21 Mar. 1791." MJB, 3026. See also MJB, 3086, 3099, 3447.

FROM JEREMY BELKNAP

Sir   Boston May 24, 1791

When I was at Exeter I left a Letter with the Secretary for your Excellency acknowledging the Receipt of £50 granted to me by the Assembly of your State as an Encouragement to proceed in my history of New

Hampshire & requesting you to make known my grateful acceptance of the same at the next meeting of the Assembly in such manner as you should think proper. It would have given me great Pleasure if my Engagements had permitted me to return home through Kingston & pay my respects to yr Excellency in person; but this was impossible.

By the assistance thus afforded me, together with what has been advanced by subscribers, I have begun the printing of the second & third Volumes of the history & hope to have them finished some time in the Course of the ensuing Summer. By the returns of subscriptions, I find so many Persons desirous of having *whole* sets, that I shall be obliged to reprint the first Volume (having not enough of the first Edition on hand to supply them all). This will put me to additional Expense; and yet I have no certainty that the number wanted will be sufficient to warrant my incurring that Expense. Could I be assured of the sale of 300 more in addition to those which are already subscribed for, I should be relieved from all difficulty.

When I made application to the Assembly in 1785 for their Countenance & assistance to this Work, it was in Contemplation by a Committee with whom I conversed to *purchase* a Number of Copies of my first Volume, to be distributed among the several towns in the state & Members of assembly, & I believe they reported in favor of such a measure; but it was not carried into Effect. Should such an idea be adopted by the Gentlemen of the Assembly at their next meeting & should they in consequence direct the Treasurer to subscribe for 300 sets & advance part of the money at the time of subscribing & pay the remainder on the delivery of the Books, I could then go forward with the work not only without fear, but with full satisfaction, & should think myself highly honoured by such a generous Patronage.

May I ask the favor of yr Excellency to communicate this proposal to the Assembly, as early in the next session as may be convenient.[1] Should they be desirous of conferring with me by letter, I shall be ready to obey their Commands as it will be inconvenient for me to attend them in person, because I am and shall be daily occupied in examining & correcting the proof sheets as they come from the Press.

I beg leave further to suggest that according to the subscription papers which at present are returned, the Number of books subscribed for in Massachusetts exceeds that in New-Hampshire, in the proportion of two to one. As I have promised to print the names of subscribers, this Circumstance may operate to the disadvantage of your State in the minds of some, as if it was not so earnest to encourage a literary work calculated for its benefit, as one of its sister states; but if what I have proposed should take place, the balance of encouragement will fall on the side of New Hampshire.

I would also beg permission to observe, that the several classes of tradesmen whom I employ in this work do not run any risque at all. The paper-maker is paid by the Rheam, the Printer by the sheet, the engraver by the hundred & for the plate, and the Book binder by the Volume. I expect to be the bookseller myself, for if I should employ any other Person he must have a Commission on the sales. I am the only one concerned whose expense is certain & whose profit is uncertain. I must pay the others for their work whether the books are sold or not; if they are sold I shall be a gainer, if not a loser. This is precisely the state of the Case & I am the more particular on this head, less it should be suggested that the advantage arising from the sale of the books will belong to the printers & booksellers, rather than to the author.

Relying on your Candour & friendship I have made this Communication & am Sir with great Respect Yr obliged & Obedient Servt.

Jeremy Belknap

RC (MeHi: The John S. H. Fogg Autograph Collection).
  1. JB complied with Belknap's request. When the question of whether the state should supply each town with a set of volumes came before the House of Representatives on 20 Dec. 1792, it was negatived. *NHSP*, 22:692–93.

FROM WILLIAM GARDNER

Treasury Office New Hampshire

Sir June 1st. 1791

I have the honor to enclose for the information of Your Excellency & the Honorable Court a Statement of the sums received for Taxes—Excise—Impost &c. from the 31st of July last (the date of my last settlement)—and the amount outstanding of each denomination.

As I do not consider myself a Candidate for this Office at the ensuing Election[1]—it is my wish that a Committee may be appointed to examine & settle my Accounts—which I shall endeavor to prepare for their inspection with all convenient speed.

The reiterated marks of confidence which I have experienced from the Honorable Court claim my warmest thanks—and I shall always feel myself happy in having oppertunities of manifesting my Zeal for the Interest of the State. I have the honor to be with the greatest respect, Sir, Your Excellency's most Obedt. & very Humble Servt.

Wm. Gardner, Treasr.

RC (Nh-Ar). Enclosure not found with letter.
  1. John Taylor Gilman was elected treasurer on 3 June. *NHSP*, 22:319. He accepted on 7 June. MJB, 2838.

In 1791 New Hampshire's chief executive was still a president rather than a governor. The general election of that spring produced a whole vote of 8,679, of which JB received 8,391, with 288 going to several other candidates whose names have been obscured from historical records. The elections in which JB participated were not party contests. JB held no formal party affiliation, but rather was, in the spirit of the times, a nationalist, an ardent supporter of the Constitution and the government under George Washington's administration. As president, JB sat in and voted with the Senate but held no power of veto over legislation. He headed the Council, but could act only with its consent.

Many, in and out of state government, could see that some revision was needed. According to a provision in the 1784 Constitution the General Court called for a convention in 1791 to consider alterations to the existing form of government. The convention met from 7 to 16 Sept. 1791, from 8 to 24 Feb. 1792, from 30 May to 5 June 1792, and finally on 5 and 6 Sept. 1792 by which time its revised Constitution had been ratified. As its last order of business the convention ordered five hundred copies to be prepared for presentation to the legislature. As engineered through the convention, principally by William Plumer, all branches were delegated increased responsibility and power. Thus was answered JB's call in the following letter for revision and strengthening of state government. Daniell, Experiment, 226–32; NHSP, 10:23–196.

TO THE GENERAL COURT

Council Chamber in Concord
the 3d of June 1791

Gentlemen of the Senate and of the House of Representatives

To meet the two Branches of the Legislature newly Elected by the free Suffrages of my Fellow Citizens, and with them to consult and deliberate on the measures necessary to be adopted for the happiness and prosperity of this State, affords me a peculiar Satisfaction at this time when the Public affairs in general wear so pleasing an aspect, after the troubles and difficulties we have had to encounter in years past. The peace harmony and good order that prevails among us: The Diminution of our late burdensome direct Taxes, the rapid increase of our agriculture & manufacturg, the freedom of Commerce & advantage of fisheries, all conspire to afford us the agreable prospect (if we are not wanting to ourselves) of future ease and Prosperity connected with Civil and Religious Liberty as the happy effects (under the Smiles of Divine Providence) of the noble Exertions of the Citizens of the United States in the great cause of Freedom and their Country and as in those Exertions the Citizens of this State in proportion to their numbers and abilities have had at least an equal Share with those of the other States in general, So they have a right to Expect in the Same proportion an Equal Share in all the advantages arising from those Exertions.

In addition to the common Business of the State which is usually transacted at this Season of the year, I beg leave to recommend the compleating the Revision of the State Laws which were in Such forwardness at the close of the last Session.

The time pointed out for the Revision of the Constitution of this State being now arrived, you will probably think proper at this Session to make the necessary arangments for calling a Convention of the State for that purpose.

The acts of Congress and Such other public papers as have come to hand Since the last Session, I shall direct the Secretary to lay Before you and if any thing further Shall occur during the Session that will require your attention, I shall not fail to communicate it to you by Seperate Message.

I have nothing further to recommend at this time but the cultivation of a Spirit of Unanimity and Harmony, of Candor and liberality of Sentiments among ourselves and the people at large, that while (as I trust) we are all aiming to promote the general wellfare, the different Sentiments that may be Entertained of the best mode to be adopted for accomplishing that desirable End, may not interrupt that Harmony and Goodwill that is so essentially necessary to the Happiness of all Public Societies. And Gentlemen you may be assured that it will afford me the most pleasing Satisfaction to be able in any degree to contribute to the real interest of my Fellow Citizens.   Josiah Bartlett

RC (NNPM).

FROM THE GENERAL COURT

May it please your excellency   June 7th, 1791

The senate and house of representatives congratulate your excellency that the suffrages of a free people have placed you in the chair of government, your constant attachment for so many years past to the concerns and best interests of the state affords us the strongest assurance that the first object of your attention is the prosperity and happiness of the people.

With particular satisfaction we receive your excellency's message to both houses communicating to us the pleasing state of our public affairs which affords us a fresh proof of the solidity of the foundation on which they rest, and of the happy consequences that have resulted from the troubles and difficulties that we have had to contend with in years past. The diminution of direct taxes the increase of our agriculture and manufactures and the expectation that our commerce and fishing will be in an eligible situation, all agree to inspire us with the auspicious prospect that joined with our own endeavours we shall enjoy ease prosperity and freedom both civil and religious.

We agree with your excellency that as the citizens of this state have had a full share in the burthens and exertions that have procured us freedom and independance they are therefore justly entitled to all the benefits and advantages resulting therefrom.

We shall renew our attention to complete the revision of the state laws and to such other objects as may be worthy of our deliberations.

The time for the revision of the constitution being now at hand we shall readily concur with your excellency in making the necessary arrangements.

We trust in all public concerns, unanimity and harmony, candor and liberality of sentiment will prevail among us and the people at Large, and that by the blessing of heaven our motives and aim may be directed to that desireable end the public good, and in your cooperation we are sure of a resource which strengthens our hopes and will justify the confidence which the citizens of this state have so unanimously placed in you.

State of New Hampshire

In the house of Representatives
June 7th. 1791.

The foregoing answer to his Excellency's message reported by a Committee chosen for that purpose having been read & considered voted, That it be received & accepted.

Sent up for concurrence.
Wm Plumer Speaker[1]

In Senate the same day read and concurred.

J Pearson Secy

FC (Nh-Ar).

1. William Plumer (1759–1850), a member of the House for Epping, had been appointed to the committee to answer JB's message to the General Court. Nathaniel Peabody had resigned as speaker of the House and Plumer had been elected in his stead. Plumer later served in the U.S. Senate and as governor of New Hampshire. Turner, *William Plumer*.

TO JOSEPH WHIPPLE

Sir   Kingstown June 28th 1791

I am to acknowledge the receipt of your favor of the 20th Instant and also of yours by Capt Salter relative to the Support of the Light House.

The reason I did not answer yours by Capt Salter was the embarrassed Situation of that business. I laid your letter before the Council and took their advice upon it, who were unanimously of opinion that as matters were circumstanced I could do nothing in the affair but lay the matter before the Legislature which I did at the last Session and a Committe of both Houses were appointed to take the matter into Consideration & report but by reason of a multiplicity of business it was omitted and nothing done.

The affair of Supporting the Lighthouse has taken a very different turn from what I was led to concieve of by the act of Congress. I did not suppose that Congress designed take the Lighthouses into their Care till they were Ceded or till they were delivered into their hands by the authority of the States, and that the States would have a just Claim against Congress according to their act for a reimbursement of the reasonable Expences they had been at for their Support till delivered up; Capt Salter who had the care of our lighthouse was paid up to March 1790 and then he entered into a Contract with the State to support it and take some small care of the stores at the Fort for £ 175 per year and on application Recd an order on the Treasury for the first half year up to Septr last and what right Capt Salter had after he had received his pay from the State to Contract with you for pay for the Same service he had done for the

State and had received his pay according to contract I will leave you to determine and whether the State is or ought to be bound by any Such Contract. I conclude the State will think they have a just claim against Congress for what they have Expended in Supporting the Lighthouse from the 15th of August 1789 till the Cession took place and it was resigned up to you and I do not conceive that I should be Justified without the voice of the Legislature in making a Settlement for a less Sum than what the State has expended, for that purpose I laid the matter before the Legislature and was in hopes some order would be taken upon it. I am sorry the affair is in such a Situation that I cannot as I conceive act anything in the affair, and I would Submit it to your consideration whether there will be any propriety in your paying Capt Salter for services he has done for, and has received his pay of, the State, and for which I Suppose the State has a just claim against the United States.

Draft (Nh).

TO TENCH COXE[1]

State of New Hampshire Exeter

Sir   June 30th 1791

Inclosed is Copy of a Resolution of the Legislature of this State authorizing us to Subscribe for One Hundred & Fifty Shares in the National Bank; also our Letter of Attorney for you to make the Subscription, which hope you will accept, but in case you cannot, that you would Substitute some Suitable person for that purpose.[2]

In case you make the Subscription please to draw Bills on us for the first Specie payment, being Three Thousand Seven hundred & fifty dollars, which Bills shall be honored on Sight; But as we are doubtful whether you will be able to dispose of Bills payable here, have wrote the Secretary of the Treasury requesting him to order your Bills on us to be taken up, and that we may pay the Money here; and hope that it may be convenient for him to make such order.

Please to send us the papers necessary to Evince the Subscription, such other information on the Subject as you may think necessary, and an account for your trouble and Expence in the business. With much Esteem We are Your Hum. Servts.

Josiah Bartlett
John Taylor Gilman

RC (PHi). In Gilman's hand, signed by JB and Gilman.

1. Tench Coxe (1755–1824), a Philadelphia merchant until 1790, was Hamilton's assistant secretary of the treasury. In 1792 he became commissioner of revenue.

2. Enclosures not with letter. A federal act supplementary to that establishing the bank delayed the opening of subscriptions to it until 4 July to give subscribers in remote areas time to subscribe. The N.H. legislature passed the resolve on 17 June, and this letter did not reach Coxe until 9 July. See his of 30 July. *NHSP*, 22:302, 359; Hammond, *Banks*, 122–23.

FROM TENCH COXE

Gentlemen   Philadelphia July 9th. 1791

I was honored this morning with your joint letter of the 30th of June covering a copy of the act of the legislature of New Hampshire of the 17th. of that month authorizing the President & Treasurer of the state to subscribe one hundred and fifty shares to the Bank of the United, and a power of attorney committing to me the execution of the Subscription. It is with sincere & very great regret that I inform you there is not at this time a probability of fulfilling even in part the intentions of the legislature & the instructions pursuant thereto, which you have been pleased to give me. The applications, which were made to the Commissioners in the morning of the fourth of July considerably exceeded the number of shares, which they were authorized to receive, so that a proportionate excision from the sums offered became necessary to an adjustment of the Business. The prices too at which the new Bank stock is selling in the Market are such as to preclude the expectation of prevailing on any of the subscribers to part with shares on the original Terms, or I would have considered the propriety of fulfilling essentially the intentions of the legislature by causing a purchase to be effected on terms precisely equal to those of the subscription.[1] With regard to the negociation of the Bills I beg leave to assure you that the requesite accomodation in the quarter you allude to would not have been wanting. Nor should I have hesitated to obtain it by my individual credit, if the course of Business had prevented its being derived by a sale of the draughts to the United States.

Altho you will perceive the chance of obtaining the Stock in any way is such as to afford no hope, I propose to retain the power a few days till the issues of all the certificates are completed, and I procure a trial to be made of the market.[2] Should I be so fortunate as unexpectedly to discover an opening, I shall cause it to be embraced without any charge of commission, which you have so politely offered as I shall be amply compensated in the satisfaction I shall feel in seeing the state of New Hampshire interested in the instution. I have the honor to be with the greatest respect, Gentlemen Your most obedient & most humble Servant.

Tench Coxe

Draft (PHi).

1. When the books were opened on 4 July, the entire $8,000,000 available to the public was oversubscribed within an hour. Active speculation had brought about such a rise in price that by August the $25.00 subscription certificates were selling at $300 or more. Hammond, *Banks,* 123.

2. Coxe returned the papers with his letter of 30 July in which he noted that the demand for bank stock had been so great "as to extinguish all hope of obtaining it on the original terms." MJB, 2875.

FROM JOHN WHEELOCK

Sir!   Dartmouth College Augt. 4th. 1791

I wrote last fall[1] and used the liberty of mentioning the wishes of the

Board, that you would accept their testimony of respect in the honours of this Seminary. My letter I fear never, reached you; but suppose the rev'd Profr Smith communicated the contents of it.

Our anniversary commencement will come on the fourth wednesday of this month: and could you find it consistent to do us the honour of being present it would add much to our happiness; and be esteemed a particular favour to the Seminary. But it belongs to us only to propose, and submit the matter to your wisdom; as you have the weighty affairs of government to occupy your attention. In sentiments of the greatest respect and esteem, I am, Sir! Your Excellency's, most Obedient, & humble servant,   John Wheelock

RC (NhD). Note with address: "Pr Honble Jonn Freeman Esq."
    1. 30 Aug. 1790.

FROM NICHOLAS GILMAN

Sir   Philadelphia October 26th 1791
    I am this day honored with your Excellencys favor of the 3d of August last[1] which accompanies a Memorial from the Legislature of New Hampshire to Congress on the subject of assumption to which seasonable attention will be paid.

    I have the pleasure to inform your Excellency that a Congress was formed on the 24th instant[2] and yesterday the President of the United States delivered a Speech to both Houses as contained in the paper which I take the liberty herewith to forward. With the greatest Respect I have the Honor to be Sir Your Excellencys Very Obedient Servant,
                                                            Ns. Gilman

RC (NhD). Clippings from the enclosed newspaper are with the letter.
    1. Not found.
    2. This first session of the Second Congress met from 24 Oct. 1791 to 8 May 1792, with New Hampshire represented
in the Senate by John Langdon and Paine Wingate and in the House by Gilman, Samuel Livermore, and Jeremiah Smith.

FROM PAINE WINGATE

Sir   Philadelphia Nov. 11th 1791
    I have received your Excellency's favour of 25th. ulto.[1] Previously to that, the President's private Secretary had informed me, that it was the Presidents wish that the members in Congress from New Hampshire would mention to him some suitable person or persons for the office of Marshal in the room of Mr. Parker deceased.[2] I had accordingly mentioned to him two persons. Since your letter came to hand I had an opportunity of conversing with the President on the same subject, when I informed him of the gentleman, whom you had recommended as a person well qualifyed for that office. He has likewise been recommended to the President by one other of the delegates at least. Who will be appointed, is at present very doubtful to me. I think the appointment cannot be a great object for any one to be anxious for; as the emoluments cannot be

considerable & the place may probably exclude the holder of it from the Legislature, if not from other state appointments. As yet nothing has been done in Congress respecting the invalid pensioners. I hope that some general regulation will be adopted in respect to all those who are justly entitled to the relief originally designed for invalids and that those from New Hampshire will participate in the benefit in common with others. This is a subject which will naturally be brought before Congress in the course of the present session by the numerous applications from all parts of the union to be admitted on the pension list as invalids. I will enclose, among some other papers, the Census which has been reported to Congress. The Marshal of South Carolina has failed in making his return it is said, be cause he could not find any person in one part of his destrict who would take the numbers, and in another the person employed did not make his return. The time for compleating & making the return from that State is now protracted to the first of March next, when it is probable the numbers in the United States will be ascertained. The Congressional business will more fully appear by the newspaper accounts than I could be able to detail in a letter. It is a very pleasing part, to me, of the Presidents speech, that no additional revenue is at this time necessary. I have reason to think however that the produce of the Excise Law in the interior parts of Pennsylvania & to the southward will fall short of what has been calculated & that there are some obstructions attending the collection.

I shall very cheerfully communicate any information of importance respecting the affairs of the general government which shall come to my knowledge, and shall be happy to receive any communications which you shall be pleased to make. I have the honour to be with sentiments of respect & esteem your Excellency's Most obedient & humble Servant.

Paine Wingate

RC (NhD). Enclosures not found.
   1. Not found.
   2. John Parker (1732–1791) of Portsmouth had been sheriff of Rockingham County since 1771. He was also marshal of the federal district court in Portsmouth at his death on 4 Oct. 1791. *NHSP*, 22:838–39, 277. Nathaniel Rogers (1745–1829), of Newmarket, was appointed to replace Parker as marshal. Rogers was a member of the Executive Council in 1791. On 15 October he had been nominated

for sheriff, but was appointed marshal on 16 November.
   George Reid (1733–1815) of Londonderry received the appointment as county sheriff. Reid, who led American troops throughout the Revolution, had taken command of the regiment under Nathan Hale when Hale was taken prisoner. *NHSP*, 22:843–44; "Vital Records of Newmarket," 6; Potter, *Military History*, 1:338.

TO THE GENERAL COURT

Council Chamber in Portsmouth
November 30th. 1791

Gentlemen of the Senate and of the House of Representatives

It affords me a peculiar satisfaction at this time to meet the two Houses of the Legislature at this Antient seat of Government of the late Province now state of New Hampshire as it brings to mind the many important Scenes through which we have been conducted in the course of a few years past and which by (divine goodness) has terminated in the happy priviledge we now enjoy of enacting such Laws as shall be most conducive to the happiness and prosperity of the state with out the controul of a foreign jurisdiction.

Indulged by Providence with so great a blessing it becomes our Indispensible duty in enacting laws and making regulations to consult the general good of the Community and to use our best endeavours both by precept and example to cultivate the principles of virtue and morality of justice and patriotism to encourage a spirit of Industry and Oeconomy and the Increase of Learning and useful knowledge through the state which will be the best means to procure a cordial Submission to the equitable Laws of the Community and greatly promote the happiness and tranquility of this rising republic.

As this is the Season of the year when the Legislature can most conveniently attend to public business I would beg leave to recommend to your consideration the propriety at this Session of making an accurate investigation of the state of the Treasury of the Sums of money due to and from the State (more especially) some accounts and demands of long standing and pointing out the mode and giving directions for calling in the one and discharging the other as soon as conveniently may be in such way and manner as will do justice to the state and to the Individuals concerned.

The time being expired for which post riders into the interior parts of the state were engaged agreably to your resolve past last winter—I beg leave to request your attention to that matter.[1]

The difficulties occasioned by the death of a high sherriff in one of the Counties will I apprehend point out to the Legislature the propriety of making a Law to prevent Similar difficulties in like cases for the future.[2]

The many embarrassments attending the levying and collecting state Taxes on unimproved wilderness lands, as the small amount of the net produce to the state when collected compared with the cost and trouble in collecting may render it worthy of your consideration whether as the affairs of the state are now circumstanced it may not be for the general advantage of the public to exempt that species of property from state taxes in future in the manner they formerly were.

Any other matters that shall occur that may require your attention I shall not fail to communicate to you during the Session and shall chearfully co-operate with you in every measure that will tend to the prosperity of our common country.   Josiah Bartlett

TR (Nh-Ar: Journal of the House of Representatives).

1. The legislature continued the postal service without alteration until June. *NHSP*, 22:411–13, 449–50.

2. An act passed on 10 December required that the deputy sheriff continue in office with the powers of sheriff. *Laws of N.H.*, 5:785–86.

TO EZRA BARTLETT

Dear Son   Portsmouth December 3d 1791

This may inform you and my family That I am well, hope this will find you & them the Same. I wish you to look in my desk in my worked pocket book and take out the paper Signed by Mr. Gardner describing the State Securities I have deposited with him to be funded and Send it to me by Colo. Eastman. You will take particular care to send the right paper, it has a Description of the notes mentioned viz in my own name & Jonathan Greeley's. In haste your affectionate   Josiah Bartlett

RC (NhExP).

FROM NICHOLAS GILMAN

Sir   Philadelphia December 12th 1791

Official dispatches are just now laid before the House from General St. Clair giving a painful account of the slaughter of the Army under his command on the 4th November by the Indians.

The plan of operation for this year against the Indians was to harass them by the Militia of the Western frontiers & drive them to the necessity of suing for peace—this plan seemed to have been pretty well executed in the successful expeditions under Scot[1] and Wilkinson—but did not produce the expected effect on the common mind of the enemy. It appears on the contrary they have been very successful in their endeavors to effect a combination with tribes far remote, who have agreed to make common cause of the war—and being amply supplied from the British Garrisons, under the cloak of an annual allowance stipulated by treaty, were in perfect condition to meet our army.

On the 4th October the Army consisting of about Two thousand Continentals & levies and some Militia march'd from Fort Hamilton on the Miami towards the Miami Towns—on the 31st October Sixty of the Militia deserted and the whole of the first Continental regiment was detach'd to bring them back and in consequence were not in the action. There is no return of the number of our Army at the time they were attack'd it consisted of the Second Continental Regiment—levies and Militia supposed about fourteen hundred with seven pieces of Artillery. The attack was made on our Camp soon after the break of day. The action continued till half after nine—an uncommon proportion of brave experienced officers were Slain. All the Matross were cut off—the Artillery was silent—the Army was routed—leaving to the enemy their Artillery—their Tents & Baggage. The route continued about Twenty nine Miles to Fort Jefferson where the remains of the Army arrived a little after sun set. Expresses were immediately dispatched to Kentuckey and large bodies of men were assembling to march to Fort Washington to take orders from St. Clair; but I fear this catastrophe will wofully prolong the Indian War in which we have already been sorely scourged for indulging an unwarrantable avidity in extending our settlements.[2]

The object of this expedition was to establish posts in the interior of the Indian Country under an Idea that little resistance would be made by the natives but an arrangement so threatning to the British fur trade has without doubt engaged the attention of people of influence in that Country and lead them to oppose our conciliatory proposals to the Indians.

The first detachment of the New-Hampshire recruits were at Pittsburg the 17th of November. With the greatest Respect I have the Honor to be Sir Your Excellencys Very Obedient Servant.   Ns: Gilman
A list of officers Killed & wounded is herewith inclosed.[3]

RC (NhD).

1. Charles Scott (c. 1739–1813) was commandant of the Kentucky district with the rank of brigadier general in 1791. He was with St. Clair on this mission and later took part in Anthony Wayne's attack at the Battle of Fallen Timbers in 1794. In 1808 Scott was elected governor of Kentucky.

At this time James Wilkinson (1757–1825) was a lieutenant colonel in the regular army. In March 1792 he was promoted to brigadier general and served under Wayne.

2. For a thorough treatise on the campaign see Kohn, *Eagle and Sword*, 113–17.

3. The list shows that thirty-nine officers were killed, twenty-two wounded (NhD). MJB, 2956.

FROM NATHANIEL PEABODY

Sir   Portsmouth Decembr 13th 1791.

From the time I had the honor of being appointed one of the Committee upon the revision of the State Laws,[1] till all the proposed Bills were prepared to lay before the Honble. Legislature and until the Several Bills had undergone the Strict ordeal of both houses, No honest efforts were wanting on the part of the Committee to Expedite an object of such Necessity & Importance. I was also reappointed with the Honble Mr. Smith to prepare an Index for the Laws—Some Necessary Forms—and to attend to a Completion of the business. But as the State had made a Contract with the printer very little was left for the Committee to do upon that head except making out a list of the Laws, and an arrangement of the order in which they were to be published, which was duly attended to by the Committee. As it was the business of the Honl. Secrety to furnish Copies, and of the printer to execute the business of his office & make an accurate Impression of the Laws according to the Copies to him Deliver'd, It was agreed by the Committee, as Mr. Smith wou'd Necessarily be at Exeter & at Portsmouth, in order to discharge his duty as one of the Commissions for stating accts. against the United States that it wou'd be saving Expence to the State for him to take Charge of Such part of the business of the Committee as related to printing the Laws, till he Shou'd go on to Congress. And that we wou'd each of us improve every favourable moment in preparing Suitable Forms for Publication.

Thus Circumstanced I paid Attention to preparing the forms only, in which I have made Some progress. And heard nothing with respect to printing the Laws only that they were in great forwardness, and that Nathl Adams Esqr. had been so obliging as to undertake forming an Index, until Since the middle of Octr. when I received a line from Mr. Smith dated at Boston the 13th. of the Same month by which I was inform'd that he apprehended Mr. Melcher had by that time well nigh finish'd printing the Laws,[2] And wished me to attend to the index—& forms—but observed that he wou'd write me more fully upon the Subject after his arrival at Philadelphia—which prevented my receiving a particular account of the Situation of the business till Just before the present Session of the Court. I wrote Mr. Adams upon the Subject—and procur'd from Mr. Melcher a Set of the Laws as Now printed. Upon examining them I found they Contain'd error, but cou'd not determine to whose acct. those errors ought to be Charged, without comparing the printed Sheets with the Original Acts, And also with the Copies Deliver'd to the printer. This being a work if accurately perform'd that wou'd require, not only much time but great Care and Attention—I therefore Applied to Mr. Adams, and had the Good fortune to persuade him to undertake the business—which arduous employment he has perform'd with great Accuracy—making Notes and observations in the margins of the printed Sheets, from which it may be determined whence the errors arose. I have examined the Several Acts, and Mr. Adams's Notes & Observations with as much Care and Attention, as the Opportunity I have had—wou'd by any means permit—And find that the printed Sheets do not agree either with the Copies, or the Original Acts—And that in Some instances there is a variation, between the Said Copies & the Said Original Acts. And however disagreeable the observation yet truth Obliges me to add that the original Acts in Some few instances have a variance with themselves.

And here Sir you will pardon me in just observing, that after the Committee for revising the Laws, had prepared the bills for the Consideration of the Honbe. Legislature many Alterations were made in those Bills, Some in one house—and Some in the other all which took place amidst a variety of Important Concerns, before they were Enacted, & which the Committee wish may be Considered as having in Some measure interrupted that Chain of Connection which they so anxiously Aim'd at preserving, not only between different parts of the same Act—but through the Whole Code. It is but Just to Observe that to Save the State Expence, the Secretary endeavoured to make many of the draughts of Bills made by the Committee, that had been, altered, & mutilated, Compare with the Acts so as to Answer for Copies, which perhaps ought to be his Apology for any inaccuracy of the Copies—and an indulgence for some of the errors of the press. Many of the variations and errors are quite unimportant—others are of such a Nature as wou'd be little or no injury, to make the Acts conformable to the printed Sheets—while some few Cases will require attention and Amendment—of this however as also of the quality of the paper the Legislature will Judge. I do myself the honr.

to present for the observation of your Excellency and the Honbe Legislature a Set of the printed Sheets of the laws, with the Notes & Observations, to which I have alluded. An Index of the Laws will be Completed Some time on the morrow which I shall do myself the Honr. to forward. But as to the various Forms proposed to be published, it will be impossible to have them Completed with any degree of accuracy this Session, Many Circumstances having Conspired to Embarrass the business. There having been many publications upon the Subject of *forms* &c.—Such as the *abridgment of Burns Justice* and others of the like Complexion that upon examination were found to be ill calculated for any other purpose than to deceive & perplex the Ignorant, and procuring money for the Editor—The Committee were therefore desirous that nothing of that Nature might be published, but what wou'd prove of the Greatest public utility.

And I wou'd take liberty to Suggest, whither it wou'd not be best to have the Laws published Immediately—And that as soon as it can be accomplished with propriety a Small, & Seperate, Book of Forms be Completed & published. With Sentiments of esteem, I have the Honr. to be, your Excelly' most obedt. and very Huml. Servt.   Nath. Peabody

RC (Nh-Ar).

1. The committee that was appointed on 23 Jan. 1790 to revise and arrange state laws and resolves included Jeremiah Smith and John Samuel Sherburne. *NHSP*, 21:730.

2. Nathaniel Adams (1756–1829), a surveyor and civil engineer of Portsmouth, was clerk of the Superior Court from 1787 until his death. He compiled the *Annals of Portsmouth* and Volume I of *New Hampshire Reports*. Bell, *Bench and Bar*, 138–39.

John Melcher (1759–1850), of Portsmouth, had taken over publication of the *New Hampshire Gazette* from Daniel Fowle in 1786 and become the first state printer in 1787. Moore, *Printing*, 510–11.

TO EZRA BARTLETT

Dear Son   Portsmouth, Decembr 16th 1791

Esqr. Page brought me yours that you gave Capt: Eastman and Silsby yours of the 14th[1] with my Socks, am very glad to hear you are all well, as you have taken Mr. Calfe's Security for what Mr. Bartlett owed me. You acted prudently and wish you to let it remain as it is, till my return. I Expected to return the last of this week but find the Court will Set the bigest part of next week, if not the week after. The going is so bad I do not expect to return till the court rises. I am in a comfortable state of health; if there should be Snow and I have a mind for the carriage shall send Stephen home for it. Tell Levi I have spoke with Col. Wentworth about the land in Warren. He says he has been offered 500 dollars for it which I told him he would not get. He offered it to me of his own accord. I Expect to see him again when he says I shall know the lowest he will take. Your brother Josiah was here last week. In haste I am your affectionate father   Josiah Bartlett

Does Lois hold Comfortable or has she had any ill turns since I left home. My love to all your brothers & sisters.

RC (NhHi).
  1. Not found.

FROM JEREMIAH SMITH

Dear Sir   Philadelphia Decr. 24th. 1791

Previous to my leaving New Hampshire I had the honour to receive your letter of the 3d of August[1] enclosing an authenticated Copy of a Memorial of the Legislature of the State to be presented to Congress on the subject of the Assumption.[2]

Your Excellency I apprehend is not unacquainted with my Opinion of the Act assuming the state debts. My sentiments have been uniform that this measure was neither dictated by policy nor warranted by Justice. It was undoubtedly reasonable that the claims of the several States for services & expenditures in the War should be adjusted on principles of equality in order that the delinquent States should be compelled to pay as well as the creditor States entitled to receive the ballances respectively due. The Idea of assuming or which is the same thing paying Ballances before Accounts are adjusted is new in theory & without precedent. It is too uncertain ground to go upon and it would be little less than a miracle if the result of the final settlement of accounts should justify this measure. If the assumption was intended to give relief to the States from the burthen of their debts contracted during the War which is the principle on which many attempt to justify it, It should have gone further and the whole of the State debts of that description should have been assumed. If it was intended only as an advance payment to the States to whom ballances would probably be due on settlements which is the only defensible ground, then the debts of those States only should have been assumed. Congress could not have been influenced by the first of these principles in assuming two hundred thousand Dollars from Delaware for they owed nothing & therefore stood in no need of relief. Nor could they have been governed by the latter principle in assuming this or the sum of two Millions two hundred thousand Dollars from Pennsylvania because it is certain that these will prove debtor States. I have for a long time puzzled my Brain to know upon what principles this measure was founded that I might have it in my power to shew that they were erroneous or that Congress had deviated from them in practice if the principles were good. For it must be apparent that the measure was unequal & unjust. The result of my enquiries has been a Conviction that in this measure they were governed by no principles at all unless those which govern jobbers & sharpers may be denominated such. It has been matter of astonishment with me that there could exist a man so weak as to be duped by the States who pressed this measure when it was apparent that the only thing they aimed at was to obtain relief from their own burthens

& that they cared not at whose expense it might be nor what injustice was done. Having thus troubled your Excellency with my sentiments on this subject and which I believe are such as generally prevailed with the members of the Legislature in framing the memorial referred to you will now permit me to observe that in my Opinion the Idea contained in the Memorial of rescinding the Act assuming the State debt is altogether, inadmissible & the thing wholly impracticable—as the rights of individuals have become involved in the public measures. These must always be held sacred.

As to the Idea of obtaining the assumption of an additional sum for New Hampshire which is the alternative proposed in the memorial it is unquestionably founded in justice. But I have my doubts of the expediency of making an application for that purpose at this time. I am afraid of opening a door thro' which so much mischief has heretofore passed. I fear were it once agreed to admit the Idea of additional assumption that the same selfish principles which led to the sacrifice of the interests of New Hampshire formerly would be found in the present House and I think it at least questionable whether the inequalities in the former assumption of which we have so much reason to complain would be likely to be diminished.

There is certainly a difference in point of praticability between preventing injust measures from being adopted & rectifying them when they are adopted.

I am aware too that those States who would have nothing to hope from an additional Assumption would urge the inexpedience of any measures which should tend to increase the public debt at present exceeding our Revenues. At a time too when from the Transactions in the West Indies & other Circumstances there is a prospect of a dimunition rather than an encrease of Revenue and a certainty that the expences of the Government especially if the military establishment be augmented as seems generally to be expected will be greatly encreased.

The still small voice of Justice will be disregarded when it leads to the encrease of a debt already too heavy.

It is to be expected too that we shall hear from our opponents that the accounts of the several States will be adjusted in a year from July next. We shall undoubtedly be exhorted to wait that event with patience. But I acknowledge there is nothing which affects my mind so forcibly on this occasion as the Consideration I have mentioned—that we shall gain nothing substantial by the application. Massachusetts Rhode Island So. Carolina & many other States are waiting with anxiety to have us move in this business. They have large sums unprovided for.

If any of the Ideas which I have mentioned & many I dare say will occur to you which I have omitted should impress your mine[3] as they do mine you will consider whether it would not be advisable to leave the matter discretionary with the delegation of the State to prefer or retain the Memorial from the Legislature as Circumstances may render expedient. As the Legislature are now in session should they be of this opinion it will be easy to frame a Resolution to that purpose. I am persuaded from the disposition I know your Excellency has to promote the interest & advantage of the state over which you preside that I shall have your forgiveness for so long a letter & that you will attribute it to an ardent desire as far as my Abilities extend to serve the interest of a State to which I feel myself so much obliged.

There is no news from the Westward of importance except that with which your Excellency is by this time well acquainted.

I shall esteem myself happy in giving you the earliest intelligence from that quarter. I am with great Respect your Excellency's most Obedt. & very hble. St.   Jeremiah Smith

RC (NhD). Smith had written also on 12 December. MJB, 2957.

1. Not found.
2. The memorial, criticizing the principle of assumption and arguing that New Hampshire was about to complete payment of its debt, was accepted by the

General Court in mid-June. *NHSP*, 22: 339–41.
3. Perhaps obviously, Smith meant "mind."

TO NEW HAMPSHIRE'S SENATORS IN CONGRESS

Gentlemen   Exeter Jany 12 1792

I have enclosed you a copy of a list of Invalids belonging to this State who have been examined by Doctors Tenney & Parker and who appear to be justly entitled to pensions; Also of four others who have not been examined by said Committee but who on application to the Legislature they think Justly entitled to pensions.[1] The original of said list, I have enclosed to our Representatives, as I suppose it will be first laid before their House. I am to request your assistance with them in carrying the matter into effect. I am with Sentiments of Respect Gentlemen Your Most Obedient & Most Humble Servant.   Josiah Bartlett

RC (Peterborough Historical Society, Peterborough, N.H.).

1. Drs. Samuel Tenney (1748–1816), of Exeter, and William Parker (d. 1796), of Portsmouth, had been appointed in June to examine invalid veterans. The General Court accepted their report on 4 January and instructed JB to forward it to Congress. Putnam, *Medical Society*, 16;

NHSP, 22:299, 475. This list has not been found, but Senators Langdon and Wingate acknowledged receipt of it in theirs of 15 February. A return of invalids dated 28 Nov. 1789 is printed in *NHSP*, 16:344–45.

Beginning at about his time, JB found himself with friends who were also avid correspondents, representing New Hampshire in the U.S. Congress. Letters that the president received from Nicholas Gilman, John Langdon, Jeremiah Smith, and Paine Wingate are often lengthy epistles that give similar accounts, especially when written only a few days apart. Hence as a rule only one of the accounts of a given period or event will be reproduced here. All are in the microfilm edition (MJB) and will be so noted.

FROM PAINE WINGATE

Sir   Philadelphia Jany. 16. 1792

I have the honor of receiving your Excellency's favour of the 2d instant,[1] and thank you for your obliging communication. I intended when
I wrote last[2] to have written to you again in a few days, but having an
opportunity before my letter went away to enclose all the information the
President had to give Congress respecting the late unfortunate defeat of
our Army, I had nothing then further to add. Within a few days past the
President has sent to both houses of Congress another message, which he
observes is in Confidence, containing the report of the Secretary for the
war department, exhibiting a plan for the future military operations. How
far this plan is expected to be made a secret I dont know; but it is of that
nature which in my opinion does not admit of secrecy; but your Excellency will judge of this and make use of my information as you see fit for
the public good. The plan in general is to increase the Continental regular troops better than five thousand men in addition to those already provided for. This increase is estimated at something more than one million
of dollars for the current year. Besides these, as many rangers woods men
and friendly Indians not exceeding one thousand, may be improved as the
President may judge necessary. The pay of the privates to be three dollars
per month & eight dollars bounty. The regulars to be inlisted for three
years unless sooner discharged. It is also suggested that the pay of the officers should be increased but this is not contained in the before estimate.
This is the general purport of the plan so far as I can recollect.[3] The Secretary of War has also reported a great number of letters and other papers
tending to shew the instructions heretofore given to the commanding officers of the late expeditions, the measures taken to accomplish peace with
the indians and the causes of our disasters. Whether they will all justify
the wisdom of our measures I will not undertake to say. That the indians
have been often irritated & injured by savage white men I fully believe
and that it was a very unfortunate calculation to commence offencive operations against them the event has proved, thô I am persuaded the intentions of the directors were pure & upright. What now is advisable to pursue is the great question and I should be in doubt what would be the
result, had I not generally if not always observed that the plans recommended are adopted. This expence our revenue can poorly afford & can,
I believe, never be repaid by the lands we are disputing about. But I am
not willing to express the disagreeable feelings I have when I think on the
subject, and will cease to add any thing further respecting it. We are informed that the British minister, who has lately been received,[4] has full
powers & instructions to adjust all disputes respecting the late treaty of
peace and it is probable that the western posts will be given up to the
united States soon. This it is hoped will have a favourable influence in restoring peace with the Indians unless they are too much elated with their
successes against our Arms to be willing to make peace until they receive
some check to bring them to reflect. The President has nominated a minister plenipotentiary to the courts of London & Paris & a resident minis-

ter to the Hague. These nominations have been consented to by the Senate but not without opposition; especially in relation to the two last the Senate was nearly equally divided. The President has also nominated two ministers with plenipotentary powers to treat with the court of Spain respecting the navigation of the Missippi which it is said Spain wish to come to a good understanding with the United States about.[5] These nominations are not yet agreed to, but it would not be surprising to me to see some persons vote to send ministers to every Court in Europe.

A bill is now in progress in the house of Representatives providing for the relief of invalid pensioners which I believe will be adequate to the wishes of the citizens of New Hampshire. A bill has passed the Senate for establishing a mint. This I fear will cost more than it is worth. Many other matters have taken up the attention of Congress, especially a host of private petioners to satisfy all of whom would be more than our treasury can afford, not to say more than it ought to. I think there is no prospect that Congress will adjourn before April if so soon. There is no suggestion of an additional revenue being called for in this session, but there will probably be some alterations made in the Excise law, which at present is generally complained of & will not be so productive as was estimated. Under all our embarrasments the public credit from some causes or other is rising & some suppose will rise considerably higher. I confess this is a mystery to me but I do not pretend to understand the arts of speculation. It may be possible that Europeans with great capitals may be willing to vest some part of their property in our funds at a rate which will pay them four or five per Cent. & on that account may buy in at the present high price or even higher, but I should suppose that few in this country would be in competition with them. The bank stock is still high & some who are considered as knowing ones, insist upon it that there is good ground to calculate upon eight or nine pr Cent upon the original stock. I think we shall have some bubles in speculations sooner or later. What will be the issue of a Bank in Portsmo. time only can determine. If all the capitals in all the banks opperating in the United States can produce a rate of interest which is expected it must be a heavy tax upon some who pay it. It is true it is creating an Ideal capital so far as the discounts exceed the real capital & thereby enabling men in business to extend their commerce or their speculations to greater lengths. This may be advantagous to some & not to others. I must ask pardon for spinning out a letter with matters of opinion instead of giving congressional intelligence. This kind of intelligence however is better detailed in the newspapers than I am able to give it. I shall only add that I am with the highest sentiments of esteem & respect your Excellencys most obedient and humble Servant

Paine Wingate

RC (NhD).

1. Not found.
2. 12 Dec. 1791 (NhD). MJB, 2959.
3. See Wingate to JB, 13 Feb. 1792, n. 1.
4. The first British minister to the

United States, George Hammond, had arrived in November 1791. Bemis, *Secretaries*, 2:30.
5. These appointments were Thomas

Pinckney to London, Gouverneur Morris to Paris, William Short to The Hague and Madrid, and William Carmichael to Madrid, Short and Carmichael to act as commissioners for a settlement with Spain before Short proceeded to The Hague. Ibid., 21, 44, 291.

FROM JEREMIAH SMITH

Sir   Philadelphia January 18, 1792

By the last Mail I was honoured with your letter of the 2d instant.[1]

A confidential communication has been made by the President of the United States to the House of Representatives relative to the Western Territory—detailing the measures taken by the executive to obtain peace with the Indians previous to the using of military force. The instructions given to those entrusted with the armed force of the union—the measures pursued by them—the causes to which the failures in that department must be attributed, and the measures deemed necessary to be adopted & pursued to retrieve our losses and misfortunes. Without this information one can be hardly capable of forming a just Opinion on this subject. I will not say that it's effect on my mind has been, a Complete justification of the Indian War or of the Conduct of those to whom it has been entrusted; but it satisfies me that *much* of the Censure so liberally bestowed on both men & measures on this occasion is undeserved. Want of Success, tho' generally the consequence of bad management, is not always so. People in general as well as Government, seem to have been in error in their Opinions respecting the lands to the westward. They have been considered as a source of Wealth to the United States and as affording *speedily* the means of extinguishing the public debt. Sufficient regard has not been paid to the just & rightful claims of the Indians to the lands they possess within the Territory ceded to us by the Treaty with Great Britain. Sales have been made of Tracts of land to which I fear we never had any just pretensions. Unjustifiable advantages have been taken in our Treaties & negociations with the natives. These people have certainly a most sensible perception of an injury. Some of the Causes of this Indian War are I fear to be laid at our door. We had no occasion, if we had any right, to meddle with, much less to sell, these western lands. But I am inclined to think the principal cause of the Indian War may justly be attributed to our friends the British. If we held those posts to which we are entitled by Treaty We might live happy (provided we were willing to be guided by justice) with the Indians.[2]

But to whatever causes this War is to be ascribed it will be our Wisdom and policy to get out of it as soon as possible.

When I have it in my power, I shall advertise you of the measures adopted for that purpose. The Aspect of our public affairs is not the most agreeable.

The disturbances in the West Indies will certainly cause a deficiency in our Revenue. It is painful to reflect, that at the same time there seems to be necessity of encreasing the expence of Government. I am sorry to observe that there seems also to be a disposition in some (& they are not a small number) to create offices merely because they have friends to fill them and to annex large Salaries to them. Direct Taxes does not appear equally inexpedient to all of us. I own I am an enemy to this mode of raising money.

The people will not clamour much against Offices & salaries as long as they are not *directly* applied to to pay these Salaries. But a direct Tax will whet the spirit of investigation & enquiry. It will be unequal & therefore burdensome.

If there be any persons from New Hampshire or Massachusetts who are in favour of such a measure—who are for building Cutters—sending fleets to block up the Algerines—for sending Ambassadours abroad at great expence without any probability of correspondent advantage & who are for drawing the money for these purposes from the frugal farmer in a hard and unequal way I must think such persons are not acquainted with the true interests of the people they represent.

I wrote your Excellency some time since on the subject of the public accounts—and which I conclude is by this time come to hand. I can add nothing material—a settlement will unquestionably take place at least a Report of such a settlement will be made in the Opinion of every body.

The act has passed continuing the powers of the Comrs. to July 93.

Virginia & Maryland accounts will not be closed in less than twelve months. I suppose they will receive Vouchers & evidence from us at any time within that period. Unless the Circumstance of one of the Comrs. being an Inhabitant of N. H. should render it unnecessary It would be advisable to have an Agent or some person specially instructed to use the evidence before the Comrs.

I believe your Excellency while conversant with the judicial Courts has not often Observed the parties in suits, tho' trifles only were in Contest, willing to send their papers & witnesses to be read by the Clerk & examined by the Court with out employing Council.

This is surely a matter of great Consequence. But I do not presume to give any Opinion on a subject in which your Excellency will no doubt have the Opinion of the Legislature in the course of the session. I shall from motives of gratitude and affection be always ready to give every information and assistance in my power. I have the Honour to be with the highest Respect your Excellency's Most Obedient & most humble Servant,   Jeremiah Smith

RC (NhD).

1. Not found.
2. For a thoughtful discussion of Anglo-American relations in the Ameri-can West and with the Indians, see Ritcheson, *Aftermath of Revolution,* 159–84.

FROM PAINE WINGATE

Sir   Philadelphia Feb. 13. 1792

I will enclose to your Excellency a News paper containing a sketch of the debates in the house of Representatives on the military bill. This bill passed that house by a majority of about ten members, and is exactly conformable to the plan of the Secretary of War and is said to be approved of by the President. The general purport of it is, to increase the military establishment, by the addition of three regiments of regular troops to the two already provided, with a squadron of horse, and such levies or militia as the President shall think necessary, not exceeding in the whole six thousand men. To which may be added a thousand friendly Indians. The pay of the privates to be four dollars pr month free of deductions & the pay of the officers to be increased, to be equal to their pay at the close of the late war. With this force, the object is, if peace should not otherwise & sooner be obtained, to march into the indian Country & establish a strong post at the miami town with a line of forts between that & our settlements. This plan did not meet the approbation of a number in both houses of Congress, who were ready to think that it would be a gulf to absorb the treasury of the united States and not probably the most expeditious mode of accomplishing the declared object which was peace with the indians. Some were only for a defencive war with a comparitively small force, merely for the protection of the frontiers while further attempts for peace should be made; Others thôt that if an offencive war was judged expedient, it should be carried on by rangers & scouting parties who might suddenly penetrate into the indian Country and make a stroke at their settlements & then retire & thereby discourage them from hostilities & induce them to peace. Under these impressions the bill came before the Senate and to try the sence of the house, a motion was made to strike out that section which provided for the raising three additional regiments of regular troops. This brôt on a debate which employed the Senate three days incessantly before the question was taken. Then it was decided in favour of striking out the section, thirteen to twelve, and the bill was committed in order to render the other parts of it conformable to that amendment. As the Senate was as nearly equally divided as they could be and as those who were for striking out the section were not all agreed in the mode of carrying on the war, it is yet very uncertain what plan will be adopted.[1] It will not be very strange if the ministerial plan should yet succeed.

It seems now to be the general opinion that an additional revenue must be sought for, but what it will be is doubtful & I think it will not be a little puzling to determine upon one that shall meet general approbation. I suppose the Secretary of the treasury will report a plan on that subject. I am told that he says we must either increase our revenue or make new loans & thereby increase our debt, both of which he considers as disagreeable, but the latter he conceives to be the greater evil of the two. I shall be glad if we do not experience both the evils. Our expences are considerably encreasing on many accounts besides that of the Indian war & our revenue, especially from the excise, has by one means or another not been so productive as was estimated. I wish we would make a proper use of our present situation & be induced to more oeconomical Ideas in our expenditures.

I will enclose a report of the Secretary of the treasury respecting the debt of the united States, by which your Excellency will see his Ideas respecting a further assumption. This is a subject which I have not heard much conversation upon and cannot say how it will meet the sence of Congress. Many seem to despair of seeing the accounts of the individual states ever adjusted & therefore they are willing to have the debts of the respective states assumed by the general government, & let that go for an adjustment. This I think would be a very unequal adjustment, however it may operate with respect to the state of New Hampshire. I should be very glad to have your opinion upon that subject. I think New Hampshire have been very injuriously treated in the late assumption and I do not expect an additional assumption will mend the evil. Thô it is proposed by the Secretary that it should not take place until the next session, yet I conclude that he means the matter should be considered & determined upon in the present. I am told by one of the clerks employed in counting the old emission money; that what was funded by N.H. has all been examined & admitted for good & held out in the amount, & a small matter over. Congress I suppose will open the subscriptions for further loans of the debt provided for by the funding system & I wish we might have a further sum to subscribe by receiving some of our outstanding indent taxes, but this is not to be expected to any considerable amount.[2]

The general proceedings of Congress your Excellency will see by the news papers better than I can detail in a letter. We have made slow progress & been pretty much divided on many questions. I please myself with the hope that we shall be able to adjourn by the beginning of April & if we should leave some business unfinished I do not think the public will suffer so much by that as to have the session protracted much longer. I have the honor to be with great respect and esteem your Excellencys most obedient and humble Servant   Paine Wingate

RC (NhD). Enclosures not found.

1. The Uniform Militia Act, passed in April and signed by Washington on 8 May, provided for the organization of all free, able-bodied, white, male citizens between the ages of 18 and 45 in the militia. A significant weakness of the act was its lack of provision for federal retaliation against noncomplying states. See Kohn, *Eagle and Sword*, 133–35.

2. According to the federal Funding Act of 4 Aug. 1790, public creditors to the United States could exchange their loan certificates, Continental paper bills, for new government stocks or bonds–two thirds to be in securities bearing six per cent interest from date of issue, one third to be in securities that would not bear interest until 1801. This was part of Alexander Hamilton's complicated plan to pay both the foreign and domestic debts of the nation and put its economy on a sound basis. Nettels, *Emergence of a National Economy*, 115.

FROM JEREMIAH SMITH

Dear Sir   Philadelphia 24 Feby 1792

On the 7th instant I received the letter which your Excellency did me the Honour to write me the 12 January.[1] The letter to the New Hampshire Representation & papers enclosed are also received. It is unfortu-

nate that these papers had not been sent forward at an earlier period—
As in that case the Invalids of New Hampshire might (as their Case seems plain) have been provided for in the Act passed the begining of this session for the relief of certain Persons therein named.

The particular applications of Invalids from all parts of the union have swelled to so great a number that immedeately upon the passing of the Act I have mentioned a Bill was brought in repealing the Resolution of limitation and making provision for the examination and enrollment of Persons entitled to Pension. This was carried through the House and it is probable will be concurred by the Senate. In Consequence of this, applications from Individuals by way of Petition are discouraged. Unless a Clause can be introduced in Senate allowing examinations already made to be good, Our Invalids will be subjected to the expence of a further examination. For I am strongly enclined to believe that Congress will not pass a special Act for them after having made Provision of a general Nature. If however my Colleagues think there is any probability of Success I am willing to make the application.

I send your Excellency by this days Mail the Report of the Secretary of the Treasury on the subject of a further assumption.[2]

Your Excellency will perceive that according to that Statement (which by the way I think is not accurate as far as respects New Hampshire) the residue of the state debts is estimated at 3,903,362 Doll. In Case this additional assumption should take place the whole sum assumed would be 25,403,362 Dollars. Upon the scale of numbers or taxation the proportion of New Hampshire would be nearly one Million whereas according to the Secretarys Report the sums assumed from New Hampshire in the whole would be only 342,501 Doll. In this second assumption according to that Report N. H. will have only 42,501 Dolls assumed whereas our proportion of the whole sum *now* to be assumed would be 150,000 Doll. nearly! So that it is apparent this second assumption so far from lessening, would greatly encrease the *inequalities* of the *former* assumption. By the Report here with transmitted your Excellency will perceive that Pennsylvania (tho' no doubt she would on just settlement found a debtor State) is receiving the interest of a large sum which she has no debt to cover. Massachusetts South Carolina & Rhode Island press the assumption—if it is agreed to I shall consider it as an omen that the accounts never will be settled.

There will then be so many states whose interest it will be to prevent it—for if the accounts can be settled in one year from next July as the Commissioners state why this haste to assume. You will perceive by the Secretary's report what use is made of the petition from our State. I expected as much—it was presented without the knowledge of Mr. Gilman or myself.

The Bill relative to a military establishment has (*in substance*) passed both Houses—some Trifling amendments are not yet decided on. It contemplates 5000 regular Troops to be raised for 3 years—authorizes the President to raise levies for 9 months in addition—to employ Indians to the number of 1000 & to call out the Militia. The annual expence of this arrangement upon the most rigid oeconomy will exceed a million of Dollars—probably it will greatly exceed that sum. As I have already (in a former letter) troubled your Excellency with my sentiments on this subject I shall forbear to add any thing; besides, I should despair of finding Words sufficiently forcible to express my disapprobation of these measures.

Mr. L——— could have prevented its passage in Senate as I am informed. I write your Excellency with great freedom because I do it with the most perfect Confidence. I shall by this Mail send you the Speeches of *Cornplanter*, the President of the United States &c. at a Conference in this City in the fall 1790. I consider the *Corn-planter's* Speech as an excellent Composition and hope (if you shall not have seen it) that it will agreeably amuse you. Before I quit the subject of Military arrangements I can not help observing that there are men in this quarter who favour the raising of a standing army because they think it will be necessary to carry into execution the laws of the union and truly I believe if these men could have the dictating of the laws to be enacted & measures to be pursued a standing army would be necessary but I persuade myself that your Excellency will concur with me in praying that our Government may speedily come to an end when Obedience to the laws must be enforced by such Means.

It is *proposed* to adjourn 1 Tuesday of April. I will add nothing to this letter already too long but that I have the honour to be with the most perfect Respect your Excellencys most Obt. hble Servant,

Jeremiah Smith

RC (NhD).
1. Not found.
2. Hamilton's report of 23 January, communicated to Congress on 7 February. Syrett, *Papers of Hamilton*, 10:537–56.

FROM NICHOLAS GILMAN

Sir   Philadelphia March 11th 1792

I am honored with your Excellency's favor of the 15th of February.[1] I take the liberty herewith to enclose an Act of Congress making provision for the protection of the frontiers, which past the Senate after a long struggle by the conversion of Mr. Hawkins of North Carolina.[2] I perfectly agree with your Excellency in opinion respecting the management of the Indians and their lands; but in the minds of some men of influence among us there appears to be a restless avidity an eagerness to extend our settlements in that Country with much greater rapidity than strict justice or policy would dictate—and however successful they may be in the end I think the inevitable consequence must be unfavorable to the atlantic States. With this impression I have never been disposed to encourage emigrations to that Country—but as settlements are made under the sanction of a Government which promises protection to all its Citizens it would perhaps be unjust to with-hold it on this occasion—but the mode of doing it is such as could never meet the approbation of my mind though supported by the proudest names. I do not think the occasion calls for five thousand standing troops with all the apparatus—parade & expence of a regular army. I hope however that the Presidents Characteristic prudence will direct to such measures as will tend to abate the honest apprehensions of many of the best friends to our Government. I don't know who is most likely to have command of the Army—Governor H. Lee of Virginia—Genl Lincoln—Morgan and others are mentioned.[3] The list of Invalids was sometime since received. I believe Congress will provide for them but I fear they will be subjected to the trouble of an other inspection in consequence of the delay in making application.

An adjournment of Congress on the first tuesday in April is in contemplation but I something dout its taking place so soon. An Act for the regulation of the Militia is gon up to the Senate but if it passes into a law without material alterations it will be as far inferior to our present State System as that is to the best that could possibly be framed—and upon this subject there is such a diversity of opinion in Congress that I am persuaded the States must attend to the subject and make laws for themselves or be intirely without a respectable militia. With the greatest Respect & Esteem I have the honor to be Sir Your Excellency's Obedient and very Humble Servant   Ns: Gilman

RC (NhD).

1. Not found.
2. "An Act for making further and more effectual provision for the protection of the Frontiers of the United States" was approved on 5 Mar. 1792. *Annals*, 3: 1343–46.
Benjamin Hawkins (1754–1816) represented North Carolina in the Continental Congress, 1781–1784, 1786, and 1787, and in the U.S. Senate, 1789–1795.
3. Henry "Light-Horse Harry" Lee

(1756–1818) was governor of Virginia from 1792 to 1795; Benjamin Lincoln was at this time collector of the port of Boston; and Daniel Morgan (1736–1802) was a businessman in western Pennsylvania. Morgan was to command the Virginia militia during the Whisky Rebellion in 1794. Higginbotham, *Daniel Morgan.*
Washington chose Anthony Wayne for the command. Kohn, *Eagle and Sword,* 125.

FROM JEREMIAH SMITH

Sir   Philadelphia March 23d. 1792

I received your Excellency's favour of the 16th. of February[1] a few days ago. The subject of additional Assumption has been called up—but little as yet has been said. I have no doubt but that it will pass & that it will be injurious to New Hampshire. Of *the evidences of State* debt which will be admitted at the loan office in payment of subscriptions I am confident we cannot have as much as our *just proportion* of the sum now to be assumed. Therefore we as a Constituent part of the United States will be loaded with a heavier burthen than that of which we shall be exonerated or as Genl Peabody once expressed himself relative to the first assumption on a Gentlemans observing that we ought to acquiesce in it as it freed us from the burthen of 300,000 Dollars, "Yes, he replied,

Your arguments are just like congratulating a man on a divorce from a young Wife & marriage to an old Hag"—but I have already written you on this subject fully. I am informed that the letters which I had the honour of writing you in December relative to assumption & accounts gave offence to some persons. I am very sorry for it. I certainly intended none because I do not recollect that I had any Idea at the time I wrote them that they would be seen by any Person but yourself & such persons as you might think proper to communicate them to. The subject of them was of a public nature and I do not remember that they contained any expressions which I would not avow in any place and before any Persons. I flatter myself that it appeared *so* to you else you would not have communicated them to the Legislature. I shall be always desirous of writing your Excellency with freedom relative to every measure that concerns the State I have the honour to represent and shall receive with great pleasure your sentiments and when your Excellency thinks proper to communicate any of my letters I am persuaded it will be such only if there are any such as will do me no dishonour & the State no disservice. There might perhaps be an impropriety in my addressing letters to the Legislature—it might be deemed officious as they are peculiarly represented here by another body. But I cannot help thinking that it is my duty to attend to the business for which I came—to possess my self of every information from my Constituents & that it is *my* duty to inform & *their* right to know how I act upon all occasions. And I cannot help giving it as my opinion in Confidence to your Excellency that those whose business it is more immediately to represent the Legislature are negligent in not corresponding with them. If they should have no communication with each other I think there is danger that the former should *forget* his dependance on the latter.

But I have already trespassed too much. I shall only add that Mr. Gilman & myself were opposed to presenting the memorial of the state & that we with Mr. L. had early agreed not to do so—but Mr. L. afterwards without consulting any body offered it. I shall make no comment on this as you are well acquainted with the *judge.*

The Representation Bill has this moment passed the two Houses—it apportions 120 members among the several States.[2] It has met with great opposition—and is considered as involving northern & southern interests. It is said by the Virginians that the President will not sign it. It gives New Hampshire 5 Members. The House will be too numerous—but I think the apportionment will be more equal than upon any other plan of representation which in the Course of this lengthy discussion has been proposed. This has been a long Session—and little business has been done—except speechifying of which we have had enough can be called business. The dispute about the Georgia election has cost the public 10,000 Dollars.[3] This is not a cheap Government. I agree with you in thinking many of its best friends begin to wax cold. I am not so sanguine with respect to its duration as I used to be. The funding & banking systems & the consequent Speculations gives great uneasiness to our Brethren at the southward who are not much interested in the funds. Stock jobbing & speculating Patriots do not bode well to the Government. I fear the public will withdraw their Confidence—Our Governmt. can proceed but a little way with out it. Duer the famous Speculator at New York has lately failed and I understand for a very large sum. It is altogether likely that many innocent people will suffer by him.

I enclose you the Secy Treasury on the Ways & means.[4] I presume an adjournment will not take place before the last of April. I am with the most perfect Respect & esteem your Excellency's most obt humble servant,   Jeremiah Smith

RC (NhD).

1. Not found.
2. The Apportionment Act, approved on 14 April, allotted four Representatives to New Hampshire. *Annals*, 3:1359.
3. James Jackson contested the reelection of Anthony Wayne as a representative from Georgia. The House heard the case from 13 to 21 March, when it declared Wayne's seat vacant and sent the resolution to the governor of Georgia.

Annals, 3:457–79.
4. Enclosure not with document. Hamilton made several reports to Congress during the spring, the one referred to here being probably that relative to raising additional revenues for the approaching year, written on 16 March, delivered the next day. Syrett, *Papers of Hamilton*, 11: 139–49.

FROM JOHN LANGDON

Sr   Philadelphia March 24th. 1792

I am honor'd with your favor of the 5th Inst.[1] by post, and observe what you Remark Touching a further assumption. My mind is fully impressed, with the Importance of the Business, and as I never suffer Myself to be absent from Senate, while a Single Question is Agitated, particular attention shall be paid to this. I feel every Attachment and Desire, that a greatful heart can possess, to Serve my State, and Contribute to it's Happiness. I often enjoy great Satisfaction, in hearing our little State spoke of in the most Respectable Terms. Indeed we deserve it, as no State in the Union according to it's Abilities, has made greater exertions.

The Settlement of the National Accounts with the Respective States, is a most perplexed peice of Business, to enter into all the particulars relative to the Subject, would far exceed the limits of a letter; Some States haveing done their duty in the most economical way, others in the most extravigant; Some Accounts well Arranged, and Vouched, others not, (and I am sorry to say that even my own State are in some measure Deficient). It will therefore be extreamly dificult to strike the ballances with any degree of Justice, and it will be full as dificult to Collect those Ballances when Struck. It would seem we have our Choice of two evils; of course we ought to take the least. This must be determined upon, when we have the further Assumption under Consideration.

In this great and extensive Confederacy, we must view Things upon a large Scale, for the good of the Union and at the same time, and of Course the good of the particular States.

The Representation Bill, has at length passed both Houses of Congress, after much debate, tho' I could have wished the number of Representatives, in the whole, had been less, yet seeing that it could not be avoided; our State has been fortunate in obtaining, five members,[2] which is to be our future Representation. You'll observe that the proportion, was made (one for every thirty thousand Inhabitants) on the Aggregate Number; in all the States.

We have also been able, as you'll see by the post office Bill, to establish a post from the Seaport, thro' the Center of the State, to Connecticut River, to meet the post from New London and Hartford in the State of Connecticut, by Winsor in Vermont, at Hanover, which I hope will meet the approbation of the State. I shall be happy in Receiving your Communications from time to time, and in paying all due attention to the Same. I have the honor to be your Excellencys Most Obt. Sert.

John Langdon

RC (NhD).
　1. Not found.
　2. Both Smith and Langdon announced that New Hampshire would have five Representatives whereas in fact she received only four, in accordance with the act. See J. Smith to JB, 23 March, n. 2.

FROM JEREMY BELKNAP

Sir　　　　　　　　　　　　　　　　　　Boston, 17 May 1792

Having completed the History of New Hampshire I expect in a few days to send Copies of the 2d & 3d Volumes elegantly bound to my Correspondent Jeremiah Libbey of Portsmo.[1] to be by him forwarded to Dover for the purpose of presenting them to the Senate & House: & having now an Opportunity by our friend Mr. Wingate I take the Liberty of enclosing to your Excellency a memorial to the Genl Court which I beg the favor of you to introduce to them at their next Session.[2] I trust the reasonableness & advantage of the request will be sufficiently apparent, and if the proposal should meet with attention I shall be ready to contract with any persons whom the Court may appoint for the delivery of such a number of the Books as they may choose to take. To facilitate the business I shall give full power to Mr. Libbey to contract in my name, unless the Gentlemen should wish to converse with me in person, in which Case I will on the shortest notice go to Dover or such other place as they may appoint.

I have been informed that when the grant of £50 was in contemplation it was supposed by some Gentlemen that the advantage of it would result to the *printers & booksellers* & not to me. Perhaps the same thing may be repeated on this Occasion. In this Case I beg your Excellency would do me the Justice to suggest that as to the Printers, Paper makers & Bookbinders, they have stated prices for their work & their bills must be paid; thus I am responsible to them for what they have done & may here after do, and that what helps me to discharge my necessary obligations to them is an advantage to them & to me. But with respect to *Booksellers*, the Case is simply this—One Bookseller in this Town has generously offered to sell as many as he can for me *gratis*. Three others have each about 1 dozen sets which they have bought of me at the usual wholesale price, & perhaps one or two more may take about as many; but they are all under engagements to me not to sell them under my stated retail price; so that in fact it is proper to consider me as the Vendor of my own work & as the only Person with whom any Contract for any number of copies exceeding 1 dozen can be made; and if any advantage is made by selling a Quantity it will accrue to me & not to any other Person or Persons, whatever. I ask your Excellency's pardon for this short intrusion on your time & beg leave to subscribe Yr Excy's most obedient humble servt.   Jeremy Belknap

RC (NhD).

1. Jeremiah Libbey (1748–1824), the postmaster in Portsmouth, was a friend of

Belknap. Libby, *Libby Family*, 62.

2. Enclosure not found.

FROM JEREMY BELKNAP

Sir   Boston June 1 1792

I had the honour of writing to you about a fortnight ago by Mr. Wingate & of enclosing a Memorial to the Gen. Court of N. Hampshire. I now beg leave to withdraw that memorial & ask the favour of you to introduce one which I now enclose, but not without your Excellency shall upon inquiry & observation judge that there is at least a probability that it will meet with a favourable reception—for it would be very mortifying to me to meet with a disappointment.[1]

The volumes which I intend to present to the Court are bound as nearly as possible like the first which I presented in 1785. I shall send them to Portsmouth next Week to the Care of Mr. Libbey. I am Sir yr most respectful & obedient Servt.   Jere Belknap

RC (NhD). Noted with address: "hond by Revd Dr. Hemmenway." The enclosure (NhD) notes that Belknap is sending copies of his second and third volumes to the Senate and House and proposes that the legislature, "at the public expense, purchase as many sets of the said History as will supply each Town in the State, & each of the public Offices with *one*." The enclosure is also dated 1 June 1792.

1. Sometime in June JB sent the memorial to the legislature under cover of the following note: "I have lately received the enclosed letter and Memorial from the Revd Mr. Belknap and now lay them before you for your consideration *& direction what answer I am to give him on the Subject*. The cultivation of Knowledge in general more especially the knowledge & history of our own Country & State in this Infancy of its National Character, is undoubtedly an object worthy the Attention of an enlightned Legislature. You will please to make such order on the Subject of the Memorial as you shall think best that I may as soon as conveniently may be inform Mr. Belknap of the result." (Nh).

There is no evidence that the legislature acted on this.

The U.S. Congress had adjourned on 8 May until November, hence JB's correspondence with those delegates had ceased for the time being. In the general election of March, JB had again won the presidency of the state against virtually no opposition, garnering 8,092 of the total 8,389 votes cast. He convened the Council on 6 June at Dover, where the General Court had determined to meet. This session lasted until 22 June. Very little significant legislation was passed, most of the twenty-six enactments being answers to petitions from individuals, towns, or specific groups. One act was passed directing the mode of balloting for and appointing of New Hampshire's electors for president and vice president of the United States, and another directing the method of electing members to the U.S. House of Representatives. Laws of N.H., 6:7–51. Nothing was done about the militia until the next session.

TO THE GENERAL COURT

Council Chamber
June 9th 1792
Gentlemen of the Honourable Senate and Gentlemen of the
Honourable House of Representatives

Among the public papers that I have received Since the last Session of the Legislature (which the Secretary will lay before you) you will please to take particular notice of "an act of Congress Relative to the Election of the President and Vice President of the United States" also of "an act apportioning Representatives among the Several States according to the first enumeration" both of which I beg leave to recommend to your early attention, as Laws for carrying Said acts into Execution so far as relates to this State will (I conceive) be proper to be passed during the present Session: I would also request your particular attention to an act of Congress intituled "an act more effectually to provide for the national Defence by establishing an Uniform Militia throughout the United States."

I have nothing *Special* further to recommend to your consideration at this time, if anything further should occur During the Session that will require your attention I shall not fail to communicate it to you by Separate Message. The General affairs of the State and any matters that were left unfinished at the close of the last Session will be before you, and you will take up such of the Business as you may think proper to be acted upon during the present Session.

The busy Season of the year coming on, will no doubt make you desirous to finish the Session and return to oversee your own particular affairs as soon as it can be done consistant with the public interest. And I shall make it my particular care to facilitate the public Business to the utmost of my power consistant with the good of the Community.

Josiah Bartlett

RC (PHC: The Charles Roberts Autograph Letters Collection).

FROM THE GENERAL COURT

May it please your Excellency—   [12 June 1792]

The Senate & House of Representatives beg leave cordially, to congratulate your Excellency, on your re-appointment, by the unanimous suffrages of the citizens, to the first Majestracy of New Hampshire; and to return their thanks for your message, pointing out the objects, which demand the attention of the Legislature the present Session.

The united voice of your fellow Citizens which has again proclaimed your Excellency the chief Magestrate of this State—while it demonstrates their most implicit confidence in your integrity and abilities, must we conceive afford you all that satisfaction which can result from the combined affection and esteem of an enlightened and virtuous people.

The two Houses have received the public papers mentioned in your Excellency's Message & perfectly agree with you that it is necessary to make immediate provision for a compliance with the several acts of Congress by you enumerated.

We shall assiduously attend to the general affairs of the State—particularly such as were before the late General Court and left incomplete—relying in the mean time on your Excellency to make such communications as you may judge worthy our deliberation. As the season of the year requires that we soon return to our private concerns it is our desire and shall be our highest object to give all dispatch to the business before us compatible with the good of the public: And in this we are confident we shall have your Excellency's most chearful concurrence.

State of New Hampshire

In the house of Representatives June 12th. 1792.

The foregoing answer to his Excellency's Message having been read and considered, unanimously voted, That the same be received & accepted.

Sent up for concurrence.

Jno. Saml. Sherburne Speaker.[1]

In Senate the same day read and unanimously Concurred.

Joseph Pearson Secy

FC (Nh-Ar).

1. John Samuel Sherburne (1757–1830) of Portsmouth had been chosen speaker of the House on 6 June. He later served in the U.S. Congress and as a federal district court judge for New Hampshire. Bartlett, "Portsmouth Families."

FROM JOHN TAYLOR GILMAN

Sir   Dover June 14th. 1792

Inclosed is a Report Respecting the Vouchers of the accounts of this State against the United States, which is respectfully submitted to your Excellency and the Honorable the Legislature, by Your Excellency's, and their Honors most Obedient Servant   J T. Gilman

RC (NhHi). Enclosures not with letter.

FROM EZRA BARTLETT AND LEVI BARTLETT

Hond. Father   Kingston, June the 17th 1792

I hereby transmit a letter to you which was handed me from Mr. Thayer. I read the contents & found it a duplicate to the one you had already received from Mr. Belknap & conceived it unnecessary to send it you by an express. Mr. Patten came here the other day with a kinsman of his a Mr. Willis Patten from Amesbury who is a Blaksmith & works in edge tools, he came to examine the situation &c. &c. of your Sweat house & Shop &c.[1] I went over & shewed him the House & Land & told him the price (30£)—he said that he woud come up again as soon as he knew that you was at home & I think it probable that he will give you that price for it—he like the situation & conveniences very well.

We have finished weeding & shall send to Stratham now soon. The Corn, Grain & fruits of the Earth look well & flourishing & your domestic affairs go on in harmony & peace.

We heard by Levi that you had taken a cold the first night that you lodged at Dover, hope that you have got better of it & have enjoyed a good state of health since. Your family are well Lois is as well as when you left Kingston. We expected you some at Kingston on Saturday but heared by Mr. Silsby that the Court expected to rise some time in this week.

If you have not a sufficiency of Cash we can transmit you some by Stephen if you shou'd think proper to send him or by any other conveyance you shall think proper. I am Your ever Dutiful & Affectionate Son
E Bartlett

The Officers of this Regiment are desirous of having this Company of Light Horse meet with them to Celebrate the 4th of July. Capt: Webster & Lt. Morril expect an invitation or Orders from the Prest. before they can make their necessary Arrangements.[2] If you sho'd think proper to give Orders accordingly I will communicate them to the Officers. I have the honor to be Sir your Dutyfull Son   L Bartlett

RC (NhHi).

1. William Patten (1749–1824) a wheelwright, opened a carriage shop in Kingston. His kinsman was Willis Patten (1770–1825), of Amesbury, Mass. The "Sweat house" was a house and shop rented from JB before 1780 by Samuel Sweat, a joiner. Baldwin, *Patten Genealogy*, 91, 138; Lacy, "Sweat Diary," 227, 230.

2. Probably Jacob Webster (see Mary Bartlett to JB, 20 July 1776, n. 3) and Nathaniel Morrill (1762–1844), of Kingston, who had served in the Revolution and were in the 7th regiment of militia. Smith, *Morrill Kindred*, 2:65–66; NHSP, 12:346–50.

TO NATHANIEL PEABODY

Sir   Kingstown July 3d 1792

I Expect a Company or two of the Militia with Capt. Youngs[1] company of Artillery &c. to meet on the plain in this Town tomorrow in the afternoon, and as you informed me that there is some damaged powder belonging to the public with or near you which will answer for exercising the artillery &c. I desire you to give order that Twenty five or thirty pounds of it may be delivered to the bearer who is sent by Capt: Young for that purpose. I should be happy to see you here tomorrow to Join in shewing some respect to the 4th of July and overseeing Capt. Websters troop of Light horse who I Expect will attend, if you can make it convenient. And am your most obedient servant   Josiah Bartlett

RC (PHi). Docketed on reverse: "July 3d 1792 Recd. of Nathl Peabody fifty pounds of gun Powder to deliver to the Presidents order. John Young."

1. There were a number of men named John Young who were of prominence in New Hampshire at this time. The editor has been unable to determine the identity of this one.

TO WILLIAM WILLIAMS

Dear Sir   Kingstown July 16th 1792

I received your favor of the 12th of March last with the enclosed Copies of your letters to Mr. Wendell, sometime the fore part of april last, and must beg your Excuse for not answering it sooner. The reason was, that I at that time was pretty much engaged in public business and beside I knew not well what to write you. I was very sensible of your friendship to Mr. W: and that it would be disagreable to you, to hear any thing to his disadvantage and I conceived that my conduct in your affair, and the hints I gave you in some of my letters, was as much as was proper for me to write on so delicate a Subject: But as I have Just now received yours of the 15th of June last,[1] wherein you wish me to be more Explicit; I will now inform you in Confidence, that from my knowledge of the man, I never had any Expectation of your recovering the money but by Coertion, and that all the trouble you take in writing to him in your benevolent and friendly manner, will be of no avail to you in procuring the money; I Suppose that it will be proper for you to determine in your own mind which is best for you, to relinquish the demand and think no more of it, or to try to recover it by Law; and you, and you only are [illegible] that point: perhaps I am mistaken and that if you were to inform him that unless the money was paid by a day which you may Set, that you would positively and without fail then put it into the Law, it is possible it might have some effect.

As to his circumstances for making payment I know nothing about it; I believe he has considerable property in lands now in his hands, and when he can by fair Speeches no longer ward off the payment of his debts he has hitherto made out to discharge them by payment.

As to an attorney in this State if you should think proper to employ one, I should reccommend the Honble Oliver Peabody of Exeter who is Judge of Probate for this County and a practising attorney in our Courts of Law, upon whose candor, integrity and fairness of mind, I think you may Safely rely.

The original letter with the receipt upon it is now in my hands upon which your affair with Mr. Wendell is founded, to be delivered as you may direct, and if you Suppose that I Esteem any little matters that I have done for you in the affair, a Trouble, you are quite mistaken, as it gives me pleasure to do any thing that will serve a Friend; however this affair of Mr. W's I think ought to be brought to a close one way or the other;

I can but admire at your Candor, Patience, forbearance & Benevolence in this affair. These are undoubtedly GODlike virtues. But, Sir, may not even those be carried to Excess and lay the persons possessed of them open to the impositions of wicked & designing men. You will please to Excuse my freedom and Believe me to be your sincere Friend & very Humble Servant   Josiah Bartlett

RC (CtHi). Note in JB's hand with address: "To be forwarded by the Stage that passes from Boston to Providence."
    1. Not found.

FROM JEREMIAH LIBBEY   Post Office Portsmouth
Sir   July 25th: 1792
    I rec'd your Excellencys favour of the 16th. Instant.[1] The Post Master General came to this Town on Thursday the 12th Instant and went away again the next day—as soon as I had oppertunity I mentioned to him Silsbys rout, and shew'd him your Excellencys Letter, and requested his determination. He answered the design of the Post was for the benefit of the State and the rout that would best answer the design ought to be attended to. The next day I again ask'd him if he had determined the rout. He said he wished your Excellency could be accomodated, but the General design of the Post must be considered. I mention'd particularly the reversing the rout agreable to your Excellencys recommendation. The Objection was that the Act said from Portsmouth to Concord and it would not be proper to make such a circuit in going, but on the return, if it would be beneficial to a number of the Inhabitants, and the time allow'd would permit it was well to do it.
    The design of this post I conceive is for the convenience of the Inhabitants of the State in general, and the more persons it accomodates the better it answers the end design'd and as Expedition is not of equal consequence with convenience, in making the Contract the consideration was, what rout could be perform'd for a given sum that would serve the largest number of Inhabitants (and as I mention'd to your Excellency in my last) I enquired of Persons that I supposed knew better than I did, what Towns were the most Inhabited &c. and what rout would be most beneficial. Your Excellency may be assured, I had no design in making the enquiry except to serve the State as I never was in either of the Towns above Exeter thro which Silsby goes to Concord.
    But Sir as the Public papers addressed to you as Chief Magistrate ought to be forwarded as soon as may be, I have agreed with Silsby, that as often as there are any such he shall on taking them, either from this Office or Exeter, Immediately deliver them or cause them to be deliverd at your House unless when the General Court are in session in that case they will be forwarded to you at Court per first Conveyance.
    I hope that this method will meet your Excellencys approbation, as it is the desire of the Post Master General that this post should be made as useful to the State as it can be, and that the public dispatches should

be forwarded with all convenient speed. I am with much respect Your Excellencys most Obedient and very Huml. Servant   Jeremiah Libbey

RC (NhD).
 1. Not found.

TO JOSIAH & EZRA BARTLETT

My dear Children   Kingstown October 18th 1792

I hope this will find you as comfortable as you Expected and have according to your desire Sent your horses that you may return home as Soon as you find your Selves able & well cleansed from the infection. I wish for your return as Soon as may be, but would by no means have you hazard your health by returning before you are able or before you are well cleansed so as not to expose others to the infection, that you may not be in too great haste for want of money I have Sent you ten dollars more by the bearer; I think it would not be advisable (even tho you should feel comfortable) to attempt to come through in a day as fatiguing or taking cold while you remain weak may expose your future healths as will too hasty a return to a full & free diet. I and my family & connexions are as well as usual. Mr. Wingate was at my house on Monday last & Spent the bigest part of the day, Says his family & Mrs. Bartlett[1] are well that it has been a very healthy time Since Josiah left Stratham, that he would have had very little to have done in the medical way had he been at home; Mr. Wingate intends to Set off Monday or tuesday next for Philadelphia. The bearer of this is Mr. Gilman who is in partnership with Dr. Tenny who goes to be inoculated.[2] Mr. Wingates Son is going to College and takes Josiah horse. From your affectionate Father   Josiah Bartlett

RC (NhHi). Addressed to Brookline.
 1. Sarah Wingate (1769–1808), second daughter of Paine and Eunice (Pickering) Wingate, had married JB's second son, Josiah, on 3 June 1792. Wingate, *Paine Wingate*, 2:535.

 2. Dr. Samuel Tenney had married Tabitha Gilman in 1788. It is not certain with which Gilman he was in partnership. Tenney, *Family*, 86–87.

FROM TIMOTHY WALKER AND EDWARD ST. LOE LIVERMORE[1]

Sir   Exeter Novr. 8 1792

We have the Honor to transmit to Your Excellency the revised Constitution of the State of New Hampshire, as enrolled on parchment by order of the Convention. We are with every sentiment of esteem Your Excellencies most obt Servants.

Timo. Walker ⎫
Edwd. S. Livermore ⎬ Comtee of the Convention
                   ⎭

RC (Nh-Ar). Written and signed for both by Livermore.
 1. Edward St. Loe Livermore (1762–1832), son of Samuel Livermore, was a lawyer in New Hampshire and Massa-chusetts. He attended the constitutional convention in 1791, served as solicitor of Rockingham County, 1791–1793, as U.S.

District Attorney, 1794–1797, and as a justice on the N.H. Superior Court, 1797–1799. After moving to Massachusetts he

was elected to the U.S. Congress in 1807 and 1809.

FROM PAINE WINGATE

Sir   Philadelphia Nov. 8. 1792

I have now the pleasure to inform your Excellency that I have brôt on safe, without any expence to the State, the New Hampshire vouchers and delivered them to the commissioners, who informed me that they were not too late but should be attended to. I was also informed that there was a good prospect that the accounts of the united States would soon be adjusted, altho' a full settlement could not be reported until after the first of March next, on account of the subscribing the state debt, the amount of which is to be charged to the respective States previously to the balances being struck.

We had two thirds of the Senators convened, on the first day of our meeting and a quorum of the other house.[1] The vice president has not yet arrived, and as Colo. Lee has resignd his seat on account of his ill health we had occasion of choosing a president of the Senate pro tempore when Mr. Langdon was elected. On the first vote Mr. Izard had eight & Mr. Langdon four votes and the rest of the votes were divided. Mr. Izard then disired that he might not be chosen as he should in that case decline, and as Mr. Langdon had one more vote than any other, he was on the next vote chosen. For the honor of the state he had my vote & perhaps from the same motive he was induced to accept the office. It is supposed that in some of the Southern states there will be an attempt to choose a new vice president, but it does not seem to be fixed who will be the most promising candidate to succeed. I believe that Mr. Adams will be as good a man as any other who may be chosen, & rather think that he will be reelected.

Our Indian affairs appear by the Presidents speech to wear an unfavourable aspect, but by an express received last evening from the westward we have agreeable information from Genl. Putnam that he has concluded a peace with some of the Western tribes and it is hoped that he will soon accomplish peace with others.[2] I am not able to recite any further particulars, as the news hath but just arrived. It is said that the Indians have been instigated & assisted in their hostilities by the Spaniards at the South & by others at the British posts westward but this may be conjecture. We have no late European news and I have nothing remarkable to communcate from this place. What Congressional information there is will appear in the news papers which I shall enclose. I have the honour to be with particular esteem and respect your Excellencys most obedient and humble Servant   Paine Wingate

RC (NhD).

1. This session, the second of the Second Congress, convened on 5 Nov. 1792 and continued until 2 Mar. 1793.

2. Washington's fourth annual address to Congress, delivered on 6 November, opened with an account of continuing

Indian hostilities on the frontier. The hope for a peaceful conclusion proved to be illusive for some time. *WGW*, 32: 205–12; Kohn, *Eagle and Sword*, 146–53.

TO NATHANIEL PEABODY

Dear Sir   Kingstown November 20th 1792

In answer to yours of this date[1] I cannot think there is a propriety in a Minister or Majestrate marrying persons without publication as the law has laid a penalty for so doing and I think it always best to Steer as near to the law as can be.

I have no doubt that a Marriage under the circumstances you mention would be a legal Marriage & binding on the parties. If from any peculiarity of circumstances it should be thought advisable for persons to marry without publication I Suppose the person Solemnizing the Marriage would take Sufficient caution against a prosecution from the persons authorised to prosecute. In haste from your friend &c. &c.

Josiah Bartlett

RC (NhHi). Addressed to "Genl N: Peabody."
    1. Not found.

FROM JEREMIAH SMITH

Sir   Philadelphia 20 Nov. 1792

I had the honor to receive your Excellency's letter of the 5th instant[1] by the last mail.

I shall not hesitate to acknowledge that your Communication gave me much pleasure.

I must be insensible indeed if I were not impressed with the most lively sentiments of Gratitude for this distinguished mark of public Confidence. I attribute the general suffrage with which I have been honored at the late election to a favourable Opinion entertained by the public of my *fidelity* & *assiduity* in their service & not to any high idea of my experience & talents. Under this impression I have the greatest Confidence that my fellow Citizens will never be disappointed in me.

Your Excellency will permit me to express my Gratitude for your personal friendship which has been as serviceable to me as it has been flattering & to assure you that I shall studiously endeavour to merit the Continuance of it.

It is now a fortnight since the session commenced & yet we can scarcely be said to have entered upon Business. By the Communications from the War Department there seems to be a prospect that the Southern Indians will remain peaceable tho' they have been on the eve of Hostilities: And a faint hope that a peace may be obtained with the Tribes now at War with us.

It would seem that every measure has been adopted by the Executive towards effecting a general pacification with the hostile Indians; & in the event of the failure of a peace (so much to be desired) of prosecuting the War with Vigour the next Campaign. I ascribe much of this to the Opposition of the minority of the House the last Session & to the Clamour of the people against this War. They have had a good effect.

At present except as to Indian Affairs every thing wears a favourable Aspect and I pray God that our prospects may continue to brighten & that we may employ all the means we possess (& no nation ever possessed more) to make our Country respectable & happy. I have the Honor to be with the most perfect esteem your Excellency's Obedt. humble Servant   Jeremiah Smith

RC (NhD).
  1. Not found.

TO THE GENERAL COURT

Council Chamber in Exeter
November 21st 1792[1]

Gentlemen of the Senate and Gentlemen of the House of Representatives

The business that more immediately requires the attention of the Legislature is, The Arrangement of the Militia and making the Laws of this State conformable to the Law of the General Government for regulating the Militia;[2] The returns that I have called for agreably to your directions, have not as yet been fully made, when compleated I shall lay them before you.

I beg leave to Suggest for your consideration whither it will not be proper at this Session, to make the necessary arrangements for introducing in to Practice those alterations in our State Constitution which have been made by the late Convention and adopted by the People.

Altho the general revision of the Laws of the State and the Several regulations that have taken place, has rendered the Situation of our public affairs more eligible than they have been in years past, yet, I conceive, that in your deliberations, you will find many regulations in the internal Police of the State, that would Still further contribute to the advantage and prosperity of the people we represent. Among the things that I apprehend would tend to that important purpose, I beg leave to mention, the opening and keeping in repair convenient roads and Bridges so as to make the transportation of articles through the State and to the public markets as convenient and easy as possible: This, I conceive, will tend to promote industry in agriculture, Trade and manufactures, which (Joined with proper Oeconomy) is the only true and genuine Source of wealth & opulence in any Country; Perhaps giving encouragement to the opening of water communications by Canals in some parts of the State might more effectually facilitate the Transportation of many Articles especially those of the heavier and more bulky kind; but whither any thing of this kind will be feasible & proper I Submit to your determination.

Every regulation that will have a tendancy to diffuse knowledge and information, and to encourage virtue, morality & patriotism among the people, especially among the Youth and rising generation, cannot fail of being abundantly useful and beneficial to the State, as it is a maxim well established "That no Republic can be lasting and happy unless accompanied with Knowledge and public virtue in the People at large."

This being the Season of the year when the general and ordinary business of the State is usually taken up and acted upon by the Legislature, I shall cheerfully attend to any other matters that you may think proper to be done at this time; and shall use my best endeavors to forward the public business with as much despatch as is consistent with that care & caution which ought to be used in transacting business of so much importance.   Josiah Bartlett

RC (NhHi).

1. The General Court met in regular session at Exeter from 21 November to 28 December. This message was sent down on 22 November with Secretary Joseph Pearson. *NHSP*, 22:638–39.

2. The condition of New Hampshire's militia at this time was noticed by the French vice-consul at Portsmouth, Jean Joseph Toscan (1752–1805), in a report on New Hampshire for the year 1792, dated 18 May 1793 and addressed to Genet, the French minister to the United States. "For six years the New Hampshire militia had been performing almost as well as the best disciplined and most drilled regular troops. At that time [1786–1787], General Sullivan, as governor of the State, was in charge. With his military mind as much as with his conviction that the safety of a Republic depends on a well organized and well disciplined militia, he had neglected nothing to inspire in them his way of thinking, and that had been all the easier for him as most of the troops still remembered very well the distinguished role they had played in the memorable Revolution which separated the United States from England. Things have changed a lot since New Hampshire has had as governor Dr. Bartlett, a man of law, elderly, not very active, a good republican and sensible, but with neither inclination or knowledge in military affairs. As a result, general reviews are rare, captains don't even have any purpose in assembling their companies other than to escape paying the fine which the law imposes. It must be said however that this lack of enthusiasm, this nonchalance is only temporary, and that the holy ardor which freedom inspires would awaken at the slightest danger to the Country." (NhHi: Toscan Papers.) Special appreciation is extended to Mr. John A. Archer for bringing Toscan's report to the editor's attention and for translating it from the French.

TO NICHOLAS GILMAN

Sir   Exeter December 5th 1792

This I Expect will be handed to you by my youngest Son Ezra Bartlett who being desirous of Seeing the Country especially the City of Philadelphia has undertaken to carry on the votes of the Electors of this State for President and vice President of the United States. He will likely tarry in the City a few days and any assistance or civilities afforded him will be gratefully acknowledged. You have I Expect been informed that you, Col. Smith & Col. J. S. Sherburne were appointd Representatives at the first election and Mr. Wingate at the Second: Certificates of your appointment are now sent on.

The votes of the Electors in this State were all for the president & vice President now in office.[1] From your friend and humble Servant

Josiah Bartlett

RC (NNPM).
   1. See the Certificate of Electors, 23 Nov. 1792. MJB, 3129.

FROM PAINE WINGATE

Sir   Philada. Dec. 12. 1792

I have received your Excellency's favours of the 5th. and 26th. ultimo,[1] and thank you for the early intelligence you have given me respecting the elections in New Hamshire, which came to hand before any other information of the elections had been received here. So far as my election implys the good will and confidence of the people at large in the State toward me, it gives me satisfaction and demands my gratitude; but I think I should not have been uneasy or mortifyed at being left out of the appointment, as I begin to feel, by my attendence here, the want of that health which I enjoyed in a more active life and cannot partake of that domestic ease and satisfaction which I believe I am fonder of than most are who come here. I hope however that I may in some measure be useful to the public and to my family by my acceptance, which will be objects of my pursuit and endeavor; and I shall be happy if in addition to these I should have the approbation of my fellow-citizens so far as it respects my public conduct.

Much has been said in the news-papers upon the Election of a vice president. The lot is now cast, and from the accounts received it is supposd beyond doubt that Mr. Adams is chosen. He has all the votes in Connecticut, New Jersey & Delaware In Maryland eight; being all who attended, and in Pennsylvania all but one, tho' it is said that some of the electors were not present & their votes of course not given. This day Mr. John Taylor of Virginia took his seat in the Senate in room of Colo. Lee who resigned. I hear that a Mr. Potts of Maryland is chosen a senator in the room of Charles Carroll resigned. Govr. Johnston of North Carolina & Mr. Bassett of Delaware decline being candidates for the next election.[2] No state has yet chosen the old member for the senate in the next congress, but three or four States have not yet made their choice. At any rate there will be about one third of the Senate new members at the next session. I will enclose some papers which I presume will be agreeable to you to peruse. The Secretarys estimate for the appropriations of the ensuing year I was obliged to enclose separately on account of its size as no franked letter may exceed two ounces in weight. The secretary of the treasurys plan for additional revenue to reduce the public debt &c. I have heard little said about. It appears to me an intricate business & I believe will undergo considerable alterations if any part of it should be carryed into effect. It is not a pleasing business to contemplate additional revenues, especially in any shape of a direct tax. I hope one good consequence will follow from the present embarrasments for further revenue, that is, that it will compel to better oeconomy in our expenditures; Tho' I despair of ever seeing it to my mind. Our Indian affairs are yet very expencive & I fear will continue to be so to a considerable degree, tho' there is some prospect that a treaty with the hostile indians may be brot about next spring. The communications upon that subject do not wear the best aspect while it gives some hope of success. Disagreeable intelligence has lately been received from Georgia of a party there of Whites killing several friendly indians. If some method cannot be devised of preventing such savage practices of the frontier people it is impossible that peace with the indians can long be preserved. Very little business has yet been compleated in congress. Several bills are now in progress and I conclude that the session will end on or before the third of March next. No news from France for the ten weeks past. I think it likely the session of the genl Court in N.H. will terminate before this will come to hand. I had like to have forgoton to mention the commissioners for settlement of the accounts of the union. They have lately reported that they expect to compleat their business by the first of July next. So far as I can conjecture the balances for or against any State will not be very great. I will thank you for any Communications you shall be pleased to make to me and am with particular esteem and friendship your Excellency's most obedient and humble Servant   Paine Wingate

RC (NhD).

1. Neither found.

2. Richard Potts (1753–1808) was elected to fill the seat of Charles Carroll of Carrollton in the U.S. Senate. Samuel Johnston (1733–1816) and Richard Bassett (1745–1815) left the Senate when their terms expired in March 1793.

FROM EZRA BARTLETT

Hond. Father   Philadelphia Decr. 19th. 1792

Dr. Gale & myself arrived here last evening without any misfortune occuring on our way except the carriage breaking down once or twice, without any injury to us. I have seen Mr. Wingate who has been very kind to us & have delivered the Packet to the vice President & have drawn my pay; (105 Dollars). The votes from Newhampshire have secured the Election of vice-President to Mr. Adams. We board at a Mrs. Smith's with Mr. Woodbury Langdon. Expect set out for Newhampshire on Monday next, but shall make some little delay on the road. Expect to inclose this in a letter to you from Mr. Wingate who with me am to dine with the vice President this day 3 oClock. I am Hond Sir Your ever dutiful Son   Ezra Bartlett

RC (NhD).

FROM PAINE WINGATE

Sir   Philada. Decr. 20. 1792

I have received your Excellency's favour of the 5th Instant[1] by your

Son, with the certificate of my appointment to Congress. I thank you for the early intelligence given me on this, as well as on former occasions. When your Son arrived here on the 18th instant in the morning we had not received any information respecting the votes in N.H. for President & vice president, & what rendered the intelligence more particularly pleasing was, that a unanimous vote in N.H. for Mr. Adams, just gave him the turning vote in favour of his Election, so that he is already elected by the several States we had then heard from. Vermont has not yet made a return; All the other States eastward of Virginia have been unanimous for Genl. Washington & Mr. Adams, excepting that the Electors of N.Y. voted for Govr. Clinton and one of the Electors of Pennsylvania, who was particularly connected with the N.Y. politicks. It is not unlikely that Mr. Adams will have some votes at the Southward tho' we have not yet heard beyond Virginia. I waited on Mr. Adams with your Son and he politely invited him to dinner the next day which he accepted. He has also got his account passed at the treasury & received his pay for coming on, so that he tarries here now only from motives of curiosity, for the sake of seeing the city for a few days. He has appeared here, I think, to advantage both in his deportment and dress and will do himself honor in the discharge of his trust. I am very glad he had this opportunity of visiting Philada & wish him a safe return. I shall enclose a letter from him in which it is likely you will have further information which you would wish for. Nothing remarkable has occurred here since my last. A motion has been pretty strenuously urged in the house of Representatives to authorise the President to commence offencive opperations against any hostile Indian tribes as he should judge expedient; but this was negatived by a majority of the house; and there is a pretty general aversion to an Indian war.

There continues a general Complaint of the Scarcity of money among the commercial Gentlemen; the Banks have either refused discounting or done it to a very small amount, & this is assigned as a reason for the Stocks falling very much. I am told that 6 pr Cents have been sold below par, tho' the newspaper represents them at 20—3s on the pound. It is supposed that the Stocks will rise again in a little time & that it is not for want of confidence in the public credit, they are low. I shall only add further that I have the honor to be with great esteem & friendship your Excellency's most obedient & humble Servant   Paine Wingate

RC (NhD).
   1. Not found.

TO DOCTOR JOSIAH BARTLETT, STRATHAM
Dear Son   Monday February 18th 1793
   This is to inform you that your Brother Levi Bartletts wife, died yesterday morning about two o'Clock and is to be buried tomorrow afternoon.[1] Should be glad you would attend the funerall if circumstances will admit. Yours &c. &c.   Josiah Bartlett

Please to call at Exeter & get two pair of mens & two pair of womens black shoebuckles & two pair of black knee buckles and take the appollo Boston newspaper at the post office at Exeter and bring with you.

P.S. A Sermon is to be preached at the house at one oclock.

RC (Mr. S. Bartlett Howard, San Mateo, Calif., 1975).

1. Levi had married Sarah Hook (d. 1793) on 6 Nov. 1791. She left a son, who died in infancy. In 1807 Levi married Abigail Stevens. Bartlett, *Genealogical*, 57.

FROM HENRY KNOX

Sir,   War Department, 23d. May 1793

I am directed by the President of the United States to address your Excellency on the following Subject. A case has lately occurred in this vicinity which required the interposition of the general Government; and as similar cases may arise in other places, it is necessary that some uniform adequate and prompt remedy shou'd be provided and operate throughout the United States.

An armed vessel of one of the powers engaged in the present war captured a Ship of another, lying in the Bay of Deleware and consequently under the protection of the United States. Both duty and honor required that the Government should cause the captured vessel to be restored, which the Minister residing here of the power whose vessel committed the aggression, has very readily undertaken to have done.[1]

But as this remedy may not be adapted to every case and especially to distant ones, some other is to be resorted to of more universal application.

The capture of vessels being generally the consequence of an attack in combat and that by an armed and foreign force is in its nature, if committed within our territory a military aggression and to be repressed by the military force of the Nation.

The standing power of the Union is its Militia, and this is everywhere at hand to correct every violation of the National protection. To your Excelency therefore as the head of the Militia of the State of New Hampshire the president of the United States confides the charge of interposing in all cases of hostility committed between the belligerent parties within the protection of your State; desiring that you would be pleased with the aid of your Militia, to detain the parties first aggressing, until you could communicate the case to the President, with the evidences in writing which may establish the facts for his ultimate decision thereon. This you may be assured of receiveing with all the dispatch circumstances may admit. I have the honour to be With great respect Your Excellency's Most obet hum. servant.

H Knox
Secy of War

RC (Nh-Ar). Marked "(Duplicate)." Written in a clerk's hand; signed by Knox.

1. The French frigate that had brought minister Edmond C. Genet to the United States had seized the British ship *Grange* in Delaware Bay. British minister George Hammond's protest led to quick restitution of the *Grange*. France had declared war on Great Britain on 1 Feb. 1793. Bemis, *Secretaries*, 2:61, 79.

In the general election of 1793 JB was again a candidate for governor. He ran into more competition than in the two previous years, but garnered 7,388 of the 9,854 votes cast. His opponents were John Langdon of Portsmouth (1,306 votes), John Taylor Gilman of Exeter (708), and Timothy Walker of Concord (382). Other candidates shared a scattering of 70 votes.

TO THE GENERAL COURT

Council Chamber in Concord
June the 8th 1793

Fellow Citizens of the Senate and of the House of Representatives

In the present Situation of our Public Affairs I have not many things of importance to reccommend to your consideration at this Time. The Settlement of the Treasurers accounts and the common and usual business of the State at this Season of the year will naturally come before you, and to them I make no doubt you will give proper attention.

I have directed the Secretary to lay before you the acts and Laws of the United States passed at their last Session, among which there is an Act "for regulating foreign coins" &c. which is to take effect after the first day of next month, and as some of the said Coins are valued somewhat different from what they are set at by an act of this State passed the 12th of February 1785 entituled "an act ascertaining the rates at which coined Silver & gold & English half pence & farthings may pass within this State" I would beg leave to reccommend it to your consideration whither some inconveniencies may not arise if the aforesaid Law of this State is not altered or Repealed.[1]

The ascertaining the amount of the debts due from this State making provision and pointing out the mode for discharging them, is I conceive a matter that will require the attention of the Legislature; whither it can with propriety be attended to at this Session is submitted to your determination.

The mode pointed out by a Law of this State for the appointment of Special Judges of the Superior Court of Judicature and for the Several Courts of common pleas in this State, has been Thought by many people not to be the most eligible method of appointing them. I would beg leave to request your attention to that matter.[2]

And, Gentlemen, if there are any other matters which from your acquaintance with public affairs and the general circumstances of the State, you may think proper to be acted upon at this time, I shall pay all proper attention to them, and all Acts and Resolves that you may think proper to pass, that will further conduce to the happiness & Prosperity of our Fellow Citizens will meet with my ready and Chearfull Assent.

Josiah Bartlett

RC (CtY).

1. Within two weeks the legislature enacted a repeal of all previous laws relating to coined silver and gold except that of 1 Sept. 1781, which allowed such coin to be used in payment of debts. *Laws of N.H.*, 6:109.

2. Possibly in response to this, the legislature acted to invest the governor "with all the rights and powers respecting issues of money, appointment of Officers, or any other matter or thing whatsoever, which were vested in, or committed to the president, or president and Council under the former Constitution, by virtue of any Laws, resolves or votes heretofore passed not otherwise provided for in and by the Constitution now in force." *Laws of N.H.*, 6:122–23.

TO THE NEW HAMPSHIRE MEDICAL SOCIETY

Concord June 19th 1793

Gentlemen of the Newhampshire Med. Society

The unexpected adress of thanks presented me by your Committee,[1] for the small Services I have been able to afford the Medical Society, I consider as an instance of the polite attention and regard they mean to pay to such persons as may in any manner endeavor to promote the public happiness.

I have long wished that the Practice of Medicine in this State (upon which the lives & health of our fellow Citizens depend) might be put under better regulations than it has been in times past and have reason to hope that the incorporation of the Newhampshire Medical Society (if properly attended to by the Fellows) will produce effects greatly beneficial to the community by encouraging Genius & learning in the Medical Science and discoraging ignorant & bold pretenders from practizing an Art of which they have no knowledge. That the members of the Society may be usefull to themselves & the public and enjoy the Exalted pleasure & satisfaction that arises from a consciousness that they have contributed to the health & happiness, not only of their respective Patients, but by communicating to others the knowledge & cure of disseases, to the general happiness of the human race, is the ardent wish of Gentlemen your very humble servt. Josiah Bartlett

TR (Mr. and Mrs. Rodney M. Wilson, Kingston, N.H., 1975). Docketed: "Copy Per L. Bartlett R. Secy."

1. JB had been president of the Medical Society since its incorporation in February 1791 (see M JB, 2770). No written document of thanks has been found.

:

FROM ALEXANDER HAMILTON

Treasury Department

Sir

November 13th 1793

The Commissioners for settling the accounts between the United States and the Individual States having made their final report to the President, dated the 29th of June 1793—I am to announce to Your Excellency, that a Balance of Seventy five thousand and fifty five Dollars has been reported by the said Commissioners *in favour* of the State of New Hampshire. I have the honor to be with respect Your Excellency's most obedient Servant

Alexander Hamilton
Secretary of the Treasy

RC (PPAmP).

FROM PAINE WINGATE

Sir   Philadelphia Dec. 6. 1793

I have taken the earliest opportunity of transmitting to your Excellency sundry Papers which I think will be gratifying to you to peruse. I have not been in this place long enough to be furnished with any political information of consequence to communicate to you.[1] By the Presidents Speech an additional revenue is supposed to be necessary in the present session of Congress.[2] What source it can arise from I have not heard suggested, nor to what amount will be requisite is yet intimated. If it should be wanted only to pay the Interest on the balances due to the creditor States as stated by the commissioner's Report, perhaps this necessity might be obviated by quoting the States according to the Census and allowing each State to pay its quota by an offset of so much of their balance or by transferring funded debt where they are Debtor States, or if they can do neither of these, then by paying their quota in Specie.[3] By this mean so much of the public debt might be extinguished which would be, I think, a desirable object.

I should be much obliged to you for your sentiments as to the kind of tax which in your opinion would be most expedient for the union in general & the State of New Hampshire in particular if a further tax should be indispensable. I shall be happy in receiving your communications on this subject and on any other matter of public or private concern. I inteded to have waited on you before I left New Hampshire to have conversed on some matters, but was prevented by a multiplicity of business which I was obliged to attend to, and which I hope will be deemed a sufficient apology. The sickness which has proved so fatal in this city seems to be pretty well gone at present, and unless something further alarming should happen of that kind, I conclude that Congress will continue their session here. We have had an uncommon fall of snow a few days since. I should judge by the appearance in the streets that there could not be less than a foot depth upon a level, but this day it is melting away again. I shall be obliged to put my enclosures under two covers, because I am not authorised by law to frank a letter exceeding two ounces in weight. With the most sincere sentiments of esteem and respect I am your Excellencys most obedient and humble Servant   Paine Wingate

RC (NhD).

1. Wingate had returned to Philadelphia for the first session of the Third Congress, 2 Dec. 1793 to 9 June 1794.

2. Wingate was referring to Washington's fifth annual address to Congress delivered on 3 December, part of which

advised that "The productiveness of the public revenues hitherto, has continued to equal the anticipations which were formed of it; but it is not expected to prove commensurate with all the objects, which have been suggested. Some auxiliary provisions will therefore, it is presumed, be requisite; and it is hoped that these may be made, consistently with a due regard to the convenience of our Citizens, who cannot but be sensible of the true wisdom of encountering a small present addition to their contributions, to obviate a future accumulation of burthens." WGW, 33:168–69.

3. On a separate sheet Wingate listed the creditor and debtor states according to the commissioners' report (MJB, 3336):

Creditor States	Dollars
New Hampshire	75,055
Massachusetts	1,248,801
Rhode Island	299,611
Connecticut	619,121
New Jersey	49,030
South Carolina	1,205,978
Georgia	19,988
Amount	3,517,584
Debtor States	Dollars
New York	2,074,846
Pennsylvania	76,709
Delaware	612,428
Maryland	151,640
Virginia	100,879
North Carolina	501,082
Amount	3,517,584

TO THE GENERAL COURT

Council Chamber
Exeter December 25th 1793

Gentlemen of the Senate and Gentlemen of the House of Representatives

Since your last Session, I have received Several official letters from the Secretary of War relative to the treatment of prizes and some other vessels, (provided they should come into the harbor in this State) which I take the liberty to lay before you for your information,[1] as it appears to me to be of importance in this delicate Situation of affairs, That the State Ligislatures should be made acquainted with the Steps taken by the Supreme Executive of the united States, to observe a strict neutrality (as far as is consistant with Treaties) between the European powers now at war, and thereby prevent giving any just ground for these States being drawn into the calamities of a war with any of them: However distinct the Federal & State Jurisdictions may appear to be, it is, in my opinion, of the greatest consequence to the stability and happiness of a government constituted like ours, that the people in general and the State Legislatures in particular, should have a proper Confidence in the propriety & rectitude of the measures adopted by the general Government, in all those important affairs in which the whole Union are deeply interested; This would prevent any very bad effects from the foreign politicks which have of late been so industriously circulated through the States.

At the request of Lieut Governor Adams of Massachusetts,[2] I now lay before you his letter inclosing a Resolve of that Legislature, in which they propose that an alteration be made in the Federal Constitution, so far, as that a State may not be compelled by a Citizen of another State to appear before the Supreme Judicial Court of the United States and answer as a Defendant in a Suit brought by him against it.

Alterations in the Federal Constitution, as it affects not only this State but all the States in the union, and may be attended with considerable effects on the General Government, will require, and I doubt not receive, your cool and deliberate attention, and whatever may be your determination on the Subject, you will no doubt observe with pleasure that the fifth Article of that Constitution has provided a Safe and easy mode of making such alterations and amendments as shall, by time and experience, be found necessary.

Since your last Session I have been requested by the Collector of the customs at Portsmouth to have the barracks at Fort William & Mary (now the property of the United States) cleared of the military Stores belonging to this State, in consequence of which I directed the Commissary General to remove and return me an inventory of them. By his letters & return to me, which will be laid before you,[3] you will see the Situation they are in and where deposited.

I would now request your attention to that matter and such further directions about them as you shall think proper.

I would beg leave to reccommend it to your consideration whither it will not be advisable at this Session to make some further provision and point out a proper mode for calling in and discharging as fast as conveniently may be, the public debts of the State, the interest of which is yearly accumulating, and as we have received official information that the Commisioners for Settling the accounts between the United and individual States, have reported to Congress a Ballance in favor of this State, of Seventy five Thousand and fifty five dollars, that sum it is to be hoped will afford us some assistance in discharging the State debts.

The present Law for the appointment of special Judges for the Several courts in this State, is attended with much inconveniency and is thought by many people not to be well calculated that purpose. Permitt me to reccommend that matter to your consideration.

As we have too often accounts of melancholy accidents taking place on days of public muster of the Militia, frequently owing to the carelessness of some, The intoxication of others, and the unhappy custom of loose and desultory firings at such times; Permit me to reccommend it to your consideration whither an additional law for regulating the Militia on muster days, might not be made, that would tend to prevent those unhappy accidents.

The examination of the inventories and such other matters as were put over for consideration to this Session will of course come before you and meet your attention, and I am happy to observe that the attention of the Legislators for sometime past to the affairs of the State and my acquaintance with the general Knowledge and disposition of the present Legislature to serve the true interests of their constituents, will make it unnecessary for me to be more particular and shall only add that it will afford me pleasure to Cooperate with them in such measures as will tend to promote the further happiness & prosperity of the people whom we represent.   Josiah Bartlett

RC (Robert A. Stein, M.D., Cincinnati, Ohio, 1977).

1. See Henry Knox to JB, 23 May 1793.

2. Samuel Adams (1722–1803), a cousin of John Adams, was lieutenant governor of Massachusetts from 1789 to 1794.

3. The commissary general, Supply Clapp, had complied. See his letter to JB of 31 July 1793 accompanied by the list of articles removed from the fort (Nh-Ar). MJB, 3302.

FROM THE GENERAL COURT

State of New Hampshire } In the House of Representatives

Jany. 2d 1794.

The Committee appointed to draught an Answer to His Excellency's Message Reported the following

Sir

It is with pleasure we receive your Excellency's Communications at the opening of the present Session, and perfectly coincide with you in sentiment, that Independent and distinct as the Federal and State Legislatures may appear, 'tis of great consequence to the stability and happiness of our Government that the People in general & State Legislatures in particular, should have such information of the measures pursued by the general Government in all the important affairs in which the United States are interested, as to enable them to place a proper confidence in their rectitude & propriety, and at all times guard them against foreign influence.

We are happy to find that measures have been taken by the Supreme Executive to preserve a strict neutrality towards the belligerent powers, so far as consistent with treaties. The subjects to which the Governor of Virginia and Lt. Governor of Massachusetts have alluded, touching the Sovereignty of Individual States, will merit our cool & deliberate attention. A further provision for discharging our public debt will be attended to, as an object of great magnitude.

The laws for the appointment of Special Judges for the several Courts in this State—An additional Act for regulating the Militia on Muster days—The examination of the Inventories, & all other matters recommended, are proper for the deliberation of the Legislature at the present Session.

And from the opinion we entertain of your Excellency's integrity and disposition at all times to serve the true interest of the State, we have no doubt of your cheerful co-opperation in all such measures as we shall adopt tending to our happiness & prosperity.

Christor. Toppan for the Committee

which Report having been Read & considered Voted that it be received and accepted.

Sent up for Concurrence

Nathl. Peabody Speaker.

In Senate the same Day Read & Concurred

Nathl. Parker Depy Secy

RC (Nh).

FROM PAINE WINGATE

Sir   Philadelphia Jany 3d 1794

I yesterday received your favour of 20th. ultimo,[1] and am much obliged by the sentiments you have been pleased to communicate. To give your Excellency any information of the present state of our national affairs I hardly know where to begin or what to say. Congress have not yet decided on many questions and those in the house of Representatives are chiefly under the injunction of secrecy. We are not without embarrassments & dangers almost on all sides; but what has made the most painfull and sudden impression on the public mind lately, is the account of a truce made between Portugal & algieres, and that a number of the cruizers of the latter are let loose on our vessels in the Atlantic. I hope that more danger is apprehended than will be realised; but at any rate it will probably subject us to very considerable expence. A treaty is to be purchased, if possible within any tollerable bounds of cost, but this is not the worst in my opinion. It has for some time been the wish of some gentlemen to establish a naval force for the protection of the commerce of the united States. And this occasion, with the present state of the European nations, has afforded an opportunity of urging with some appearance of success, the necessity and expediency of equiping immediately some frigates & other armd vessels in the united States. This measure if gone into will subject us, it is probable, to an expence of more than a million of dollars in the outfit and it will not be strange if it should be nearly that annually, so long as the country shall be able or willing to bear it. This is an evil in my opinion to be avoided; especially as it may have a tendency to draw us into a war under the Idea of protecting the honor of our flag resenting injuries & a thousand other excuses for quarrelling where there is pride & ill humour on the other side to excite to action. I believe the house of Representatives will be nearly equally divided on the question to provide a naval armament, unless the difficulty of finding the ways & means should discourage some from the attempt.

The communications which by the last post I enclosed to you will give you as extensive an Idea of our situation in regard to France & Great Britain as I am able to give. It is expected that the french minister will be recalled; but how far he may gain credit & have influence with the ruling powers in France to injure us in their esteem is uncertain. If the national convention is as mad as their minister it would not be strange if they should declare a war against us; but this does not seem to be apprehended. England has not discovered any very friendly disposition towards us excepting in words, but this does not seem to be the time for us to be very resentful. Spain, it is supposed by some, who are the best knowing of her disposition, is the most likely to come to a rupture with the united States. The Messisippi, & their influence with the southern Indians to be hostile to us, will probably induce the quarrel when ever it shall come.

As to the war with the Western Indians nothing I believe is expected to be accomplished this winter and I think we have very little else to calculate upon, but the continuance of that war with an increasing expence. There can be no doubt but that the success of the late proposed treaty with the Indians was defeated by the influence of Agents in the British interest; but I do not know that it can be charged directly on the British government. The Spanish territory on one side, the British on another both unfriendly & the Indians on the West and the Algerinnes on the Ocean both hostile together with the disturbed state of Europe generally, which more or less affects our commerce, has placed the united States in a very critical and precarious situation. All these combined will perhaps rendor necessary some cautionary provisions for our defence. The increase of our Arsenal stores and some defence of our harbours seems to be thôt indispensable. If to these should be added a Naval equipment, the expence must I think, exceed any resources in the power of the united States, excepting a recourse to credit. But I will not dwell on these disagreeable Ideas any longer. This Country has so often even from its beginning, experienced almost miraculous deliverances, that I will still hope that we shall yet be under the protection & blessing of heaven. I will mention one small circumstance in our favour in the post office department. That department, which by the extension of the post roads was expected to be an expence, has neated to the government in the last year about 24 thousand dollars. And our other revenues taken collectively have equalled hitherto their estimated value.

I have enclosed from time to time sundry newspapers to Dr. Bartlett at Stratham & desired him to forward to you which I hope he has done. We have no late European News. Mr. Jefferson has resigned his office as Secretary of State, I believe principally from a desire of retirement. Mr. Edmund Randolph is appointed in his room.[2]

I shall direct this letter to Exeter supposing that it will find you attending the Generall Court there. I desire my respectful compliments to any of my friends at Court and am with particular esteem and respect your affectionate friend & most humble Servant.   Paine Wingate

P.S. This letter may not be proper to expose to general view as it has relation to some confidential matters, thô I do not know that I have said any thing inconsistent with the injunction of secrecy.

RC (NhHi).
1. Not found.
2. Randolph served as secretary of state

from 2 Jan. 1794 to 19 Aug. 1795.
BDEB, 272.

FROM PAINE WINGATE

Sir   Philadelphia Janr. 28. 1794
I have this day received your Excellency's favour of the 14th Instant[1] and am very glad to find that my first pamphlet is come to hand, and hope that mine of the 18th has also been received containing the correspondence with the British minister. I shall now enclose in a letter accompanying this a continuation of the Presidents communications, which will contain interesting information, this day published. I will also enclose the

report of a committee on the Algerine affair. This subject has produced long debate in the house of Representatives and was carryed in the affirmative by a small majority. I think there is some probability that it will not finally prevail. A negotiation with the Algerines is now in train and there is some hope that a treaty may be effected. Portugall also has discovered more disposition to protect our commerce than was at first expected. Spain may from motives of Interest do the same. On the other hand A Navy if attempted must cost a certain & very great expence & its efficacy after all must be uncertain. The situation of our resources can poorly afford the undertaking. It is not likely that the estimates in the report will be adequate to the expence. The President has already purchased & ordered to be purchased warlike stores to a considerable amount & it seems to be taken for granted that some of our sea ports must be put into a state of defence, this will be an extra expence as much as we can well afford. As to the probability of the united States being drawn into the war, I think it is diminishing. Every body in Congress professedly deprecates it. Mr. Madison's resolutions which I will also enclose have been considered by some as not having a favourable tendency to a tranquil state with great Britain. They have been the subject of debate in the house for ten days and the question is not yet decided. I rather think they will be rejected in a day or two more, as inexepident and unseasonable at the present moment. But it is supposed the house will be very near equally divided. The Nothern members are generally opposed & the Southern generally in favour of them. The news papers will no doubt give you some Idea of the debate in which some severe recriminations are thrown out against great Britain & sentiments favourable to France.[2]

Congress have yet passed but one Act & that of no importance concerning the national flag.[3] When there will be an end of the Session it will be difficult to conjecture. There are hosts of private petitions. If every body who wants his salary increased or compensation allowed should be gratifyed, the treasury of the united States would be insufficient for the purpose. I can only add that I am with sentiments of particular esteem & respect your Excellency's most obedient & humble Servant.

Paine Wingate

RC (NhD). Enclosures not found.

1. Not found.

2. Congressman James Madison had introduced on 3 January seven resolutions designed to offer more favorable terms of trade to nations having commercial treaties with the United States. As friction increased in the spring between the U.S. and Great Britain, other, more stringent resolutions were enacted. *Annals*, 4:155–59.

3. On 13 January an act was approved altering the national flag to include fifteen stripes and fifteen stars. *Annals*, 4: 1417.

TO THE GENERAL COURT

Gentlemen of the Legislature,   Exeter January 29th 1794

After having served the public for a number of years according to the best of my abilities in the various offices to which I have had the honor to be appointed; I think it proper before your adjournment to signify to you, and through you to my fellow citizens at large—That I now find myself so far advanced in life, that it will be expedient for me, at the close of the present year, to retire from the cares and fatigues of public business, to the repose of a private life. With a grateful sense of the repeated marks of trust and confidence that my fellow citizens have reposed in me, and with my best wishes for the future peace and prosperity of the State, I am, Gentlemen, Your Most Obedient, and very Humble Servant.

Josiah Bartlett

Reprinted from *The New Hampshire Gazette* (Portsmouth), 22 February 1794. This letter was received on 7 February according to the Journal of the House, 1790–1794, pp. 649–50 (Nh-Ar).

TO WILLIAM WILLIAMS

Dear Sir   Exeter February 19th 1794

Your letter of the 30th of last month[1] with blank power of attorney I have received and as soon as the Legislature rises, which I hope will be in a few days, I Shall deliver your papers into the hand of the Honble Oliver Peabody of this Town, upon whose honor abilities & integrity you may Safely rely to transact the business agreably to your directions; what Mr. W.'s circumstances are at present I am not able to Say, but I fear it will be more difficult to procure it at this time than it would some years past;[2] It is time those affairs were Setled, as we all are advancing in years; for my part I feel myself so far advanced in life that I have signifed to the Legislature that I shall decline any farther concern in public business at the expiration of the present year.

You are much mistaken if you think that I consider any little Matters that I have or may do for you a burthen, as it will really afford me pleasure provided it will be of any advantage to you.

The affairs of France appear to me to be in a very alarming & critical Situation and their conduct in many things unjustifiable; but as many of the accounts we receive of their conduct come through the hands of their implacable enemies and when I remember the Brittish account of our conduct during the revolution, I am apprehensive that some things are aggrevated, and that they may have better reasons for some of their conduct than at present appears to us and after all I am perswaded that all these affairs are in the hands of a Supreme overruling Being who can and I believe will bring real good out of this apparent Evil. With my best wishes for your happiness I am Sir (in haste) your friend and humble Servant   Josiah Bartlett

RC (CtHi).
1. Not found.
2. The concern was over a debt owed to Williams by John Wendell. See JB to Williams, 21 Mar. 1791.

FROM THE GENERAL COURT

May it please Your Excellency   20 February 1794

The Senate & House of Representatives having received your letter addressed to them, and through them to their fellow Citizens, expressing your desire at the close of the present Year of retiring from the cares and fatigues of public business to the repose of private life, and your grateful sense of the repeated marks of confidence reposed in you by your fellow Citizens—Beg leave to assure your Excellency that we entertain the most grateful sentiments of your many important services equally honourable to yourself and acceptable to us—And in returning you our sincere thanks for your eminent exertions during a long and distressing war, and since the establishment of an honourable peace, we do no more than express the sentiments of our fellow Citizens.

Accept Sir our ardent wishes that you may find in retirement all that felicity which is the result of fidelity & integrity—That your future days may be easy comfortable and happy, as your former have been useful—And that you may finally meet the rewards of your public and private virtues.

FC (Nh-Ar).

TO THE GENERAL COURT   Council Chamber Exeter

Gentlemen of the Legislature   February 22nd 1794

All the acts and Resolves that have been presented to me by your Committe this Session have received my approbation and Signature.

                              Josiah Bartlett

RC (Nh-Ar).

FROM PAINE WINGATE

Sir   Philadelphia Feb. 24. 1794

I have received your Excellency's favour of the 30th ultimo,[1] and thank you for the communication of your sentiments contained therein. It is very true the situation of our Country has been extremely critical and embarrassing and many mortifying abuses have been received from the belligerent powers; but I do not feel so apprehensive of our being drawn into the European quarrels, as I have sometimes been. The recal of Gennet and the arrival of his successor (M. Fauchet who was received by the President last Saturday)[2] affords a pleasing hope that we shall keep on peaceable terms with his nation. It is not yet known what is the temper or character of the new minister; but Gennet's conduct being reprobated by the present ruling power in France, it is assumable that one of different sentiments from him has been sent. France is in a deplorable condition, such as must shock the feelings of humanity to reflect on; but it seems to be the prevailing opinion that they will support themselves against their enemies internal & external and finally settle down into an orderly & free government. And this I believe would be for the interest,

& is the general wish of the Americans; but more than our good wishes and friendly professions it will probably not be expedient for us to afford. Even this may afford umbrage to some of the other nations; but I think cannot be the excuse of a quarrel. There has been no late information made known from our minister at London tho' dayly expected. I cannot but hope that the misunderstand[3] between this country and Great Britain will be amicably adjusted by negotiation. This I do not expect so much from motives of friendship & justice on their part as from interest. How far Spain may be actuated by the like motive of peace is more doubtful; but I have such an aversion to war at all times and especially in our present situation, that I should be disposed to submit to many injuries & abuses that did not manifestly endanger our existence as a nation, rather than appeal to the sword. We have lately had some flattering information that the western hostile Indians are desirous of peace & wish it may prove true. A party of our troops have advanced & taken a post at St. Clair's battle ground, but it is not thôt that it will be practicable for them to advance farther this winter. The proceedings of Congress will generally be better known by the newspapers than I am able to communicate in a single letter. The resolutions on commercial regulations, which I enclosed in my last, after about three weeks debate, were postponed by the advocates of them until March & I believe will go no further. They were thôt by many to be unseasonable & hazardous in their tendency at least. The first proposition was agreed to by a majority of 5, but it was pretty well known that a majority would not agree in the next proposition. The subject of a naval armament has likewise taken up much time of debate in the house of Representatives & was carried by a majority of only two. This subject is yet further to be agitated in the progress of a bill and as the house is so near equally divided it is very much uncertain what will be the issue. Those in favour of the measure urge the necessity of protection of our commerce against the Algerines and those against suppose the mode is inadequate to the purpose and will be attended with certain & permanent & great expence & that the desired protection may be obtained in some more eligable way. To defray the expence of the navy it is proposed to increase the duties on those articles which now pay 7½ pr. Cent to 8 or 8½ pr. Cent & to lay higher duties on certain enumerated articles chiefly on luxuries & those the manufacture of which we would encourage among ourselves. The increased duty on Salt was not agreed to. You will see by the foregoing that Congress are much divided in sentiment and I think there is too much of a party spirit prevailing on most questions. There is a jealousy & animosity often apparent and I am sorry to say in my opinion injudiciously excited, which is not favourable to the well being of government. I suppose such tempers will exist more or less in public bodies & the increase of numbers generally increases this evil.

I am sorry that your bad health & fatigue in public business has induced you (as I hear) to decline serving any longer in your present station, tho I can easily conceive from my own feelings that retirement to private ease & domestic enjoyment is to be coveted after experiencing the toils of public life. I wish your Excellency the enjoyment of health & every domestic happiness & am with the highest sentiments of respect & friendship your Friend & humble Servant   Paine Wingate

P.S. It is said (& I believe by good authority) that Genl Knox has resolved to resign his office at furtherst in April next. The reason I hear assigned is that his salary does not maintain him. Some conjecture that Colo. Pickering will succeed him.

RC (NhD).

1. Not found.

2. Jean Antoine Joseph Fauchet was in the United States as French minister from

February 1794 to July 1795. Bemis, *Secretaries*, 2:105, 184.

3. Misunderstanding.

FROM PAINE WINGATE

Dear Sir   Philada. April 2d. 1794

Since I wrote to your Excellency on the 24th of Feby, the face of our public affairs has been changing frequently; so that it has been difficult to form any fixed opinion what would be expected next. Sometimes, by appearances, war was generally apprehended as almost unavoidable; and then we were again flattered with the hopes of the continuance of peace. At present we have those hopes revived more strongly than they have been for some time past. The destruction of our commerce abroad, especially in the West Indies had filled almost every mind with gloom; and those who had been the immediate sufferers, many of them considering themselves as ruined, were irritated to the highest degree and were impatient that some measure whould be taken by government to prevent at least further spoliation on our commerce, if redress could not be obtained for past injuries. There was such a ferment in the public mind, especially in the commercial Towns, that they seemed ready for any vigorous measures, even should they lead to certain war. During this state of things Congress have laid an Embargo for thirty days which took place on the 26 of March.[1] They have provided for the defence of our principal harbours, and for the increase of our military stores & warlike apparatus. And Bills are ordered to be brôt into the house of Representatives, for raising a regiment of Artilery consisting of 800 men to man the fortifications on our harbours; and to call on the Executives in each state, to organize, arm and have ready on any emergency a select corps of Militia proportioned according to the number of white inhabitants, amounting in the whole to eighty thousand men. And further it is proposed to provide for raising under certain restrictions 25,000 men as Continental troops; but this last measure I hardly think will prevail at present. I consider this parade of continental troops & perhaps of the 80,000 militia as designed more for appearance of readiness for war than from any expectation of using them. There has been another motion which has produced considerable debate, that is the sequestration of all British debts in america, to be held as a pledge for the indemnification of our losses by seizing & condemning our vessels. This motion is postponed at present & is doubtful which way it would be decided if brôt to issue. The late news from London gives hope that G. Britain is not disposed for war with the united States, however they may have abused us; and it is urged that by avoiding on our part any irritating measures, (however Justifiable) we shall be more likely to obtain indemnification of the past injuries & preserve the peace which is of the greatest importance to the prosperity & happiness of this country. It has been very difficult to determine what were the views of great Britain, whether they wished for an open rupture with the United States. Their professions, so far as we have known them by our minister at London have been pacific, & it is not easy to conceive how it can be for their interest to be at war with us. And from the late intelligence, it is believed by most, so far as I can judge, that there is more reason to expect that Gr. Britain is not in earnest for war with us, than we before were ready to suppose. I shall be happy to have this expectation realised, as I consider war in our circumstances the greatest evil that can well befall us. The preparations for defence which have been judged necessary, will involve in considerable expence & there is a committee appointed to report the ways & means. As yet I cannot conjecture what kind of Revenue will be proposed. I have given you very imperfect Ideas of our affairs suggested in great haste & will enclose some newspapers and must beg an apology for my not writing any oftener as I have been at a loss what information to give & have very little leisure to write. It is uncertain when Congress will adjourn; but I think my affairs will require my returning home by the first of May at furthest. I am with particular respect and esteem your Excellency's affectionate friend & most humble Servant   Paine Wingate

RC (DLC: Miscellaneous Manuscripts).
1. The resolution laid "an embargo on all ships or vessels in the ports of the United States, bound to any foreign port or place, for the term of thirty days." *Annals*, 4:531.

TO [SUPPLY CLAPP]

Sir   Kingstown April 9th 1794

I have received a letter from the Secretary at War inclosing the resolve of Congress for fortifying sundry Ports and harbours of the United States[1] and informing me that an Engineer will as soon as possible be appointed and sent to Portsmouth for the purpose of fortifying that harbour &c. &c. and then Says "If the State of Newhampshire is in possession of any good Cannon of and above the Caliber of Eighteen pounds and which could be appropriated to the fortifications within Said State a return of them is requested together with the condition of their Carriages and apparatus in order that their necessary repairs be provided without delay."

I am Sir to request you to make out a return of Cannon &c. agreably to the above request and transmit the same to me as Soon as may be.

Atho I have no authority to dispose of any of the cannon belonging to the State yet it is my opinion that the Legislature will consent to do it as they are to be used for the protection and defence of the State.[2]

Draft (NhD).
1. The act, which specifically included Portsmouth, was approved on 20 Mar. 1794. *Annals*, 4:1423–24.

2. See letter to Henry Knox, 14 Apr. 1794.

TO [HENRY KNOX]   State of Newhampshire
Sir   Kingstown, April 14th 1794

In answer to yours of the 24th of last month,[1] requesting to know, whither the State of Newhampshire is in possession of any good Cannon of and above the caliber of Eighteen pounds and which could be appropriated to the fortifications within the said State would inform you that the Commissary of the State has made a return of one Eighteen pounder, four 24 do and 3—32 do that are good, that the Carriages are so decayed that he does not think them fit to be trusted. Those Cannon at this time are not in use and I believe the Legislature will readily dispose of them to the United States for the purpose of defending the Harbor in this State.

Draft (NhD).
1. Not found.

FROM PAINE WINGATE

Dear Sir   Philadelphia Ap. 23d. 1794

I have to thank your Excellency for your favour of the 22d ultimo,[1] which I had the pleasure of receiving on the next day after I wrote my last to you. We have most of the time since then been in such a state of uncertainty as to political affairs that I hardly knew what to write. I will now in the little time which I can improve for writing this, give you some account of matters, and the enclosed papers must supply the defects of the letter. Congress have almost during the whole session been perplexed and in a considerable degree of ferment, owing to the wars in Europe and the injuries our citizens have Sustained by the belligerent nations, especially by that of great Britain. In the commercial towns the losses have been so great that it is not strange there should be the highest degree of resentment in the breasts of the immediate sufferings, and this fire has been communicated to others. Add to this, the old dispute about the in-execution of the treaty of peace with Great Britain & the injuries we are Sustaining by the Algerines & Indians which are imputed more or less to British influence. And if we further consider a natural sympathy which this Country has for France struggling almost against all Europe in a cause somewhat simalar to what this country has experienced and in which that nation afforded important aid. Under all the foregoing circumstances and many others that might be suggested it is not strange that there is prevailing in this country a bitterness of spirit against G. B. which is not very compatible with a state of neutrality and will render it almost impossible to preserve peace with that country. There are however many cool reflecting persons, sensible how much we may loose by war & how little we can expect to gain by it, are averse to the Idea & wish to preserve peace & endeavour to obtain justice by negotiation. The President has accordingly appointed Mr. Jay an Envoy extraordinary to G. B. who, I believe, if any Man can, will bring our disputes to an amicable adjustment.[2] But this plan of negotiating does not satisfy all the hot-headed ones among us. A measure in the house of Representatives, which I will enclose appears to me to be the dictate of too much passion and very unseasonable at the very moment of appointing a negotiator. This Resolution I cannot believe will eventually become a law. I do not think the President would approve of it if it should be passed in the two houses. And I have heard it suggested that Mr. Jay would not undertake the negotiation embarrassed with that resolution. The newspapers I shall enclose will give the latest European news we have received here. From which it will appear that the French have recovered almost all they had lost during the last campain, and that the combined Armies have suffered heavy losses. However the prospect is that the present year will afford a new scene of distress & horror by increased vigour in prosecuting the war on all sides. Our Situation in this Country is not without embarrasment independent of our controversy with G. B.

The prospect of peace with the Indians has wholly vanished, & but little is expected this year from Genl Wayns opperations.[3] The Southern Indians are likewise very troublesome. You will see by a report of a committee on ways & means what taxes are contemplated, but how they will finally be agreed upon is very doubtful. There is considerable business yet to be done before Congress will probably adjourn; but I have been here longer than I expected & cannot be content to stay more than ten days from this time when I purpose to ask leave of absence & hope to have the pleasure of returning home. I think it likely that I shall pass thro' Haverhill & Shall be able to wait on you on my return and Shall be happy then to give you such further communications as may be in my power. In the mean time I will only add that with Sentiments of particular esteem and respect I am your Excellency's most obedient humble Servant,   Paine Wingate

RC (NhD). Enclosures not found.

1. Not found.

2. John Jay, then chief justice of the U.S. Supreme Court, was commissioned as special envoy to Great Britain on 19 April, sailed on 12 May, and arrived on 8 June. His negotiations ended on 19 November with the signing of the Jay Treaty. Bemis, *Secretaries*, 2:119.

3. Wayne's operations remained quiet during 1794. Kohn, *Eagle and Sword*, 182.

TO RHODA TRUE

Dear Daughter   Kingstown April 28th 1794

I hope this will find you in a comfortable State of health and your conections; By a letter that you wrote to your Sister Lois Sometime past you appeared to be much alarmed by a Spitting of Blood and wished for my advice about it. I have had no opportunity to Send to you Since, and if I had, have so imperfect a knowledge of your particular Situation that I should not be able to give you much advice about it, hope Dr. Bartlett who I understand has seen you gave you the necessary & proper advice.

The raising and Spitting Blood by women under obstructions is often times not attended with much danger unless continued for some time and I am in hopes there is less danger from it than your fears; your Brother Levi is of the same opinion and says he has had several women in that Situation lately, from which no bad consequences has arisen nor to be feared; he wishes me to tell you not to be too much frighted about it as he thinks you are too apt to be; However, tho' I hope you have got over your fears about it as Col. Webster[1] (by whom I send this) informs me that he did not hear but that you were well as usual, yet I shold be glad to hear more directly from you.

Your friends and relations here are as well as usual except Ezra who has had Something of a slow remitting fever for some days which I hope will not last long. You wrote Lois that you did not know but you might come down this Spring. I should be very happy to see you here if your health and other circumstances will allow it, but if your lungs continue weak and there is danger of raising more blood, I should fear that riding on horseback so long a Jorney would Scarcely be advisable, unless great care is taken by making short Stages and not making too much haste.

I wish you to write as soon as you can and inform us of your health; Esqr. Freeman of Hannover is to meet the Council at Exeter the fourteenth of next month perhaps you may find an opportunity to write by him if not before. And am your affectionate Parent.   Josiah Bartlett

RC (Mr. Warren A. Reeder, Hammond, Ind., 1975).
  1. Probably Col. David Webster. See 26 Feb. 1780, n. 1.

TO EZRA BARTLETT

Dear Son   Kingstown Tuesday 22nd July 1794

Your Brother Levi returned here last Sunday Evening and found your Brother Josiah here and he Josiah has agreed to come here next Sunday evening and to Set out on Monday to See your Sister and will probably be there monday evening or tuesday before noon, however you will tarry till after his arival if any thing should happen to prevent his arriving there so soon as is expected.

Remember my Love to Mr. True & his Connections and in a Special manner to your Sister True and let her know that she has my Sincerest love and best wishes and tho the State of my health discourages me at this season of the year from undertaking a jorney to See her yet I shall Spare no cost for doing every thing in my power to contribute to her advantage. By your brothers account I Suspect she is too much Sunk & too low in her Spirits, for by comparing all the Symtoms of her disorder,

I still entertain hopes that there is a good probability that She may recover her former health. At this hot season of the year her being confined to her bed will have a tendancy to keep on her relaxation & weakness; the more her strength will permit her to keep from bed or set up in the bed that the refreshing air may surround her, I think would likely be for her advantage however you will be best able to judge of her Strength & how much she can bear; Remember me to Sally and let her take care of her own health, our family & connections are much in the Same State of health as when you left us. Our haying & havesting goes on pretty well; had a small matter of rain on Sunday but the ground Still very dry and parched. Yours Affectionately   Josiah Bartlett

Wednesday forenoon

I have Sent for your Sister True, Some Cucumbers & pears, the pears hardly ripe and a few ears of the forwardest green corn I have tho hardly fit for use, I hope it will be larger when Josiah Sets off. I shall endeavor to Send Some whortleberris by him. If there is any thing else wanting that I can procure for her send word by Dr. Gale and also how your Sister is. Yours ut Supra   J Bartlett

RC (NhHi). Postscript: RC (Lloyd L. Wells, M.D., Manchester, N.H., 1975).

FROM EZRA BARTLETT   Salisbury Septr Thursday 25th. 1794
Dearly Beloved Father   Thursday 8 oClock eveng

I am exceeding sorry to be under the necessity to inform you that after I wrote you on Sunday[1] Mrs. True continued to grow weaker & weaker every Day since. Yesterday she grew weak very fast & had two small abscesses brake in the lungs & the matter came into her mouth so fast that it almost suffocated her, & at night was very weak indeed. I sat up with her all night with two Women & she rested better than I expected she wou'd, but has not taken any food since night before last. I went to lay down this morning about 7 oClock & was call'd up at 9 oClk by the family who supposed Mrs. True to be dying being very much convulsed —has got better of that turn & at 12 oClock Noon & went up & laid down & slept 1½ hours & was call'd to her since which she has had 3 or 4 spells of being convulsed the Neighbours being here all this afternoon—in those convulsed spells pulsation is scarcely perceptible at the wrist & at other times the heart & Arteries vibrate so fast as almost to leave no distinct pulsation. I think that she can't continue long perhaps she may 24 Hours & may be not half an hour & I wish that a Brother & Sister wou'd come up immediately if they have not already sat out, which I hope they have from what I wrote you on Sunday last by Mr. Garland.

Mrs. True has her senses as well as ever but has not strength sufficient to expectorate the matter that lays rattling in her throat. I have been so stupid as not to think of sending express 'till now & at this time all the young men are all gone about 2 miles off to a raising am Just inform'd that Mr. Jono. Fifields Son will set off immediately with this. I am Your Sorrowful & Afflicted Son   Ezra Bartlett

RC (Mr. and Mrs. Rodney M. Wilson, Kingston, N.H., 1975).
1. Not found.

TO EZRA BARTLETT

Dear Son   Kingstown September 26th 1794

I received on Tuesday last your letter of last Sunday giving a more melancholy account of Mrs. Trues Situation. Sally was desirous of going up but a horse could not be procured, yesterday I got mine from Stratham and Josiah & Sally intended to Sett off in a day or two, But this morning Mr. Fifield arrived with the melancholy account of your Sisters death: We would all wish to shew our respect to your Sisters remains by attending the funeral if possible, Tho no advantage to her will accrue from it. I have sent to notify your Sister Greely and shall send to Josiah to inform him, whither any of them will be able to come to the funeral I cannot Say; I Sincerely Condole with Mr. True on the melancholy occasion and hope it will work for his & our real good. I rather Expect Some of your Brothers or Sisters will be up to the funeral, but think they cannot be there till the forepart of the day of Sunday whither they can come up or not (for it is Something Sickly). I Suppose you will return next week. In haste from your affectionate Parent   Josiah Bartlett

p:s: I have given Mr. Fifield three dollars which with one dollar he says you gave him he is contented with for his Journey down.   J Bartlett

RC (Mr. and Mrs. Rodney M. Wilson, Kingston, N.H., 1975).

The above is the last letter found among JB's correspondence. His extant papers from this time are chiefly receipts, which suggest that he was putting his affairs in order. In February he wrote the will that follows. In his "Memoirs" (NhHi) Levi writes that his father was reading his paper, the Apollo, *at Gilman Gale's tavern in Kingston on the morning of Tuesday, 19 May 1795, when he suffered a paralytic stroke affecting his left side. JB was immediately taken by stage to his house, where Dr. Levi Gale and Dr. Amos Gale, Jr., attended him. During the early afternoon he suffered a second stroke, went into convulsions around sunset, and died early in the evening. He was buried on the 23rd in the cemetery behind the church in Kingston.*

JOSIAH BARTLETT'S WILL   [25 February 1795]

I Josiah Bartlett of Kingstown in the County of Rockingham and State of Newhampshire Esquire, being at this time of a sound mind, Do make & ordain this my last Will and Testament, that is to Say, Firstly I Commit my Soul into the hands of GOD its great and benevolent Author and my body to the Earth to be buried in a decent manner. And as to my worldly Estate I give devise & dispose in the following manner and form viz

first   I give to my beloved Daughter Mary Greeley and to her hiers and assigns forever, the undevided half of about forty acres of land in Kingstown aforesaid commonly known in the family by the name of the Jemson place. I also give her the right of land in the Township of Warren in County of Grafton in Said State that was laid out to the original right of Joseph Blanchard (except the first devision lot which I have before disposed of) I also give her one hundred & fifty dollars of my six per cent Stock in the books of the loan office in Portsmouth the interest of which is now payable, but this last is to be considered to be in full satisfaction for about one hundred dollars of State Security which I had of her to be loaned with my own, and promised to be accountable to her for the same.

2ndly   I Give to my beloved daughter Lois Bartlett and to her hiers and assigns forever, about Thirty acres of land in Kingstown aforesaid at the westerly end of my Young place (so Called) begining at the westerly end of the land I bought of Josiah Judkins and runing & extending Easterly carrying the whole width of my said land till it comes to the ditch or Canal that was lately dug a Cross my land to vent the water from the little Pond into Exeter river. I also give her the undevided one third part of about Twenty acres of land that I bought of Charles Hunton in Kingstown aforesaid called in the family the Hunton Meadow; I also give her the remainder of my six percent Stock now on intrest Books of the loan office aforesaid being about five hundred & [   ] three dollars, I also give her one of my best cows & five Sheep also that she have all the House hold furniture that I bought for her and given her.

3dly   I Give to my beloved son Levi Bartlett and to his hiers and assigns forever the following pieces of land in Kingstown aforesaid viz about two or three acres of land which he has now in his possession being formerly part of my home place, also about Twenty three acres of land that I bought of Mary Gilman by three Several Deeds, commonly called the Merrill place. I also give him fifty acres of land in Said Town which I bought of Jonathan Fifield called in the family the Rockrimmon pasture, he paying such legacies as in this will I shall order him to pay.

4thly   I Give to my beloved Son Josiah Bartlett and to his hiers and assigns forever, Two whole original rights of Land in the Township of Warren aforesaid viz the original rights of Andrew Wiggan and of John Marsh. I also give him the whole of my three pr Cent Stock in the funded debt of the united States in the Loan office at Portsmouth.

5thly   I Give to my beloved son Ezra Bartlett and to his hiers and assigns forever the following lands in Kingstown aforesaid viz the whole of the lands I now own that I bought of Nathan Sweat also the Easterly end of the Young place (so Called) adjoining to it viz begining at the highway at the easterly and runing westerly carrying the whole width of my said land till it comes to the Southwest Corner of land Joseph Calef bought of Daniel Colcord, from thence South westerly to the northwest corner bound of the aforesaid land that I bought of Nathan Sweat. I also give him about forty acres of land laying on the Easterly Side of the highway near the meeting House that I bought of James Prince and his wife. I also give him the undevid two thirds of the before mentioned land that I bought of Charles Hunton. I also give him the undevided one half of the before mentioned Jemson place, he paying the Legacies I shall herein order him to pay. I also give him the whole of my home place not before disposed of, with the building and appurtenances thereto belonging on the Conditions & limitations following viz that my Two daughters Lois Bartlett and Sarah Bartlett shall have, use, and occupy my now dwelling house Barns and other buildings with the privilidges and appurtenances thereto belonging as they may want for their own use and occupancy, not exceeding one third part of each, so long as they or either of them shall live single & unmarried; I also give the said daughters during Said time the use & occupancy of one acre and an half of land at the northeast Corner of said homeplace also one quarter part of the apples &c. growing on the fruit trees in said home place yearly during said time the said land & buildings to be kept fenced & in repair by the said Ezra Bartlett.

6thly   I give to my Beloved Daughter Sarah Bartlett and to her hiers and assigns forever one right of Land in the Township of Warren aforesaid viz all the lands that is laid out to my own original right in said Town: I also Give her the Remainder of my land in the Young place so Called in Kingstown aforesaid viz begining at the ditch or canal at the easterly end of land given to my daughter Lois and extending Easterly carrying the whole width of my said land till it comes to the land I have given to my son Ezra. I also give her fifty dollars to be paid her by my son Ezra within two years after my decease. I also order that the said Sarah Bartlett shall be fitted out with Household furniture equivalent to what I have before given to my other daughters and to have one Cow and four Sheep to be done by my son Ezra Bartlett unless it shall be done by me before my decease.

7thly   I give to my beloved grandchildren Josiah Calef & Miriam Calef children of my daughter Miriam Calef deceased the whole of my deferred Six pr cent Stock in the funded debt of the United States to be equally devided between them. I also give to the said Josiah Calef the whole of the lands I now own in the Township of Wentworth in the County of Grafton aforesaid being the whole of the lands belonging to my own original right in said Town; and to the said Miriam Calef I give one good feather bed & beding in Stead of one I formerly gave to her mother and was returned to me after her decease. I also order that all other household furniture that I had given her mother that was returned to my house and shall remain at my decease be returned to the said Miriam also all her Mothers wearing apparel &c. that shall remain to be delivered to her. I also give her one hundred dollars to be paid her when she shall arive at the age of Eighteen years by my son Levi Bartlett and my will is and I hereby order that if the said Josiah or Miriam should die before they arive at the age of Twenty one years without lawful issue, that the survivor shall be intitled to what I have willed to the deceased.

8th   I give to my beloved grandchild Josiah Bartlett True and to his hiers and assigns forever being the son of my daughter Rhoda deceased, one hundred acres of Land in the Township of Salisbury being the lot No. forty in the first range which I bought of Ebenezer Page viz in Salisbury in the County of Hillsborough & State aforesaid, I also give him one hundred and fifty dollars provided he shall live to the age of Twenty one years to be then paid him, one half by my son Levi Bartlett and the other half by my son Ezra Bartlett.

9thly   I order that all the lands in the Township of Sutton in said State that shall belong to my Estate at my decease shall be equally devided between my two Sons Levi Bartlett and Ezra Bartlett to assist them in paying the aforementioned legacies.

10thly   I order that all the provisions that shall be in my house & Cellar shall be for the use of Such of my Children as shall live in my family at my decease; My wearing aparel I order to be devided among my three Sons, My printed books on law Physick & Surgery I give to my Son Ezra, all my other printed books I order to be equally devided among all my Children that shall be living at my decease; That all my household furniture (Excepting what I have before disposed of and one large Silver table spoon which I give to my grandaughter Miriam Calef) I order to be devided one third to my son Ezra Bartlett and the other two thirds to be equally devided between my three daughters, Mary, Lois, & Sarah.

Item   All the rest and remainder of my Estate not otherways disposed of both real and personal, I give to my son Ezra Bartlett and order him to pay all the Just debts and demands against my Estate and to pay the funeral charges and the cost of Settling my Estate and all legacies & bequests for which no other provision is made and to put up decent gravestones at my Grave.

And lastly I Do hereby Constitute and appoint my Said Son Ezra Bartlett sole Executor to this my last will & Testament hereby revoking all other and former wills by me made and Ratifying and confirming this to be my last will and Testament. In witness whereof I have hereunto Set my hand and Seal This 25th day of February one Thousand Seven hundred and ninety five.

Josiah Bartlett

Signed sealed pronounced
and declared by the Testator
to be his last will and
Testament in presence
of us who Signed as
Witnesses in his presence
Jacob Webster
Thomas Elkins
Benjamin Sanborn
John Brown

Rockingham ss. June 3rd. 1795. This Will was proved in common Form by the oath of Thos. Elkins Benja. Sanborn and therefore approved & allowed By Saml. Tenney, Jud. Prob.

MS (Register of Probate, Rockingham County, Exeter, N.H.).

Calendar of Correspondence Not Printed

[1751]

25 July
From Hannah Kent. RC (Mr. & Mrs. Rodney M. Wilson, Kingston, N. H.). Sends price list of medical supplies. MJB, 21.

1756

18 March
From Daniel Rogers. RC (Mr. & Mrs. Rodney M. Wilson, Kingston, N. H.). Note, with invoice for medical supplies. MJB, 53.

1759

26 April
From Daniel Rogers. RC (Mr. & Mrs. Rodney M. Wilson, Kingston, N. H.). Encloses invoice for medical supplies. MJB, End of Roll 1.

1762

19 May
From Timothy White. RC (Mr. & Mrs. Rodney M. Wilson, Kingston, N. H.). Sends bill for services. MJB, 128.

1763

4 April
From Josiah Gilman. RC (Mr. & Mrs. Rodney M. Wilson, Kingston, N. H.). Note of explanation with medical supplies. MJB, 147.

1764

12 May
From Josiah Gilman. RC (Mr. & Mrs. Rodney M. Wilson, Kingston, N. H.). Note, with mace and cinnamon oil. MJB, 159.

1768

5 December
To Nathaniel Folsom. RC (NhHi). Explains inability to meet with Folsom to referee a legal case. MJB, 281.

1771

4 November
From Micha Hoit and Joshua Plumer. RC (Mr. & Mrs. Rodney M. Wilson, Kingston, N. H.). Agree to continue case. MJB, 416.

1772

4 May
From Nathaniel Peabody. RC (Mr. & Mrs. Rodney M. Wilson, Kingston, N. H.). Encloses a rule of reference. MJB, 441.

2 September
From Abel Davis. RC (Nh). Informs that work ordered by JB is completed. MJB, 461.

1773

18 March From Nathaniel Folsom. RC (Mr. & Mrs. Rodney M. Wilson, Kingston, N. H.). Informs that JB has been appointed by Superior Court to settle several disputes. MJB, 484.

1774

6 June To John Dudley. RC (NhHi). Encloses a legal rule of reference. MJB, 544.

14 September To Overseers of Boston. TR (MHi). Town of Kingston sends 100 sheep to the Boston poor in appreciation of their difficulties. MJB, 553.

16 September From Overseers of Boston. TR (MHi). Expresses thanks for the sheep sent. MJB, 555.

1775

22 February From Isaac Rindge. From facsimile in *Daughters of the American Revolution Magazine*, 51 (September 1927), 672. Notifies that Governor Wentworth has withdrawn JB's commission as justice of the peace. MJB, 586.

26 April From John Collins. RC (Mr. S. Bartlett Howard, San Mateo, Calif.). Informs that Americans have disarmed the British garrison at New York City. MJB, 595.

21 July From Nathaniel Huntoon et al. RC (NhD). Asks JB's intervention with Committee of Safety to get firearms for Unity. MJB, 605.

4 September From John Sullivan. From *Letters by Josiah Bartlett*, 21–25. Urges confirmation of appointment of Alexander Scammell and closer congressional regulation of the army hospital. MJB, 616.

9 September To the N. H. Committee of Safety. RC (Nh-Ar). Sends news of sympathy for America in London. MJB, 686.

7 October To Matthew Thornton. RC (Nh-Ar). Requests account of supplies and census, and suggests strengthening provincial defenses. MJB, 696.

11 October To Mary Bartlett. RC (NhHi). Notes his recovery from smallpox inoculation. MJB, 697.

[12 October] From William Whipple. *Letter not found.* Referred to in a letter from Timothy Walker, Jr. to Whipple, 15 Oct. 1775, RC (Nh-Ar): "Your Letter to Coll Bartlett will be forwarded tomorrow morning by the Post."

6 November To Mary Bartlett. RC (NhHi). Expreses hope to return home soon. MJB, 705.

11 November From John Langdon. RC (PHi). Instructs JB to disperse $15,000 of Continental money to New Hampshire. MJB, 707.

21 November The N. H. Committee of Safety to JB and John Langdon. Draft (Nh-Ar). Requests grant from Congress to cover military expenses. MJB, 713.

27 November	To Mary Bartlett. RC (NhHi). Repeats hope of returning home before winter. MJB, 715.

1776

8 January	To Mary Bartlett. RC (NhHi). Notes that he must remain in Philadelphia until another delegate arrives from New Hampshire. MJB, 740.
8 January	To John Langdon. TR (DLC: Force Transcripts). Extends congressional permission for Langdon to send a vessel to Europe and return with military supplies. MJB, 742.
9 January	To the Committee of Safety. RC (DLC: New Hampshire Manuscripts). Sends congressional resolve; notes Congress will probably sit through the winter. MJB, 744.
13 January	To the Committee of Safety. From Force, *American Archives*, 4th ser., 4:568. Sends congressional resolve re military pay. MJB, 746.
23 January	Credentials to Congress. RC (DNA:PCC). MJB, 751.
24 January	To the Committee of Safety. RC (Nh-Ar). Sends $12,500 from Congress for military expenses. MJB, 754.
8 February	To Mary Bartlett. RC (NhHi). Tells of health, weather; hopes to be relieved soon. MJB, 767.
13 February	Secret Committee to Benjamin Harrison, signed by JB et al. From *Calendar of Virginia State Papers*, 8:125–26. Authorizes Harrison to load the *Fanny* with export goods. MJB, 774.
19 February	Secret Committee to Several Merchants, signed by JB et al. RC (DNA: PCC). Agreement for the merchants—John Alsop, Francis Lewis, Philip Livingston, Silas Deane, and Robert Morris—to ship produce to Europe and use proceeds to purchase supplies needed for Continental use. MJB, 779.
26 February	To Meshech Weare. RC (MeHi: The John S. H. Fogg Autograph Collection). Transmits congressional resolves for each province to promote the manufacture of salt petre and gunpowder. MJB, 783.
26 February	From John Langdon. RC (MeHi: The John S. H. Fogg Autograph Collection). Encloses sketch of harbor showing shipbuilding docks. [Printed in *NDAR*, 4:79]. MJB, 781.
2 March	To Meshech Weare. RC (Nh-Ar). Assures that several New Hampshire matters are before Congress. MJB, 785.
8 March	To John Langdon. TR (DLC:Force Transcripts). Encloses shipbuilding dimensions; tells of military promotions. MJB, 788.
24 March	From William Whipple. RC (NhD). Relates general news of Congress, illness of Gov. Samuel Ward. MJB, 812.
11 May	From Mary Bartlett. RC (NhHi). Tells of health and weather. MJB, 827.

23 May	From Mary Bartlett. RC (NhHi). Says that they have finished planting. MJB, 835.
27 May	From John Langdon. FC (John Langdon Letter Book, Capt. J. G. M. Stone Private Collection, Annapolis, Md., 1976). Notes that the *Raleigh* was launched on 21 May. [Printed in *NDAR*, 5:265]. MJB, 836.
29 May	From Mary Bartlett. RC (NhHi). General news from home. MJB, 839.
[June]	Draft of Articles of Confederation in JB's hand. (Nh). MJB, 841.
3 June	Secret Committee to Richard Harrison, signed by JB et al. RC (PHi). Authorization for disposal of proceeds of voyage. MJB, 851.
4 June	To Meshech Weare. From Force, *American Archives*, 4th ser., 6:708–09. Conveys congressional resolution to send reinforcements to Canada. MJB, 856.
7 June	From Mary Bartlett. RC (NhHi). Comments on health, cold weather, ship launchings. MJB, 858.
8 June	From Mary Bartlett. RC (NhHi). Acknowledges receipt of letters of 18 and 28 May. MJB, 860.
10 June	From Mary Bartlett. RC (NhHi). Thanks him for newspapers; comments on weather and apples. MJB, 864.
14 June	To [Meshech Weare]. RC (DLC). Sends $20,000, half for New Hampshire, half for John Langdon. MJB, 868.
[17 June]	To [Mary Bartlett]. RC (NhHi). Fragments of a letter describing Philadelphia and Congress. MJB, 871.
18 June	Meshech Weare to JB and William Whipple. TR (DLC:Force Transcripts). Authorizes delegates to support a declaration of independence. MJB, 876.
21 June	From Mary Bartlett. RC (NhHi). Notes that flax and apples are doing poorly. MJB, 878.
26 June	To John Langdon. TR (MH: Sparks Transcripts). Informs of Langdon's appointment as naval agent. MJB, 887.
26 June	To Meshech Weare. From Force, *American Archives*, 4th ser., 6:1082. Urges the raising of troops for the Canadian expedition. MJB, 888.
6 July	From Mary Bartlett. RC (NhHi). Comments on weather, corn, powder mill at Kings Falls, and order for interest due on paper money. MJB, 900.
6 July	From John Langdon. RC (NhHi). Expresses gratification upon appointment as agent. Comments on military activity and legislature. MJB, 902.

29 July — From Mary Bartlett. RC (NhHi). Discusses health of family and Kingston men "gone to Canada." MJB, 916.

5 August — From Mary Bartlett. RC (NhHi). Reveals that all is well. MJB, 920.

5 August — From John Langdon. FC (John Langdon Letter Book, Capt. J. G. M. Stone Private Collection, Annapolis, Md., 1976). Relates news of naval captures, congratulates on success of war. MJB, 922.

7 August — From Mary Bartlett. RC (NhHi). Comments on the British; harvest keeping everyone busy. MJB, 924.

13 August — From John Langdon. FC (John Langdon Letter Book, Capt. J. G. M. Stone Private Collection, Annapolis, Md., 1976). Writes of naval officers and John Roche. MJB, 930.

20 August — Secret Committee to the Governor of Hispaniola. TR (Archives Nationale Marine, B7, vol. 458, Archives De France, Paris). Encloses a printed copy of the Declaration of Independence and solicits amicable commerce between Hispaniola and the United States. MJB, 937.

26 August — To Mary Bartlett. RC (NhHi). Tells of a ride from Philadelphia to Chester and the weather. MJB, 938.

9 September — To John Langdon. TR (DLC: Force Transcripts). Names congressional delegates sent to General Howe re Generals Sullivan and Sterling. MJB, 953.

13 September — Secret Committee to the Maryland Council of Safety. TR (MdAA). Requests a supply of gunpowder for naval agents. MJB, 961.

13 September — From Mary Bartlett. RC (NhHi). Hopes JB will be home soon and will not forget her "Circumstances." MJB, 962.

14 September — From John Langdon. RC (NhD). Encloses long letter about cannon and announces several naval appointments. MJB, 966.

14 September — From John Langdon. FC (John Langdon Letter Book, Capt. J. G. M. Stone Private Collection, Annapolis, Md., 1976). Discusses his problems in getting guns for the ship. [Printed in *NDAR*, 6:815–16]. MJB, 967.

16 September — To Mary Bartlett. RC (NhHi). Says his health is getting precarious, expects to set out for home soon via Connecticut. MJB, 973.

16 September — From Pierse Long. RC (NhD). Discusses problems of enlisting men, praises Theophilus Dame. MJB, 976.

20 September — Secret Committee to William Bingham. TR (PHi). Authorizations and instructions for commercial transactions. MJB, 980.

21 September — Secret Committee to Thomas Cushing. FC (MHi). Announces authorization for *Boston* and *Raleigh* to sail the New England coast in pursuit of *Milford*. MJB, 981.

[23 September]   From John Langdon. FC (Capt. J. G. M. Stone, Annapolis, Md.). Extract. Asks that Congress consider an appeal in a privateer case of Capt. Tobias Lear. MJB, 983.

24 September   Secret Committee to William Bingham. RC (PHi). Instructs as to disposition of cargo on *Betsey*, Capt. William Stevens. MJB, 986.

24 September   From Ebenezer Thompson. RC (NhD). Indicates that facts about military operations are scarce in New Hampshire. MJB, 987.

27 September   Secret Committee to John Ross. From J. Jay Smith and John F. Watson, *American Historical and Literary Curiosities*, 2nd ed., rev. (Philadelphia, 1847). Orders purchase of various types of cloth. MJB, 991.

27 September   From Mary Bartlett. RC (NhHi). Incomplete. Notes that all are well except Rhoda. MJB, 988.

30 September   From John Langdon. RC (NhD). Requests advice of Congress relative to property of passengers and seamen taken in prize ships. MJB, 992.

30 September   From William Whipple. RC (NhD). Tells of rumors about war, hopes to reach Philadelphia by 20 October. MJB, 994.

7 October   Congressional Committee on Clothing to the Convention of New York. RC (NN:Emmet Collection). Sends $10,000 to purchase clothing. MJB, 999.

7 October   From John Langdon. FC (John Langdon Letter Book, Capt. J. G. M. Stone Private Collection, Annapolis, Md., 1976). Says Whipple is about to set out for Congress, Langdon awaits instructions for fitting out ships. MJB, 998.

8 October   From Mary Bartlett. RC (NhHi). Urges JB to preserve his health, to return home as soon as possible. MJB, 1001.

9 October   To Nathaniel Folsom. (Copy from the *Daily Umpire* [Portland, Maine], 4 May 1850; found among papers of Mr. & Mrs. Rodney M. Wilson, Kingston, N. H., 1978). Hopes that three regiments will be raised to relieve Ticonderoga. Expects that the clothing allowance enacted by Congress will aid in recruiting men. Found too late to film.

10 October   Congressional Marine Committee to Commodore Esek Hopkins. FC (DNA:PCC). Postscript signed by JB is in RHi. Orders Hopkins to cruise against British ships on coast. [Printed in *NDAR*, 6:1201]. MJB, 1004.

11 October   Committee on Clothing to Gov. Nicholas Cooke. RC (R-Ar). Asks amount of money needed to clothe state troops. MJB, 1005.

13 October   Secret Committee to Nicholas and John Brown. RC (RPJCB). Instructs that cloth and blankets be delivered to General Mifflin. MJB, 1008.

13 October   Marine Committee to John Bradford. RC (MB). Orders assistance to Nathaniel Falconer. [File copy printed in *NDAR*, 6:1248]. MJB, 1006.

13 October   Marine Committee to John Langdon. RC (MdBJ). Orders assistance to Nathaniel Falconer. [TR printed in *NDAR*, 6:1248]. MJB, 1007.

13 October   Secret Committee to Thomas Mifflin. RC (DLC: Continental Congress Collection). Recommends having cloth made into uniforms and notes that more tents have been ordered. [Extracted in *NDAR*, 6:1246]. MJB, 1009.

15 October   To Mary Bartlett. RC (NhHi). Notes that his health is improved, he expects to return home soon, that there is little cloth to be purchased and brought home. MJB, 1011.

18 October   Secret Committee to Andrew Limozin. RC (CtY). Authorizes sale of cargo, especially flaxseed, from the *Mary* out of New London, in Europe by Limozin and Continental agent Thomas Morris. MJB, 1013.

21 October   Secret Committee to William Bingham. RC (PHi). Advises as to several cargoes exported and also as to the supplies wanted in return. MJB, 1016.

[23 October]   Marine Committee to the Governor and Committee of Safety of North Carolina. RC (MdAN Museum). Informs of their order to Esek Hopkins to sail against British vessels in Cape Fear River. MJB, 1017.

7 December   To Levi. *Letter not found.* Cited in Robert F. Batchelder Autographs Catalog 23 (November 1978), No. 51. Notes the Rev. Thayer to be ordained 18 December; that Levi was suffering with lame leg.

10 December   From Nathaniel Folsom. RC (NhExP). Orders JB to prepare regiment to march. MJB, 1044.

1777

4 January   From Azor Orne. RC (Nh-Ar). Encloses a letter and papers from Gen. William Heath revealing favorable military news. MJB, 1083.

11 April   From Ezra Currier. RC (NhD). Encloses a return of Continental Army enlistees from East Kingston. MJB, 1148.

27 April   From William Whipple. RC (NhD). Relates news of Congress, hopes his replacement has been chosen. MJB, 1166.

5 May   To the Selectmen of Kingston. RC (DLC: Miscellaneous Manuscripts). Urges that the town fulfill its quota of militia. MJB, 1184.

8 May   From Samuel Kelly. RC (Nh-Ar). Notes that he will resign his militia captaincy and asks JB to appoint a time for a new election. MJB, 1186.

10 July	N. H. Committee of Safety to Mass. Committee of Safety. TR (DNA:RG 45). Signed by JB as chairman *pro tem*. Transmits letter of Gen. Arthur St. Clair at Ticonderoga to Joseph Bowker, president of the Vermont Convention, revealing that British had opened campaign on Lake Champlain. MJB, End of Roll 2.
11 July	From Artemas Ward. RC (Nh-Ar. Sent to the attention of Josiah Bartlett). The Massachusetts Council has ordered militia reinforcements to Ticonderoga.
12 August	From Nathaniel Folsom. RC (NhD). Gives news from Congress and that Howe is not far from Philadelphia. MJB, 1233.
5 October	From Silas Hedges. RC (Nh-Ar). Informs about progress made against counterfeiters in Massachusetts. MJB, 1251.
30 October	From Nathaniel Folsom. RC (NhD). Encloses copy of letter from Jacob Duché to General Washington, hopes JB will return to Congress soon. MJB, 1253.

1778

[January]	To Capt. Robert Stewart [Stuart]. *Letter not found.* Extracted in *The Collector*, 51 (June 1937), Item 1844. Orders a return of Newton's men for the Continental Army by 9 February.
2 January	From Nathaniel Folsom. RC (NhD). Discusses his attitude toward military officers. MJB, 1283.
March	To Nicholas Gilman. *Letter not found.* Cited in *The Collector*, 56 (August 1943), Item 413. Orders money to Capt. John Hale to pay his men.
11 March	To William Whipple. TR (MH: Sparks Transcripts). Encloses vote of legislature regarding Whipple's allowance while serving in Congress. MJB, 1305.
11 March	From John Wentworth, Jr. RC (Nh-Ar: Weare Papers). Requests a brief time to consider appointment as a delegate to Congress. MJB, 1306.
11 March	From William Whipple. RC (Nh-Ar). Argues that pay for delegates to Congress does not cover expenses, therefore declines. MJB, 1307.
27 March	From Meshech Weare. RC (Nh-Ar: Weare Papers). Directs JB to complete enlistments in his regiment and prepare them to march westward. MJB, 1314.
2 April	From Joseph French, Jr., and David Poor. RC (Nh-Ar). Signifies their determination to resign their militia commissions in Hampstead. MJB, 1316.
27 April	From Jeremiah Dow. RC (NhHi). Regrets his inability to muster the men of Salem for Continental service. MJB, 1321.
27 April	From Capt. Robert Stuart. RC (NhD). Return of men enlisted from Newton.

16 May	From Mary Bartlett. RC (NhHi). Relates conditions of family, neighbors, weather. MJB, 1326.
22 May	From Mary Bartlett. RC (NhHi). Notes her impatience in not hearing from him since he left. MJB, 1330.
26 May	To Mary Bartlett. RC (NhHi). Brief note sent by a man going to Boston. MJB, 1333.
27 May	From John Langdon to JB and John Wentworth, Jr. *Letter not found.* Extracted in George D. Smith, "Rare & Fine Books," [n.d., 64pp., 270 items], p. 48, item 218. Refers to naval affairs.
28 May	From Mary Bartlett. RC (NhHi). Informs that General Court adjourned owing to outbreak of smallpox. MJB, 1336.
1 June	To Mary Bartlett. RC (NhHi). Says York healthier than Philadelphia, but lodgings hard to find. Mentions lottery. MJB, 1340.
13 June	From Mary Bartlett. RC (NhHi). Discusses Rhoda's illness. MJB, 1351.
15 June	To Meshech Weare. RC (MHi). Asks for compliance with Congress's need for troops to defend Rhode Island. MJB, 1353.
18 June	From Benjamin Thurston. RC (NhD). Comments briefly on several matters, discusses explosion at powder mill in Andover, Mass. MJB, 1356.
20 June	From Mary Bartlett. RC (NhHi). Discusses Rhoda's illness, asks about lottery results. MJB, 1361.
3 July	From Mary Bartlett. RC (NhHi). Tells of Rhoda's continuing ill health and of other general news. MJB, 1372.
3 July	From Meshech Weare. RC (NN:Emmet Collection, No. 1973). Assures that he will try to answer president's letters more punctually. Encloses grant request to Congress. MJB, 1371.
4 July	From Samuel Philbrick. RC (NhD). Complains about raising troops and about speculators. MJB, 1374.
6 July	To Mary Bartlett. RC (NhHi). Expresses deep concern for Rhoda's health, sends news of Congress. MJB, 1375.
9 July	From Elihu Thayer. RC (NhD). Comments generally on the *Ranger*, community health, weather and crops. MJB, 1383.
10 July	To Mary Bartlett. RC (NhHi). Reports fine health. MJB, 1384.
17 July	From Mary Bartlett. RC (NhHi). Reports family is well, crops abundant. MJB, 1396.
20 July	To Mary Bartlett. RC (NhHi). Expresses great concern at lack of news from home. MJB, 1400.
20 July	To William Whipple. TR (DLC:Force Transcripts). Discusses the reception of Gerard and negotiations with British commissioners at New York. MJB, 1404.
24 July	From Mary Bartlett. RC (NhHi). Assures that Rhoda is recovering. MJB, 1406.

27 July   To Mary Bartlett. RC (NhHi). Expresses relief that Rhoda is better, comments briefly on other news. MJB, 1408.

31 July   From Mary Bartlett. RC (NhHi). Tells of Rhoda's improving health and rainfall relieving the drought. MJB, 1412.

2 August   From William Whipple. RC (NN:Emmet Collection, No. 1543). Comments at length on Frenchmen and the French fleet, more briefly on soldiers, Silas Deane, and farmers. MJB, 1417.

3 August   To Mary Bartlett. RC (NhHi). Comments on weather and on Gerard. MJB, 1418.

7 August   From Mary Bartlett. RC (NhHi). Says weather hot and rainy, militia going to Rhode Island. MJB, 1423.

9 August   To Mary Bartlett. RC (NhHi). Discusses the health of Charles Chace and John Wentworth, and reception of French minister. MJB, 1426.

11 August   To Mary Bartlett. RC (NhHi). Expresses apprehension at slow receipt of letters from home. MJB, 1428.

12 August   From Samuel Philbrick. RC (NhD). Relays news as received about the war. MJB, 1430.

14 August   From Mary Bartlett. RC (NhHi). Describes the weather, health of children. MJB, 1431.

20 August   From Mary & Lois Bartlett. RC (NhHi). Gives general news, hopes JB will be home soon. MJB, 1442.

21 August   To Mary Bartlett. RC (NhHi). Informs that Charles Chace and John Wentworth are returning at once to New Hampshire. MJB, 1444.

31 August   To Mary Bartlett. RC (NhHi). Appreciates news from home, hopes delegates will soon be sent to relieve him. MJB, 1458.

3 September   From Mary Bartlett. RC (NhHi). Notes that New Hampshire volunteers had returned before the engagement at Newport, R. I. in August. MJB, 1460.

8 September   To Mary Bartlett. RC (Mr. & Mrs. Rodney M. Wilson, Kingston, N. H.). Hopes to return home in November. Mentions the Saratoga Convention. MJB, 1464.

8 September   To Meshech Weare. RC (NhD). Discusses money, Vermont question, and appointments to Congress. MJB, 1465.

10 September   From Mary Bartlett. RC (NhHi). Expresses relief that JB intends to return home in fall. MJB, 1467.

12 September   To Mary Bartlett. RC (NhHi). Encloses newspaper, says he is very busy in Congress. MJB, 1469.

15 September   From Pierse Long. RC (NhD). Requests assistance in obtaining debts from overseas and support for himself and family. MJB, 1476.

18 September	From Meshech Weare. From *American Clipper* (June 1938), 282–83. Wants money to supply troops. Not filmed.
19 September	From Mary Bartlett. RC (NhHi). Notes that all are well, Miriam and Rhoda are gone to the beach. MJB, 1478.
20 September	To Mary Bartlett. RC (NhHi). Expects to leave Philadelphia by first of November. MJB, 1480.
24 September	From Mary Bartlett. RC (NhHi). Relates that Miriam is ill following trip to sea. MJB, 1483.
28 September	To Mary Bartlett. RC (NhHi). Tells that Dr. Benjamin Rush has been near death, is recovering. MJB, 1491.
29 September	To William Whipple. TR (DLC:Force Transcripts). Urges Whipple to hurry to Congress. MJB, 1492.
1 October	From Mary Bartlett. RC (NhHi). Wishes him a safe trip home. Most people well, weather warm and pleasant. MJB, 1520.
3 October	From Samuel Philbrick. RC (NhD). Discusses politics in Grafton towns and plight of Nathaniel Hovey. MJB, 1522.
5 October	To Mary Bartlett. RC (NhHi). Notes his health is improving after illness, still expects to be home in November. MJB, 1523.
10 October	To Meshech Weare. RC (MHi). Sends $150,000 for the state. MJB, 1530.
14 October	From Mary Bartlett. RC (NhHi). Wishes him a safe journey. This is Mary's last letter. MJB, 1532.
17 October	To Mary Bartlett. RC (NhHi). Relates good health and impending departure from Congress for home. MJB, 1534.
27 October	To John Langdon. RC (Mr. Donald M. D. Thurber, Detroit, 1976). Urges that state legislatures resolve to vest Congress with full power to make peace, contract foreign alliances, and conduct the war. MJB, 1542.

1779

9 January	To William Whipple. TR (DLC:Force Transcripts). Discusses the depreciation of money and Sullivan's request for reinforcements at Rhode Island. MJB, 1573.
9 January	From the N. H. Committee of Safety. RC (NhHi). Directs JB to return by 15 February a list of those men from his regiment who had enlisted to serve in Continental service for three years or duration of the war. MJB, 1575.
13 January	From William Whipple. *Letter not found.* Abstracted in Charles F. Libbie, "Catalog of Collection of E. H. Leffingwell," (Jan. 6, 1891), Item 3217. Writes of finances, effects of *Common Sense*.
27 February	To William Whipple. TR (DLC:Force Transcripts). Regrets news of enemy victory to the south, urges that naval ships at Boston get to sea. MJB, 1592.

28 February   From William Whipple. RC (NhD). Discusses the calling in of money, Silas Deane's problems, and foreign diplomacy. MJB, 1594.

23 March   From William Whipple. RC (NhD). Asks for opinion about levying additional tax. MJB, 1600.

6 April   From William Whipple. RC (DLC: Continental Congress Collection of Edmund C. Burnett, "Burnett Photostats"). Transmits congressional resolutions, requests more news from home. MJB, 1610.

14 April   From William Whipple. RC (PHi). Rails against those who want to give up the war. MJB, 1611.

19 April   To William Whipple. TR (DLC: Force Transcripts). Informs that Peabody and W. Langdon are appointed to Congress. Discusses enlisting militia and depreciation of money. MJB, 1612.

27 April   From William Whipple. From *American Antiquarian*, 2 (September 1871), 108. Comments on congressional recommendation to raise regiments of Negroes in the south. Not filmed.

May [1779]   From Meshech Weare. RC (Nh-Ar). Reports that Woodbury Langdon will probably not fulfill his appointment as a delegate to Congress. MJB, 1615.

3 May   To William Whipple. TR (DLC: Force Transcripts). Again requests Pennsylvania laws respecting treatment of Loyalists. MJB, 1616.

24 May   From William Whipple. *Letter not found*. Extracted in *The Collector*, 58 (August–September 1945), Item 2660. Hopes to send the Pennsylvania laws by next post.

3 July   From Nathaniel Peabody. RC (MHi). Notes jealous spirit between southern and eastern states. MJB, 1648.

3 July   From William Whipple. RC (NhD). Encloses the only law of Pennsylvania he can find "respecting the Fugitives & other disaffected Persons." MJB, 1650.

12 July   From William Whipple. RC (NhD). Reports the congressional committee to the N. H. Grants has returned. MJB, 1653.

20 July   From Nathaniel Peabody. RC (NhD). Assures that the Penobscot expedition will prove successful. MJB, 1656.

27 July   From William Whipple. RC (NhD). Discusses reports from Europe, assures of victory in the war. MJB, 1662.

3 August   From Nathaniel Peabody. RC (NhD). Encloses a few papers and notes that Whipple has consented to tarry longer at Congress. MJB, 1665.

10 August   From William Whipple. RC (NhD). Expects to return home in October; news from South good; expects to have a successful report from Penobscot. MJB, 1671.

17 August	From Nathaniel Peabody. RC (NhD). Expresses anxiety about Penobscot, quotes letter of 26 May from Benjamin Franklin at Passy, France. MJB, 1675.
24 August	From William Whipple. RC (NhD). Comments on American publications and events in Europe. MJB, 1679.
31 August	From Nathaniel Peabody. RC (NhD). Sends newspaper, dreads authentification of Penobscot failure. MJB, 1680.
21 September	From Nathaniel Peabody. RC (NhD). Encloses circular letter from President John Jay; urges virtuous citizenry effort to win war. MJB, 1685.
29 September	From Nathaniel Peabody. RC (NhD). Marked "No. 9." Encloses a copy of Gen. John Burgoyne's letter to George Germaine of 20 Aug. 1777. MJB, 1686.
5 October	From Nathaniel Peabody. RC (NhD). Says Whipple left Philadelphia; enemy's movements reported. MJB, 1690.
12 October	From Nathaniel Peabody. RC (NhD). Marked "No. 11." Reports no news; encloses papers and a journal. MJB, 1692.
18 October	From Nathaniel Peabody. RC (NhD). Comments on many points, notes that 2 December is to be observed as day of thanksgiving. MJB, 1693.
9 November	From Nathaniel Peabody. RC (NhD). Comments on foreign affairs. MJB, 1709.
30 November	From Nathaniel Peabody. RC (NhD). Marked "No. 16." Reports William Whipple's appointment to newly-created board of admiralty. MJB, 1718.
24 December	From Nathaniel Peabody. RC (NhD). Supports increased taxes, complains about high cost of living in Philadelphia. MJB, 1731.
25 December	To Nathaniel Peabody. RC (MB). Asks that congressional treasury records be checked for $100,000 supposedly sent to New Hampshire in 1778 but never received. MJB, 1733.

1780

17 March	From Nathaniel Peabody. RC (NhD). Notes rumors of a British peace proposition. Reports that $200,000 charged to New Hampshire in July 1778 was mistake. MJB, 1764.
13 May	To Nathaniel Peabody. *Letter not found.* Extracted in *The Collector*, 57 (May 1946), Item J1084. Expresses belief that Peabody would have already left Congress.
28 June	From Meshech Weare. RC (NhD). Orders all soldiers, militia and army, at Kingston to be mustered, paid, and sent to Worcester. MJB, 1792.
6 August	From Nathaniel Peabody. RC (NhD). Lengthy diatribe against those prolonging the war. MJB, 1802.
21 September	From Nathaniel Peabody. RC (NhD). Reports that he is in ill health and Folsom is on way home. MJB, 1811.

1781

19 April   To Col. Jonathan Chase. RC (MnHi). Orders raising of two companies for defense of western frontier. MJB, 1891.

1 August   JB and John Dudley to Simeon Ladd. RC (Nh-Ar). Orders to keep prisoner John Sinclere Gibson in safe custody and bring him before next meeting of Committee of Safety. MJB, 1928.

26 September   To Daniel Gordon. FC (Nh-Ar). Orders dispatches delivered to Col. Daniel Reynolds and his officers to march to Charlestown. MJB, 1938.

26 September   To Daniel Reynolds. FC (Nh-Ar). Orders to march from Springfield, Mass. to Charlestown, N.H. MJB, 1937.

27 September   To Francis Blood. FC (Nh-Ar). Orders to acquire beef and bread for troops at Charlestown. MJB, 1939.

27 September   To Daniel Reynolds. FC (Nh-Ar). Instructs that supplies should be obtained at Charlestown. MJB, 1943.

28 September   To Gen. Benjamin Bellows. FC (Nh-Ar). Informs about troops moving to Charlestown. MJB, 1945.

28 September   To Charles Johnston. FC (Nh-Ar). Informs of troop movements. MJB, 1946.

2 October   From Samuel Hunt. RC (Nh-Ar: Weare Papers). Requests instructions on supplying troops with beef. MJB, 1950.

4 October   From Francis Blood. RC (Nh-Ar: Weare Papers). Lists beef supplied to army. MJB, 1951.

5 October   From Meshech Weare. RC (Nh-Ar). Stresses the need for ammunition. MJB, 1952.

6 October   To Francis Blood. FC (Nh-Ar). Sends £300 to purchase flour for army. MJB, 1953.

6 October   To Samuel Hunt. RC (RPJCB). Orders to supply Col. Reynolds' regiment. MJB, 1954.

23 November   To Abraham Bayley et al. RC (Nh-Ar). Subpoena to testify against Robert Young before Committee of Safety. Found late.

27 December   To Jonathan Martin. FC (Nh-Ar). Sends warrants for several arrests. MJB, 2036.

27 December   To Robert Smith. FC (Nh-Ar). Sends warrant for arrest of Benjamin Giles. MJB, 2037.

29 December   From Roger Enos and Ira Allen. RC (DNA: PCC, Item 40). Encloses commission to attend General Court on behalf of Vermont. MJB, 2040.

1782

20 April   To Isaac Williams. FC (Nh-Ar). Orders supplies issued to recruits of Capt. Jeremiah Fogg. MJB, 2113.

27 April   To Benjamin Bellows. RC (DLC: Peter Force Collection). Requests that he supply new recruits if Hunt cannot. MJB, 2114.

27 April   To Ephraim Stone. FC (Nh-Ar). Requests his presence at Exeter to settle payrolls. MJB, 2115.

27 April   To Isaac Williams. FC (Nh-Ar). Orders exchange of rum for bread for troops. MJB, 2116.

27 April   To Isaac Williams. FC (Nh-Ar). Requests that he secure beef for Fogg's recruits. MJB, 2117.

21 August   From John Taylor Gilman. RC (NhD). Thanks for letters, lacks news, sends newspapers. MJB, 2249.

1783

11 January   To Nicholas Gilman. FC (Nh-Ar). Orders receipt of certain certificates. MJB, 2306.

5 February   From Phillips White. RC (MeHi: The John S. H. Fogg Autograph Collection). Discusses the Vermont controversy. MJB, 2314.

4 March   From John Taylor Gilman. *Letter not found.* Extracted in Robert F. Batchelder Autographs Catalog 21 (March 1978), #179. Encloses something from Dr. Rush, anticipates that peace will soon be final.

8 April   From Phillips White. RC (NhD). Requests a depreciation table from New Hampshire. MJB, 2335.

9 August   To George Gains and Nathaniel Folsom. FC (Nh-Ar). Requests that he inspect and dispose of state's salt beef. MJB, 2357.

3 November   From Meshech Weare. RC (DLC: Peter Force Collection). Regrets his inability to attend next session of General Court. MJB, 2373.

1784

23 January   To Nathaniel Adams. FC (Nh-Ar). Requests him to inspect papers of Superior Court re counterfeiting cases. MJB, 2399.

10 February   From Jonathan Blanchard. RC (NhD). Notes his decision to travel on to Congress at Annapolis by stage from Boston. MJB, 2403.

18 February   From Jonathan Blanchard. RC (NhD). Notes arrival in New York to attend Congress. MJB, 2404.

1 March   From Jonathan Blanchard. RC (NhD). Informs of attendance at Congress and of dining with President. MJB, 2410.

25 March   To John Langdon et al. FC (Nh-Ar). Supports their position on reciprocal commercial conditions with foreign nations. MJB, 2419.

28 March   From Levi Bartlett. *Letter not found.* Extracted in Argosy Book Stores Catalogue #453 (1959), Item 10. Relates medical news from Andover, Mass.

1786

9 February — To John Dudley. RC (NhHi). Acknowledges receipt of a rule of the court. MJB, 2487.

20 June — From John Pierce. RC (NhD). Warns of blank securities stolen and counterfeited. MJB, 2494.

17 October — From Woodbury Langdon. RC (NhHi). Sends a load of salt, freighted courtesy of Langdon's commercial boat. MJB, 2504.

15 December — From John Abbot. RC (University of Alabama in Birmingham). Returns book of Franklin's letters on electricity. MJB, 2510.

1787

20 December — To John Dudley. RC (NhHi). Informs that parties to a legal dispute will meet. MJB, 2538.

1789

8 January — To William Duty. *Letter not found*. Listed in *The Collector*, 56 (March–April 1943), 78. "On Legal matters."

2 February — To John Dudley. RC (NhHi). Suggests they go together to Salem on legal matter. MJB, 2580.

1790

17 January — To Nicholas Gilman. *Letter not found*. Extracted in *The Collector*, 57 (October–November 1944), Item E 1363. Congratulates Gilman on reappointment to Congress.

4 February — To Joseph Pearson. RC (Nh-Ar). Requests salary be sent per his son. MJB, 2618.

13 March — Agreement with Ebenezer Kelley. MS (Nh). Kelley agrees to work for JB for eight months. MJB, 2623.

2 June — From William Gardner. RC (Nh-Ar). Encloses statement of tax money received. MJB, 2630.

8 June — From Phillips White. RC (Nh-Ar). Resigns as judge of probate for Rockingham County. MJB, 2634.

11 June — From William Gardner. RC (Nh-Ar). Requests that his accounts be settled. MJB, 2641.

11 June — From Benjamin Goold. RC (Nh-Ar). Resigns militia command. MJB, 2639.

14 June — From Oliver Peabody. RC (Nh-Ar). Declines appointment as state solicitor in Rockingham County. MJB, 2644.

23 June — From George Hough. RC (NhD). Asks to be awarded contract to print Journals of House of Representatives at his Concord printing office. MJB, 2654.

1 July — To Col. Hacket. *Letter not found*. Abstracted in Dodd & Livingston Autograph Catalogue, #7 (April 1912), 3. Asks for cannon fire in honor of Independence Day.

22 July   From John Dennett. RC (Nh-Ar). Resigns militia command. MJB, 2660.

28 July   From Thomas Kittredge. RC (Nh). Sends bill for £12 for boarding JB's sons. MJB, 2663.

29 July   From Joseph Pearson. RC (NhD). Encloses order for sum from Gov. John Wentworth's estate. MJB, 2664.

20 August   From Jeremiah Smith. RC (NhHi). Requests JB's assistance in court case. MJB, end of Roll 3.

23 August   From John Pickering. RC (Nh-Ar). Accepts appointment as chief justice of Superior Court. MJB, 2674.

24 August   From John Odlin. RC (Nh-Ar). Resigns militia command. MJB, 2675.

30 September   From William Page. RC (NhD). Notes expenses in trial of Judge Woodbury Langdon. MJB, 2681.

4 October   From John Langdon. RC (NhD). Notes that he will soon leave for Philadelphia. MJB, 2682.

8 October   Unsigned letter. RC (Nh-Ar). Advises against filling vacancies in 5th militia regiment immediately. MJB, 2683.

11 October   From Joseph Pearson. RC (NhHi). Encloses militia commissions for JB's signature. MJB, 2684.

12 October   From Ebenezer Thompson. RC (Nh-Ar). Recommends James Hearsey for justice of the peace for Strafford County. MJB, 2686.

12 November   From Samuel Livermore. RC (Nh-Ar). Accepts appointment to Congress. MJB, 2704.

20 November   From John Dudley. RC (NhHi). Informs of time and meeting on legal matter. MJB, 2708.

1 December   From John Pride and Thomas Mathews. RC (Nh-Ar). Send resolutions of Virginia Assembly applying to U. S. Senate to hold open sessions. MJB, 2711.

9 December   From Nicholas Gilman. RC (NhD). Sends newspaper containing President's address to Congress. MJB, 2714.

11 December   To Joseph Pearson. RC (Nh-Ar). Orders bounty payment to Col. Hobart. MJB, 2716.

13 December   From Hercules Mooney. RC (Nh-Ar). Resigns as justice of the peace. MJB, 2717.

1791

[1791]   From Levi Bartlett. RC (NhHi). Asks JB to take care of his horse. MJB, 2727.

[January 1791]   From George Jerry Osborne. RC (Nh-Ar). Requests remuneration for printing done for state. MJB, 2731.

2 January   From Richard Champney. RC (Nh-Ar). Resigns as coroner. MJB, 2732.

6 January   From Samuel Draper. RC (Nh-Ar). Resigns militia command.

15 January   From John Sullivan. RC (NN: Emmet Collection, No. 1929). Recommends Oliver Whipple for Superior Court justice. MJB, 2745.

15 January   From Oliver Whipple. RC (NhD). Solicits seat on Superior Court vacated by Woodbury Langdon. MJB, 2746.

17 January   From Christopher Toppan. RC (Nh-Ar). Declines appointment to state Senate. MJB, 2749.

27 January   From Paine Wingate. RC (NhD). Sends news from the frontier. MJB, 2754.

9 February   From Oliver Whipple. RC (NhD). Seeks appointment as attorney general in case John Prentice should resign. MJB, 2763.

16 February   From William Gardner. RC (Nh-Ar). Deplores cut in salary for services as Treasurer. MJB, 2782.

4 March   From John Sullivan. RC (NhD). Suggests Joseph Whipple as source of answer about a settlement. MJB, 2797.

10 March   From Samuel A. Otis. RC (Nh-Ar). Transmits journals of U. S. Senate. MJB, 2798.

18 March   From Joseph Whipple. RC (Nh-Ar). Sends agreement with Titus Salter for maintenance of the lighthouse at Portsmouth. MJB, 2802.

4 April   From John Beckley. RC (NhD). Sends two copies of journals of House of Representatives. MJB, 2807.

10 April   From John Hubbard. RC (Nh-Ar). Encloses claims against estate of Breed Batchelder. MJB, 2810.

13 April   From Jeremy Belknap. FC (MHi). Expresses thanks for New Hampshire's publication grant of £50. MJB, 2811. RC (NhExP) dated 14 April.

25 April   From Joseph Pearson. RC (NhD). Encloses order to Oliver Olcott for JB's signature. MJB, 2812.

6 May   To Moses Dow. *Letter not found.* Abstracted in Paul C. Richards Autographs, Catalogue No. 63, Item 203. Notified Dow of his election to state Senate.

7 May   From John Pickering. RC (NhD). Sends papers for "Mr. Williams." MJB, 2813.

11 May   From Joshua Wentworth. RC (Nh-Ar). Suggests regulation of fees for pilots. MJB, 2814.

11 May   From Joseph Whipple. RC (Nh-Ar). Asks for settlement of his account for upkeep of lighthouse. MJB, 2815.

16 May   From Noah Lovewell. RC (Nh-Ar). Informs that militia commission to John Gosse had been destroyed by weather. MJB, 2817.

17 May	From John Cram. RC (Nh-Ar). Recommends Robert Tibbets to be justice of the peace of Pittsfield. MJB, 2818.
17 May	From Benjamin Sias. RC (Nh-Ar). Resigns as justice of the peace in Pittsfield. MJB, 2819.
29 May	From Woodbury Langdon. RC (Nh-Ar). Notes that vouchers were not included with state claims against United States. MJB, 2827.
1 June	From Nathaniel Parker. RC (Nh-Ar). Resigns as receiver of non-resident state taxes. MJB, 2830.
3 June	To the General Court. RC (Nh-Ar). Encloses report of committee charged with funding old Continental money. MJB, 2835.
7 June	From John Taylor Gilman. RC (Nh-Ar). Appreciates appointment as Treasurer. MJB, 2838.
11 June	From Amos Shepard. RC (Nh-Ar). Notes vacancies in his militia regiment and suggests replacements. MJB, 2842.
15 June	From Richard Ayer. RC (Nh-Ar). Resigns militia command. MJB, 2846.
15 June	From Asa Herrick. RC (Nh-Ar). Resigns militia command. MJB, 2847.
16 June	From Nathaniel Rogers and Christopher Toppan. RC (Nh-Ar). Decline committee appointments. MJB, 2850.
20 June	From Joseph Whipple. RC (Nh-Ar). Suggests that some person be appointed to witness the settlement of contract regarding expenses for maintenance of lighthouse. MJB, 2870.
28 June	From John Taylor Gilman. RC (Nh-Ar). Sends news just received about Bank of the United States. MJB, 2859.
29 June	From Joseph Whipple. *Letter not found.* Extracted in George D. Smith, Autograph Letters Catalog, n.d., 288 pp., Item 34. Discusses lighthouse.
[July 1791]	From David [Bryant?]. RC (Nh-Ar). Favors restoration of Joseph Welch to office. MJB, 2861.
12 July	From Samuel Ashley. RC (Nh-Ar). Resigns judicial seat. MJB, 2865.
12 July	From Samuel Ashley. RC (Nh-Ar). Recommends Thaddeus Mc-Carty for judiciary. MJB, 2867.
12 July	From William Page. RC (Nh-Ar). Nominates officers for militia. MJB, 2868.
16 July	To John Hancock. *Letter not found.* Extracted in Paul C. Richards, Autographs, Catalogue No. 53. Item 5. Acknowledges receipt of act of Massachusetts legislature.
24 July	From Amos Shepard. RC (Nh-Ar). Testifies as to his credentials for appointment to rank of brigadier. MJB, 2872.

30 July   From Tench Coxe. RC (Nh-Ar). Regrets the impossibility of procuring bank stock for New Hampshire on original terms. MJB, 2875.

4 August   From John Jackson. RC (Nh-Ar). Resigns as inspector of pot and pearl-ash. MJB, 2877.

14 August   To John Wheelock. RC (MeHi: The John S. H. Fogg Autograph Collection). Regrets inability to attend commencement. MJB, 2879.

15 August   From Phillips White. RC (Nh-Ar). Recommends Joseph Merrill to be justice of the peace for South Hampton. MJB, 2880.

22 August   From J. White. RC (Nh-Ar). Testimonial letter on behalf of Joseph Welch. MJB, 2881.

30 August   From William Page. RC (Nh-Ar). Asks for blank militia commissions. MJB, 2882.

10 September   From Jonathan Freeman. RC (Nh-Ar). Asks JB to forward enclosed militia commissions. MJB, 2884.

19 September   From John Taylor Gilman. RC (Nh-Ar). Suggests that a bill of Continental paper be funded. MJB, 2887.

5 October   From John Langdon. RC (NhD). Recommends William Simpson for sheriff of Rockingham County. MJB, 2924.

7 October   From Paine Wingate. RC (NhD). Recommendation of Col. Simpson for Rockingham sherrif. MJB, 2925.

8 October   From Jonathan Cass. RC (NhD). Solicits for appointment as Rockingham County sheriff. MJB, 2926.

8 October   From Paine Wingate. RC (NhD). Recommends Nathaniel Rogers for sheriff. MJB, 2927.

14 October   From Nathaniel Peabody. RC (NhD). Recommends James Macgregore for sheriff. MJB, 2929.

22 October   From Nathaniel Peabody. RC (NhD). Agrees to serve as sheriff himself, if appointed. MJB, 2934.

11 November   From Nicholas Gilman. RC (NN: Emmet Collection, No. 463). Discusses the office of Marshall, invalid pensioners, and militia regulations. MJB, 2936.

15 November   From George Gaines. RC (NhD). Confirms arrangements for JB's stay in Portsmouth during legislative session. MJB, 2939.

1 December   From John Taylor Gilman. RC (NhHi: Treasurers' Warrants). Encloses general statement of Treasury. MJB, 2943.

7 December   From James Macgregore. RC (Nh-Ar). Discusses settlement of state accounts. MJB, 2947.

8 December   From Ebenezer Britton. RC (Nh-Ar). Resigns militia command. MJB, 2950.

12 December   From Jeremiah Smith. RC (NhD). Sends account and news from frontier. MJB, 2957.

12 December	From Paine Wingate. RC (NhD). Sends news from army on frontier. MJB, 2959.

1792

15 January	From Nicholas Gilman. RC (NhD). Comments on Indians in west and on invalid pensions. MJB, 3002.
15 February	From John Langdon and Paine Wingate. RC (NhD). Acknowledge receipt of list of invalids as examined by Drs. Tenney and Parker. MJB, 3016.
12 March	From William Williams. RC (NhD). Discusses personal financial situation. MJB, 3026.
22 March	From Nicholas Gilman. RC (NhHi). Relates news from Congress. MJB, 3030.
6 April	From Jeremiah Smith. RC (NhExP). Sends news of Congress. MJB, 3037.
10 April	From Thomas Jefferson. RC (NhD). Sends copies of two acts of Congress. MJB, 3039.
28 April	To? *Letter not found.* Printed in George D. Smith Autograph Catalog, #107 (February 1951), Item 30. Certifies return on estate of Breed Batchelder.
15 May	From Benjamin Bellows. RC (Nh-Ar). Resigns militia commission. MJB, 3042.
23 May	From Daniel Gould. RC (Nh-Ar). Resigns militia commission. MJB, 3049.
1 June	From Samuel A. Otis. RC (NhD). Sends journals of U. S. Senate. MJB, 3054.
2 June	From Samuel Adams. RC (Nh-Ar). Resigns militia commission. MJB, 3056.
4 June	From George Aldrich. RC (Nh-Ar). Resigns militia commission. MJB, 3057.
6 June	From Nathaniel Adams. RC (Nh-Ar). Sends volume of printed state laws. MJB, 3058.
16 June	To Ezra Bartlett. RC (Mr. & Mrs. Rodney M. Wilson, Kingston, N. H., 1975). Notes that he is well, expects to return home next week. MJB, 3066.
3 July	From Jonathan Smith. RC (Nh-Ar). Resigns militia command. MJB, 3082.
3 July	From Nathaniel Peabody. *Letter not found.* Extracted in John Heise Autograph Catalogue, 2460, n.d., Item 373. Regrets inability to attend July fourth commemoration.
11 July	From Jeremiah Libbey. RC (NhD). Discusses postal route between Portsmouth and Concord. MJB, 3084.
12 July	From Oliver Johnson. RC (Nh-Ar). Resigns militia command. MJB, 3085.

26 July   From Joseph Pearson. RC (Nh). Sends blank orders for JB's signature. MJB, 3089.

4 August   From John Wheelock. RC (NhD). Invites JB to commencement MJB, 3092.

13 August   From Joseph Pearson. RC (NhD). Transmits list of military accounts. MJB, 3094.

3 September   From William Williams. RC (NN: Emmet Collection, No. 693). Expresses appreciation of JB's intervention in affair with John Wendell. MJB, 3099.

28 September   From Woodbury Langdon. RC (PHi). Offers to take vouchers to Philadelphia to settle New Hampshire's claims against the Federal government. MJB, 3103.

2 October   From Ezra Bartlett. RC (NhHi). Informs that he and Levi are recovering well from inoculation. MJB, 3106.

12 October   To Joseph Pearson. RC (Nh-Ar). Sends twelve signed blank orders. MJB, 3109.

13 October   From Timothy Walker. RC (NhD). Solicits use of cannon for regimental muster at Concord. MJB, 3110.

22 November   From John Taylor Gilman. RC (Nh-Ar). Encloses statement of state treasury. MJB, 3128.

26 November   From Jeremiah Smith. RC (NhD). Recommends his brother John for a justice of the peace in Hillsborough County. MJB, 3134.

28 November   From Jeremiah Eames. RC (NhHi). Sends letter relating to American-Canadian boundary. MJB, 3137.

3 December   From John Weeks. RC (Nh-Ar). Request additional justices of the peace around Exeter. MJB, 3142.

6 December   From William George. RC (Nh-Ar). Resigns as coroner for Grafton County. MJB, 3147.

13 December   From Oliver Peabody. RC (NhHi). Announces additional account in estate of Stephen Holland. MJB, 3154.

21 December   From Nathaniel Peabody et al. RC (Nh-Ar). Report of committee to survey state line. MJB, 3167.

22 December   From Nicholas Gilman. RC (PP). Says Levi arrived in Philadelphia, sends news of Congress. MJB, 3168.

1793

[1793?]   From John Wheelock. RC (NhD). Introduces E. W. Phelps. MJB, 3180.

5 January   From George Hough. RC (Nh-Ar). Asks payment of account be delivered to Thomas Stickney. MJB, 3183.

8 January   From Samuel Hale and Isaac Waldron. RC (Nh-Ar). Recommend John Cate for packer of beef for Barrington. MJB, 3184.

21 January	From Samuel Tenney. RC (NhD). Recommends himself for appointment as recorder of deeds for Rockingham County. MJB, 3186.
22 January	From Woodbury Langdon. RC (Nh-Ar). Discusses accounts of state with United States. MJB, 3189.
7 February	From Joshua Wentworth. RC (NhHi). Asks that letters from Philadelphia be forwarded. MJB, 3197.
11 February	From Oliver Peabody. RC (Nh-Ar). Notes that dividend payment from New Hampshire Bank awaits JB's order. MJB, 3203.
20 February	From Joseph Cilley. RC (Nh-Ar). Declines militia command. MJB, 3207.
6 March	From Joseph Pearson. RC (NhHi). Encloses an order for sum due town of Northwood. MJB, 3208.
4 April	From Thomas Bartlett. RC (Nh-Ar). Recommends Jonathan Cilley as brigade inspector. MJB, 3225.
17 April	From Oliver Peabody. RC (Nh-Ar). Informs that payment of bank dividend awaits JB's order. MJB, 3226.
18 April	From Daniel Norris. RC (Nh-Ar). Declines militia appointment. MJB, 3227.
1 May	From Samuel A. Otis. RC (NhD). Sends Senate journals. MJB, 3229.
7 May	From Ebenezer Brewster. RC (Nh-Ar). Recommends Rufus Graves for brigade inspector. MJB, 3231.
13 May	From Amos Shepard. RC (Nh-Ar). Suggests uniform for militia. MJB, 3238.
31 May	From Samuel Works. RC (Nh-Ar). Resigns militia command. MJB, 3245.
3 June	From John Prentice. RC (Nh-Ar). Resigns as attorney general. MJB, 3248.
4 June	From Oliver Whipple. RC (NhD). Solicits office of attorney general. MJB, 3249.
5 June	From Oliver Peabody. RC (Nh-Ar). Resigns as probate officer for Rockingham County. MJB, 3250.
10 June	From Gideon Granger. RC (Nh-Ar). Asks that he be allowed to purchase unlocated lands. MJB, 3254.
8 July	From Supply Clapp. RC (Nh-Ar). Requests orders to clear barracks at Fort William and Mary. MJB, 3296.
15 July	From Joshua Wentworth. RC (NhD). Requests information re estate of Mr. Eddy. MJB, 3297.
18 July	From Oliver Peabody. RC (NhD). Informs about state's dividend from New Hampshire Bank. MJB, 3298.
24 July	From Thomas Bartlett. RC (NhD). Requests blank commissions for use in recruiting militia field officers. MJB, 3299.

29 July   From Edward St. Loe Livermore. RC (NhD). Resigns as solicitor for Rockingham County. MJB, 3301.

31 July   From Supply Clapp. RC (Nh-Ar). Encloses list of stores removed from barracks of Fort William and Mary. MJB, 3302.

10 August   From Michael McClary. RC (NhD). Fears militia standards cannot be procured. MJB, 3311.

14 August   From Michael McClary. RC (PHC: Charles Roberts Autograph Collection). Requests return of companies of light horse. MJB, 3313.

27 September   From Benjamin Bellows. RC (Nh-Ar). Resigns office of justice of the peace, Walpole. MJB, 3323.

27 September   From The Massachusetts Society for promoting Agriculture. RC (Nh). Certificate of admission. Found too late to film.

27 September   From Stephen Peabody. RC (Nh). Recommends William Cogswell to be justice of the peace.

30 September   From Daniel Newcomb. RC (Nh-Ar). Resigns judiciary commission. MJB, 3324.

4 October   From William Page. RC (Nh-Ar). Forwards petition to JB. MJB, 3328.

28 November   From John Calfe. RC (NhD). Recommends James Neal. MJB, 3334.

16 December   From John Price et al. RC (Nh-Ar). Recommend James Day for inspector of pot and pearl ashes at Portsmouth. MJB, 3340.

1794

1 January   From Daniel R. Rogers. RC (Nh-Ar). Resigns as inspector of pot and pearl ashes. MJB, 3356.

1 January   From Moses Leavitt. RC (Nh-Ar). Recommends Joseph Dow for brigade inspector. MJB, 3358.

1 January   From Paine Wingate. RC (NhD). Encloses pamphlet of "interesting communications." MJB, 3360.

6 January   From William Gardner. RC (Nh-Ar). Expresses concern for his compensation. MJB, 3368.

17 January   From John Langdon. RC (NhD). Recommends Richard Cutts Shannon for justice of the peace at Portsmouth. MJB, 3382.

18 January   From Paine Wingate. RC (NhD). Relates general news from Congress. MJB, 3386.

20 January   From John Hubbard. RC (Nh-Ar). Recommends Samuel Crosby for register of probate for Cheshire County. MJB, 3388.

26 January   From Peleg Sprague. RC (Nh-Ar). Recommends Samuel Crosby for register of probate. MJB, 3394.

February	From Gov. Richard Dobbs Spaight. RC (Nh-Ar). Encloses North Carolina resolutions re cases of individuals vs. states before Federal Supreme Court. MJB, 3412.
11 February	From John Prentice, John Calfe, and James Macgregore. RC (Nh-Ar). Recommend Samuel Moore of Candia for justice of the peace. MJB, 3434.
24 February	To the President of the Senate of the United States. RC (DNA: RG 46; Records of the U. S. Senate, Petitions and Memorials). Transmits a memorial of the General Court respecting the power of the United States re each individual state. MJB, 3452.
25 April	From Michael McClary. RC (NhD). Asks if JB will be at next General Court session. MJB, 3477.
25 April	From Daniel Rollins. RC (NhHi: Militia Miscellaneous Papers). Return of 2nd regiment. MJB, 3479.
1 May	To Joseph Pearson. RC (NhHi). Orders payment to Philip Tilton. MJB, 3482.
15 May	From Joseph Peirce. RC (Nh-Ar). Resigns judiciary and militia commissions. MJB, 3487.

Selected Bibliography

MANUSCRIPTS

"An Abstract of the Kingston Church Records of Kingston, New Hampshire."
    1947. NhHi. [Typescript.]
Bartlett, Agnes. "Portsmouth Families." 8 looseleaf notebooks. NhHi.
Dudley Papers. NhHi.
Gale, Charles B. "Gale Family Records: Bartholomew Gale Line." NhHi.
Folsom, Mrs. Wendell. "Cemetery Inscriptions of Exeter." NhHi. [Typescript.]
Hammond, Priscilla. "Gravestone Inscriptions, Salisbury, N. H." 1933. NhHi.
    [Typescript.]
———. "Vital Records of Kingston, New Hampshire, 1681–1823." 1935.
    NhHi. [Typescript.]
Hampstead Town Records. Microfilm. Nh.
Kingston Church Records, 1725–1844. NhHi.
Kingston Town Records, 1732–1808. 4 vols. NhHi.
Miscellaneous Manuscripts. NhHi.
MJB. "The Papers of Josiah Bartlett." Microfilm, 7 rolls. New Hampshire His-
    torical Society, 1976. [See *Guide to the Microfilm Edition of the Papers
    of Josiah Bartlett (1729–1795)*, Edited by Frank C. Mevers. Concord:
    New Hampshire Historical Society, 1976.]
New Hampshire Loyalists. Transcripts from the Records of the Commission
    for Enquiring into the Losses and Services of American Loyalists, 1783–
    1790, preserved in the Public Record Office, London, England. Nh.
New Hampshire Province Deeds, 1630–1770: and Rockingham County Registry
    of Deeds, 1770–1824. 239 vols. Nh-Ar. [Province Deeds microfilmed
    by The Genealogical Society, Salt Lake City, Utah. Indexes on micro-
    film.]
New Hampshire Revolutionary Pension Records. 64 vols. + 7 supplemental
    vols. + 3 index vols. NhHi. [Typescript.]
Paine, R. T., Collection. MHi.
PCC. Papers of the Continental Congress. DNA.
Portsmouth Town Records. Microfilm. Nh.
Records of the Bar in the County of Grafton & State of New Hampshire. NhHi.
Sandown Town Records. 2 vols. NhHi.
State of New Hampshire, "Account of Salt Petre." NhHi.
Toscan Papers. NhHi.
Vital Records of Newmarket, N. H. NhHi. [Typescript.]
Weare, Meshech, Papers. Nh-Ar.

PRINTED PRIMARY SOURCES

*Annals of the Congress of the United States: The Debates and Proceedings in
    the Congress of the United States.* 42 vols. Washington: Giles and Sea-
    ton, 1834–1856. [The printing used employs running heads on both recto
    and verso pages reading "History of Congress."]

Batchellor, Albert S., and Metcalf, Henry H., eds. *Laws of New Hampshire,* *1689–1835.* 8 vols. Manchester and elsewhere, 1904–1920.

Bouton, Nathaniel, ed. "Records of the New Hampshire Committee of Safety," *Collections of the New Hampshire Historical Society,* 7 (1863), 1–339. [The journal of the Committee of Safety is printed also in *Laws of New Hampshire,* 4: 575–883.]

Boyd, Julian P., ed. *The Papers of Thomas Jefferson.* 19 vols. to date. Princeton: Princeton University Press, 1950– .

Burnett, Edmund C., ed. *Letters of Members of the Continental Congress.* 8 vols. Washington: The Carnegie Institution, 1921–1938.

Butterfield, Lyman H., et al., eds. *Diary and Autobiography of John Adams.* 4 vols. Cambridge, Mass.: Harvard University Press, 1961.

Cornish (N. H.) Bicentennial Commission. *General Jonathan Chase (1732–1800) of Cornish, New Hampshire: His Papers.* Cornish: Cornish Bicentennial Commission, 1977.

Evans, Charles, Shipton, Clifford K., and Bristol, Roger C. *American Bibliography: A Chronological Dictionary of all Books, Pamphlets and Periodical Publications Printed in the United States of America, 1639–1800.* 13 vols. + Index + Supplement. Chicago, Worcester, and Charlottesville, 1903–1970.

Force, Peter, ed. *American Archives: . . . A Documentary History of the Origin and Progress of the North American Colonies.* 4th series, 6 vols.; 5th series, 3 vols. Washington, D. C.: M. St. Clair Clarke and Peter Force, 1837–1853.

Hammond, Otis G., ed. *Letters and Papers of Major-General John Sullivan.* 3 vols. Concord: New Hampshire Historical Society, 1930–1939.

The Historical Magazine. 23 vols. 1857–1875.

JCC. Ford, Worthington C., et al., eds. *Journals of the Continental Congress,* *1774–1789.* 34 vols. Washington, D. C.: Government Printing Office, 1904–1937. See also Harris, Kenneth E., and Tilley, Steven D., comps., *Index: Journals of the Continental Congress, 1774–1789.* Washington, D.C.: National Archives and Records Service, 1976.

Jewell, E. P. "A Curious Relic" [Log of the *Ranger,* 18 Aug. 1778–2 Mar. 1779], *The Granite Monthly,* 5 (1881–1882), 64, 100, 129, 244, 340, 407.

Lacy, Harriet S. "Samuel Sweat's Diary, 1772–1774," *Historical New Hampshire,* 30 (1975), 221–30.

Letters by Josiah Bartlett, William Whipple, and Others. Philadelphia: Henry B. Ashmead, 1889.

"Memoir of the Hon. Joseph Badger," *New Hampshire Historical Society Collections,* 6: 124–31.

NDAR. Clark, William B., and Morgan, William J., eds. *Naval Documents of the American Revolution.* 7 vols. to date. Washington, D. C.: Government Printing Office, 1964– .

New-Hampshire Gazette (Portsmouth), 1756–1899. Published under various titles and occasionally at Exeter.

NHSP. Bouton, Nathaniel, et al., eds. *Documents and Records Relating to New Hampshire.* 40 vols. Concord and Manchester, 1867–1940. [New Hampshire State Papers.]

Paullin, Charles O., ed. *Out-Letters of the Continental Marine Committee and Board of Admiralty.* 2 vols. New York: The DeVinne Press for the Naval History Society, 1914.

Shipton, Clifford K. and Mooney, James. *National Index of American Imprints*

Through 1800: The Short-title Evans. Worcester: American Antiquarian Society, 1969.

Slade, William, Jr. *Vermont State Papers; Being a Collection of Records and Documents . . . of Vermont.* Middlebury: J. W. Copeland, 1823.

Syrett, Harold C., et al., eds. *The Papers of Alexander Hamilton.* 24 vols. to date. New York: Columbia University Press, 1961– .

Vital Records of Amesbury, Massachusetts, to . . . 1849. Topsfield, Mass.: Topsfield Historical Society, 1913.

Vital Records of Haverhill, Massachusetts. 2 vols. Topsfield, Mass.: Topsfield Historical Society, 1910.

Vital Records of Salisbury, Massachusetts. Topsfield, Mass.: Topsfield Historical Society, 1915.

Walton, E. P., ed. *Records of the Council of Safety and Governor and Council of the State of Vermont.* 8 vols. Montpelier: Steam Press, 1873–1880.

WGW. Fitzpatrick, John C., ed. *The Writings of George Washington from the Original Manuscript Sources, 1745–1799.* 39 vols. Washington: Government Printing Office, 1931–1944.

Wharton, Francis, ed. *The Revolutionary Diplomatic Correspondence of the United States.* 6 vols. Washington: Government Printing Office, 1889.

SECONDARY SOURCES

Akers, Charles W. "New Hampshire's 'Honorary' Lieutenant Governor: John Temple and the American Revolution," *Historical New Hampshire,* 30 (1975), 79–99.

Alden, John R. *General Gage in America.* Baton Rouge: Louisiana State University Press, 1948.

Aldrich, Edgar. "The Affair of the Cedars and the Service of Colonel Timothy Bedel in the War of the Revolution," *Proceedings of the New Hampshire Historical Society,* 3 (1902), 194–231.

Allen, Gardner W. *A Naval History of the American Revolution.* 2 vols. Boston and New York: Houghton Mifflin Co., 1913.

The American Pioneer, A Monthly Periodical . . . of the Logan Historical Society. 2 vols. Chillicothe and Cincinnati, 1842–1843.

Baldwin, Thomas W. *Patten Genealogy.* Boston, 1908.

Barker, Ellen F. *Frye Genealogy.* New York, 1920.

"Bartlett Genealogy," *The Essex Antiquarian,* 7 (1903), 1–17.

Bartlett, Levi. *Genealogical and Biographical Sketches of the Bartlett Family in England and America.* Lawrence, 1876.

Bayley, Jacob. *Account of the Thirteenth Gathering of the Bailey-Bayley Family Association.* n.p., 1911.

BDEB. Sobel, Robert, ed. *Biographical Directory of the United States Executive Branch, 1774–1971.* Westport, Conn.: Greenwood Publishing Co., 1971.

Belknap, Jeremy. *History of New Hampshire.* 3 vols. Philadelphia and Boston, 1784–1792.

Bell, Charles H. *The Bench and Bar of New Hampshire.* Boston: Houghton Mifflin and Co., 1894.

———. *History of the Town of Exeter, New Hampshire.* Exeter, 1888.

Bell, Whitfield, Jr. *John Morgan, Continental Doctor.* Philadelphia: University of Pennsylvania Press, 1965.

Bemis, Samuel F., ed. *The American Secretaries of State and Their Diplomacy.* 18 vols. to date. New York: Alfred A. Knopf, 1928– .

Biographical Directory of the American Congress, 1774–1971. Washington, D. C., 1971. [Used often, but not cited.]

Boardman, Anne C. *Robert Calef of Boston and Some of His Descendants.* Salem, Mass.: Essex Institute, 1940.

Boatner, Mark M., III. *Encyclopedia of the American Revolution.* New York: David McKay Co., 1966.

Brewster, Charles W. *Rambles About Portsmouth.* 2 series. Somersworth, N. H.: New Hampshire Publishing Co., 1971–1972. [Facsimile of 1873 edition.]

Briggs, Vernon L. *Genealogies of the . . . Families . . . of Kent . . . 1295–1898.* Boston, 1898.

Brighton, Raymond A. *They Came to Fish.* 2 vols. Portsmouth, N. H., 1973.

Burleigh, Charles. *The Genealogy of the Burley or Burleigh Family of America.* Portland, Me., 1880.

Burnett, Edmund C. *The Continental Congress.* New York: The Macmillan Co., 1941.

Bush, Martin H. *Revolutionary Enigma: A Reappraisal of General Philip Schuyler of New York.* Port Washington, N.Y.: 1969.

Butterfield, Lyman H. "Benjamin Rush, the American Revolution and the American Millenium," in *Physician Signers of the Declaration of Independence,* edited by George E. Gifford, Jr. New York: Science History Publications, 1976, 18–42.

Butters, Avery J. "New Hampshire History and the Public Career of Meshech Weare, 1713–1786." Ph.D. dissertation, Fordham University, 1961.

Cappon, Lester J. et al. *Atlas of Early American History: The Revolutionary Era, 1760–1790.* Princeton: Princeton University Press, 1976.

Carrington, Henry B. *Battles of the American Revolution, 1775–1781.* New York, 1876.

Carter, N. F. *History of Pembroke, New Hampshire.* 2 vols. Concord, N. H.: 1895.

Cash, Philip. "Oliver Wolcott of Litchfield: A Temperate Revolutionary," in *Physician Signers of the Declaration of Independence,* edited by George E. Gifford, Jr. New York: Science History Publications, 1976, 43–69.

Chapman, George T. *Sketches of the Alumni of Dartmouth College.* Cambridge, Mass., 1867.

Chase, Benjamin. *History of Old Chester, from 1719 to 1869.* Auburn, N.H., 1869.

Chase, Fannie S. *Wiscasset in Pownalborough.* Wiscasset, Me., 1967.

Chase, Frederick. *A History of Dartmouth College and the Town of Hanover, New Hampshire.* 2 vols. Cambridge, Mass., 1891.

Child, William H. *History of the Town of Cornish, New Hampshire, 1763–1910.* 2 vols. Concord, n.d.

Clapp, Ebenezer. *The Clapp Memorial: Record of the Clapp Family in America.* Boston, 1876.

Clark, George L. *Silas Deane: A Connecticut Leader in the American Revolution.* New York: G. P. Putnam's Sons, 1913.

Clark, William B. *Lambert Wickes, Sea Raider and Diplomat.* New Haven: Yale University Press, 1932.

Cleaveland, Nehemiah. *The First Century of Dummer Academy.* Boston, 1865.

Colby, James F. *Manual of the Constitution of the State of New Hampshire.* 2nd ed. rev. Concord, 1912.

Currier, Harvey L. *Genealogy of Richard Currier*. Newport, Vt., 1910.

Daniell, Jere R. *Experiment in Republicanism: New Hampshire Politics and the American Revolution, 1741–1794*. Cambridge, Mass.: Harvard University Press, 1970.

———— "Lady Wentworth's Last Days in New Hampshire," *Historical New Hampshire*, 23 (1968), 14–25.

Dearborn, John J. *The History of Salisbury, New Hampshire*. Manchester, 1890.

Dexter, Franklin B. *Biographical Sketches of the Graduates of Yale College, 1701–1815*. 6 vols. New York and New Haven, 1885–1912.

DNB. Stephen, Leslie, et al., eds. *Dictionary of National Biography*. 63 vols. + 7 supplements. New York: Macmillan and Co., 1885–1971.

Dodge, Levi W. "Colonel Joseph Whipple and his Dartmouth Plantation," *The Granite Monthly*, 15 (1893), 20–31.

Dover Historical Society Collections, 1 (1894).

Dow, Joseph. *History of the Town of Hampton, New Hampshire*. 2 vols. Salem, Mass., 1893.

Emery, William M. *The Salters of Portsmouth, New Hampshire*. New Bedford, Mass., 1936.

Estabrook, William B. *Genealogy of the Estabrook Family*. Ithaca, N. Y., 1891.

Estes, J. Worth. "Dr. Hall Jackson and the Purple Foxglove: Medical Practice and Research in America 1760–1820." MS. NhHi. [Photocopy of typescript.]

———— "Honest Dr. Thornton: The Path to Rebellion," in *Physician Signers of the Declaration of Independence*, edited by George E. Gifford, Jr. New York: Science History Publications, 1976, 70–98.

Farmer, John, and Moore, Jacob B., eds. *Collections, Historical and Miscellaneous and Monthly Literary Journal*. 3 vols. Concord, 1823.

Ferguson, E. James. *The Power of the Purse: A History of American Public Finance, 1776–1790*. Chapel Hill: University of North Carolina Press, 1961.

Fitts, James H. *History of Newfields, New Hampshire*. Concord, 1912.

Folsom, Elizabeth K. *Genealogy of the Folsom Family*. 2 vols. Rutland, Vt., 1938.

Foss, Gerald D. *Three Centuries of Freemasonry in New Hampshire*. Somersworth, N. H.: New Hampshire Publishing Co., 1972.

Fowler, William M., Jr. *Rebels Under Sail: The American Navy During the Revolution*. New York: Charles Scribner's Sons, 1976.

Fox, Charles J. *History of the Old Township of Dunstable*. Nashua, 1846.

French, Jonathan. *Reminiscences of a Fifty-Years Pastorate*. Portsmouth, 1852.

Fuess, Claude M. *Andover: Symbol of New England*. Andover, Mass., 1959.

Gale, George. *The Gale Family Records*. Galesville, Wisc., 1866.

George, Nellie P. *Old Newmarket, New Hampshire: Historical Sketches*. Exeter, N. H., 1932.

Gillman, Alexander W. *Searches into the Gillman or Gilman Family*. London, 1895.

Gilman, Arthur. *The Gilman Family*. Albany, 1869.

Greeley, George H. *Genealogy of the Greely-Greeley Family*. Boston, 1905.

Greene, Evarts B., and Harrington, Virginia D. *American Population Before the Federal Census of 1790*. New York: Columbia University Press, 1932.

Griffin, S. G. *A History of the Town of Keene*. Keene N. H., 1904.

Gruber, Ira D. *The Howe Brothers and the American Revolution*. New York: Atheneum, 1972.

Hammond, Bray. *Banks and Politics in America*. Princeton: Princeton University Press, 1957.

Hawke, David F. *Paine*. New York: Harper and Row, 1974.

Heitman, Francis B. *Historical Register of Officers of the Continental Army During the War of the Revolution*. 2nd ed. rev. Washington, D. C., 1914.

Higginbotham, Don. *Daniel Morgan: Revolutionary Rifleman*. Chapel Hill: University of North Carolina Press, 1961.

———— *The War of American Independence: Military Attitudes, Policies, and Practice, 1763–1789*. New York: The Macmillan Co., 1971.

Hills, William S. *The Hills Family in America*. New York, 1906.

Hurd, D. Hamilton. *History of Hillsborough County, New Hampshire*. Philadelphia, 1885.

Jackson, Russell L. *The Physicians of Essex County*. Salem, Mass.: The Essex Institute, 1948.

Jaffe, Irma B. *John Trumbull: Patriot-Artist of the American Revolution*. Boston: New York Graphic Society, 1975.

Jensen, Merrill. *The Articles of Confederation*. Madison: University of Wisconsin Press, 1940.

———— *The New Nation: A History of the United States During the Confederation, 1781–1789*. New York: Alfred A. Knopf, 1950.

Johnson, Allen, and Malone, Dumas, eds. *Dictionary of American Biography*. 22 vols. + 4 supplements. New York: Charles Scribner's Sons, 1928–1950. [Used often, but not cited.]

Kaplan, Sidney. *The Black Presence in the Era of the American Revolution, 1770–1800*. Greenwich, Conn.: New York Graphic Society, 1973.

Kelly, Giles M. *A Genealogical Account of the Descendants of John Kelly of Newbury, Massachusetts*. n.p., 1886.

Kingsbury, Frank B. *History of the Town of Surry, Cheshire County, New Hampshire*. Surry, N.H., 1925.

Kirsch, George B. "Jeremy Belknap: A Biography." Ph.D. dissertation, Columbia University, 1972.

Kittredge, Mabel T. *The Kittredge Family in America*. Rutland, Vt., 1936.

Kohn, Richard H. *Eagle and Sword: The Federalists and the Creation of the Military Establishment in America, 1783–1802*. New York: The Free Press, 1975.

Lee, William. *John Leigh . . . and His Descendants*. Albany, N. Y., 1888.

[Leonard, L. W., and Smith, Samuel A.] *Genealogy of the Family of William Smith of Peterborough, N. H.* Keene, N.H., 1852.

Libby, Charles T. *The Libby Family in America*. Portland, Me., 1882.

Mayo, Lawrence S. *John Langdon of New Hampshire*. Concord, 1937.

————*John Wentworth, Governor of New Hampshire, 1767–1775*. Cambridge, Mass.: Harvard University Press, 1921.

Merrill, Nancy. "Nathaniel Folsom," *New Hampshire Profiles*, 25 (March 1976), 24.

Mevers, Frank C. "Congress and the Navy: The Establishment and Administration of the American Revolutionary Navy by the Continental Congress, 1775–1784." Ph.D. dissertation, University of North Carolina, 1972.

————"Josiah Bartlett," in *Physician Signers of the Declaration of Indepen-*

dence, edited by George E. Gifford, Jr. New York: Science History Publications, 1976, 99–121.

Moore, John W. *Historical Notes on Printers and Printing.* Concord, 1886.

Morgan, William J. *Captains to the Northward: The New England Captains in the Continental Navy.* Barre, Mass., 1959.

[Morgan, William J., ed.]. *Maritime Dimensions of the American Revolution.* Washington, D. C.: Naval History Division, 1977.

Morison, John H. *Life of the Hon. Jeremiah Smith, LL.D.* Boston, 1845.

Morison, Samuel E. *John Paul Jones: A Sailor's Biography.* Boston: Little, Brown and Co., 1959.

Morrison, Leonard A. *The History of Windham.* Boston, 1883.

NEHGR. *New England Historical and Genealogical Register.* 131 vols. to date. 1847–

NHGR. *New Hampshire Genealogical Record.* 7 vols. 1903–1910.

NHHS, *Collections. Collections of the New Hampshire Historical Society.* 10 vols. 1824–1893.

NHHS, *Proceedings. Proceedings of the New Hampshire Historical Society.* 5 vols. 1872–1912.

Nebenzahl, Kenneth, and Higginbotham, Don. *Atlas of the American Revolution.* New York: Rand McNally & Co., 1974.

Nettels, Curtis P. *The Emergence of a National Economy, 1775–1815.* New York: Holt, Rinehart and Winston, 1962.

Noyes, Harriette & Henry. *Genealogical Record of Some of the Noyes Descendants.* 2 vols. Boston, 1904.

Noyes, Harriette E. *A Memorial of the Town of Hampstead, New Hampshire.* Boston, 1899.

Odiorne, David W. *Genealogy of the Odiorne Family in America.* 2nd ed. rev. Ann Arbor, Mich., 1967.

Oliver, Nancy Elaine Briggs. "Keystone of the Federal Arch: New Hampshire's Ratification of the United States Constitution." Ph.D. dissertation, University of California, 1972.

Page, Elwin L. "Josiah Bartlett and the Federation." *Historical New Hampshire*, 2 (October 1947), 1–6.

———*Judicial Beginnings in New Hampshire, 1640–1700.* Concord: New Hampshire Historical Society, 1959.

———"Rider For Freedom: Josiah Bartlett, 1729–1795." MS. NhHi.

Palmer, John F. *General von Steuben.* New Haven, 1937.

Parker, Edward L. *The History of Londonderry.* Boston, 1851.

Parsons, Charles L. "The Capture of Fort William and Mary, December 14 and 15, 1774," *Proceedings of the New Hampshire Historical Society*, 4 (1906), 18–47.

Patterson, Samuel W. *Horatio Gates.* New York, 1941.

Peckham, Howard H., ed. *The Toll of Independence: Engagements & Battle Casualties of the American Revolution.* Chicago: University of Chicago Press, 1974.

Pell, John. *Ethan Allen.* Boston: Houghton Mifflin Co., 1929.

Pierce, Frederick C. *Batchelder, Batcheller Genealogy.* Chicago, 1809.

Potter, Chandler E. *The Military History of the State of New-Hampshire, 1623–1861.* 2 vols. Baltimore, 1972. [Reprint of the 1868 edition which was part of the report of the state adjutant general.]

Preble, George H. *History of the United States Navy-Yard, Portsmouth, N. H.* Washington, 1892.

Proctor, William L. *A Genealogy of Descendants of Robert Proctor.* Ogdensbury, N. Y., 1898.

Putnam, Hamilton S. *The New Hampshire Medical Society: A History.* Milford, N. H., 1966.

Rich, Wesley E. *The History of the United States Post Office to the Year 1829.* Cambridge, Mass.: Harvard University Press, 1924.

Ritcheson, Charles R. *Aftermath of Revolution: British Policy Toward the United States, 1783–1795.* Dallas, Tex.: Southern Methodist University Press, 1969.

Runnels, M. T. *A Genealogy of Runnels and Reynolds Families in America.* Boston, 1873.

Russell, Alice and George F. "Town Officers of Atkinson, N. H., 1775–1783." MS. NhHi.

Sanborn, V. C. *Genealogy of the Family of Samborne or Sanborn . . . .* n.p., 1899.

Saunderson, Henry H. *History of Charlestown, New-Hampshire, The Old No. 4.* Claremont, N. H., 1876.

Scott, Kenneth. "Colonial Innkeepers of New Hampshire," *Historical New Hampshire,* 19 (1964), 3–49.

———"Colonel Stephen Holland of Londonderry," *Historical New Hampshire,* 3 (March 1947), 15–27.

Secomb, Daniel F. *History of the Town of Amherst, Hillsborough County, New Hampshire.* Somersworth: New Hampshire Publishing Co., 1972. [Reprint of 1883 edition.]

Shryock, Richard H. *Medicine in America: Historical Essays.* Baltimore: The Johns Hopkins University Press, 1966.

Sibley, John L., and Shipton, Clifford K. *Biographical Sketches of Graduates of Harvard University, 1713–1771.* 17 vols. Cambridge, Mass. and Boston, 1873–1975.

Silsby, George H. *Silsby . . . Silsbee Genealogy.* 3 vols. NhHi. [Typescript.]

Smith, Annie Morrill. *Morrill Kindred in America.* 2 vols. New York, 1931.

Smith, Page. *John Adams.* 2 vols. Garden City, 1962.

Smith, Paul H. "Time and Temperature: Philadelphia, July 4, 1776," *The Quarterly Journal of the Library of Congress,* 33 (October 1976), 294–99.

Sprague, William B. *Annals of the American Pulpit.* 7 vols. New York, 1859–1861.

Squires, James Duane. *The Granite State of the United States.* 4 vols. New York: The American Historical Company, Inc., 1956.

———*The Story of New Hampshire.* Princeton: D. Van Nostrand Company, 1964.

Stackpole, Everett S. *Swett Genealogy, Descendants of John Swett of Newbury, Mass.* Lewiston, Me., n.d.

Stark, Caleb. *History of the Town of Dunbarton.* Concord, 1860.

Stearns, Ezra S. *Genealogical and Family History of the State of New Hampshire.* 4 vols. New York, 1908.

———*History of Plymouth, New Hampshire.* 2 vols. Cambridge, Mass., 1906.

———*History of the Town of Rindge, New Hampshire.* Boston, 1875.

Stevens, Charles E. *Noah Emery of Exeter.* 1886.

Temple Bicentennial Commission. *A History of Temple, New Hampshire, 1768–1976*. Dublin, N. H., 1976.

Tenney, M. J. *The Tenney Family*. 2nd ed. rev. Concord, N. H., 1904.

Thacher, James. *American Medical Biography*. 2 vols. New York: Da Capo Press, 1967. [Reprint of 1828 edition.]

Thompson, Dorothea M. "Enoch Poor," *New Hampshire Profiles*, 25 (March 1976), 48.

Thompson, Mary P. *A Memoir of Judge Ebenezer Thompson of Durham, N. H.* Concord, N. H., 1886.

Thurston, Brown. *Thurston Genealogies*. 2nd ed. rev. Portland, Me., 1892.

Tilton, Francis T. *History of the Tilton Family in America*. 1 vol. in 8 numbers. 1927–1928.

Toner, J. M. *The Medical Men of the Revolution*. Philadelphia, 1876.

Turner, Lynn W. *William Plumer of New Hampshire, 1759–1850*. Chapel Hill: University of North Carolina Press, 1962.

Upton, Richard F. *Revolutionary New Hampshire: An Account of the Social and Political Forces Underlying the Transition from Royal Province to American Commonwealth*. New York: Octagon Books, 1971. [Reprint of 1936 edition.]

Vaughan, Dorothy M. *This Was a Man* [William Whipple.] 1964.

Waite, Otis F. R. *History of the Town of Claremont, New Hampshire*. Manchester, N. H., 1895.

Walker, Joseph B. *A History of the New Hampshire Convention*. Boston, 1888.

———*New Hampshire's Five Provincial Congresses, July 21, 1774—January 5, 1776*. Concord, N. H., 1905.

Wallace, Willard M. *Appeal to Arms: A Military History of the American Revolution*. New York: Harper & Brothers, 1951.

———*Traitorous Hero: The Life and Fortunes of Benedict Arnold*. New York, 1954.

Waters, Thomas F. *Ipswich in the Massachusetts Bay Colony*. 2 vols. Ipswich, 1905–1917.

Weis, Frederick L. *The Colonial Clergy and the Colonial Churches of New England*. Lancaster, Mass., 1936.

Wells, Robert V. *The Population of the British Colonies in America before 1776: A Survey of Census Data*. Princeton: Princeton University Press, 1975.

Wentworth, John. *The Wentworth Genealogy: England and America*. 3 vols. Boston, 1878.

Wheeler, Edmund. *The History of Newport, New Hampshire*. Concord, 1879.

Whittemore, Charles P. *A General of the Revolution: John Sullivan of New Hampshire*. New York: Columbia University Press, 1961.

Whittier, Charles C. *The Descendants of Thomas Whittier and Ruth Green*. Rutland, Vt., 1937.

Wickwire, Franklin and Mary. *Cornwallis: The American Adventure*. Boston: Houghton Mifflin, 1970.

Wilderson, Paul W. "Protagonist of Prudence: A Biography of John Wentworth, the King's Last Governor of New Hampshire." Ph.D. dissertation, University of New Hampshire, 1977.

———"The Raids on Fort William and Mary: Some New Evidence," *Historical New Hampshire*, 30 (1975), 178–202.

Index

THIS BOOK

Was composed by G&S Typesetters Inc.

and printed and bound by Murray Printing Company

The text type is 10 point Sabon

with annotation set in 8 point.

The designer was Richard Hendel.